W95CN396S4610C

USER INTERFACE DESIGN

PRENTICE HALL INTERNATIONAL SERIES
IN INDUSTRIAL AND SYSTEMS ENGINEERING

W. J. Fabrycky and J. H. Mize, Editors

USER INTERFACE DESIGN

Ray E. Eberts

Purdue University

PRENTICE HALL, Englewood Cliffs, New Jersey 07632

Library of Congress Cataloging-in-Publication Data

Eberts, Ray E.
   User interface design / Ray E. Eberts.
       p. cm. -- (Prentice Hall International series in industrial
and systems engineering)
  Includes bibliographical references and index.
  ISBN 0-13-140328-1
  1. User interfaces (Computer systems) I. Title. II. Series.
QA76.9.U83E23 1994
004'.01'9--dc20

                   93-29743
                   CIP

Acquisitions editor: Marcia Horton
Editorial/production supervision: Joan Stone
Copy editor: Nikki Herbst
Cover designer: Design Solutions
Production coordinator: David Dickey
Editorial assistant: Dolores Mars

 ©   1994 by Prentice-Hall, Inc.
A Paramount Communications Company
Englewood Cliffs, New Jersey 07632

Printed in the United States of America

10 9 8 7 6 5 4 3 2 1

ISBN 0-13-140328-1

Prentice-Hall International (UK) Limited, *London*
Prentice-Hall of Australia Pty. Limited, *Sydney*
Prentice-Hall Canada Inc., *Toronto*
Prentice-Hall Hispanoamericana, S.A., *Mexico*
Prentice-Hall of India Private Limited, *New Delhi*
Prentice-Hall of Japan, Inc., *Tokyo*
Simon & Schuster Asia Pte. Ltd., *Singapore*
Editora Prentice-Hall do Brasil, Ltda., *Rio de Janeiro*

CONTENTS

Chapter 6. Hazards to Conducting and Interpreting HCI Experiments   126

SECTION VI. ISSUES IN HCI (APPLICATION OF APPROACHES)

Chapter 22. Feedback and Help Messages   521

Chapter 23. Menu Displays   539

PREFACE

The material in this book can be used for undergraduate or graduate courses in industrial engineering, computer science, experimental psychology, or management information science (MIS). I have arranged the book in a modular style divided into six main sections. The sections chosen for teaching will depend on the interests and backgrounds of the students. Section I is an introduction and is useful for all groups. The last section, Section VI, discusses applications and how the material from the middle four sections, the four approaches to user interface design, can be used in these applications. Each of the chapters in this last section concentrates on one of the four approaches. Section II is on the empirical approach which discusses how user interface design should use good experimental design techniques to test users during software development. Section III is on the cognitive approach and discusses some of the major cognitive theories and the applications which have been developed from these theories. Section IV is on the predictive modeling approaches and discusses how modeling techniques can be used to predict execution times, learnability, mental workload, and consistency before an interface is prototyped. Section V is on the anthropomorphic approach and discusses techniques to make the user interface design more human-like in character. Industrial engineering students would be most interested in Sections III and IV; computer science students would be most interested in Sections II and III; psychology students would be most interested in Sections IV and V; and MIS students would be most interested in Sections III and V.

This book has grown from the courses I teach in industrial engineering at Purdue University and the industrial contacts I have had over the years. I have used previous versions of the material in the book to teach students and professionals from Purdue, AT&T, DEC, NTT (Japan's telephone company), and NEC. The people from these courses have offered many important suggestions which have been incorporated in the book. My engineering students at Purdue have especially nudged the material from cognitive engineering theories to the applications that they enjoy and to the development of job-based skills that they need.

I have taught the material from this book in two different courses at Purdue to two different audiences. First, I have used the material to teach an undergraduate laboratory course in cognitive-based human factors. The section on predictive modeling techniques assists the students in performing tasks analyses for any product design. The chapters on experimental design allow the students to understand how to evaluate the needs of customers and design products to meet those needs. I find that affordances and constraints from Chapter 21 are fun to teach in this course because of the many examples that can be used. The computer-based products used as examples in this book provide useful application examples because the successful products are always well human-factored and customer based. Other product designs can follow these examples.

Second, I have used the material in this book to teach a graduate-level course in interface design. This course concentrates on the theories and especially how the cognitive and anthropomorphic theories can be translated into interface designs. I also teach the students how to program interfaces in this course by teaching the Motif widget set. They enjoy seeing how the theories are transformed into actual designs, but I have not tailored the book to any particular interface language. It could, however, be used in conjunction with Motif, as I do, or with Macintosh (HyperCard) or PC-based (Windows) interface languages. Good popular books exist for these languages and could be used in conjunction with this book. These other books do not, however, teach the proper techniques of interface design.

There are many people to thank. Gavriel Salvendy and Ferd Leimkuhler provided important support at Purdue University. Mitch Tseng, at Digital Equipment Corporation (DEC), allowed me the opportunity to work with DEC in the summers, exposing me to interesting industrial applications. Drs. Kamae and Endo, directors of the NTT research labs in Yokosuka, Japan, provided me with some time to work on the concepts in the book while I was on sabbatical. Katsuhiko Ogawa was a gracious and generous host during the Japan visit, exposing me to Japanese practices in this area and patiently answering questions about Japanese life. Gerry Nadler provided me with support during the second half of my sabbatical at USC, allowing me a place to write while viewing the San Gabriel mountains. Yei-Yu Yeh tested an earlier version of the book on her students at the University of Wisconsin and many important suggestions came from this. The staff at Prentice Hall—Marcia Horton, Joan Stone, Nikki Herbst, and Dolores Mars—provided the needed support to produce a book of this scope.

Finally, the book could not have been written without the support of my family. My in-laws, Philip and Iris Gray, provided a place to set my computer while I worked on the book in the midst of the Rocky Mountains in Montana. My parents, Harry and Dorothy Eberts, always provided the examples to motivate me to take on such a task. My two sons, Wescott and Russell, missed out on some baseball games with their father, but always seemed to understand. The book could not have been done without my wife, Cindy, who was always there to help and, among other things, to offer suggestions and help with the index.

Ray Eberts
Lafayette, Indiana

USER INTERFACE DESIGN

CHAPTER 1

INTERACTING WITH COMPUTERS

INTRODUCTION

In the last few years, as more people use computers, a greater emphasis has been placed on effective human-computer interaction. Back in the 1950s, it was predicted that 10 computers would handle our country's data processing needs. In 1991, it was estimated that 15% of American homes have computers in them. The use of computers is even more widespread in the workplace, of course. Estimates are that 50 million Americans now work with computers on their job. Table 1-1 contains data from the U.S. Census Bureau of computer use on the job in 1984 and 1989. Computer usage in all types of jobs has risen dramatically in those five years; in 1989 over 56% of the managers and professionals surveyed used computers on the job (some types of jobs are not reported in the table). A recent survey estimated that there were over 2.7 million computers in the approximately 100,000 public schools in the United States; this is almost a hundred-fold increase from 1980 and represents about one computer for every 16 students. The estimated cost for this is $4 billion per year. Recent magazine articles have questioned whether this investment has been cost effective because of the supposed decrease in quality of American schools during the computerization age, but there are certainly many other reasons for the education problems.

Even consumer products are computerized. Most of us have VCRs or we use microwaves. We have copying machines at work or school with multiple functions. We may have found that automatic teller machines (ATMs) are more convenient than human tellers. Even our automobiles have computer chips in them to control some aspects of the car. When examining these consumer products, it would be difficult to find someone in the modern world who has not interacted with some kind of computer or computer keyboard, be it a copy machine or an ATM. The effect of this rapid increase in the number and availability of computers is that the computer, especially the design of the computer interface, must be made for everybody instead of just the professional or computer hobbyist.

Often we tend to think that merely computerizing a manual task will make the task easier to perform. But sometimes, if the interface is not designed correctly, computerizing the task makes it more difficult and time-consuming. Hansen, Doring, and Whitlock (1978) found that a computerized class examination took students as much as 100% longer to finish than did the typical paper-and-pencil test. In analyzing the task, they found that much of the extra time was spent in trying to figure out how to use the machine. Similarly, Kozar and Dickson (1978) found that students took more time making decisions if the relevant information was presented on a computer screen rather than on paper. Finally, Gould (1981) found that writing a letter on a word processor required up to 50% more time than writing a letter by hand. The process of interacting

1

Chap. 1 Interacting with Computers

TABLE 1-1
The number of workers in the work force using computers in 1984 and 1989 (from the U.S. Census Bureau).

Occupation	1984 Total (Millions)	1984 %Work Force	1989 Total (Millions)	1989 % Work Force
Managerial, professional	9.418	39.0	16.696	56.2
Tech. sales, admin. support	11.728	38.7	18.461	55.1
Service	0.774	6.2	1.368	10.2
Precision production, craft, repair	1.289	10.3	2.016	15.3
Operators, laborers	0.877	5.5	1.563	9.5

with computers has been difficult. Advances have been made in usability since these studies have been reported, but the point is that computerization of a process will not guarantee increased efficiency.

The computer must be designed so that it is easy to use. To make computers easy to use, designers concentrate on the interface between the computer and the computer user, which is often referred to simply as "the interface." Designing an effective interface requires more than just a knowledge of how the hardware or the software of the computer works. The designer must also understand how a person works. Thus, the study of designing an effective interface, often referred to as human-computer interaction research, requires an expertise in two knowledge areas, computers and psychology. In recent years, much research has been devoted to how humans interact with computers.

Computer Sales and Worker Productivity

If the computer is difficult to use, then it will not be used at all or it will not be used effectively. This has two implications: sales of computerized products will drop, thus affecting the economy; and productivity, for those using computers, will also drop. Some evidence exists that sales of computer equipment are starting to slump, and productivity of white collar workers, the ones most likely to use computers for a variety of jobs, is also stagnant.

Office automation is a big business which is very important to the economies of several different countries. On the whole, the information industry is a $500 billion industry, but recently it has shown signs of slumping. In the 1980s, the business was growing at 20% a year; but in 1990, the growth had fallen to 6% a year. Part of the earlier growth was due to companies buying computer equipment. In the 1980s, corporations bought about 57 million personal computers at a price of about $98 billion (McCarroll, 1991). The slump in the computer industry can be attributed to other factors besides difficult-to-use computers. As any industry matures, the high growth rates of earlier years cannot be matched. By emphasizing easy-to-use computers, however, the computer industry could be revitalized, resulting in new products and new growth as older more difficult to use machines are replaced.

Computers are becoming more and more important in the workplace, and, consequently, they have a larger effect on the productivity of the workers. In many of the jobs taken over by computers, the human becomes a monitor, decision maker, and problem solver instead of a controller or material handler. Service-oriented jobs increasingly form a larger percentage of the total jobs. If the service job is selling hamburgers at the local fast food restaurant, then the cash register can be computerized to determine the prices and track the inventory. If the service job is a high management job, then the manager can utilize the computer to assist with decision making. Typically top management tends to be older and not as familiar with computers. Since managers must also be effective people managers and maintain a sense of control or intelligence, they may be reluctant to ask for help from the clerical staff and lower management. These higher-level managers will utilize computers only if the programs are designed effectively.

Computers in the workplace must be easy to use so that white collar productivity can be increased. It is disturbing to note that as offices have been computerized, productivity has fallen. As reported in the Los Angeles Times, Stephen Roach, a senior economist with Morgan Stanley & Co., estimated from federal statistics that office productivity since 1973 has decreased by 7% while factory productivity has increased 51%. The effectiveness and productivity of computer usage has to be increased. Much effort has been spent on increasing productivity of blue collar workers, and this effort has paid off with large productivity increases. More effort needs to be devoted to increasing productivity of white collar workers, a group of workers which is becoming larger and larger. One way to achieve these increases is to improve the usability of computers. Increased emphasis needs to be placed on the interface design and the environment in which the computer is used. The increase in office computerization and the concomitant fall in white collar worker productivity is just a correlation, not a cause-and-effect relationship, and could be due to other factors such as the growth in the number of white collar workers or even a difficulty in measuring white collar productivity, an activity which does not always result in an identifiable or measurable number of products. The overall trend, though, is discouraging, and the problem must be addressed. Designing more effective interfaces for the workplace is one way to address this problem.

Just as white collar productivity is difficult to measure, productivity around the home is even more abstract and difficult to measure. Anecdotal and personal evidence seems to indicate that home consumer products are becoming more and more difficult to use, resulting in more time needed to operate these machines and increased levels of frustration in doing so. With microwave ovens, very few people use all the functionality available. VCRs are an entire story to themselves. While comedians joke about the flashing 12s on the VCR, many people have had major problems setting the time on their VCR clocks. We can set time on an analog watch or a clock but have trouble with a VCR. Many people also have trouble programming the VCR to record programs.

Even the sound, which should be simple on a VCR, can cause problems. I owned a hi-fi stereo VCR for over a year, enduring terrible sound quality, until I learned that I initially had pushed the wrong buttons for the sound. One of the buttons can be placed either on or off for "hi-fi/normal mix." As most people would, I chose the "on" position because a mix sounded like it should be better than one alone. After trying several combinations to try to fix the sound problems, I reread the instructions and came across this: "When playing back a tape containing the same soundtrack on both hi-fi and normal audio tracks, a slight time lag is sensed between the two soundtracks, probably with some distortion, in the ON position. Therefore, in such a case, use the OFF position." I found, through experience, that almost all commercial tapes have the soundtrack on both tracks, and the distortion was fairly large. I estimated that I spent probably about 10 hours trying to fix this problem, and many more hours were spent in frustration over the product. Consumer products should be simpler to use.

The trends in computer sales and productivity are discouraging, but the fact that these machines have not reached their potential is also disturbing. Home computer use increased initially, probably because people learned how to use some simple programs at work, such as word processing, database programs, or spreadsheets, and then bought home computers to do these tasks at home. Home computers potentially could be used for many other functions besides these typical applications. In the schools, initially there was much concern that the computer's potential for teaching would not be realized and, like television, would be reduced to entertainment such as video games. Many clever and easy to use programs have been written to teach school children important learning concepts. More potential exists.

More Emphasis on Usability

In the past, little emphasis was placed on the software running the interface because economically viable hardware could not support complex software. In the 1950s, 90% of the cost of a computer system was in hardware and the rest was software. Today, the costs are just the opposite. Many of the early personal computers had 16K or 32K of internal memory (the amount of instructions that can be kept in memory at one time). An early version of the Apple Macintosh, a computer which has been popular because of its ease of use, contained 40K of internal memory just to run the operating system. This complexity in the operating system, which correspondingly makes the computer easy to use, could not have been supported by the hardware of the early computers. In the past, designers were constrained by what could be done; now designers can think about what should be done.

Without the hardware limitations, the user interface has become more important and, thus, more of the effort is being placed on software usability. With the memory constraints of the early computers, emphasis was placed on the functionality of the code and the user had to be a computer expert to run the program. Very few lines of the computer code were concerned with the user interface. Now, the percentage of lines of codes just for the user interface is increasing. In 1984, Smith and Mosier (1984) estimated that the user interface required 30-35% of the lines of code; a more recent estimate places it at 47-60% (MacIntyre, Estep, and Sieburth, 1990). About 29% of the cost for software development is invested in the user interface for high-resolution workstations incorporating icons and a mouse; less is needed, about 17% of the cost, if the computer does not offer high-resolution graphics capability (Rosenberg, 1989).

Given the increased emphasis and cost of the user interface, is usability worth the cost and the effort? In recent years, for a product to sell or be used, the interface must be well designed. Advertising executives are aware of this. When a computer product is advertised, its "user-friendliness" will be emphasized or its "ergonomical design" will be touted. A television commercial from a large computer company a few years back showed psychologists dressed in white lab coats analyzing the ease of use of computer systems as normal people used them. Another commercial showed two executives talking about the power of the two different computer systems. The one executive pointed out that the system he purchased was more powerful because people were using it, and enjoying themselves in the meantime. Another advertisement showed people analyzing a report from a company and, because of the quality of the graphics in the report, they wrongly concluded that it was from a large company. The commercial then revealed the report's origins to be from a one-person company with an easy-to-use computer.

Besides selling products, this popularization of ease of use of computers has another effect: it produces rising expectations for the user interface. Whereas a few years ago users would be content with a program containing the needed functionality, even though it was difficult to use, this is no longer the case. People have discovered from past experiences with good interface designs that if time is put into the interface design, the program can be easy to use. Anything less is unacceptable, since users are becoming more sophisticated which places additional pressure on companies to design good computer products. Increased user sophistication also places additional pressure on producers of in-house products. Just because you are designing a program for in-house use only does not mean good interface design principles can be violated. Because of the rising expectations, potential in-house users will not put up with poor designs any more than the regular consumers will.

Has the programming effort and the increased cost improved usability? Even though examples were provided earlier for how computers were difficult to use, anybody who has been using computers for more than five years would almost certainly agree that some computer products for specific applications have become more usable. Concrete evidence of improved usability is difficult to find, though, because of the difficulties in measuring usability. One area in which good records have been kept over the years is in the design of computer-assisted instruction (CAI) lessons. CAI uses the computer to present instructional materials to students. One of the problems with incorporating CAI in teaching programs is the difficulty and the amount of time needed to write a good CAI program. With the changing hardware configurations, the programs need to be updated continually.

Much of the work in CAI has been research oriented so that measurements of

TABLE 1-2
Increases in productivity for programming CAI courseware measured according to the number of hours needed to program one hour of instruction

Language	Dates Available	Batch or On-Line	Hours/ Hour	References
FORTRAN	Before July 1967	Batch	2286	Avner (1979)
Authoring	Before Oct. 1968	Batch	615	Avner (1979)
Authoring	After 1968	On-Line	151	Avner (1979)
Authoring with menus and prompts	1984	On-Line	8	Fairweather and O'Neal (1984)

various parameters of the production of the task are available. One such measurement has been the number of hours taken to author an hour of computerized instruction. If the interface is designed well, then increases in productivity of the CAI programmers should be seen. Table 1-2, from Eberts (1985), contains examples of authoring times over the past 20 years. As can be seen, a large decrease in interaction times occurred when a switch was made from FORTRAN, a general all-purpose language, to an authoring language which was designed specifically for CAI applications. Another improvement happened when the computer system changed from a batch-oriented system (sending a complete job to the computer and receiving feedback only on the complete program) to an on-line interactive system (line-by-line feedback is provided). A third improvement appeared when the authoring language was equipped with menu displays and prompts which help tell the user what to do. Similar examples of improvements could probably be seen in other

specific examples of human-computer interaction tasks. This example shows that large productivity increases can be achieved with the successful application of good human-computer interaction principles.

ILLUSTRATIONS OF USABILITY PROBLEMS

With so much emphasis on ease of use, one might wrongly conclude that the problems in usability either do not exist anymore or are being attacked on all fronts. The problems have not all been solved. I know of someone who received a bill for minus $10 (which means that the company owed this person $10), but he kept on being billed for what was owed to him. These kind of errors have in the past been attributed to computer or machine errors. A very simple programming fix would have solved this problem. Many people still refuse to use computer systems because of these kinds of errors in software design.

To illustrate this problem further, consider the following example. Most software produced by the large software companies generally will be easy to use because they have the resources to invest in the interface and they realize that their product will not sell unless it is easy to use. Software designed for more specialized tasks sometimes places more emphasis on functionality than usability.

Consider the card catalogue system in a large library. In the past, card catalogues have been a physical entity in a physical location in the library. Traditional card catalogues in libraries are being replaced by interactive computer systems. These on-line library systems offer the potential to greatly increase the speed and access with which relevant documents can be identified by the library patron. Instead of having to travel to the physical location of the traditional card catalogues, it is now possible, if one has a computer terminal in the office, to determine whether the book is available without leaving your desk. The on-line system also is easier for the librarians because they quickly can make insertions or deletions to the on-line database of books without having to update paper card files.

If one thinks about the traditional card catalogues, however, they have many aspects which make them easy to use. When using a card catalogue system, the user can easily look around, just through head movements, and see the location of all the cards in the drawers and the cabinets. When using an on-line system, how does the user browse through the parts of the book database? In addition, the user has only a small window on the book database; most computer screens can only hold information from one index card of the traditional system at a time. With a card catalogue system, the user can look around the room and easily identify the categories, such as by-author or by-title, in which the books are classified for searches. With an on-line system, the user is not always aware of all the categories. With a card catalogue system, the methods of operation such as opening a drawer and fingering through the cards is obvious by the design of the drawers and the cards. A handle on the drawer provides an "affordance" (see Chapter 21) to imply that the drawer is meant to be opened. Once in a drawer, the user easily can determine that the cards can be manipulated to find the one needed. With an on-line system, such affordances are not necessarily available to the user. How does one find the right location? How does one search through each entry? With a card catalogue system, the user easily can determine how many cards and therefore books are available from one author by looking at the length of the cards under that entry. With an on-line system, such a natural method of conveyance of number of entries is not always available. With a card catalogue system, the user utilizes logical operations such as "and" and "or" without realizing it. With an on-line system, the user would have to specify these operations exactly. Any on-line system which replaces the old system would have to be better than the old system in order to make progress.

Smith and Janosky (1985) performed a study to determine how well university students could use an on-line catalogue system similar to the one just described. In the study, 30 subjects were provided with instructional material normally available to a user of an on-line library system. This included off-line help (see Figure 1-1),

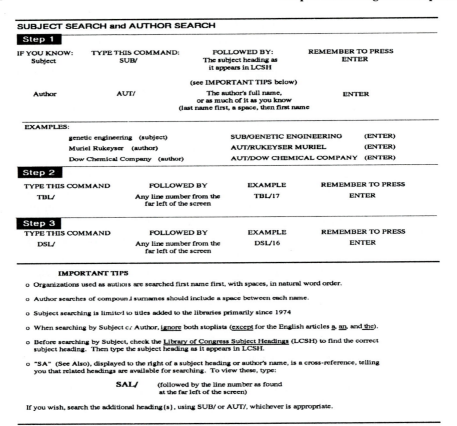

Figure 1-1. Example of off-line help from the study on usability of an on-line cataloguing system (reprinted from Smith and Janosky © 1985 IEEE).

```
HELP.  YOU MAY CALL UPON MESSAGES, WHICH WILL REMIND YOU ABOUT THE COMMANDS...
SEARCHING CONCEPTS, AND CODES USED....................PLEASE TYPE THE MESSAGES
BELOW EXACTLY AS LISTED AND PRESS THE ENTER KEY.
.....HELP-AUTHOR                HELP-FBR                    HELP-STOPLIST........
.....HELP-AUTHOR-TITLE..... ...HELP-OHI...................HELP-SUBJECT.........
HELP-BROWSE...................HELP-OHM....................HELP-TITLE............
HELP-CALL-NUMBER.............HELP-PERIODICALS...........HELP-TITLE-CHANGE....
HELP-CORPORATE-AUTHOR........HELP-PERIODICALS-CURRENT...HELP1................
```

Figure 1-2. Example of on-line help from the study on usability of an on-line cataloguing system (reprinted from Smith and Janosky © 1985 IEEE).

on-line help (see Figure 1-2), and a stop list (a list of words that cannot be included when searching by the title of a document). The subjects were required to find the following information.

1. What are the titles of the books in this catalogue written by Thomas S. Eliot?

2. What is the call-number for the book *Studies in the Design of*

Mass Transit by Giffin?

3. Find all books on the subject of television, cable.

4. In what library can you find the journal article:

   Swets, J.A., "The Relative Operating Characteristic Curve," *Science*, 1973, *182*, 990-1000.

5. What is the call-number for *How It Was*?

To determine any errors and the reasons for such errors, the subjects were told to think out loud as they performed the searches. This method of recording the subjects' verbalizations of mental processes is called the verbal protocol method and is used often in experiments in which people are required to solve problems or make decisions. All interactions with the computer were stored in a file on the computer.

The off-line help which was provided to the users, shown in Figures 1-1 and 1-2, looks as though it would be helpful. The information is nicely divided into areas on the document and proceduralized into three steps for performing the tasks. The steps are highlighted and, thus, differentiated from the rest of the document to make them stand out. Examples are provided for each of the steps. Important tips are provided at the bottom of the page. For the on-line help, some assistance is provided to remind the user of all the commands and how further help can be found. On the surface, it appears the system designers were concerned about the users and provided some means of assistance to them.

If you closely examine the help provided, however, you can begin to see

how problems might ensue. For the on-line help, the instructions say to type the messages exactly as listed. But what does this mean? Each of the listings has dots following it. Are these to be included? The HELP-AUTHOR and HELP-AU-THOR-TITLE commands are the only ones which have five dots in front of them. Are these five dots to be included, or are these dots merely to set these commands off in some way? For the off-line help, the users clearly are told the steps but are not provided with the meaning of the steps. What do TBL and DSL represent? Why do these steps have to be performed? This document is intended to provide people with a sequence of steps but not any understanding of the steps.

The subjects in the experiment had difficulty performing the five searches. Table 1-3 contains the number of errors and the average times for the 30 subjects across the five searches. The author reports that some of the subjects took as long as 60 minutes to complete some of the individual searches.

Why did the subjects in the experiment have such difficulty with these searches? The computer commands recorded in the file and the protocols can provide information about the difficulties and ways in which the system can be improved. First, consider searching for the T. S. Eliot books. Twenty-four of the subjects tried to use the on-line help before starting, and 15 of them made errors. Four entered HELP-AUTHOR-TITLE because they did not know whether terms like author or title referred to information already known or information desired. Four entered HELP-ELIOT because they did not know whether the word AUTHOR was one that should have been typed ex-

TABLE 1-3

Average times and success rate (the proportion of subjects completing the task) for the five subjects in the on-line library experiment

Search	Success Rate	Time(min.)
1. T S Eliot	0.58	17.1
2. Call-number for Giffin book	0.24	13.6
3. Television, cable books	0.44	13.3
4. Library for Swets article	0.00	16.2
5. Call-number for How It Was	0.00	5.0

actly or should have been substituted with the name of the author. Four others failed to include the hyphen in the command.

Other errors occurred because of misunderstandings about how the system was to be used. A common error was to enter the author's name in the wrong order (T S Eliot was entered instead of Eliot T S). Another common error occurred while trying to find all the screens for the Eliot search. The books filled up 23 screens, each of which had to be accessed. A severe limitation with computer displays is that they typically can have only 24 lines of information. To access the screens, the subjects typed PG1 to get the first screen, PG2 for the second screen, and PG3 for the third screen. Twenty more screens had to be accessed. What should be entered for the fourth screen and succeeding screens? Think about this for a minute or two.

The obvious choice would be to enter PG4, PG5, and so on for the next screens. If you entered this then you would get an error and the computer would tell you INVALID PAGE OR LINE NO. If you received this error you would probably assume that no more pages were available and you would give up. We already know, however, that 20 more pages on T S Eliot are available. The error message is misleading. Having this sequence of steps and then not allowing PG4 is like walking up three steps and then the designer has made the fourth step just slightly higher. No matter how many times you use those steps, many times you will trip over them. The designer of a house or building would not want to do this deliberately, yet the designer of this software has done something similar.

If PG4 does not work, then some users may hypothesize that hitting the RETURN key would move to the next page. Or perhaps hitting a down arrow key would perform the needed operation. Some computer keyboards have function keys which say "page up" or "page down." None of these will work.

Have you given up? The correct answer is PG+ for the fourth and succeeding pages. Can you think of any reason for using this command? It may save one line of programming code, so a couple minutes of programming were saved. But think about the amount of time that this error consumes. If you think of all the users making this mistake and total the time for the mistake, the loss in productivity becomes quite large and the programming time needed to fix this error becomes inconsequential. Program designers have to think about the consequences of user errors also. Many people would think that only three screens existed for the Eliot query. This may seem unimportant because what could be the possible consequences? One consequence would be that more than 80% of the books by T. S. Eliot are in the library but unknown to the library patrons. This may not be a life-threatening problem or have a significant effect on the national economy, but if similar mistakes were made for nuclear power plants or industrial databases, then the effects of these errors would be much worse.

Other errors were made by the users. For one of the queries, no one got it correct. By now, you probably have gotten the idea that the computer interface must be designed carefully so that the user is not tripped up along the way.

COST/BENEFIT ANALYSIS

The anecdotal evidence of the previous illustration indicates there are problems in usability. Why fix the problems? Do the potential benefits outweigh the costs? Why not let the users make some mistakes? In other words, it may cost too much to fix the problems. The realities of the workplace and the marketplace, developing software tools and marketing products, may not allow the time and money needed for usability improvements. Although there has been much emphasis in recent years on improving quality in products, arguments against increasing the quality of software products are heard over and over again and are too often accepted by software developers and managers. A method for analyzing the costs and benefits of usability is needed.

A cursory analysis of the preceding illustration would indicate that a better design for the library system would result in many tangible benefits. First, training costs could be reduced. We would assume that the librarians operating the system would have to go through fairly extensive training in order to learn how to operate the library system. In making it easier to use, the training time and costs for librarians could be reduced. Second, for a well designed system, the librarians would spend lesser amounts of time answering questions from the users than if the system was poorly designed. This may mean that a staff size could be reduced or the librarians could concentrate on other useful tasks. Third, we would expect that the users would require less time in order to operate the system. This decrease in time would be a function of not having to read and reread the instructions and faster recovery from errors. Relatively large universities have potential user bases of up to 50,000 people. Any decrease in time to use the system would have a potentially large effect on overall productivity of the users. Finally, a less tangible effect would be the willingness of people to use the system and the library. Without this willingness, any kind of needed library research may not occur. The potential benefits are large.

The costs of incorporating these improvements would be in added development time and increased costs due to personnel. For the added development times, we would expect that the number of

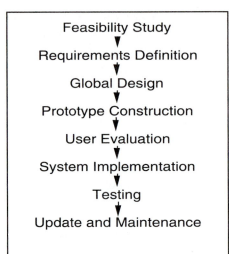

Feasibility Study
▼
Requirements Definition
▼
Global Design
▼
Prototype Construction
▼
User Evaluation
▼
System Implementation
▼
Testing
▼
Update and Maintenance

Figure 1-3. The eight stages in the computer system design development cycle without incorporating human factors (Mantei and Teory, 1988). (Copyright 1988, Association for Computing Machinery. Reprinted by permission.)

lines of code would have to be increased in order to make the interface simpler. A possibility is that the developers may want to perform some studies and tests on the usability of the system. These tests would result in further changes. Experts may have to be added to the staff, or consultancy fees may have to be paid to consultants to evaluate the software. In other words, the whole design process may have to be changed in order to make the system more usable. These changes in the life cycle of the product potentially can be expensive. Will the benefits outweigh the costs?

Stages in the Design Process

Mantei and Teory (1988) have developed a cost/benefit analysis for incorporating human factors issues in the software life cycle. Based upon previous work, they indicated that the typical development

stages in a prototyping life cycle included the eight stages shown in Figure 1-3. The first stage is the feasibility study to determine whether any other products are available on the market for performing the task and how feasible it is to develop the software if no existing products are available. During the updates, new feasibility studies may be performed as the functionality of the program is changed or increased. Second, a requirements definition is performed. In this stage, the functionality and the kinds of tasks to be performed by the software are determined. With feedback from the users, and further updates, the requirements may change over the life of the product. Third, the global design is specified by decomposing the tasks into modules. In addition, an overall concept for the interface will be specified. Fourth, a prototype, which is a preliminary version of the proposed software, is built quickly. Several rapid prototyping tools have been developed in recent years to facilitate this stage. Not all the functionality is included in the prototype. Fifth, users interact with the prototype and provide informal comments to the designers in the user evaluation stage. If the comments are extensive, and the users dislike the prototype, a new requirements definition may be required. Sixth, the full system is implemented. Seventh, testing of the full system occurs. Any errors in the design are corrected and the programmers must ensure that there are no dead ends in the program. More system implementation may be required. Finally, some errors may be missed in the earlier stages and corrections have to be implemented in the update and maintenance stage. Improvements may be implemented in later updates.

Any development costs that occur

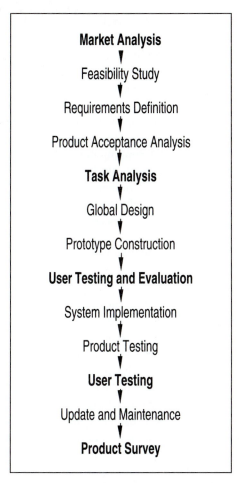

Figure 1-4. Additional stages, needed from that observed in Figure 1-3, to incorporate human factors in design (Mantei and Teory, 1988). (Copyright 1988, Association for Computing Machinery. Reprinted by permission.)

during these eight stages can be considered typical for the life cycle of a software product. If the software is to have a human-factored design, then this life cycle will have to change, and these changes will reflect additional costs for improved usability. Mantei and Teory (1988) argue that five more stages are needed (see Figure 1-4). Preceding the feasibility stage is a market analysis. This analysis focuses

more on the current users, called the focus group, to determine their needs and perceptions of the present method of performing the task. In this kind of study, users may be asked to perform several tasks using their current system. These sessions would be videotaped, comments elicited, and the results analyzed.

Second, a quick mock-up of the system will be analyzed in the product acceptance analysis stage. Users, possibly the same focus group as in the previous stage, will be shown the mock-up. Comments will be elicited either informally or formally through surveys and questionnaires. Chapter 4 includes some methods for designing questionnaires and performing survey studies such as these.

Third, a task analysis is performed. This stage determines how a person thinks about the tasks to be performed and whether or not the software design will be compatible with that thinking. In some cases, the user may form a mental model of the task (see Chapter 7). Many of the techniques discussed in Section III of this book can be utilized. More formal techniques for task analysis are discussed in Section IV.

Fourth, users are tested on the prototype in the user testing and evaluation stage. Projected users will perform a cross-section of tasks for the intended system. The experimental techniques outlined in Chapters 4 and 5 can be used to run the experiment. The experimenter should avoid the hazards discussed in Chapter 6. User testing, following the system implementation and product testing, is similar; the difference is that this later stage tests users on a more complete version of the software than the prototype.

Finally, the last human factors stage is the product survey. Once the product is on the market, users are surveyed to determine what they like and dislike. The surveys and questionnaires, discussed in Chapter 4, will also be used in this stage except, this time, they are used on the final product.

Usability Analysis Methods

To determine the cost of human factors usability studies, the analyst must determine the cost of each of these six new stages. Mantei and Teory (1988) indicate that the tangible costs of these stages can be decomposed into the following costs: the cost of running the focus groups, building product mock-ups, initially designing a prototype, making a prototyping design change, purchasing the prototyping software, running the user studies, creating a user study environment (laboratory), and conducting the user survey. These costs will vary depending on the available personnel and equipment. For example, if the equipment and personnel are in place to perform usability research, then the cost will be less. If not in place, the cost will be higher.

Mantei and Teory (1988) indicate that there are three potential benefits for performing the usability studies: reductions in user learning time, in user errors, and in the cost of maintaining the system. The reduction in learning time can be calculated by the following equation:

$$\text{savings/year} = (\text{turnover}) \times (\text{training time saved}) \times (\text{wages}) \quad (1.1)$$

The turnover is important because this is the number of new people who must be trained. The training time saved and the wages should be obvious. Many times the training time saved will have to be approximated. As an example for the library system, let's say that a better system can save each student about 30 minutes in training time. At a large university, the entering freshman class will be about 5000 students, and these are all potential users. Determining the wages of students is not obvious, but let us estimate that the students could be spending this time at a part-time job which pays $10/hour. The potential savings are as follows:

$$\text{savings/year} = (5000) \times (.5) \times (\$10)$$
$$= \$25,000 \quad (1.2)$$

We also need to estimate the training times for the librarians which would be more extensive. Let's say that the turnover for librarians would be about 10 a year. Each librarian would have to go through a two-week training program to learn the system inside and out. With a more usable system, let's say that that training program can be reduced by half. Each librarian earns $500 a week. So, with 10 employees saving a week each, the potential savings per year is $5,000.

To estimate the cost of errors, the errors per year and then the costs per year are estimated. Errors per year can be estimated from:

$$\text{errors/year} = (\text{no. of employees}) \times (\text{P[error]}) \times (\text{scenarios/hour}) \times (\text{hours/year}) \quad (1.3)$$

The P[error] can be estimated or determined empirically. The P[error] was calculated in the Smith and Janosky (1985) study at 71%. This is probably high, because the searches were chosen to be difficult in the study. We will place the error, instead, at a very conservative 10%, which should not seem unreasonable based upon use of a similar system. A scenario, in this case, would be a search through the database. The study showed that each search required an overall average of 13 minutes. This means that about 4.6 searches could occur in an hour. We would expect that in a typical 12 hour library day, 7 days a week, 4 people would be using the system. If we assume, discounting holidays and break times, that the system would be used 320 days out of the year, then the number of hours of use in the year would be approximately 3840 hours. The errors per year can now be calculated as follows:

$$\text{errors/year} = (4) \times (.1) \times (4.6) \times (3840)$$
$$= 7065.6 \quad (1.4)$$

The cost/year can be estimated as follows:

$$\text{cost/year} = (\text{errors/year}) \times (\text{hours/error correction}) \times (\text{wages/hour}) \quad (1.5)$$

The errors/year were estimated above. The hours per error correction can be determined from the data. Let's assume that each error requires 10 minutes to fix. We will use the same wage scale as previously. The cost becomes

$$\text{cost/year} = (7065.6) \times (.167) \times (\$10)$$
$$= \$11,799.60 \quad (1.6)$$

The cost savings in maintenance of the system is more difficult to calculate. Once a version of the software is released, changing it becomes more costly than if

these kinds of changes were caught at the beginning. As an estimate, we will use the costs calculated by Mantei and Teory (1988). The formula for early changes, if made before implementation, would be

$$\text{early cost} = (\text{hours/change}) \times (\text{no. changes}) \times (\text{wages/hour}) \quad (1.7)$$

Assuming 25 changes at 8 hours per change for programmers earning $40 an hour, the early cost is calculated as follows:

$$\text{early cost} = (8) \times (25) \times (\$40)$$
$$= \$8,000 \quad (1.8)$$

Assuming that a later change will take four times as long, the design change savings (DCS) is calculated as follows:

$$\text{DCS} = (\text{late cost}) - (\text{early cost})$$
$$= 4 \times (\text{early cost}) - (\text{early cost})$$
$$= 4 \times \$8,000 - \$8,000$$
$$= \$24,000 \quad (1.9)$$

Remember that the total savings can be calculated by the following sum:

$$\text{total savings} = \text{reduction in learning time} + \text{user errors} + \text{maintenance costs} \quad (1.10)$$

Using the particular measures for these three items from the library example above, the total savings are summed as follows:

$$\text{total savings} = \text{savings/year} + \text{cost/year of errors} + \text{design change savings} \quad (1.11)$$

Finally, the calculated dollar amounts can be inserted as follows:

total savings = ($25,000 + $5,000)
$$+ \$11{,}799.60 + \$24{,}000$$
$$= \$65{,}799.60 \qquad (1.12)$$

Perhaps this is a conservative cost estimate. Putting a price on user frustrations and nonuse of the system are intangible costs which cannot be calculated easily. Mantei and Teory (1988), using a similar analysis, conclude that usability studies are cost-effective for medium-sized or large projects.

The Mantei and Teory (1988) analysis was concerned mostly with developing software in-house for use by employees within a company. If a company is in the business of selling software, then the concerns become somewhat different. The question becomes one of whether or not the new product will sell better than an existing product that the company may already have on the market. This is emphasized in a study by Karat (1991). The analysis is fairly simple. Assume that the existing software sells 5000 copies a year. If the prediction is that the new product will sell 25% more copies than the existing software because of enhanced usability, and the cost of the software is $200, then the increased revenue would be as follows:

Revenue = software cost x percent
increased x sales of old units
$$= \$200 \text{ x } .25 \text{ x } 5{,}000$$
$$= \$200{,}000 \qquad (1.13)$$

In many cases, predicting the percent increase could be difficult because of other factors involved, such as compatibility with existing hardware and market penetration to date. The above equation provides, however, an idea for how much

money could be spent on usability and the potential return. Spending contingencies could be developed from the preceding equation.

Another tangible benefit from usability studies is to make transference between software products easy (Karat, 1991). If a new product is being introduced, and we know that users can already use an existing product, then decreases in training time would be achieved if the new product was similar to the old product so that it did not have to be learned anew. Karat has shown that the cost benefits of designing products in this way can be extensive.

Business Case Data

Karat (1992) has recently completed three business case study analyses of the cost and benefits of usability analyses for internal and external products. For the first study, Karat reports that the usability analysis involved task analysis, screen design, three iterations of usability tests, results reporting, and recommendations for redesign. This whole process required seven months, and, by including all business-related expenses in the costs, the usability analysis was determined to be $20,700. If the usability engineering had not been performed on the product, then the first design iteration (out of three) would have been incorporated in the final project. To determine the productivity increase due to the human-factored design, productivity using the first iterative design could be compared to productivity using the third and final design. The gains due to increased productivity were estimated to be worth $41,700 for a 1:2 cost-benefit ratio. This is a conservative estimate because, as pointed out by Karat, other benefits could accrue due to users becoming more productive after increased use, reductions in user training, reductions in errors, and reduced maintenance costs, all of which were not included in the analysis.

The second case study performed by Karat (1992) was also for an internal computer project. This project involved many of the same usability analyses as the preceding project but was a larger project requiring 21 months for completion. The costs for completing this study were about $68,000. Benefits were again determined by how much more productive the users were when comparing the first iteration of the product to the final human-factored product after the analysis. In the first year of use, the increased productivity resulted in a savings of $68 million, resulting in a 1:100 cost-benefit ratio.

The final case study examined by Karat (1992) was based on data reported in the literature. A large copy machine company was losing market share because their products were judged by the customers to be unreliable and difficult to use. Many of the reliability problems were, instead, problems of usability. In other words, the customer would think that a feature had broken when in fact it was being used incorrectly. Increased costs occurred due to the unnecessary service calls. Whereas usability studies had been performed on these earlier copiers, they were ignored until the loss of market share made the management decide that usability was important. The products then started to be designed taking into account the recommendations of the usability analyses, and over three years, the market share increased. Over this time period, the

increase in revenues amounted to about one billion dollars. Karat estimated that the cost of performing the usability studies was about $2 million which resulted in a cost-benefit ratio of 1:500.

These studies show the importance of usability studies in computer product design. Not only can the studies save money, but the survival of a company's product line may be dependent on ease of use.

SUMMARY

The discussion in this chapter has outlined some of the problems that occur when using computer systems. The data on the time to generate CAI lessons indicated that large time savings have been achieved when the interface and interaction are designed effectively. The data on the cost/ benefits of performing usability studies indicate that clear cost savings have been achieved through good interface design. The rest of this book provides the approaches, models, and theories for improving the human-computer interaction.

The following chapters show how the interface can be, should be, and has been designed to be easy to use. These chapters are based upon four approaches to human-computer interaction. In the first part of this book, the principles of the four approaches will be explained. After this, specific applications of these approaches will be provided.

QUESTIONS

1. Think of some examples of computer interaction tasks which have been poorly designed. Explain why you believe they are poorly designed, some

of the errors that one typically makes when performing these tasks, and possible ways to fix the design.

2. In the example of the on-line library system, how would you phrase the error message of PG4 so that it is not misleading? How would the computer differentiate between this kind of error and an error that is really an invalid page number?

3. For each of the errors that occurred for the library system, indicate how you would design the system so that people would not make these kinds of errors.

4. From the cost/benefit studies, what are the three potential benefits for performing usability studies? To answer this question, think back to the example about cost savings for the library systems, and the sources for those savings.

5. Assume that the P[error] in equation 1.3 is either .25 or .01. All other values in the library example are the same as reported. Perform the calculations again to determine the total savings (equation 1.12) with the new values for the P[error]. Discuss the cost/benefits of systems with these error rates.

6. Assume that a library has a turnover rate for librarians of only 2 librarians per year. All other values are the same as reported for the example. Calculate a new value for total savings (equation 1.12) based on this turnover rate.

7. According to this chapter, the following stages in product development would occur for human-factored products:

   1. Market analysis
   2. Feasibility study
   3. Requirements definition
   4. Product acceptance analysis
   5 Task analysis
   6. Global design
   7. Prototype construction
   8. User testing and evaluation
   9. System implementation
   10. Product testing
   11. User testing
   12. Update and maintenance
   13. Product survey

   a. Which of the stages listed were added to the normal development cycle in order to "human factor" the product?

   b. If the cost of performing the normal development cycle stages was $30,000, the cost of performing the additional human factors stages was $20,000, and the benefit due to the increased usability of the product was $120,000, what is the cost/benefit ratio for including the human factors in the design?

CHAPTER 2

INTERFACE WIDGETS

INTRODUCTION

This textbook is not meant to teach the principles of computer programming as applied to interface design. Instead, the purpose is to present the conceptual approaches, experimental methodology, theories, and models needed to design good interfaces. To facilitate understanding of the latter parts of this book, some basic aspects of computer interface programming will be presented, such as the structure of a program and the building blocks of an interface display.

In the early days of computer use, programming the interface was of no concern, because there was no interface. The user did not interact directly with the computer. Instead, each line of computer code would be written on an IBM card (remember "Do not fold, spindle or mutilate"?) using a card punch machine, and the stack of cards would be given to a computer operator. The cards would go through a card reader to be entered into computer memory. Of course, with this method, feedback was far from immediate. To receive the feedback, you or the computer operator would fetch the results of your program, which had been printed on a line printer. In many cases, the output from the program would not be seen until one or two days later; if you were lucky, you had access to a card reader and a line printer so that the turnaround time was faster. Any stupid errors could be catastrophic due to the long turnaround time. Applications that we now take for granted, such as word

processors or spreadsheets, made no sense in this kind of computer environment. Pity the person who, while carrying the cards, dropped them so that they all got out of order. For a large program, placing them back in order again was an arduous task.

The interface was not with the computer, but with the computer operator who handled the cards. These people were knowledgeable and willing to try to solve most problems. This was especially helpful since frequently you did not know enough to ask a specific question.

Large advances in usability occurred when the card punch machines were removed and the users were allowed to communicate directly with the computer through a terminal, sometimes referred to as a CRT (cathode ray tube) or, in the more general case, as a VDT (visual display terminal). This system still had many carryovers from the old card system. Using a VDT, each line on the screen corresponded to a card. The set of cards was referred to as a file which was stored on some kind of computer storage device. The computer could now understand a few simple commands which could be entered on a line of the VDT. Output was no longer sent only to a line printer, but was now sent to the computer screen or to a file which could be scrolled down the screen as the user saw fit.

Although this was certainly an advance over the computer cards, this method caused problems in comprehension. A computer program became an abstract entity which could no longer be seen or touched. No longer was a line of computer code a tangible object such as a physical card with holes punched in it. Now it was just electrons exciting the phosphor on the screen which, when scrolled off the screen, possibly no longer existed. With cards, the order of the statements in the program could be changed by physically removing a card from the stack and placing it in front of another card. With the VDT, moving the lines of code around was no longer a physical action on a tangible object; instead, you had to give a command to a line editor which would cause something to happen in your program. Many times, you were not quite sure whether the command had the intended effect. With a stack of cards, you could store them in some place in your office, find them when needed, and use them over again. If you no longer needed the card stack, you could just throw them in the wastepaper basket. If you decided that you threw away the wrong cards, you could retrieve them easily. With the VDT, you had to understand the abstract concept of a computer file, which contained the lines of code and was stored in an unseen storage device. You had to have some method of listing all the files that you had stored. You had to have some method of throwing away a file and making sure that you threw away the correct one. Deleting files could be a serious problem that was too easy to execute; recovering from mistakes was now very difficult. All this required specific understanding of the intricacies of the computer system. With the removal of keypunch cards and computer personnel, interacting with the computer became more removed from the familiar common place physical world.

With the VDT, the computer would provide some kind of feedback on incorrect actions. This feedback was not nearly as detailed or flexible as that received from the computer operators of the past method. More often, no method for providing help was offered to the user at all.

Computer users were so happy with the faster turnaround time, they did not notice what they were losing by using the VDTs. When interacting with a computer no longer used tangible objects, such as cards, but occurred through abstract concepts, such as commands, the user could not be sure exactly where the program was or how to manipulate the objects in the program. The computer now used an interface to communicate with the user, but oddly this interface had not changed much from the past ones; the human interpreters were just removed. Users could only communicate through text, numbers, and commands.

Obviously, one aspect missing from these command-based interfaces was the feeling that you, as a computer user, were interacting with tangible objects which could be manipulated physically. After all the problems incurred with command-based interfaces, some software developers started to realize that user comprehension would possibly be enhanced if the objects manipulated by the user looked and acted more like physical ones. To realize these concepts, computer companies began to manufacture bit-mapped displays so that each pixel on the VDT could be controlled. Computer input and output were no longer restricted to the usual 80 columns and 24 rows of 5x7 matrices of dots which were used for the characters. With the bit-mapped displays, the dots could be used for characters or they could be used for graphics. Objects could now be represented on the screen to appear in a physical form to be manipulated by the user.

Whereas the characters were the building blocks of the early VDT interfaces, computer programmers could now think in terms of other kinds of building blocks for interfaces besides just characters. Thus, the concept of a widget was developed. A widget is a building block for an interface, and it can correspond in appearance to some sort of object which can be manipulated. An example of a widget is the box which may appear on your screen asking you if you really wanted to delete the file you specified. A widget can also be the box of menu items which appears on the screen or the menubar at the top of the screen. Most modern interfaces are composed of these widgets. So, in many ways, computer interaction has come full circle. In the earliest days, the users were manipulating the physical objects of the computer cards. Now, through the interface design, users manipulate graphical representations on the computer screen. Of course, the modern interfaces, composed of computer widgets, can perform many more tasks than could be performed through interaction with early computers. Understanding the widgets is a good beginning for understanding how to design modern interfaces. Beyond this chapter, much of the rest of the book discusses the theories and ideas for how to use the widgets effectively.

THE PROGRAMMING CONTEXT

Programming a user interface has many concepts in common with general programming. For the most part, when programming, the pathways through a program are set with little deviation. In programming a highly interactive interface, because the user initiates the path, a set pathway through the program cannot always be determined a priori by the programmer, and, thus, the pathway choices for the user should not be limited by characteristics of the program. Providing the user with the feeling of choice or freedom in using the interface is an important aspect of a good interface design. If you have programmed in languages such as FORTRAN or C, you learned to program providing one pathway through the code. This kind of thinking must be changed when programming interfaces.

Only recently have specific functions and widgets for interface design been developed. One of the most important milestones in interface programming has been the development of the X Window functions (see Jones, 1988, for more information on X Window functions). Development of these functions represented a cooperation between the major computer companies who were manufacturing large workstations. Workstations, usually having large bit-mapped display screens of high resolution, represented a challenge for interface designers because of the flexibility allowed by the large screen and the graphics capability of the bit-mapped displays. Trying to avoid the mistakes of the past, especially the compatibility problem for the machines built by different vendors, the computer companies combined resources and agreed upon a standard set of functions which could be used for interface design on any of the machines. Since the X Window functions were placed in the public domain, wide availability of the functions was ensured and the interface designer had only to pay for the distribution media (the disk or tape containing the functions and any documentation needed).

The X Window functions are low-level functions written in the C programming language that can be called by other functions. Only the very serious interface designer would program directly with X Windows. Built on top of the X Window functions are higher-level functions such as the widgets; one of the most widely used widget sets is Motif. Other widget sets are also available. Most interface designers would use the widget set exclusively, instead of the X Window functions, when programming.

Other widget sets are also available. Digital Equipment Corporation (DEC) used the X Window functions to develop their own look and feel for interface design called DECWindows. These contain a general widget set. One of the most popular widget sets, Motif, was developed by the Open Software Foundation, which includes many of the largest computer companies, including IBM, DEC, and Hewlett Packard (HP). Motif is also built on the X Window functions and, since the software is also in the public domain, is virtually free. For the Macintosh, programming in HyperCard can be accomplished in much the same way as using the X Window functions and widgets. For the IBM PC, Microsoft Windows contains a widget set with many of the same characteristics as the X Windows widget set, although not as powerful. In UNIX, a set of functions called Curses was developed at a fairly early date, and this set of functions contains some of the same characteristics as these other widget sets.

Many of these widget sets resemble each other and require similar programming structures. The exception is the Apple Macintosh HyperCard programming. In this case, the interface designer does not really write a program, with lines of code, but rather enters the HyperCard environment where the system can prompt the designer for setting up the interface. This kind of environment is easy to program so you can get an interface running quickly, but the ease of use trades off with flexibility in what can be accomplished. Instead of discussing these specialized environments, we will discuss the more typical and more generalizable interface programming environment, such as X Windows, which is just a part of the normal programming environment. In such a generalized situation, a typical program would have the following structure:

- Providing header information

- Initializing the program

- Creating the widgets

- Realizing the display

- Building an infinite loop with callback routines

Each of these parts of the program will be explained in more detail.

Providing Header Information

In a normal program, specialized functions from general libraries will be included so that the programmer does not have to program these functions each time they are used. When programming with widgets, the widgets will be located in these special libraries of functions and subprograms. The programmer must indicate in the program at the beginning that these widgets from a specialized library will be included. In addition, in an interface design program using X Windows, all the X Window libraries must be included. The form for calling these libraries is specific to the particular application.

Initializing the Program

Initializing the program is specific to the particular application program also. Most interface functions require that the first executable statements in the program be used to initialize the computer for using the functions. In the X Windows environment, this initialization statement performs many tasks. The interface functions must obtain information from the computer about the kind of machine it is, the size of the screen, and other information about how to store the program information in memory.

Creating the Widgets

Each widget in the widget set will have its own name. A widget is usually a function which must be called by the program. In the function call, several parameters can be included. If unspecified by the calling program, the parameters will revert to default values. The programmer has some control over these widgets through specification of the parameters. As an example, a typical widget may have parameters for size, location on the screen, background color or pattern, foreground color or pattern, name of callback function, and the nesting of the widgets which is referred to as a parent-child relationship. Not all of these functions may be present in all systems or for all widgets; these are just examples.

The concept of parent-child relationship is very important for interface programming and other kinds of object-oriented programming. These kinds of relationships are especially important for programming ease with building block units such as widgets; by using them, much programming code can be eliminated. In a parent-child relationship, the child widget is defined only in the context of the parent widget. Let's say that we have a widget which displays information about the file directory. This could be just a square widget that allows the directory of files to be scrolled. A child widget, in this case a scroll bar, could be placed in a vertical orientation on the right side of the display widget. The coordinates of the child scroll bar widget would be defined only in the context of the parent display widget. This saves programming code because if the display widget is moved, then the child scroll bar widget also moves automatically; its coordinates do not have to be specified again because its frame of reference of the parent widget has not changed. If a parent-child relationship did not exist, then the coordinates of both the parent and the child would have to be specified. With the parent-child relationship, only one of them has to be specified. In addition, a child widget can only be displayed if the parent is already or simultaneously displayed; if a parent is removed from the screen then the child widget is also removed automatically from the screen; and, in most cases, the child widget would have to be placed in the window of the parent widget. These are only some of the useful functions of the parent-child relationship.

Another important aspect of this part of interface programming is the specification of the callback routine for a particular widget. The widgets that you create will be waiting for certain events to occur. As an example, for the text widget, it will wait for the user to type on the keyboard so that text can be entered in the widget. Other events, with other peripheral devices, will be ignored by the text widget. The callback routine specifies what to do when each of these events occur. Some widgets may not be waiting for any events, such as the display widget, and some may be waiting for multiple events. The callback routines provide the interface programmer with much flexibility in how the program responds to user interaction events.

When the widgets are being created, they are not displayed on the screen. In fact, the part of the program that the user will interact with has not even begun yet. This kind of programming style has its advantages. The programmer should try to perform everything that can be done initially outside the loop of the main program. The consequence of failing to perform these setup activities outside of the main loop is that the user may have to wait unnecessarily for the system to respond. Creating widgets and other setup activities take time and computer resources. When interacting with the interface, the program should be designed so that it runs as fast as possible so that the user receives almost immediate feedback for his or her actions. By taking the time at the beginning of the program for creating the widgets, the loop where the interactions occur can happen much faster.

Realizing the Display

As mentioned previously, creating the widgets causes nothing to appear on the screen. Before any widgets appear, the display must be realized. This has the effect of displaying the initial information at the beginning of the interactive display and for mapping the rest of the widgets. Many of the widgets will only appear through the callback routines after the appropriate events occur. Realizing the display could be time-consuming. Remember, it is better to consume this time before the interaction starts instead of delaying the feedback once the user is interacting with the computer system.

Building an Infinite Loop with Callback Routines

In normal programming, placing the program in an infinite loop is to be avoided. The program should have some specific starting point, and, once it carries out all its functions, it should stop. In interface programming, though, the program intentionally is placed in an infinite loop. The program itself does not determine when the interaction is over. This determination is left to the user: some event must be specified by the user to terminate the program. In the meantime, the interactive program is polling and buffering the user events and performing the appropriate callback routines. Polling occurs when the program checks all the input devices to determine if an event has occurred.

An event is anything that the user does. An event could be hitting a particular key, or just any key, on the keyboard. It could be moving the mouse so that the cursor on the screen is inside some widget. An event might be pressing a mouse button without releasing it. A separate event could be releasing a button on the mouse. If other input devices are available, then the events could be dependent on these devices.

In the loop, the program will wait for these events and buffer (record in computer memory) the event and the widget in which it occurred. If the widget has a callback routine and the event has been specified, then the program will carry out the code from that part of the callback routine. As an example, the purpose of an event may be to display another widget on the screen. If the event occurs, and the callback routine correctly specifies the needed function, then the widget will be displayed on the screen.

One of the most difficult parts of programming an interface is for the programmer to "give up" control of the program to the user. Some programmers would like to have absolute control over the program and specify only certain pathways that the program can go. The trick is to let the user have control, and to anticipate all the possible interactions so that the user is not placed in a situation that cannot be recovered from. Anticipating all these occurrences, especially for complicated programs, can be very difficult. Good programmers are able to anticipate, and let the user exercise the freedom of choices instead of the programmer.

TYPES OF WIDGETS

Different interface programming packages may have different widget sets. A surprising number of them contain similar kinds of widgets, so that one can think of a generic widget set which is applicable to most interfaces. The following widgets have been chosen as being representative of that generic class. With this set, almost any kind of interface programming can be

performed. Before examining some of these widgets, however, some of the basic concepts and terminology for interface design should be reviewed.

Defining Some General Concepts

Starting with the VDT, the total display area on the terminal is often referred to as the screen. Some of the early VDTs had screens in which only characters could be displayed, and those characters had to appear in an 80 column by 24 line matrix. These kinds of VDTs will not be considered in the rest of the book, because of the inflexibility of the display and the difficulty in designing good, usable interfaces. Bitmapped displays, in which each dot, or pixel, on the screen can be controlled, provide the flexibility needed for good interface designs. A typical bitmapped display will have a resolution of 256 x 256 pixels. A workstation display, which allows more flexibility and better interfaces, typically has a resolution of about 1000 x 1000 pixels.

The screen can be divided into windows. Most modern interfaces allow several windows to be displayed at one time. As an example, on an Apple Macintosh, computer files can be stored in folders. When displaying a list of the folder contents, the contents of each of the folders would appear in a separate window (see Figure 2-1). Some of the more powerful workstations allow multiple processes to occur on a screen. As an example, the user may be performing word processing in one of the windows, and then decide that a spreadsheet is needed to perform a function needed for a particular piece of text. Instead of exiting the word processing and then starting the spreadsheet ap-

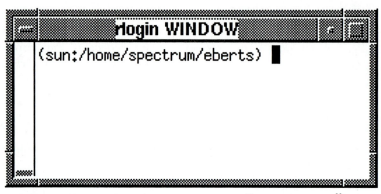

Figure 2-1. Each window usually has a border and a title ("rlogin WINDOW"). The small box in the upper right corner is used to make the window bigger; the small dot to the left of the box makes the window smaller when clicked. The dash (-) in the upper left corner is used to open up a menu with various functions such as lowering, raising, and closing the window. The window size can be changed by placing the mouse in the border, holding down the mouse button, and moving the mouse in the direction for the resize.

plication, if the workstation can perform multiple processes, the spreadsheet can be started from another window while keeping the word processing running (see Figure 2-2). This provides a great deal of flexibility to the user.

The window in which specialized functions can occur is the widget. The widget may look for certain events which can occur through the peripheral input devices. Most computer systems use two devices: the keyboard and a mouse. Most people computer users are familiar with a mouse. It fits in the hand and can be moved on the table top to position a cursor on the screen. Since the mouse is usually used to point to objects on the screen, such as a particular character, the cursor often appears as an arrow on the screen to signify this pointing function. If using the mouse for drawing, then the cursor often appears as a cross hairs or some other form needed for drawing. Often, the shape of the cursor will change depending on the application and what is being done. The cursor, when controlled by the mouse, is

sometimes called a sprite, to differentiate it from a cursor controlled by the keyboard in a word processing situation.

The mouse usually has one to three buttons on the top of it. Pressing and releasing a mouse button is called a mouse click. Some users have difficulty remembering the functionality of multiple buttons on the mouse because this functionality will often change with the context. Most interfaces will try to limit the specific functionality of different button clicks to simplify the interface for the user. More information about using the mouse can be found in Chapter 19.

The other common input device used in a computer system is the keyboard. The keyboard usually includes the alphanumeric characters. Many keyboards also include cursor control keys, designated by arrows, which can move a cursor on a screen. Some keyboards include a help button, page up and page down buttons, some kind of editing commands, a numeric keypad, and other general function keys.

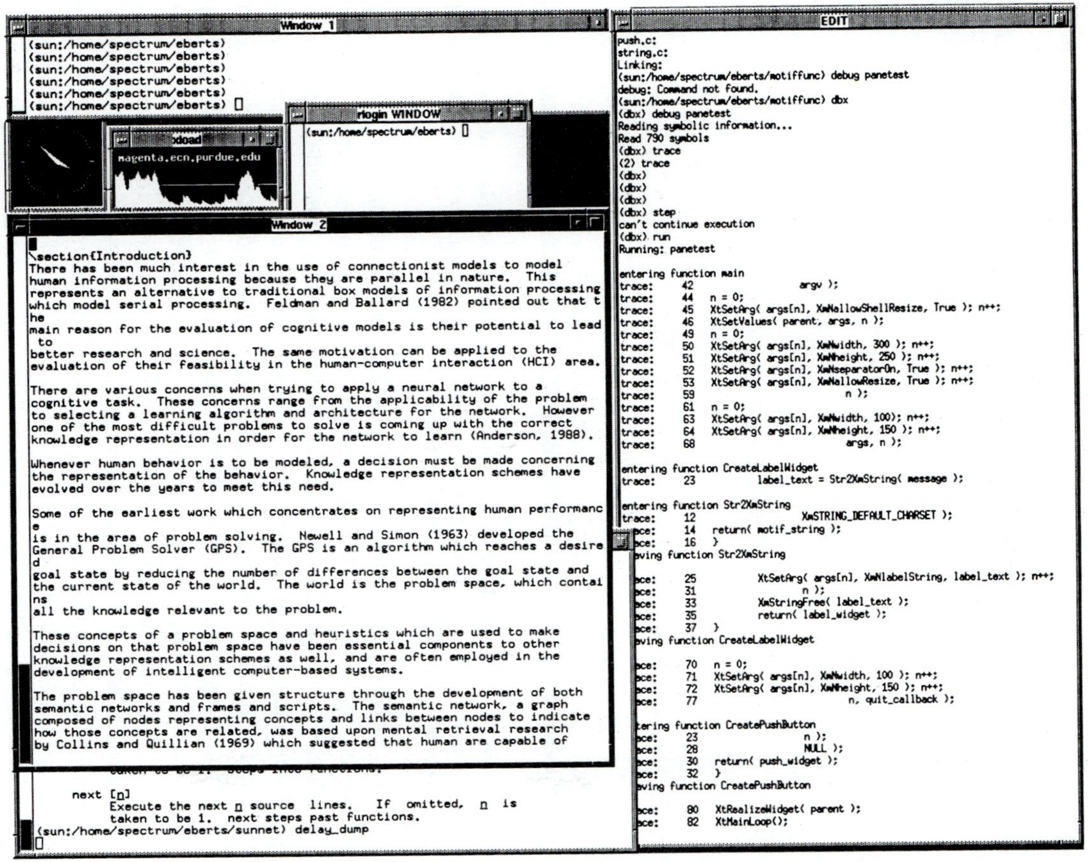

Figure 2-2.
Some workstations can perform multiple functions simultaneously in different windows. In this figure, word processing is occurring in the left window and a computer program trace and debugging is running in the right window.

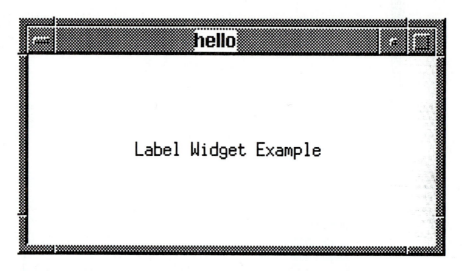

Figure 2-3. An example of a label widget. A label widget like this would usually be included as a child in some parent widget. In this way, it could provide a title for the parent widget but would accept no events if the cursor was in this widget.

Other input devices are available but are not as common. A touch screen, in which the user interacts with the computer through touching the screen, is becoming more popular. Additional peripheral devices, and a comparison of them, are discussed in Chapter 19.

In summary, events could be any of the following: typing a specific key, typing any key, moving the mouse cursor into or out of a window, pressing the mouse button, releasing the mouse button, and clicking on a mouse button. If an event occurs in a widget which the widget is not looking for, then that event will be ignored. The widgets are defined by what can occur in the window of the widget.

Label Widget

The label widget is probably one of the simplest widgets. It does nothing except provide a label for another widget, the parent widget. This kind of widget would

not expect to have any events associated with it; nothing would happen if a mouse button is clicked inside this label because a callback routine is not needed nor is it specified. It does provide a good example for how interface design can be based upon the widget building blocks in that even something as simple as a label would be a separate entity. Most of the widget sets have a label widget; Motif, Hyper-Card, DECWindows, and the X Toolkit all have the label widget. An example of a label widget appears in Figure 2-3.

Form Widget

A form widget does not really stand by itself but exists merely to contain other widgets. It makes optimal use of the parent-child relationships, which were discussed earlier. The form widget is set up to contain child widgets; child widgets could be placed at the top, bottom, left, or right of the form. As an example, labels could be placed at the top and bottom of the form widget. The parent-child relationships are used in that as the form widget moves, the child widgets also move; as the form widget is resized, the child widgets are also resized. Like the label widget, the form widget has no callback routine so that it is not waiting for events to occur in it. Other widgets could be attached to it, however, that would wait for events.

List Widget

The list widget is used to select an item from a list. The list of items will appear in a window. The user can select the appropriate item by moving the mouse and the mouse cursor; as the mouse cursor moves over the items, the current item is highlighted. A selection is made by clicking the mouse button. As an alternative on some systems, the item can be selected by hitting the up and down arrow keys on a keyboard; the highlighted item is selected by hitting the ENTER key. If the list contains more items than can fit in the window, then a scroll bar widget must appear on the side of the window (see the next section). As with all scroll bar widgets, the user can move the list up and down by clicking the arrow keys.

If the number of items is fairly small, then the list widget is appropriate. If too large, and thus too much time is needed for scrolling through the list, then the file selection widget or a variant of it may be useful (see the discussion of file selection widgets in the dialog widgets). Another alternative is a dialog widget in which the user types the name of the item instead of choosing it from a list. The list widget would be used most often for selecting a

file from the file directory. An example of a list widget appears in Figure 2-4.

Scroll Bar Widget

The scroll bar widget cannot really stand on its own but must be used in conjunction with other widgets to perform scrolling functions. In many cases, the main window of a widget will have too much information to appear in the limited window space. To access the other information, the text must be scrolled. The scroll bar widget has several parts to it (see the right part of Figure 2-4): an up arrow, a down arrow, a scroll box, and a moving elevator. Scrolling can be done in one of two ways: using the arrows or using the scroll bar. When the arrows are clicked by the mouse, then the text moves in the appropriate direction. If the button on the mouse remains in the down position while on an arrow, then the text will continue to scroll in that direction.

The other scrolling method involves the scroll box and the moving elevator. The scroll box area represents all the text. If the desired location of the text is halfway through the text, then the mouse button would be moved halfway down the scroll box, the mouse button pressed, and then the text will scroll to that position. When the text reaches that position, then the scrolling stops. Other locations can be reached by placing the mouse at the appropriate position in the scroll box.

The moving elevator represents the text moving to the location. If the moving elevator is 25% down the scroll box, then the user knows that the text displayed in the window has approximately 25% of the remaining text preceding the window and 75% after the window. In some widgets,

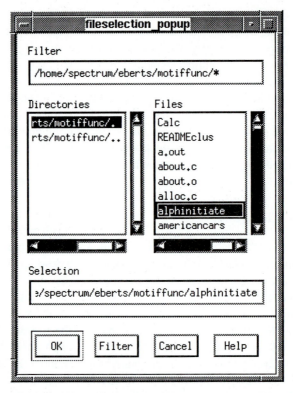

Figure 2-4. An example of two list widgets (the two widgets in the middle of the window) and corresponding scroll bar widgets to the right and at the bottom of the widget. In the list widget, the list appears from top to bottom in the window. The scroll bar widgets include two arrows, the rectangular elevator close to the bottom arrow, and the scrollbox rectangle which includes the arrows, the elevator, and the space in between. The size of the elevator gives a general indication of how big the displayed items are when compared to the rest of the items not displayed. Since the elevator for the right list widget is about a tenth of the scroll bar space, this means that about 10% of the items are displayed currently. The position of the elevator indicates the position of the displayed items from the list. Since the elevator is at the top, this means that about nine-tenths of the items precede those displayed. The up and down arrows can be clicked to move to the items preceding those displayed. The file name that is highlighted, alphinitiate, is the item that is currently selected and would be chosen if the OK button is clicked.

the elevator will change size depending on the percent of the text in the window. If a high percentage of the text is in the window, then the moving elevator will be large; if a small percentage, the elevator size will be small.

A problem with scrolling the text is to determine what is up and what is down. Does up mean that the text should move in an upward direction on the screen, or does it mean that the user desires to get to a location up towards the top of the document? The scrolling directions will not be the same under these two ways of conceptualizing the scrolling. With the use of a scroll bar, we think of the text as being stationary and the window of the widget moves over the stationary text. Thus,

Figure 2-5. The push-button widget, labeled "quit," appears on a form widget. If the mouse button is clicked while the cursor is in the push-button widget, then the event associated with the push-button widget has occurred and the callback routine will be initiated. For this particular push button, the event will exit the application.

clicking an up button means that the moving window will move up towards the top of the text and, conversely, the movement of the text scrolling on the screen will be in a downwards direction. The moving elevator helps to alleviate these direction problems. The position of the elevator indicates the position of the text which is displayed on the screen. If the elevator is at the top of the scrollbar, this indicates that the window is at the top of the text. If at the bottom, then the text displayed in the window is at the bottom of the text.

Push-Button Widget

One of the simplest of the interactive widgets is the push-button widget. All widget sets have some form of the push-button widget. For this widget, the programmer would usually specify a label to be placed on the button, the parent of the push button (possibly a form widget), and

then the callback routine. If the mouse button is clicked while the cursor is in the push-button widget, then the callback routine is called. This routine specifies the action to take on the event. As an example, an action could be to exit the program, which would be one possible way to get out of the program and terminate the loop. See Figure 2-5 for an example of a push-button widget.

Toggle Switch Widget

In a toggle switch widget, the user has a set of choices which must be made. The widget responds in much the same way that a real toggle switch would respond: it can be in one of two positions. If the mouse is clicked while the cursor is in the box, then the box is highlighted and the switch is turned on. If the mouse is clicked again in the box, then the switch is toggled to the off position. In some cases, the box provides feedback by turning color, or

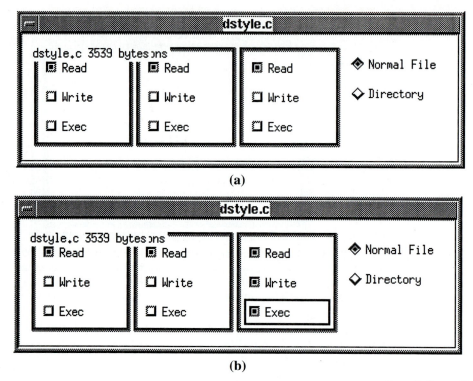

(a)

(b)

Figure 2-6. An example of toggle switch widgets for the three boxes displaying "Read," "Write," and "Exec." In (a), the read buttons have been toggled on. In (b), all three buttons have been toggled on for the third box.

black, when on, and white when off. In other cases, an "X" is placed in the box when on and no "X" is in the box when off.

Toggle switch widgets are a very powerful widget form which should be considered often by the interface designer. An alternative to using this widget is to display choices made through a list widget, as an example. Each choice must be made separately in this case. Using a toggle widget is much faster for those choices that have two positions: off or on. By displaying a control box with these toggle positions on them, choices can be made quickly and the feedback provided by the toggled switches is an effective means to determine quickly the current

state. An example of using toggle switches occurs in word processors. For a paragraph, the user may want to indicate that the paragraph is indented/not indented, that a page break occurs or does not occur at the beginning of the paragraph, or that the spacing is single or double spaced. All of these choices could be made using a control panel with toggle switches (see Figures 2-6a and 2-6b).

Radio Box Widget

The radio box widget is related to the toggle switch widget described in the preceding paragraphs with one difference. This widget gets its name from some older

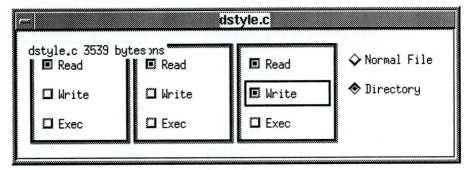

Figure 2-7. An example of a radio box widget for the "Normal File" and "Directory" buttons. Only one of these buttons can be on at a time. In Figures 2-6a and 2-6b, when the "Normal File" button is clicked on, the "Directory" button would be turned off automatically.

designs of radios and electronic equipment having a series of push buttons. Each push button could be pushed in to the on position; but when this was done, the previous button which was on would automatically be pushed out, returning to the off position. If another button was pushed on, then the button on previously would revert back to the off position. One button would always have to be on, and only one button.

The widget is designed to look much like a radio box. Each of the functions has a circle beside it. In the on position, the circle is usually filled in; in the off position, the circle is empty. The mouse cursor is usually moved to the circle and the mouse button is clicked. The circle becomes filled in, to indicate it is on, and all the other circles or buttons are empty. This has the appearance of a physical button being pressed and the previously on button being popped out to the off position.

The radio box widget can and should be used when one, and only one, function can be turned on at a time. It eliminates any problems or errors users may have in trying to turn on more than one function when it is impossible to do so. It also saves

time over the typical toggle switch in which one switch would have to be toggled off and another toggled on to achieve the same result.

The radio box widget should be used over toggle switches if the operation being performed can only be in one mode at a time. As an example, some kinds of software require that characteristics of the user's system be specified before the software can run. Aspects such as amount of memory, size of screen, color or monochrome terminal, and processor speed would all need to be specified. In each of these four cases, one and only one answer would be correct. A radio box, with four separate sections, could be created to perform these operations. See Figure 2-7 for an example of a radio box widget.

Paned Window Widget

This widget looks like a window pane, with a sash. The sash can be raised or lowered in order to change the size of the view through the window. Child widgets can be arranged vertically in the window area. As the sash of the window is raised, the size of the child widgets is increased. As the sash of the window is lowered, the

(a) 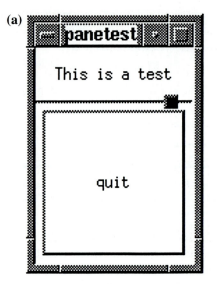   (b)

Figure 2-8. An example of a paned window widget. In (a), the child widget (labeled "quit") has been raised, and in (b), the child widget has been lowered. Control is achieved by moving the mouse cursor to the small box tab just above the child widget. When the mouse button is pushed down, the window is raised and lowered as the mouse is moved in the vertical direction. Control is relinquished when the mouse button is released.

size of the child widgets is decreased. Usually the sash has some kind of control bar that the user would control by placing the mouse in the bar, pressing the button, and then moving the sash with the button in the down position. When the button is released, the control of the sash is relinquished. Figure 2-8 shows examples of the paned window widget when the child widget is raised and lowered.

Dialog Widgets

A dialog occurs when the computer asks the user a question and the user must respond in some way. The dialogue could be as simple as to indicate that the information in the window has been read, or it can be used to ask the user to make some kind of choice. The dialog widget usually consists of text and push-button widgets.

Some widget sets have many different kinds of specialized dialog widgets. For others, the programmer must make these specialty dialog widgets by combining several widgets.

One kind of common dialog is a warning dialog widget. When the user attempts to perform an action which is potentially harmful and cannot be recovered from, then a good interface design would provide a warning to the user which must be responded to before the action can proceed. As an example, deleting a file could be harmful if the user needs to keep that file. Formatting a disk will destroy all the files on a disk and, thus, is extremely harmful if the disk is formatted unintentionally. A warning dialog widget will include some kind of text, usually asking "Are you sure?" and then displaying two push-button choices: "OK" and "Cancel."

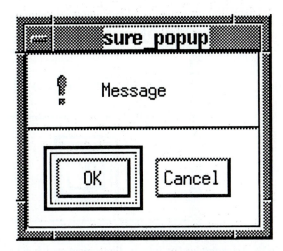

Figure 2-9. An example of a dialog widget. Any message could be placed at the top of the widget. An example would be asking the user whether or not the application should be exited. The user should be warned if potential actions make error recovery difficult.

The "OK" button can be clicked if the action is acceptable. The "Cancel" button can be clicked if the action was unintended and, thus, harmful. Usually a default button, the "OK," is also specified. A default button means that the button will be activated upon selecting the ENTER key which is convenient if the user's hands are already on the keyboard; reaching for the mouse and clicking the button would take extra time. Although responding to this warning dialog widget requires extra time, potentially harmful actions can be avoided. Some users find these warnings annoying; for others, if it has served its purpose, they are glad to have had an extra chance to avoid serious problems. Figure 2-9 shows an example of a dialogue widget.

An information widget can provide the user with information which is nonessential but useful. Whereas the warning widget warned the user about the consequences of the action and allowed a way out, the information widget provides in-

formation which could prove useful but does not have to be responded to immediately. As an example, an information widget could tell the user that some e-mail (electronic mail) has arrived. It could be used to tell the user that the computer system will be going down later in the day. On some systems that have calendars, an information window could inform the user about a meeting scheduled to begin in 10 minutes.

This kind of widget usually pops up on the screen. It normally includes the text, providing the information, and one push button labeled "OK." The push button is usually defaulted so that a button click or a keyboard return will remove the window. Including the push button ensures that the user receives the information. Especially on large workstations, many users may leave the workstation on the entire time while performing other non-computer work. Leaving the information displayed for a certain amount of time would not ensure that the information

Figure 2-10. An example of an information widget, which is a class of the dialog widget. For this information widget, only one button, "OK," is displayed on the screen, so that the window will not be removed until the user signifies that it has been read by clicking the "OK" button. This forces the user to acknowledge the information in the window before any other commands can be performed.

actually was read because the widget may be removed automatically while the user is performing other noncomputer tasks. Some information widgets may also include an auditory beep to alert the user who may not be attending to the visual display. An example of an information widget is shown in Figure 2-10.

An error dialog is much the same as an information widget except for the intent of the information. Similar to the information widget, this widget contains text and a push button. It informs the user of errors that have occurred on the system, out of control of the user, although it may not provide the user with information about how to recover from the error. Figure 2-11 shows an example of this kind of widget. Once again, the user must acknowledge the message by clicking the "OK" button or by hitting the ENTER key.

A working dialog widget informs the user that the program is busy perform-

ing some time-consuming operations. The widget states that the program is working at this point and provides push buttons to allow the user to cancel the program if desired. An option is to provide a push button to indicate that the window has been read (an "OK" button) and a "Help" button to provide further assistance. Such a working dialog is useful because the user loses control of the system when a program is performing a time-consuming operation. Without this kind of feedback on what is occurring in the background, the user may think that the system has crashed or stopped. In this kind of situation, the user could try to reboot or restart the machine which would destroy the operation; therefore, the user should always be provided with as much feedback as possible. However, requiring a response from the user to indicate that the working dialog widget has been read is not essential and could become irritating to

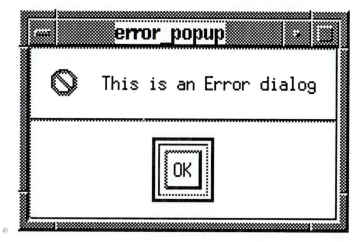

Figure 2-11. An example of an error dialog widget. An unspecified error has occurred on the system, and the user has been notified. To remove the window, the user must click the "OK" button or hit the ENTER key.

the user. Figure 2-12 shows an example of this kind of widget.

The prompt dialog asks the user a question and provides a space for the answer, which is entered through typing on the keyboard. The entry required is usually only one word that is to be terminated by hitting the ENTER or RETURN key. A typical use of this kind of prompt dialog widget is as a spelling checker. In a spelling checker, the computer reads all the words in a piece of text and compares the words to a dictionary of words. If no match is found, the computer prompts the user to indicate if the word is right and, if not, to enter the corrected word in the

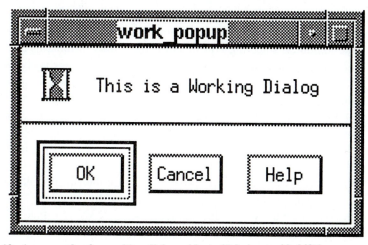

Figure 2-12. An example of a working dialog widget. Help is provided if the user needs it.

space provided. Other applications are available. An alternative to this kind of dialog widget is to use a menu widget (described in a later section). Menu widgets can be used when the number of alternatives is small because all the alternatives must be listed and the user makes the choice by pointing with the mouse. Obviously, with many choices, the search time, either visual or through scrolling on the screen, would be too long. In the above spelling checker example, including all possible words menu style as an alternative to typing the correct word would be impossible. If the number of choices was small, such as entering the name of a month, then using a menu widget is a viable alternative. Push buttons can also be included on the widget, such as "OK," "Cancel," and "Help." The "Cancel" will remove the widget from the screen without responding to the prompt, and the "Help" will provide further assistance. The "OK" button will usually be the default so that the user can either enter the response by hitting the ENTER key or by clicking the mouse on the "OK" button.

The file selection widget is a type of dialog widget that assists with one of the most common kinds of tasks performed on the computer: selecting a file or listing file names. The user must select a file when using a word processor, when using a drawing program, or when choosing an application program. In many cases, the user may want to browse through a listing or directory of the files to determine what files are available or what has happened to the file space since the last operation.

Many of the older command-based interfaces required that the file name be entered through the keyboard. The two advantages to this method were (a) the

files can be filtered, and (b) if the directory size is large, entering the file name through the keyboard could be faster than pointing to the file with a mouse. For filtering, symbols can be used to select a certain class of files. As an example, the $*$ symbol is usually used as a substitute for all possible character combinations. In UNIX and DOS, which can have a prefix and then a suffix after a dot (.) in the file name, a directory of $*.*$ files would include all possible files and a directory of $*.for$ files would include all the files with the .for suffix, such as test.for and program.for (the for suffix is usually used to indicate a FORTRAN program source code). Usually the symbol ? will provide a substitution for just one character in the file name. Thus, a directory using test?.for would include test1.for, test2.for, and so on, but would not include test10.for. This kind of filtering can be very useful, especially when searching through a large number of files.

Some of the newer operating systems require that all file selections be performed by pointing to the file. The advantage of this method is that only those files which already exist can be pointed to, thus eliminating the possibility of a typing error. The disadvantage, however, is that filtering is difficult and listing all the files in a large file space can be time-consuming. In this case, it is critical that the user organize the files in a hierarchical manner. The Apple Macintosh system allows the use of folders to organize files. As an example, the user may want to include all the FORTRAN files in a folder called FORTRAN, so that when searching for a FORTRAN program the folder would only have to be opened. In command-based

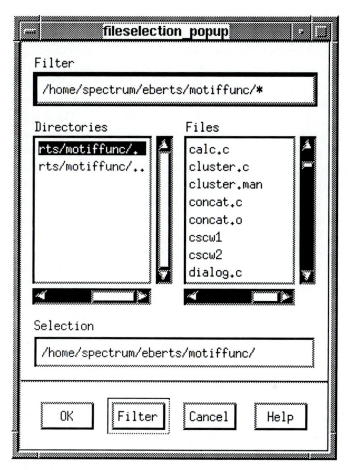

Figure 2-13. An example of a file selection widget. This is a conglomeration of several other widgets. The file filter at the top allows the user to enter the special characters to filter files. The widget in the center allows files to be selected through pointing.

operating systems such as UNIX and DOS, the user also has this option through the use of subdirectories. Without easy use of filtering, however, it is even more important that the hierarchical file structure, afforded through the use of folders, be used.

A file selection dialog widget can be used to accommodate the best aspects of command-based and direct manipulation interfaces (see Figure 2-13). The main window on the widget displays the list of files. Since most file spaces would have more files than could be placed in the window, a scroll bar on the right side is needed. The rectangle indicates the position on the scroll, and the mouse can be clicked on the up or down arrows to scroll in either of these directions. A file can be selected usually by double-clicking on the line corresponding to the file. The window at the top indicates the filter that can be used. Usually the same kinds of symbols used for command-based displays, the * and the ?, can be used in the filter. The filter is entered through the keyboard, and the filtered files are displayed in the large window. Any files can be selected in the appropriate manner. Finally, a file can be selected through the keyboard also. The window towards the bottom of the widget is a selection widget. It displays the currently selected widget that is pointed to in the large window. Also, by moving the mouse cursor to point to this window and then clicking the mouse, characters can be entered through the keyboard. When a RETURN is entered, or the mouse is clicked on the "OK" push button, then the entered file will be chosen. Many of the same buttons seen for the other dialog widgets, with the same functions, are also included in this widget. A new button, the filter button, can also be used to perform the filter specified in the top window. As can be seen, this type of file selection dialog widget includes most of the convenient functions from the command-based and direct manipulation operating systems. It also uses many of the other widgets discussed previously.

Text Widgets

A common function performed on a computer is text editing. When writing a computer program, the text for the lines of code must be entered and the editor must allow some way to change the characters. Writing a manuscript or a report is a common usage for text editors. Many computer applications are packaged to look like a form that needs to be filled out. If a database of customers' addresses is kept, then the program may appear as a form with slots for the customer's name, street address, city, and state. If an address changes, the database user would like to move to the appropriate slot and make the change directly. Instead of programming specialized text editors whenever one of these applications occur, many interface design systems include text widgets.

The simplest form of the text widget is a single line of text appearing in a window. The widget will display enough room to enter text on only a single line. For this widget, text can be entered and then changed once it is entered. Typical text editing commands include insert, delete, copy, and cut and paste. Selecting the text to delete, cut, or copy is also a typical function, and selecting can usually be performed by either the mouse or keyboard. For mouse text selection, the mouse cursor is placed at the beginning of the text to be selected and the mouse button is pressed down. While keeping the button down, the mouse cursor is moved to the end of the text to be selected, and, as it is moved, the text between the beginning and end is highlighted. When the mouse button is released, the highlight stays on and that text is now selected. As an example, issuing the delete command will delete the highlighted text. Text selection can often be performed using function buttons also. As an example, a particular function button may select the current word, and a different function button may select the entire paragraph. Single-line text widgets are especially useful when several are combined. Several could be used for the form example given previously; separate widgets would be displayed for the name, street address, city, and state. When combined, the text editing operations would appear to allow the user to directly change, delete, or add information on a form (see Figure 2-14).

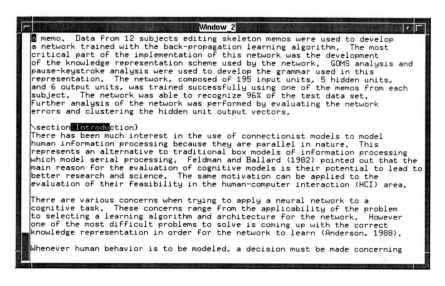

Figure 2-14. An example of a text widget. In this example, the user has highlighted a part of a word by moving the mouse cursor to the beginning, pressing the mouse button, then moving to the end, and releasing the mouse button. The highlighted characters can be operated on through the use of editing commands such as delete or move.

With multiline text widgets, some method of navigating through the text must be used. Many times, the text will be too large to fit in the window provided. The main difference between the single-line and multiline text widgets is that the multiline widgets will include some text navigation ability, usually in the form of a scroll bar. They can appear on the right side of the window, for moving up and down, and on the bottom of the window, if needed, to move right and left. Once the desired text is in the window, the same editing commands and text selection techniques as discussed in the single-line case can be used in the multiline widget.

Menu Bar Widgets

Menus are an important part of interface design and will be discussed in more detail in Chapter 23. Several different kinds of widgets are available to build different kinds of menus. One of these widgets is the menu bar. The menu bar widget is a long rectangle which extends the length of the window either at the top or bottom of the window. Several push buttons can be present on the bar. Usually two push buttons would always be present: Help and Quit (or Exit). The Help button will allow the user to obtain assistance specific to the context. The Quit button will allow the user to exit the particular program at any time. Other buttons, specific to the function being performed, will also be included on the menu bar. If the number of functions that have to be performed is small, then the menu bar is a good method for choosing the function.

Command-based interfaces have generally accommodated large numbers of functions by requiring that the user enter the command through the keyboard.

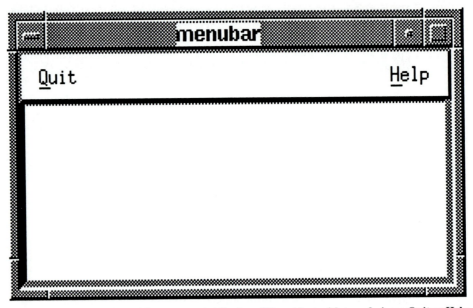

Figure 2-15. A menu bar widget appears at the top of the widget with two choices: Quit or Help. The items can be selected by pointing and clicking with the mouse or by typing the first letter of the menu item. The first letter is underlined to indicate that it could be entered for selection.

This demands, however, that the user be able to recall from memory the name of the command. The menu bar is easy to use because the user only has to recognize the command name, since it will be displayed on the menu bar, instead of recalling it. A selection on the menu bar can usually be made in two ways: by moving the mouse cursor to the function name and clicking, or by entering the first letter of the function name on the keyboard. For the latter method, sometimes the names have to be changed so that each function name has a unique starting letter. Figure 2-15 contains a menu bar with only two items.

If the number of functions is large, then a hierarchical design of the functions, through the use of pull-down menus, is needed. These will be discussed in the next section.

Pull-Down Menu Widget

As mentioned in the previous section, the menu bar will not be able to accommodate a large number of choices. If the number of items is larger than can be displayed across a menu bar, as would occur in many applications, then the items must be designed in a hierarchical fashion using the pull-down menu widget (see Figure 2-16). For a pulldown menu, the categories of the items are displayed on a menu bar at the top of the window. The user moves the mouse to the category desired and pushes the mouse button. While the mouse button is down, the functions under that category name pop up on the screen, under the category chosen. As the user moves the mouse cursor down the displayed items, while keeping the mouse button down, the

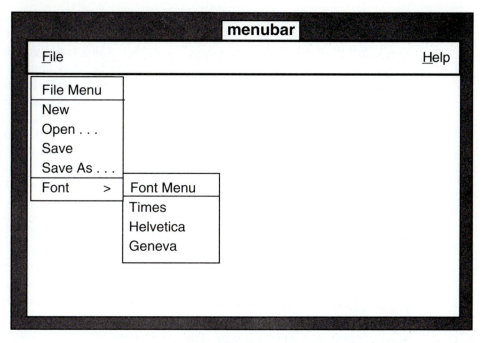

Figure 2-16. A pull-down menu is displayed. In this example, the user has already selected the category "File" by moving the mouse cursor to that item at the top of the display and pressing the mouse button. When this operation is performed, the pull-down menu appears. With the mouse button down, the mouse cursor is moved to the bottom of the menu. At the bottom, another level in the hierarchy is used so that the menu to the right appears automatically. When the mouse button is released, the item that is highlighted, through the use of the box, is selected.

choice is highlighted. When the mouse button is released, the highlighted line is chosen. In some applications, another level of the hierarchy is needed. In this case, a further window is popped on the screen as a choice is highlighted. The mouse is then depressed and the mouse must be moved to this section of the menu display, where the mouse button is released and the choice is made.

Pull-down menus are a very effective means of choosing functions and commands. The interface designer must be careful, however, to choose the correct menu category names so that the functions are all located in their logical place. In some cases, functions could be included under one category or another, so that the user may have difficulty finding the correct category to search. Ideally, the number of levels should be restricted to just one pull-down menu per category.

Of course, the larger the mouse movement, the longer the interaction time. Usually, the most popular menu items are placed at the top of the pull down menu to reduce mouse travel time. Mouse movement time can also be reduced by providing the users with an option on the menu size and number of functions. Some systems provide a user with the choice of long pull-down menus or short ones. The long menus would include functions not normally used. The short menus would include the most popular commands and functions, and their use would thereby reduce search time and mouse movement.

WIDGETS AND CONSISTENCY

The use of widgets in interfaces can provide a consistent "look and feel" to the interface design. The dialog widgets presented in this chapter provide such an example when using the Motif toolkit. After some experience, users would recognize easily the information, error, working, and prompt dialog widgets. Users would learn to expect text widgets to have scroll bars and would be familiar with their functionality. One of the most important reasons to use the widgets as building blocks for interfaces is because they provide a consistency to the design. The users do not have to learn anew what each of the widgets can do if a new application is performed. Researchers and developers of user interface designs generally agree that consistent designs should improve the user's productivity by leading to higher performance with fewer errors which in turn generally lead to improved user satisfaction with the system (Nielsen, 1989).

One of the easiest ways to incorporate consistent interfaces is to make use of the "look and feel" aspects of the toolkits which are available for the different kinds of computers. For the Apple Macintosh, HyperCard provides a toolkit of widgets which can be used to construct interfaces utilizing pull-down menus, dialog boxes, mouse manipulations, and iconic representations. Microsoft Windows provides many of the same features for IBM PCs and compatibles. For engineering workstations, many interface designers would use X Windows and the associated toolkits

such as the X Toolkit and Motif. An advantage of X Windows is that it is highly portable. A disadvantage is that the designer must be fairly proficient in the C programming language because all the widgets are called as functions from a C program. This programming context makes it different from HyperCard or Microsoft Windows, but with these latter two, the interface designer would still have to learn the pseudo-programming languages associated with the two toolkits. If one already knows C, then X Windows is easy to incorporate. Other computers, such as Next, also have advanced interface design packages available with them.

If a user has an Apple Macintosh and an application is being prepared for this user, then anything that uses something other than the toolkit available for the Macintosh will be unacceptable to this user. Similarly, for users running Windows on an IBM PC or compatible, applications outside of Windows will be unacceptable. The number of incompatible operating systems is shrinking, as the computer market weeds out some of the competition, so that any new application program can be limited to a Macintosh and IBM PC or compatibles and the designer would still be able to please a good share of the market. As the large workstations become cheaper and more accessible, the X Window toolkits should increase in use and application programmers will also have to consider this environment. For professional computer users, X Windows has a strong market presence. The users know that the interface can be done more simply, making it consistent with other applications. Lack of using the "look and feel" characteristics of the toolkits and widgets sends a message to the user that not much thought or time went into the interface. Consequently, even if the functionality of the application program is good, the application has a high chance of not being used or appreciated.

There are still many interface design issues which must be considered, even in the context of using one of the toolkits. In addition, research on user interfaces is rapidly changing how people think about the design, so that what is in use today may not be used too much in the future. Finally, Grudin (1989) argues that consistency can sometimes conflict with ease of use and learning, and that consistency should not be the main focus in these potential conflicts. Many more issues besides consistency of the interface must be considered in the design.

Some of the consistency issues will be revisited throughout the rest of the book. Models that will be considered later in the book can be used to determine and calculate the cognitive consistency of computer-based tasks: Reisner's (1981) use of formal grammars in analyzing interfaces (Chapter 17), work on Task-Action Grammars (TAG) (Payne and Green, 1986) (Chapter 17), the use of productions to measure the overlap in required knowledge among tasks (Bovair, Kieras, and Polson, 1990; Kieras and Polson, 1985) (Chapter 16), and the GOMS (Goals, Operators, Methods, and Selection rules) (Card, Moran, and Newell, 1983) (Chapter 14) and related task analyses such as Natural GOMS Language (NGOMSL) (Kieras, 1988) (Chapter 15).

SUMMARY

This chapter has outlined briefly some of the aspects of programming interfaces which are different from typical programming structures and methods. Many of the specialized interface design programming packages incorporate widgets, which are the building blocks for interface designs. When using a widget package, an interface is designed by specifying the widgets and the actions associated with the widgets. Typically the actions occur in programming functions called callback routines.

Merely knowing the building blocks is not enough to design effective and easy-to-use interfaces, though. One must also know how to build with these blocks. In this chapter, some of the design principles were discussed, in terms of when to use one widget and when to use another, but the reasons for using them were not presented. Guidelines are not always effective either, because the guidelines can and should change as the technology changes. The underlying principles or theories upon which guidelines are constructed are the most effective means for determining the guidelines, based upon the current technology, and for guiding future designs and research. Because of this, the rest of this book discusses these approaches to the interface design, with little emphasis on the guidelines and a greater emphasis on the underlying principles.

QUESTIONS

1. Design an interface on paper, using the widgets discussed in this chapter, for the following tasks.

   a. Ordering a meal from your favorite fast food restaurant.

   b. Choosing features you would like to have in a new car.

c. Receiving and sending electronic mail (e-mail).

2. A storyboard is an artistic sketch of scenes in a movie. Storyboards have been used by screen writers and movie directors to outline the scenes from a movie before filming begins. For *Raiders of the Lost Ark*, George Lucas and Steven Spielberg discussed the movie concept, and thus formed a visual image of the film concept, by drawing a storyboard for each of the crucial scenes. Performing this exercise is important for determining how the whole movie will fit together.

In a movie storyboard, each sketch of a scene is accompanied by a textual description of what will occur in the scene and how this scene relates to other scenes in the film. A complete storyboard can save time and money because many of the details are considered before filming begins.

Storyboards can also be used for interface design. In this kind of storyboard, each separate screen from the interface is sketched. Each action, such as a button press, is listed, along with a reference indicating which screen would appear due to the action. Such a storyboard provides a complete description of the interface, and any changes can be made to the interface design before programming begins. Design storyboards for the tasks listed in parts a-c of problem 1.

3. What is a bit-mapped display, and why is it useful for programming interfaces?

4. Why are the X Window functions becoming the standard for interface design of workstations?

5. List the five parts of a typical program structure containing a user interface. Indicate the functionality and purpose of each of the parts.

6. Why is a widget created and then displayed (realized) in two different steps?

7. Explain why the parent-child relationships used in X Windows makes coding the interface more efficient.

8. Explain the differences between an interface design toolkit language, such as Motif, and regular programming languages such as C or Fortran. Discuss the differences in the structure of the code and the statements in the languages. Explain the usefulness of widgets when compared to the statements available in regular programming languages.

CHAPTER 3

FOUR APPROACHES TO HUMAN-COMPUTER INTERACTION

INTRODUCTION

Several different methods have been used by human factors specialists, psychologists, engineers, and computer scientists for designing computer interfaces that are easy to use. Many of these solutions have been dependent on advances in hardware or technology, are very memory consumptive, and are dependent on processing speed. One theme will continue throughout this book: simplicity is difficult to implement. The price of computer memory has gone down at an amazing rate so that memory-consumptive processes, such as direct manipulation interfaces, can be implemented. A few years ago the computing power needed to do this would have been out of the price range of the novice computer users who most needed it. Advances have been made in display technology so that graphics and bit-mapped displays are now possible. This has increased the possibilities for displaying information. Other technologies such as voice recognition, voice output, touch displays, and pattern recognition are making advances quickly and could possibly be incorporated into the interface to a higher degree in the near future. Predicting the kinds of features in future interface designs is difficult.

Books written on human-computer interaction (HCI) emphasizing the technology and not the theory or approaches would be out of date in a very short time. Technology-specific texts and courses become obsolete before students can implement their knowledge in the business and academic areas. This book places little emphasis on the technology of HCI except as illustrations of applications. Instead, this book places an emphasis on the theories and approaches to HCI. Theories change, but not as rapidly as the technology, because any new theory will have to account for the data from the old theories. The approaches to HCI will remain relatively invariant over time. When new technology becomes available, past approaches can be applied. Knowing the approaches and the theories ensures that a student's knowledge will not become obsolete but can continually be applied to the new challenges.

In reviews of the area of HCI, the methods have been categorized into four general approaches (Eberts, 1987; Eberts and Eberts, 1989). These will form the basis for this book. The four approaches are the empirical approach, the cognitive approach, the predictive modeling approach, and the anthropomorphic approach. When categorizing the methods into these four approaches, the divisions between the approaches are not always clear; some studies fall into several categories. As an example, many of the predictive modeling methods and theories are based upon cognitive theories and, thus, could be classified under either approach. This categorization scheme is beneficial for organizing the wide range of material on this topic and for identifying ways to apply the different approaches to new problems.

In the next paragraphs, each of the four approaches to HCI will be discussed briefly. In the remainder of the book, sections will be devoted to each of the approaches and chapters within the sections will be devoted to the subapproaches. In the last section of the book, examples of applications of the approaches to important topics are discussed. For each of the approaches, the problem of HCI is seen in a different light: for the empirical approach, the various potential interactive methods are evaluated by testing them; for the anthropomorphic approach, ways must be found to make computers as easy to interact with as humans; for the cognitive approach, the interaction with the computer should be designed so that it assists human problem-solving instead of impeding it; and for the predictive modeling approach, the tools must be developed to predict which of the interactive methods will be the best before they are prototyped and developed.

THE EMPIRICAL APPROACH

Many different choices have to be made for designing the interface. When designing a system that queries the user, the designer can choose between menu displays, fill-in-the-blank, parametric, or direct manipulation displays. In database searches, the designer must choose between logical OR or AND searches or searching by paging through the database. The designer has a wide choice of input devices such as keyboard, voice, mouse, or touch display, just to name a few. Since all of these methods and devices have already been developed, the problem is to

decide on which one to choose. By incorporating the empirical approach, the correct choice depends on the results of experimentation. In some cases this means being able to intelligently interpret the results of experiments run by someone else or being able to run the experiment yourself.

The methodology of this approach should be familiar to researchers who perform behavioral studies. First, the items to be tested are identified. These items usually correspond to the different levels of an independent variable (the variable being manipulated by the experimenter). Next, a task which corresponds closely to the real-world task but is controllable in a laboratory situation is identified. The choice of the task determines the kinds of dependent variables that will be used and measured. Finally, the experiment is carried out in a well-controlled environment so that factors other than the independent variable do not vary from condition to condition. The results are then analyzed to determine the statistical significance of the results. The methodology of the approach as applied to human-computer interactions has been outlined by Shneiderman (1980), Moher and Schneider (1982), and Embley (1978).

Under the empirical approach, the interface designer would be required to design, implement, and analyze the results from empirical studies. As an experimenter, the designer must ensure that the experimental variables are not confounded and that the results are interpretable and generalizable to other situations. In addition, the designer could also play a role as a keeper of the database which has been built up from this approach. The designer must also be familiar with the experimental designs used in the database so that the generalizability of the results can be predicted.

The advantage of the empirical approach is that it offers an alternative to intuition in determining the best design. Since humans use the computer systems, the characteristics that are easiest for the human to use should be the ones incorporated in the design. One means of gauging the effectiveness of the empirical approach is to examine whether intuition is disconfirmed through the empirical studies. Such has been the case in experiments which have shown that graphics are not always better than text-based displays (Power, Lashley, Sanchez, and Shneiderman, 1984; Stern, 1984) and courteous error messages are not better necessarily than hostile error messages (Shneiderman, 1982). Many times intuition will be confirmed through the empirical studies.

The empirical approach also has some disadvantages. Those with backgrounds in behavioral research are aware of the dangers of improperly designed experiments. As an example, Sheil (1981) did an extensive literature review on empirical research for computer programming tasks. He concluded that a large percentage of the studies had some kind of methodology problem associated with them which made the applicability of the results questionable. A related problem occurs in the designs used. The majority of the studies use novice subjects in one or two hour experiments. The generality of this research can be questioned. Merely looking at a brief summary of the results of a set of experiments without critically examining the whole experiment can be misleading.

The final disadvantage of the empirical approach is the lack of theoretical guidance. The experiments which will be reviewed under this approach were designed, for the most part, to solve some particular need at the particular time; they are need-driven instead of theory-driven. In many cases this is quite appropriate. To fill in the missing links, such as how a novice changes to an expert, guidance from a theoretical orientation is needed. All of the experiments that need to be done to cover all the applications cannot be performed. Without a theoretical perspective, when a new device or display mode is developed, the experiments must be performed all over again to determine how the new method compares to the old. The approach cannot be used to suggest novel designs, only to test extant designs. Many of the methods for the other approaches, on the other hand, take a theoretical perspective.

The empirical approach will be explained in more detail in Section II. Chapter 4 in that section examines the methodology of the empirical approach in explaining how to execute an effective design. The different experimental designs commonly used for human-computer interaction studies are discussed in Chapter 5. This chapter is most useful for someone planning to run an experiment, but it also includes useful information for evaluating other research which may already be reported in the research literature. Chapter 6 examines the common hazards which occur in human-computer interaction experiments. How to recognize the hazards and methods available to alleviate the hazards are discussed. This chapter is intended to guide the interpretation of experiments. All experiments should be designed to avoid these hazards.

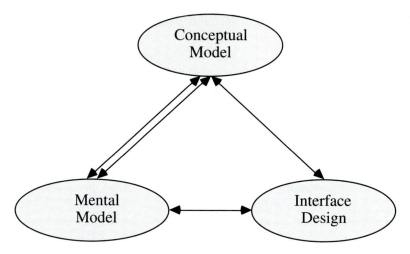

Figure 3-1. Conceptualization of the design of human-computer interfaces.

THE COGNITIVE APPROACH

For the cognitive approach, theories in cognitive science and cognitive psychology are applied to the human-computer interface to make the processing of information by both the human and the computer easier and more efficient. The cognitive theories state how humans perceive, store, and retrieve information from short- and long-term memory, manipulate that information to make decisions and solve problems, and carry out responses. The overall goal of the cognitive approach can be stated pictorially as in Figure 3-1. Three concepts are important. First, the conceptual model is a description of the computer system in engineering terms so it is accurate, consistent, and complete. Second, the mental model is the model the user forms of how the computer system works; this mental model guides the user's actions and behaviors. Third, the mental model is built up through interactions with the interface design, which can include the display representation and the documen-

tation. As one example, if the display presents information so that the developed mental model is inaccurate, then computer interaction problems occur. The designer's goal is to try to choose the information to represent on the display and in the documentation, and make connections to the user's prior knowledge so that the mental model, like the conceptual representation, is accurate, consistent, and complete.

The cognitive approach views the human as being adaptive, flexible, and actively involved in interacting with the environment to try to solve problems or make decisions. This approach has been concerned with applying specific theories to the human-computer interactions. Theories which have been applied include those on analogical reasoning and metaphors, spatial reasoning, problem solving, attentional models, and connectionist or neural network models. Brief discussions of these main theories follow; more detailed discussions are in Section III.

Analogies and metaphors are an important kind of learning and are used often in teaching. In teaching, the instructor chooses some concrete situation the student is familiar with and presents the new information in terms of how it relates to the old familiar information. One of the most popular examples of using analogies in teaching is to say that light acts like particles in some situations and like waves in other situations. Neither is totally correct but it does help the student develop a concept of light by using familiar information built up through interacting with particles or waves. Similar procedures are used in human-computer interaction. For a novice, the new information to be learned is the computer system itself. The old familiar information must be conveyed to the user through the interface design. Often, the analogy or metaphor used is a desk top. This desk top is conveyed to the user through graphics on the computer screen. The user is assumed to know how to manipulate objects on a real desk top. To understand how to use the computer, the user needs only to transfer the knowledge about real desk tops to the metaphorical desk top on the computer screen. Supposedly, this approach reduces the learning time because the user need not learn all the concepts again; the user merely applies existing knowledge to the new task.

Many kinds of problems to be solved require the manipulation of images. For example, Bower (1972) found groups of subjects instructed to use imagery were better than a no-imagery control group at solving certain kinds of problems. In a three-term series problem (e.g., Al is taller than Bob; Bob is taller than Carl; who is the tallest?), Huttenlocher (1968) found subjects solved the problem by visualizing the size of the people and then deciding from the visual image which person was taller. In other kinds of problems, research has shown that imagery is used to determine which object is larger (Moyer, 1973); imagery is used to determine if objects in different orientations are rotated or reflected from a standard (Cooper, 1975; Cooper and Shepard, 1975); and people have the ability to zoom in on items in an image to obtain more detail. Many of these abilities are developed through interaction with items in the world. The computer can provide this kind of image manipulation experience for a user through the use of interactive graphics.

Generally, for the cognitive approach, human-computer interaction is seen as presenting problems which have to be solved by the user. Thus, many of the problem-solving theories which have been developed in cognitive psychology can also be applied to the human-computer interaction task. Newell and Simon's (1972) theory of problem solving has been influential in this area. Under this conceptual scheme, problem solving can be evaluated as a series of interconnected goals and subgoals in a hierarchy. Formal models have been derived from this theory in order to understand human-computer interaction processes (e.g., Bovair, Kieras, and Polson, 1990; Card, Moran, and Newell, 1983; Kieras and Polson, 1985).

Attention is required when the human processes information. Since humans cannot process or apply attention to all the information being received through the senses, attention is often viewed as having limited capacity (Moray, 1967) or as a processing resource of limited availability (Kahneman, 1973). The human must, therefore, consciously or unconsciously decide which pieces of information will be attended to. More recently, refinement of this undifferentiated resource theory of attention has resulted in the conception of multiple resource "pools." Under this theory, tasks interfere if they pull resources from the same resource pool (e.g., Navon and Gopher, 1979; Wickens, 1980, 1984a). This multiple resource theory of attention has important implications for the design of human-computer tasks, especially the design of tasks in environments, such as a nuclear power control room or an aircraft cockpit, where the operator must process information from several different sources and make multiple responses. In these situations, the operator is required to time-share or perform more than one task at a time.

Finally, neural network or connectionist theories are becoming an important concept in cognitive science and cognitive psychology. Under these theories, human information processing is conceptualized as occurring in parallel and distributed throughout the system (e.g., Rumelhart and McClelland, 1986). Earlier approaches to human information processing emphasized the structural aspects of information processing by conceptualizing processing as occurring in a sequence of stages. Formal computer models, called connectionist models or neural networks, have been developed to simulate these parallel distributed human processes. Although these have not been applied extensively to human-computer interaction tasks, the potential for such applications exists.

For the cognitive approach, the interface designer must be familiar with theory and advances in cognitive psychology. Such a person needs to be able to apply theoretical perspectives to concrete situations in human-computer interaction tasks. Thus, the designer must be a theoretician and an engineer, in addition to a designer, to apply the theories.

The advantage of the cognitive approach is that it views the user as a flexible, adaptive information processor who is actively trying to solve problems when using the computer. This approach has also been used to suggest which design may be appropriate and easy to use instead of merely testing the design after it has been finalized (e.g., Bewley, Roberts, Schroit, and Verplank, 1983). The success of this approach has been realized in the interface for the Xerox Star, which was the predecessor of the popular Apple Macintosh. The Apple Macintosh has, in turn, been very successful and is known for its ease of use. Other possibilities for "cognitively styled" designs exist and have been implemented. The only possible disadvantage is that some of the terms used in this approach may not be well defined and specific enough to offer suggestions for human-computer interface designs.

In Section III, each of the cognitive theories which have been applied to HCI problems so far will be discussed. Chapter 7 discusses mental models, which is a concept often applied to interface design. Chapter 8 discusses human information processing theories which include the older discrete stages models and the newer connectionist theories. Related to this discussion is Chapter 13, which explains a predictive model, called the Model Human Processor, which is based upon human information processing theories. Chapter 9 introduces the theories based upon neural networks or connectionist models and presents some new research directions from these theories. Chapter 10 discusses analogies and metaphors which have been very influential for interface designs. Chapter 11 discusses the applications of graphics based upon theories of spatial reasoning. Finally, Chapter 12 discusses the applications of attentional theories, especially for complex situations in which an operator may become overloaded mentally.

THE PREDICTIVE MODELING APPROACH

The purpose of the predictive modeling approach is to try to predict performance of humans interacting with computers, which is similar to the predictions engineering models make for physical systems. Just as in civil engineering, where a bridge would not be built until all the modeling is complete to determine its structural viability, the predictive modeling approach can be used to determine if an interactive design is viable in terms of usability before it is prototyped. Four general classes of predictive modeling techniques will be discussed: information processing models, GOMS and NGOMSL models, rule-based production systems, and grammars.

The Model Human Processor, developed by Card, Moran, and Newell (1983), was designed to parameterize aspects of human information processing theories so that time and error predictions could be determined based upon the information which needed to be processed by a computer user. As in most human information processing theories, the model hypothesized that information would be processed through three stages: the perceptual, cognitive, and motor stages. By analyzing the information which needed to be processed, and the cycle times for this processing to occur in each of the

stages, time predictions can be made. Because the information packages which have to be processed are so small, the model is most applicable to very simple tasks and not complex tasks. The other models are more applicable to complex tasks.

The GOMS model was developed by Card, Moran, and Newell (1983) based upon the earlier work by Newell and Simon (1972) on human problem solving. The Newell and Simon work was mentioned previously in connection with cognitive problem solving. GOMS stands for Goals, Operators, Methods, and Selection of rules, which is descriptive of how the model works. GOMS has been applied extensively to the use of text editors. Usually when working with a text editor, the user has some kind of goal in mind, such as taking out a piece of text and inserting it elsewhere. Thus, the first letter of GOMS stands for goals. Next, the user knows the operators, or the editing commands in this example, which can be used to accomplish the goals. Thus, the second letter of GOMS stands for operators. Third, methods or procedures are needed to carry out the operators and in many cases the user has multiple methods to choose from. As an example, the user may scroll down the screen by hitting an arrow button or by hitting a "Page Down" function key. Finally, when the user has a choice of methods, certain rules can be followed for which method to choose. As an example, if the target text is close to the present cursor, the user would hit the arrow key; if the target text is farther away from the present cursor, the user would hit the "Page Down" key. NGOMSL, which stands for the Natural GOMS Language, was devised by Kieras (1988) to remove some of the ambiguities in the GOMS model and to allow the modeling language to be more natural.

A rule-based production system is a concept which has come out of artificial intelligence, especially from the work on expert systems. It is a programming technique or language that can be used to store knowledge about an entity and then process that knowledge to solve problems or make decisions based upon the environmental conditions. The structure of this language is in terms of if-then rules. The if part of the rule is used to determine if an environmental condition is true. Usually in a production system, the processor will read a sequence of rules starting from the first and continue on down until the condition (the if part) is true. When a condition is true, then the environment is changed through the processing of the antecedent (the then part of the rule). This antecedent will change the state of the system, that which is true, so that when the conditions of the rules are tested once again then new rules may fire. Production systems have been used to model human cognitive processes (Anderson, 1976). Since human-computer interaction can be characterized as a problem-solving task, using production systems to model human cognitive behavior when interacting with a computer is a logical step to take. This technique has been refined for human-computer interaction tasks by Kieras and Polson (1985) and later by Bovair, Kieras, and Polson (1990). In particular, the goals, methods, operators, and selection rules from the GOMS model can be converted into if-then rules which can then be used to model the behavior. Through these modeling techniques, the usability of interactive programs can be determined by ana-

lyzing the complexity of the program through the number of rules needed or analyzing the transfer of one program to another through the overlap of rules.

Finally, the usability of interactive programs has been analyzed in terms of the cognitive grammars that describe the program. Cognitive grammars were developed to describe the grammars of languages, that is, the rules which govern the usages of the language. If interactive programs are conceptualized in terms of an interactive language, then cognitive grammars can also be used to describe the human-computer interaction task. Applications in human-computer interaction tasks have been performed by Reisner (1981) and Payne and Green (1986, 1989). Grammars have many characteristics of the production systems discussed above. Once again, they are useful for analyzing the usability of the programs before the programs are prototyped.

For the predictive modeling approach, the interface designer must be familiar with the existing models and the techniques to apply these models to various tasks. When implementing these models, the designer would perform many of the functions that other kinds of engineers perform: considering the possible designs, modeling the task for the designs, and choosing a design based upon quantitative predictions from the model. Thus, for this approach, the human factors engineer is a modeler.

These models present a significant advance in our ability to predict which design is better. They have the advantage that they can make fairly accurate error and time estimates for a task, in some of the cases, and these can be used to predict how the user will perform a particular task. The fit of the model's predictions with actual data has been quite accurate.

The major disadvantage of these models is that the implementation involves some interpretation of the task. Two modelers modeling the same task using the same technique could come up with different models. In many cases, more than one analysis for the same task can occur. Some of the later models have been specified explicitly so that this problem is less likely than it may have been with earlier models.

All four classes of the models mentioned above will be discussed in more detail in Section IV of the book. Chapter 13 discusses the Model Human Processor, which is based upon a parameterization of human information processing. Chapters 14 and 15 discuss the GOMS and NGOMSL models. These models emphasize the prediction of time and errors for interaction tasks. Chapter 16 discusses the application of production systems to human-computer interaction tasks. In this case, the emphasis is on predicting transfer from one program to another or determining the complexity of an interactive task. Chapter 17 discusses the cognitive grammars. Emphasis is placed on complexity and consistency analyses.

THE ANTHROPOMORPHIC APPROACH

The word anthropomorphic can be defined as the application of human qualities to nonhuman entities. Under this approach, the designer uses the process of human-human communication as a model for human-computer interaction. The logic is as follows: humans can communicate effectively, for the most part, between themselves, so the source of the problem with human-computer communication must be that the computer does not act enough like a human to carry on an effective interaction. Therefore, if the computer is provided with the right humanlike qualities, the interaction can be more effective. Several qualities can be applied to the computer: natural language, voice communication, help messages, tutoring, and friendliness.

"User-friendly" is a term which currently is used to describe computer products. Defining the term is difficult; determining if one system is more friendly than another is even more difficult. The term has been used so often to describe products that it has lost much of its meaning. Defined within the context of the anthropomorphic approach, the meaning of the term can become clearer. In essence, the term means that the computer will interact with the user much the same way one human would interact with another human. In particular, the interaction will be easy, communication will occur naturally, mistakes and errors will be accepted and mutually fixed, and assistance will be given when the user is in trouble. The importance of these characteristics can be demonstrated by examples of systems which failed to incorporate them. Several glaring and common examples of user-*unfriendly* systems exist. In such systems, errors can be difficult or impossible to recover from without clearing everything from the screen and starting over from the beginning. An unfriendly system requires the use of cryptic commands instead of more natural commands. In an unfriendly system, error messages are vague (e.g., "illegal entry") and contain no advice on why the error occurred or how to recover from the error. Finally, in an unfriendly system, common sense is not used. Examples of this were given in the first chapter. Sending bills for negative payments does not make sense to the person receiving them. A person would not communicate errors to another person by saying "Invalid page number." A system is user-unfriendly if it requires responses or utilizes commands that are unusual in normal human communication.

Another term which is utilized often with the anthropomorphic approach is "natural." Like user-friendly, a definition of naturalness is difficult. Several researchers have speculated on how to define natural. Naturalness is understood to be present if the human and computer act as partners (Press, 1971), if the natural language interaction is "graceful" (Hayes and Reddy, 1983), if the computer has some ability to critique the users' plans (Langlotz and Shortliffe, 1983), and if the computer can be introspective by providing the user with its underlying "thinking" or an image of its underlying process (Fitter, 1979).

Full application of the human-human communication analogy to human-computer interaction is impossible at this time. The success of this anthropomorphic approach is dependent on advances in technology and on further study of artificial intelligence, because many kinds of human-human interactions cannot occur in current human-computer interaction. The computer only "knows" what it receives from the user through input devices; it has very limited perceptual properties if it has any at all. Many of the important human-human interaction cues cannot be perceived by the computer. The

human can pick up on visual cues, such as loss of eye contact, which may indicate stress, or voice inflections which may indicate irritability. When another human perceives stress or irritation, normal kinds of communication may be altered so that the stress or irritability level can be reduced. A computer does not have this ability and so cannot be completely user-friendly.

Three methods are used currently in the anthropomorphic approach. In the first method, humans interacting with each other are used as a model and a means for gathering information. This human-human interaction can either be studied in a controlled laboratory setting or in a less controlled nonlaboratory setting. The data from this kind of research can be used to specify the appropriate parameters of the computer system which is to be designed. The second method is more intuitive. For this method, the human-computer task is compared with a human-human interaction task to try to look for mismatches. The mismatches can be corrected through the use of a variety of applications of technology such as natural language, voice input, and artificial intelligence. Finally, in the third method, researchers contend that each possible computer application may have a natural design associated with it. Generalizing the designs, so that they are applicable to many different problem areas, will make interfaces difficult to use.

What kinds of features should be included in the human-computer interaction interface? By analyzing and observing humans interact, the same features can be incorporated in computers to increase their user-friendliness. There is little excuse for designing a computer system where the error messages are cryptic and the system is unforgiving of mistakes. Most of these improvements would take only a few lines of extra code for the programmer to implement them.

Some users, especially expert users, may not want systems that are overly friendly and wordy. These user-friendly systems may be inefficient for users familiar with these tasks. Research investigating how to adapt the system to the level of the user has addressed this issue. In these studies, the interaction mode would be different for an expert and a novice.

Another advantage to the anthropomorphic approach is that it can be used to create a novel design for computer interfaces instead of following the lead of other disciplines as has occurred with the empirical approach. By performing a task analysis which looks at the mismatches between human-human interaction, suggestions can be made for the improvement of the interface.

A logical extension of this approach can also be made. Findings from academic fields that do research in human-human interaction, such as social psychology, can be applied to human-computer interaction to advance the computer field. An example of this is the application of Kelly's (1955) construct theory from psychoanalysis to the automated acquisition of expert knowledge in the design of an expert system (Boose, 1984). Other social psychology theories, such as the theory of telling (Lewis and Cook, 1969), which analyzes one-way communication, and a theory of conversation (Pask, Scott, and Kallikourdis, 1973), could be also be applied under this approach.

The anthropomorphic approach is overly dependent on technology advances. As emphasized previously, "natural" is complicated. Some advances in natural language processing and voice recognition have been made, but these features are difficult to implement in most computer systems.

Another problem is that natural and friendly may not always be the best design. Achieving natural systems has been a goal of the anthropomorphic approach. Should computers be natural? A few experiments have addressed this issue from a position of the design of command names. The experimental evidence has not always been supportive of naturalness in computer systems.

One set of experiments (Scapin, 1981) compared command names that were natural with command names that used computer terminology and, thus, were computer-oriented. In a free recall memory task, inexperienced subjects could more easily recall the functions of the computer-oriented words than the functions of the natural words. The natural words may have had other connotations to the subjects, besides the computer applications, and, thus, differentiating the computer context from the natural context may have been difficult. The computer-oriented words may have had less interference from other meanings.

In another experiment, Dumais and Landauer (1981) investigated the possibility of having novices choose the command names that were the most natural to them. The experimenters found that using commands is more complicated than just trying to recall what they are; the specificity of the name must also be taken into account. The novices, not being familiar with the task, chose natural names that were nonspecific. As they acquired expertise, the nonspecific command names could be misleading. Naturalness may not be a good substitute for specificity.

The concept of natural language interaction has also been criticized. An experiment by Small and Weldon (1983) compared natural language interaction to a specialized query language in database retrieval searches and found that subjects worked faster with the specialized query language; no differences in accuracy were found. Other researchers and practitioners have argued that natural language may be inappropriate for a computer system. As Shneiderman (1980) states, "When people want a discussion they go to other humans, when they want precision and speed they go to a computer." Other reasons why natural language may be inappropriate for computers, according to Shneiderman (1980), are that the overhead for creating and maintaining a natural language interface could be applied more appropriately to other tasks, and users may form unrealistic expectations of the computer's power. The latter was validated experimentally when Jenkins (1984) found that operators of a nuclear power plant thought that the expert system controlling the plant "knew" more than it actually did. By using natural language, the computer may appear to be smarter than it actually is.

The anthropomorphic approach is most often used in the task analysis stage to determine the important communication stumbling blocks. These specifications can then be used in the design of the system. Thus, for this approach, the interface designer is a task analyzer and possibly an experimenter.

The anthropomorphic approach will be discussed in more detail in Section V of this book. This section is divided into four chapters. Chapter 18 examines the use of human-human interaction as specifying the parameters for the computer interface. Chapters 19 and 20 discuss the methods used for designing natural interfaces, and these methods have been divided into hardware methods (Chapter 19) and software methods (Chapter 20). Chapter 21 discusses how the interface design should be tailored according to the particular application.

THE INTEGRATION OF THE FOUR APPROACHES

As emphasized throughout this chapter, the role of the interface designer changes depending on the approach. Traditionally, the designer has taken a narrow role in the total interface design process. By defining that role under the four kinds of approaches, a method to integrate the approaches and expand the roles can be determined. The product design cycle of Mantei and Teory (1988) was discussed in Chapter 1 and illustrated in Figure 1-4. The four approaches are especially relevant within this design cycle for some of the stages. The most relevant stages are: task analysis, global design, prototype construction, user testing and evaluation, and final user testing. Different approaches can be taken in these five stages.

In the task analysis stage, the anthropomorphic and the predictive modeling approaches can be invoked. For the anthropomorphic approach, the human-computer interaction task should be analyzed so that it is as close to a human-human interaction as possible. This can be done by either intuition or by running experiments to specify the important variables. For the predictive modeling contribution, the models can be used to analyze the task in terms of the predicted time to perform the task and make the anticipated errors.

In the global design stage, all four approaches can be used. From the anthropomorphic approach, the specifications from the task analysis could be implemented. From the cognitive approach, the designer must be aware of the conceptual representation of the system and must design the display so that the user's mental model becomes an accurate reflection of the conceptual representation. For the predictive modeling, several alternative designs can be evaluated through the models to determine which can be eliminated quickly as being too complex, too difficult, or too long. A database search of the experiments which have been performed in the past to differentiate between the chosen designs can be performed. This search would have to take into account the generalizability of these previous experiments to the present situation.

The prototype construction stage would be performed to implement the design suggestions from the previous stages. No direct human factors involvement would be required. Ideally, depending upon the amount of resources available, several different design possibilities would be prototyped. If few resources are available, then the process could be terminated at this stage and results of the predictive modeling and database search would have to be adequate.

In the two user testing stages (user testing and evaluation and final user testing), the different prototypes or the constructed systems would be tested, under the empirical approach, to determine which design is the best. The results from these

tests should be similar to that predicted by the predictive models and from the cognitive approach evaluation. If these do not match, then the generalizability of the experiments, the tasks analysis using the predictive models, and the cognitive breakdown of the tasks should be evaluated to determine why the discrepancy has occurred. Further experiments and analyses may be required.

The next four sections of this book discuss the four approaches in more detail. The last section of this book examines how the four approaches can be applied to specific design issues.

SUMMARY

The four approaches to HCI—empirical, predictive modeling, cognitive, and anthropomorphic—used throughout this book were introduced and discussed in this chapter. These four approaches provide a structure for how to approach the problem of designing a user interface. The approaches provide different perspectives and insights on how a human will interact with a computer.

Often user interface design concepts are discussed through the principles of design. The problem with this approach is that a new principle is needed in each context for each task and design. As the technology changes, new principles must be formulated. From the perspective of this book, principles can only be formulated when the four approaches, along with the associated theories, are applied to a specific task or design. A user interface designer, therefore, must understand the approaches and theories along with the task.

To emphasize this concept of designing user interfaces, the book is organized in the following way. The first four sections discuss, in some detail, the four different approaches to user interface design summarized in this chapter. The final section of the book (Chapters 21-25) examines several computerized tasks and demonstrates how design principles can be formulated from the approaches and theories.

QUESTIONS

1. Consider how each of the four approaches is similar. For the following, discuss the similarities between the pairs of approaches.

   a. Empirical - Cognitive

   b. Empirical - Predictive modeling

   c. Empirical - Anthropomorphic

   d. Cognitive - Predictive modeling

   e. Cognitive - Anthropomorphic

   f. Predictive modeling - Anthropomorphic

2. For the six pairs in the previous question, discuss how each of the four approaches is different.

CHAPTER 4

EXPERIMENTAL METHODOLOGY

INTRODUCTION

In Chapter 1, the stages of human-factored designs for computer systems, including the interface design, were discussed. These stages can be used to determine the experimental techniques which must be mastered by interface designers. This chapter discusses these experimental techniques in the context of the development stages. Mantei and Teory (1988) contend that five stages relevant to the human factors of design are needed: market analysis in which users may be asked to perform several tasks using their current system; the product acceptance analysis stage in which comments on a mock-up will be elicited either informally or formally through surveys and questionnaires; a task analysis stage which determines how a person thinks about the tasks to be performed and whether or not the software design will be compatible with that thinking; the user testing and evaluation stage in which formal experimental techniques are used to evaluate the product; and the product survey stage in which users are surveyed to determine their likes and dislikes about the marketed product.

Each of these five additional stages has some kind of empirical evaluation associated with it. The product acceptance stage and the product survey stage both use questionnaires and surveys as the testing technique. These will be discussed in the next section. Market analysis can use informal experimental techniques based upon observation and description. The task analysis stage can use several

different techniques such as the formal predictive models of Section IV or other kinds of descriptive statistical techniques which will be discussed only briefly. Formal experimental design using the experimental method is used in the user testing and evaluation stage. The scientific method will be discussed in some detail, as this should be used for formal experiments.

The experimental techniques used in interface design are varied and can range from very rigorous techniques to informal techniques. Academic research is often focused on the rigorous techniques using the experimental method in controlled environments. This method is good because cause-and-effect relationships between features of the interface design and usability can be determined. This method can, however, be costly, and the results can be so narrow, for example, a yes/no choice about whether one design is better than another, that it may not be beneficial to product developers (Landauer, 1987). On the other hand, the informal techniques can provide important observational and descriptive information about the interface design, but, the results may be unstable and not generalizable to other users and environments.

The following discussion will start with the most rigorous method, the experimental method, and move on to more informal methods such as questionnaires and informal experimentation. Much of the discussion on the experimental method has been adapted from Eberts, Smith, Dray, and Vestewig (1982).

EXPERIMENTAL METHOD

Several components are involved in designing an experiment. The experimenter must formulate a research question, design the experiment so that the results are interpretable, choose the independent variable(s), and choose the dependent variable. In this section, the issues related to making these choices are discussed. The important interactions that occur among the various design-related components are then discussed. The purpose of this section is to provide designers and experimenters with a discussion of the issues and the interactions between the components which must be considered when designing an experiment that will address the research question and avoid potential problems.

Formulating the Research Question

The research question is used to direct the research and experimentation. Many of the issues addressed in the following sections should already be considered when the research question is formulated. In particular, the issues considered in the next sections, such as the design of the experiment, the choice of independent variables, the control of potential confounding variables, and the choice of a dependent variable, should all be considered when formulating the research question. Many of these issues will be discussed in the next sections.

The target group of users should be identified by the research question. Several potential target groups users can be identified: novices with no previous computer experience, experts on a particular computer system, experts on com-

puter systems in general, or users who have experience with other similar kinds of software. An interface design cannot usually be targeted towards all these groups at once because trade-offs have to be made in the design. By considering this issue in the formulation of the research question, characteristics of the subjects in the experiment will be determined.

A critical component of the research question is the comparison to be made. In human-computer interaction research, many times the comparison will be obvious. If a new interface is developed, it must be better than the best existing interface, so the obvious comparison will be between the new interface design and the existing interface design. The comparison could become more complicated if the target group of users is also stated in the research question. In particular, the research question could state explicitly that the new interface design may be best for a certain class of users, when compared to this class of users using the old interface design.

The observation and measurement must be explicitly stated in the research question. It is not enough to ask whether one interface will be better than the other; the research question should also state in what way they will be compared. In particular, the interfaces can be compared in terms of time and errors (other examples of measurements are provided in the section on dependent variables). How they are compared will be important in the design of the experiment.

As should be evident from this discussion of the research question, experimentation can only be conducted when the experimenter has previous information available. The experimenter must know the strengths and weaknesses of the newly developed interface. The experimenter should have information about the older interface with which the new is to be compared. Any previous research reports on the older interface should be consulted. The overall purpose for developing the new product should be understood by the researcher. The experimenter must know how performance on these interfaces has been measured in the past, and which measurements may be relevant to the purposes of the present research. The experimenter must know characteristics of the users and how they might react to the different interfaces being tested. Therefore, a good experimenter, through prior reading and research, is not often surprised by the outcome of the experiments.

No single experiment is expected to totally address all the research issues. Especially when performing theoretical work, as opposed to product development, an experiment will pose as many questions as it answers. If the experimental results do not turn out as expected, then new research questions can be formulated to determine why this occurred. Experiments cannot be conducted in isolation from the body of research preceding it and the possible research succeeding it.

Considerations in the Design of an Experiment

The experimental method is the set of procedures used throughout diverse science areas to establish scientific facts. A scientific fact is established when clear cause-and-effect relationships can be shown. To show a cause-and-effect relationship, it must be shown with certainty that a particular factor will cause an effect

in behavior. For example, suppose you wish to show that a particular interface design (the factor) will cause an improvement (the cause) in user performance. It is possible that an effect could occur without establishing a clear cause-and-effect relationship. The researcher must differentiate between the possibility that the effect occurs merely because two things happen to regularly occur together, or the preferred possibility that there is a controlling relationship.

The experimental method is used to establish clear cause-and-effect relationships by showing that the one experimental factor, and only that factor, could have caused the effect observed in the data. This factor is often referred to as the independent variable or sometimes as the treatment. All the other factors, known as the extraneous variables, that could have caused the effect must be discounted through the experimental design, the experimental environment, and careful experimentation. An important way in which these extraneous factors can be discounted is by showing that the cause-and-effect relationships between the independent variable and performance still occur when the extraneous factors are held constant or are absent altogether. An extraneous factor is called a confounding variable when it affects one of the treatment levels and not the others. In this case, the experimenter cannot determine if the differences between conditions are due to the treatment or to the confounding variable. When using the experimental method, the trick to performing an effective, interpretable experiment is to show that confounding variables have not occurred.

The experimental method uses the following procedures to determine cause-

and-effect relationships. First, the subjects (or participants in the experiment) are divided into comparable groups, usually by randomly assigning subjects to groups. If the groups are comparable initially, then any observed differences during testing cannot be due to group-related variables.

Second, the treatment is applied to one or more of the groups. The treatment is the manipulated factor, or independent variable, that is allowed to be different across the groups. It is the factor that will be assumed to cause the effect. In most interface design experiments, the treatment will be the different interfaces which are being considered. The treatment can have several different levels. If two interface designs are being compared, the treatment will have two levels: interface type 1 and interface type 2. Also, a single interface design or several designs could be compared to a control group. The subjects in the control group would use a traditional interface design so that this group could be compared to the group(s) provided with the new interface designs.

Third, the experiment should be implemented in a controlled environment. The experimenters should be able to control the environment so that potential confounding variables can be eliminated or held constant.

If the groups are comparable initially, and the treatment is the only factor allowed to vary across groups, then observed differences between groups must be due to the effect of the treatment. A clear cause-and-effect relationship has been established.

To use the experimental method, the experimenters must have a controlled environment and be able to manipulate the factors. Some researchers believe that a controlled environment is too sterile and not at all like the real world. This reservation is referred to as ecological validity. Additionally, it is not always possible to experimentally manipulate variables. Astronomy, for example, has progressed without being able to manipulate the important factors experimentally. If experimenters believe that a controlled environment is too sterile, or if it is impossible to manipulate factors experimentally, then they should use techniques other than the experimental method.

The cause-and-effect relationship in the experimental design, and the potential problem of confounding variables, is illustrated in Figure 4-1. In the figure, the treatment could be three different interface designs used by the subjects, and the confounding variable could be having experts as subjects when novice subjects are expected. The top two illustrations show clear cause-and-effect relationships. In (a), the treatment levels are all the same initially. A treatment is applied at each level. The confounding variable has been eliminated—it does not vary within or between the treatment groups—possibly by having novice subjects in all groups. Since the confounding variable has been eliminated, it is not applied to the treatment levels, and therefore the performance differences can only be accounted for by the application of the treatment. In (b), the confounding variable has an equal effect on all treatment groups. This could occur by having a mixture of novices and experts in each group, with the average expertise level within a group the same for all. Since the confounding variable has an equal effect on all groups, performance differences are due only to the different levels of

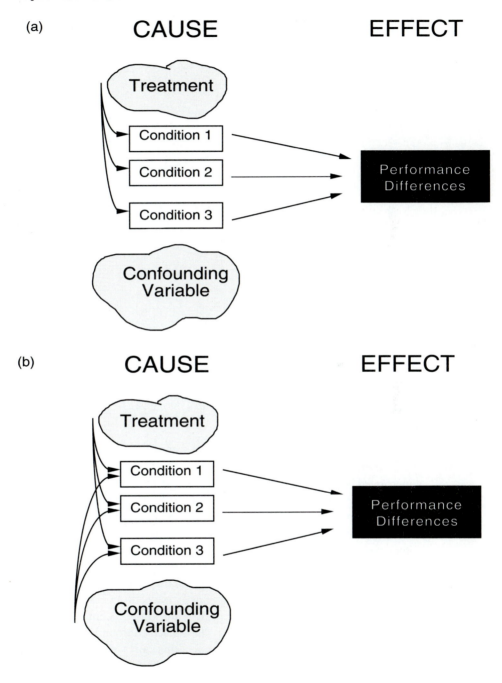

Figure 4-1. Illustration of the experimental method. Figures (a) and (b) show clear cause-and-effect relationships but (c) does not. The results from (c), shown on the next page, cannot be interpreted and the experiment is useless.

(c)

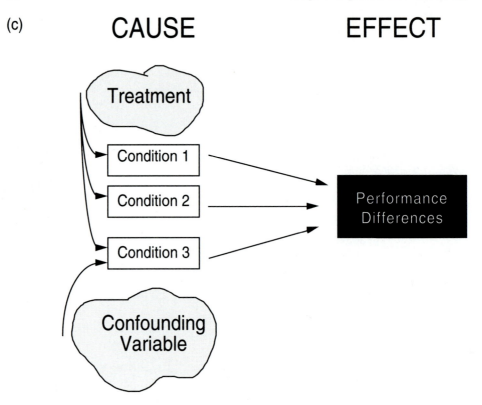

Figure 4-1 (cont.)

the treatment. In (c), the experiment has been confounded and the results cannot be interpreted because the confounding variable has been applied to one group but not the other two. This could occur by having experts in one group and novices in the other two. Performance differences are due to the treatment and also the confounding variable. One cannot determine if group 3 is better because of the effect of the third treatment level or because of the effect of the confounding variable. The experiment cannot be interpreted.

The choice of an experimental design partly depends on the kinds of confounds that are likely to occur in the experiment. Remember that a confound, or

confounding variable, is an uncontrolled factor that is allowed to vary along with the treatment, and it could affect the results and the interpretation of the results. When a confounding variable occurs and cannot be measured, it is impossible to tell whether any observed changes are because of the treatment alone or whether the confounding factor has made an important contribution. In discussing confounds, the kinds of confounds are first identified. Each confound should be eliminated, and this can be done in one of three ways: by holding it constant thereby eliminating its effects, by measuring it, and by manipulating it. These three possibilities will be discussed in the last three sections.

Identifying Confounds. The potential confounds can be grouped into two broad categories: design-related confounds and implementation-related confounds. The implementation-related confounds are discussed later. Design-related confounds are those confounds that could occur because of a poorly designed experiment. The following six confounds could occur because of poor design (the first four were taken from Cook and Stanley, 1979).

- History—The observed effect might be caused by some event that took place during the course of the experiment, when this event is not the treatment of research interest.

- Maturation—The observed effect might be caused by the respondent's growing older, wiser, stronger, etc., during the course of the experiment, and maturation is not the treatment of research interest.

- Test-Retest Familiarity—The effect might be caused by factors associated with taking a test a number of times.

- Instrumentation—The effect might be caused by a change in the measuring instrument during the course of the experiment.

- Comparability of Groups— The effect might be caused by initial differences between the groups instead of differences attributed to the treatment.

- Amount of Training— The amount of training can be improperly chosen so that an effect seen at one time period might not be seen at another time period.

These six confounding variables can be controlled by incorporating the correct procedure or construct in the design.

Eliminate the Confound or Hold It Constant. The experimental designs using the experimental method assume that a controlled environment is used. In a controlled environment, possible confounds are eliminated by controlling the stimuli the subjects will come into contact with. In a controlled environment, confounding variables are eliminated or held constant by ensuring that all subjects in all groups are treated exactly the same. Randomly assigning subjects to groups is one method for holding constant potential confounding variables that might be related to individual differences. This method is actually more useful for controlling implementation-related confounds. Part (a) in Figure 4-1 was an example where the potential confound was eliminated, by using only novice subjects, and part (b) was an example where the potential confound was applied equally to all the treatment levels, by having a combination of novice and expert subjects in each condition.

Measure the Confound. It must be shown that the possible confounds were actually eliminated or held constant. This can be done by measuring the effects of the confounds. Pretest-posttest designs will show whether the groups were the same initially. If the groups are not the same, then the pretest will measure the confound of noncomparable groups and allow a meaningful interpretation of the results. A control group can be used to measure the possible confounds of history, maturation, instrumentation, and test-retest familiarity effects. During the course of the experiment, the subjects can change in some way that is not because of the treatment. If a control group is used that has the same experiences as the treatment group, the effects of this confound can be determined. Finally, the effects of confounds can be measured by statistical techniques. Analysis of covariance is one technique. Post hoc blocking and post hoc analysis of covariance are statistical techniques to measure effects of certain kinds of confounds after the experiment is completed.

Manipulate the Confound. The possible confounding variable can be manipulated as an experimental variable so that it can be measured. Variables other than the treatment can be manipulated. A randomized block design will block out a potential confounding variable (such as the amount of experience for a subject) and experimentally determine whether it has an effect (see Chapter 5 for this design).

Real-World Constraints. When choosing a design, the experimenters must also consider real-world constraints. Time, money, and subjects are limited resources. The effects of potential design-related confounding variables could be eliminated mostly if the resources available to perform the experiment were unlimited. As an example, multiple groups of subjects could be tested for long periods of time. The experimental designs, and how they vary in cost, are considered further in Chapter 5.

Choosing the Independent Variable

The independent variable is manipulated in the experimental design through the application of the treatment to the different treatment levels, or conditions, in the experiment. The independent variable should be the only manipulation varying between the treatment conditions. If some other factor varies, then, as discussed in the previous section, a confound occurs and the results can be invalidated.

The most obvious independent variable is the interface design or the features of an interface design. If the research question is to determine which design, a command-based or direct manipulation interface, is fastest to use, then the interface design is the treatment with two levels (command-based or direct manipulation). If the research question is to determine how long a help message should be (4, 8, or 12 lines) to be most comprehensive to the user, then the treatment is the help message with 3 levels (4, 8, or 12 lines). For human-computer interaction research, the interface design features are usually the main variable of interest.

An experiment can have more than one independent variable. One of the most common independent variables, other than the interface design, is practice or training. One kind of interface design may be better for people at the very beginning because it is easy to learn. Over time, little improvement may be seen in this interface. Another interface design may be difficult to learn, but once learned, may be fast to operate. With these different interfaces, depending on the practice and training time, different conclusions would be made. By including training time as an independent variable, then the conditions under which one interface would be better than another could be demonstrated explicitly.

Characteristics of the user, often considered as a possible confound, could be included as another kind of independent variable. There are many subject-related effects which could possibly confound the results in human-computer interaction research: expertise level of the subject (novice or expert), amount of training on the interface, cognitive abilities of the users, or experience on other interface designs. As indicated previously, these possible effects can be eliminated (by holding them constant), randomized between the conditions (the effects will cancel out), measured, or manipulated as an independent variable.

As an example of controlling the effect through manipulating an independent variable, consider again the comparison of direct manipulation to command-based interfaces. A one-factor experiment would have the one independent variable (interface design) with two levels (command-based and direct manipulation). Many interface designers believe that experts prefer and find it easier to use command-based displays and novices prefer and find it easier to use direct manipulation displays. With one independent variable, and with the subjects' expertise levels varying within the conditions, then the confounding variable of expertise would have an effect on performance. A good experimental design would try to control the confounding variable in the ways mentioned in the previous sections. In particular, if only the one independent variable is used (the interface design), then this possible expertise confound can be either controlled, by using subjects who are all novices or all experts,

or it can be randomized between the groups, by having both expert and novice subjects and randomly assigning them to the different treatment conditions.

The two solutions of holding the confounding variable constant or randomizing its effect between the conditions may not be totally satisfying to the experimenter in addressing the research question. If the effect is held constant, then the generalizability of the results will be limited. Using the example, if novices participated in the experiment, then the results could only be generalized to novice users; the experiment would say nothing about experts. If the confounding variable is randomized between conditions, then the variance in the data could increase. Increased variance could hide any possible effects due to the treatment or independent variable. The possibility of increased variance could also increase the cost of the experiment because more subjects would be needed to find the effect.

If a possible confound, such as expertise level, may be important to the results and interpretation of the experiment, then the experimenter should consider manipulating this possible confound, thus making it another independent variable. The result of using two or more independent variables in an experimental design is a potential interaction in the results. With only one independent variable, the result will be a possible main effect where, for example, one could conclude that people performed better on the direct manipulation display than on the command-based display (see Figure 4-2). With two or more independent variables, the results could become more complicated and possibly more interesting. As an example, with an interaction one could

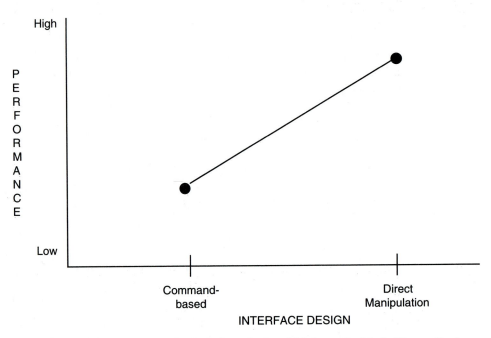

High

P
E
R
F
O
R
M
A
N
C
E

Low

Command-based　　　　　　　Direct Manipulation

INTERFACE DESIGN

Figure 4-2. In this experiment only one independent variable is manipulated. The results show a main effect, that one interface design is better than the other.

conclude that the experts perform better on the command-based display and the experts and novices perform about the same on the command-based display (see Figure 4-3).

　　Many experimenters will try to design experiments to find an interaction. Interactions are more interesting, because one of the purposes of experimentation is to consider the conditions under which one interface design will be better than another. Also, an interaction can provide more validity to the results. It is possible that with just a main effect someone could argue that one condition was designed so poorly that people could not possibly perform very well on it. With an interaction, the results show that some people can perform well on the interface design, thus refuting the argument of poorly designed conditions.

Choosing a Dependent Variable

A dependent variable is used to measure performance. Four kinds of measures are useful in interface design experiments. Quantity of performance (speed) is used typically to measure performance. This could be used to determine the amount of time needed to perform a task with different interface design features. Quality of performance (accuracy) is also used typically in human-computer interaction research. Some interface designs may be easier to use than others, and this ease of use could be reflected in the number of errors. There is usually a trade-off between time and errors. As subjects perform faster, they will make more errors. Because of this, both should be measured so that treatment conditions do not trade off the two differentially. A third measure

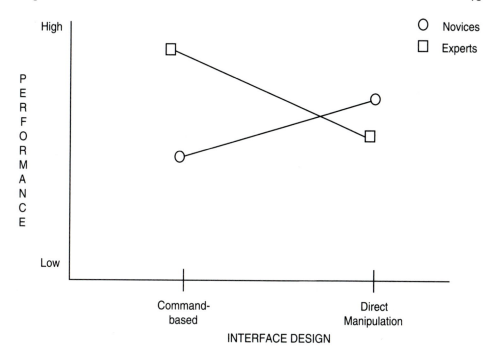

Figure 4-3. In this experiment two independent variables are manipulated. The results show an interaction between the two. Experts are better than novices on the command-based system, but little difference between the groups occurs on the direct manipulation system. This result could be more interesting than just a main effect, because the results show that performance is dependent upon expertise level.

to be used is frequency of events. For a frequency, a simple count is performed. As an example, the experimenter may measure the number of times that help messages are requested as a measure of ease of use. Some statisticians argue that the analysis of variance techniques discussed in this chapter and the next cannot be used with frequency data. As an alternative, one would perform a chi-square test or use a log-linear model, both discussed later.

A final category of dependent variable, used quite often in human-computer interaction research, is the preference rating. Sometimes subjects will be required to use several different interface designs and decide which one is preferred. This dependent variable is more subjective than the others and should be used with caution. However, when performing product research for marketing, preferences often are valid measures because of the relationship to buying decisions. Preferences, as a dependent variable, will be considered in more detail in a later section of this chapter.

Most dependent variables will fall into one of these four categories. As an example, the experimenter may wish to measure comprehension of the information presented on different interface designs, such as a display with 80 columns and one with 40 columns. To do this, the experimenter could design questions based upon the information which was read from the displays. In answering these questions, the experimenter would measure the time to answer plus the number of errors in reading comprehension. The dependent measure ultimately is related to time and errors, in this case.

A dependent variable should satisfy two criteria: it should be a realistic or valid measure of performance and it should be an objective measure. To be a realistic measure, the dependent variable should predict accurately future performance on the interface design. Subjects who score high on the dependent variable in the experiment should perform consistently well on the interface design in the future. Subjects who score low on the dependent variable in the experiment consistently should perform poorly on the interface design in the future. This seems a fairly intuitive or even trivial matter. It is, however, very difficult to achieve in practice. To validate how realistic the dependent variable is, it should be correlated with an overall measure of performance after the experiment is over. Experimenters rarely have the time, means, or expertise to perform this validation, however. Experimenters should always consult experts in the area, if the experimenter is not one already, for suggestions on the best ways to set up valid measurements of performance in the experiment.

The second criterion of a good dependent variable is that it should be as objective a measure as possible. Several experimenters should be able to measure performance and come up with the same score. An example of an objective measure is the time taken to interact with an interface design. Time should be measurable with little difference in scores across several experimenters, especially if time is collected by the computer internally. An example of a nonobjective, or subjective, measure is a rating by an experimenter on how well the subject utilized the features of an interface. Different experimenters may disagree on what constitutes good utilization of the features and they would thus give different scores to the same utilization. If subjective measures such as ratings are used, the experimenters should define beforehand the criteria that will be used for giving low and high scores, and they should double check, using correlations between the raters, to make sure that raters give reliable ratings.

Examples of important experimental designs for human-computer interaction research are provided in Chapter 5. Some of the experimental design analysis considerations are also discussed. The hazards associated with improper use of the experimental method are discussed in Chapter 6. The subsequent sections in this chapter examine some of the informal experimental techniques, such as the use of questionnaires, which does not require the rigorous application of the experimental method. These techniques can provide the interface designer with important information about the use of interface designs.

QUESTIONNAIRES

From the stages of human-factored usability studies (refer back to Figure 2-2), the market analysis and product survey stages both can involve the use of questionnaires. Questionnaires are developed to determine and measure any kind of subjective behavior such as evaluations, judgments, comparisons, attitudes, beliefs, and opinions (Meister, 1986). For market analysis and product survey, the researchers must determine how users feel about the current products (market analysis) so that they can correct perceived problems in the new product, and how users feel about the new product after it is designed (product survey) to determine if the previously perceived problems have been corrected. Most of the time, in the marketing of computer-based products, attitude toward the problem may be the main determinant of whether someone will buy it. In industry, for an internally designed and maintained product, attitudes toward the use of the product may be a main determinant of whether or not the product will be used.

An alternative to the use of questionnaires is to interview the people one-on-one. This has the purpose of making the process more personal, and the format is very flexible. If the user voices an opinion not considered previously, then the interviewer can be flexible enough to follow up on that opinion and ask additional questions, possibly eliciting more information from the user.

Questionnaires can be evaluated on reliability, validity, and factor loadings. Reliability refers to the probability that a questionnaire item will be answered the same way on two or more administrations of the items. Reliability can, thus, be measured from 0 (no reliability) to 1.0 (perfect reliability). To determine reliability, sometimes a questionnaire will contain duplications of items--the duplications do not always have to be worded exactly the same--and reliability can be determined by correlating the responses between the duplicate items. Alternatively, the questionnaire, or parts of the questionnaire, can be administered separately at two different times. Correlations

between items can again be determined to assess reliability. If the questionnaire has few items, then reliability should be determined by separate administrations because the duplicates may be too obvious and too easy for the interviewed subjects to check on their own reliability.

Validity refers to how well the questionnaire measures what it is supposed to assess. Obviously, a questionnaire which supposedly assesses usability of interfaces, but leads to erroneous conclusions because of the composition of the questionnaire would be useless itself and dangerously misleading. Validity can be difficult to determine, however, several methods can be used. In one method, experts answer the questionnaire items and then these items are correlated with non-experts. Another technique uses an independent objective measure of the item and compares this to the response to the questionnaire item. As an example of an objective measure, validity could be determined by evaluating how many of the people actually bought or used the product compared to how many people rated the product as one they would like to buy. Many questionnaires will be used without determining a measure of validity.

The third method to evaluate questionnaires is in terms of factor loadings. For the factor loadings, an assumption for questionnaire designs is that one or more factors may underlie the answers that people provide. As an example, several of the items may assess directly an underlying factor of the software; other factors may assess directly an underlying factor of the hardware. If these two were termed different factors, then those items that assess hardware would all be highly correlated with each other and not correlated with software. Similarly, the items that assess software would all be highly correlated and not correlated with the hardware items. By examining these patterns of interactions, the underlying factors could be determined. A statistical technique, called factor analysis, is available for doing this. Factor analysis determines the number of factors which may be underlying the items; the researcher then has to examine the factors and name them. The analysis also determines how each item loads on the factor, or, in other words, how each item measures the underlying factor. The loadings can range from -1.0 to 1.0. A final questionnaire can be designed to include only a subset of items included in the original questionnaire because some of the items may load on the same factors, and including them would only provide redundant information. The factor loadings can be used to determine which items should be included in the final questionnaire. By performing a factor analysis, the number of items in a questionnaire can be reduced, thus increasing the time efficiency of the experimentation.

Several general classes of questionnaire items are available. One class is the open-ended item. An open-ended questionnaire item is somewhat like an interview except that the user writes down the answers to questions on a piece of paper or, if designed for the computer, the answers can be entered through the keyboard. The answers are not restricted—they are open-ended—so that much information can be gathered. As an example, the user may be asked to write down any errors that occurred in the use of a particular interface. Some problems exist with these kinds of items. The user may feel it requires too much effort to answer these

kinds of questions and then he or she would take the easy way out by saying no errors occurred. Also, the user may not remember if errors occurred. Finally, the items, because they do not force the user to make a specific choice, cannot be coded easily for statistical analyses. Open-ended questionnaire items are not very reliable.

The second type of questionnaire uses closed-ended items which can be of two types: multiple choice and rating scales. Most people are familiar with multiple choice items, where a question is asked or a statement is presented and several possible answers are provided. Multiple choice answers are easy to score and analyze, although alternative answers must be designed carefully so as to be plausible answers representing some kind of misperception. For most evaluations of users' attitudes, however, no correct answer is needed; the users' attitudes can be evaluated instead.

The other form of closed-ended questionnaire uses rating scale items. These are numerical values assigned to alternatives. Rating scales have all the advantages of closed-ended questionnaires with the additional advantage that traditional statistical techniques, such as analysis of variance considered in the next chapter, can be used to analyze the answers. Usually rating scales incorporate a Likert scale which is characterized by a set number of choices, usually 5, 7, or 9. The number of choices is always odd so to provide a clear center point. Each of the numbered values is anchored by an adjective which describes the attitude of the interviewee to the question item. Typical scales, with the adjectives at each point, are provided in Figure 4-4. The scales can either be continuous, in which case the

Never	Seldom	Sometimes	Generally	Always	

Largely Unacceptable	Barely Unacceptable	Borderline	Barely Acceptable	Largely Acceptable	

Wholly Unacceptable	Largely Unacceptable	Borderline	Largely Acceptable	Wholly Acceptable	

Completely Inadequate	Considerably Inadequate	Borderline	Considerably Adequate	Completely Adequate	

Totally Inadequate	Very Inadequate	Barely Inadequate	Borderline	Barely Adequate	Very Adequate	Totally Adequate

Decidedly Disagree	Substantially Disagree	Slightly Disagree	No Preference	Slightly Agree	Substantially Agree	Decidedly Agree

Strongly Disagree	Disagree	Slightly Disagree	No Preference	Slightly Agree	Agree	Strongly Agree

Figure 4-4. Examples of Likert scales with possible adjectives at each of the markings.

interviewee places a mark along the scale, or they can be discrete, in which case the interviewee chooses one of the numbers. The continuous scale answer can be analyzed by taking a ruler and determining the real number associated with the mark. This technique has some advantages statistically because most statistics require continuous values as part of the distribution assumptions.

One important aspect of questionnaire design is in the wording of the item. People can be encouraged to respond one way or the other based upon the phrasing of the question. To evaluate the questionnaire, the wording must be evaluated also. Generally, the question should be as neutral as possible and should not go into great detail or background. Meister (1986) suggests that negative words should be avoided and, if used, should be emphasized either through underlining or by use

of italics. Of course, no double negatives should be used. Meister (1986) also presents some examples of how the question can be loaded or biased to get the respondents to respond in a certain way. As an example, the following are loaded questions: "Experts have suggested . . . , do you approve of this?" or "Is this new equipment better than the old because it is less fatiguing or are they about the same?"

Questionnaires have some advantages over the interview technique. Questionnaires are more likely to produce frank answers than interviews because the interviewee is anonymous. Many times with interviews, the interviewees are reluctant to criticize the product because they may feel that they would get into trouble for being too critical. Additionally, questionnaires are less expensive because they can be administered to several people at the same time. If the questions are closed-ended, then the items can be evaluated statistically, allowing comparisons of different systems.

Examples of Questionnaires for HCI Evaluations

Specific questionnaires for evaluating computer systems and interface designs have been developed. LaLomia and Sidowski (1990) reviewed some of the questionnaires under two general classes: user satisfaction with computer systems, and computer literacy and aptitude. For each of the questionnaires, they evaluated the reliability and validity. In the following discussion, only the best questionnaires will be reported; more can be found in the LaLomia and Sidowski article.

User Satisfaction. Knowledge of user satisfaction would be useful in the product acceptance and product survey stages. For product acceptance, the questionnaire could be used to determine that which is wrong with the current system and what could be improved with the new to-be-developed version. For the product survey stage, conducted after the prototype has been developed, the questionnaire could be used to determine if some of the problems have been corrected, and to compare the new system to the old one.

LaLomia and Sidowski (1990) report five questionnaires which have been developed to address user satisfaction. Each questionnaire addresses slightly different aspects of usability and different kinds of equipment. Because of these different foci, it is difficult to compare directly the different questionnaires. However, one of the best and most versatile questionnaires appears to be the Questionnaire for User Interface Satisfaction

(QUIS) developed by Chin, Diehl, and Norman (1987, 1988).

QUIS has 27 items using a 9-point Likert scale. According to LaLomia and Sidowski (1990), the items test overall reactions to software (6 items), evaluation of characters on the screen (4 items), use of terms and information throughout the system (6 items), learning to operate the system (6 items), and system capabilities such as speed (5 items). The reliability of the test was found to be 0.94. Validity was tested by how well the items discriminated between PC systems that were liked and disliked. In all cases, the means were higher for the liked systems than for the disliked systems, thereby providing evidence for the validity of the questionnaire.

A factor analysis was performed on 96 users from a PC users' group. The factor analysis was administered on 90 original items and, by determining the underlying factors and the factor loadings for each of the items, the 90 items were reduced to the 27 items on the final questionnaire. Four underlying factors were identified: learning, terminology and information flow, system output, and system characteristics. Each of the 27 questions loads on one of the four factors.

Computer Literacy and Aptitude Scales. Computer literacy provides an indication of the computer expertise of a person. Computer aptitude refers to the predictions of performance in a training program for computers or a student in a computer course at a school or university. The main function of these scales for human-computer interaction research would be their use in conjunction with other experimentation. Computer expertise of a subject in a controlled laboratory experiment could be an important factor in determining usability of interface designs. An expert might perform best on one interface design, whereas a novice might perform best on a different interface design. This kind of information can be important in the interface evaluation. Computer literacy questionnaires could be used to divide the subjects into expert and novice groups so that this factor could be controlled experimentally.

All of the six scales which constitute the questionnaire and are reviewed by LaLomia and Sidowski (1990) are very specialized, so that determining one overall questionnaire that would be best in all situations is difficult. Of the six scales, three of them measure computer literacy and these would be the most useful for human-computer interaction research. The Standardized Test of Computer Literacy (STCL) (Montag, Simonson, and Maurer, 1984) measures three computing skills in individuals: computer applications, computer systems, and computer programming. The Computer Literacy Examination: Cognitive Aspect (CLECA) (Cheng, Plake, and Stevens, 1985) covers computer terminology, computer language commands, writing computer programs, components of computers, writing algorithms, math concepts, and history of computers. It was developed specifically for Apple II computers. The Cassel Computer Literacy Test (CCLT) (Cassel and Cassel, 1984) was designed to be given before and after computer training to assess the effectiveness of the training.

Both the CLECA and the CCLT are restricted to certain kinds of computer literacy; for the CLECA the restriction is literacy on Apple II computers, and for the CCLT, the literacy restriction pertains to the content of the particular content of the

training course. If this is too restrictive, the tests still have some usefulness in that the test items could possibly be examined to determine how they could be modified to other specific computer systems or situations. The STCL is more general, and it will be discussed in more detail.

According to LaLomia and Sidowski (1990), the STCL has 80 multiple-choice items divided into computer systems (29 items), computer applications (28 items), and computer programming (23 items). The items included in the final test were selected based upon a literature review and survey results of computer experts on their opionions of what constitutes computer literacy. Reliability was found to be 0.87. No validity testing was performed and no factor analysis was reported.

Conclusions. Very few systematic reviews of questionnaires have been performed. The LaLomia and Sidowski (1990) review is useful, however, and should be consulted for more information. The questionnaires discussed above or those from the review article can be used to determine some aspects of usability and computer literacy. The exact tests are useful because the reliability and, in some cases, validity can be reported. For some of the computer literacy tests, the obtained scores can be compared to norms developed from large samples of people. As an example, the percentile of the score could be determined, based upon all high school students. This could be very useful information, especially when trying to justify whether the subjects were characteristic of a certain class of users. The questionnaire items can also be modified to make them more specific to the particular aspect tested. If this is done, though, the original reliability and validity scores are no longer valid and must be determined again.

INFORMAL EXPERIMENTATION

The methodologies of informal experiments are too numerous to list, but they still form an important part of human-computer interaction research. Informal experimentation is especially important in the early stages of research to describe the behavior of users. These descriptions can be used later in more rigorous experimentation. In the beginning of the experimental process, though, the researcher may not know what to expect, and resulting information from descriptive studies can be quite useful. In addition, because experimentation using the experimental method is mostly limited to answering a yes/no question, for example, whether one interface design is better than another, informal experimentation can provide much richer information. The informal experimentation may try to determine if the person looks confused, the kinds of problems encountered, and the kinds of verbal questions asked of the experimenter. These would all have to be described mostly through qualitative analyses.

Perhaps one of the most restrictive aspects of the experimental method is that the environment be controlled so that no extraneous variables, or confounds, are allowed to vary with the treatment conditions. In the observational method of gathering data, behavioral changes are observed and recorded in the natural environment. The researcher has no control over the environment, so this method has the disadvantage that treatments cannot be applied and confounding variables are not held constant or eliminated. Some re-searchers believe that being able to observe events in the natural environment is more important than the disadvantages inherent in this technique.

Two techniques are often used to measure performance in informal experimentation: transcripts and videotape. With transcripts, the subjects are encouraged to talk while they are performing the task. These verbal responses are recorded, and written transcripts are typed and saved. Hypotheses about subject behavior can be confirmed by including sections of the transcript. The problem with this method is that the evidence is anecdotal. If the researcher has preconceived notions about what will occur, then the parts of the transcript fitting these preconceived notions can be included in the report and any disconfirming parts of the transcript can be ignored. This may be unintentional bias on the part of the experimenter. With enough information, practically any hypothesis could be supported if the experimenter does not make a conscious effort to be fair in the evaluations and receptive to alternative explanations and hypotheses.

Videotape can also include a verbal transcript in addition to the visual information. The visual information could be very important in an evaluation of the experiment. Looks of confusion, motions which are nonproductive, and interactions between people in the experiment are all examples of visual information providing some clues to usability of an interface. Videotapes have many of the problems associated with transcripts in selecting the important and nonbiased aspects of behavior.

If using informal experimentation techniques, the researcher should be aware of the drawbacks of the technique. These drawbacks should be considered when comparing informal data gathering methods to the experimental method. The experimental method is devised to determine cause-and-effect relationships between the environment and behavioral events. This requires a controlled environment and control over the extraneous variables. In informal experimentation, the environment should be controlled as much as possible so that the effects of extraneous variables are reduced.

In the experimental method, dependent variables are supposed to be as objective as possible. Many of the measurements in an informal experiment are subjective, and the researcher has great latitude in what is deemed significant behavior and what is not. Effort should be made by the researcher to ensure that the measurements used, even though very subjective and qualitative, are as nonbiased as possible.

Replication of the results of the experiment is important in any scientific pursuit. In a report of the experimentation, enough detail should be provided so that another researcher in another laboratory would be able to perform the experiment and replicate the results. The report for informal experimentation should contain the same kind of detail so that it could be replicated in some form also.

Most formal experiments are evaluated in terms of statistical comparisons between the treatment conditions. The statistics provide some indication of the probability that this result could be found just due to chance instead of the treatment effect. Statistics are very difficult to apply in informal experimentation because the measurements are often subjective.

Deciding whether to use formal or informal experimentation involves a trade-off. Formal experimentation provides cause-and-effect relationships, objective measurements, replicable results, and statistical analyses. These can also be criticized as being too controlled and sterile, the measurements being irrelevant to important user behavior, and the statistics only providing one-dimensional yes-no information. On the other hand, informal experimentation can be very subjective, vulnerable to the biases of the researcher, and not replicable.

Informal experimentation should be designed so the rich information obtained is not too subjective or biased. It should not be used just because the researcher does not wish to invest the effort to be more rigorous. Transcripts and videotapes can be used to determine objective measures. By reading the transcript or by watching the videotape, frequencies of events can be observed and counted. As an example, utterances can be categorized into positive and negative categories by some operational definition. The researcher could then go through and count the number of positive and negative utterances. Several different observers could be utilized, and the results from each of the observers could be correlated to determine the goodness of the operational definition. As another example, behaviors on the videotape could be categorized into those that are productive and those that are nonproductive. Once again, the frequency of the events in each category could be determined by one or more observers. In many cases, the informal experimentation techniques can be made more rigorous, with a little more effort, without losing the richness of information inherent in these designs.

Some textbooks provide information on conducting these informal experiments. Texts such as Campbell and Stanley (1966) and Cook and Stanley (1979) can be consulted if the experimenter wishes to use naturalistic observation or informal experimentation.

SUMMARY

This chapter has discussed the experimental method, the design and use of questionnaires, and informal experimentation techniques. The next two chapters discuss in more detail the experimental designs, with some discussion of statistical techniques, and then the hazards associated with running and interpreting experiments. All of these techniques can be used at different times during the product development cycle.

QUESTIONS

1. Consider the following experiment. Two work schedules are being tested in a production task. In work schedule A, people work for 2 hours and then take a 20 minute break. In work schedule B, people work for 1 hour and then take a 10 minute break. People are tested on a computer data entry task for speed and accuracy. The subjects in the experiment were hired from a temporary employment service in Lafayette. Schedule A was run in April, and schedule B was run in May. In May, many Purdue students join the temporary employment service. All subjects were chosen randomly, from those available at the time, for each of the two schedules.

a. What is (are) the independent variable(s) in the experiment?

b. What is (are) the dependent variable(s) in the experiment?

c. A confound occurs in this experiment. From the six confound types discussed in Chapter 4, what kind of confound is it? Explain why it occurs.

d. How should the experiment have been conducted to eliminate the confound?

2. Indicate if the following remarks refer to validity, reliability, or factor loadings of questionnaires.

    •   All items are correlated, through a statistical technique, to determine this.

    •   Can be used to reduce the number of questionnaire items by eliminating the ones which measure the same thing.

    •   It may measure something, but not what it was supposed to.

    •   A perfect score on this measure would be 1.0.

    •   Items are repeated on the questionnaire in order to measure this.

    •   Uses an independent objective measure of the item and compares this to the response on the questionnaire item.

3. Consider the following questionnaire item (a person would respond along

a 7-point Likert scale to determine if they agree or don't agree with the statement):

Most people believe that questionnaire items are not subjective.

a. Name *two* things that are wrong with the wording of this questionnaire item.

b. Rewrite the questionnaire item so that it avoids the two problems you identified in part a.

4. Go to the library and choose an article on HCI research from a journal such as *Human-Computer Interaction*, the *International Journal of Human-Computer Interaction*, or the *International Journal of Man-Machine Studies*. Answer the following questions about this article.

a. What is the research question?

b. What is the independent variable?

c. What is the dependent variable?

CHAPTER 5

EXPERIMENTAL DESIGNS AND ANALYSIS

INTRODUCTION

The choice of an experimental design depends on many factors. Choosing the correct design is very important so that the results can be interpreted and the research question can be addressed. In human-computer interaction research, there are about 18 basic experimental designs commonly used. The following provides the rationale and a procedure for choosing one of the 18. The procedure is divided into two parts. In the first part, the design issues are discussed. In the second part, summaries of each of the 18 designs are provided. Each design has a particular statistical analysis associated with it which will be discussed in the last section.

Some texts will use flowcharts to explain how to choose an experimental design after addressing a few basic questions. Flowcharts are useful, but perhaps a better way to conceptualize the choice of an experimental design is in terms of a matrix. Figure 5-1 presents the matrix of the 18 basic designs. There are six rows divided into within-subject and between-subject designs. A further division occurs depending on the number of independent variables, or factors, that are to be manipulated. The columns are divided into three parts depending on the use or nonuse of practice or learning as an independent variable.

EXPERIMENTAL DESIGN ISSUES

Four experimental design issues represent decision points which must be addressed before choosing an experimental design: within- or between-subject designs; whether to control the potential effects of extraneous variables; whether an important interaction could occur; and when to evaluate performance. When decisions have been made concerning the four design issues, then a unique experimental design can be selected. During the decision process of determining the appropriate experimental design, the design issues do not have to be considered in a set order, since they are independent of each other; the following presentation of the order in the decisions is just one way to carry out the procedure.

The following procedure for choosing the experimental design is based upon an elimination process on the components of the matrix of Figure 5-1. After making decisions about the four design issues, several parts of the matrix can be eliminated. A single design will remain upon resolution of the four issues, and that experimental design will best answer the research question under consideration.

During subsequent discussion of the design issues, the main independent variable will be different interface designs or features of interface designs. Of course, this will not always be the important variable, or the only one, in human-computer interaction research, but it would be the most likely one. A second factor that will be used in the example is individual differences between the subjects, such as expertise level. For different research questions, other factors or variables may be important in the research question besides

		X	Y	Z
	WITHIN	Test	Test-Retest	Multiple Test
A	1 factor			
B	blocked			
C	2 factor			
	BETWEEN			
D	1 factor			
E	blocked			
F	2 factor			

Figure 5-1. A representation of the 18 basic experimental designs which can be used in human-computer interaction research.

the variables of interface design or individual differences. The appropriate experimental design can be selected using the logic of the following procedure.

Design Issue—Within- or Between-Subject Design

Experimental designs can be divided into within- and between-subject designs. Consider the case when the independent variable, the possible interface designs, has two levels: interface A and interface B. To compare the two, subjects must use the devices. How the subjects are divided between the two interface designs determines whether or not a within- or between-subjects design is used.

For a within-subjects design, each of the subjects will use both interface design A and B. For the between-subjects design, one group of subjects will use interface design A and another separate group of subjects will use interface design B. Each of these possibilities has advantages and disadvantages which must be weighed and considered subjectively. The decision only

becomes easier when the experimenter is very familiar with the relevant research and theories in the area.

The first consideration in evaluating within- and between-subjects designs is equality between the subject groups for the interface designs. So that no confounds occur, the two groups must be equal in how they interact with the interfaces. For the within-subjects design, the groups are the same on the interface designs simply because they are the same people. For the between-subjects design, equality of the groups cannot be assumed automatically because the two groups are comprised of different individuals. To help ensure equality for a between-subjects design, one may have to rely on randomization. This is a critical issue, and randomization should be done very carefully. Each subject must be randomly assigned to one of the two groups so that any potential confounding variables due to individual differences within a treatment condition would be dispersed randomly across groups. The fewer the subjects in the group, the more likely that the groups will be different in some way. With more subjects, randomization will work better. For a between-subjects design where few subjects are used, the experimenter may try to determine all possible ways that the subjects can be different (male/female, type of job, experience, etc.), match and pair subjects on these characteristics, and randomly assign one from each pair to each condition. The resulting between-subjects correlated samples design is an excellent solution to the problems created by small sample sizes and individual differences.

The second consideration when choosing within- or between-subjects design is whether or not experience with one interface will affect performance on the other. For example, assume that an experiment is being run to determine whether a graphics organization of the information is better than a textual organization of the material, and in this experiment, a within-subjects design is used where each subject operated and was tested on both the graphics and the textual displays. Does using one of the displays affect performance on the other? Maybe when the subjects perform on the graphics display it provides them with ideas for mentally organizing the information in the textual display, thus creating a behavioral carryover effect from one experimental condition to the other. We would assume that the subjects would not have generated these ideas without the previous experience on the other display. Because of this prior experience, we may expect to see few differences between the conditions, which may not be due to the interfaces being equivalent, but rather to subjects being "contaminated" by exposure to the other interface design. If each subject

operated and was tested on only one interface design, as in a between-subjects design, then this "contamination" problem would not occur. If the experimenter has reason to believe that experience on one interface will affect performance on the other, then the between-subjects design must be used.

Even if there is no reason to suspect carryover effects, the order in which subjects do the two tasks must be split evenly. This results in third consideration for within- and between-subjects designs, which is concerned with experience and transfer. For a within-subjects design, the subject has to operate one of the interface designs first. If the experiment was designed so that interface A was always operated before interface B, and the results showed that B was better than A, then these results could be due to B actually being better than A or it could be due to the experience factor of subjects performing better because they have been performing the task longer by the time they use B. If B was operated first, then we would expect A to allow better performance. Of course, a way to solve this problem for within-subjects designs is to have half the subjects use A first and the other half use B first. This actually introduces another independent variable into the design which can be controlled. In this case, you may need more subjects because of the introduction of this factor of order. Proper statistical analysis will be able to determine if the ordering of the interfaces had an effect. Even in a between-subjects design, the collection of data requires a random ordering of the two groups. Data should never be collected for all of one level and then for all of the second.

The choice of a within- or between-

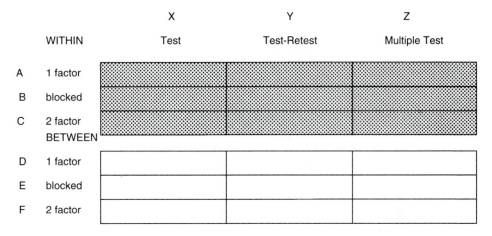

Figure 5-2. For illustration purposes, a between-subjects design has been chosen. Based upon this decision, all the within-subjects designs can be eliminated, and this is illustrated by blacking out rows A, B, and C.

subjects design is a subjective decision. The experimenter should perform the task to get some intuitive idea about whether subject "contamination" might occur. But more important, the experimenter also needs to bring to the research any knowledge from other experimentation or theories. If the theory states that subjects will form a conceptualization of the problem which will transfer to another interface design, then this information would indicate a between-subjects design would be best.

For the procedure illustrated in Figure 5-1, if a within-subjects design is chosen, then the experimenter can eliminate rows D, E, and F from the figure. If a between-subjects design is chosen, the experimenter can eliminate rows A, B, and C. Just for the purpose of illustration, let's say that a between-subjects design was chosen. Figure 5-2 shows how rows A, B, and C have been blacked out based upon this decision to use a between-subjects design.

Control the Potential Effects of Extraneous Variables?

In Chapter 4, a discussion of possible confounding variables revealed that three things could be done to control these potential effects of extraneous variables: the variable could be controlled by making it an independent variable, it could be eliminated by holding it constant, or it could be reduced by randomizing it between conditions. Each of these has advantages and disadvantages and each possibility has implications for choosing a particular experimental design.

First, consider eliminating the potential confound by holding it constant. As an example, let's say that expertise may affect performance on the task. If expertise is allowed to vary between the conditions, then the variability in the dependent variable would be increased so that effects due to the treatment may be difficult to find.

Holding the potential confounding

variable constant also reduces the generalizability of the results. As an example, if all subjects are novices, the results could only be generalized to novices. The experimenters would not have any information about the effect of the treatment on experts, and so the results could not be generalized to experts. This restriction may be desirable in some cases if the interface is targeted towards a certain user group, such as automatic teller machines being targeted to novices. However, if the target group of users is more diverse than the subjects in the experiment, then the results cannot be generalized to the diverse parts of the group, and the experimentation may have to be conducted again using those other users to generalize the results correctly.

Second, the experimenter could consider reducing the effect of the potential confound by randomizing the effect between the treatment conditions. This possibility was discussed in connection with the previous design issue of within- and between-subjects designs. The consequences are that more subjects would be needed and high variability within the groups would result. These effects could be circumvented by matching the subjects on the confounding extraneous variables. This could be done before or after the data are collected. It is more difficult to match beforehand.

Third, the experimenter could consider controlling the potential confound as an independent variable. This would partial out the variability, which was a problem in the randomization solution. It is possible that the experimenter may be interested in the effect of this variable on performance anyway. As an example, if expertise does have an effect on the results, then determining if one interface is better than another, conditional on the expertise of the users, would be important information. As mentioned in Chapter 4, designing an experiment to obtain an interaction between the factors has desirable consequences in the interpretation of results. The main disadvantage is that the experiment becomes more costly. More subjects would be needed, and the design and interpretation would be more complicated.

For the procedure illustrated in Figure 5-1, if the choice is to control the potential confound, then rows A and D can be eliminated or blacked out because a new factor would have to be introduced. The factor can either be blocked or it can be a separate independent variable. If the choice is to eliminate the effect or randomize it, then rows B, C, E, and F can be excluded, because only one factor would be incorporated in the experimental design. For the illustration, let's say that the experimenter decided to control the potential confound. In Figure 5-3, row A had already been eliminated. Because of this new choice, row D can now be blacked out also.

Importance of an Interaction Effect

If the experimenter has decided to control the possible confounding variable, then this design issue of interaction effects must be considered. On the other hand, if the possible confound is eliminated or randomized, this design issue does not have to be considered.

If the possible confound is varied as an independent variable, then the experimenter has two choices: make it a factor or block it out. The differences between

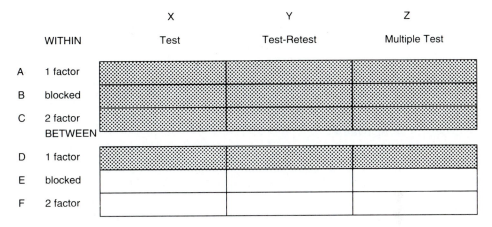

Figure 5-3. For illustration purposes, the experimenter has decided to control the potential confounding variable by including it as a factor in the experiment. By this choice, the experiment now has more than one factor, so that rows A and D can be blacked out or eliminated. Since row A had already been blacked out, this figure shows how D has now been blacked out also.

these two consequences are as follows. If it is a factor, then the experiment will have at least two factors in it, possibly more depending on whether training is a factor, and an interaction between interface device and the factor can be analyzed. As indicated in Chapter 4, this interaction may be important to the interpretation of the results. The experimenter may wish to know if one interface will be better under some conditions while the other interface may be better under other conditions.

If the extraneous variable is blocked out, then an interaction cannot be found and a design called a randomized block design will result. For this kind of design, the experimenter can still determine if the blocked variable had an effect on interface performance, but the interaction of this blocked variable and the interface factor cannot be determined. Blocking the variable is useful because it can remove some of the variability from the error term, thus improving the likelihood of finding effects of the treatment variable. Blocking should only be done when there is a good

reason to assume that the particular variable being blocked will affect performance. Blocking a variable which has no effect results in a larger error term, and the effects of the treatment may not be discernable. A randomized block design is cheaper to run than a factorial design with an interaction because fewer subjects are required. For a randomized block design, a minimum of one subject per cell is needed.

Once again, the design decision is subjective, but it requires careful consideration of the issue. The experimenter can make a good decision by performing extensive background work. This involves searching the research literature to find other similar experiments which may or may not have found an interaction. In addition, background work includes a working familiarity with the theoretical considerations, so that expected results could be hypothesized based upon the theories. Preliminary experimentation may be fruitful in providing information for making the final design decisions.

If the experimenter decides an inter-

		X Test	Y Test-Retest	Z Multiple Test
WITHIN				
A	1 factor			
B	blocked			
C	2 factor			
BETWEEN				
D	1 factor			
E	blocked			
F	2 factor			

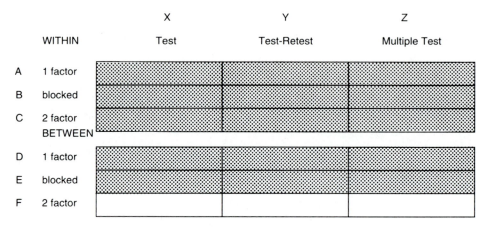

Figure 5-4. In the illustration, the experimenter has decided that the interaction is important in the results. By this choice, rows B and E can be blocked out. Since B has already been blacked out, then E has been blacked out in this figure.

action effect is important to addressing the research question, then a complete factorial experiment must be used and rows B and E can be eliminated, if they have not already been blacked out (rows A and D must have been eliminated already in order to consider this design issue). If a randomized block design is to be used, the interaction is unimportant, so rows C and F can be eliminated. For the illustration, let's say that the experimenter decided that the interaction is important. In Figure 5-4, row B has already been blacked out. Row E must now be eliminated.

When to Evaluate Performance

The last choice considered in this section is when to evaluate the performance of the users on the interfaces. From Figures 5-1 to 5-4, the choice considered in this section is whether to choose an experimental design from column X, Y, or Z. Figure 5-5 shows an illustration of a design from column X. In this case, the subjects in the experiment are practiced on the interface for some set period of time, t, and then they are tested. The test could involve determining how fast they are performing the

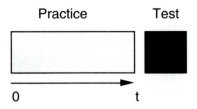

Figure 5-5. An illustration of the "test" design of column X. Subjects are practiced at a set time, t, before they are tested.

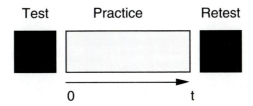

Figure 5-6. An illustration of the "test-retest" design of column Y. Subjects are tested initially on the interfaces, then practice is provided, and subjects are finally tested again.

task or their comprehension of the task after using the interface. Any of the dependent variables mentioned in Chapter 4 could be used in this test. The practice time, t, could range from 0 to some higher number. The practice time should be chosen based upon the situations in which the interfaces are designed. If the interface is designed to require no practice for its use, then t can be equal or close to 0. An example of this would be the interface for an automatic teller machine. If the interface is designed to be used repeatedly, so that practice becomes an important issue, then t can be much higher. An example would be the interface for a word processor or for a computer operating system. In most experimental cases, however, t is limited by the amount of resources available for conducting the experiment. It is costly and time-consuming to conduct an experiment incorporating large amounts of practice. If practice is limited, the results of the experiment can only be generalized to these small amounts of practice.

Figure 5-6 shows an illustration of an experimental design for the test-retest situation of column Y. This is similar to Figure 5-5, with the difference being that a test before practice is given to the subjects. The initial test can be used to establish that the groups of subjects are the same at the beginning of the experiment,

and consequently, any differences seen in the retest would be due to practice and learning from interacting with the different interfaces.

The test-retest experimental design is also good for determining the effects of practice on performance of the interfaces. People may learn faster on one interface when compared to another which could be a very beneficial aspect of the interface. Figure 5-7 shows a graph of a hypothetical situation where one interface is faster to learn than another. In this case, the test and retest would have to measure the same dependent variable. The groups do not have to be the same initially, because the interaction of interface design and practice time provides the important information about whether one interface can be learned faster than another. It would be desirable to show that the groups are the same initially; otherwise it could be argued that people who exhibit high performance initially can naturally learn faster than the others.

The test and retest do not have to measure the same dependent variable. As an example, the research question may address whether one interface allows people to perform faster than another interface. The initial test could collect typing speeds for both groups to show that potential execution time differences on the retest could be due to ease of interaction

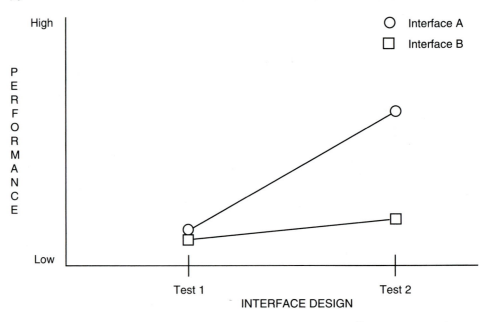

Figure 5-7. An example of different practice effects determined from a "test-retest" experimental design. The important part of the graph is the interaction; subjects using interface A learn at a faster rate than those on interface B.

instead of inherent typing speed differences between the groups of subjects. As another example, the experimenters may want to demonstrate how one group of subjects can be classified as experts and another group as novices. To show this, information could be collected on the initial test, possibly through a questionnaire, on various aspects of expertise. The retest could test performance characteristics of the interface. If the test and retest are different dependent variables, then two separate analyses of the results would be performed and, essentially, the analysis on the performance data (the retest) would be the same analysis as used in the "test" design. If the test and retest are the same dependent variable, then practice could be treated as an independent variable and the experiment would incorporate multiple factors. These analysis issues will be

considered further in the next section.

With a "test" and a "test-retest" design, we would need to assume that the functions relating performance to practice are linear or at least parallel for the different interfaces being tested. If this assumption is not true, then the results could be misleading. It is possible that performance on different interfaces will peak at different training times. As a hypothetical example, consider the performance on two interfaces (see Figure 5-8). The performance measure shown is the hypothetical performance on the interfaces taken continuously over time. In most cases, the experimenter would not have this continuous performance measure but would only be able to sample at certain times.

In Figure 5-8, some kind of performance, such as time to execute the task, is represented on the vertical axis. On the

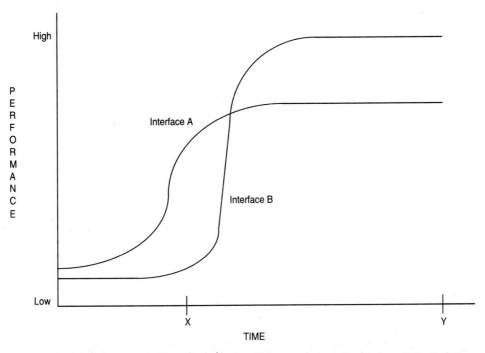

High

P
E
R
F
O
R
M
A
N
C
E

Interface A

Interface B

Low

X

Y

TIME

Figure 5-8. An illustration of differential practice effects on two interface designs. Interpretation of the results would be different depending on whether subjects were tested at time X or time Y.

horizontal axis, the practice time is represented. As can be seen, performance on interface A peaks early and then levels off. Performance on interface B will require practice and so will not peak until a later time. The intervals in which to sample performance could be important. If performance was sampled at time X, performance would be higher for interface A and the experimenters would conclude that interface A was better than interface B. If subjects had practiced for a longer period of time, however, to time Y, performance would be higher for interface B. The experimenters in this case would conclude that interface B was better than interface A because they would not have the information on the preceding part of the function. Knowing the whole form of the function, by testing subjects at differ-

ent practice times, would be advantageous in this situation. If subjects were tested at times X and Y, then an interaction would be observed. The experimenter could conclude that interface A was best for short amounts of practice and interface B was best after longer periods of practice.

Figures 5-9 and 5-10 show other hypothetical examples of how training time could affect interpretation of the results. In Figure 5-9, the earlier training time, X, would be too brief to show that a difference in performance (as occurs at time Y) between the interfaces exists. If the subjects were tested at both times X and Y, then the interaction could be seen. From the interaction, the experimenter could infer that interface A is only better than B at high amounts of practice. In Figure 5-10, if subjects are trained for a

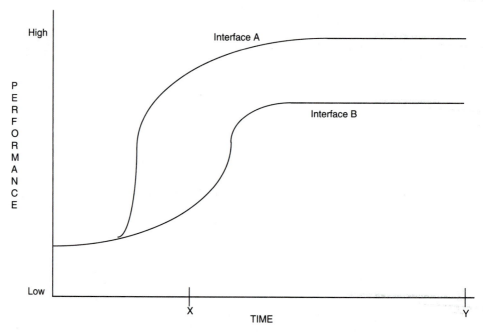

Figure 5-9. Another illustration of differential practice effects on two interface designs. Performance differences between the interfaces would be seen only at time Y.

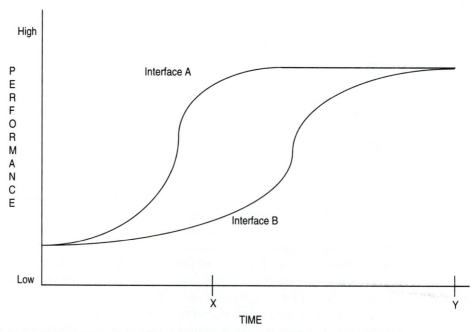

Figure 5-10. Another illustration of differential practice effects on two interface designs. Performance differences between the interfaces would be seen only at time X.

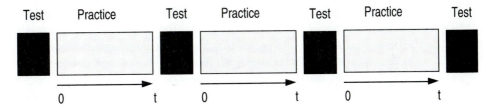

Figure 5-11. An illustration of the "multiple test" design of column Z. Subjects are tested multiple times in order to determine the form of the function relating performance to practice.

longer period of time, time Y, the performance for the two interfaces will be about the same. Only at the shorter practice time of X would differences be seen between the interfaces. Interface A is probably more valuable overall because subjects can learn faster on it, as illustrated by the differences at time X.

Unless the interface is tested continuously during the training, the experimenter cannot know the underlying function. If the shape of the functions representing performance during training is different, then the experimenter should try to test at close enough time periods to determine the form of that function. On the other hand, if the shape of the functions is known to be similar, or linear, then the time periods between tests can be longer. Here again, the experimenter would have to bring in prior knowledge in order to make this kind of decision. A pilot experiment, which is a test experiment with only a few subjects, might be needed to determine the underlying functions.

If the underlying functions are assumed to be different, then the multiple test design of column Z from Figure 5-1 should be used. In this design, performance can be tested as often as needed depending on the resources available. Figure 5-11 provides an illustration of the multiple test design where tests are taken

three times. The practice time, t, between the tests, can range from 0 to a high number, but it should be small enough to capture the form of the function. Including a test before practice begins is optional. In order to analyze the results, especially the important interaction between practice and interface design, the dependent variable measurement used all during the test times must be the same.

Providing the subjects with long practice times on an interface before the test is performed could be a costly procedure. For a typical interface design, such as an operating system or a word processor, the amounts of practice could be enormous. Replicating this in the laboratory is virtually impossible or prohibitively expensive. An alternative to these long practice sessions would be to provide some practice, not as much as would be received in the real world, and then look for trends in the data. If one interface is getting progressively better than the other, then this trend might be projected, with caution, into the future. One can never be certain, however, when the divergence might occur.

The choice of practice time is one of the thorniest questions in human-computer interaction research, as well as other kinds of human factors research. Most experiments are designed so that the subjects have very little time to learn how to use the interface. Consequently, the experiment can only be interpreted in terms of the short-term effects of the interface design. If one interface is found to be better than another, and the subjects have little practice on it, then the results can only be generalized to the initial stages in the use of the interface. The experiment cannot determine whether the situation is likely to change over time. The interface determined to be best initially may not be the best interface after considerable practice with it.

Decisions made concerning when to evaluate performance require extensive literature review, preliminary investigation, and a thorough knowledge of the theoretical implications. One obvious choice to some of these decisions may not be apparent at the outset of the experiment. The experimenter should also always try performing the tasks on the interface to get a feel for whether practice and learning will have a significant impact on performance. A researcher must bring as much background information as possible into the design considerations of the experiment.

The procedure from Figure 5-1 can be used for the experimental design choice of when to evaluate the performance. If resources only allow one test, then the designs in column X could be chosen. If it is important to test for comparability between groups, or to test for practice effects assuming that the functions are linear or parallel for the interface designs, then the designs in column Y can be used. If the form of the function relating practice to performance cannot be predicted, and is assumed to be nonlinear or nonparallel, then the designs in column Z can be used.

For this illustration, we can assume that the form of the function is nonlinear so that multiple tests are needed. In this case, columns X and Y can be eliminated; this has been shown in Figure 5-12.

Experimental Design Choice

If the procedure has been followed correctly, only one of the cells in the figure should remain white. In the example, the experimental design has been chosen based upon which cell remains after all the others have been eliminated. The chosen design is a between-subjects design with the following three factors: interface design, a factor such as subject expertise, and a factor for the multiple tests. Methods to analyze these designs are considered in the next section.

ANALYSIS OF RESULTS

Contrary to what might be expected, analyzing the results through the use of statistics is one of the easiest parts of conducting an experiment. The process of formulating a research question, choosing an experimental design, and interpreting the results are more difficult issues requiring decisions based upon prior knowledge, experience, and research. The analysis of results plays a central role in this whole process. The research question should be addressed, and the experimental design should be chosen, to facilitate the analysis of results. Each experimental design must be coupled with the appropriate statistical test. Finally, the experimenter must be able to interpret the results correctly and generalize the results to the correct situations. This last point is probably the most difficult part of the process. Only through

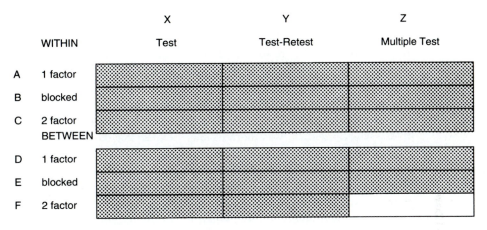

	WITHIN	X Test	Y Test-Retest	Z Multiple Test
A	1 factor			
B	blocked			
C	2 factor BETWEEN			
D	1 factor			
E	blocked			
F	2 factor			

Figure 5-12. In the illustration, the experimenter has decided that the multiple test design is needed to determine the underlying practice functions. With this choice, columns X and Y can be blacked out.

a clear conceptualization of the result analysis process, and through an understanding of the underlying statistics, can experimenters interpret the results correctly. In some cases, an interface designer may not actually run an experiment, but the research literature must be reviewed. The researcher must know the terminology used in statistics to better understand the experiment and its implications.

This part of the chapter is not meant to be a substitution for a normal statistics text. The information available on statistical tests is too vast to include and discuss with any degree of completion in a chapter. Instead, the purpose is to provide an introduction to the issues in statistics and the underlying concepts. If you understand the basics, you can always consult statisticians or statistics books for more unusual statistics problems.

Rationale for Using Statistics

Since usability studies for computer systems are designed to determine if people can use one design better when compared to others, this kind of experimentation must use human subjects. Based upon this premise, the rationale for using statistics is very simple: people are different from each other. It would indeed be a dull world if everybody was the same. Look around you, though. Obviously, people are different. What is worse, in terms of analyzing results from experiments, is that this variability between people can only be described as random variability. Predicting the differences between people is difficult because of this random component. Some days a person will randomly have a bad day, and unfortunately this may occur during an experimental study. On the other hand, some days may be going well for a subject and everything in the experiment is done correctly. We cannot expect that everybody coming into an experiment will react to the treatment in the same way. Even though the treatment may be carefully controlled, the way people react to the treatment may appear to be random. But what does all this have to do with statistics?

If everybody behaved the same, then experimentation would be easier and the interpretation of the results would be simpler. If two interfaces needed to be evaluated, we would simply find just two people (since everybody is the same), have them use the interfaces, and then test them to see which interface was more usable. For the test, the interface which scored the highest would be the best. Since we assumed that everybody behaved identically, then we would not need to have extra subjects for verification of performance on a particular interface and thus no further analysis would be needed. The assumption that everybody is the same is of course outlandish, yet some researchers implicitly accept this assumption by employing improper research techniques by using just one or two experimental subjects per group, and then analyzing the results by examining the means (the average scores).

The variability between people, and the resulting variability in the testing of human subjects, is the principal reason for using statistics. If an experiment is conducted with several subjects in each condition, we would expect that the means would be different between the interfaces just due to individual random differences between the subjects or due to random fluctuations in performance, not due to inherent usability differences between the interfaces. However, if the means between the performance scores on the different interfaces were high enough, at some as yet undetermined level, then we would expect that the differences in the performance scores of the groups using the interfaces are probably due not only to variability between the people or random fluctuations but also to differences in the usability of the interface designs. Statistics allow us to separate the variability of the subjects from the variability due to the treatment of interest, such as the different interface designs.

A Numerical Illustration

Starting with a numerical example is perhaps the best way to explain the use of statistics, and a particular statistical technique called analysis of variance (ANOVA) which is used in all of the 18 experimental designs. In the example, we have three interfaces, A, B, and C. The time needed to complete the task in seconds is being used to measure the usability of the interfaces. Table 5-1 shows some sample data for three subjects on the three

TABLE 5-1
Numerical example for time (sec.) for performing a task on each of three interfaces

Observation	Interface A	Interface B	Interface C
1	24	24	11
2	19	25	14
3	22	21	17
Mean	21.67	23.33	14.00

interfaces. Each subject gets tested on each of the three interfaces, resulting in nine data points.

When the data are examined, we see there is some variability between the groups; the groups range from a mean of 14.00 to 23.33. There is also some variability within a group also, for example, subjects using interface A range from a low score of 19 to a high score of 24. Similar variability is noticed for the other two interface designs also. In order to determine if one interface is better than another, we need to be able to determine if the variability between the groups is due to actual differences in the performance on the interfaces or due to random variability. Random variability could be due to individual differences between the subjects. For example, some kind of distraction could occur for a subject during the experimentation, thereby affecting the time, or a subject could just happen to make the right guesses in the task which would decrease the time on the task. These are just some of the possibilities which could cause the random variability. In the statistical analysis, the random variability, within the interface conditions, must be separated from the between-group variability, which represents the differences due just to the interface designs.

Before a person can fully understand statistics, they must understand what the data points in Table 5-1 mean. What is a number, in the statistical sense? A number is composed of several effects which, when summed together, produce the numbers in each cell of Table 5-1. Actually, the effects can be conceptualized in two ways: as an effect from the population, or as an estimate of this population effect from the sample taken in the experiment. The

population effects are always designated by Greek letters. When performing experiments, the main emphasis is on the population; the experimenter must make inferences from the sample used in the experiment to the population. Of course, the exact value for the population is rarely known. For interface design experimentation, the population is all the people who use the interface or could potentially use the interface. Testing the whole population of users is impossible, and as a result we will never have exact values for the population effects. Estimates of the population effects can be found from the sample tested in the experiment, and these estimates are one of the goals of statistical analysis.

For illustration purposes, assume that, as some all-knowing person, you know the exact values for the population effects. Of course, this is only a hypothetical situation in that you cannot know everything about the whole population of users and potential users. By pretending that you know these things, the statistical concepts are easier to demonstrate.

What is a number, in a statistical sense? One component of a number from Table 5-1 is the average time taken to perform the task no matter which interface is used. A person needs a certain amount of time to perform the task no matter what kind of interface is provided. This component, call the population effect, is termed μ. Because each number in each of the cells of the table uses the same task, μ is a component of each. Let's assume, in the hypothetical situation, that μ is equal to 20.

Some of the interfaces can be expected to be easier to use than others. In other words, there should be a treatment

μ - population effect

TABLE 5-2
The effects due to random variability for each data point

Observation	Interface A	Interface B	Interface C
1	$\varepsilon_{11} = 3$	$\varepsilon_{12} = 0$	$\varepsilon_{13} = -4$
2	$\varepsilon_{21} = -2$	$\varepsilon_{22} = 1$	$\varepsilon_{23} = -1$
3	$\varepsilon_{31} = 1$	$\varepsilon_{32} = -3$	$\varepsilon_{33} = 2$

effect of interfaces on performance. The population treatment effect will be termed τ_j, and each of the interface designs, for j = 1, 2, and 3, will have a different value for its effect, depending on its usability. In the hypothetical situation for the population, we will assume that $\tau_1 = 1, \tau_2 = 4$, and $\tau_3 = -5$. So, interface C should be the easiest to use because it takes less time, compared to the average, to perform the task on this interface. The effect τ was referred to earlier as the between-group variability, and this is the effect that we would like to isolate to demonstrate that one interface is better than another.

One more component is left, and that is the random variability. In this case, each data point in Table 5-1 should have some kind of random component to it, due to, among other things, individual differences, random attentional changes during the task, or random distractions which may have occurred during the experimentation. This random component, or random effect, in the population will be called ε. The individual values for the hypothetical ε are contained in Table 5-2. Since we need to describe the ε's for each individual data point, each point will be addressed as ε_{ij} where, in this case, both i and j run from 1 to 3.

The preceding example has shown that each number is really composed of several effects: μ, or the overall mean; τ, or the treatment effect; and ε, or the random variability. Table 5-3 illustrates how the numbers from Table 5-1 can be decomposed into these components. Each

TABLE 5-3
Example of how each data point can be decomposed into an effect for μ (the first number in the sum), an effect for τ (the second number in the sum), and an effect for ε (the third number in the sum)

Observation	Interface A	Interface B	Interface C
1	20 + 1 + 3 = 24	20 + 4 + 0 = 24	20 - 5 - 4 = 11
2	20 + 1 - 2 = 19	20 + 4 + 1 = 25	20 - 5 - 1 = 14
3	20 + 1 + 1 = 22	20 + 4 - 3 = 21	20 - 5 + 2 = 17

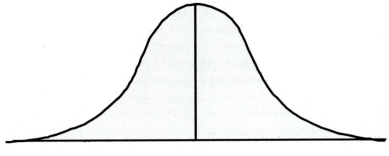

Normal Distribution

Figure 5-13. A representation of the normal or Gaussian distribution. Each distribution can be described by its mean and variance.

number has a μ effect; each column, for the different interface designs, has a τ effect; and each number has a random effect, ε.

If you were all-knowing and therefore knew the values for these population effects, then there would be no need to perform the statistics. We would be able to say, from what we knew, that performance on interface C was the fastest, and performance on interfaces A and B was about the same with B slightly better than A. But in reality we do not know these population values, so we must estimate them. That is the role of statistics.

Estimating Population Parameters

The statistical problem is to separate the μ and the τ's from the ε_{ij}'s when the data from the sample is available and we do not know the population effects exactly. These estimates can only be determined through a variety of assumptions about the underlying population values. The most important assumptions are about the underlying distribution of values. For those not familiar with probability terms, a random variable, such as the ε_{ij}'s, cannot be described individually, but it can be described in terms of overall characteristics, such as its mean value, its range, and its general shape. Many random variables have a distribution which is usually described as a normal or Gaussian distribution. A normal distribution is characterized by its bell shape (see Figure 5-13), and this distribution can be described mathematically. The central point of the distribution is called the mean, and for a symmetrical distribution like this, half the population values will fall above and half will fall below the mean. The amount that the values are spread out is called the variance of the distribution and is often designated as σ^2. Some distributions will be spread out, and some will be relatively thin. By knowing the mathematical equation for the curve, and knowing the mean and variance of the distribution, you can describe each separate distribution completely.

The first assumption, for estimating the population values, is that the ε_{ij}'s are random and can be described by a normal distribution. We will assume that this normal distribution has a mean of 0 and a variance that will be described as σ_τ^2. Similar assumptions can be made for the τ_j, depending on how the treatment levels, in this case the interface designs, were chosen. If the treatment was chosen for specific reasons, such as interface C is the new interface and interfaces A and B are the examples of interfaces performing the same functions, then the treatment levels will be called fixed. Since these are all fixed points, not chosen from a population of possibilities, then we do not have to consider a distribution. If the treatment levels were chosen randomly from a population of possibilities, then we would have to make assumptions about the population from which it was chosen, similar to that done for the ε_{ij}'s. Most levels in factors will be fixed, because we have specific reasons for choosing them. Many times the subjects used in an experiment will be a factor in the analysis, and since these subjects will have been chosen at random from a population of possibilities, this would be an example of a random factor. Subjects is probably the only factor which would ever be random in most human-computer interaction research. With τ as a fixed factor, however, we make the assumption that the sum of the τ_j's over j is equal to 0.

The analysis is changed slightly if the factors are fixed or random, in a way that will not be discussed at this point. Additionally, the interpretation of the results will change. With a random factor, the results can be generalized to the population of possibilities from the factor. As an example, if subjects is a random factor in the experiment, then the results could be generalized to the population of people from which the sample used in the experiment was taken. The generalizations are not as broad for fixed factors. If specific, fixed interface designs are chosen for the fixed factor, and the results show that one interface is better than another, then the results could only be generalized in terms of the interfaces tested and not a population of all possible interfaces. This generalization makes sense for the purposes of most human-computer interaction research.

With these assumptions, estimates of the population parameters can now be made. A good estimate of the population mean would be the mean of the entire sample. This mean can be found by summing all nine data points and then dividing by N, or 9. This grand sum of the sample is designated as $\overline{Y}..$ and has a value of 19.67 (the bar above the Y indicates that it is a mean, and the two dots mean that the values have been determined by collapsing or summing over the i rows and the j columns).

Estimates of the τs can be found by determining how much the means for each interface deviate from the grand mean. The interface means, or the column means, will be designated as $\overline{Y}_{.j}$ for j running from 1 to 3. The estimate for τ_1 is as follows:

$$\text{est } \tau_1 = \overline{Y}._1 - \overline{Y}..$$
$$= 21.67 - 19.67$$
$$= 2.00 \qquad (5.1)$$

The estimates for τ_2 and τ_3 are found in a similar way. Table 5-4 contains a summary of these estimates and compares these estimates to the population values from the hypothetical situation in which the population values were known. As could be expected, the estimates of the τ's are close to the real values, but they deviate slightly (of course, we would never know these "real" values).

The ε_{ij}'s can be determined by subtracting the column means from each of the data points. Table 5-5 shows how each of the effects is removed in order to find

TABLE 5-4

The estimate of the τ_j, and a comparison of this estimate to the hypothetical τ_j

Observation	Interface A	Interface B	Interface C
1	20 + 1 + 3 = 24	20 + 4 + 0 = 24	20 - 5 - 4 = 11
2	20 + 1 - 2 = 19	20 + 4 + 1 = 25	20 - 5 - 1 = 14
3	20 + 1 + 1 = 22	20 + 4 - 3 = 21	20 - 5 + 2 = 17

the ε_{ij}'s. This satisfies the assumption that the sum of the ε_{ij}'s should be 0.

Separating Random Effects from Treatment Effects

Table 5-4 showed that the treatment effects varied, resulting in the conclusion that performance on the task was dependent on the interface used. In the hypothetical situation, we assumed that a treatment effect existed. If no treatment effect occurred, then the τ_j's would be 0. As shown by Table 5-4 also, the estimates of τ, from the sample data, are not exactly the same as the real value of the τ's in the population. It is possible to have estimates of the τ's which are not exactly equal to 0, but

vary from one to the next. How close to 0 does it have to be before we can say that the performance differences between the interfaces were due only to random variability and not the treatment effect?

As an illustration that the estimates of the τ's can be not-equal to 0, but perhaps close enough to 0 so that we cannot infer performance differences between the interfaces, consider the calculations in Table 5-6. In this table, in the hypothetical situation where the population values are known, each of the τ's has been set to 0, reflecting no performance differences when using the interfaces. The column means still vary from one another, and the estimates of the τ's, in Table 5-7, show that they are not exactly equal to 0 nor are

TABLE 5-5

The estimates for the ε_{ij}'s by subtracting the column means from the data points

Observation	Interface A	Interface B	Interface C
1	24 - 21.67 = 2.33	24 - 23.33 = 0.67	11 - 14.00 = -3.00
2	19 - 21.67 = -2.67	25 - 23.33 = 1.67	14 - 14.00 = 0
3	22 - 21.67 = 0.33	21 - 23.33 = -2.33	17 - 14.00 = 3.00

TABLE 5-6
The hypothetical effects when the τ's are set to 0, reflecting no performance differences between the interfaces

Observation	Interface A	Interface B	Interface C
1	$20 + 0 + 3 = 23$	$20 + 0 + 0 = 20$	$20 + 0 - 4 = 16$
2	$20 + 0 - 2 = 18$	$20 + 0 + 1 = 21$	$20 + 0 - 1 = 19$
3	$20 + 0 + 1 = 21$	$20 + 0 - 3 = 17$	$20 + 0 + 2 = 22$
mean	20.67	19.33	19.00

they as high as the estimates for τ when a treatment effect was still present in the data. A statistical analysis should be sensitive enough to show that performance differences had occurred for the data from column 3 of Table 5-7, but not for the data from column 2.

In column 2 of Table 5-7, the variations in the τ's are due only to the random effect, while the variations in the τ's of column 3 are due to variations in the treatment effect plus the random effect. The random effect is often termed the random error. The statistical analysis should be able to differentiate the treatment plus random effect from the random effect alone. This can be accomplished by

estimating a reasonable value for the random effect, using the estimates of the treatment effects discussed earlier, and then comparing the size of the treatment plus random effect to the size of the random effect alone. If the sizes are about the same, then the treatment effect would be close to 0 and no performance differences between the interfaces could be inferred from the data. If the treatment plus random effect is much larger than the random effect alone, then performance differences between the interfaces could be inferred.

Remember that statistics uses the estimates of the population values for making the inferences so that when comparing the effects, inferences from the

TABLE 5-7
The estimate of the τ_j when $\tau_j = 0$ compared to the estimates of τ_j when not equal to 0 and to the hypothetical τ_j

Interface	j	est τ_j when $\tau_j = 0$	est τ_j when $\tau_j \neq 0$	hypothetical τ_j
A	1	1.00	2.00	1
B	2	-0.34	3.66	4

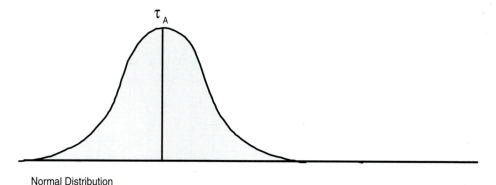

Normal Distribution

Figure 5-14. The normal distribution for the observations from performing on interface A.

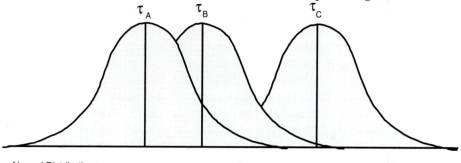

Normal Distributions

Figure 5-15. Performance on the other two interfaces, B and C, are also normally distributed.

populations must be compared. Obviously, the population values will not be a single value or number; one would not expect everybody to perform exactly the same. Consequently, the population values will be distributed over a range of values. By comparing the characteristics of the distributions, the important effects can be analyzed.

Analysis of variance can be understood through the following steps. First, we can assume that the set of performance measures on an interface will be normally distributed. Using the sample data from Table 5-1, we would assume that the three performance scores generated by the three subjects on interface A come from a population of normally distributed values, as

could have occurred in Figure 5-14. In that example, the mean of this hypothetical population distibution occurs in the middle of the curve because the distribution is symmetrical; this mean is designated as τ_A. Performance on interfaces B and C would also be normally distributed with means of τ_B and τ_C for the two interfaces (see Figure 5-15).

In the second step, the mean of the means from the distributions (the means of τ_A, τ_B, and τ_C) must be found, and this grand mean is designated as μ (see Figure 5-16). The arrows in the figure show the amount each of the distribution means differs from the grand mean.

In the third step, the set of the deviations of the τ's from μ (the arrows in

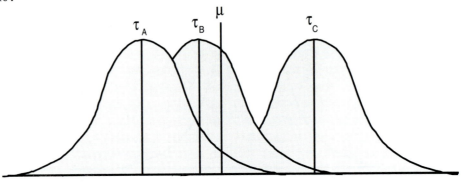

Normal Distributions

Figure 5-16. The mean of the means from the three distributions is shown and labeled as μ.

Figure 5-16) can be considered as a set of variances. Figure 5-17 shows how the set of all these variances can also be represented as a distribution of values. This distribution is called a chi-square distribution, and it is different from the normal distributions in that it is no longer symmetrical about a mean. Analyses have shown that the variances from normally distributed data are described by a chi-square distribution. Mathematical formulas have been devised to describe the characteristics of the chi-square distribution.

The shape of the chi-square distribution will change according to how much the means of the distributions (the τ's) differ from the grand mean (μ). If there are performance differences due to the three interfaces, then the means will be far away from the grand mean and the chi-square distribution will be spread out. In Figure 5-17, the distributions at the top of the figure are separated, and so one could expect that the interface design, either A, B, or C, would have an effect on performance. Figure 5-18 shows a hypothetical situation in which the distributions are not very separated. Only small performance differences have occurred. The chi-square

distribution at the bottom of the page shows how the distribution is more compact; it is not spread out as much as that observed in Figure 5-17. These differences between the means may not be large enough to cause reliable performance differences between the three interfaces. The overlap of the distributions indicates that performance differences may not occur very often. The statistics should be able to show the differences between the situations depicted in Figures 5-17 and 5-18. In Figure 5-17, we would be likely to say that the differences between the interfaces was reliable or significant; from the situation in Figure 5-18 we would be likely to say that the differences are not reliable or are nonsignificant.

Since the performance differences are reflected in the dispersion of the chi-square distribution, this can be used to indicate the significance of the differences in the interface designs. A chi-square distribution which is highly dispersed will reflect significant performance differences; a chi-square distribution which is not dispersed will reflect nonsignificant differences. Where can the line be drawn between high and low dispersion of the vari-

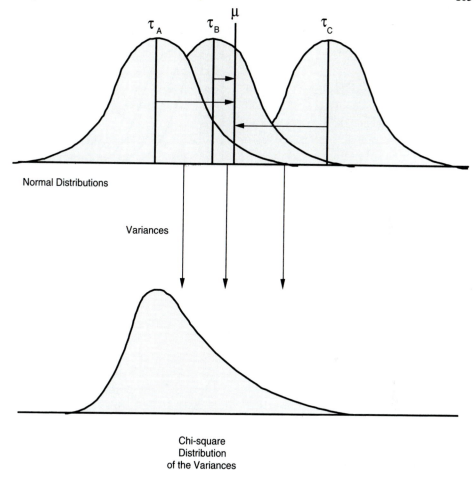

Normal Distributions

Variances

Chi-square
Distribution
of the Variances

Figure 5-17. The deviations of the distribution means from the grand mean can be represented in a chi-square distribution.

ances? Remember that some dispersion in the distribution would be found due to the random effects in the experiment, not due to the treatment effects. If a treatment effect exists, as is likely in that depicted in Figure 5-17, then the dispersion of the chi-square distribution should be due to both treatment and random effects. If little or no treatment effect is present, as depicted in Figure 5-18, then the dispersion of the distribution should be due only to random effects. If we could find an independent

measure of the dispersion of the chi-square distribution which could be expected due only to the random effects, then we could compare the distributions of Figures 5-17 and 5-18 to this random-effects distribution to see if they are the same or different.

Figure 5-19 shows how an independent measure of the dispersion of the chi-square distribution can be found for the random effects. The same three normal distributions from Figure 5-17 are shown. In the experiment used for this

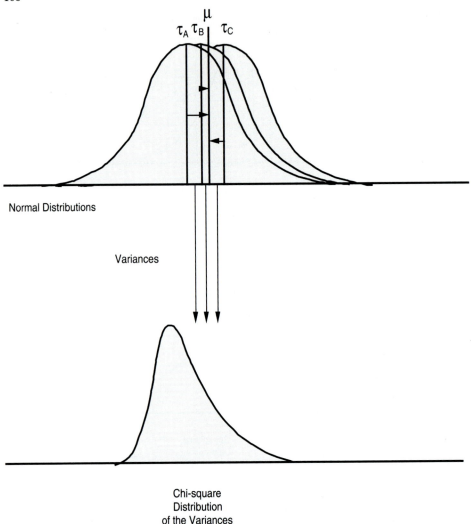

Figure 5-18.

Normal Distributions

Variances

Chi-square
Distribution
of the Variances

Figure 5-18. If the distributions of performance scores for the interfaces are close together, then the chi-square distribution will have a low dispersion.

example, the performance of three subjects is recorded on each interface design. The score for the three subjects is shown by the three diagonal lines, other than the distribution mean, for each of the three distributions. The variances due to random effects only can be estimated and calculated by considering the variations in the distances of the three scores within the

distribution to the mean of the distributions (the τ's). These distances are represented by the ε's in the figure. Those variances are distributed according to the chi-square distribution at the bottom of the page. This distribution represents an estimate of the dispersion which could be expected only due to the random effects, not the treatment effects. The treatment

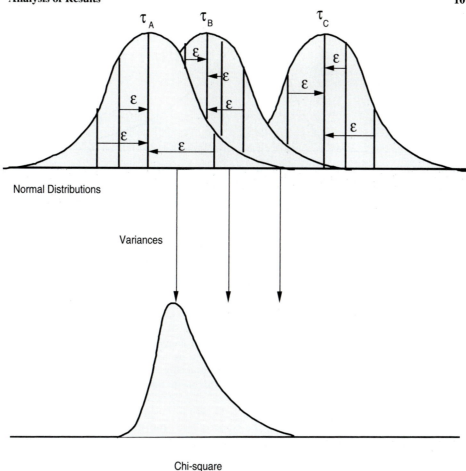

Figure 5-19. The random effects can be calculated by determining the differences between the performance scores and the mean within a distribution. These differences are represented in a chi-square distribution.

effects do not enter into the calculations in this case because all the variances are determined within a normal distribution at the top of Figure 5-19. The treatment effect is only present when the normal distributions are compared between themselves.

The magnitude of the differences between the performance scores on the three interface designs can be determined by comparing the chi-square distributions which represent the treatment plus random effects to the chi-square distribution which only represents the random effects. This is shown in Figure 5-20. The chi-square distribution from Figure 5-17, representing the treatment plus random effects, is shown at the top of the figure, and the chi-square distribution from Figure 5-19, representing the random effects only,

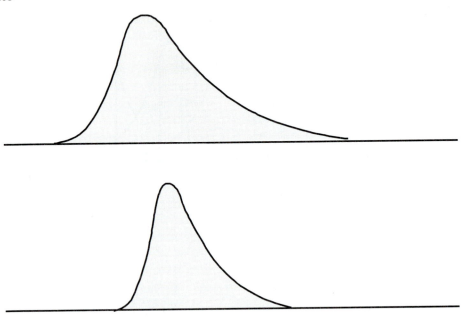

Figure 5-20. The chi-square distributions are compared. The top distribution, from Figure 5-17, represents the treatment plus random effects in the experiment. The bottom distribution, from Figure 5-19, is a representation of the random effects. Because the top distribution is more highly dispersed than the bottom distribution, this means that the treatment effects in the experiment are probably significant.

is shown at the bottom of the figure. By comparing them in this way, one can see clearly that the dispersion for the distribution at the top is much greater than the dispersion for the distribution at the bottom. Therefore, one could conclude that a treatment effect is present, because it is causing the greater dispersion in the top distribution, and that the interfaces cause performance differences.

If there is little or no treatment effect, then one could expect that the treatment plus random effects distribution would look similar to the random effects distribution. Figure 5-21 shows the comparison between the chi-square distributions from Figure 5-18, which represents small performance differences between the interfaces (at the top of the figure), and

the chi-square distribution from Figure 5-19, which showed the estimate of the random effects distribution. When comparing these two chi-square distributions, you see that they are about the same. This should have been expected because both distributions are due mainly to the random effects differences; the treatment effects are so small in the top distribution that they are hardly noticeable.

The next section shows how to perform numerical calculations for the conceptual ideas presented in this chapter. In particular, the comparison of the distributions in Figures 5-20 and 5-21 can be considered to be a ratio of distributions. On the top of the ratio is the distribution for the treatment plus random effects and on the bottom of the ratio is the distribu-

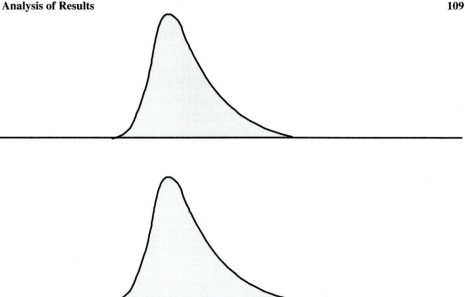

Figure 5-21. Two other chi-square distributions are compared. The top distribution, from Figure 5-18, represents a situation in which the treatment effects are small or nonexistent. The bottom distribution, from Figure 5-19, represents the random effect. Since both distributions are highly similar, the dispersion from both distributions is probably due to just random effects and not a treatment effect.

tion for the random effects only. If the treatment effect is large, increasing the dispersion of the distribution at the top, then the ratio would be much greater than 1. If the treatment effect is small or absent, then the ratio of the two distributions would be close to 1. Mathematicians have worked out the form of this ratio of distributions, the ratio of the two chi-square distributions, and it is called the F distribution. Statistics books have tables in them to indicate if the treatment differences reflected in the F distribution could be due to chance or actual differences. The higher the F value, the higher the probability that a treatment effect is present.

The illustrations of the distributions can also be used to show the advantages of reducing the random effects due to good experimental techniques. As an example, if the room in which the experiment is conducted is too noisy, then this could cause performance of the subjects to fluctuate. If the random effects are reduced, then the normal distributions will be thinner, less dispersed. In Figure 5-22, the means of the distributions are the same as in Figure 5-17, but the random effects have been reduced. The variances of the ε's, when mapped to the chi-square distribution at the bottom of the figure, are less dispersed. If this distribution for the random effects was used in the calculation of the F-ratio, then it would be more sensitive to finding the treatment effects.

Sample Calculations

At this point, the background material should be in place for performing calculations of the treatment effect. From the illustrations in Figures 5-18 through 5-20,

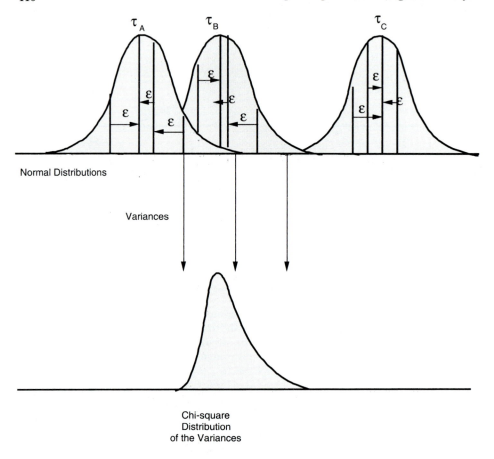

Figure 5-22. **If the experiment is conducted so as to reduce the random effects, the chi-square distribution will have low dispersion. This will increase the chances of finding treatment effects if they are actually there. It makes the statistical tests more sensitive to the effects.**

the meaning of a variance should be clear. All of the variances in those figures are used to determine the amount of the deviations from a mean. A variance can be defined as the squared sum of the deviations of a value from the mean, divided by the degrees of freedom associated with the calculation. The degrees of freedom is difficult to understand on an intuitive basis, but it represents the number of components in its calculation that are free to vary. In the example, totals for the treatment are 65, 70, and 42. The total of these totals is

177, with a total mean of 59. The sum of the deviations of the column totals from the total mean must be 0. If you already know two of the totals, say 65 and 70, and you know the total mean, 59, then the sum of the deviations from the total mean is

$$(65 - 59) + (70 - 59) = 6 + 11 = 17 \quad (5.2)$$

Knowing this, and knowing that the totals of all these deviation must be equal to 0, the following must be true:

$$17 + (x - 59) = 0$$
$$x - 59 = -17$$
$$x = 42 \qquad (5.3)$$

The variable x refers to the remaining column mean and could be determined by knowing two of the three column means. Therefore, the degrees of freedom is 2, because if either of the two values is known, then the third value is already known. If k represents the number of levels of the treatment, then the degrees of freedom is k - 1.

To differentiate the treatment plus random effect from the random effect, an estimate for both of these effects is needed. An estimate for the treatment effect is easy because that had been calculated in Table 5-4 by subtracting each column mean from the grand mean. From this, the variance of the treatment effects, often termed the between-group variance or s_B^2, could be calculated by squaring the effects and dividing through by the degrees of freedom. The official calculation is

$$s_B^2 = \frac{\sum\limits_{j=1}^{k} n_j (\overline{Y_{\cdot j}} - \overline{Y_{\cdot\cdot}})^2}{k-1} \qquad (5.4)$$

where n_j is the number of observations in each of the columns, and k is the number of columns, or the number of levels of the treatment. The n_j term is needed because we are finding the effect for each of the nine data points in the table. Because each of the data points in each of the columns has the same column mean, it is more efficient to just use the column means once, and then multiply that value by 3. The alternative would be to subtract 19.67 from a column mean three times, but this

would be a waste of time. From the above equation, the part on the top of the fraction is often termed the sums of squares. This is an important value, and it will be used when further discussing some of the analysis techniques.

Using the values from Table 5-4, the calculation of s_B^2 is as follows:

$$s_B^2 = (3(21.67 - 19.67)^2$$
$$+ 3(23.33 - 19.67)^2$$
$$+ 3(14 - 19.67)^2)/2$$
$$= \frac{148.67}{2}$$
$$= 74.32 \qquad (5.5)$$

If the differences between the levels of the treatment are large, then the τ_j's will be different and, thus, s_B^2 will be large.

Next, an estimate for the random effect alone is needed. A good estimate is the variability, or variance, between the subjects within a treatment level. This variance is often called the within variance, or error variance, and is designated as s_W^2. This variance can be determined from the ε_{ij}'s which were calculated earlier and displayed in Table 5-5. This variance is calculated by

$$s_W^2 = \frac{\sum\limits_{j=1}^{k}\sum\limits_{i=1}^{n_j} (Y_{ij} - \overline{Y_{\cdot j}})^2}{N-k} \qquad (5.6)$$

where N is the total number of data points (9) and k is the number of treatment levels (3). In this case, N - k is the degrees of freedom for this term. Using these values, and the values for the ε_{ij}'s from Table 5-4, s_W^2 is found as follows:

$$s^2_W = ((24 - 21.67)^2 + (19 - 21.67)^2$$
$$+ \ldots + (14 - 17)^2)/6$$

$$= \frac{39.33}{6}$$

$$= 6.56 \qquad (5.7)$$

By taking the ratio of s_B^2 over s_W^2, the size of the effect can be determined. This ratio is called the F-ratio because it utilizes the F distribution. The F-ratio for the sample data is

$$\frac{74.32}{6.56} = 11.33 \qquad (5.8)$$

As discussed earlier, if this ratio is much larger than 1.0, then the treatment plus random effect is much larger than the random effect alone, and we can infer from the data that the treatment has a significant effect on performance.

Rather than using phrases such as "much larger than" or "close to 1," more precise terminology would be desirable. In statistics, the probability terminology provides this preciseness. If we assume that there is no treatment effect, and therefore only random error for both between and within variance, then the F distribution can be used to determine the probability that the obtained F-ratio was a result of just random error or random error plus the treatment. As the F-ratio increases, this probability value, called the p-value, decreases. Therefore, a low p-value indicates the probability is low that the result could have occurred by random error alone without the influence of the treatment.

The F-ratio for the sample data was found to be 11.33. Each F-ratio has a particular p-value associated with it, al-

though when reporting the results of experiments, the p-value is not usually reported exactly, but rather it is reported as being less than some reference number. The F distribution used for a certain experiment is actually a family of F distributions with slightly different shapes, depending on the degrees of freedom for the variances of the top and bottom parts of the ratio. The degrees of freedom for the between variance is one less than the number of treatment levels (3) for a final value of 2. The degrees of freedom for the within variance is the total number of data points (9) minus one minus the degrees of freedom of the between variance (2). This is calculated to be 6. When a table is consulted for an F-ratio of 11.33 with 2 and 6 degrees of freedom, the associated p-value is less than 0.01. This is usually reported as $\underline{F}(2,6) = 11.33$, $\underline{p} < 0.01$. The probability is very low that the large effects were just random effects and not due to the treatment.

Most experimenters like to be fairly certain that the treatment had an effect. As an example, putting a product on the market may be very costly, and the developers would like to be fairly certain that the new design is better than the old. Before the experiment starts, the experimenter should determine the risk involved in making a mistake in saying that a treatment effect occurred when it actually did not occur. Then the experimenter must state the probability of this error occurring which is at an acceptable level. The acceptable error rate, set before the experiment begins, is referred to as the α-value. Setting an α-value is a subjective decision and can best be explained through an example. If the risk of an error is high, due to high development costs down the road, then the α-value should be low before proceeding with the development. If the risk is low, due to low development costs, then the α-value can be higher before proceeding with the development. In most human-computer interaction research, the α value is usually set at 0.05, which involves a medium risk. For less risky experimentation, the α value is sometimes set at 0.1. If the p-value calculated from the data is less than the α-value, then the experiment has been successful at showing that the treatment had an effect at an acceptable error rate. In this case, the effects of the experiment would be called significant. If the p-value is above the α–value, then the effects are called nonsignificant. The literature from other similar experimentation should be read before setting an α-value to get an idea what other researchers have determined to be an acceptable risk level by their choice of α.

The preceding example showed that this analysis of variance method was successful at separating the variability due to the treatment from the variability due to random error. If the variability in the τ's is just due to the random error, then the F-ratio should be low. As an example of this, consider the values from the third column of Table 5-7, the estimates of the τ's when τ is equal to 0. The between-group variance can be determined by using these new estimates of τ:

$$s_B^2 = \frac{3(1)^2 + 3(-0.34)^2 + 3(-0.67)^2}{2}$$

$$= \frac{4.69}{2}$$

$$= 2.35 \qquad (5.9)$$

The between-group variance is much lower

in this case, as it should be because the τ's from the population are actually 0. With this change in the data, the within-group variance does not change because this variability was not removed from the data points; s_w^2 is still equal to 6.56. Using these new values, the F-ratio is

$$\frac{2.35}{6.56} = 0.36 \qquad (5.10)$$

Obviously, this is a low value, and it signifies that the results are not significant. Any variability in the treatment conditions was only due to random variability and not an effect of the treatment. The analysis of variance successfully separates the treatment effect from random variability.

The process for calculating the F-ratio can be simplified greatly by using computational formulas found in all statistics books. One does not have to estimate the τ's and the ε's to find the within- and between-groups variances. To obtain a conceptual understanding of analysis of variance, however, it should have been helpful to do the preceding exercise.

TYPES OF STATISTICAL ANALYSES

Each of the experimental designs of Figure 5-1 has a statistical test associated with it. Many analyses of variance techniques are available for analyzing human-computer interaction experimentation. In the preceding discussion, only one of the techniques, a one-factor analysis of variance, was discussed. Depending on the number of factors and the kinds of effects, the analysis of variance can be tailored to the experimental design.

The analyses of variance techniques differ depending on the effects removed from the error term, or the random variability. Possible effects which can be removed are those due to the different factors, those due to blocked variables, and those due to interactions. These issues will be considered in the next two sections.

Removing Blocked Effects from the Error Term

Sometimes effects which are not due to random variability are placed inadvertently in the error term. But if these have a systematic effect on performance, then they are not random and should be removed from the error term. A new F-ratio could be determined for these effects to see if they are significant. If the error term is reduced by removing the variability which can be accounted for systematically, then the F-ratio could increase and the test would be more sensitive for finding the effects. If the systematic variation is not removed from the error term, then the size of the error term could mask any effects due to the treatments.

One method in which an effect can be removed is to block the effect in a randomized block design. If some variable has an effect on performance, then this effect can be removed by estimating the effect, similar to that done for estimating the effect for the interface design. As an example, consider the data from Table 5-1. Let's say that the expertise of the nine subjects in the experiment varied, and this expertise level had an effect on performance on the interfaces. For each of the three interfaces, each of the three subjects in a treatment level varied as novice, average, and expert. The same data points from Table 5-1 have been reorganized to show the levels of expertise in the rows of Table 5-8.

In Table 5-8, the between-group variance, due to the different interface designs, has not changed, but now the row information is meaningful. In the previous examples, the variability due to expertise level was just combined with the random error in the within-group variance. Looking at the data, it appears that expertise level has an effect on performance, so all the variability originally assigned to the random error term is not really random

TABLE 5-8

Numerical example for time (sec.) for performing a task on each of three interfaces, blocked by expertise level

Expertise Level	Interface A	Interface B	Interface C	Mean
Expert	19	21	11	17.00
Average	22	25	14	20.33
Novice	24	24	17	21.67
Mean	21.67	23.33	14.00	19.67

because some of it varies systematically. That part of the within-group variance which varies systematically should be removed from the error term.

Estimating the effects due to expertise level, and then removing this effect from the error term, is similar to estimating the τ_j's from the previous section. The new effect can be designated as τ_i, for i running from 1 to 3, and can be estimated by subtracting each of the row means from the grand mean, as follows:

est τ_1 = 17.00 - 19.67 = -2.67
est τ_2 = 20.33 - 19.67 = 0.66
est τ_3 = 21.67 - 19.67 = 2.00   (5.11)

By squaring each of these values, summing the squares together, and multiplying this sum by 3 (because each estimate is from 3 data points), the size of the effect due to expertise can be calculated as follows:

effect = 11.56 (3) = 34.68   (5.12)

Remember that this part, without dividing out the degrees of freedom, is called the sums of squares for the effect. The sums of squares is used when removing the effects from the variance.

Since the expertise effect is systematic variability, the amount of this effect can be subtracted from the old random error sums of squares to obtain a new random error value. The old error value was 39.34, so the new error value is

39.34 - 34.68 = 4.68   (5.13)

In a randomized block design, the F-ratios corresponding to the effects should be calculated with just the random error term as the estimate of random variability.

Therefore, the F-ratio will change, due to the new error term and different values for the degrees of freedom. The F-ratio for the interface design is now

$$\frac{148.67/2}{4.66/4} = 63.56$$ (5.14)

The F-ratio has increased greatly, and the associated p-value will be much lower than that calculated when not using the randomized block design. We can now say that interface design has a significant effect on performance, $F(2,4) = 63.56, p < 0.0001$.

The F-ratio for the expertise level is

$$\frac{34.67/2}{4.66/4} = 14.82$$ (5.15)

This effect is significant, $F(2,4) = 14.82$, $p < 0.01$. If this effect is not significant, then there would have been no reason to block out the effect because, based upon past research, you should have had an idea of whether or not it would be significant. If not significant, the p-value could actually increase, when compared to the nonrandomized block design, because of the loss of degrees of freedom. An exercise at the end of this chapter illustrates this concept.

Removing Effects of Factors and Interactions from the Error Term

Other effects could also possibly be removed from the error term. In the two-factor designs, three effects are present: the main effects from the two factors and the effect of the interaction between the two factors. An example of an additional factor would be the multiple tests of the

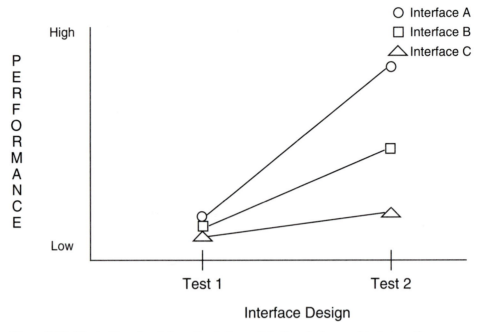

Figure 5-23. **Illustration of an interaction between interface designs and tests over time.**

experimental designs of Figure 5-1. These effects can be estimated in the same way as that discussed for the interface and expertise effects. A difference with the two-factor design is, however, that an interaction effect can occur. An interaction happens when the effect of one of the factors, such as the interface design, is different at the levels of the other factor, such as the first and second test. As an example, significant differences between the interface designs may exist for the second test but not for the first test (see Figure 5-23). This interaction also represents a systematic variability which can be removed potentially from the error term. Most two-factor designs remove the effect of the interaction from the error term; a blocked design like that discussed in the previous section does not remove the effects of potential interactions.

If the systematic variability is inter-active in nature, then a randomized block design may not be the best design, because it assumes no interaction. If there is an interaction present, these systematic effects are lumped in with the random error, thus decreasing the sensitivity of the test. This design also misses the potentially interesting effect of the interaction. To correct this problem, more data would have to be collected than that shown in Table 5-8 for the randomized block design, because now the two-factor design requires a minimum of two observations in each of the nine cells. Without this additional data, the random error term cannot be calculated. Increasing the number of observations could potentially increase the cost of the experiment. The decision to use a design with an interaction is one which requires consideration of previous results and theoretical implications, as discussed in Chapter 4.

TABLE 5-9
Numerical example for time (sec.) in a repeated-measures design where subjects are repeated over interface designs

Subjects	Interface A	Interface B	Interface C	Mean
Subject 1	14	16	6	12.00
Subject 2	22	25	14	20.33
Subject 3	29	29	22	26.67
Mean	21.67	23.33	14.00	19.67

Removing Effects Due to Differences in Subjects

A special analysis technique, called repeated measures, is often used in research utilizing humans as the subjects in the experiment. The data considered in the previous sections all had nine subjects in the experiment, with data from each of the nine subjects in each of the nine cells accounting for the nine data points. An alternative way to conduct the experiment would be to have three subjects use each of the three interface designs. In this case, the observations from the subjects are repeated over interface design. Hence, the term "repeated measures" describes this kind of design and analysis.

When conducting experiments on interface designs, the individual differences between the subjects over the interface designs would be uninteresting; the interface designs would be the most important factor. However, one subject might happen to be fast, while another subject might happen to be slow. The most interesting aspect of the experiment should be the change in performance of a subject from one interface to another. If the fast subject has the same pattern of results as

the slow subject, only faster, then this is the important part, rather than the fact that a subject is faster or slower than another. Repeated measures are designed to remove the effects of individual differences from the estimation of the error term for the interface designs.

Removing the individual differences from the error terms is similar to removing the effect of the blocked variable from the error term. The example data from Table 5-9 show the same overall trends of the other data in the previous tables: Interface C is performed faster by all the subjects. This example exhibits large individual differences between the three subjects even though the means for the interface designs are the same as previously. Since the column means and the grand mean are all the same, the size of the treatment effect, the τ_j's, is the same as that considered in the previous cases for the data on the three interfaces.

Since the data points have changed somewhat from the previous tables, the ε_{ij}'s must be calculated anew to determine a value for the error term. Recall that the ε_{ij}'s can be calculated by subtracting the τ_j's from each of the data points. This has been done in Table 5-10. The variability

TABLE 5-10
Determining the estimates for the ε_{ij}'s by subtracting the column means from the data points for the repeated-measures design

Subjects	Interface A	Interface B	Interface C
Subject 1	14 - 21.67 = -7.67	16 - 23.33 = -7.33	6 - 14.00 = -8.00
Subject 2	22 - 21.67 = 0.33	25 - 23.33 = 1.67	14 - 14.00 = 0
Subject 3	29 - 21.67 = 7.33	29 - 23.33 = -5.67	22 - 14.00 = 8.00

between these data points can be determined by summing the squares of the ε_{ij}'s for all i and j, and then dividing through by N (9) - k (3), or 6. The sum of squares is 329.33, and the s_w^2 is 54.89. Because of the individual differences between the subjects, this is considerably higher than the 6.56 which was seen for the first set of data.

Individual differences can be determined by the overall performance level of the subjects over all the levels of the repeated factor, in this case, the levels of the interface design. These individual differences should be separated from the random variability, because this variability is not really random, it is due to the systematic differences between the subjects. The effect for the individual differences can be estimated in much the same way as the blocked effect was estimated in the previous sections. The individual differences effect can also be designated as τ_i and be determined by subtracting the grand mean from the row means as follows:

τ_1 = 12.00 - 19.67 = -7.67
τ_2 = 20.33 - 19.67 = 0.66
τ_3 = 26.67 - 19.67 = 7.00   (5.16)

The effect for the individual differences

can be found by summing the squares of the individual effects above, multiplying the sum by 3, and then dividing by 2. The sum of the squares is (multiplied by 3) 324.79, and s_B^2 is 162.40.

The true random variability can be determined by separating the effect due to individual differences from that which was termed the random variability effect earlier. Mathematically, this is done by subtracting the individual differences sum of squares from the original error sum of squares, as follows:

$$329.33 - 324.79 = 4.54 \qquad (5.17)$$

The 4.54 represents the true error term, when calculating the effect due to interface design. The F-ratio for interface designs can be calculated as follows:

$$\frac{148.67/2}{4.54/2} = 32.75 \qquad (5.18)$$

The interface design factor is highly significant, $F(2,4)=32.75, p<0.0001$. Except for rounding error, this effect would be the same as that seen when the randomized block design was used.

If the analysis was not performed correctly as a repeated-measures design, then the error term would contain both the true random variability and the effect due to individual differences. This sum of squares would be 329.33. The F-ratio would be calculated as follows:

$$\frac{148.67/2}{329.33/6} = 1.35 \qquad (5.19)$$

This is nonsignificant (NS), $F(2,6) = 1.35$, NS. The reason it is nonsignificant is that the estimate of the random variability is inaccurate. The estimate should only contain the variability which cannot be accounted for by any other effects. Since the repeated-measured analysis showed that some of the variability could be accounted for by individual differences, the estimate of the random variability for the repeated-measures design is more accurate and more sensitive for finding the effects.

The repeated-measures design is similar to the randomized block design except for one thing: the individual differences effect is a random effect and the blocked variable will most likely be a fixed effect (see the previous section in this chapter that discusses fixed and random effects). For reasons beyond the scope of this discussion, this means that an F-ratio can be found for the blocked effect, which is fixed, but an F-ratio cannot be found for the random effect, the subjects, which is repeated over another factor. In most cases, the experimenter uses a repeated-measures design because it is known and accepted that individual differences will occur, and no useful information is derived by changing the design so that individual differences can be measured by an F-ratio. If individual differences, such as expertise, is an experimental factor that needs to be investigated in a repeated-measures design, then the design should be modified by the addition of subjects to each cell of the experimental matrix.

Mapping the Eighteen Experimental Designs into Statistical Analysis

Each of the 18 experimental designs considered in this chapter can be analyzed according to some of the statistical techniques discussed in the previous section. In most cases, the statistical analyses are more complicated than those discussed previously, and statistics books should be consulted for how to apply the correct test. The purpose of this section is to indicate which kind of test should be associated with each of the designs, so that a statistics book could be consulted after already knowing the terminology. All the analyses incorporate analysis of variance (ANOVA), and they can be divided into four kinds: one-way ANOVA, two-way ANOVA, repeated measures, and randomized block.

One-Way ANOVA . This is the simplest analysis, and it is used only for the one-factor between-groups design (see Figure 5-24). The analysis is the same as that considered from the data in Table 5-1. One factor, such as interface design, has several levels. Each cell in the design has a different subject. In the example from Table 5-1, each of the nine cells had a different subject. The only F-ratio determined is the one for the interface designs.

Two-Way ANOVA . This analysis differs from the one-way ANOVA in that two factors are manipulated in a between-groups design (see Figure 5-25). A second factor may be expertise of the subjects, for example. The subjects could be grouped

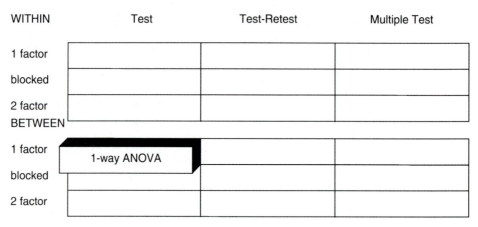

Figure 5-24. The experimental design in which a one-way analysis of variance is used.

into expertise levels, and the number of levels of expertise determines the number of levels of this second factor. Each subject would use each of the interfaces. An important aspect of this design would be the hypothesized interaction between the two factors, or, in the example, the interaction between interface design and expertise level. If no interaction was expected, then the experiment could be better analyzed by using a randomized block design, blocking the expertise level, thus not determining the interaction.

Repeated Measures. Figure 5-26 shows that repeated measures are used for 10 of the 18 experimental designs. Each of the 10 designs is slightly different from each other.

The within-groups one-factor design in the "test" column of Figure 5-26 is the same as the repeated-measures design illustrated in the previous section. The subjects participate at all levels of the factor, the interface design, so that subjects are repeated over interface design. The individual differences of the subjects

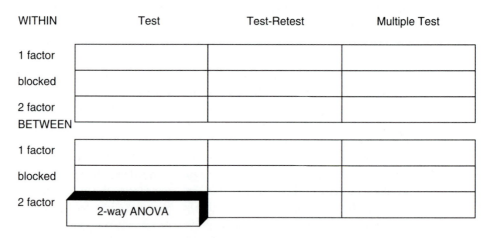

Figure 5-25. The experimental design in which a two-way analysis of variance is used.

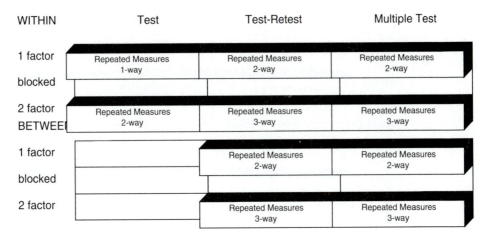

Figure 5-26. The experimental designs in which repeated-measures analyses are used.

are removed from the error term, in this kind of design, and an F-ratio can only be found for the interface designs factor, not the subjects effect.

The within-groups one-factor designs in the second ("test-retest") and third ("multiple test") columns of Figure 5-26 are essentially the same design, with the only difference being the number of levels for the test factor. In this design, subjects are repeated over both interface design and tests. F-ratios can be determined for the interface design, the tests, and the interactions between the interface design and the tests. Individual differences can be removed from all these effects. Statistics books should be consulted for the exact form of the test and the error terms used for each of the effects.

For the within-groups two-factor designs of Figure 5-26, another factor, possibly expertise level, is introduced into the experiment. In the case of expertise level, subjects would only be repeated over interface designs and not over the expertise level. Three effects could be determined: interface design, expertise

levels, and the interaction between interface designs and expertise level. Individual differences can only be removed, however, from the error term which is used to calculate the F-ratio of the interface designs. It should be obvious why subjects cannot be repeated over expertise level. A subject can only be at one expertise level during the course of an experiment; he or she cannot be reincarnated as someone else at another expertise level.

The three-way repeated-measures designs of columns 2 and 3 of the two-factor within-groups row of Figure 5-26 are both the same design. A third factor, tests, is introduced, resulting in the following effects which can be analyzed: interface design, expertise level, tests, interaction between interface design and expertise level, interaction between interface design and tests, interaction between expertise level and tests, and the three-way interaction between interface design, expertise level, and tests. The subjects factor is repeated over interface design and tests, so that individual differences could be removed from the error terms for

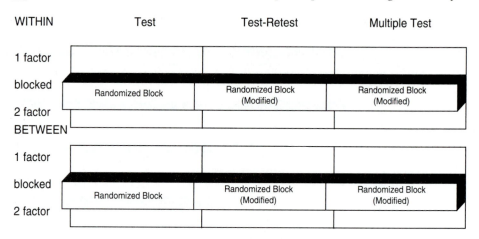

Figure 5-27. The experimental designs in which randomized block designs are used.

those two factors, plus any interactions which contain both of the factors in which the subjects factor is repeated over.

The between-groups designs of Figure 5-26 utilize slightly different repeated-measures analyses. The second and third columns of the one-factor between-groups designs use the same analysis. In this analysis, because different subjects are used for each of the interface designs, the subjects factor is repeated only over the tests factor. Individual differences can only be removed from the error term used to determine the F-ratio for the tests factor. This design can calculate the following factors: interface design, tests, and the interaction between interface design and tests.

The two-factor between-groups design of Figure 5-26 introduces another factor, such as expertise level, into the experimental design. Once again, subjects can only be repeated over tests, but not over the other two factors of interface design and expertise level. Effects can be calculated for all those considered for the three-way repeated-measures design from the within-groups row.

Randomized Blocks. Randomized block designs are used when the interaction between the blocked variable and the other factors is unimportant. The randomized block for the "test" column of the between-groups design (see Figure 5-27) is the same as that analyzed in the previous section and shown in Table 5-8. In that design, interfaces was the factor, and expertise level was blocked. No interaction can be found between the two effects. If an interaction is important, by having an effect on the data or the interpretation of results, then the two-factor design should be used.

The randomized block designs of the between-groups designs for the second and third columns combines features from the between-groups one-factor design with a blocked effect. The only difference between the one-factor design of the row above and the randomized block designs in Figure 5-27 is that a blocked variable is included in the design. This blocked variable is never used in an interaction with another factor.

The randomized-block analyses of the within-groups design of Figure 5-27 are all the same as the one-factor row analyses except for the addition of the blocked variable. For the first column, an F-ratio for the blocked variable can be calculated, and, like the one-factor case, an effect for the interface designs can also be determined. For this analysis, subjects is repeated over interface designs, so that the error terms should be chosen appropriately. This has no effect on the blocked variable, however. For the second and third columns, the analyses are the same as those used for the row above, except for the addition of the blocked variable.

SUMMARY

This chapter discussed 18 typical designs used for conducting experiments in human-computer interaction research. These are typical designs; more designs could be included for more esoteric experimentation or tests of theories. In most of the cases, these 18 designs will address most research questions. A procedure was provided for deciding which design may be best for addressing a particular research question. Each design decision has implications for the analysis and interpretation of the results.

Next, important issues in statistical analyses were discussed. Having a good basic understanding of these issues is critical for analyzing the experiment and interpreting the results. Statistical analyses are used to separate the effects due to the variable of interest from the random error. If the effect is large enough in relation to the random error, then the effect is a significant effect and therefore not just due to the random variability.

Only randomness should be included in the random error term. Techniques were discussed for separating the random error from other kinds of variability which could be identified. In a randomized block design, variability from some effect is blocked out and removed from the random error. For repeated-measures designs, variability due to individual differences between subjects can be removed from the error term. These techniques make the tests more sensitive by only testing the experimental effects against true random error. If these techniques are not used, nonsignificant results could result due to some identifiable effect being lumped with the random error.

The 18 experimental designs were then mapped into statistical tests. Procedures were not provided for how to perform all of the analyses, but once a conceptual understanding has been established for each design, these tests can be found in most statistics books. Calculating the necessary F-ratios is quite easy; understanding what the numbers mean and how to interpret the data is the difficult part.

In the next chapter, some of the hazards of experimental research will be discussed. Comprehension of these hazards is easier once the basis for the statistical tests has been established.

QUESTIONS

1. Modify the graph of Figure 5-7 to show results in which (a) the two groups are different initially; (b) the subjects using interface A learn faster than subjects using interface B; and (c) this interaction could not be explained by saying that those subjects who are high performers initially will learn faster than lower performers.

2. Consider the data in the table at the bottom of the page. Perform a randomized block analysis on the data. Find the F-ratios for the expertise level, the blocked variable, and the interface design. What happens to the F-ratio for interface designs when compared to the case when expertise level is not blocked out? Why does this happen?

3. Consider the following experiment. Two interfaces are being tested for a database application. One interface, the graphical interface, uses Venn diagrams (see Chapter 24) to allow the users to enter the logical relationships. The other interface, the textual interface, uses words such as AND, OR, and NOT to specify the logical relationships. The experimenter feels that practice on the graphical interface would be beneficial to the users of the textual interface because they would not know how to construct Venn diagrams from the text. The experimenter also felt that the spatial ability of the subjects, as measured on a standardized test, could affect how people perform using the interfaces. The score on the standardized text was then used to place the subjects into two groups: high and low spatial. The experimenter was particularly interested in the interaction between the the factors.

a. What is (are) the dependent variable(s)?

b. What is (are) the independent variable(s)?

c. What are other extraneous variables which could have an effect on performance?

d. For a test such as this, how much practice do you think should be provided for the subjects?

e. Which experimental design would you use?

4. Consider the following experiment. A company wishes to determine which kind of automatic teller machine (ATM) design is the easiest to use. They are considering two possible designs: placing the label on the button for the different functions or placing buttons beside a video display unit (VDU). The VDU design has the advantage of fewer buttons because the labels can be changed on

Expertise Level	Interface A	Interface B	Interface C	Mean
Expert	19	21	17	19.00
Average	22	25	14	20.33
Novice	24	24	11	19.67
Mean	21.67	23.33	14.00	19.67

the VDU depending on the functions needed. The labeled button design would require more buttons but may be easier to use because the button/function mapping does not change. Answer the following questions pertaining to this experiment.

a. What is (are) the dependent variable(s)?

b. What is (are) the independent variable(s)?

c. What are other extraneous variables which could have an effect on performance?

d. For a test such as this, how much practice do you think should be provided for the subjects?

e. Which experimental design would you use?

CHAPTER 6

HAZARDS TO CONDUCTING AND INTERPRETING HCI EXPERIMENTS

INTRODUCTION

This chapter contains descriptions of eight common hazards to conducting and interpreting experiments in human-computer interaction. These hazards should be avoided when conducting experimentation in this area. Also, when reading experiments performed by other people, the methodology and interpretation of the results should be read critically to determine if any of the hazards occurred which might invalidate some of the results or conclusions. In fact, Sheil (1981) performed a survey of the experimentation in the related area of research on computer programming tasks and determined that a large percentage of the studies had some kind of methodology problem associated with them which made the applicability of the results questionable.

Experiments should be conducted properly, and the experimentation reported in journals and conference proceedings should be read carefully to determine that none of these hazards have occurred. Most journal articles are refereed, which means that they are accepted only after peer review. Most conference proceedings are not refereed so that little control exists for bad experimentation. This is not saying that all conference proceedings papers are bad; the point is that the reader should be knowledgeable about experimentation when reading any kind of experimental research.

Some of the problems with empiri-cal research can be summarized according to common hazards which may occur. For each of the eight hazards that follows, examples are provided in the context of human-computer interaction research. Then, a discussion is provided for why it is a hazard and how it can be avoided. The formats for these hazards have been taken from Eberts, Smith, Dray, and Vestewig (1982).

HAZARD 1—RESEARCH QUESTION IS PHRASED IMPROPERLY

This hazard is actually related to all the hazards. If the experiment does not start with a clear research question, then the experiment will not seem to address any particular question, thus being ill-defined and poorly formulated. Some experiments seem to address a question, but it may be the wrong question.

Examples

Following are examples of poor or wrong research questions. Perhaps the research question which is most addressed for interface design is: Is this new interface effective? This can be the start of a research question, but it must be elaborated more until the question is specific enough to guide the research. What is meant by effective? Is the interface supposed to be fast or should it produce few errors? Do the users prefer to use this interface? The term "effective" must be operationalized through some kind of performance which can be measured.

If measuring effectiveness, some kind of comparison has to be made. It is possible that the experimenter is interested in comparing two possible designs to each other to determine which is best. Or, the experimenter could compare a new interface design to the standard interface in the field to determine if the new interface provides any performance benefits over the other. Recall from Chapter 4 that the basis of experimentation is the experimental method. For the experimental method, treatments are provided to two or more conditions so that the only thing which varies between conditions is the treatment. Evaluations can be made only by comparing interface design features for two or more treatment conditions.

If measuring effectiveness, the experimenter must determine for whom the effectiveness is targeted. Experts may find the new interface effective and novices may not. An interface which is best for one group may not be effective for another.

Another often-used research question which is poorly defined is: How do people perform on this interface? This is more of a qualitative question than a quantitative question. Qualitative questions are useful, especially in the early stages of experimentation or interface design, but these kinds of questions can usually be defined further to make them easier to test. The kind of performance should be decomposed into specific hypotheses which can be tested. As examples, one hypothesis could be that the subjects will not spend as much time on one particular part of the task as is done usually on the target task

with other interfaces. To test this, the frequencies of use of each kind of command can be determined. Another hypothesis could state that the interface can be performed easier than others and with less assistance. To test this, the number of times that the help messages are used and the type of help message utilized can be measured. Another hypothesis could state that less mental processing of the items on the interface is needed. To test this, the pauses between performing different parts of the task can be measured. A final hypothesis could state that the subjects use different strategies with different interface designs. To test this, the experimenter can try to determine the kinds of strategies used by asking the subjects what they are doing at each point in the task. One of the most difficult and challenging aspects of experimentation is to hypothesize about how subjects may be behaving with the different interfaces and determine methods to test those hypotheses.

Why Is This a Hazard?

If the research question is ill-defined, the experiment may be designed so that concrete results cannot be determined and the experiment will be inadequate to make the kinds of decisions it is intended to address. Many times an experiment will be conducted, the experimenter will observe the subjects performing the task, and the results will be analyzed, but after the experiment has been terminated, from the results or from prior observations during the experiment, the experimenter may determine that certain measures, such as pauses between events, should have been collected to address some of the hypotheses. When the experiment is over, these measures may be impossible to reconstruct. With careful planning prior to experimentation, and correct phrasing of the research question, much time can be saved. In some cases, pilot studies should be conducted on a small number of subjects so that these kinds of costly mistakes do not occur.

How Can This Hazard Be Avoided?

The research question is just not a matter of determining a simple question that is addressed. Much behind the scenes work should go into the formulation of the question. The experimenter should have a very good idea about what will happen in the experiment and how the results should turn out. As an example, if months or years have been spent on designing a new interface, then the experimenter has a good idea that the new interface will be better than the old interface. The development effort should have been based upon some perceived need. Based on the past evaluation, the experimenter should have a good idea about how the new interface will be better than the old; this can be used to determine the dependent variables. The background work is very important to the research question. The experimenter should know the theories and the prior experiments that have been performed. The results of the experiment should not be surprising if this background work has been performed properly.

It may be difficult to understand the reason for performing research if the results are already known. Each experiment, however, answers some questions, but other questions, not considered previously, can be determined from unexpected results. These unexpected results can lead to further hypotheses and further experimentation. In addition, some of the results may not turn out exactly as expected. The experimenter would then have to look at the results and make new hypotheses and generate new research questions. One experiment is usually inadequate to address any important research issue. Your experiment should be a part of a bigger research effort, either in your own lab or as part of the research literature in your area. A good experiment answers some of the questions. A better experiment answers some of the questions and poses many more questions that can be addressed through further experimentation.

HAZARD 2—IMPORTANT VARIABLES ARE NOT CONTROLLED

An experimental design is intended to separate the effects of the variables of interest, the independent variables, from the effects of other variables. A confound occurs when some other variable is allowed to vary at the same time as the independent variable.

Examples

Unfortunately, many examples exist of confounds occurring. One of the most difficult things to control is the prior training of the subject groups. If a new interface design is being tested by comparing it to an old design, then prior training for the subjects could be different. Subjects may have experience on the old design or something similar to the old design, and no experience on the new design or anything similar to the new or old design. The old design could be shown to be better just because of the prior experience. New subjects, with no experience on either, could perform better on the new design. This is a confound, because prior experience has been allowed to vary with the treatment conditions of interface design.

Another problem is that the subjects in the different groups may be treated differently. A company may have much time and money invested in a new interface. The experimenters may have many reasons to show that the investment has been beneficial. They could then treat the subjects being tested differently on the new interface than the subjects on the old interface. Many times these differences may not be overt on the experimenters' part; they may not even know that they are treating the groups differently. The subjects could, however, pick up on cues, such as enthusiasm, indicating that the designs could be different and so should be performed differently. Some measures, such as user preferences, could be affected greatly by these unintentional cues. The more objective measures would be less likely to be affected by these cues. This is a confound, because the treatment of the subjects in the different groups varies along with the levels of the independent variable.

Other differences could exist in how the experiment is conducted. The skill levels could be different for the subjects in the different groups. Different ways of selecting the people for the conditions could have been done inadvertently. For instance, volunteers could have been used for one group and paid personnel could have been used for another group. Or, in a more subtle case, the first people to arrive could be assigned to one treatment and the last people to arrive to another

treatment. The first group could have characteristics which may be inducive to better performance. Finally, the circumstances of testing could have been different. One test could have been given in a small, noisy, overcrowded room, and another given in a spacious, quiet room. These different environments could affect performance.

Why Is This a Hazard?

One problem is that an uncontrolled variable can simulate a treatment effect when there really is no treatment effect. Differences between groups owing to different treatment by the experimenters might look like they were caused by the type of interface design tested.

A second, closely related problem is that an uncontrolled variable can counteract the effect of a real treatment effect. In the prior example, if the subjects had more experience with the old design, then performance comparing the new and old might be the same. The experience counteracts the performance enhancements of the new design.

A third problem is that the uncontrolled variable will increase the variance of the results, hiding any effects that may actually occur. The more variance, the more difficult it is to find the underlying effects. The experiment will be more precise, and more likely to determine the real effects, if the variance is reduced as much as possible. The discussion in Chapter 5 showed that F-ratios are determined by taking the ratio of the treatment effect due divided by the random variation. If the random variation is high, due to sloppy experimentation, then the F-ratio will decrease. This decrease could place the F-ratio below the α value which is considered safe for showing significant results.

How Can This Hazard Be Avoided?

Before the experiment is designed, the experimenter should list all the variables that might influence behavior. This may be a very long list. No single experiment can control all variables, but the experimenters should be aware of potential confounds before they occur so that they can be anticipated and their effects reduced. Three methods can be used to control each variable: randomization, holding the variable constant or eliminating it, or manipulating the variable.

Randomization means distributing the effect of the variable over treatment conditions so that there are only chance differences between the groups. The subjects should be assigned randomly to the treatment conditions. This is easy to do procedurally, but the problem is that randomization does not reduce the variability in the results. With small numbers of subjects in each group, the probability increases of having unequal groups across some kind of measure.

The variable can be held constant or eliminated. To do this, all treatment groups are chosen to be identical with respect to the variable. As an example, if experience is a potential confound, then all groups could have the same experience level. This has the effect of reducing the variability in the results, thus increasing the possibility of finding the experimental effect. It has the added effect, however, of reducing the generalizability of the results to only that tested in the experiment. To continue with the example, the general-

izability of the results would be confined to the potential users of the same experience level as tested in the experiment.

The variable can be manipulated. It can be treated as an independent variable or a blocked variable so that it varies in known ways. Its effects are then distinguished from the effects of other independent variables by statistical techniques such as analysis of variance and randomized block designs. The advantage of manipulating the variable is that it reduces the variability in the results, and important information could be determined by examining the interactions which may occur. The disadvantage of this approach is that it is more difficult to conduct, and the results may be more difficult to interpret.

HAZARD 3—AN INAPPROPRIATE SAMPLE IS USED

The people selected as subjects for an experiment should be representative of a larger group of users. The results can only be generalized to people with similar characteristics to those tested.

Examples

Many interfaces, such as word processors and database packages, are designed for expert users. When evaluating them experimentally, however, training someone to become an expert is difficult or even impossible. So, instead of experts, novices are used as subjects. One interface may be better than another experimentally, but the results can only be generalized to the characteristics of the groups which were tested. In the above example, the results would only be generalizable to novices; experts could have completely different results.

The problem also occurs in the opposite direction. Within a company, experiments are many times performed on company employees who may have more computer experience than the target group of users. Since the company employees have computer experience, the results could not be generalized to computer naive subjects.

Why Is This a Hazard?

This is one of the most common hazards which occur in human-computer interaction research. The results of an experiment could be misleading if the results are generalized to the wrong potential group of users. A product could be developed, with the experimentation only on novices, and then experts may not buy it or continue to use it. When evaluating experiments, the researcher must be careful to determine the characteristics of the subjects.

How Can This Hazard Be Avoided?

Avoiding this hazard is difficult, especially on the problem of expertise. The experimenter should try to demonstrate that the subjects in the experiment have been stabilized at some performance level and that performance is not still becoming better as the important experimental results are collected. Many experiments can be criticized as not allowing sufficient time for the subjects to become proficient at the task. Perhaps this hazard cannot be avoided as much as it can be reported honestly. The experiment should report honestly the training that was provided to the subjects and the potential limitations of the generalizability of the results.

HAZARD 4—NOT ENOUGH SUBJECTS ARE USED

Decisions about sample size are made typically rather informally. Experimenters talk to one another, read reports of similar studies, and so forth. Usually, there is at least some consensus among experimenters regarding the minimal sample size desirable. In human-computer interaction research, finding enough subjects with the desired traits may sometimes be difficult. As an example, finding people who have no computer knowledge, or the desired level of computer knowledge, may be difficult. In practice, the number of subjects is often determined by the number of available, appropriate personnel. This may lead to testing too few subjects.

Example

It is possible that two experiments may have the same mean differences between the interface devices but, because of differences in sample size, the differences may be significant statistically in one experiment and not in the other. If an effect exists, it is more likely to be found when the sample size is larger.

How Can This Hazard Be Avoided?

The easiest way to avoid this hazard is to have large sample sizes. This is not always possible, though, because of limitations in the number of subjects available and because more subjects will cost more money to run. The art of experimentation is to try to determine how to find the potential underlying effects with the least amount of resources (that is, time or money).

Trade-offs exist between three aspects of experimentation: the sample size, the variability, and the size of the potential effect. Generally, the more variability which may occur, the larger the sample size needed. The larger the expected effects, the smaller the sample size needed. Other decisions, discussed in this chapter and the previous one, are also important in the context of sample size. Recall that the variability can be reduced by eliminating or holding a potential confounding effect constant. More variability in the results is expected if the potential confound is randomized between the groups. As an example, if the sample size is small due to resource or subject population problems, then the experimenter may decide to hold a potential confound constant, e.g., all subjects have the same experience level, instead of randomizing this potential effect between the conditions.

Determining potential variability or the potential size of the effect is a subjective decision. Again, the more information that can be brought into the situation, the better. Theories and previous experimentation are all sources for this kind of information. Previous experimentation can also provide a guide for the minimal sample size that can be used in a particular area. In human-computer interaction research, the minimum sample size usually considered in an experiment is six subjects in a group. More typically, the research literature will show that between 10 and 12 subjects usually are included in a treatment condition. Before designing an experiment, the researcher should read the experimentation from similar experiments to determine the number of subjects used.

HAZARD 5—TESTING IS ADMINISTERED IMPROPERLY

If testing is not administered properly, then two things could occur which would make the results of the experiment difficult to interpret. First, the variability of the results may be increased due to sloppy experimentation. Second, the two or more treatment groups may be treated differently so that a confound is introduced to the results.

Examples

The experimental room should be designed so that it is as free from distractions as possible. If not, the distractions could disrupt performance. If the experimental room is not isolated, then other people moving around, noise from telephones, and noise from other people's conversations could all provide distractions. As another example, sometimes equipment failures occur, and these are distracting events to the subject. Finally, the experimenter could be uncertain about how to run the experiment and exhibit confusion in the instructions. In this case, the subjects would not know what is required of them during the experiment.

Why Is This a Hazard?

Distractions due to poor design of the experimental environment, even if the distractions are the same for all treatment conditions tested, may not alter the relationships between the final results, but they will increase the variability which could possibly mask underlying effects. The sample size may have to be increased in order to find underlying effects.

For equipment failures, if a new untested interface design is being compared to a standard tested interface design, then the equipment failures would not only increase the variability in the results but could be confined mostly to one treatment condition: the new interface design. If confined to this one condition, the experiment is confounded and the results would be difficult to interpret. The differences could be due to one interface being better than the other, or they could be due to disruptions because of the equipment failures in the one condition. Alternatively, the equipment failures for the new interface device could hide any benefits from the interface.

Instructions to the subjects must be set before the experimentation begins. If not stable, then these could be another source of variability in the experiment and the results. The experimenter must be especially careful for the first treatment condition run. If poor instructions are provided in the first condition run, and the instructions are polished and refined for the later conditions, then any differences between conditions could be due to instructions and not the treatment. This introduces a confound in the experiment and the results would be difficult to interpret.

How Can This Hazard Be Avoided?

This hazard should be relatively easy for an experimenter to avoid. If the experimental room does not block out distractions, then a room should be designed that does. Even though this may be expensive, the costs could be justified through many

potential savings: poor experimentation could mean that another experiment has to be run; misleading results could harm performance and sales of the product; or conclusions that a product shouldn't be marketed when the product should be marketed because of its good design.

An interface design should not be tested experimentally if the design is not stable and relatively bug-free. Program failures do occur, however. The experimenter should keep a log of everything that happens during the experiment, including equipment failures. If, after the experiment, the results are nonconclusive or different from expectations, then the log can be examined to determine if these results could be due to equipment failure.

All experimenters should be well trained before the experiment begins. The experimental procedures and instructions should be very clear. If several experimenters are conducting the experiment, then it is even more imperative that the procedures and the training of experimenters be well planned and consistent. The experimenters should practice by running pilot subjects or other experimenters through the experiment. One experimenter should not be confined to running subjects from one treatment condition while another experimenter runs subjects from another treatment condition. The two experimenters could conduct the experiment differently, and this would introduce a confound in the experimental design.

HAZARD 6—AN IMPROPER ANALYSIS IS USED

Each of the experimental designs has a certain analysis associated with it. The analysis has been matched to the design.

In addition, each of the analyses discussed in Chapter 5 has certain assumptions associated with it that should be adhered to if used properly.

Examples

One of the assumptions of the parametric statistical tests is that the underlying distribution of scores should be normal. A normal distribution is found usually for dependent variables such as time to perform the task and the Likert scales of questionnaires. Under the strict assumptions of parametric tests, in many cases the dependent variables cannot be assumed to have a normal distribution. Frequencies, such as number of errors or number of help messages used, are not considered to be normally distributed. The percent correct measure is not normally distributed.

Another example of the problem is not using the correct statistical test, especially repeated-measures designs for human-computer interaction. One of the principles of analysis of variance is that the correct error term has to be used. If subjects are involved in the experimentation, as they are in this area, and they are tested repeatedly over one level of another independent variable, then the repeated-measures design should be used.

Why Is This a Hazard?

Using the wrong statistical test, or applying it incorrectly, can invalidate the statistical results of the experimentation. If the assumptions due to distributions are not adhered to, then the other assumptions of the test are invalid and the results would be difficult to interpret.

The repeated-measures design actu-ally increases the chances of finding the underlying effects. In this kind of design, every subject serves as his or her own control. The sensitivity of the test is increased. The hazard with not using the repeated-measures design, when it should be used, is that statistical significances may not be found when they could be found with the proper test. This was demonstrated in the Chapter 5 examples.

How Can This Hazard Be Avoided?

If the distribution assumptions are not satisfied, then two alternatives exist. First, nonparametric tests not having the distribution assumptions can be used. For frequency data, such as number of errors, the chi-square test should be used. The problem with using the nonparametric tests is that some of the important information, such as interactions between the independent variables, cannot be determined. In turn, the kinds of questions which can be addressed by the experimentation is limited.

The second alternative is to transform the data so that the distribution is normal. As long as all the data are subjected to the transformation, then this is accepted practice. One of the most used transformations is for percentage data, which are not distributed normally because of the ceiling at 100%. A transformation often used is to take the inverse hypotenuse tangent of the percent score. This has the effect of stretching out the high scores, while keeping the middle to low scores constant. Parametric statistics could then be used on these transformed scores because they more closely follow a normal distribution.

In practice, many experimenters use

parametric statistics, such as analysis of variance, on frequency data. Although this is incorrect, it seems to be accepted practice in many cases. Research on parametric statistical tests has shown that the tests are fairly robust in violations of the distribution assumptions. The experimenter should examine the data, especially the frequency data, to determine the shape of the distribution. If the distribution assumption does not appear to be violated to a great degree, then the parametric tests can be used with the resulting increase in information of the test. If the assumption is violated, by having many low scores or many scores around a certain frequency, then the use of the parametric statistical test becomes more problematic.

The hazard of not using the repeated-measures design, when it should be used, can be avoided easily by choosing the correct design. The only problem may be that some statistical packages for the computer may not contain this version of the test. Statistics books usually explain how the input can be altered so that a repeated-measures analysis is used.

HAZARD 7—NULL EFFECTS ARE INTERPRETED INCORRECTLY

A null effect occurs when no differences are observed between the treatment conditions. These results are difficult to interpret. Recall that the experimental method was devised to isolate one variable, and that if differences occurred, the effects could be attributed to the one variable that was varying between the conditions. If a null effect occurs, several possible reasons exist for why no differences occurred. It cannot be attributed to one variable, as it could if significant differences were found.

Example

An experiment is conducted comparing a new interface design to an old one. The results show no statistical differences between the two designs, and, indeed, the examination of the group means show that they are very similar. The experimenter interprets the results to mean that the two interfaces are the same and that the new interface should not be marketed.

Why Is This a Hazard?

That the two interfaces are the same is only one possible interpretation, and it could be a true and accurate interpretation. But the experiment cannot be designed to isolate this conclusion from all the rest. The conclusion that the experiment shows no difference is fine, but it should not be concluded that the interfaces are the same. There are many reasons why the results could show no difference between interfaces; many of these conclusions have no relationship to equality of the interfaces. This is a hazard because the experimenters could concentrate on the interfaces, and why they are not different, instead of concentrating on any problems that may have occurred in the experimental design. It is possible that the experiment was conducted poorly, and, if conducted properly, differences between interfaces could be determined.

How Can This Hazard Be Avoided?

If null effects occur, the experimenter must not interpret the results solely in terms of equality of the interfaces. Many of the other hazards have possible reasons, other than the treatment, for results to turn out the way they do. With Hazard 2, a confound may have occurred. If the confound caused one condition to be better than it should have been with no confound, the improvement may result in equal performance for the two interfaces. Therefore, no differences would be seen, but this would not be due to equality of the interfaces.

With Hazard 4, it's possible that not enough subjects were used. The statistical tests, and the variability within a group of subjects, are dependent on the number of subjects used. If the results showed no differences between interfaces, it is possible that more subjects would be needed to find the differences. Once again, the lack of differences may not be due to the equality of the interfaces.

Hazard 5 occurs when the treatments are adminstered poorly. This could result in a confound occurring, as discussed with Hazard 2. It could also result in the variability in the conditions being so high that any true differences between the interfaces would be dwarfed. Lack of differences could be due to high variability because of poor experimental procedures and not due to equality of the interfaces.

Hazard 6 occurs when the wrong statistical test was conducted. The results could be significant if the proper test was used. Lack of statistical significance does not mean that the interfaces are equal; the correct test should be used.

HAZARD 8—RESULTS ARE GENERALIZED BEYOND THE PARTICULAR CONDITIONS TESTED IN THE EXPERIMENT

An experiment cannot test all possible scenarios. Extreme caution should be exercised in generalizing results.

Example

An experiment is conducted to test two different interfaces on ease of use. The results show that one interface takes longer to perform complex tasks than the other but no differences occur for simple tasks. The experimenter concludes that one interface is easier to use for complex tasks and the other is easier for simpler tasks. Further examination of the task revealed that these differences could be due to the nature of the interface and not ease of use. An analysis indicated that the execution time, due to using a keyboard, could be expected to be longer for complex tasks because more keystrokes were needed. For the other interface, the predicted execution time would be the same for both tasks.

These results should be interpreted in terms of the physical time needed to enter the information instead of the more global concern of ease of use. Just because the physical time is longer does not mean that the ease of use is different. If an interface using a keyboard requires you to enter an abbreviation such as "rem" and another requires you to type the full word "remove," this does not mean that one is easier to use than the other. It is faster to enter abbreviations, but users may have a more difficult time remembering which abbreviation to enter (e.g., "rm" or "rem"). The results should be interpreted cautiously.

The example discussed under the confound hazard can also be used here. The results can only be generalized to a population of users similar to that tested in the experiment. If the experiment used novices, then the results can be generalized to novices. If the experiment used experts, then the results can be generalized to experts. A common hazard occurs when the results are generalized to a group not represented in the subject sample.

Why Is This a Hazard?

Sometimes the only part of the experiment that the audience will attend to is the interpretation of the results and the conclusions. All parts of the experiment must be examined to determine how the results can be generalized. The conclusions can be misleading if interpreted incorrectly.

How Can This Hazard Be Avoided?

The conclusions are controlled by the experimenter. The experimenter should be aware of all the interpretation implications of the decisions made when designing and conducting the experiment. Conditions should be placed on the interpretation based upon some of the factors considered above. If not conducting an experiment, but reading experimentation from others, the practitioner should read the report of the whole experiment, and not just the abstract or conclusions, to determine if the interpretations follow from the design decisions and the results.

SUMMARY

These three chapters, 4, 5, and 6, have explained some aspects of experimentation and the scientific method. These chapters have concentrated on the scientific method because it is the most rigorous kind of experimentation, providing the clearest results and interpretations. As emphasized in Chapter 4, this is not the only possible means for conducting experi-

ments. In the early stages of experimentation, studies could be conducted in which subjects are observed under various kinds of conditions. This could provide some important information which could be used in the interface design. Under these conditions, however, it is also likely that some of the hazards may occur, making the results difficult to interpret or meaningless.

Researchers should be aware of these eight hazards when conducting HCI experiments. Additionally, when performing literature reviews of HCI research, the experimental methods should be read closely to determine if any hazards occurred in the reported experimentation and, thus, if the results can be generalized to the situations in which you are interested.

QUESTIONS

1. Go to the library and choose an article on HCI research from a journal such as *Human-Computer Interaction*, the *International Journal of Human-Computer Interaction*, or the *International Journal of Man-Machine Studies*. Answer the following questions about this article.

   a. Did any hazards occur in the experimentation? If so, list the hazard and indicated how it occurred.

   b. For any hazards listed in part a, how could the hazard be avoided?

   c. For any hazards listed in part a, how should the interpretation of the experimental results be changed in regard to the hazard?

2. Explain how hazards could occur if questionnaires and information experimentation, as described in Chapter 4, are used for the experimentation.

3. One of the most common hazards is when the null effects are interpreted incorrectly (Hazard 7). In some cases, the experimental design can be used to limit the number of interpretations for the null effects so that the only viable interpretation is that there are no differences between two interface designs. Consider the following experiment. Two interfaces, A and B, were tested on both novices and experts. The experiment was run in exactly the same way when the novices and the experts were tested (same number of subjects, same method, same instructions, etc.). The results showed that novices performed better on interface A than on B; no differences between the interfaces were shown for the experts. In other words, the null effect was found for the experts but not for the novices.

Answer the following questions based upon the interpretation of the null effect of interface design when the experts were tested.

a. A possible interpretation for the null effect is that not enough subjects were used. Is this a viable interpretation for this design? Why or why not?

b. A possible interpretation for the null effect is that the treatments were administered poorly. Is this a viable interpretation for this design? Why or why not?

c. A possible interpretation for the null effect is that a confound may have occurred. Is this a viable interpretation for this design? Why or why not?

d. Besides the interpretations of parts a through c, are there any other possible interpretations of the null effects which should be considered?

CHAPTER 7

MENTAL MODELS

INTRODUCTION

For the cognitive approach to human-computer interaction, theories in cognitive science and cognitive psychology are applied to the human-computer interface to make the processing of information by the human easier and more efficient. The cognitive theories have as a starting point concepts of human information processing outlined in Chapter 8. Similar to other human-based tasks, the computer user perceives, stores, and retrieves information from short- and long-term memory, manipulates that information to make decisions and solve problems, and then carries out responses.

Interacting with a computer through the interface is a cognitive activity on the part of the user. The user must remember many things and then be able to implement and execute the appropriate commands. The user must retain cognitive information about the particular system or program, for example, that "dd" will erase a line on one text editor or that the function key "F3" will erase a line on another editor. The user must also know about how to interact with computer systems in general by having a cognitive model of how computers behave, and knowing how to cognitively decompose a task into workable units. This division between specific and general knowledge has been termed as a division between syntactic and semantic information (Shneiderman, 1987).

To address cognitive behavior in more detail, consider, as an example, that you wish to reorder some of the paragraphs in a memo, originally prepared using a word processor, to make the memo more readable. Norman (1986) would say that the user would work in sequence through the following seven stages:

- Establishing the goal (to reorder the paragraphs in the memo to make it more readable).
- Forming the intention (the user may intend to move paragraph 1 behind paragraph 2).
- Specifying the action sequence (this particular word processor may require that the user highlight paragraph 1, use a menu to "cut" the paragraph, move the cursor behind paragraph 2, and then use the menu to "paste" paragraph 1).
- Executing the action sequence (execute the above steps).
- Perceiving the system state (if the word processor shows the changes as they occur, then the user perceives the screen and reads the changed memo).
- Interpreting the state (the user determines the consequences of the changes).
- Evaluating the system state with respect to the goals and intentions (the user evaluates whether the reordered memo makes it more readable).

These stages do not have to be performed sequentially. As examples, multiple intentions may be formed before an action sequence is determined. If the evaluation determines that the goal has not been satisfied, then new intentions are constructed by the user.

THE INTERFACE DESIGN PROCESS

The interface designer must try to understand the cognitive activities of the user in order to design an effective and easy-to-use interface. The interface design process utilizing the cognitive approach can be shown pictorially in Figure 7-1 (this is the same as Figure 3-1). Three concepts are important. First, the conceptual model is a design model maintained by the designer of the computer system or the interactive program, in engineering or programming terms, so that it is accurate, consistent, and complete (Norman, 1986, later referred to this as the Design Model). In this design, if it is done carefully, the designer should consider the user's task and capabilities. Many of the capabilities of the user, in terms of human information processing and cognitive functioning, will be considered in more detail in later chapters.

Mental Model Definition

The mental model is the model that the user forms of how the computer system or program works; this mental model guides how the user structures the interaction task (Norman, 1986, later referred to this as the User Model). The mental model is built up through interactions with the display representation which provides the user, along with off-line documentation, the only view of the conceptual model. Norman referred to the display representation and the documentation together as the System Image.

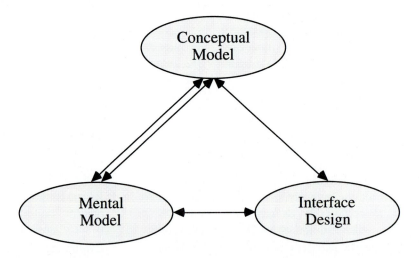

Figure 7-1. The design process for human-computer interaction tasks. The programmer uses a conceptual model to design the task, this conceptual model is conveyed to the user through the display representation, and the user must form a mental model of the task which is as close to the conceptual model as possible.

The goal for an interface designer is to try to choose the information to represent on the display so that the mental model can, like the conceptual model, be accurate, consistent, and complete. Norman emphasizes that the design should allow the conceptual model of the system to be explicitly intelligible and consistent. A test of the success of an interface is a comparison of the user's mental model to the conceptual model.

Norman (1986) argues that some tasks lend themselves better to explicitly displaying the conceptual model to the user. A general rule is that the more specialized the application, the better the conceptual model. Software such as spreadsheets, some database programs, and drawing programs, as a few examples, are relatively easy to convey to the user if the design is considered carefully. The flip side is that general-purpose programs, such as large operating systems, are very difficult to convey to the user. One way to solve this problem of using general-purpose programs is to design everything to be special purpose. This line of thinking is considered further in Chapter 21.

The Central Role of the Mental Model

The mental model formation is key to understanding methods that can be used to design effective interfaces for computer users. Many review articles and books have been written in an attempt to define the mental model (Carroll, Mack, and Kellogg, 1988; De Kleer and Brown, 1981; Gentner and Stevens, 1983; Goodstein, Andersen, and Olsen, 1988; Johnson-Laird, 1981; Rouse and Morris, 1986; and Wilson and Rutherford, 1989). A good definition of a mental model has been

difficult to state because it can mean so many different things in different contexts. Generally, a mental model can be conceived as the users' understanding of the relationships between the input and the output so that a user could predict, after the development of a mental model, the output which would be produced for the possible inputs. Stated in a slightly different way, the mental model can be "run" and users can predict the output which would result from some kind of input.

Wilson and Rutherford (1989) review research and thinking on the representations used in mental models. They differentiate the mental model from other kinds of representations used in psychology and elsewhere, such as schemas (Rumelhart, 1980), frames (Minsky, 1975), and scripts (Schank and Abelson, 1977), by stating that mental models are the utilization of these other representations in a dynamic situation. Schemas, frames, and scripts are relatively permanent and can be stored and activated in memory, whereas the mental models can be thought of as temporary data structures utilizing the more permanent structures.

Norman (1983) has made some observations on the kinds of mental models that users utilize when interacting with machines. Norman states that mental models are incomplete, unstable, unscientific, and parsimonious. Furthermore, he found that the ability to "run" them is severely limited and no firm boundaries exist between the separate mental models. In observations made of calculator users, he found that the subjects always took extra steps or declined to take advantage of features of the calculator. As an example, he found that subjects wrote down partial results when they could have been stored in memory, they hit the clear key several times to clear the calculator before each problem, and they would not use memory for often-occurring constants. Thus, their mental model of the calculator was rather elementary and they did not use the calculator to its fullest advantage.

The mental model is important to human-computer interaction in two ways. First, methods have been researched to enhance the development of an accurate mental model of the computer system. Some of this research and these ideas will be reviewed. Second, determining the form of the mental model can be important in interface design. Techniques have been developed to acquire knowledge from people about their mental models of the task. If knowledge acquisition is performed on experts, then interfaces can be designed that are compatible with these mental models. When novices use the interface, then they should develop mental models similar to those of the experts. These knowledge acquisition techniques will also be reviewed.

DEVELOPMENT OF AN ACCURATE MENTAL MODEL

In the case of human-computer interaction, the users should develop an accurate mental model of how the computer works. They should be able to understand the relationships between the input, such as typing a command, and the output, or what the computer does with the command. After interacting with the computer over a period of time, the users should be able to predict the output that would result from each kind of input. Three techniques which can and should be incorporated in computer interfaces have been shown to be effective in helping to develop accurate mental models of the system: active interaction with the computer, the use of metaphors and analogies to explain the system, and the use of spatial information to convey the conceptual model.

Active Interaction

Much of the research on active or passive interaction with a system has been examined for operators understanding physical systems. This research can be applied to computer systems in general.

Young compared three groups of subjects on their ability to detect a change in the system's output function. A change would occur when the input device, a joystick in this case, controlled the system in a different way from the normal control. The three groups of subjects were: (1) an active group which actually controlled or interacted with the system; (2) an inactive group which actively controlled the system during the first part of a trial, but after a short time control was disconnected and they were shown the same output that was seen and generated by the active group; and (3) a passive group which monitored the display that the active controllers controlled. Young found that the active and inactive groups were much better than the passive group in the time it took to detect a change in output; the active group was slightly better than the inactive group. He concluded that the active group develops an accurate mental model of the control elements of the sytem, the passive group must rely on pattern recognition to do the task, and the inactive controllers were acting on the basis of control in the early part of the trial. These results show evidence for the importance of interactive control in developing an accurate mental model of a system.

Kessel and Wickens (1982) studied the differences between controllers and monitors, similar to Young's study, with the added purpose of trying to localize the effect of the development of an accurate mental model. They found, like Young (1969), that the active controllers were better than the passive controllers, but they also found that the chance to interact with the system helped direct the attention of the subjects to the relevant cues and information on the display. Kessel and Wickens concluded that the development of an accurate mental model could be due to operators being able to hypothesize an effect and then test that effect by an input. The passive controllers were not able to use a hypothesis-test strategy to develop the internal model.

Active control of the system is important so that computer users can hypothesize and then test those hypotheses for how the system works. The interface should be designed to enhance this activity. In particular, the interface should be designed so that the user can explore how the system works. Exploration behavior can be enhanced by ensuring the user that errors are not costly and can be recovered from easily. If the user thinks that an error may cause a problem that cannot be recovered from, then exploration would cease. Exploration behavior can also be enhanced by symbols and words on the screen. The user can explore these symbols and words if it is obvious that they might do something. There is nothing more intimidating and inhibiting than to get on a computer system and see a blank screen (see Figure 7-2). It is much better if the computer screen displays some of the applications available. The direct manipulation displays, discussed in Chapter 11, encourage active exploration through easy error recovery and by symbols displayed on the screen. The interaction should always be designed so that the user is encouraged to explore other possible ways to perform a task.

Metaphors and Analogies

A second method for developing an accurate internal model is to provide the subjects with an analogy or metaphor about how the system works. The general approach taken is to specify how knowledge of a familiar sitaution can be applied to a new situation, thus explaining some aspect about how the system works. As an example, storing information on a computer disk is analogous to storing files in a filing cabinet. This method is generally used to quickly orient someone about how the computer system works.

Mayer and his associates have investigated the use of analogies as a training method for novices on computer systems. The general approach taken is to provide the novices with a concrete model of how the system works. As an example, in the Mayer and Bromage (1980) experiment, they told the subjects in the experiment that computer input operated like a ticket window in that only one number could be processed at a time, that computer output was like a message pad next to a telephone, and that executive control was similar to a shopping list and pointer arrow. The subjects given this concrete model were compared to a control group which did not receive the model. Mayer found, through several experiments (Mayer, 1975, 1976a, 1976b, 1978, and

(a)

(b)

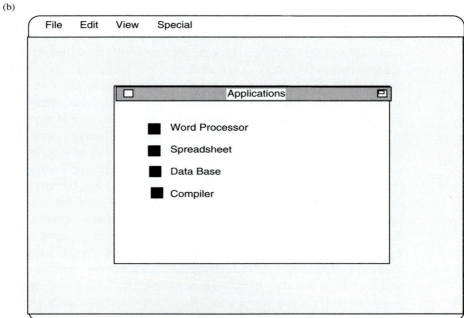

Figure 7-2. A blank screen can be intimidating to a user. As in (a), most command-based systems use a blank screen to start out with; the user does not know where to begin. A screen that has the applications listed (b) invites the user to explore.

1980), that the concrete model group performed better on tasks which required creative transfer of their knowledge to novel situations or tasks that required the integration of several pieces of knowledge. The control group performed as well as the model group on retention tasks.

For most situations, users must be trained on several metaphors to account for how a system operates. Rumelhart and Norman (1981) found that in the teaching of an edit system, one metaphor by itself could cause misconceptions about how the edit system worked. To get around this problem, they had to construct three metaphors that explained different aspects about the system. Similarly, Mayer and Bromage (1980) used the three metaphors to teach subjects the input/output characteristics of the computer system. Stevens and Collins (1980) found that expert tutors probably have multiple conceptual models that are relayed to the students when trying to teach how a complex system works.

The use of metaphors and analogies has been a very important method for helping computer users develop an accurate mental model of the system. Chapter 10 discusses some of the many metaphors which are used currently in computer systems. Some metaphors are more effective than others. The long-term usefulness of metaphors is not known. Carroll and Thomas (1982) warn that even though the metaphor provides a useful overview of the system, there may be a time when the metaphor is no longer useful. The main use of the metaphor seems to be to get novices used to the system so that they can use it, interact with it, and learn more about how it works along the way. The metaphor would help to get the novices

started on the active exploration of the system so that an accurate mental model can be developed.

Spatial Models

Many of the most effective and accurate mental models seem to be spatial in nature. If decisions have to be made about the effect an input will have on the system, the user seems to run through a mental simulation of the event by visualizing or envisioning the results of a control input (De Kleer and Brown, 1981; Hollan, Stevens, and Williams, 1980). Similarly, Bainbridge (1974) concluded from verbal reports that operators keep a mental picture of the current state of the system which provides the context for predicting future events. Through the acknowledgment of the existence of visualization, envisionment, or the mental picture in the mental model, the implication is that an accurate mental model can be developed if novices use an interface incorporating graphics. Hollan et al. (1980) incorporated interactive graphics and animation in the design of the STEAMER simulator for the Navy with the idea that these graphics would later be incorporated in the students' mental model of the system. Chapter 11 discusses STEAMER and other spatial applications for computer systems.

Another related method to help develop an accurate mental model is to show clearly the cause-and-effect relationships between the input and the output. In analyzing simple electrical circuits, De Kleer and Brown (1981) provide many possible mental models that must be developed to understand the circuit. They conclude that the clear display of the cause-and-effect relationships is important.

KNOWLEDGE ACQUISITION

The previous section discussed methods to enhance the development of accurate mental models through the proper display of information. Some overall guidelines for displaying information were presented: active interaction, metaphors and analogies, and spatial representations. Valuable information about what to display can also be acquired from task experts. We would assume that the mental model they have developed of the task is accurate. If this mental model can be acquired from these experts, through knowledge acquisition techniques, then this would provide important information about how the interface should be designed. In other words, designing the interface based upon knowledge acquired about experts' mental models is a method to communicate an accurate mental model to novices.

From work done on studying experts in process control tasks, Lees (1974) states that "... it is well-known, for example, that a pilot may be skilled in flying but may give a quite erroneous account of the control linkages in the aircraft." In other words, the pilot may be an expert at the task but may not be able to explain how the task is carried out. Another problem is that the task may be done automatically and, thus, not be accessible by conscious processes. In fact, this is a problem that has been studied for some time; Woodworth (1938) cites evidence that conscious content of verbal reports disappeared with extended practice. Despite these problems, methods ranging from the problem-solving techniques of Newell and Simon (1972) to a clinical psychology theory (Kelly, 1955) have been developed to elicit knowledge from experts.

Protocol Methods

To help guide the knowledge acquisition, psychological theories about human behavior are often used. The information processing theory of Newell and Simon (1972) has been used extensively. Recently, techniques from psychotherapy have also been adapted to elicit information from experts. Both of these techniques will be discussed.

Following the influential Newell and Simon (1972) book, the expert is often modeled as an information processor who is presented with a problem that must be solved. The information used for solving a problem is viewed as passing through three successive stages (Newell and Simon, 1972) or a problem space. The problem space is the state of knowledge at a particular point in time. Strategies, procedures, and operations are used to transform the knowledge state to match that of the desired goal state. Several strategies may be needed and several subgoals may be formulated to solve the more complex problems.

The Newell and Simon (1972) approach has been used extensively as a framework for acquiring knowledge from experts and is often referred to as the protocol method (for a general review of this method see Ericsson and Simon, 1980). For the protocol method, experts are given a problem to solve and are asked to verbalize what they are doing as they try to solve the problem. They are asked to verbalize their strategies used, the kind of prior knowledge that they are using, and their goals and subgoals as they move through the task. The method requires motivated experts who can easily verbalize what they are doing. The interviewer, or so-called knowledge engineer, also plays a significant role because he or she must know when to prompt the expert if it is felt that steps are being left out. The information processor model can be used as a framework for understanding the protocols and, thus, can be used to determine what kind of information is needed and if any important information is being left out.

The expertise transfer system (ETS) (Boose, 1984) is another protocol method based on an interviewing technique used in psychotherapy by Kelly (1955) to elicit information from clients. An important part of the technique is to have the client list underlying elements (the knowledge base) and then have the interviewer ask a series of "why" questions to determine the superordinate and subordinate relationships. The result of this kind of interview is an understanding of the hierarchical relationship of the elements and the reasons for using the elements.

ETS has been developed to automatically interview the expert and help construct and analyze an initial knowledge base for the problem. In ETS, knowledge is elicited from the information sources (the experts), placed into an information base, analyzed and organized into knowledge bases, and then combined with other knowledge bases to form a knowledge network. ETS tests the knowlege for sufficiency and necessity and will ask the expert to fill in any missing parts. As pointed out by Boose (1984), evaluating the success of ETS and other similar techniques is difficult; inappropriate constructs are easy to weed out, but there is no guarantee that all the important knowledge has been elicited from the expert.

Although a knowledge engineer is trained to elicit information from experts, these techniques ultimately rely on the experts being able to verbalize their expertise. Several problems exist with the method of data collection:

Interpretation—The knowledge engineer must interpret the protocols so that his or her biases are not inserted into the data.

Completeness—The expert may leave out important steps in the problem-solving task.

Verbalization Assumption—An implicit assumption of these methods is that the procedures and data can be verbalized; some may not be amenable to verbalization.

Problem with Experts—Expert skills are often automatized and, thus, may be difficult to verbalize or to interpret.

The knowledge engineer is usually aware of these problems and tries to work around them. Asking the expert and taking protocols is still the most-used knowledge acquisition method.

These techniques can be used for interfaces that utilize knowledge bases, often termed intelligent interfaces. As an example, a knowledge base can be incorporated into an expert discourse interface. An example of such an interface is the MYCIN program (Shortliffe, 1974; Davis, Buchanan, and Shortliffe, 1976) which offers expert advice on the diagnosis and treatment of infectious blood diseases. Given a set of data, MYCIN will provide a user with a diagnosis. Most physicians would then like to know how MYCIN arrived at the diagnosis. A module was designed in which the user could interact with MYCIN by asking questions about how it reached its diagnosis; these questions would include mostly "why" type questions. As pointed out by Card (1989), these queries were limited in that MYCIN could not justify its rules or explain how it derived the ordering of its hypotheses. It provides an example, however, of using acquired knowledge from experts in the design of a system that can discourse intelligently with a person. In this case, the acquired mental model of the expert is used as the conceptual model of the system.

Card (1989), following earlier work done by Sheridan and Verplank (1978), has described the range of possibilities for how a human could communicate with an intelligent machine (see Figure 7-3). At the top of the figure, the human performs the whole task; at the bottom of the figure, the computer performs the whole task. In between these two extremes, the human can check the actions of the intelligent computer and, sometimes, the human must approve the action before it can be executed. This figure demonstrates the ranges of complexity in combining a human with an intelligent machine. Because of these complexities, successful commercial applications of these types of programs have not been fully realized.

Another application of the protocol methods of knowledge acquisition to HCI design is in modeling user performance. The GOMS (Card, Moran, and Newell, 1983) technique (see Chapter 14) very closely follows the Newell and Simon (1972) approach for modeling problem solving, although in this case, the problem is how to perform some task on the computer. Consequently, protocols are obtained to determine the goals, the methods or steps to accomplish the goals, the operators used in the procedures (e.g., keystrokes), and the rules to select between possible methods for performing the task. The formal modeling technique takes the knowledge acquired from the protocols and provides, basically, a model of the user's mental model for performing the task. These techniques are discussed and explained in Chapter 14. Similarly, protocols can also be used in the NGOMSL (Chapter 15) and the Production System (Chapter 16) models. By specifying the mental model of a user in these predictive models, they can be used to predict behavior of the users and they can be used to revise the interface designs.

Scaling Techniques

Another knowledge acquisition method is the use of scaling techniques to organize knowledge into dimensions or clusters. These statistical methods arrange the individual items into spatial representations or hierarchical clusters. Once the knowledge is obtained in this way, it can be represented on the user interface according to dimensions or clusters. Thus, the method used by experts to organize their knowledge can be represented on the screen so that novices could come to represent the knowledge in the same way. Such a representation can provide an "ideational scaffolding" (Ausubel, 1968) in which to place the knowledge as the novice user acquires it. Since this scaffolding is similar to that of the experts (remember, the structure was acquired from the experts) one could expect that the novices will be able to generate these structures and models faster than if they had to acquire them through trial and error. With trial and

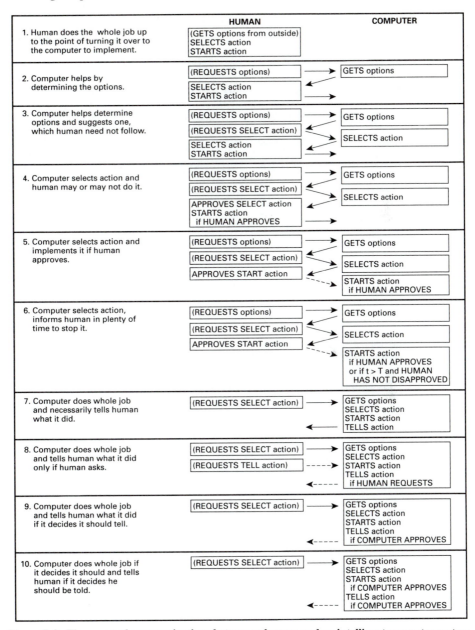

	HUMAN		COMPUTER
1. Human does the whole job up to the point of turning it over to the computer to implement.	(GETS options from outside) SELECTS action STARTS action		
2. Computer helps by determining the options.	(REQUESTS options)	→	GETS options
	SELECTS action STARTS action		
3. Computer helps determine options and suggests one, which human need not follow.	(REQUESTS options)	→	GETS options
	(REQUESTS SELECT action)		SELECTS action
	SELECTS action STARTS action		
4. Computer selects action and human may or may not do it.	(REQUESTS options)	→	GETS options
	(REQUESTS SELECT action)		SELECTS action
	APPROVES SELECT action STARTS action if HUMAN APPROVES		
5. Computer selects action and implements it if human approves.	(REQUESTS options)	→	GETS options
	(REQUESTS SELECT action)		SELECTS action
	APPROVES START action		STARTS action if HUMAN APPROVES
6. Computer selects action, informs human in plenty of time to stop it.	(REQUESTS options)	→	GETS options
	(REQUESTS SELECT action)		SELECTS action

	APPROVES START action		STARTS action
			  if HUMAN APPROVES
			  or if t > T and HUMAN
			    HAS NOT DISAPPROVED

7. Computer does whole job and necessarily tells human what it did.	(REQUESTS SELECT action)	→	GETS options SELECTS action STARTS action TELLS action
8. Computer does whole job and tells human what it did only if human asks.	(REQUESTS SELECT action)	→	GETS options SELECTS action
	(REQUESTS TELL action)	----→	STARTS action TELLS action if HUMAN REQUESTS
9. Computer does whole job and tells human what it did if it decides it should tell.	(REQUESTS SELECT action)	→	GETS options SELECTS action STARTS action TELLS action if COMPUTER APPROVES

10. Computer does whole job if it decides it should and tells human if it decides he should be told.	(REQUESTS SELECT action)	→	GETS options
			SELECTS action
			STARTS action
			  if COMPUTER APPROVES
			TELLS action
			  if COMPUTER APPROVES

Figure 7-3. The range of communications between a human and an intelligent computer system (from Card, 1989, reprinted with permission of publisher).

error, the novice would most likely have to reorganize the model at some point when it is discovered that the early knowledge structures were inaccurate.

As an example of a scaling technique, consider the acquisition of knowledge about the location of cities in the United States. If you were given the pair

CITIES	Atlanta	Boston	Chi.	Dallas	Denver	Hous.	L.A.	Miami	N.Y.	Seattle	D.C.
Atlanta		1108	708	822	1430	791	2191	683	854	2625	818
Boston	1108		994	1753	1998	1830	3017	1520	222	3016	448
Chicago	708	994		921	1021	1091	2048	1397	809	2052	709
Dallas	822	1753	921		784	246	1399	1343	1559	2131	1307
Denver	1430	1998	1021	784		1034	1031	2107	1794	1341	1616
Houston	791	1830	1091	246	1034		1541	1190	1610	2369	1365
Los Angeles	2191	3017	2048	1399	1031	1541		2716	2794	1134	2646
Miami	683	1520	1397	1343	2107	1190	2716		1334	3303	1057
New York	854	222	809	1559	1794	1610	2794	1334		2841	237
Seattle	2625	3016	2052	2131	1341	2369	1134	3303	2841		2843
Washington, D.C.	818	448	709	1307	1616	1365	2646	1057	237	2843	

Figure 7-4. The driving distances between 10 cities are represented in matrix form and can be used in a multidimensional scaling program.

"San Diego/New York" and told to assign a number from 1 to 7 which represents the distance between the pairs, you would probably assign this pair a 7. If given the pair "New York/Philadelphia," you would probably assign the pair the value of 1. If several pairs are rated, then a good range of values would be found. With n cities, all possible pairs would be $n(n + 1)/2$ pairs; for 20 cities this would mean 210 pairs. The subject in this experiment would have to provide ratings on all 210 pairs.

Multidimensional Scaling. Two statistical programs, multidimensional scaling (MDS) and cluster analyses, are typically used to scale the data. The MDS analysis scales the data into two or more dimensions so that the actual distances are as close as possible to each of the values in the pairs. The data from the cities should fit a two-dimensional structure.

Figures 7-4 and 7-5 illustrate this technique. Figure 7-4 shows a matrix of cities where the numbers represent the driving miles between any pair (for example, Chicago and Atlanta are 708 miles apart by car). In an MDS analysis, these distances between the pairs would be the input for the program. Figure 7-5 shows the output from an MDS program where the cities are spaced so that the distance between any pair, from the matrix, is scaled accurately (for example, the distance in the figure between Chicago and Miami, 1397 miles, is approximately twice that of Chicago and Atlanta, 708 miles). Sometimes the axes must be rotated to accurately represent the directions on the map, but the directions represented in Figure 7-5 seem accurate for this analysis. As can be seen, this representation is close to an actual two-dimensional United States map.

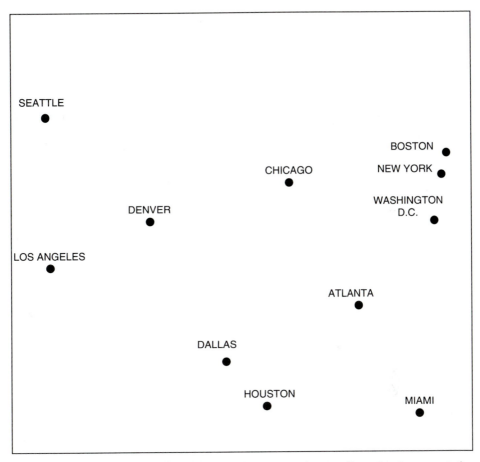

Figure 7-5. The result of a multidimensional scaling program is a two-dimensional representation of the driving distances between cities.

An MDS analysis will only provide a mapping of the data; it does not provide an interpretation. An experimenter would have to look at the plot of the data and try to interpret the dimensions. Since two dimensions are represented in Figure 7-5, this interpretation is fairly simple. Obviously, the horizontal dimension can be interpreted as the east-west dimension, and the vertical dimension can be represented as the north-south dimension. The subject who provided the pair ratings should look at the scaled data to provide his or her interpretation of the dimensions.

For most data, the dimensional representation is not as obvious as it would be for the United States map data. In fact, we did not need to do an MDS analysis to know what a map of the United States looked like. Other kinds of data, such as commands in an operating system or statements in a computer language, do not have such an obvious dimensional structure. In those cases, and others like them, the choice of the number of dimensions and the interpretation of the dimensions is important. Several techniques are available for choosing the number of dimensions and for

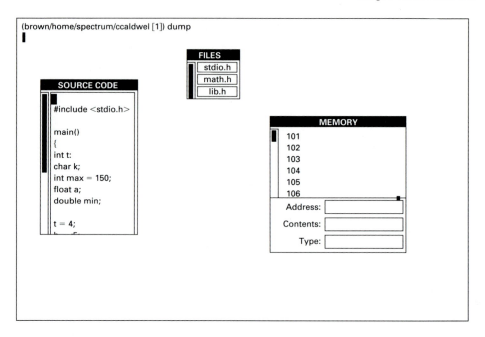

Figure 7-6. Three dimensions were present in the MDS analysis for the similarities between C programming commands. The three dimensions were represented in the user interface design by placing the items from the dimensions in different spatial locations.

rotating and fitting the axes to the data. These issues are beyond the scope of this discussion; other references should be consulted (e.g., Kruskal and Wish, 1978).

The MDS analysis provides a spatial representation of the information. If a subject thinks that two entities are related, then those entities will be clustered together. If two entities are unrelated, then they will be separated by a larger distance. Sometimes groups of items fall into identifiable clusters.

Little systematic work has been done on mapping the acquired knowledge described by the MDS analysis into features for an interface design. One research effort has examined mapping the acquired knowledge about programming languages into an interface design. In this study by Caldwell and Eberts (1989), novices and experts were given pairs of C program-

ming language statements and asked to rate them. These data were analyzed by an MDS program to determine the spatial and dimensional structure of the data. This spatial structure was then mapped directly into a spatial representation on the computer screen for teaching programming languages. As an example, the MDS analysis showed that operations (e.g., arithmetic and logical operations), output, and computer memory were the dimensions; the interface was designed to show these entities in separate spatial locations (see Figure 7-6). The interface seems to capture the experts' knowledge so that novices can develop similar mental model structures for programming languages through their work on the interface.

Clustering. An alternative to an MDS analysis of the data would be to use a cluster analysis on the data. Figure 7-7

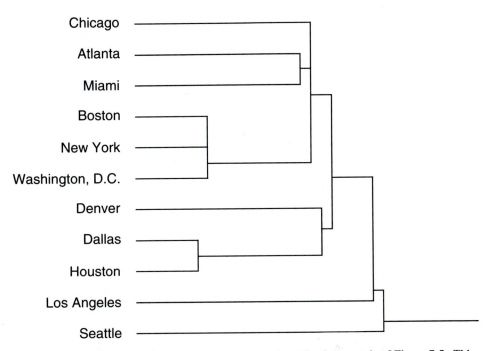

Figure 7-7. The cluster analysis of the city distances from the data matrix of Figure 7-5. This illustrates how the distances, by tracing down the lines from one cluster to another, corresponds to the driving distances between the cities. Categories of cities are also apparent in the representation.

uses the city distances matrix data from Figure 7-5 to show the differences between cluster analysis and MDS. In the figure, the distances are no longer represented as a Euclidean distance, as they were in the MDS analysis, but are represented by the pathway from one item to the next. The tree structure of the cluster analysis also shows the category relatedness among the items. Just like the dimensions of the MDS analysis had to be interpreted by the subject, so the clusters must also be interpreted.

From Figure 7-7, several meaningul clusters are apparent. Two major clusters are divided with Washington, D.C. above the break and Denver below the break. The top cluster represents cities east of the Mississippi and the bottom represents cit-

ies west of the Mississippi. Other smaller clusters also appear. Boston, New York, and Washington, D.C. are all clustered together and could be interpreted as east coast cities. Dallas and Houston are clustered together and could be interpreted as southwest or Texan cities. The number of clusters, and the kinds of clusters, are important for understanding how a person organizes the information.

A cluster analysis is just an alternative organization to the MDS analysis of the data. The MDS emphasizes the dimensional and spatial structure of the data, and the cluster analysis emphasizes the categories in the data. Sometimes data do not have a clear dimensional and spatial representation so that cluster analysis should be used.

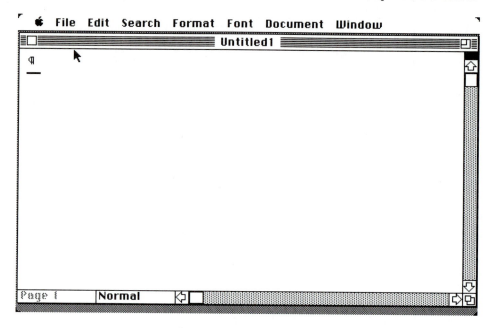

Figure 7-8. The clustering of the menu items in Microsoft's Word word processor. Menu items are chosen by finding the category of the items at the top of the screen. The menu items when the menu is pulled down should be good representatives of those category types.

A good example of data which would have a cluster representation instead of a dimensional structure is commands from an operating system. The clusters from an analysis of these commands could be used to determine how the items should be clustered in menu displays, such as for word processing. Figure 7-8 shows the menu item headings for the Word word processor. Each of the headings, such as "File" and "Edit" represent categories of the menu items, and these categories should correspond to identifiable clusters from a cluster analysis.

Consider the data in Figure 7-9 in which the menu items from the Word word processor have been rated in terms of dissimilarity (a 1 means highly similar and a 7 means highly dissimilar). In Word, open, close, save, and delete are "File" commands; cut, copy, and paste are "Edit"

commands; character, section, and styles are "Format" commands; and spell, outline, and index are "Document" commands. A cluster analysis should find a similar structure when someone familiar with the program rates the dissimilarities between the menu items.

The cluster analysis of the menu item ratings of Figure 7-9 is shown in Figure 7-10. The clusters are very similar to the structure of the menu commands for Word. One of the differences, though, is that styles was clustered with the "Document" commands instead of the "Format" commands. This makes some sense, because the styles have an effect on the structure of the document.

Cluster analysis is one method that could be used to decide which items should be clustered together for menu displays. Roske-Hofstrand and Paap (1986) have

COMMANDS

	open	close	save	delete	cut	copy	paste	char.	section	styles	out.	spell	index
open		1	2	3	6	6	6	6	7	7	6	6	7
close	1		1	2	5	6	7	6	6	7	7	7	7
save	2	1		5	6	5	5	4	6	7	5	7	7
delete	3	2	5		2	5	6	7	7	7	6	6	7
cut	6	5	6	2		2	3	5	5	7	7	7	7
copy	6	6	5	5	2		2	4	4	7	7	7	7
paste	6	7	5	6	3	2		4	6	7	7	7	7
character	6	6	4	7	5	4	4		2	4	7	7	7
section	7	6	6	7	5	4	6	2		6	7	7	7
styles	7	7	7	7	7	7	7	4	6		6	7	7
outline	6	7	5	6	7	7	7	7	7	6		1	1
spell	6	7	7	6	7	7	7	7	7	7	1		1
index		7	7	7	7	7	7	7	7	7	7	1	1

Figure 7-9. Ratings of the dissimilarities between commands used in a word processing program.

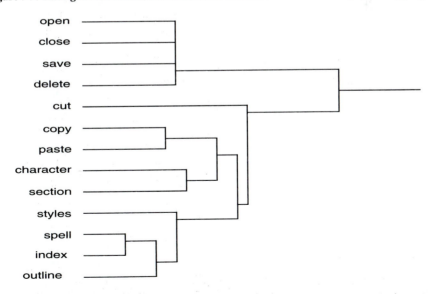

Figure 7-10. Cluster analysis of the commands from Figure 7-9. Each of the clusters should represent a category which is used as a header in the menu structure. Compare these clusters to the menu headers of Figure 7-8.

used a cluster analysis program to determine the organization of menu items in an airplane cockpit.

Another use of clustering analyses, and MDS analyses also, is in the documentation or on-line help accompanying interactive computer programs. Clustering analyses have examined how the clusters change with changes in skill level (e.g., Cooke and Schvaneveldt, 1988, used a related network anaysis program called Pathfinder). As an example, McKeithen, Reitmen, Rueter, and Hirtle (1981) found that novices rated computer language statements on surface features such as mnemonics or the number of characters in the statement. As the novices gained some experience, they rated the statements according to function, but the clusters were very concrete; they could only be interpreted in the context of a program. For experts, the structure was more abstract than it was for the novices, and it represented the meanings of the statements. By comparing the knowledge of the novices to that of the experts, the documentation and on-line help could be designed to fill in the gaps and assist the transitions of novices to experts. In fact, a program called Pathfinder that determines the network relationships has been used to acquire and represent the knowledge from computer users in the design of a UNIX help system (McDonald, Dearholt, Paap, and Schvaneveldt, 1986).

At the end of this chapter, two exercises have been provided for determining the clusters and the subsequent appropriate display of information. In the first example, function cash registers are analyzed. Function cash registers are being used increasingly in restaurants and other businesses. For a function cash register,

the price of each item is entered by hitting a key, labeled by item name, instead of hitting the keys for the digits of the price. If the number of items is relatively low, then function cash registers are useful. Ease of use can be increased by organizing the keys into clusters of related items. The clusters could be determined through a clustering analysis of how people rate pairs of items. In this case, the cluster analysis is manifested in the positioning of keys on a keyboard instead of items on a computer screen.

The other example at the end of the chapter is to perform a clustering analysis on the commands in a word processor. Experts would probably tend to cluster the items in ways that are similar to the word processors used by them. Novices may have different ways of clustering the information.

Both MDS and cluster analyses are methods to determine the mental models of computer users. The representations of these mental models provide information about how the users organize the mental models; the procedural information, very important to a mental model, is missing from these techniques. The protocol method is good for determining the procedures but probably poor for determining the structure of the mental models. Both techniques can be combined to obtain a more complete picture and representation of the mental models.

Pattern Recognition Techniques

Knowledge can be acquired from the user through pattern recognition techniques. Each user may have a different pattern of interacting with the system. This information can be used for several purposes:

designing a user signature for security of computer use in place of passwords and other methods; acquiring knowledge to place in an expert system; and describing the mental models or structures of the data. Three pattern recognition techniques will be discussed: statistical techniques, neural networks, and filters.

Statistical Techniques. Statistical techniques use statistical measures to identify patterns in users' behavior. In the last few years, research has been conducted on identifying computer users through the latencies between keystrokes. A review of some of the techniques illustrates the different statistical measures that can be used for this pattern recognition problem.

The simplest measure is the mean or the average of the latencies. Gaines, Lisowski, Press, and Shapiro (1980) used the means of log-transformed latencies between two keystrokes, the keystroke digraph, to identify individual users. In this line of research, two methods on the performance of the technique are used to gauge success: the impostor pass rate, or the percentage of invalid user attempts accepted; and the false alarm rate, or the percentage of times that the valid user is denied access. The method of the means of the digraph latencies resulted in a 0% impostor pass rate and a 4% false alarm rate. Refinements to the technique limited the number of digraphs which had to be examined.

Umphress, Williams, and Leggett (Leggett and Williams, 1988; Umphress and Williams, 1985) used a tolerance analysis with standard deviations as the statistic to identify users according to keystroke digraphs. They organized reference digraphs into a 27 x 27 matrix (the 26 letters and the blank), with the row

being the first character in the digraph and the column being the second character in the digraph. Each cell in the matrix contained a latency corresponding to the row and column characters. An overall standard deviation of the latencies was used as a reference measure. Test data were then gathered through typing tasks. If the means in the test data were within 0.5 standard deviations of the reference latency means, then the user passed the verification test. The best method using this technique resulted in an impostor pass rate of 5% and a false alarm rate of 5.5%.

A third technique (Joyce and Gupta, 1990) used latencies from users typing in only their name. A "signature" was obtained by examining the latencies between each of the keystrokes in the name. As a comparison of the test data to the reference, they organized the latencies into vectors of the means for each of the digraphs. A simple distance metric was used to determine if the reference and test vectors were close enough to be a valid user. The metric summed the absolute values of the differences between each individual latency on the reference and on the test to calculate a single value for the match. This vector and distance metric technique resulted in an impostor pass rate of 0.25% and a false alarm rate of 16.67%. These three methods show that a variety of statistical techniques can be used in matching the reference keystroke patterns to the test patterns.

Neural Networks. Another pattern recognition technique is the use of neural networks. Neural nets are described in detail in Chapter 9. A neural network determines the weights on a network so that some kind of input pattern can be mapped to the appropriate output pattern.

Using the keystroke example from above, the keystroke latencies could be mapped to individual users; if an output exceeded a threshold then the user could be verified. Various techniques are used for knowledge acquisition using neural nets.

Gallant (1988) developed a neural network for medical diagnosis problems. Experts were given the symptoms and asked to produce the diagnosis. These input/output pairings were used for training the neural network through the values for the connection weights. A method was developed to transform the network and connections into rules used for a traditional expert system. Performance on the neural network compared very favorably to human performance on this reduced problem. For the knowledge acquisition, physicians were provided with the symptoms and they supplied the diagnosis. The rules could then be generated for further diagnoses. Using these examples to extract rules is a much simpler process than a protocol analysis. At the end of this procedure, the acquired knowledge can be stored as rules in a production system (see Chapter 16 for a discussion of production systems).

NETtalk (Sejnowski and Rosenberg, 1987) was a pioneering research effort to show that a neural network can exhibit many of the same learning characteristics as humans. NETtalk was trained from speech production examples to produce spoken words. The network was composed of three layers: an input layer representing the alphabetic characters in words; a hidden layer representing combinations of letters; and the output layer representing the spoken sound. After training, the weights connecting the nodes in each of the layers are set so that the letters can be mapped to the appropriate spoken sound for the words.

The hidden units were analyzed to determine if the training produced letter categories similar to that which would be produced after human learning. By using a cluster analysis program, Sejnowski and Rosenberg were able to provide meanings that were linguistically plausible for many of the hidden units. One of the most striking aspects of their cluster analysis was that two main clusters formed according to vowels and consonants; other subclusters were also meaningful. In another example, a more complete analysis of the structure of the hidden units revealed by NETtalk was performed (Rosenberg, 1987). This analysis used multivariate analysis, hierarchical clustering, and factor analysis to determine the internal structure of the hidden units. The model was able to distinguish between vowels and consonants. For the vowels, it was able to distinguish articulatory features, such as vowel height and place of articulation, even though these features were not used in the encoding for the model. Similar to the clustering and MDS discussion earlier in this chapter, the organization of the knowledge is captured. Whereas the earlier methods required ratings on all the pairs of items, the neural network obtains similar data through the training examples.

A problem with the above knowledge acquisition technique is that it provides only the structure and organization of the information and not the procedures. Villegas and Eberts (1992) have been exploring methods to obtain both aspects of the mental model from neural network data. This research used a neural net to map the commands generated by a user from a text editor into the goals that were

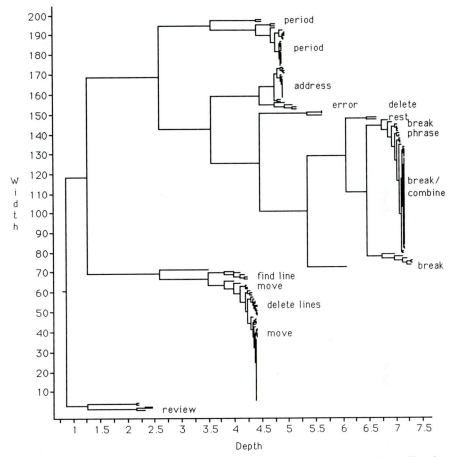

Figure 7-11. The cluster analysis of the performance of the user on the text editor. The clusters reveal how the user organizes the editor commands.

being performed. A cluster analysis similar to that done by Rosenberg (1987) for NETtalk generated the way in which the users organized the commands in the context of the text editor task. Figure 7-11 shows the output from the cluster analysis, and clear clusters of commands can be seen. The procedural knowledge acquisition was examined through the transitions between goals over time. This transition analysis is illustrated in Figure 7-12 for one of the subjects and 7-13 for a different subject in the experiment. As can be seen from these figures, each of the subjects has a different procedural mental model for performing the task. The differences in the representations show graphically how the two subjects differ.

The pattern recognition acquisition of knowledge from computer users can be applied to human-computer interaction in many ways. The applications for the statistical techniques is obvious: it can be used as part of the security system of a computer. Passwords are common on present systems, but passwords can be stolen and sometimes the user forgets the password, especially after not using the

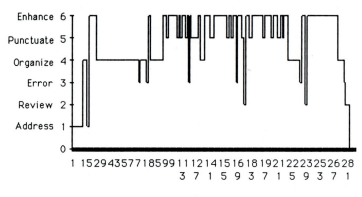

Events

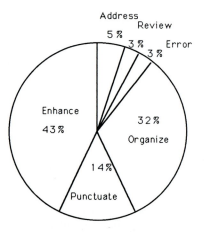

Figure 7-12. A mental model for subject 1 is shown. This should be compared to subject 2 in Figure 7-13. The transition analysis at the top of the page shows how the subject jumps from goal to goal. The pie chart at the bottom shows the percent time the subject spends in each goal. Each subject has a different signature when comparing this figure to Figure 7-13.

computer for a long period of time. Access to the computer through keystroke latencies may be a less intrusive method for security.

The knowledge acquired through the neural net can be used in a similar manner to some of the other applications discussed previously. Certainly the cluster analysis from the neural net is similar to the cluster analyses generated from paired items. Both can be used in determining how to cluster items on the display; the neural net may be advantageous because the data are collected in a direct manner by asking the person what would happen in various situations. The transition analysis can be used to determine more information about the user's mental model which can be used in help messages for critiquing the user's plans and strategies for determining how

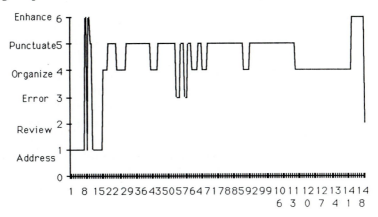

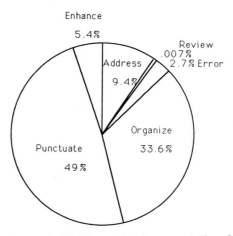

Figure 7-13. The mental model from subject 2. The graphical representation of this mental model should be compared to the mental model of subject 1 in Figure 7-12. As can be seen, subject 1 spends more time enhancing and subject 2 spends more time punctuating.

they could be performed more efficiently (e.g., Eberts, Villegas, Phillips, and Eberts, 1992).

Filters. A filter recognizes a pattern and then filters the different patterns into categories. A user with an accurate and useful mental model should be able to recognize patterns in the modes of interaction so that each command or interaction method is not seen as a separate entity. The Task-Action Grammar model, dis-

cussed in Chapter 17, determines the patterns or schemas in an interaction language and makes predictions about which ones are the most usable. Such a model can analyze a task and predict how a user will perform. For acquiring knowledge, a filter should be able to do the reverse process; it should be able to take data from the user and determine if the user is recognizing interaction mode patterns.

Siochi and Hix (1991) designed a

filter to determine information about users' mental models for a task. Specifically, they designed a filter which could map a class of inputs into the syntax of an interaction language. As an example, the interaction language may be designed so that a number input is followed by two commands, or NUMBER, COMMAND, COMMAND. Any other syntax will not work. The filter of Siochi and Hix was designed to determine if the mental model of the user included the correct syntax and, thus, whether or not the mental model corresponded to the conceptual model of the system. The filter could map all numbers into the NUMBER category and all commands into the COMMAND category. By examining the results of the filtered interaction transcripts from the users, Siochi and Hix could determine if the interface was successful in conveying the conceptual model to the user.

SUMMARY

The concept of the mental model is essential for determining effective techniques and methods for interface design. The display representation should be designed so that the users can develop accurate mental models; the mental models can be compared to the underlying conceptual model of the computer system. Some techniques have been studied to determine the best methods for developing accurate mental models of the underlying computer processes. These include designing the interface so that users can interact actively with it, using metaphors and analogies to explain concepts, and using spatial relationships so that users can develop capabilities for mental simulations. Being able to predict the output

from a given input is important for developing accurate mental models.

Some interfaces are designed based upon the knowledge acquired from expert users. Since the interfaces mimic the mental models of the experts, novice users should be able to develop accurate mental models through interaction with them. Knowledge acquisition techniques were reviewed, and some of the applications were discussed. Verbal protocols are used in some of the predictive models to predict user behavior. Scaling techniques can be used for the spatial layout of interfaces and for deciding how display information, such as menu items, should be categorized. Pattern recognition techniques have been used for identifying individual users for computer security systems. More research can be done on mapping the mental models of experts, obtained through knowledge acquisition techniques, to actual display features.

The chapter has highlighted the need for effective techniques to allow the user to develop an accurate mental model of the computer system; much of the cognitive-based research on human-computer interface design can be categorized according to these techniques. Some of the following chapters use these categorizations to organize the material on cognitive approaches and predictive models to human-computer interaction. Several cognitive-based techniques have been developed for determining how to best develop accurate mental models for the user through effective interface design. Researchers say that users form a mental model of a task through the application of metaphors and analogies (see Chapter 10) or through the imposition of a spatial model (see Chapter 11). Other cognitive-based theories have stressed methods for formally representing the mental models of users by specifying the procedures needed for a user to interact with a computer. One set of approaches defines the procedures for breaking goals into subgoals (see Chapters 14 - 16). Another approach specifies how grammatical rules can be formed from the syntax of the interface commands (see Chapter 17). Formal models have been formulated to define the relationships between an interface design and the procedures of the mental model which will be developed (see Chapter 15). These theories can be used to organize the vast and growing literature of the cognitive aspects of human-computer interface design, and they can be used for understanding how to design a usable interface. Each of these approaches will be discussed in more detail in the following chapters.

QUESTIONS

1.   Many fast-food restaurants now use function cash registers where the operator pushes a button for "French Fries" instead of typing in the digits of the price. The location of the buttons on the function cash register are important in the speed of use. Those items that are related should be clustered together on the cash register. Go to a fast-food restaurant and record all the items on the menu. Then place all those items in pairs and ask someone to rate the similarities between the pairs. Most statistical packages have clustering and MDS programs in them. Take the data and find the dimensional structure of these items in an MDS package, and find the clusters from a clustering program. Have the subject interpret the dimensions and the structures. Discuss how the dimensions and structures could be used to place the items on the cash register. Which of the two analyses, MDS or clusters, was the most useful for organizing the items?

2.   Do a similar analysis as you did in question 1 for the commands in database and spreadsheet programs. Have subjects rate the similarity of the commands and use these data for MDS and cluster analyses. Compare the clusters and dimensions to existing packages to determine the matches and mismatches between the menu structures and the data structures and clusters.

CHAPTER 8

HUMAN INFORMATION PROCESSING

INTRODUCTION

Human information processing has been a dominant theoretical position or paradigm in American experimental and cognitive psychology since the early 1960s. To understand and apply this theory in human-computer interaction, one must, of course, first understand the theory. Many excellent review books and chapters about the human information processing theory have been written over the years (Lachman, Lachman, and Butterfield, 1979; Keele, 1973; and Wickens, 1984, 1987). Without exception, these articles equate human information processing with discrete stages models. In these models, information is processed by the human through a sequential series of stages. Recently in cognitive psychology, discrete stages models have been criticized and other models have been explored. The most promising of these alternative models are neural network models (also called connectionist models) in which information is assumed to be distributed and processed in parallel (see Chapter 9). Discrete stages models emphasize the structure of information processing, whereas neural network models emphasize the process of information processing, particularly the dynamics and the learning aspects. Only recently have applications based upon the neural network models occurred in human-computer interaction, and more can be expected to occur in the near future.

Since the discrete stages models have matured over the years and many articles have been written about them, the theo-

retical aspects will be reviewed only briefly. The sources mentioned earlier can be referenced for more detail. As this model has matured, it has been used increasingly in applications, and so the first part of this chapter will concentrate on some of those applications. A primary application area has been determining the compatibilities between stimulus and response. Another main application area for the discrete stages model has been using the Model Human Processor for predicting the times needed for processing displayed information. The Model Human Processor will be reviewed in detail, because this represents a critical advancement in modeling techniques. Examples using this model to predict times for various display configurations of computers will be presented.

DISCRETE STAGES MODELS

A model is useful because it is a synthesis of experimental data from many different experiments. A model is also a simplification which does not always do complete justice to the research that preceded the formulation of the model. When discussing human information processing models, the previous research will not be discussed in detail; only the model will be explained. Information processing models have been classified into three categories (Haber, 1974): perceptual, memory, and problem solving. Table 8-1 lists some of the well-known discrete stages models. Two models will be presented in more detail. The Wickens (1984a) model repre-

TABLE 8-1

Information processing models

Model Type	Authors	Year
Perception	Garner, Hake, and Eriksen	1956
	Broadbent	1958
	Sperling	1963
	Sperling	1967
	Card, Moran, and Newell	1983
Memory	Shiffrin and Atkinson	1969
	Norman and Rumelhart	1970
	Atkinson and Juola	1973
	Schneider and Shiffrin	1977
	Shiffrin and Schneider	1977
	Card, Moran, and Newell	1983
	Wickens	1984a
	Cowan	1988
Problem Solving	Newell and Simon	1972
	Card, Moran, and Newell	1983
Network	Hebb	1949
	Quillian	1968
	Collins and Quillian	1969
	Collins and Loftus	1975
	Smith, Shoben, and Rips	1974

sents a later model incorporating much of the previous research on the structure of human information processing. It provides a good reference point to consider the compatibilities between stimuli and responses and how these compatibilities can be utilized in equipment and interface design. The Model Human Processor (Card, Moran, and Newell, 1983, 1986) will be the other model discussed. It can be used to determine the timing characteristics of human information processing and to predict which alternative interface designs will be the fastest to operate. After the consideration of these models, and the basic principles of discrete stages models, the applications will be discussed.

The Wickens Human Information Processing Model

Figure 8-1 illustrates a model of human information processing. In this initial discussion, ignore the values from the Model Human Processor. These will be discussed in the next section. For a dis-

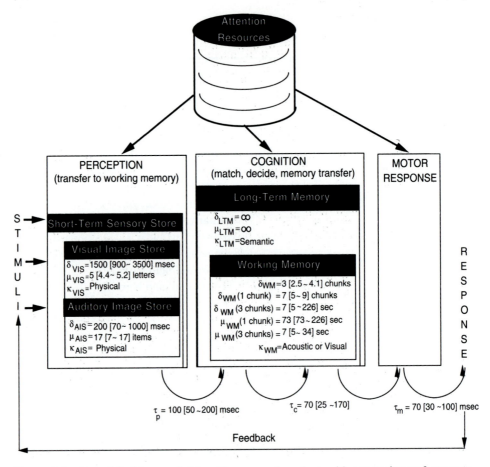

Figure 8-1. A model of human information processing along with processing and memory parameters from the Model Human Processor.

crete stages model such as this, stimuli are believed to be transformed as they pass through the three stages of processing within the human (the three large boxes in the figure). These stages are conceived as discrete, which means that a later stage cannot begin processing until a prior stage is completed. Processing occurs in the order specified by the arrows. Processing can continue in the cognitive stage for successive iterations. For the percetual and response execution stages, iterations do not occur. Each of these boxes will be explained.

Stimuli enter the human processing system and are stored in a temporary memory or sensory store. The iconic short-term store is for visual stimuli, and the echoic short-term store is for auditory stimuli. In these storage memories, the stimuli are represented in their physical form. The stimuli will decay if not further processed. The iconic and echoic stores have different decay rates. These decay rates and the storage capacities of the memories will be discussed further for the Model Human Processor.

Not all information from the short-term sensory store will be perceived by being processed at the next stage. Long-term memory is used to identify appropriate stimuli for perceptual encoding to occur. At this stage, identified in the model as perception, the stimuli are either detected, recognized, identified, or categorized. The number of stimuli perceived will be limited by the amount of attentional resources available and the amount allocated to this stage.

Cognitive processes, such as decisions and response selections, occur in the next stage. This stage has two memories associated with it: long-term memory and working memory. Working memory is very limited, while long-term memory provides a permanent storage system. To make decisions, a human may compare two or more stimuli recently perceived and maintained in working memory or comparisons might be made between recently perceived items and information retrieved from long-term memory. Attentional resources are required to perform these mental operations.

Finally, the response chosen in the cognitive stage is executed in the motor stage. A response can be a hand movement, an eye movement, a head movement, or some other kind of motor response. Attentional resources are also required at this execution stage. The consequence of the response is called feedback which may be either intrinsic or extrinsic. Feedback is important for monitoring and improving performance.

Model Human Processor

The Model Human Processor (Card et al., 1983, 1986) is an excellent model for applied research because the capacity,

duration, and memory code parameters of the model are all defined. Refer again to Figure 8-1 and the parameters associated with the memories and processing cycles.

First, consider the memory parameters. Two of the subsystems, perception and cognition, have memories associated with them; the motor system does not. The characteristics of all the memories are described by three parameters: storage capacity, decay constant, and code type. Storage capacity, μ, refers to the amount of material or information which can be stored in a particular memory such as iconic memory. The decay constant, δ, indicates how long information stays in a memory. Code type, κ, refers to the representation type of the stimuli. Five codes have been distinguished: two physical sensory codes for the visual and auditory short-term stores, two codes for working memory (visual and acoustic), and a single code for long-term memory (semantic). Codes are important for compatibility issues and for comparing similar codes in working memory.

Each numerical value for a parameter has a typical value (listed first), and within the brackets are the range values derived from experimental results. Sometimes the typical value is referred to as the Middle Man value, the low value in the range as the Fast Man value, and the high value in the range as the Slow Man value.

The perceptual system has two short-term sensory stores or memories: the visual information store (VIS) and the auditory information store (AIS). The code is still physical at this stage of processing. Memory decay rate for the visual memory is 200 [70-1000] msec, whereas for the auditory memory the rate is slower at 1500 [900 - 3500] msec. The memory capacity for the two short-term stores is different as well. The visual memory capacity is 17 [7-17] letters, and the auditory capacity is 5 [4.4-6.2] letters.

The cognitive subsystem has three information codes: acoustic, visual or semantic, depending on the memory system. Working memory codes are either acoustic or visual, and long-term memory codes are semantic. The decay rate for working memory without attention is 7 [5-226] sec. For 1 chunk the decay rate is 73 [73-226] sec, and for 3 chunks the decay rate is 7 [5-34] sec. The storage capacity is 7 [5-9] chunks. Long-term memory has no decay rate, since the model assumes no erasure from long-term memory. The capacity is thought to be unlimited as well.

The processor parameter, τ, is the cycle time or the amount of time required to process the smallest unit of information in a particular subsystem. Processor time is needed to transfer information from one subsystem to the next. The cognitive subsystem is different from the others in that processing cycles can occur within this stage as the information is transformed, matched, and used for decision-making.

Each subsystem has a different numerical value for the parameter. The cycle time of the perceptual processor is 100 [50-200] msec., the cognitive cycle time is 70 [25-170] msec., and the motor system processor time is 70 [30-100] msec.

Basic Tenets of Discrete Stages Models

There are basic assumptions about information processing which are not always explicitly stated; therefore, six of the major tenets of this theoretical position will be discussed. How they apply to human-computer interaction tasks will also be examined briefly. For the most part, these tenets apply to almost all of the major models in Table 8-1. Keep in mind that a specific model will have additional assumptions which make it unique from other models of information processing.

The first tenet states that perception is not immediate. Instead, humans process stimuli or information and the information undergoes functional transformation. The earlier theoretical positions in psychology concentrated on the causal relationships between stimulus and response. Characteristics of the stimulus and characteristics of the human such as past experience or individual differences were manipulated in order to study the subsequent effect on observable behavior. There was little attempt to hypothesize about unobservable events which might be occurring within the human between the onset of the stimulus and the response. Thus, the assumption that perception is not immediate is a fundamental one for information processing. This is important for understanding human-computer interaction, because many theories try to determine how the information presented on the interface is transformed and mentally manipulated by the user. The cognitive approach takes the view that users actively process the presented information.

The second tenet assumes that the processing of information requires time. The time between the onset of the stimulus and the execution of the response is called reaction time. Reaction time has been both the dependent or measurement variable in research as well as the experimental or independent variable. Reaction time serves as the principal tool for determining the characteristics of the processing stages. As a dependent variable, reaction time can be used in a variety of experimental situations; it is not limited to research on discrete stages theories. Chapter 4 on the experimental approach showed how reaction time is a very important dependent variable for the study of human-computer interaction. The Model Human Processor uses these times for small information processing events to measure the time needed to process tasks.

Mental chronometry can be considered the third major tenet of information processing. The characteristics of the stages such as their identification, the temporal sequence, duration, and descriptions of the processing, or the functional transformations of the stimuli occurring in a stage are studied. Again, this tenet is very important for the Model Human Processor.

A fourth tenet deals with the transformation of information which was alluded to in the first tenet. As discussed in the specific models, the internal representation or codes vary depending on the time or on the stage of processing. The concept of coding does not appear in psychology (Lachman et al., 1979) prior to the classic work in communication theory (Shannon and Weaver, 1949). This has now become a key concept in cognitive psychology and cognitive engineering. For human-computer interaction tasks, understanding the codes at each stage will assist the interface designer in developing compatible codes which can then be displayed to the user.

The fifth tenet of limited capacity refers to limits of both time and space. The limits of time occur because of the duration of the information in any particular stage (Keele, 1973), transformation of the stimulus into different codes, and memory retrieval, all of which involve processing

time. The space limits were described first in communications theory as channel capacity (Shannon and Weaver, 1949). Channel capacity means that there is a definable number of signals which can be transmitted and received without error on a particular channel during a fixed amount of time. A more updated description of space limits would be processing resources (Keele, 1973). There are limits to how much information can be processed and to how many tasks can be done in concurrence. For human-computer interaction applications, the designer must be concerned that the user not be overloaded in terms of information which must be processed.

The sixth tenet defines the unit of information. Originally, the bit was conceived as the information metric which had the advantage of being dimensionless or not dependent upon the physical nature of the stimuli (Shannon and Weaver, 1949). A bit was formally defined as the number of binary questions required to differentiate which event would occur. The probability of each event was important as well. Information was calculated in terms of the average probability of an event occurring. The bit as the primary metric for information processing was replaced by a new metric after 1956 when the unit of information was redefined from the bit to the chunk (Miller, 1956). The chunk is a familiar unit of organized stimulus material. Learning plays an important role in the formation of these chunks. Chunks are key to the problem of informational bottlenecks because they allow more information to be processed without surpassing the channel capacity of the processor. Reading is a good example of this. Young readers begin by reading one letter at a time, and as they grow more proficient they break the symbols into words or chunks. Finally, an advanced reader chunks in phrases and relies on context to anticipate the forthcoming material to be read. Miller's (1956) contribution was not just in terms of the identification of human channel capacity as seven plus or minus two items. This contribution to information processing was the recognition of the importance of prior experience (long-term memory) in guiding perception of current events which determines how chunks will be formed. The ability of people to chunk information must be considered when designing the interface.

APPLICATIONS AND EXAMPLES

Human information processing has been applied to human-computer interaction tasks in many ways. First, the discrete stages model has been used for determining compatibility of stimulus and response across the different stages and for predicting and accounting for effects due to workload. Second, the Model Human Processor has been used as a model for making time predictions about tasks based upon the design of the task so that, as one application, two or more designs can be modeled, the time needed to complete the task can be calculated, and decisions on the best design can be made before the design prototype stage. Both kinds of applications will be considered.

Discrete Stages Applications

For the discrete stages models, two main application areas have occurred: determining compatibility between the stimulus and response, and using the model as a

means of specifying pools of attentional resources which can, in turn, be used to indicate the kinds of tasks which can be performed together and the kinds of tasks that have to be performed separately. This latter application area has been used in the analysis of cognitive workload effects.

The compatibility between stimulus and response has been termed S-R compatibility, and this area has been recently reviewed (Proctor and Reeve, 1990). The basic premise of S-R compatibility is that information will be processed faster if the stimulus is compatible with the needed response. The stimulus and the response can be manipulated through display design so that this theory of compatibility has important implications for human-computer interaction.

As an example of S-R compatibility outside of human-computer interaction, consider the three configurations of stove tops in Figure 8-2. In configurations B and C, S-R compatibility is high, and in configuration A, S-R compatibility is low. In B and C, the stove top has been designed so that the controls are in the same spatial relationships as the burners. In A, the burners are laid out in a square but the knobs are laid out in a line from left to right. It is easy to see that the left two knobs correspond to the left two burners and the right two knobs correspond to the right two burners, but determining which knob corresponds to the front and rear burners, without reading the label, is impossible. The position of burners and knobs does not allow for front and rear compatibility. In B, the compatibility has been maintained by moving the burners so that they can be considered from left to right just as the knobs are configured. In this configuration, the leftmost knob cor-

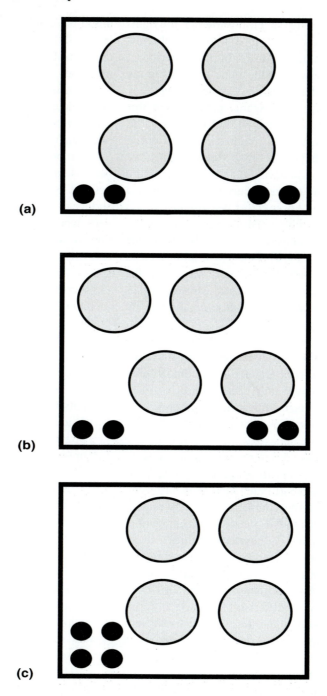

(a)

(b)

(c)

Figure 8-2. Three configurations of stove tops demonstrating different stimulus-response compatibilities.

responds to the leftmost burner, the rightmost knob corresponds to the rightmost burner, and so forth. In configuration C, the burners are the same as in A but the knobs have been redesigned so that they have the same spatial pattern. For this design, seeing which knob corresponds to the burner is easy without having to look at the labeling. For all three designs, we would assume that B and C would require less time to process information and would result in fewer errors because of the S-R compatibility. To use configuration A, one would have to process the knobs, the burners, and the labels to be able to use it. This would require more steps than the other two configurations. More examples and discussion of S-R compatibility are presented in Chapter 21.

Recently, the concept of S-R compatibility has been extended by introducing the concept of S-C-R compatibility (Wickens, Sandry, and Vidulich, 1983), which stands for stimulus-central processing-response compatibility. This approach emphasizes the role of cognitive mediators, between the stimulus and response, in information processing. Whereas S-R compatibility theories emphasize the compatibilities between the stimulus and response, S-C-R compatibility emphasizes the compatibilities between the stimulus and central processing, and between central processing and response.

An important part of the S-C-R theory is that different tasks have different representation codes associated with them. The theory has shown that the code of representation of a task is important for theoretical explanations of human performance in complex situations. If a task has a certain code associated with it, then this code may have an effect on the total compatibility, from the stimulus through the central processing of the task to the response.

Once the representation code of a task is determined, then the task environment can be designed so that S-C compatibility and C-R compatibility are high. For S-C compatibility, the type of input must be considered. Four types of input can be defined by a 2 x 2 matrix formed by the auditory and visual modalities and the verbal and spatial primary perceptual codes (Wickens, 1984). The four types are (1) text (visual modality, verbal code); (2) speech (auditory modality, verbal code); (3) sound localization and pitch (auditory modality, spatial code); and (4) analog picture (visual modality, spatial code). For tasks with a verbal representation code, the most compatible input was speech (Wickens et al., 1983). For tasks with a spatial representation code, the most compatible input was visual analog. Thus, by knowing the representation code used in central processing, the compatible stimulus input can be specified.

For C-R compatibility, only two types of response output were investigated (Wickens et al., 1983): manual responses (such as a key press or a joystick input) and speech. The writers stated that matching verbal processing with speech output and matching spatial processing with manual output results in the highest compatibility. This was based on the assumption that most manual responses were spatial in nature and that most speech responses were verbal in nature.

The usefulness of S-C-R compatibility in terms of specifications for interface design hinges upon the ability to specify the representation code of the task. If the task can be specified as a verbal task, then the information should be displayed using speech and the response should also be a speech response. If the task can be specified as a spatial task, then the information should be displayed using analog pictures and the response should be manual. If the task is a combination of verbal and spatial, then presently the theory loses its predictability.

S-C-R compatibility theory was expanded by stating that the code of representation in central processing may be only one aspect of the importance of maintaining this compatibility (Eberts and Posey, 1990). The mental model formed by operators when performing a task is important for the central processing. Recall from Chapter 7 that a mental model is constructed when an operator attempts to internalize how a system works and the parameters that control the system. The mental model can be considered in more detail than just the code of representation, as considered previously (Wickens et al., 1983). As an example, one can consider the task/action pairings (Payne and Green, 1986; and Reisner, 1981), the goal structures constructed for a task (Card et al., 1983, 1986; and Kieras, 1988), the spatial representation (Caldwell and Eberts, 1989), or the metaphors used (Carroll, Mack, and Kellogg, 1988). Examples of research techniques have been presented (Eberts and Posey, 1990) that could be used to acquire the form of the mental model, for example, the task/action pairings, the goal structures, or the spatial representations. Any kind of interface design should be compatible with this acquired knowledge about the mental model.

Model Human Processor Applications

The Model Human Processor (Card et al., 1983, 1986) has been designed similar to an engineering model so that the task can be analyzed, parameters of the task can be specified, time values can be assigned to the parameters, and the total task time can be calculated. Several examples with particular applications for human-computer interaction tasks are provided in Chapter 13. These examples include calculations for simple reaction time, for complex reaction time, for predicting the amount of time needed to choose a menu item, and for predicting execution times for function and digit cash registers. Only one example is included in this chapter to show the generalizability of the Model Human Processor to S-R compatibility problems. The example is on calculating the time needed for the burner/knob compatibility problem considered earlier.

Consider the three stove top configurations discussed earlier for S-R compatibility and illustrated in Figure 8-2. For the calculations, the timing will be started after a pan is placed on any burner and the operator must determine which knob to turn. We will assume that the operator has never used this particular stove before. We will also assume that the hand movement times are minimal and inconsequential to the predictions. We will start with configuration C because it is the easiest. The steps and the parameters needed are as follows:

1. τ_p perceive burner by transferring from visual image store to working memory a verbal code of placement of burner (e.g., bottom right burner)

2. τ_c decide to execute eye movements to knobs

3. τ_m execute eye movements to knobs

4. τ_p perceive knobs by transferring from visual image store to working memory the verbal code of the knob (e.g., bottom right burner knob)

5. τ_c match verbal codes of burners and knobs

6. τ_c decide on response (yes: turn on burner; no: go back to step 5)

7. τ_m movement to turn on burner

Steps 4 through 6 would be performed (4+1)/2 times on an average, because four burners are on the stove, we assume that the pan is randomly placed on one of the burners, and we assume that the operator is performing a serial exhaustive search to look for the pan (i.e., each is looked at sequentially, and the search stops when the pan is seen). The average time to perform this task for configuration C is:

$$\text{total time} = \tau_p + \tau_c + 5/2\ (\tau_p + 2\tau_c) + 2\tau_m \tag{8.1}$$

Inserting the times from the Middle Man values, we find that:

$$\begin{aligned}
\text{total time} &= 100 + 70 + 5/2\ (100 + 2(70)) \\
&\quad + 2(70) \\
&= 910 \text{ msec.} \tag{8.2}
\end{aligned}$$

Configuration B would have the same time calculation. The only slight difference would be that the working memory store would be in terms of the one-dimensionality of the layout: the burners and knobs would be encoded as first, second, third, and fourth.

Configuration A would require slightly different calculations from the other two. Two different processing sequences are plausible. In the first, the operator would read the label and then perceive the knob and execute the response. To do this, step 4 would be to perceive the label of the knob instead of perceiving the knob directly and assigning a label. This method also would require two extra steps from the previous procedure inserted after step 6 but before step 7:

6a. τ_p decide on eye movement corresponding to verbal code of knob label in working memory (e.g., move eyes to the bottom right)

6b. τ_c execute eye movements to the knob

These two steps would require 170 msec. extra so that the total time would be 1080 msec. using this procedure.

The second plausible procedure would be for the operator to first localize the side of the burner, either left or right, and then to determine if the front or back burner is being used. The steps and parameters for this procedure are as follows:

1. τ_p perceive burner by transferring from visual image store to working memory a verbal code of the left-right position of the burner

2. τ_c decide to execute eye movements to knobs in the direction of the verbal code in working memory

3. τ_m execute eye movements to knobs

4. τ_p perceive two knobs by transferring visual image store to working memory a verbal code of the left-right position of the knobs

5. τ_c match first (or second) knob position to burner position

6. τ_c decide on match (yes: go to next step; no: go to step 5)

7. τ_m execute eye movement

8. τ_p perceive burner by transferring from visual image store to working memory a verbal code of top-bottom position of the burner

9. τ_c decide to execute eye movements to knob labels in direction of left-right code stored in working memory

10. τ_m execute eye movements to knobs

11. τ_p perceive label of knob by transferring from visual image store to working memory a verbal code of top-bottom label of knob

12. τ_c match first (or second) verbal code of knobs to burner

13. τ_c decide on match (yes: execute response; no: go back to step 12)

14 τ_m execute response

Steps 5 through 6 and 12 through 13 would each require $(2 + 1)/2$ steps because, in the first case, the left-right position is being considered, and in the second case, the top-bottom position is being considered, and, since the search is serial and exhaus-

tive, an average value is chosen. The equation summarizing the above is

$$\text{total time} = 4\tau_p + 2\tau_c + 4\tau_m + 3/2(4\tau_c) \tag{8.3}$$

By inserting the Middle Man values of the parameters, we get

$$\begin{aligned} \text{total time} &= 4(100) + 2(70) + 4(70) + 6(70) \\ &= 1240 \text{ msec} \end{aligned} \tag{8.4}$$

Comparing this time with the previous value for configurations B and C, we would predict that the incompatible configuration A would require a maximum 330 msec. more to perform the task.

No matter which procedure is used, configurations B and C would require about the same time to operate and configuration A would be the slowest. This prediction matches that of the analysis using S-R compatibility. The Model Human Processor is useful because it makes explicit time predictions not made by the S-R compatibility analysis.

Using the Model Human Processor to perform a task analysis results in plausible values and corroborates evidence from other areas, such as the stove top analysis and the analysis performed on reconstructing Fitts' Law (Fitts, 1954). The method for applying the model is not invariant. Other people analyzing the task may specify different steps for the same task. Others may have different models for different kinds of people. The stove top analysis showed that two different sequences of steps were plausible. A large problem with the method is the large range of values possible. For the above analyses, we only inserted the Middle Man values without considering the range of values. If the range of values was considered, in many cases, especially tasks requiring a large number of steps, the ranges would overlap to a high degree, limiting the predictability of the analysis. As an example, if the task has a perceptual processor, a motor processor, and 10 cognitive processors, then the Middle Man value would be 870 msec., with ranges from 330 msec. (for the Fast Man model) to 2000 msec. (for the Slow Man model). Thus, this range of values would make it difficult to predict and test the exact number of cycles which may be occurring in a process. Within the 330-2000 msec range, assuming only one perceptual and motor processor, and assuming Middle Man values, the number of cognitive processors in that range would be from 3 to 27. For complex tasks with many cognitive processors, the Model Human Processor loses its predictability.

The use of the Model Human Processor also depends on accepting the assumptions of the discrete stages model. As the next chapter shows, some of these assumptions are beginning to be attacked, especially assumptions that processing in each stage must be completed before the next stage begins. This assumption is central to accepting the values from a task analysis using the Model Human Processor. The model assumes that the time parameters are additive. If processing is incomplete in a stage, the values would not be additive and other task analysis methods would be needed. The neural net models in the next chapter present some alternatives to performing task analyses using a discrete stages model.

A Chunking Application

One of the important concepts of human information processing is that of chunking information. A chunk is a meaningful unit of information and can vary in size depending on the individual. As an example, consider the following sequence of letters:

ATTIBMDEC

An American with a technical background would easily recognize these as three chunks of information corresponding to the companies AT&T, IBM, and DEC. Without this background, a person would have to remember all nine letters so that the chunk size would be 9. Consider another sequence of letters:

NTTNECNHK

A Japanese with a technical background would recognize these as three chunks of information corresponding to the large Japanese companies NTT, NEC, and NHK. Without this kind of background, the chunk size would be 9 corresponding to the number of letters in the sequence.

Chunking can be utilized in many kinds of human-computer interaction tasks. As an example from Card et al. (1983), consider saving a file. The Model Human Processor shows that one chunk of information can be maintained in memory longer than three chunks of information. Thus, if a user were saving a file which was named with three random characters representing three chunks, such as RDE, then this file could only be maintained in working memory for 7 sec. If, instead, the file was given a meaningful name, such as CAT, then it is stored in only one chunk and the file could be maintained in working memory for 73 sec.

Similar analyses could be performed for command names. Command names should have meaningful names which can easily be stored as one chunk of information. Let's say that a user wishes to change the name of a file. Perhaps a good name for this command is RENAME. Because this is all one word, the user would be able to store this sequence of 6 characters as one word. A poorer choice for the name would be something like CHNGNM. Although this is also 6 characters, a novice user may have difficulty storing this as only one chunk. With experience in using this command name, though, the user could come to encode it as only one chunk.

SUMMARY

In this chapter, human information processing was discussed in terms of the traditional discrete stages models. The applications have shown how these models can be used for equipment and interface design by considering the compatibilities between the stimuli and responses. Other applications showed how variants of these models could be used for making time predictions for various configurations of equipment design. In the next chapter, a new modeling technique, neural network modeling, is discussed. This modeling attempts to use a neural analogy to accomplish parallel distributed processing. In initial application efforts, this technique has been applied to many areas of interface design. More applications of the Model Human Processor are discussed in Chapter 13 when considering the predictive modeling capabilities of this model.

QUESTIONS

1. S-R compatibility is important in many kinds of designs. Consider a room that has two separate lights in it.

You are connecting the two light switches to the two lights. Answer the following questions, through drawings, about S-R compatibility. In the three drawings, the perspective is from the top of the room looking down. You may want to read all three questions before you start with the first one.

a. Draw the lights, and the connections between the switches and lights, to demonstrate S-R compatibility.

b. Draw the lights, and the connections between the switches and lights, to demonstrate S-R incompatibility.

c. Draw the lights to demonstrate a situation in which S-R compatibility could not be achieved no matter which mapping was made between the connections and the lights.

2. Answer the following questions about S-C-R compatibility. In an airplane, a fault warning system is being developed to warn the pilot, as an example, when a problem may be occurring with one of the engines. By talking to the pilots, the designers find that the pilots represent this problem in their own heads by thinking of the problem as occurring in some spatial location. In other words, they would have an image of the plane in their head and picture the location of the problem in that image. Knowing this information about the "C" in the S-C-R compatibility, answer the following two questions about S-C-R compatibility for this design problem.

a. Name the modality and the code for the input to maintain S-C-R compatibility. From the example, the input would provide the pilot with the information about where the problem is occurring when a problem occurs.

b. Name the type of response output which would maintain S-C-R compatibility. From the example, the output would be provided to the pilot so that the pilot's response could start correcting the problem.

3. Answer the following questions about human information processing and the Model Human Processor.

a. Which of the three subsystems in the Model Human Processor does not have an associated memory?

b. Name the three codes of representation, the κ, for how information can be represented in WM and LTM.

c. In which of the memories do all decision and matching processes occur?

4. Answer the following questions about S-C-R compatibility. When driving a car, the code of representation for speed is different depending on the particular task. For the following questions, consider these two tasks: (1) glancing at the speedometer to find how far you are from your desired speed; and (2) setting the speed when using a cruise control.

a. For task 1, would the code of representation be spatial or verbal? Justify your answer.

b. Based upon your answer in part a, and from the four input choices (text, speech, sound localization and pitch, and analog picture), which two kinds of inputs (the "S" part in S-C-R compatibility) would be compatible with this code?

c. Which kind of response would be most compatible with the input and code of representation used in parts b and c?

d. For task 2, would the code of representation be spatial or verbal? Justify your answer.

e. Based upon your answer in part d, above, and from the four input choices, which two kinds of inputs would be compatible with this code? Justify your answer.

f. Which kind of response would be most compatible with the input and code of representation used in parts d and e?

g. Use the Model Human Processor to determine the execution time for the simple task of checking the speedometer to determine if you are going the correct speed and then making the appropriate response. Specify each step.

CHAPTER 9

NEURAL NETWORK MODELS

INTRODUCTION

The neural network models, sometimes referred to as connectionist models, are another method used to model human information processing. This has been a very active research area in cognitive science, biological sciences, and computer science in recent years. Many of these models are now being applied to human-computer interaction applications. In this chapter, criticisms of the discrete stages models will be considered, neural networks will be described in general terms, a specific model will be discussed in detail, and then applications will be considered.

NEURAL NETWORKS AND INFORMATION PROCESSING

For human information processing, the shift from discrete multistage models, discussed in the last chapter, to connectionist networks has some practical implications beyond a mere change in cognitive architectural structures. In psychology, prior to information processing, learning was a major topic of interest. Earlier theoretical positions in psychology, such as early behaviorism, stressed learning as opposed to hypothetical constructs of mental activities. Discrete stages models have not addressed the acquisition of long-term memory information very well. The immediate concern for interface design is that discrete stages models do not adequately address issues of skilled learning, or how a user changes from being a novice

to being an expert. Expertise or skilled learning is very critical to the cognitive engineering modeling of human-computer interaction. Connectionist models have appeal because of their ability to model expertise. Network models, unlike discrete stages models, can and do address learning.

Several criticisms of the discrete stages model of human information processing, reviewed in the last chapter, have been listed (Fodor and Pylyshyn, 1989) which have led some researchers to search for new models of human information processing, such as the neural network models that are considered in this chapter. These arguments can be categorized into six dealing with the basic serial computer assumption of discrete stages (arguments 1 through 4) and the "all-or-none" assumption of stage processing (arguments 5 and 6). These six arguments are summarized in the following paragraphs.

First, one of the assumptions of the discrete stages model is that the brain operates similar to serial computers. A problem with this assumption is that a computer can execute computer instructions in nanoseconds, whereas neurons take tens of milliseconds to fire. Typically, human tasks, such as recognizing a word, take less time than a second for the processing. A present-day computer, to perform the same kind of task, would require many thousands or even millions of instructions. For a word-recognition task with the physiological time constraints of neurons, a human would only be able to perform serially about 100 instructions, which is an inadequate number for performing the task. In contrast, if the brain operated in parallel, then the task could be performed. The neural network models considered in the next section operate in parallel. This has many possibilities for human-computer interaction. Presently, computer systems are very slow in recognizing handwriting or facial expressions, to name two examples. By operating in parallel, similar to humans, computers can conceivably recognize patterns such as handwriting or voice and, thus, interaction could occur in these modes.

Second, again attacking the assumption that humans operate like serial computers, it has been shown that humans have the ability to recognize large-capacity patterns from thousands of alternatives. If one had to search through memory as a serial computer searches, then the complexity would overwhelm the machine. Since humans can do this easily, some researchers believe that knowledge must be stored and processed differently in people than in computers. In exploring different knowledge storage and processing schemes, such as those associated with connectionist models, then the computer capacity may be increased which would have an effect on the kinds of interactions available.

Third, discrete stages models have shown little progress in dealing with processes that are nonverbal or intuitive. Many skilled behaviors, such as walking, are not open to conscious reasoning and cannot be described verbally. The computer has been structured to operate in a linguistic mode and thus has difficulty modeling nonverbal or intuitive processes. This is another case where the assumption of humans operating like serial computers

may be invalid. For human-computer interaction tasks, the computer could become more intuitive which would enable more intelligence to be available in the interaction.

Fourth, another characteristic of computers is that decision processes and memory are highly localized. As examples, if one line of code is destroyed in a program, the program will not work. Or if a value in memory is destroyed by overwriting that memory location, it cannot be retrieved. This is in contrast to people suffering from local brain damage where performance will not be destroyed but will vary gradually with the extent of the damage. Since the processing is distributed spatially, damage is less catastrophic and the brain can handle noisy signals. Discrete stages models, based on the serial computer assumption, cannot handle these problems easily. Neural network models are relatively insensitive to damage and noise. As examples, parts of a neural network were destroyed but it could still perform cognitive functions (Anderson, J. A., 1983); parts of a neural network for producing speech were destroyed yet it still functioned (Sejnowski and Rosenberg, 1987); and for a vision neural network with noisy characters, the characters could still be classified correctly (Fukushima, 1988).

One of the assumptions of the discrete stages model is that processing occurs as "all-or-none." For the discrete stages models, processing in one stage must be completed before processing can occur in the next stage. A research literature review found that this assumption was not always valid (McClelland, 1979). A Cascade Model was proposed (McClelland, 1979) where processing cascades, so one stage does not have to be completed before information can be processed at another stage. This model was a precursor to the neural network models considered in this chapter. For those cases in which the "all-or-none" processing in a stage is invalid, then the Model Human Processor of Chapters 8 and 13 cannot be applied.

Points 5 and 6 address criticisms of the "all-or-none" assumption. Fifth, cognitive processes are never rigidly determined or precisely replicable but seem to have a random component to them. With the "all-or-none" assumption, no mechanism for randomness is available. Neural network models, on the other hand, would account for randomness based upon the randomness available at a neuronal biochemical or electrical activity level.

Finally, when humans are unable to perform a task perfectly, they do not quit but do something that can be perceived as reasonable. Computers based on the "all-or-none" assumption do not show this characteristic. The neural network models are good at pattern recognition and thus are able to find the good solutions even though they may not be perfect solutions. Interface designs should be able to interpret the reasonable responses of the users and assist in finding the correct response. Present interface designs have little capability for doing this.

GENERAL DESCRIPTION AND BACKGROUND

Like discrete stages models, even though some assumptions of connectionist or neural network models are specific to the individual model, several are shared across the various models. Neural network models are considered to have the follow-

ing seven features (Rumelhart and McClelland, 1986):

- A set of processing units
- A state of activation
- An output function for each unit
- A pattern of connectivity among units
- A propagation rule for propagating patterns of activities through the network of connectivities
- An activation rule for combining the inputs impinging on a unit with the current state of that unit to produce a new level of activation for the unit
- A learning rule whereby patterns of connectivity are modified by experience

Figure 9-1 illustrates some of these features of the models using neural-like representations.

Features of Neural Networks

The set of processing units are the nodes in the network. These nodes are usually organized into input and hidden layers. The input layer is the representation of the pattern which needs to be recognized. Depending on the application, these units in the input layer can represent different concepts. In visual pattern recognition tasks, they could represent visual features such as letter features, letters, words, and

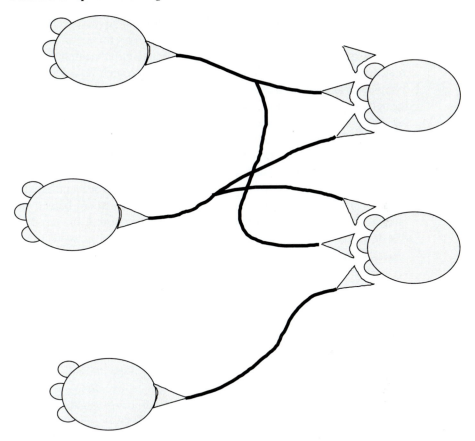

Figure 9-1. Neural network models are based upon how neurons are connected to each other in the human nervous system. This simple figure represents the neurons (the large ovals) and the connections between them. If a neuron receives enough electrical activity, then it fires, causing other neurons to fire on down the line.

phrases (Fukushima, 1987, 1988a, 1988b; Fukushima, Miyake, and Ito, 1983). For general programs not specific to a particular application, they represent abstract elements over which meaningful patterns can be defined. The nodes in the hidden layer have the same characteristics as those in the input layer although they may not represent a meaningful concept. The hidden layer is needed for mapping some complex conjunctions and disjunctions of input nodes into the output nodes. A node in an output layer is similar to nodes in the input and hidden layer except that an output node is not connected to any higher processing layers. All the processing in neural nets is carried out by these units with no executive control over them. The unit simply receives input from neighbors, combines all inputs using a specified function, and computes an output value to pass on to the neighboring units in the next level. Under this scheme, several units can be activated at any particular time so that parallel processing can occur.

The state of activation of the system

at any time t can be represented by a vector, **a**(t), where each of the N units in the network corresponds to a value in the vector (Rumelhart and McClelland, 1986). The pattern of activation determines what the network is representing at any particular time. The vector values can be discrete, continuous, or stochastic, either bounded or unbounded. For discrete values, the vector value is usually either 0 or 1, representing on or off. Continuous values can be activated as any real number. Stochastic values could be a function of a defined probability distribution. The neural nets described in the following applications take on continuous values bounded between 0 and 1. Because values of 0 and 1 can have undesirable effects on the learning algorithms, values of 0.1 and 0.9 were used for off and on, respectively.

Each unit, except the input units, will receive activation from its neighbors in the preceding layer of the network. The units sum all the input activity and, if the value exceeds some threshold, outputs signals to its neighbors. The function relating the input values to the output determines the strength of the output of the units. The functions depend on the model used and the purpose of the model. Rumelhart and McClelland (1986) identify common functions such as the identity function, step threshold functions, continuous threshold functions, and stochastic functions based upon some probability distribution.

The pattern of connectivity is important to how the information is processed. Humans usually process information in a combination of top-down and bottom-up processing. For bottom-up processing, the inputs to the network represent perceptual units such as letter features in vision

or phonemes in speech recognition. These low-level units are combined into larger units until a meaningful high level unit is output, such as a word. For top-down processing, the input to the network is some kind of context which is used to activate the lower-level units. As an example, if the overall context was animals and the network received input of three letters with "C" and "T" the only ones which could be identified, then the middle letter "A" would be activated instead of "U" because of the top-down activation. Some neural network models use either bottom-up or top-down processing alone or a combination of the two. The pattern of connectivity is established by determining the weights or strengths associated with the connections between the units. In most models, the input to the unit is a weighted sum of the separate inputs from each of the individual units. The weights can be excitatory, a positive value, or inhibitory, a negative value. A weight of 0 would represent no connection between two units. The weights are usually represented as a matrix of weights in which the units to be connected are from the rows and columns of the matrix. The knowledge of the neural network is represented in the weights between the connections. When a neural network learns, it changes the weight values so as to produce input/output pairings corresponding to the values observed for the training examples.

The rule of propagation states how the matrix of connection weights is combined with the output values of the units to produce a net input for each type of input into a unit. Generally, the matrix of weights is multiplied by the output vector to determine the net input. Two types of inputs are usually considered, the excitatory and inhibitory inputs, so that separate net input values would be determined for each.

An activation rule states how the net inputs of each type impinging on a particular unit are combined with one another and with the current state of the unit to produce a new state of activation. Two useful activation rules are decay or saturation over time. For decay, the activation is descreased over time and for saturation the activation is increased over time.

Learning Rules

One of the important aspects of neural networks is that the network can change according to experience by modifying the patterns of interconnectivity. Three kinds of modifications can occur: the development of new connections, the loss of existing connections, and the modification of the strengths of connections that already exist. Little work has been done on the first two, but these first two can be considered a special case of the third one if a new connection is considered established when the weight becomes nonzero and a disconnection occurs when the weight becomes zero (Rumelhart and McClelland, 1986). Most of the important learning rules are based on that of Hebb (1949) who stated, simply, that when one unit receives input from another unit, and both are highly active, then the connection weight between the two units should be strengthened. In practice, this simple rule can take on many forms. The equation most approximating that of Hebb is

$$\Delta w_{ij} = g(a_i(t), t_i(t))h(o_j(t), w_{ij}) \qquad (9.1)$$

where Δw_{ij} is the change in weight for the connection from unit u_j to unit u_i at time t.

The equation represents the product of two functions, g() and h(). The g() function has parameters corresponding to the activation, $a_i(t)$, of u_i, and a teaching function, $t_i(t)$. The h() function has parameters corresponding to the output value, $o_j(t)$, of u_j, and the connection strength between the two units, w_{ij}. Variants of this include the following. If the teaching function is not specified, then the functions g and h are proportional to their first arguments and the change in weight is:

$$\Delta w_{ij} = \eta a_i o_j \qquad (9.2)$$

where η is the constant of proportionality representing the learning rate. If the amount of learning is taken to be proportional to the difference between the actual activation achieved and the target activation provided by a teacher (this is often called the delta rule), then the equation is

$$\Delta w_{ij} = \eta(t_i(t) - a_i(t))o_j(t) \qquad (9.3)$$

A further variant is the following rule which was specified by Grossberg (1976):

$$\Delta w_{ij} = \eta a_i(t)(o_j(t) - w_{ij}) \qquad (9.4)$$

These are the main learning rules; others exist for more specialized situations. Through application of the Hebbian learning rules, the neural network determines the connection strengths between the nodes so that the input-output relationships in the training examples are captured. After training, test data can be propagated through the trained network so that the model can recognize input patterns by mapping them to output nodes using the existing connection weights established during learning.

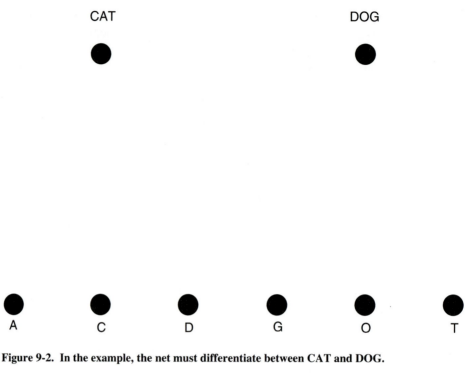

Figure 9-2. In the example, the net must differentiate between CAT and DOG.

Advantages

The main advantage of the neural network approach to human information processing is that the processing occurs in parallel and is distributed. This solves many of the problems in using the serial computer model analogy for human information processing. Another advantage is that these models are very good for pattern recognition. Solutions can be found based upon partial information.

NEURAL NET EXAMPLE

Understanding the operation of a neural net or connectionist model is difficult in the abstract, as stated above. By providing concrete examples, the understanding becomes a bit easier. A concrete example is provided below.

Propagating Inputs Through the Net

Consider a neural net which has alphanumeric characters as its input and the net provides a means to identify words, the output, from the letters. As a starting point, let's say that the net must differentiate between the words CAT and DOG, as in Figure 9-2. From the preceding discussion, the first thing to be considered is the structure of the network. We will make it as simple as possible at this point by having the input layer, corresponding to individual letters, at the bottom of the net and the output layer, corresponding to the two words, at the top of the net. In this simple example, no hidden layer is provided.

From this example, we know that when the net "perceives," in some way, the letters C, A, and T, the net is supposed to recognize that combination of letters as

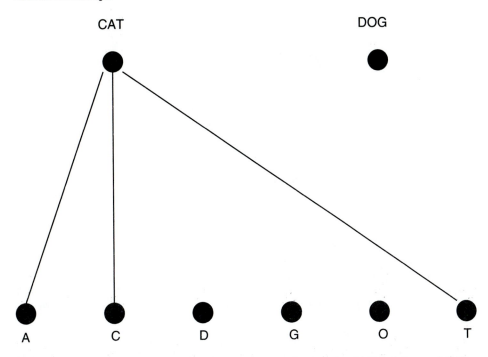

Figure 9-3. Connections are made between the individual letters for CAT and the word CAT.

the word CAT. One way to indicate this is to draw connections between the input letters C, A, and T, at the bottom of the net, to the output word, CAT, at the top of the net. This is done in Figure 9-3. We can perform a similar operation for mapping the letters D, O, and G into the word DOG. This is done in Figure 9-4.

So far, the connections only represent excitatory connections, which means that whenever the input occurs, the connection provides an indication that the word may have occurred. The analysis so far has ignored possible inhibitory connections. An inhibitory connection between a letter and word would indicate that the presence of the letter means that the word should not be activated. An inhibitory connection can be represented in a figure, following standard electrical engineering practices, by a line with a perpendicular line at the connection. These inhibitory connections can be differentiated from the excitatory connections by putting an inverted arrow at the end of the lines from Figure 9-4. A new figure, with the inhibitory connections and the new representation of the excitatory connections, is shown by Figure 9-5.

Now, numerical values can be assigned to the connections between the letters and the words, and these values can replace the function of the inhibitory and excitatory connection lines. The connection weights can take on any value, but it is convenient to limit the weights to be between -1 and +1. A negative value indicates an inhibitory connection, and a positive value indicates an excitatory connection. The absolute value of the weight shows the strength of the connection. The connection weights are labeled

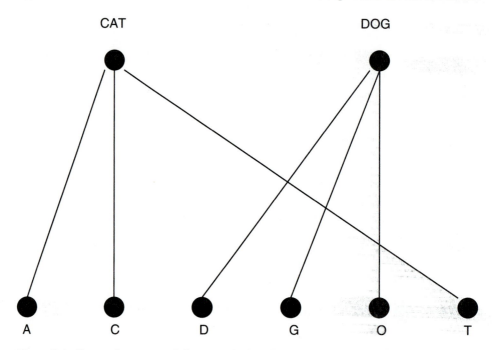

Figure 9-4. Connections are made between the individual letters for DOG and the word DOG.

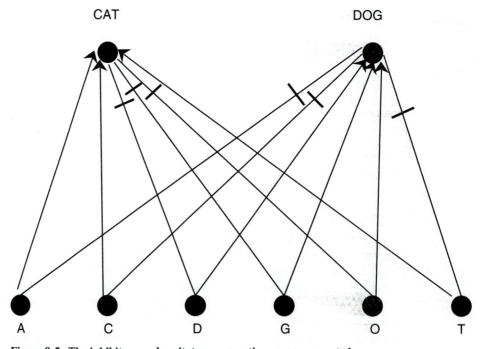

Figure 9-5. The inhibitory and excitatory connections are represented.

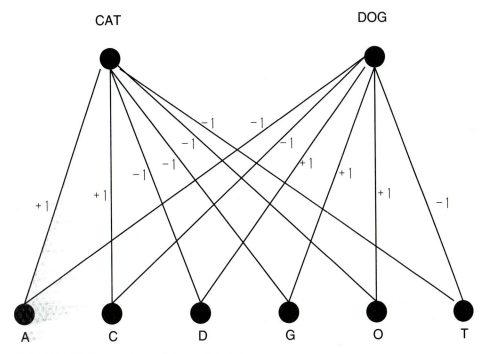

Figure 9-6. The connection weights are labeled.

in Figure 9-6. Reading the weight values is difficult in this kind of figure. An easier way to represent these values is in matrix form (the pattern of connectivity, item 4, from the previous discussion). The matrix is shown in Figure 9-7 with the two outputs as the columns and the six inputs as the rows. This representation increases the readability and is especially needed for more complex nets.

	CAT	DOG
A	+1	-1
C	+1	-1
D	-1	+1
G	-1	+1
O	-1	+1
T	+1	-1

Figure 9-7. The net represented in matrix form.

The net is now completely specified to map input letters into output words to determine which of the two words is presented. Let's first present the net with the word CAT and determine what happens. Under the input values of Figure 9-8, the three letters of CAT are represented. With this input, the net can determine a numerical value for the output by taking the input values, multiplying these values by the appropriate connection weights, and then summing all of these values that map into the output units. In the example, since C, A, and T are input, we will assign the corresponding input units an activation of 1 for each. Since D, O, and G are not input, we will assign those corresponding input units an activation of 0 for each. Each of these input units has connections to the output units. The activation values from the input units are multiplied by the con-

Figure 9-8. The input to the net is represented by the bottom row of letters.

nection weight for each of the connections. Looking at the first unit, A has an activation value of 1. This value is multiplied by +0.33 for the connection to CAT and -0.33 for the connection to DOG. For the next unit, C has an activation value of 1 and is multiplied by +0.33 for the connection to CAT and -0.33 for the connection to DOG. We can continue on down the line. The next step is to sum all of these products to determine an overall activation value for the CAT and DOG output units. For CAT, this sum of products is

$$1*0.33 + 1*0.33 + 0*-0.33 + 0*-0.33 \\ + 0*-0.33 + 1*0.33 = 1 \qquad (9.5)$$

For DOG, this sum of products is

$$1*-0.33 + 1*-0.33 + 0*0.33 + 0*0.33 \\ + 0*0.33 + 1*-0.33 = -1 \qquad (9.6)$$

For this input, the net would show that the letters C, A, and T map into the word CAT and not the word DOG.

Mathematically, it is much easier to represent the above operation using matrices and matrix algebra. Instead of specifying that the letters A, C, and T were input specifically, we can represent the same thing by using an input vector with vector elements corresponding to each of the six input units. For the letters in CAT corresponding to the positioning of the input units in the figures, the following input vector represents the A, C, and T pattern of letters:

$$[1, 1, 0, 0, 0, 1]$$

A "1" means that the input unit is present, and a "0" means that the input unit is not

$$\begin{bmatrix} 1 & -1 \\ 1 & -1 \\ -1 & 1 \\ -1 & 1 \\ -1 & 1 \\ 1 & -1 \end{bmatrix} \qquad [\,1\ 1\ 0\ 0\ 0\ 1\,] = [\,3\ \text{-}3\,]$$

Figure 9-9. The input vector is multiplied by the matrix of strengths.

present. Other values besides the 0 and 1 can be used, but, considering that the other values range between -1 and +1, keeping an upper bound of 1 is sensible. For the letters corresponding to DOG, the input vector would be

[0, 0, 1, 1, 1, 0]

Using matrix algebra, the activation values for the two output values can be determined by multiplying the matrix of strengths by the input vector. This operation is shown in Figure 9-9. To briefly review this matrix operation, the first column of values from the strength matrix is multiplied by the values in the input vector the same as was done above for the CAT input of equation 9.5. This results in a value of 1. The second column of the strength matrix, representing the connections to the DOG output, is multiplied by

the input vector the same as was done for equation 9.6.

Once the net is set up with the values, then other input values can be propagated through it, and the net is good at identifying words on partial information or ambiguous information, as indicated in the introduction to this chapter. Let's consider the situation when the input vector is the following:

[0, 0, 1, 1, 0, 0]

This would be the same as receiving the letters D and G, missing the middle letter. Can the net still identify the word based upon this partial information? Propagate the input vector through the net, by multiplying the connection weight matrix by the input vector, and output values can be determined. This is done in Figure 9-10. As can be seen by the output vector, the net

$$\begin{bmatrix} 1 & -1 \\ 1 & -1 \\ -1 & 1 \\ -1 & 1 \\ -1 & 1 \\ 1 & -1 \end{bmatrix} \qquad [\,0\ 0\ 1\ 1\ 0\ 0\,] = [\,2\ \text{-}2\,]$$

Figure 9-10. Partial information from the word DOG, missing the letter O, is propagated through the net.

O A T

Figure 9-11. The word, which is digitized and then propagated through the net, is ambiguous being either CAT or OAT.

determines that the evidence supports the case that the word DOG was presented.

The net can also operate under ambiguous information. Let's say that the net is connected to a vision machine and the input of Figure 9-11 is received. The net can clearly determine that the letters A and T were presented, but it does not know whether the first letter is an "O" or a "C". The probability of it being either of these letters is 0.5. In this case, the following input vector would be propagated through the net:

$$[1, .5, 0, 0, .5, 1]$$

The output vector resulting from the matrix multiplication of the weight matrix with the input vector is

$$[0.66, -0.66]$$

Since the CAT output is highest, the net would recognize the input as CAT. Once again, the net is able to identify that the word is CAT even though the conclusion is based upon partial information.

The net also should be able to indicate when it cannot recognize a word. Let's say that the word GOAT is received by the net. The input vector for GOAT would be

$$[1, 0, 0, 1, 1, 1]$$

When the weight matrix is multiplied by this input vector, the output vector is

$$[0, 0]$$

Obviously, the net would conclude that this word could not be identified.

The example above is a very simple example used to explain some of the concepts behind neural nets and connectionist models. Obviously, the real systems would not be this clean or simple and would contain a larger vocabulary of words. Many neural nets also have a hidden layer, between the input layer and the output layer, because in some cases finding an input/output mapping is impossible without this hidden layer. In addition, very simple functions were used. Rumelhart and McClelland (1986) indicated that the activation of the units could take on discrete, continuous, or stochastic values at any particular time. To simplify the above example, the activation value of the units was always discrete. Also to simplify the explanation, the timing values were not considered. In a typical case, the input vector would activate the input unit and then this would decay over time. If the letters C and A were received and then T was received later, C and A may have decayed, depending on the function and the timing, before the T was received. This timing mechanism could also be used to determine the ordering of the letters in the words. Ordering information was not available for the simple example above.

Training the Net

One feature obviously missing from the above example is the learning function. As indicated in the introduction to this chapter, one of the big advantages of neural nets over other kinds of modeling techniques is its ability to learn. From the example, the connection weights between the input and output layers were provided and not learned by the net. In practice, the neural net would have to learn the value of those weights from examples supplied to the net. This learning process is usually referred to as training the net. When training the net, it must be provided with example mappings of input to output.

Rumelhart and McClelland (1986) provided many learning rules which could be used to train the net. The most popular and easiest to apply is the delta rule of equation 9.3, and repeated here:

$$\Delta w_{ij} = \eta(t_i(t) - a_i(t))o_j(t) \qquad (9.3)$$

where Δw_{ij} is the change in the weight value for any connection i and j; η is the learning rate; $t_i(t)$ is the target activation of unit u_i at time t; $a_i(t)$ is the actual activation of unit u_i at time t; and $o_j(t)$ is the output value of unit u_j at time t.

To start training the net, the user would have to first specify the structure of the net: how many input units, the number of hidden units, and the output units. Using the same example as previously, there are six input units, no hidden units, and two output units. Next, the user would have to indicate the learning rate, η. A high number indicates a fast learning rate, and a low number indicates a slow learning rate. For a fast learning rate, the net will learn faster but at the expense of having less of a memory of the previous values and the possibility of jumping over a solution to the training examples. For a slow learning rate, the net will learn slower, but it will have a larger memory of the previous states and a better possibility of not missing the optimal solution. The correct learning rate can only be determined from experience. For this example, we will choose a value of 0.5. Next, the user

would have to specify the training examples of the correct mappings of input units to output units. From the previous example, these training examples could be represented by the following two vectors:

$$[1\ 1\ 0\ 0\ 0\ 1\ 1\ \text{-}1]$$
$$[0\ 0\ 1\ 1\ 1\ 0\ \text{-}1\ 1]$$

For the two vectors, the first six elements are the input layer corresponding to CAT, for the first vector, and DOG, for the second vector. Elements 7 and 8 in the vector represent the output units. As can be seen, element 7 represents the word CAT because the letters A, C, and T map into this output unit, and element 8 represents the word DOG. Because of the characteristics of the learning rule, the 0 is replaced with a low number such as 0.1. With a 0 the weights will not change for some of the connections. The new training vectors are, therefore, as follows:

$$[1\ 1\ 0.1\ 0.1\ 0.1\ 1\ 1\ \text{-}1]$$
$$[0.1\ 0.1\ 1\ 1\ 1\ 0.1\ \text{-}1\ 1]$$

The net must try to learn how to set up the weights so that these mappings can be achieved. It may have to cycle through many trials before it can learn the correct mapping. In some cases, the net may not be able to converge on a solution for the mappings.

Let's run through an example of how the net would learn the connection weights based upon the training examples provided to it. A typical neural net program would provide the net with a random value for all the connection weights to begin with. For this example, let's say that the net begins with all the connection weights set randomly to 0.2. To simplify

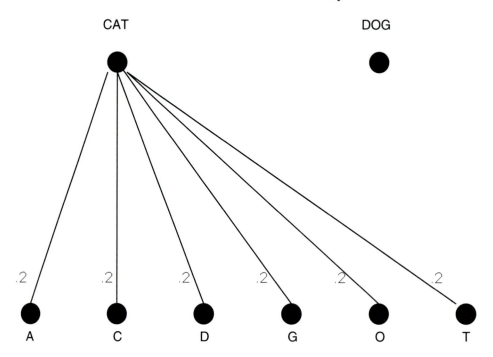

CAT   DOG

.2   .2   .2   .2   .2   .2

A   C   D   G   O   T

Figure 9-12. The initial state for training the net where all the connection weights are set to a value of .2.

this example, let's just consider training the connection weights for those connections between the input layer and the output node corresponding to CAT (see Figure 9-12); the connections to the DOG output node would be very similar in the training characteristics.

To train the net, look back to the delta learning rule. The first value we need to determine is the activation of unit u_i at time t. This unit corresponds to the

CAT output node and can be determined by using the first training vector and the random weights assigned to the connections. This can be determined by the multiplication of the two vectors in Figure 9-13, resulting in a value for the CAT node, $a_i(t)$ from the delta rule, of 0.64. The delta rule can now be applied to determine the change in weights. First, consider the rule for the first (A), second (C), and sixth (T) connections, going from left to right,

$$\begin{bmatrix} .2 \\ .2 \\ .2 \\ .2 \\ .2 \\ .2 \end{bmatrix} \qquad [\,1\ 1\ 0.1\ 0.1\ 0.1\ 1\,] = [\,0.64\,]$$

Figure 9-13. The connection weights are multiplied by the training vector for CAT.

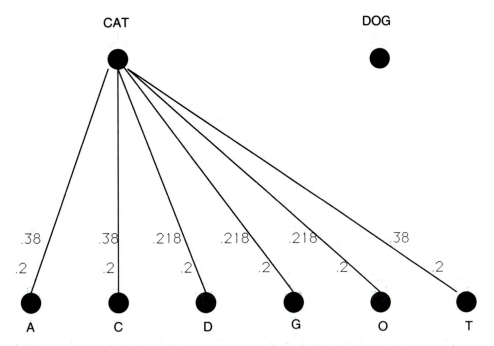

Figure 9-14. The new weights after one example from the training set is learned by the net.

of Figure 9-12. Recall that η is 0.5, t_i is 1 (this is the target value of the CAT node for the particular input vector, the seventh element in the input vector), a_i as determined above is 0.64, and o_j corresponds to the value for the input node. Since C, A, and T are turned on, o_j is 1 for the first, second, and sixth nodes. So, the change in the weights is

$$\Delta w_{ij} = 0.5(1 - 0.64)1 = 0.18 \qquad (9.7)$$

For the third, fourth, and fifth nodes of Figure 9-12, the only changes are that a_i is -1 and o_j is 0.1. The change in these weights is

$$\Delta w_{ij} = 0.5(1 - 0.64)(0.1) = 0.018 \qquad (9.8)$$

Since the resulting numbers from equations 9.7 and 9.8 are delta changes to the weights, these numbers must be added to the existing weights. The values for the

connections for the first, second, and sixth connections are $0.18 + 0.2$ or 0.38. For the third, fourth, and fifth connections, these values are $0.018 + 0.2$ or 0.218. These new weights are represented in Figure 9-14.

To continue the learning, the second training example vector is used. Multiplying the current connection weights by this vector is represented by the matrix algebra of Figure 9-15. The value 0.768 becomes the new value for a_i. Applying the delta rule for the first, second, and sixth nodes, we get

$$\Delta w_{ij} = 0.5(-1 - 0.768)(0.1) = -0.088 \quad (9.9)$$

Applying the delta rule for the third, fourth, and fifth nodes, we get

$$\Delta w_{ij} = 0.5(-1 - 0.768)(1) = -0.884 \quad (9.10)$$

These changes in the weights are then

$$\begin{bmatrix} 0.38 \\ 0.38 \\ 0.218 \\ 0.218 \\ 0.218 \\ 0.38 \end{bmatrix} \quad [\, 0.1 \;\; 0.1 \;\; 1 \;\; 1 \;\; 1 \;\; 0.1 \,] = [\, 0.768 \,]$$

Figure 9-15. The matrix algebra representation used for learning the second example from the training set.

added to the previous weights, resulting in values of 0.292 and -0.666 (see Figure 9-16). A learning cycle is completed when the neural network has worked through all the training examples. Since only two training examples are present in this case, the first learning cycle is now completed.

The learning continues for another cycle. Once again, the first training example vector is used and a_i is determined

from the matrix multiplication of Figure 9-17. The delta rule is applied to the first, second, and sixth connections as follows:

$$\Delta w_{ij} = 0.5(1 - 0.676)1 = 0.162 \qquad (9.11)$$

The same rule is applied to the third, fourth, and fifth connections as follows:

$$\Delta w_{ij} = 0.5(-1 + 0.676)(0.1) = 0.016 \quad (9.12)$$

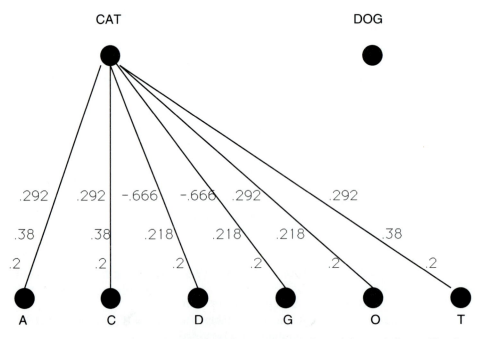

Figure 9-16. The new weights after the second example from the training set is learned by the net. This completes one iteration through the training set.

$$\begin{bmatrix} 0.292 \\ 0.292 \\ -0.666 \\ -0.666 \\ -0.666 \\ 0.292 \end{bmatrix} \quad [\,1\ \ 1\ \ 0.1\ \ 0.1\ \ 0.1\ \ 1\,] = [\,.676\,]$$

Figure 9-17. The matrix multiplication for the first training example in the second iteration of the training cycle.

When these changes in weight values are added to the appropriate current weights, the new connection weight values are those shown in Figure 9-18.

The second training example can now be used and a_i, determined from the matrix multiplication of Figure 9-19, is -1.814. The two delta rules, respectively, for the first, second, and sixth connections and for the third, fourth, and fifth connections, are

$$\Delta w_{ij} = 0.5(-1 + 1.814)(0.1) = 0.041 \quad (9.13)$$

$$\Delta w_{ij} = 0.5(-1 + 1.814)(1) = 0.407 \quad (9.14)$$

These connection weights are shown in Figure 9-20.

At this point, one can see the weights are converging on a pattern similar to the one logically chosen in the first part of this example where the connection weights were 0.33 and -0.33. In the present ex-

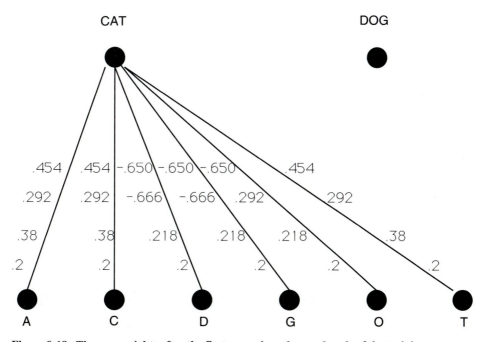

Figure 9-18. The new weights after the first example and second cycle of the training set.

$$\begin{bmatrix} 0.454 \\ 0.454 \\ -0.650 \\ -0.650 \\ -0.650 \\ 0.454 \end{bmatrix} \quad [\,0.1 \ \ 0.1 \ \ 1 \ \ 1 \ \ 1 \ \ 0.1\,] = [\,-1.814\,]$$

Figure 9-19. The matrix multiplication for the second training example in the second iteration of the training cycle.

ample, if the cycles were continued until cycle 8, the connection weights that were -0.33 in the first example would be -0.409; the weights that were 0.33 are now 0.367. The output for the CAT input would be 0.978 with these weights; for the DOG input, the output would be -1.117. This matches fairly closely the target values of 1 and -1, and, thus, the neural network exhibits learning for how to map the inputs to the appropriate outputs.

In this example the network needed only around eight cycles to learn the appropriate connection weights from the provided training examples. In most situations, however, the pattern to be learned would be much more difficult and the net would need hundreds or even thousands of cycles in order to obtain an acceptable solution. In some cases, the patterns are so difficult and similar to each other that the net cannot converge on a solution. Obvi-

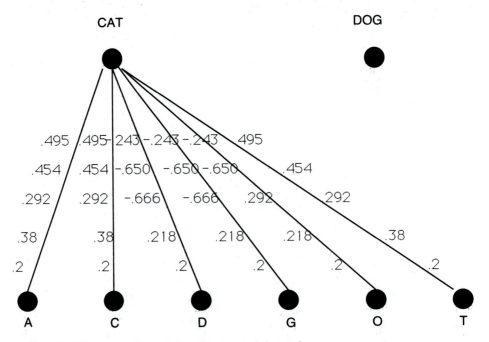

Figure 9-20. The connection weights after two training cycles.

ously, providing such an example in this book would serve no useful purpose. Showing the simple example, with learning occurring in two cycles, is useful for providing the reader with an understanding of how neural nets can learn.

Many variants of neural nets exist. Many times, neural nets will be provided with a specific architecture in order to simulate a particular class of problems. As an example of this, the neural net called CAP1 (Schneider and Detweiler, 1987) was developed specifically to model human information processing and human learning. It was designed to be realistic in terms of cognitive functioning and physiology, and it can be used to understand and explain cognitive phenomena. Table 9-1 contains a list of the assumptions of the CAP1 model and how these assumptions have a basis in the physiological system.

TABLE 9-1

Assumptions of the CAP1 model and their relationships to physiological characteristics

Assumption	Physiology
1. Processing occurs in a network of modules having a similar structure but differing in their inputs and outputs	Similarity to structures of cortical hypercolumns from neurophysiology
2. Local specialization of function, i.e., given module specializes in processing a small set of stimuli	A small region of the cortex specializes in processing a particular class of processing
3. Knowledge is stored in the connection weights between neural-like units in the system	Strength of connection at synapse assumed to change with learning
4. The connection rates may change with a variety of rate constants (high rates change quickly, low rates slowly)	Existence of over 50 neurotransmitters with time courses ranging from 1 msec to 30 min
5. Modulatory control system that regulates flow of information among modules produces attentional phenomena	No physiological analogue, but behavioral analogue

APPLICATION EXAMPLES

Much of the work on neural networks has been performed as basic research in cognitive science or computer science. Some applications have begun in several different areas, and the number of these applications should increase in the near future. Neural networks have been applied in some areas of human-computer interaction. Many of the neural network models have been designed so that they mimic human information processing and can be successful in areas, such as machine learning, machine vision, and machine speech recognition, that have been studied with other kinds of artificial intelligence techniques.

Direct Applications to Human-Computer Interaction

In recent years, several applications of neural networks to human-computer interaction problems have been researched. These applications all involve some sort of pattern recognition, because this is the strength of neural networks. Applications include recognizing handwriting and gestures, recognizing cognitive goals during a human-computer interaction task, recognizing inefficient commands input by the user, recognizing the identity of a user for security purposes, and filtering information from e-mail messages or bulletin boards.

Recognizing Handwriting and Gestures. Some of these applications in this area are reviewed in Chapter 20. In particular, neural nets have been used to recognize hand gestures through touch screen. Instead of inputting characters through a keyboard, a user could draw on a touch

screen a representation of the character or words. Since much variation could occur in this task, a neural net interpretation of the characters is especially useful because of the net's capabilities to recognize patterns, to fill in missing infomation, and to interpret ambiguous characters in the context of a word. This application would be useful for people, such as the police, who must input data out in the field. Instead of using paper and pencil, data could be input on a small portable computer by writing on the screen.

Another application of handwriting and gestures has occurred at MCC's Human Interface Laboratory. MCC is a consortium of several U.S. computer companies who cooperate on the development of computer systems. This lab developed a rapid interface prototyping tool which could be used to develop interfaces. For this tool, a developer would draw the interface on a touch screen using a simple stylus. As an example, a rectangle could represent a push button. A neural net would interpret the drawings and clean them up. Using the example of the rectangle, if the neural net recognized this representation as a rectangle then the neural net would help to redraw it as a rectangle, with straight lines, parallel sides, and right angles at the corners. The neural net could help to interpret the functionality of some of the drawings also. This tool has the capability of decreasing the development time of interfaces through this neural net tool.

Recognizing Cognitive Goals in an HCI Task. In human-computer interaction, text editing is a commonly performed task, but typically the computer cannot understand the strategies of the users. A neural net which could evaluate the strategies, or the goals used to perform a task, could then be used to offer suggestions for how to improve the efficiency of the strategies.

Research by Villegas and Eberts (1992) was directed toward creating and evaluating a neural network which identifies user strategies in the performance of a text-editing task. The data used in this research were from a study which examined memo-editing strategies of users. The users were required to address the memo, delete extraneous lines, punctuate the memo, and make any enhancements they thought would be appropriate. The keystrokes and interkeystroke times for 36 memos (three memos from 12 subjects) were collected and stored.

Previous research (Robertson and Black, 1986) suggests that goal planning occurs at major pauses between keystrokes and, thus, the data were broken down into pause-to-pause units, enabling the events which complete a goal to be demarcated by the pauses. The events between the pauses became inputs for a neural network, and the high-level goals were chosen as outputs. For example, two of the outputs were addressing the memo and adding punctuation, and two of the 39 inputs identified were deleting a line and adding a phrase. Thus, a grammar was developed, using cognitive modeling, for application of the neural network.

A network was trained on the first of three memos from a subject for mapping low-level operators, like those described previously, to cognitive goals. For the training set, this mapping was determined initially by the researchers so that the net could be trained. After training, the network was presented with test data composed of the second and third memos

edited by the subjects, data never before provided to the net. Results indicated that the network's performance rate in identifying the cognitive goals on the test data was quite high at an average of 96% correct. By identifying the strategies of users during text editing, this research shows the feasibility of developing real-time decision aids which can track the progress of subjects, recognize inefficiencies, and offer solutions. Follow-on research can be directed toward developing a system that can identify the cognitive strategies of users on-line in real time. Intelligent help messages could be developed to provide feedback to the subjects about the efficiency of their cognitive strategies. This method could also be applied to determine cognitive strategies for other kinds of complex tasks.

Recognizing Inefficient Commands Input by Users. Research has been performed to provide intelligent help systems to offer assistance to UNIX users on how to perform the operating system commands more efficiently (Eberts, Villegas, Phillips, and Eberts, 1992). In this research, five UNIX tasks which could be performed efficiently or inefficiently were chosen for the experimentation. The five tasks involved concepts such as how to pipe an output to an input, how to use command parameters, and how to send output directly to a file. The inefficient methods for performing these tasks were collected from users in an initial experiment.

From the initial experiment, a neural net was trained on the inefficient examples so that it could recognize the inefficient commands and map that input to advice on how to perform the command sequence more efficiently. In a second experiment, code from the neural net was used to

To check who is on the system, and sort the names alphabetically, you can use one command line.

type who | sort

or

f | sort

who and f will look up the people on the system, and the sort command will sort the names alphabetically.

The pipe (|) indicates that you should use the output from who or f as input to the sort command.

Figure 9-21. Example of the help provided to users when the neural net determined that the task was being performed inefficiently.

monitor the users' behavior to propagate patterns of commands through the net, while the subjects were performing the five tasks, to determine if an output threshold was reached and, thus, that a more efficient command sequence could be used. Real-time assistance was provided to the users by displaying a window, through the X Window system on a workstation, which either displayed a more efficient method to perform the command or indicated that the user had chosen one of the most efficient methods (see Figure 9-21). The main advantage for the neural net condition was that it helped the users find the most efficient method to perform the task. The neural net was able to find the most

efficient commands, and users input these commands 81% of the time. This performance can be compared to a control condition in which the efficient commands were found without the neural net only 31% of the time. In addition, the variance between the users on the tasks was reduced. This means that the neural net condition did not have much of an effect on the best users, but it helped to ensure that the worst users did not get stuck on the task.

Recognizing the Identity of Users. A problem in computer interfaces, especially with networked systems, is to provide security so that unauthorized users cannot access sensitive information or destroy files on a computer system. Typically, security is achieved by requiring each login to be accompanied by a password. A problem with passwords is that they can get stolen, or, in some cases, broken. Other systems are being developed that monitor the behavior of users instead of relying only on passwords. With these kinds of systems, even if an intruder breaks into a system by accessing an authorized user's password, it is doubtful that this intruder could mimic the same kinds of behavior as the authorized user. If the computer system could recognize when behavior deviated from the norm, then the intruder could be caught.

Digital Equipment Corporation (DEC) has incorporated such a system for their VMS operating system. One of the main components of user behavior when using VMS is the length of the command names used. In VMS, a user has a wide choice of command names to use for a single command. The operating system only requires that enough characters of the command name be entered so that it is unique from other command names. As an example, for DIRECTORY, the user would only have to enter DIR or any longer version of the name. Just entering D would not be adequate because other commands start with D. By knowing the preferences for users on command names, the security system for DEC can recognize when intruders may have broken into the system.

An alternative method for recognizing intruders would be to use neural nets. In a neural net, patterns of usage for users could be mapped to the identification of individual users. When someone is using the computer under a particular login and password, the neural net could monitor the user and map the inputs to the user ID outputs. If the threshold of the net output for the user who is supposed to be on the system is not high enough, then the net could recognize that this is not the user who should be on the system under that ID and password. The net could even identify who the user may be, based upon the other outputs. Finlay and Beale (1992) have been working on developing a neural net for a similar security application.

Neural Nets as Information Filters. One of the biggest information-sharing problems is that of disseminating information to the people who will find it useful, without distracting others who will find no value in its contents. Assuming that people use the same pattern of words when writing about a particular topic, neural nets could be used to recognize those word patterns to automatically select, classify, route, and prioritize information people receive. This possibility was tested by using a neural net to classify messages used in a particular newsgroup (Habibi and Eberts, 1992).

In this research, a neural net was trained to recognize a dictionary of words in messages that the user has indicated in the past would be useful. In the dictionary filter, the words in a message represent the input and the relevance of the message represents the output. As an example, if a certain pattern of words was of interest to the user in the past, then this message would have a high relevance for the output. If a pattern of words was of no interest to a user in the past, then these messages could be mapped to a low-relevance output. Based upon the output, a message could be prioritized for the user as being relevant or irrelevant.

In the Habibi and Eberts research, methods were examined for constructing the dictionary filter. A neural net was developed for mapping the word inputs to the relevancy of the messages. On new messages, the net was found to have a high accuracy rate, in some cases, only having one mistake out of 64 in the mappings. This kind of method could be used for other messages, such as e-mail.

Peripheral Applications to Human-Computer Interaction

Many neural network applications have only a peripheral association with human-computer interaction. In this area, neural networks have been applied to cognitive training issues and knowledge acquisition. Cognitive training can be used to train a neural net on a computer interaction problem before the software is developed, to understand how well humans may be able to learn without having to go to the expense of testing humans. Knowledge acquisition has been discussed in Chapter 7; it can be used to determine the kinds of human knowledge structures so that the interface can be designed to be compatible with this knowledge.

In training cognitive skills, the training itself can be performed in several different ways. Traditionally in human factors, the best training method has been determined through manipulating the training variables in an experiment using human subjects. This procedure can be expensive and time-consuming. Neural network research offers an alternative approach which is less costly and less time-consuming, at least after the cost of the initial setup. Neural network models are, for the most part, learning models based upon aspects of human learning and information processing. If human learning and the training environment can be modeled, then the different training techniques could be tested using the neural network model instead of running an experiment. This has been done in two general cases, outside the realm of human-computer interaction tasks. This kind of methodology can certainly be applied to human-computer interaction tasks, and one example of this will be discussed.

The general cases of using neural nets to investigate learning have occurred with NETtalk and CAP1. NETtalk, a model of speech learning, was used to examine different methods of training words which could possibly be applied to human learning (Sejnowski and Rosenberg, 1987; Rosenberg and Sejnowski, 1986). Two training methods are possible: massed or distributed training. In massed training, one word would be trained on several trials and then another word would be introduced to be trained on several trials. In distributed training, the two words would be alternated on successive

trials. The researchers found that distributed practice was much better than massed practice, and they were able to explain why this occurred by examining the changes in connection weights that occurred with the different training techniques. By distributing practice, the learning rule was able to find a more global minimum for the entire set of words, while for massing practice the minimum found was more local for the specific patterns.

CAP1 (Schneider and Detweiler, 1988) was used to determine the best methods to train someone in skill acquisition of dual tasks, that is, tasks that must be performed at the same time. The issue was the relative advantages of training someone on the single tasks and then transferring them to the dual task as compared to training exclusively on the dual task situation. In examining how the neural network model CAP1 would handle dual task training, and how this would differ from single task training, seven activities of dual task training were identified that did not occur in single task training: (a) shedding and delaying tasks and preloading buffers; (b) letting go of high-workload strategies; (c) utilizing noncompeting resources; (d) multiplexing over time; (e) shortening transmissions; (f) converting interference from concurrent transmissions; and (g) chunking of transmissions. By observing the simulated network, this research shed some light on controversies related to this particular training issue. A future goal would be achieving the ability to predict optimal points for shifting from single task practice to dual task practice.

For the application of neural net learning simulation to human-computer interaction tasks, Tanaka, Eberts, and Salvendy (1991) were interested in modeling the consistency of interface designs. A consistent interface design can mean one of two things: (a) users will be able to transfer from one interface to another with little problem; and (b) the users may be able to alternate between different interfaces. The transfer between interfaces has been studied by Polson and his associates (Polson, Bovair, and Kieras, 1987; Polson, Muncher, and Engelbeck, 1986; and Polson, 1988). Transfer occurs when a user learns one interface design and then transfers to a different interface without returning to the original. The Polson research showed that two or more interface designs are consistent if the overlap of interface features is high. Much of this research, and the models for predicting transfer, are discussed in Chapter 16.

Tanaka et al. (1991) were interested in user performance when alternating between interfaces. This is different from the transfer situation because the user does not abandon the original interface, as in the transfer situation, but will use both interfaces alternately. They predicted that, in the alternating sequence, interfaces with high overlap of features would be inconsistent and difficult to use; this is just the opposite finding from the transfer situations.

Instead of training humans on this problem and looking at the results, a time-consuming and expensive proposition, Tanaka et al. used a neural net model to simulate the learning of the users. This simulation showed that the same task can be considered consistent or inconsistent depending on how it is sequenced during training or use. If the overlap of features for the tasks was high, then the simulation showed that the interfaces could be considered consistent in the transfer tasks, as

was demonstrated experimentally by Polson (1988), but inconsistent in the alternating tasks.

Another issue in human-computer interaction has been knowledge acquisition from experts for the design of interfaces. This was considered in Chapter 7 in the discussion about acquiring knowledge about the mental models of users and then designing the interface to be compatible with that knowledge. As indicated in Chapter 7, typically knowledge acquisition has occurred through protocol analyses or through some more automated methods (Garg-Janardan, Eberts, Zimolong, Nof, and Salvendy, 1987). A drawback to these techniques has been the inability of the domain expert to report all mental activity which is necessary for determining the mental steps or procedures. Neural network modeling is a possible improvement in this area because the domain expert can be given only a series of examples and from them the expert produces the solution to the examples. The neural network, through its learning function, determines the connection weights that would produce the results specified by the domain expert. Knowledge acquisition using neural nets was discussed in Chapter 7 and will not be repeated here.

Another area of applications of neural nets for human-computer interaction tasks is in the realm of artificial intelligence. Neural nets are adept at recognizing patterns so that applications have occurred in visual and auditory pattern recognition tasks. Some of these areas have been applied to interface designs, and more applications can be expected in the future. A few of these will be discussed.

One of the primary applications of

neural networks has been in machine vision. Neocognitron (Fukushima, 1987, 1988a, 1988b; and Fukushima et al., 1983), a model of visual pattern recognition, tries to be faithful to physiological brain functions and human information processing. It can learn to recognize visual patterns and is especially adept at recognizing patterns with partial information. In recent years, companies have been developing interfaces, based upon this technology, in which the user interacts with the computer not through a keyboard but through handwriting or even head movements. To perform these tasks, especially identifying the head movements, the neural net must be able to use visual pattern recognition to interpret the movements.

Also, NETtalk (Sejnowski and Rosenberg, 1987), discussed previously, has been designed to learn to produce speech from English text . This has many possibilities in terms of providing feedback to users. PARSNIP (Hanson and Kegl, 1987) is a neural network which learns natural language grammar after being exposed to natural language sentences. PARSNIP was trained syntactically on sentences of 15 words or fewer. Once trained, it was able to syntactically label words in the trained sentences and it was able to successfully generalize the syntactic labels to new sentences. Natural language interfaces, discussed further in Chapter 19, have been researched but have not been commercially successful because of the large amount of processing which has to occur to interpret natural language. Perhaps a neural network approach to natural language interfaces, along the lines of PARSNIP, will prove fruitful in the future.

A related artificial intelligence application is that of problem solving, decision making, and diagnosis. Neural nets have been designed to assist with diagnosis problems. Medical clinical trial data were examined in a neural network application (Irani, Matts, Long, and Slagle, 1989) which was trained to provide diagnoses. The network acquired knowledge from the training examples and, after training, performed favorably compared to a panel of human experts, to a statistical analysis technique, and to an expert system. The researchers complained, however, that the hidden units were difficult to identify and that they needed some better method to specify the structure of the networks (e.g., how many layers and how many hidden units) to fully utilize the network.

SUMMARY

Neural networks can be used to model how people process information. Besides being a good model for this, they can also be used in many applications in human-computer interaction tasks. Some of those applications have been discussed in this chapter. It is expected that more applications will become available in this area in the near future. Some of these applications, such as for interpretation of writing on notebook-size computers, are now commercially viable. Much room exists for many more commercially viable applications in the future.

QUESTIONS

1.   Propagate the word GOT through the network provided in the example. What are the values for the two outputs?

2. Perform the computations for the two learning cycles using an input vector which has vector elements of 0 instead of 0.1.

   a. What happens to the weights in this case?

   b. Why is this a problem for the learning situation?

3. Perform the computations for learning cycles 3 through 8 to determine how the weights change.

   a. For neural network programs, the error is usually calculated by the root mean square. This can be calculated by taking the difference between the target value for the input vector and the output and then squaring the difference. Calculate the root mean square error for the eight learning cycles.

   b. Graph the results of the learning in part a by placing the learning cycle number on the horizontal axis and the error on the vertical axis.

4. Run through eight learning cycles of the training examples with different learning rates of 0.25 and 0.75.

   a. What are the differences between characteristics of learning for these different rates?

   b. What are the advantages and disadvantages of a fast learning rate as compared with a slow learning rate?

5. Identify some of your own behavior when using a computer system that a neural net may be able to determine and differentiate from the behavior of other users. How quickly does your behavior change as you become more proficient at the tasks?

6. Think of other examples of human-computer interaction tasks that require pattern recognition, and specify how neural nets could be used for these tasks.

CHAPTER 10

METAPHORS AND ANALOGIES

INTRODUCTION

Metaphors and analogies are an important kind of learning used quite often in teaching. In teaching, the instructor chooses some concrete situation with which the student is familiar and presents new information in terms of how it relates to the old familiar information. One of the most popular examples of using analogies in teaching is to say that light acts like particles in some situations and like waves in other situations. Neither is totally correct, but it does help the student develop the concept of light by using familiar information which may have been built up through interacting with particles or waves.

Gentner and Gentner (1983) found that the kinds of analogies used by subjects in an experiment determined the kinds of mistakes that were made in problem-solving tasks. They found that people very often form an analogical model of electricity based upon either a water flow analogy or a teeming crowd analogy. By analyzing the analogies, Gentner and Gentner determined that the water flow analogy would be better for predicting the effects of a battery on an electrical circuit, and the teeming crowd analogy would be better in predicting the effects of a resistor on the circuit. The results indicated that the predictions were fairly accurate and that the analogy used can affect how people think about a task. Related to analogies is learning by example. Again, new knowledge is created by giving subjects a concrete example of its use. Anderson, Greeno, Kline, and Neves (1981) found that learn-

ing by example was an effective approach for learning algebra skills.

Computer interfaces incorporate many metaphors in order to make the computer more usable. Some of these metaphors will be discussed in this chapter. One of the most important metaphors, discussed in the next section, is the desktop metaphor.

THE DESKTOP METAPHOR

One of the most used metaphors and one of the most successful has been the desktop metaphor. To incorporate a metaphor, the user must be able to apply old, familiar knowledge to a new situation. The old knowledge must provide a reasonable match to the new knowledge. When discussing computer interfaces, of course, the new knowledge to be acquired is how to use the computer to perform tasks. Since many of the tasks performed on a computer were done, in the past, with paper and pen on a desk top, a natural metaphor was that of the desk top.

To illustrate how the desktop metaphor works, consider your own desk top without a computer on it. What are the essentials of a desk top for performing work? You would need some surface to work on which is fairly clear of other materials. You need something to write on, such as paper. You need something to write with, such as a pen or pencil. If you are organized, then you have some way to organize the papers you have already written on, for example, you might have a set of folders in which to store the papers.

You may have a filing cabinet or drawers in which to store the folders. The papers that you are working on currently may still be on the desk top. You need the ability to move the papers into a folder and to move the folders into a storage unit. You need to have the ability to move a paper to the work area so that work can be done easily on it. You may also have other items such as a calculator, a clock, an appointment book, or a calendar on the desk top within easy reach. Although not on the desk top, the garbage can beside the desk can perform the important function of helping you keep the desk top clear of useless material.

Most people are familiar with how to manipulate these items on the desk top, at least at this time. In a few years, maybe, computers will become so prevalent that the old familiar desktop manual operations will no longer be familiar, having been replaced by computer operations. Anyway, we can expect that most people would probably know how to perform these operations manually.

For a metaphor, we must try to find a match between the familiar information and the new information. Figure 10-1 shows how such a match could occur between the desk top and the computer display and operations. The computer screen is analogous to the desk top. In other words, the computer screen is the work area in which the objects can be placed and manipulated. The objects on the desk top can be depicted by icons which look like papers and folders. By moving the mouse so that its screen pointer is pointing to a paper sheet or a folder, the object can be selected; this is similar to pointing to an object with your finger or reaching to touch an object. Grasping an object has the analogous computer operation of pressing a mouse button while pointing to an object. With the button pressed, as the mouse is moved from position to position, the object on the screen is also moved. The user can arrange items on the desk top: paper sheets can be placed in folders, or sheets can be moved to the trash can so that they are thrown away. Folders can be opened by placing the mouse cursor on a corner of the folder and then pressing the mouse button (this is called a mouse click).

Analogous to a filing cabinet or, at least, a drawer within a filing cabinet, are the disks in which the folders and paper sheets (files) are stored permanently. A computer may have several hard disks, each representing a separate drawer. The floppy disks that can be inserted in the computer and then removed and stored outside are other examples of drawers. Figure 10-1 shows an example of two hard disks on the right of the screen: the internal disk is on the top and the external disk is below it. An icon of a diskette, inserted into the disk drive of the computer, is depicted below the external hard disk drive.

An important operation for the desktop metaphor is the direct manipulation of objects on the screen. This means that to perform a computer operation, the user does not have to go through a secondary operation but can manipulate an object directly. As an example, a folder may have to be identified by name. On a desk top, we would perform this operation by taking a pen or pencil and writing the name of the folder directly on the folder. This is a direct manipulation of the folder in the real world, an operation that we expect to be possible with real-world items. We should be able to do the same opera-

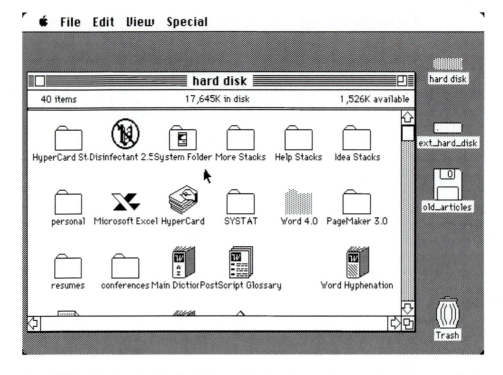

Figure 10-1. An example of a desktop metaphor used on a computer screen (from an Apple Macintosh). The contents of the hard disk are shown on the screen. Files are represented as icons and folders look like representations of folders. On the right, a hard disk, an external hard disk, and a diskette are represented on the screen. The trash can, for deleting files, is represented at the bottom right of the screen. At the upper left, the words are pull down menus which can be used for functions to be performed on the files and folders.

tion on the computer using the desktop metaphor. This is usually done by moving the mouse pointer to the tab in which the name of the folder usually appears (see Figure 10-2). The mouse button can then be clicked to initiate the action and the name can be typed in directly from the keyboard. As the keys are pressed, the user can see the result on the folder tab.

For computer interfaces not utilizing direct manipulation or the desktop metaphor, this folder naming operation would be indirect through the use of secondary operations. As an example, a menu item could be picked for entering the folder name. A cursor would then appear for where the typing could begin. The user would type in the folder name. When the ENTER key was hit, the name would then appear on the folder tab. This is indirect in that the place for entering the name is different from the position on the folder in which it will ultimately be placed. Since we do not do these kinds of operations on a desk top, to make the analogy to a computer completely sensible, we must not force the user to perform these indirect functions on the computer. (One could argue, however, that we could possibly write the name on a sticker and then trans-

(a)

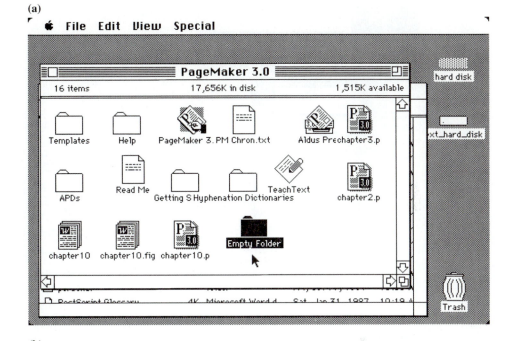

(b)

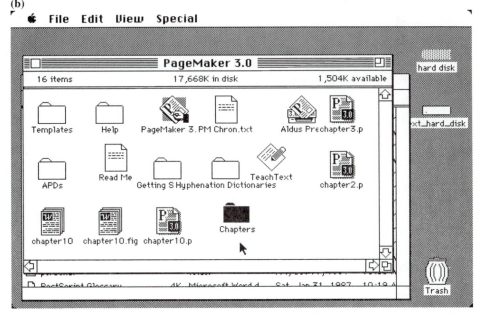

Figure 10-2. An example of entering the name of a folder using the desktop metaphor (from an Apple Macintosh). In (a), the empty folder has just been created by choosing a function from the "File" pull down menu. In (b), the folder name has been changed to "Chapters" by highlighting the words "Empty Folder" with the mouse and then typing in the new name.

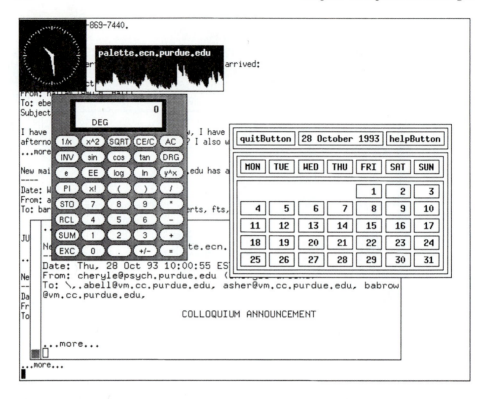

Figure 10-3. An expansion of the desktop metaphor for large screen displays. This screen has a calculator and an appointment book. It was created from the Motif window manager using the X Windows functions.

fer the sticker to the folder. If this was done on the computer, the interface would have to show clearly that this was a sticker being written on.)

Many of the large-screen workstations (19 inch and larger) have an environment in which more objects can be placed permanently on the screen, because of the larger work area. These screens usually include an analog clock in one corner of the display (see Figure 10-3). A calculator, designed to appear like a calculator by having the same shape and function as a real calculator, can also be put on the desk top. The calculator buttons are "pushed" by moving the mouse button to the button and clicking and, in addition, sometimes

the buttons can be activated by typing the digits from the keyboard. Some interfaces utilizing the desktop metaphor also have an appointment book connected to a calendar (see Figure 10-4). A date from a traditional-looking calendar can be clicked so that an appointment book, segmented by the half hour, appears on the screen. Appointments can be entered directly into the "book" at the appropriate time slot. Some even come with alarms which will display a message and sound a tone as the appointment time approaches. The entries can be accessed and changed at any time.

The desktop metaphor has been a very successful means for designers to increase the usability of the interface. A

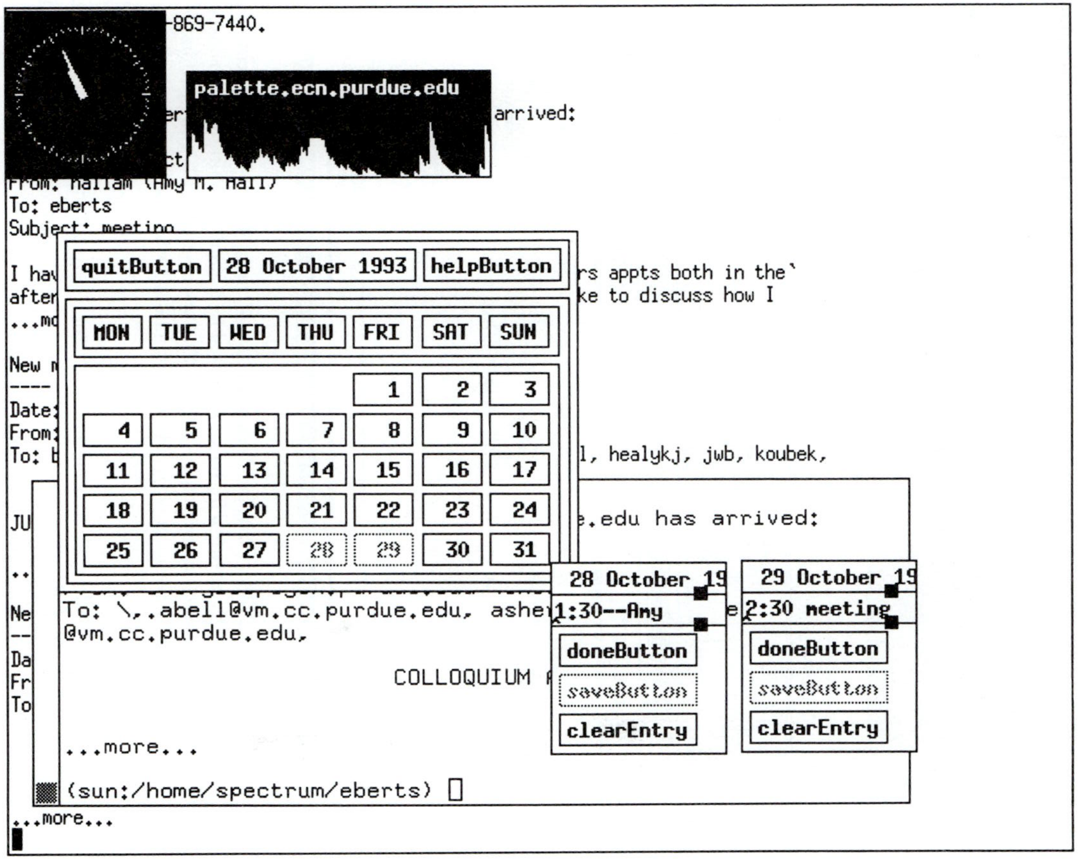

Figure 10-4.
An example of an appointment book from Motif. Notice how the calendar begins with Mondays on the left, which does not follow the analogy most users would expect.

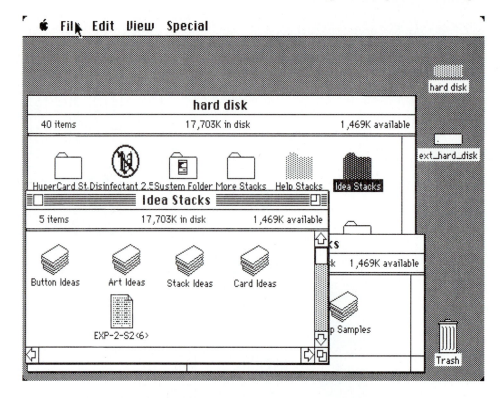

Figure 10-5. Folders can be stacked on top of each other. In the Macintosh interface, this is accomplished by having a folder represented by a window. Windows can obscure other windows to convey the stacking principle. Folders that are opened are highlighted in the window in which they are stored. The topmost window is designated by highlighting the border and by being on the top of the stack.

user must merely realize that the computer screen is like a desk top, and know how to perform some simple operations such as grasping and clicking, in order to know how to use many of the complete functions of the interface. The user would not have to know, therefore, specifically how to delete a file through formal training or through reading the manual. Instead, the user would just have to know that the trash can is where the file to be deleted must be placed, know how to grasp a file, and know how to move it to that location. This could be determined from prior knowledge that the user has of the functions of a

trash can. Certainly, features like the calculator or the appointment book would also be simple extensions of existing knowledge.

Consistent Use of the Metaphor

The designer of an interface must be careful to maintain the metaphor on the interface so that it is consistent. Sometimes this does not occur. The Apple Macintosh utilizes a desktop metaphor, but, in some cases, it is inconsistent (see Figure 10-5). As an example, the Macintosh interface always provides a representation of the

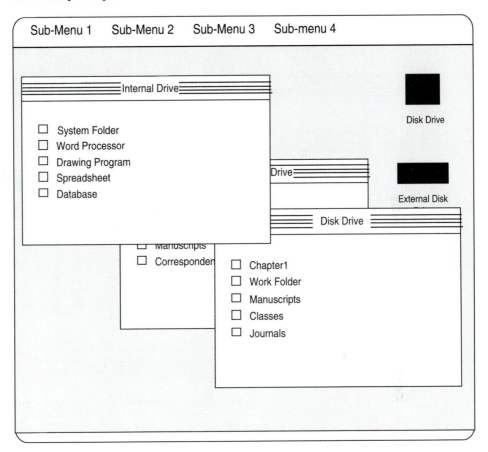

Figure 10-6. The stacking of folders on the desk top before the applications program was entered.

files in a folder or on a disk by using a windowing system. The contents of each folder will appear in a separate window. Windows can be overlapped so that only the topmost windows may be seen at any time. This is analogous to laying folders on a desk top and seeing only the topmost folder(s) completely, and only parts of other folders which may be underneath.

Applying the desktop metaphor, the user would expect that any folders stacked on the desk top would maintain their positions unless manipulated by the user. This does not always occur with the Macintosh operating system, however. In particular,

if the user has several folders stacked on the desk top (see Figure 10-6) and then performs an application, such as using the spreadsheet, once the application is finished the folders should have the same stacking arrangement as before the application. If the folders are from different storage devices, the ordering of the stacks may not be the same. When an application is finished, the Macintosh operating system restacks the folders as follows: folders off the internal hard disk, folders off any external hard disks, and then folders off any diskette. If a folder from the hard disk was originally on the top of the stack

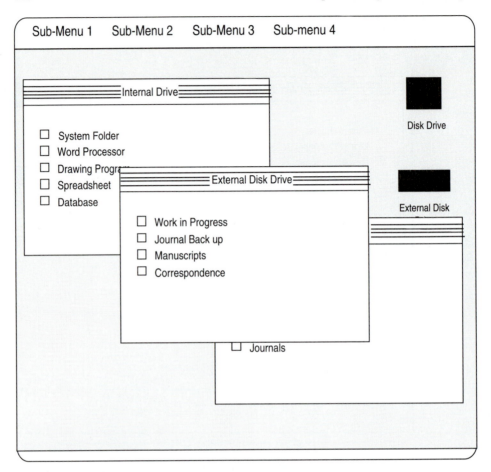

Figure 10-7. The stacking of folders on the desk top after the application program was exited. The stacking order has changed, due to restacking the folders disk by disk.

before the application was entered, this folder will now be on the bottom of the external disk and the diskette folders (see Figure 10-7). A user could predict the restacking by knowing how the Macintosh restacked the folders according to storage device; this is different from what could be expected if the desktop metaphor was used consistently.

Consistently applying the desktop metaphor for the Macintosh would require more memory and more code; the computer would have to store the overall place-

ment of the folders. The Macintosh system is used because the placement of folders is stored directly on the separate disks, instead of in a central location. The code would have to be changed to change the stacking procedure. If a metaphor is used, however, consistency is important and should be maintained even if it requires larger memory requirements and more computer programming code. Usability, maintained through consistent use of the metaphor, is more important than saving memory or code.

Metaphor Matches

One of the characteristics of a metaphor is that a perfect match never exists between the known task (such as the desk top) and the target task (such as the computer operations). A problem with using a metaphor is that for some operations no match will be found or the match will be clumsy. As an example, how would the computer operations for ejecting a disk from the computer be performed based upon the desktop metaphor? There is no analogous operation on the desk top itself. The only possibility would be to go to a filing cabinet and remove the drawer and place the drawer on the desk top. On one interface, however, ejecting the disk is performed by moving the disk icon to the trash can and then releasing the button. A novice, however, may be reluctant to "trash" the whole disk, thinking that all the files might be deleted.

Another problem for the desktop metaphor is that it cannot easily incorporate some of the features in interfaces which are now becoming prevalent. Many of the current interfaces include many of the tasks that a secretary may perform, such as keeping an appointment calendar, answering the phone, operating a fax machine, and using electronic mail (e-mail). If the metaphor is confined to a desk top, then, unless the desk top can accommodate the secretary, the metaphor will no longer work. Recently, the desktop metaphor has been incorporated into a more encompassing office or room metaphor.

In an office metaphor, different applications can be located in different rooms or areas of the office. The work that may be performed by a secretary, such as the examples listed above, could be located in an outer room. If these applications were to be performed, such as reading e-mail, then the user would move to the outer office by moving on the screen.

One of the interesting problems with using an office metaphor is how to navigate between the rooms. Researchers at Xerox (Clarkson, 1991) have been investigating this problem through an interface that they call "Rooms." They are investigating a virtual environment (see Chapter 11) in which the screen takes on the perspective of the visual scene as the user moves through it. As an example, picture yourself walking through a room in the physical world. As you move forward, far away objects become larger, and thus appear closer, and you can walk past the close objects so that they are no longer seen. When turning to the right, the objects that were in front of you are now on the left side in the periphery. When turning to the left, the objects in the front move to the right. This same kind of visual experience occurs in a virtual environment, except the images on the screen correspond to the view. When moving forward, the objects in front become larger; when moving to the right, the screen images move to the left; and when moving to the left, the screen images move to the right. Using this metaphor, if you know how to walk through the world, then you know how to navigate through the display.

In the Xerox Rooms interface, the user can "walk" through doors to get to the different rooms. Certain kinds of applications and data may be stored in certain rooms. As an example, you, as the user, may decide that you need an "Accounting" room to store spreadsheet applications and the files that go along with this application. To run this application, you would not have to find the spreadsheet on a list of files from a directory, but instead you would "walk" through the virtual environment to the "accounting" room and then perform this application. Performing a directory on the list of files would now become an obsolete and meaningless task.

The office or rooms metaphor can be expanded in many ways. Xerox has incorporated a "pocket" capability in their metaphor. Files or other sources of information can be placed in a pocket and then carried from room to room. Also, they introduced the concept of multiple doors. The front door is used in a normal way but the back door can be used to return to the room from which the user came.

OTHER INTERFACE METAPHORS

Most software packages use metaphors to make them more usable. In this section, some of the interfaces which use metaphors are discussed and illustrated. This section is divided into experimental investigations of metaphors and commercial packages using metaphors.

Experimental Investigations of Metaphors

One of the earliest attempts to use analogies for computer-based tasks was that of Mayer (1975) to teach computer programming skills to novices. In his experiments, Mayer told the subjects that computer input was similar to a ticket window, output was similar to a message pad, control structures were similar to a shopping list with a pointer, and computer memory was similar to an eight-space erasable blackboard. Analogies helped the user produce

programming code for novel tasks, that is, tasks different from those on which they were trained. Additionally, he found that the subjects with lower Student Aptitude Test (SAT) scores benefitted more than those with high SAT scores; the high scorers may use analogies naturally or may not need analogies to impose a structure on the information.

An experiment by Rumelhart and Norman (1981) highlights some of the advantages of metaphors in teaching novices about using the computer, but it also highlights some of the problems associated with the use of metaphors. In this experiment, a metaphor was used to teach novices how to use an editing system. The subjects were told first that the editor was analogous to a secretary, in that they give the secretary commands and text to type. This allowed the subjects to perform some of this task, but it caused a problem in that the subjects thought that the editor should be as intelligent as a secretary and be able to differentiate between the commands and text. To get around this problem, a second analogy, the tape recorder analogy, was used to indicate to the subjects that the editor is put into record mode and faithfully records everything until it is told to stop by issuing the appropriate command. This analogy was useful for solving the first problem but introduced another problem by not being able to account for the delete command. As a third analogy, the subjects were told that using the editor was similar to filing information in a filing cabinet, in that cards could be inserted or removed. A conclusion was that analogies could be useful for teaching novices about computer systems.

The above experiment can also be used to highlight the problem with analo-

TABLE 10-1
Standard metaphors used for interface designs (adapted from Carroll et al., 1988)

Application Area	Systems	Metaphor	Exploits Knowledge of
Word and text processing	WordStar, Word	Typewriting	typewriting, typing paper, keyboard
Advanced document composition (i.e., desktop publishing)	PageMaker, Etude, Star	Document	types of graphical text objects and their attributes, logical structure of documents
Idea organizers and outline systems	NoteCards, Maxthink	Outline	structure/decomposition of ideas often using further metaphors (index cards, frames)
Forms-based business applications	SBA, OBE, ALL-in-1	Business forms	codification of business activities in forms, organization of information, information items, report generation
Spreadsheets	VisiCalc, Lotus 1-2-3, Excel	Ledger sheet	matrix-structured numerical data
Object-oriented programming environments	Boxer, Rehearsal World, Alternate Reality Kit	Physical world	physical objects and systems, their attributes, appropriate actions
Drawing and painting	MacPaint, MacDraw, PC Paint, PC Draw	Paper, pens, and palettes	paintbrushes, pens, erasing, drawing
Operating environments for personal	Star, Macintosh, X Windows workstations	Desk top	office organization and work procedures
Database	QBE, OBE, DBase III, ALL-in-1	Table of data	matrix-management structured data: rows, columns

gies and metaphors: finding a perfect match between the old information and the new information may be difficult. If a perfect match is not found, then the user could inappropriately overextend the analogy as the subjects did when ascribing intelligence to the text editor. In using metaphors and analogies in the interface design, the designer must be careful that the user not need to learn too many metaphors. If they do, then the user has to remember which metaphor to apply in which situation, the extent of each of the metaphors, and how one metaphor may or may not apply in a certain situation.

Metaphors in Commercial Software Packages

Carroll, Mack, and Kellogg (1988) list many other computer operations in which metaphors and analogies are used. Some of these metaphors are listed in Table 10-1; the list has been extended from the

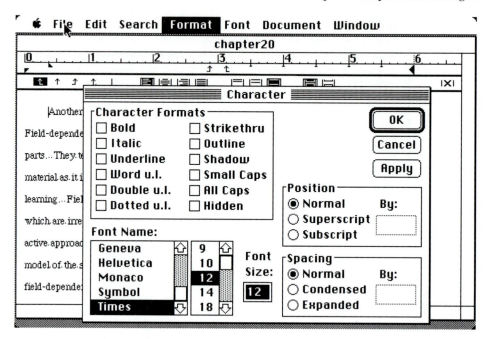

Figure 10-8. In a word processing system, such as Microsoft Word, many of the page setup capabilities of the typewriter are used analogously on the computer.

Carroll et al. list to include other applications. Many of the word processors use the metaphor of typewriting, typing paper, and the keyboard to make it easier to understand text editing. This metaphor is a bit awkward for some aspects of text editing. In Chapter 14, the differences between using space keys with typewriters and computers are discussed; the two are not equivalent and cause errors for novice computer users. Many other parts of the metaphor are maintained. The concept of tab stops and tabbing are the same. The idea of changing fonts and the point size of the characters is maintained (see Figure 10-8). Of course, computer text editing allows the user capabilities, such as spell-checking, beyond that which can be performed on a normal, noncomputerized typewriter.

Desktop publishing makes extensive use of the metaphor of cutting and pasting pictures and text to a page layout. In fact, in PageMaker, many terms, such as leading (pronounced "ledding"), which may only be known in the publishing business, are used to preserve the metaphor. Leading refers to the spacing between the lines and is derived from the old typesetting machines which had different sizes of lead to use for the line spacing. It is even more confusing if the user pronounces it as "leeding" and thinks that it may mean the spaces that are in front of, or "lead," the first line of a paragraph. If a user of PageMaker tries to determine how to vary line spacing by looking through the menus, trouble could occur if the term "leading" is not recognized (see Figure 10-9). Preserving the typesetting metaphor is admirable, but it presupposes that the user has more knowledge than may be realistic.

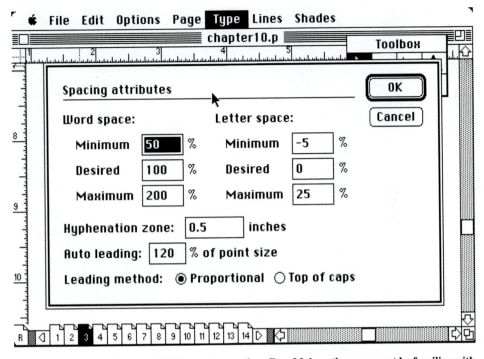

Figure 10-9. In a desktop publishing system such as PageMaker, the user must be familiar with typesetting terms in order to understand the metaphor.

For the next application area, idea organizers and outline systems, the computer can be used similarly to index cards or an outline on a piece of paper. For real index cards, a person may write on the card and then place the card in a file to be quickly accessed. NoteCards uses this metaphor for storing and organizing information on a computer (see Figure 10-10).

For certain business applications, the screen format will be designed to look like standard business forms so that the user need only move to the area on the form and input the appropriate information. Since people are so used to filling in forms, having to do this task more than we would probably like to, the business form as a metaphor is easy to understand and use. These business forms allow the user to move to different locations on the form and fill in the information as instructed (see Figure 10-11). A computerized business form can be better than a paper business form if the computer performs simple checks on the inputted information. As an example, if a box in the form is used for filling in a Social Security number, the computer can check to determine if all the characters are digits and whether or not nine digits are entered.

Similar to the business form applications, spreadsheets use the metaphor of a ledger to structure the numerical data in matrix form. A big advantage of spreadsheets is that numbers can be entered in a column, as an example, and then all the numbers in the column can be summed. If a number is changed in the column, then the sum will change automatically. As on a ledger, numbers in a certain location in

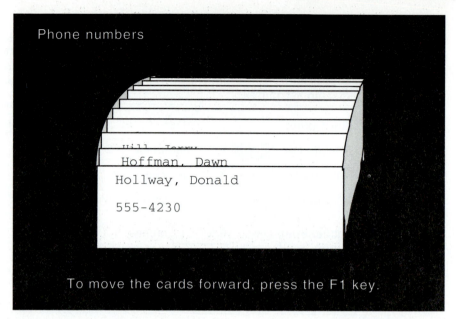

Figure 10-10. NoteCards uses the metaphor of index cards to store and organize information.

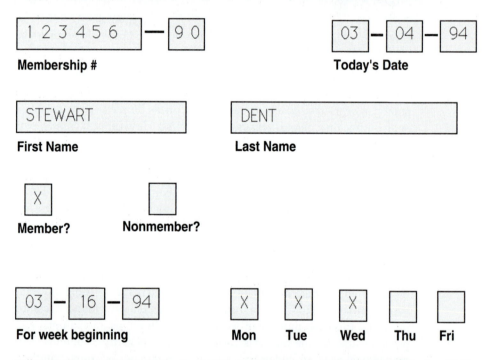

Figure 10-11. An example of using the metaphor of a business form for a computer display. Fields (the darkened boxes) can be used for entering information. Xs are used to choose among the possibilities.

| File | Edit | Formula | Format | Data | Options | Macro | Window |

| C13 | | =(C12*D4)+C12 |

pension

	A	B	C	D	E	F
3			Current balance	54494.44		
4			Growth salary	0.06		
5			Current monthly	675		
6			# months/year	12		
7			interest	0.11		
8						
9		Year	Yearly contribution	Accumulation	Salary	
10	1	1990	$8,586.00	$72,187.04	$50,800.00	
11	2	1991	$9,101.16	$88,713.61	$54,200.00	
12	3	1992	$9,647.23	$107,573.27	$57,452.00	
13	4	1993	$10,226.06	$129,053.56	$60,899.12	
14	5	1994	$10,839.63	$153,475.52	$64,553.07	
15	6	1995	$11,490.00	$181,197.45	$68,426.25	
16	7	1996	$12,179.41	$212,619.18	$72,531.83	
17	8	1997	$12,910.17	$248,186.69	$76,883.74	
18	9	1998	$13,684.78	$288,397.39	$81,496.76	
19	10	1999	$14,505.87	$333,805.89	$86,386.57	
20	11	2000	$15,376.22	$385,030.40	$91,569.76	
21	12	2001	$16,298.79	$442,759.96	$97,063.95	

Figure 10-12. An example of a computerized spreadsheet using the metaphor of a ledger.

the matrix can be used in other calculations elsewhere on the spreadsheet. The metaphor between the ledger and the computerized spreadsheet works when entering and deleting numbers. It does not work as well, however, when the user has to set up equations to calculate series of numbers. Figure 10-12 shows an example of the ledger metaphor used in a computerized spreadsheet.

Object-oriented programming enables programming to be easier by endowing the parts of a programming language with attributes. Just as objects in the physical world have certain attributes, so do the parts of the programming language. As an example, a chair is an object in the physical world. All chairs have certain features, such as legs, possibly arms, and most likely a back. A chair is a kind of furniture, and so it carries over the characteristics that we know about furniture in general. Object-oriented programming uses a similar system. The widgets discussed in Chapter 2 are an example of objects in an object-oriented programming environment. As an example, a push button widget has certain features such as a button, a label on a button, and then an action in the callback routine once the button is pushed or clicked by the mouse. The push button will be part of another widget, such as a form widget, and so it would take on a parent-child relationship with this widget. In reviewing some of the other widgets in Chapter 2, the extent of the use of metaphors in object-oriented programming can be seen.

Drawing and painting programs use, naturally, the metaphor of drawing or painting on paper with pencil, pen, or paintbrush. The metaphor is fairly accurate for most painting programs in that the user can pick up a brush by moving the mouse

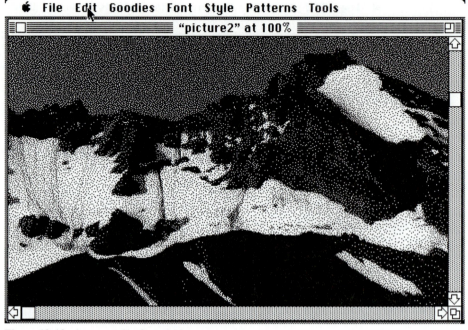

Figure 10-13. An example of a painting program.

cursor to a brush icon and holding down the mouse button (see Figure 10-13). If color is available, the user can choose a color similar to dipping the paint brush in the paint. An advantage of the computerized paint program is that the paint color can be easily changed. The drawing programs do not follow as closely the metaphor of drawing on paper. Typically, to draw a rectangle on the computer screen, the user will click on a rectangle icon, move the mouse to a starting position, hold the mouse button down, move to the position for the opposite corner of the rectangle, and then release the mouse button (see Figure 10-14). The form of the rectangle is shown on the screen as the mouse is moved between the mouse button push and release. With paper, the operation is not quite so simple. We would have to use a ruler, draw along the straight edge, and then measure where the

rest of the lines would be. The drawing programs also allow objects to be moved around easily, an operation that cannot be performed with a single sheet of paper.

The last two application areas, the desktop metaphor and databases, have been discussed or will be discussed elsewhere in this book. The desktop metaphor has been discussed previously in this chapter; the database application area will be discussed in Chapter 24.

THEORY FOR USING METAPHORS

To help clarify the effectiveness and ineffectiveness of metaphors for learning how to use the computer or to perform computerized tasks, Carroll et al. (1988) have formulated a theory of metaphor use. In the theory, three stages in metaphorical reasoning are defined: instantiation, elaboration, and consolidation.

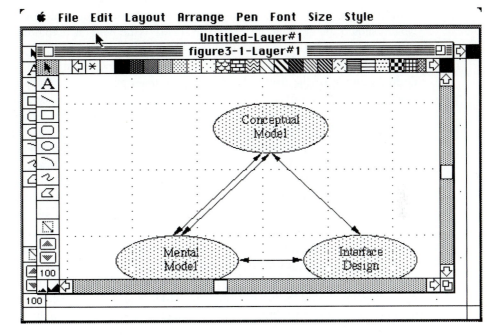

Figure 10-14. An example of a drawing program.

Instantiation is the recognition or retrieval of something known which can be targeted to the new computerized domain. In an interface design, screen features or words should be conveyed to the user so that the appropriate metaphor can be instantiated. Sometimes this is done through the use of icons or pictures. In the desktop metaphor, icons of folders would assist the instantiation of a desk top for the user.

The second stage, elaboration, involves the generation of inferences about how an instantiated source can be applied to the target domain. An important aspect of this stage is exploration of possible ways, based upon prior knowledge, in which the metaphor could be applied. This stage is also used to identify the mismatches between the source domain and the target domain.

The third stage, consolidation, con-solidates the elaborated metaphor into a mental model of the target domain itself. At this stage, the new mental model is not the same as the original metaphor; it is a new entity which accounts for the matches and mismatches between the source and the target domains.

Based upon the above stages, Carroll et al. (1988) suggest that four steps are involved when designing interfaces using metaphors: the identification of candidate metaphors; the detailing of the metaphor/software matches with respect to representative user scenarios; the identification of likely mismatches and their implications; and the identification of design strategies to help users manage mismatches. Application of the desktop metaphor to these four steps can help to illustrate this design process.

The first step is the identification of candidate metaphors. Carroll and Thomas

(1982) suggest some general features which should be present in candidate metaphors. First, they suggest that the emotional tone of the metaphor match the desired attitude of the user. As an example, they say that you would not want to use the metaphor of a funeral, but may instead choose a parade metaphor. Second, if more than one metaphor is needed to explain a system, then the metaphors should not be too dissimilar; a similar theme should form the basis for all the metaphors. As an example, a common theme for several metaphors could be office machines; office machines should not be combined with analogies to the "human like a machine," if at all possible. Third, the metaphor should be as exciting as possible, especially for routine work. As an example, they suggest that some of the characteristics of games could be incorporated into the metaphor so that the interface becomes dynamic and actively involves the user in the scenario. Other researchers, such as Carroll (1982) and Malone (1981), have also explored how to incorporate games into the interface.

An important feature of candidate metaphors, emphasized by Carroll, Thomas, and Malhotra (1980), is the spatial nature of the metaphor. In an experiment, they tested people on solving problems by using a spatial office layout metaphor or using a temporal scheduling problem with no spatial referent. Results showed that people using the spatial metaphor were much better at solving the problem than those using the temporal layout. When examining the metaphors from Table 10-1 and thinking about other metaphors, it is difficult to find any metaphors which are not spatial in nature. Perhaps the capability of manipulating an image is important

for understanding analogous situations. This issue will be explored further in Chapter 11.

The candidate metaphors depend on the main purpose of the application program. Candidates for an operating system will be different from candidates for a desktop publishing system. The desktop metaphor is a prime candidate because it captures the manipulation of documents (stacking and moving), the work that must be performed on a document (writing and calculations), and the storing of documents (use of file cabinets and drawers). Other possible candidates are to use the office metaphor which was discussed previously. This would be useful if the tasks require some kind of intelligence, and the computer is capable of performing intelligent tasks. For this metaphor, each office area would house resident experts who could be called upon to help process the information. A final metaphor which could be used could be a factory metaphor. In this case, the information is manufactured; it is changed into the desired form. In the following discussion, two of the scenarios, the desktop and the office metaphor, will be discussed. Three of the typical applications—text editing, spreadsheets, and drawing—will be considered in those two contexts.

The second step is to detail the metaphor/software representations for certain user scenarios. For the desk top, the metaphor specifies that program applications will occur if the application is placed in the work area of your desk. Thus, on the computer, this translates into accessing the appropriate application file on the desk top and then placing it in the work area by double clicking the mouse on the application. Thus, text editing, using the spreadsheet, and drawing can occur by locating the file on the desk top and activating the application through mouse clicks. Finding the appropriate application file occurs by visually searching the files on the desk top and possibly opening and closing file folders to search in them.

For the office metaphor, navigation occurs by walking through the office building. Each of the application programs may be located in different rooms. The text editing application may be in a secretary's office; the spreadsheet may be in an accountant's office; and the drawing program may be in a graphic artist's office. One of the benefits of this metaphor is that another application, such as a painting program, can also be located in the graphic artist's office.

The third step is to identify some of the mismatches that are likely to occur. For the desktop metaphor, a mismatch will occur when all the items on the desk top will not fit on the desk window. Typically, if this occurs, the user must scroll through the items on the window in order to locate the file. This really has no analogous function on an actual desk top. The problem with ejecting diskettes has already been discussed. A diskette seems to be very specific to a computer, with no analogous feature on the desk top.

The office metaphor solves the mismatch problem of scrolling when too many files are available. For Xerox's Rooms, at least, all items are located by "walking" and searching. Many different files can be located in the different rooms, and so the area of the usable screen is no longer limited to just those items that can be fit on the screen. Walking around and finding items is a process which fits in the metaphor. The office metaphor also seems to

have a problem with an equivalent action to ejecting the diskette. With a diskette in the drive, this would allow the materials on the diskette to be placed in the appropriate locations of the rooms. When the diskette is removed, all those materials in all the different rooms will disappear simultaneously. If a user "walks" to the room expecting to find the material which was on the diskette, this cannot be easily explained, in the context of the metaphor, when the materials are missing due to the diskette having been removed.

The final step is to design some interface strategies to help the user manage the mismatches. These strategies are typically included in the documentation for the current systems by indicating how the interface operations may not fit into the metaphor. In the future, these strategies need to be designed as on-line help so that the kinds of mismatches and problems may be averted before they are encountered.

This approach addresses directly the problem with metaphor mismatches and courses of action to minimize the seriousness of the problem. Carroll et al. claim that, if designed properly, metaphor mismatches can actually help the user gain greater insight into the computerized task by allowing the user to understand what can and cannot be done, although no experimental evidence is provided for this. The interface must be designed, however, so that the mismatch is isolable, and a salient course of action should be available. The user must also be provided with assurances, through the design, that explorations of metaphor extensions, and therefore identification of mismatches, can occur without penalty. This can be achieved through the use of "undo" commands or by not having the computer respond to actions which are not possible.

SUMMARY

The advantage of metaphors is that they are useful for allowing novices to quickly learn the computer system through the application of a source domain to the target domain (the computer). The disadvantage is that mismatches between the source and the target are inevitable. During the elaboration stage, the user must feel free to explore and identify possible mismatches. If this is allowed, then the user can elaborate the initial metaphor into a new and accurate mental model of the computerized task.

Most of the discussion in this chapter has been about how the metaphors and analogies can be used to guide the display of information. Analogies are also useful in other ways. One use is in generating design ideas before the ideas are implemented in the computer display (MacLean, Bellotti, Young, and Moran, 1991). MacLean et al. present many examples where innovative design ideas came as a result of discussing extensions of the metaphor or analogy. The analogy provided the designers with creative ideas which probably could not be generated without considering the analogy. In some cases, implementing the analogy on the display may be secondary to the role analogies play in helping to generate ideas.

Metaphors are most effective if they are spatial in nature, that is, if they utilize graphics for their instantiation. The next chapter discusses the use of graphics in interface designs.

QUESTIONS

1. Find examples of how a metaphor has been applied inconsistently to an interface.

2. Try to think of a better way to eject a disk rather than moving the diskette icon to the trash can. What would be an analogous operation on the desk top?

3. Use the office metaphor to explain how the following tasks would be represented on the display:

    a. Deleting a file
    b. Copying a file
    c. Changing the name of a file
    d. Reading e-mail
    e. Sending e-mail
    f. Addressing and sending a fax

4. Think about the role of menu displays on computers and the analogous role of menus in restaurants. In many cases, these roles are very different. How can menu displays on a computer be improved by implementing some of the ideas from actual menu use in restaurants? You may want to compare some of your ideas to those generated by Norman and Chin (1989).

CHAPTER **11**

SPATIAL REASONING AND GRAPHICS

INTRODUCTION

In an interesting article, Ferguson (1977), a professor of history, states that: "Pyramids, cathedrals, and rockets exist not because of geometry, theory of structures, or thermodynamics, but because they were first a picture—literally a vision—in the minds of those who built them." He goes on to say that in the sixteenth and seventeenth centuries many of the most influential thinkers encouraged the visual nonverbal study of machines as a backlash against some of the wordy books being studied at that time. Ferguson presents many examples of how scientists and engineers have used mental pictures in their discoveries: for example Galton's claim that he only thought using visual images, and Einstein's claim that he rarely thought in words at all. Ferguson's conclusion is that "Much of the creative thought of the designers of our technological world is nonverbal, not easily reducible to words."

If much of the creative thought is nonverbal, how do we provide information to designers to support creativity? To be compatible with this creative thought, the display of information on a computer screen should be spatial, or make use of computer graphics. It is possible that the computer, which has been so adept at processing text and symbols, can now be used to enhance nonverbal processing of information. One of the main goals of this chapter is to determine how computer graphics can be used, and how they are sometimes misused, in the display of information on a computer screen.

Graphics and spatial representations exhibit many similarities to the metaphors and analogies reviewed in the preceding chapter. In almost all cases, the metaphors and analogies provide a spatial representation of the information which can be mapped easily to graphical displays. The desktop metaphor, cutting and pasting for desktop publishing, business forms, and spreadsheets can be depicted graphically on the screen, and the metaphors help in specifying the information organization. In other cases, though, spatial representations can be used without an organizing metaphor. Organizing the graphics by depicting the physical representation of the system or operation is one technique that is used. An interesting possibility is to use graphics for those tasks not usually considered spatial in nature.

Some experiments indicate that having the ability to make use of the manipulation of spatial information may make human-computer interaction tasks easier to perform. In particular, Gomez, Egan, and Bowers (1986) found that those people who scored high on spatial ability tests could learn how to use line and screen editors better than those who scored low on spatial ability. In another area, Molzberger (1983) found that computer programmers often form a mental picture of the program before they actually start to develop the code. Supposedly, high spatial ability would also make this task easier.

Many times, an assumption is made that graphics will always make a task easier. As can be seen from a quick review, this is not the case. Tullis (1981) and Bury and Boyle (1982) have demonstrated that graphics are better than text display on some measures; however, the Stern (1984) and Power, Lashley, Sanchez, and Shneiderman (1984) experiments showed that other presentation modes such as text can be better. Merely presenting information in a graphics display will not enhance user performance. The graphics have to be chosen carefully.

The decision to use or not to use graphics depends on task characteristics. If the operator is looking for trends in a set of data, then graphics may be appropriate. If the operator needs to perform precise calculations, then text in tabular form may be most appropriate. This has been demonstrated by Benbasat, Dexter, and Todd (1986) in a marketing problem. In another experiment (Umanath and Scamell, 1987), information was presented in a bar chart or in table form. If the task involved a spatial component, such as the pattern of the results, then the graphics bar chart display was better. If the task involved textual information, such as the recall of particular facts, then the graphics display held no advantage over the textual table presentation.

The use of graphics in metaphors and analogies has been discussed in the previous chapter. In this chapter, other applications of graphics will be discussed: the use of graphics in direct manipulation displays, the use of graphics to make the invisible visible, use of graphics for representing physical systems, and some investigations of using graphics for nonspatial or abstract knowledge. In addition, the kinds of tasks and situations in which graphics are used appropriately will be discussed.

DIRECT MANIPULATION DISPLAYS

Direct manipulation displays are an important application of the use of graphics and spatial reasoning. Many of the most successful commercial software and computer products have been based upon direct manipulation display ideas: full-screen editors (Word, WordStar, etc.), spreadsheets (VisiCalc, Lotus 1-2-3, and Excel), and computer operating systems (Xerox Star and Apple Macintosh). The windowing techniques used by many workstations, such as X Windows and DECWindows, also utilize ideas from direct manipulation displays.

Merely having graphics displayed on the screen is inadequate to achieve a feeling of direct manipulation, though. As with other applications of graphics, the graphics must be placed into an input and output interaction environment which fully utilizes its possibilities. It is important that the graphics be combined with input devices and appropriate software design to allow the user to have a feeling of directly manipulating objects on the screen. Shneiderman is generally credited with coining the term direct manipulation, and he says that these kinds of displays have the following characteristics (Shneiderman, 1987):

- continuous representation of the objects and actions of interest

- physical actions or labeled button presses instead of complex syntax

- rapid incremental reversible operations whose impact on the object of interest is immediately visible

An Example of Direct Manipulation Displays

Probably the best way to illustrate the differences between direct manipulation displays and command-based displays is to consider an example. The following example is from research performed on interacting with databases by Eberts and Bittianda (1993). Database applications are discussed in some detail in Chapter 24. Database retrievals can be very difficult because the user must have a good knowledge of the data and the commands to retrieve that data. Often the database retrieval will require the use of complex syntax. The user often must have some knowledge of logical operators such as AND, OR, and NOT.

As an illustration of the difficulty of the syntax, consider the following database retrieval problem:

Find the names and respective cities of all those projects that have a name starting with an alphabet letter between "B" and "Q."

To perform this task using a command-based interface (for an example, see Figure 11-1), the user would determine that the query concerns the "Projects" relation and that the fields to be output are jname (name), for the name of the project, and jcity (city), for the city of the project. For the interface, the user would type

Retrieve unique (Projects.jname, Projects.jcity)

at the bottom of the display in order to retrieve the appropriate fields. Then on the next line, the user would type

where Projects.jname = "[B-Q]"

to restrict the project names to only those between B and Q. If any part of the syntax is wrong, such as leaving out parentheses or using the wrong kinds of parentheses, then the computer will not accept the entry. If the designation of the fields is wrong, then the computer will perform the wrong search and the user may get erroneous information.

The same task can be performed using a direct manipulation display. In this display for database retrievals (see Figure 11-2), graphics are used for representing the structure of the information and a mouse along with the keyboard are used for manipulating the data. The metaphor of a filing cabinet can be used for organizing the database concepts and for organizing the graphical display. The metaphorical relationships between the filing cabinet and the database are as follows: the cabinet is analogous to the complete data structure of the database; the drawers in the cabinet are analogous to the broader divisions of data structures; the folders are analogous to the actual data sets; and the sheets of paper in each file are analogous to the records in the data sets.

For the direct manipulation interface, using the same problem as that described above, the mouse would be moved to point to the Parts drawer and then clicked to open the drawer (see Figure 11-3). As soon as the mouse is clicked, folders appear on the desk corresponding to jname, jcity, and jpart. The user would point and click with the mouse on jname and jcity.

```
┌─────────────────────────────────────────────────────────────────┐
│                    DATA RETRIEVAL SYSTEM                          │
│                                                                   │
│                         ┌──────────────┐  ┌──────────────┐        │
│                         │     View     │  │     Exit     │        │
│                         └──────────────┘  └──────────────┘        │
│            ┌──────────────────────────────────────────────┐      │
│            │                  THE  DESK                     │      │
│            │                                                │      │
│            │                                                │      │
│            │                                                │      │
│            │                                                │      │
│            │                                                │      │
│            │                                                │      │
│            │                                                │      │
│            │                                                │      │
│            │                                                │      │
│            │                                                │      │
│            │                                                │      │
│            │                                                │      │
│            │                                                │      │
│            │                                                │      │
│            │                                                │      │
│            │                                                │      │
│            └──────────────────────────────────────────────┘      │
│                         Query  Command                            │
├───────────────────────────────────────────────────────────────  │
│  Retrieve unique (Projects.jname, Projects.jcity)                 │
├───────────────────────────────────────────────────────────────  │
│  where Projects.jname = "[B-Q]"                                   │
└─────────────────────────────────────────────────────────────────┘
```

Figure 11-1. An example of a database retrieval problem using a command-based display.

These folders would then immediately be highlighted by a change in shading (see Figure 11-4). Finally, the mouse would be moved to the fill-in area of the jname folder and the user would type "[B-Q]". This is similar to writing with a pen or pencil on the folder (see Figure 11-5).

This direct manipulation display has the characteristics listed earlier from Shneiderman (1987). By placing the drawers and folders on the screen, this enables a continuous representation of the objects and actions of interest. Much of the difficult syntax is removed by allowing button clicks on the drawers and folders, and by allowing physical actions such as writing directly on the folder. Probably most important, the impact on the object of

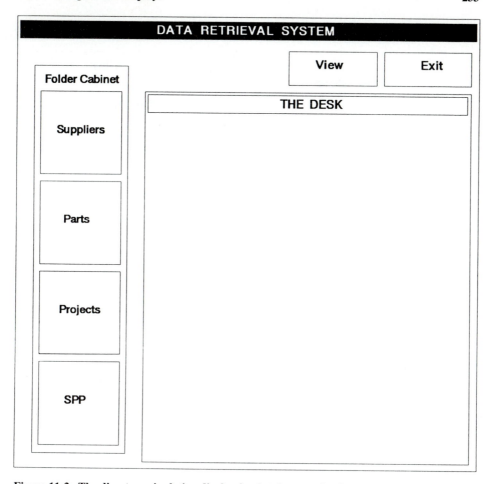

Figure 11-2. The direct manipulation display for database retrievals.

interest is immediately visible in that the drawers are opened immediately, the folders are placed immediately on the screen, and the user can see directly how the fields are limited by writing the limitations on the relevant folder.

Other Direct Manipulation Display Examples

The first direct manipulation display, although this term was not used at that time, is generally credited to be the Sketchpad by Sutherland (1963). In that early appli-

cation, the goal was for the user to converse with the computer not through textual commands but through graphics-based line drawings. The lag between this early implementation of some of the direct manipulation ideas and later applications was due to hardware constraints. Direct manipulation requires much memory and sophisticated graphics usually performed on bit-mapped displays. These hardware constraints were not overcome at a reasonable cost until the early 1980s.

Shneiderman lists several other examples of direct manipulation displays

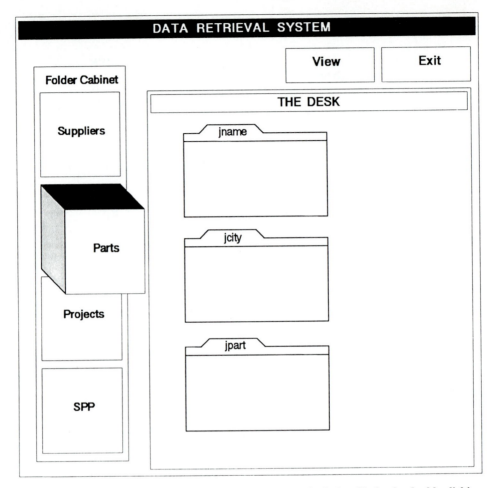

Figure 11-3. The Parts drawer is opened on the direct manipulation display by double clicking on the drawer.

that were explored by him and his colleagues. For addresses, a Rolodex-type display was designed so that the addresses appeared to be on cards on the screen. The cards were searched by moving a joystick which corresponded to a person thumbing through the cards as the cards rotate in a circle. Card searching and maintenance could be performed by displaying a graphics representation of a card and then searching through each card again using a joystick. Other examples include full-

page display editors often referred to as WYSIWYG (What You See Is What You Get) displays wherein changes are made directly to a document and these changes are seen immediately. Spreadsheets, such as Excel, VisiCalc, and Lotus 1-2-3, have many of the same characteristics as the WYSIWYG display editors. Video games, which are highly interactive, are another example of direct manipulation displays, and the popularity of these games is an indication of how other kinds of direct

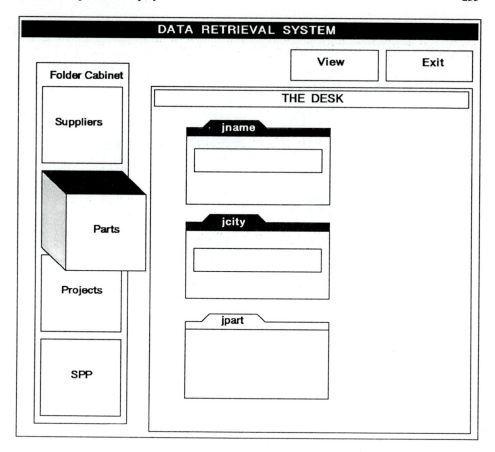

Figure 11-4. The appropriate folders are clicked and opened.

manipulation interfaces can even be fun to use. In computer-aided design (CAD) systems, the designer directly draws and manipulates objects on the screen. The Apple Macintosh and Xerox Star interfaces are examples of direct manipulation displays for computer operating systems. Shneiderman (1987) provides an example of how the command-based DOS operating system can be changed to a direct manipulation interface. Other examples, such as STEAMER and Rasmussen's work on process control displays, are discussed later in this chapter.

Why Are Direct Manipulation Interfaces Successful?

What are the possible reasons for the success of direct manipulation interfaces? One of the premises of the cognitive approach is that if interface designers know how people think then interfaces can be designed to be compatible with those ways of thinking. This applies to direct manipulation interfaces. As discussed in the Cognitive Approaches section of Chapter 3, people have an ability to think in terms of visual images and to manipulate those

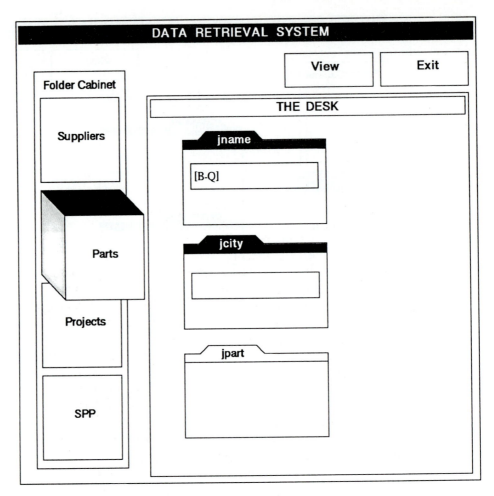

Figure 11-5. The mouse is moved to the fill-in area of the folder where the database items are limited to the letters listed.

images in the head. Several examples of those manipulations were provided. Direct manipulation displays perform similar functions, only this time the objects to be manipulated are on the screen instead of in the head. Hutchins, Hollan, and Norman (1986) make a similar statement in their claim that direct manipulation displays are in a form that directly supports our normal way of thinking and amplifies our knowledge of the domain. Shneiderman (1987) also points to the importance of spatial manipulations for problem solving in general.

Hutchins et al. (1986) claim also that a direct manipulation display is no longer recognized as an interface. Instead, the user feels as if she or he is interacting directly with the domain and, thus, directly engaging the problem of interest. The user no longer has to worry about artificial means of performing a task, through the syntax of commands, but can deal directly with the problem to be solved.

Shneiderman (1987) bases the success of direct manipulation displays on his syntactic/semantic model. Syntactic knowledge is the device-dependent information about the computer system. The user must remember the name and form of the command, such as DIR to perform a directory, or using the ESCAPE key to get out of an insert mode. These kinds of commands are dependent on the computer and the application. Some applications extensively use function keys which may have different uses in different applications. Some operating systems may use DIR for directory, others may use LS, and still others may allow both. In many cases, the syntactical knowledge appears to be arbitrary to the novice user; it is difficult to understand, and because of the need to memorize this kind of knowledge, it is easily forgotten.

Semantic knowledge is general knowledge about how the computer system works. Shneiderman (1987) claims that it is hierarchical in structure. It is another way to understand the structure of computer interaction which will be described in other terms in succeeding chapters. The GOMS model (Card et al., 1983) (see Chapter 14) has levels corresponding to the operators, methods, and goals. Or, using this model, human-computer interaction can be explained in terms of the unit tasks. The NGOMSL model (Kieras, 1988) (see Chapter 15) emphasized the hierarchical structure of the goals in relation to the methods and the steps in a method. Shneiderman (1987) says that semantic knowledge is composed of computer concepts which include objects and actions. Objects are the items that can be manipulated. Actions are the goals, methods, and operators which can be used to manipulate those objects. Since this kind of semantic knowledge is general, it can be transferred to other computer systems, is highly organized, and is relatively easy to remember and maintain in memory.

Since having computer interfaces that utilize semantic knowledge rather than requiring much syntactic knowledge is desirable, the success and ease of use of direct manipulation displays can be understood in this context (Shneiderman, 1987). Direct manipulation displays engage the computer objects and actions directly. The objects are displayed directly on the screen. Each action produces a comprehensible result which can be seen immediately on the screen. There is no need to remember seemingly arbitrary syntactic rules because this kind of knowledge is used rarely.

The Benefits and Problems of Direct Manipulation Displays

Shneiderman (1987) claims that direct manipulation displays have the following benefits:

- Novices can learn basic functionality quickly, usually through a demonstration by a more experienced user.

- Experts can work rapidly to carry out a wide range of tasks, even defining new functions and features.

- Knowledgeable intermittent users can retain operational concepts.

- Error messages are rarely needed.

- Users can immediately see if their actions are furthering their goals, and, if not, they can simply change the direction of their activity.

- Users experience less anxiety because the system is comprehensible and because actions are so easily reversible.

- Users gain confidence and mastery because they are the initiators of action, they feel in control, and the system responses are predictable.

Hutchins et al. (1986) dispute the claim that experts would be able to perform tasks faster on direct manipulation displays than with command-based displays because of the long amounts of time needed to manipulate a mouse, which is usually the preferred input device for direct manipulation displays. No empirical evidence, though, was offered for this statement. Ziegler and Faehnrich (1988) have reviewed the empirical evidence for direct manipulation displays when compared to command-based displays and found two kinds of differences between the interfaces in initial use: direct manipulation displays were executed faster for complex tasks and after experience; and for most tasks, subjects preferred the direct manipulation display over the others.

Collecting empirical results for direct manipulation displays is difficult. Comparing performance differences across two or more interface designs is also difficult. With different interfaces, the predicted execution times are different and, thus, hard to compare (see the question at the end of Chapter 13 for applying the Keystrokes Model to predicting execution times for the two kinds of interface). Generally, if the command-based interface requires many keystrokes, then the predicted execution time would be higher than for a mouse-based display which just requires pointing. Matching the pointing and clicking with the keystrokes to ensure equivalent execution times would be very difficult. The results are confounded if nonequivalent predicted execution times are used.

One way to get around this problem is to ask the users their preferences for the displays. In this way, responses will not be confounded with predicted performance times. User preference responses are also problematic, however, especially when comparing a new technology, such as direct manipulation displays, to older technologies, such as command-based interfaces. Determining what aspects of the task the users are responding to is a challenge. If the users know that the direct manipulation interface is the newer design, with fancier graphics and more expensive equipment, then they may be responding to these aspects of the task instead of any overall preference for use. On the other hand, some users may prefer the older familiar designs, such as the command-based interfaces, merely because they have more experience with them. Different users may base their judgments on novelty or familiarity, which would increase the variance of the responses, further increasing the difficulty of interpreting preference results.

Shneiderman (1987) mentions some of the other potential problems for direct manipulation displays. One of the main problems is understanding the meaning of the graphics representations. The picture of an object, using an iconic representation, may have several meanings or ambiguous meanings. On the other hand, a verbal description may not be so vague. In some cases, the graphics representation may even be misleading. Some of these problems were discussed in the previous chapter when analyzing metaphors and analogies. Since most direct manipulation displays utilize metaphors, the same problems apply for direct manipulation displays.

OTHER APPLICATIONS FOR GRAPHICS

Graphics have been used in many other kinds of applications. One of the problems with using graphics is knowing when and how to use them. The next sections survey several ways in which graphics have been implemented successfully.

Graphics for Information Organization

One of the uses for graphics in human-computer interaction tasks is in the organization of information. The pictures represented by the graphics can provide a natural way to organize the material. If the same information could be organized without the use of graphics, then similar advantages would be seen. In many cases, well-organized computer displays using text in table form show many of the same advantages as do graphics (Dickson, DeSanctis, and McBride, 1986).

As an example of the use of graphics to organize information, consider the following experiment. Tullis (1981) was designing interface displays so that the operators could quickly and accurately

diagnose problems on telephone lines. Four different kinds of displays were studied. The narrative display (see Figure 11-6) used complete words and phrases interspersed with measured electrical values. Any characteristics representing bad conditions would precede any representing good conditions, and the order varied with the context. This kind of display was very unorganized. The structured display (see Figure 11-7) placed key information in a box at the top of the results and clearly separated the logical categories of the data. The detailed characteristics were presented in a fixed, tabular form. The graphics display (see Figure 11-8) was similar to the structured display but added a schematic of the telephone line. Good, bad, or marginal conditions were represented anywhere in the schematic by shape coding where a filled-in space stood for good, a cross-hatched space for marginal, and an open space for bad. The color graphics condition was the same as the black and white but used color coding instead of shape coding to represent the conditions.

In the experiment, eight employees of the telephone company were tested. Performance was evaluated by giving the operators multiple-choice questions with each screen to determine characteristics of their decision making. Both time and accuracy were recorded. All subjects participated in each of the conditions.

For the accuracy data, the trend in the data favored the graphics displays, but these differences were nonsignificant statistically. The experiment had a problem with ceiling effects in that the scores were too high so that fluctuations in performance may have been obscured.

For the time results, statistically significant results occurred. The response

```
TEST RESULTS     SUMMARY:  GROUND

        GROUND, FAULT T-G
        3  TERMINAL DC RESISTANCE
           >  3500.00 K OHMS T-R
           =     14.21 K OHMS T-G
           >  3500.00 K OHMS R-G
        3  TERMINAL DC VOLTAGE
           =      0.00 VOLTS T-G
           =      0.00 VOLTS R-G
        VALID AC SIGNATURE
           =      8.82 K OHMS T-R
           =     14.17 K OHMS T-G
           =    628.52 K OHMS R-G
        LONGITUDINAL BALANCE POOR
           =     39    DB
        COULD NOT COUNT RINGERS DUE TO
           LOW RESISTANCE
        VALID LINE CKT CONFIGURATION
        CAN DRAW AND BREAK DIAL TONE
```

Figure 11-6. The narrative display from the Tullis (1981) study. Reprinted with permission from <u>Human Factors</u>, Vol. 23, No. 5, 1981. Copyright 1981 by the Human Factors and Ergonomics Society, Inc. All rights reserved.

```
        ✳✳✳✳✳✳✳✳✳✳✳✳✳✳✳✳✳✳✳✳✳✳✳✳✳
        ✳                        ✳
        ✳    TIP GROUND      14K  ✳
        ✳                        ✳
        ✳✳✳✳✳✳✳✳✳✳✳✳✳✳✳✳✳✳✳✳✳✳✳✳✳
```

```
DC RESISTANCE          DC VOLTAGE          AC SIGNATURE

  3500 K T-R                                   9 K T-R
    14K T-G             0 V T-G               14K T-G
  3500 K R-G            0 V R-G              629 K R-G


    BALANCE                              CENTRAL OFFICE

    39 DB                                VALID LINE CKT
                                         DIAL TONE OK
```

Figure 11-7. The structured display from the Tullis (1981) study. Reprinted with permission from <u>Human Factors</u>, Vol. 23, No. 5, 1981. Copyright 1981 by the Human Factors and Ergonomics Society, Inc. All rights reserved.

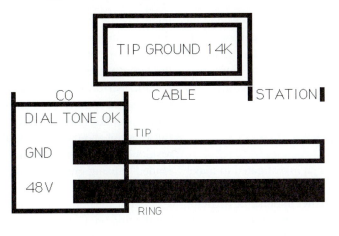

TIP GROUND 14K

CO   CABLE   STATION

DIAL TONE OK

TIP

GND

48V

RING

DC RESISTANCE	DC VOLTAGE	AC SIGNATURE	BALANCE
3500 K T-R		9 K T-R	39 DB
14 K T-G	0 V T-G	14 K T-G	
3500 K R-G	0 V R-G	629 K R-G	

Figure 11-8. The graphics display of Tullis (1981). Reprinted with permission from <u>Human Factors</u>, Vol. 23, No. 5, 1981. Copyright 1981 by the Human Factors and Ergonomics Society, Inc. All rights reserved.

times for the two graphics conditions were significantly faster than for the narrative. After practice, the structured condition was not significantly different from the graphics and it was better than the narrative.

Tullis (1981) also collected questionnaire data on the subjects' preferences for the different conditions. The preferences were in this order: color graphics, black and white graphics, structured text, and then the narrative. Statistical analyses of these data showed that the adjacent pairs were not different from each other but the nonadjacent pairs were. As an example, the color graphics was significantly better than the structured or the narrative display but was not better than the black and white graphics. The black and white graphics condition was rated significantly better than the narrative but not better than the structured text.

The implications of this experiment are that graphics can enhance performance when they provide an organization to the information to be displayed. Text can achieve some of the same results as long as it is structured; when the information changed depending on the context (in the narrative condition), then performance suffered. The advantage of the use of graphics is that the subjects can understand the structure faster than text, even if the text is structured. In the experiment, the structured text condition became as good as the graphics conditions only after some practice.

One of the important aspects of the use of graphics is the preference of users for these kinds of displays. These preferences do not always translate into performance improvements but they certainly can be very important when considering the attitudes of users toward the displayed information, and they are also important considerations in marketing decisions. Performance can be the same with graphics and text, but people may not buy a machine or software unless it has graphics capabilities.

Making the Invisible Visible

Methods have been investigated to make invisible operations visible to the users so that they could better understand difficult concepts such as computer languages (Caldwell, 1993; Caldwell and Eberts, 1989; DuBoulay, O'Shea, and Monk, 1981). These examples follow from ideas articulated by Bayman and Mayer (1983, 1984) that one of the reasons people have trouble with computer programming or using a calculator is there are so many invisible operations occurring behind the scenes. If these invisible operations were made visible, then performance might be enhanced. Bayman and Mayer investigated the use of simple instructional techniques on paper for making the invisible visible. DuBoulay et al. and Caldwell and Eberts have investigated the use of spatial graphics on a computer terminal.

The Bayman and Mayer (1983) study investigated the kinds of invisible operations novice computer programmers thought occurred in a computer programming language. By asking what was happening behind the scenes, Bayman and Mayer found that these novices had many misconceptions about these computing concepts. They concluded that instructional techniques explaining these invisible operations were needed. In the next paper, Bayman and Mayer (1984) investigated how to present instructional materials for calculator users so that they could

have a better understanding of the invisible operations of a calculator. By presenting some of the users with simple line drawings of the memory buffers in a calculator, performance was enhanced and the misconceptions were corrected. Although neither of these studies presented information about computer displays, the results and recommendations can be extended to using graphics on computer interfaces.

For the computer programming application of Caldwell (1993), the researchers acquired knowledge of C programming from computer programming experts and then used this acquired knowledge for guidance in the kinds of information to display on the screen. For some computer programming statements, many operations are hidden from the programmer; the novice programmer especially finds this confusing. As an example of the kinds of invisible information that can be made visible, the experts had a good representation of what happens in computer memory when variable values are placed in an array or when arrays are dimensioned. Novices have difficulty with this concept, especially for integers and floating points which require different numbers of slots in memory.

An example of how the invisible computing operations were made visible in the Caldwell research can help to illustrate these concepts. From acquiring the knowledge from the expert programmers, Caldwell found that this knowledge could be divided into three sets: commands which affect the flow of control; features which perform data operations; and the manner in which commands could be combined to obtain more complex statements. These features were then used for

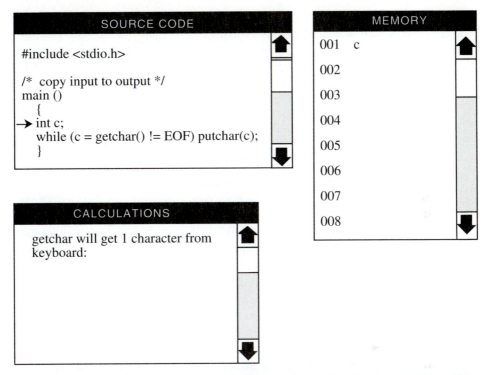

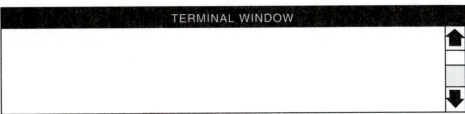

Figure 11-9. The overall representation of the programming task.

the elements and widgets of a graphics display which could be used by novice programmers to organize their knowledge of programming (see Figure 11-9). The flow of control, which is represented in the figure, is depicted in the display as a separate window (the source code window) and the user can examine the flow as the program is working. The data operations are represented through a memory window so that the user can see memory allocation as it occurs through the graphi-cal representation of memory slots. Finally, animation is used to represent input/output and the movement of data from one area to another, such as into the output window.

As an example of the graphics and animation on the display, consider the simple program in the upper lefthand window of Figure 11-9 in which the program identifies a keystroke from the keyboard and assigns the number of the keystroke to the variable c. The while loop will identi-

fies keystrokes until an end-of-file character which is entered on the keyboard.

The programmer can move down
the statements of the programming code to
see the invisible computer operations at
each step. In the **int c** statement, the
computer needs to set up slots in memory
for storing the value for the c variable.
When this statement is executed, a slot is
reserved in memory, and this can be seen
clearly through the graphics representation in the upper right-hand memory window of Figure 11-9.

The next part of the computing task
is to go through the loop in the **while**
statement. Loops such as these are often
difficult for novices to understand. By
clearly illustrating the invisible operations,
they are more easily comprehended. From
the example, the programmers must understand that a character is obtained from
keyboard input (refer to the middle window in Figure 11-9). Next, the computer
interprets the keystroke and determines its
ASCII number (each character has a different ASCII code associated with it). In
the example, the character which was
entered from the keyboard is 119. This
number will be placed in the memory slot
which has been specified for the c variable
(the darkened space in the upper righthand
window). This operation includes many
operations which would be difficult for a
novice computer programmer to understand; this display explains these hidden
operations.

The next statement, **putchar**, is also
an amalgamation of several invisible
operations. Putchar will take the value
stored for c in memory, convert this ASCII
code back into a character, and then output
this character on the screen. In the calculations window, one can see that the char-

acter w has an ASCII code of 119 (see
Figure 11-10). So, putchar converts the
119 into the character w, and prints the
character on the screen. The character w
is moved to the terminal window so that
the programmer can see clearly that it will
appear on the screen. This loop continues,
with all the characters being moved to the
terminal window, until an end-of-file
character is entered on the keyboard.

Figure 11-11 shows another program
illustrating a source of confusion for novice programmers. In most programs, such
as c shown here, the variables have to be
dimensioned and each variable type may
require a different number of slots to store
a variable. As an example, an **int** type
requires twice as much room and slots as
does the **char** type. By looking at the
spatial size of the variable, one can see
clearly that **int** requires twice as much
memory as does **char**.

An experimental investigation of this
display has shown that making the invisible operations visible was very beneficial
for novice computer programmers. They
were able to form a much more accurate
mental model of the task than those not
provided with the display. Instead of
trying to determine a visual representation
of the task through trial and error, the
display provides the programmers with a
clear and accurate representation of the
task through the use of graphics and animation.

Graphics for Representing Physical Systems

The use of graphics for representing physical systems can be placed into the context
of S-C-R compatibility which was reviewed in Chapter 8. Recall from this

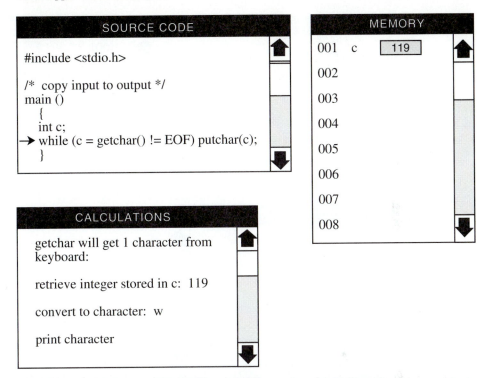

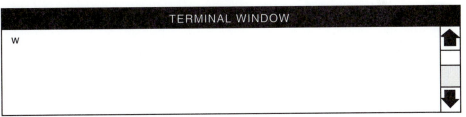

Figure 11-10. The putchar statement will convert the number 119 to the corresponding character (w) and print this character on the screen (from Caldwell, 1993).

previous chapter that the code of the central processing must be determined so that the stimulus and response can be designed to be compatible with that code. If the system being represented on an interface has a simple physical reference, as would occur for any physical system such as a manufacturing facility or a car, then the central processing code is spatial. For the stimulus, or the display representation, to be compatible with central processing, the display must use graphics, or an analog picture. To continue the compatibility to the response stage, the response must be a manual response. The best kind of response would be to point to the graphical object on the display with a pointing device such as a mouse.

In the past, displays have often been designed with hardware or software con-

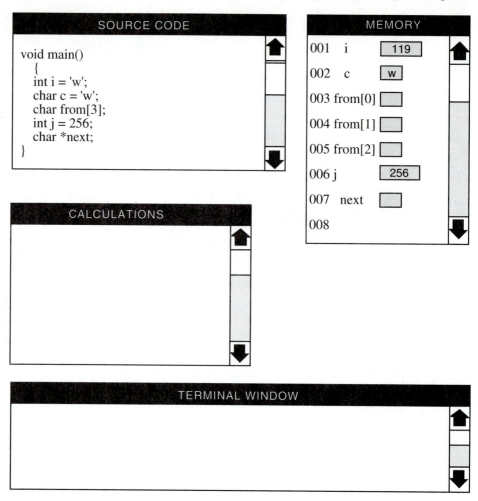

Figure 11-11. This simple program shows how different variable types take up more or fewer slots in memory. The int types take twice as many slots as the char types.

straints in mind. Using text, even for spatial information, has always been easiest. The S-C-R compatibility theory shows that this can cause problems if the task is represented spatially; the stimulus will be incompatible with the central processing. Correcting this incompatibility was always left to the user. The user would have to perform mental transformations on the data to get it into a form which is compatible with central processing. Mental transformations require time to perform, and can be a source of errors if the transformation is performed incorrectly. Thus, to reduce time and errors, S-C-R compatibility must be considered. In the following discussion, several examples are provided where physical systems have a spatial code and then the interface is designed to be compatible with the representation.

STEAMER was a CAI (computer-assisted instruction) program developed by the Navy to teach students how to control a steam propulsion plant such as would be found on board large ships (Stevens, Roberts, and Stead, 1983). Training in propulsion engineering is judged by naval officers to be one of the greatest training problems in the Navy. The purpose of a shipboard steam plant is to convert heat into electricity and to turn the ship's propellor. The collection of operating procedures runs to two or more four-inch thick volumes. The operational system is quite large and contains thousands of complex components. Mistakes due to misconceptions can cause expensive damage and even death. The design of the interface used for the training is, therefore, quite important.

The interface used for the simulator makes heavy use of graphics. The complex components of the steam plant are simulated through the use of color graphics and animation. Students can inspect and manipulate the steam plant through this graphics interface.

STEAMER was designed so that the student could develop a conceptual understanding of the system. The developers of STEAMER felt that the steam plant operation was too complex to learn by rote. This observation was corroborated by examining how experts think and talk about steam plants. In an analysis of experts performing the task, Hollan, Stevens, and Williams (1980) concluded that the experts had a spatial representation of the plant that was used to solve problems. In terms of S-C-R compatibility, this means that the code of representation of the central processing of the task was spatial. If the experts had to solve a problem, they could run a mental simulation on the spatial model. Instruction should be geared, through the graphical design of the interface, so that the students could come to mentally simulate the operation of the system. So novices could quickly develop this ability, they designed the interface so that the students could easily manipulate graphics on the computer. STEAMER was an important advancement for two reasons: it was one of the first interfaces to utilize interactive color graphics and it was developed based upon experts' conceptual models of the task.

Another application of using graphics to represent physical systems is the work of Rasmussen (1985) on interface designs for process control tasks. The process control systems, such as the energy plants studied by Rasmussen, are so complex that all the system cannot be represented on one screen. A solution to this problem is to design the interface in levels so that a user can get more detail by successively zooming to these different levels. The design problem is to determine the levels which should be used; Rasmussen based his levels on operator interviews and his experience in the process control industry. Figure 11-12 shows an example of one of his displays. The levels chosen by Rasmussen range from very low-level information, such as valve settings or steam and water flow, to high-level information, such as company profits and plant safety, with the operators concentrating mostly on the high-level information but accessing the low-level information as needed for decision making and problem solving. This research is based upon interviews and experience; surprisingly little empirical research has been performed on the effectiveness of

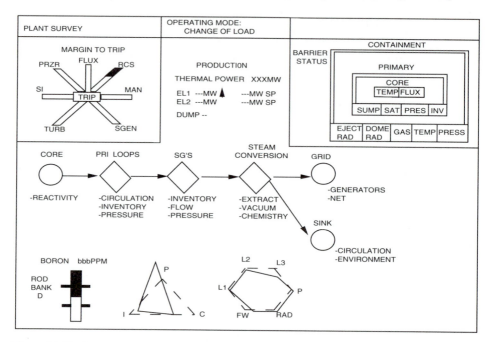

Figure 11-12. An example of a graphics display for a nuclear power plant. This is the overview that the user would see of the plant. More detail can be found by clicking the mouse on any of the items (reprinted from Rasmussen © 1985 IEEE).

these kinds of displays. In a different example for flexible manufacturing systems when the effectiveness of graphics was tested (Sharit, 1985), graphics did not necessarily enhance performance.

In conclusion, a physical system, with an obvious spatial referent, should be represented using computer graphics so that the S-C-R compatibility can be maintained. The work on steam plant expert operators indicated that these people performed the task spatially; the computer display should augment these spatial abilities, especially for novice users. Because some of these systems are so complex, however, a display technique such as designing in different levels, and then providing the capability to move around the different levels, is needed and has been provided by some of the existing displays.

Graphics and Icons

One of the most popular uses for graphics is in icons. An icon is a graphical representation on the screen representing some object or function. Since the introduction of the Xerox Star, and the success of the Apple Macintosh, interface designers have incorporated icons into the interface design. As an example of icon use, consider Figure 11-13 which shows the file directory on an Apple Macintosh. Each of the files is represented by an icon. The icon displays the kind of file that it is. A folder, representing a subdirectory, has an icon associated with it that looks like a folder. Each application file, such as the text in a Microsoft Word file, has its own distinct icon developed by the application programmers. By just glancing at the screen,

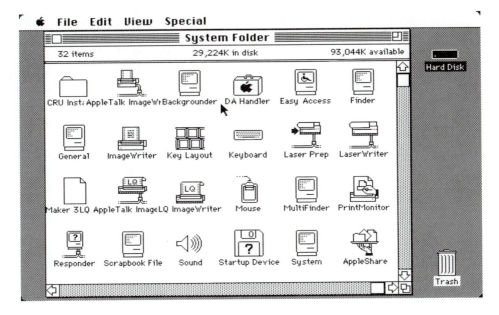

Figure 11-13. An example of the file structure of the Apple Macintosh. This interface makes extensive use of icons.

the type of file can be determined supposedly by the icon associated with the file. As an example of another type of icon, the Apple Macintosh displays an icon for a wastepaper basket at the bottom right of the screen. Again, by glancing at the screen, the user can understand the meaning of the delete function (throwing a file into the waste basket).

There are many reasons from cognitive psychology for why an icon representation of an object or function may be appropriate. Research has shown that people can recall and recognize very large numbers of pictures (Paivio, 1971). In fact, research on the recognition of pictures by Standing, Conezio, and Haber (1970) showed that people recognized 2650 pictures with a hit rate of 0.95 or better. Recall and recognition for words is much worse. More recent work has shown, however, that recall and recognition for

words and pictures is closer if the pictures incorporate line drawings, are black-and-white, and the stimulus sets for the pictures are similar. Along the same lines, Dallett, Wilcox, and D'Andrea (1968) found that recognition performance could drop to around 70% if the pictures are similar. Palmer (1975) showed that in some cases, line drawings of pictures could not be determined without a context. Using icons can utilize this good memory recognition for pictures; but the icons should be developed based upon the research on picture recognition.

As Switchenko (1985) points out, many of the icons used for interfaces incorporate features which make them quite indistinct, not optimizing fully the properties of pictures which make them easier to recall and recognize. Many of the icons are black and white, they incorporate mostly line drawings, and they are usually about the same size. Experimentation on icons, when compared to textual icons, confirms some of Switchenko's contentions. Rohr and Keppel (1984) compared graphical icons to verbal commands and found no performance differences, in terms of time and errors, between the two. The only difference was that more help messages were requested in one of the conditions for commands as compared to icons.

In another study, Guastello and Traut (1989) compared preferences and perceived meaningfulness for verbal icons, graphics icons, and combined verbal and graphics icons. They found that the subjects did not prefer one set over the other. They did find, however, that the combined icons were perceived to be more meaningful than the other two. The verbal and graphics icons were about equal in meaningfulness.

The experimental results have been somewhat ambiguous on the benefits of icons. Switchenko (1985), in a review of the research literature, found that icons may be useful and enhance performance only in some situations. First, the icons should be developed to incorporate as many distinctive properties of pictures as they can. As an example, the icons should be different colors, different shapes, different sizes, and incorporate shadings. Basically, the representation of icons should get away from line drawings. Second, there seems to be a "directness" factor involved. If the icons can depict the object directly, then they are more useful. Using analogies for icon depictions are less direct. Using icons for abstract functions, such as in text-editing functions, are much more indirect.

A possible solution to some of these problems with icons is to animate them.

This animation would be especially useful for dynamic tasks, such as using a painting program. In a painting program, the user typically chooses an icon to set the mode for performing a dynamic task. As an example, an icon can be chosen for drawing an oval. This icon typically has only an oval represented in the icon. This must represent the mode, that is, drawing the oval, and also the procedure for drawing it. To draw an oval, the user must move the pointer of the mouse to the starting location, press and hold a mouse button, move the cursor of the mouse to the ending location (the oval changes size accordingly), and then release the mouse button for the final oval. An animated icon can illustrate the procedure for drawing the oval besides just indicating the mode for the oval. Baecker, Small, and Mander (1991) designed animated icons for painting programs similar to that described above and found that some novice users could not understand static icons but all novices could understand how to perform the functions using the animated icons. This research only investigated animated icons for the painting program. It is possible that animated icons would not be useful for representing static tasks.

As with other aspects of computer graphics, merely employing icons in the computer interface design will not enhance usability; the icons must be used correctly. Simple black-and-white line drawings may not be effective; the icons must have more picture qualities in them to enhance recognizability. Sometimes the icons should be labeled with verbal descriptions to make them more understandable. In addition, for representations of dynamic processes, animated icons can be used.

Providing Graphics to Visualize Information

One of the new challenges of a computer system is presenting the information so that people can walk through, and then come to visualize, the data. This follows from the Ferguson (1977) paper discussed at the beginning of the chapter which stated that engineers and technologists must be trained to think nonverbally. Being able to "walk around" in the engine of a car, and then internalize that imagery, could be useful for thinking of new future design modifications for the engine. Some techniques to perform this data visualization function have been discussed in other chapters. Chapter 10 discussed the use of a metaphor for walking around and exploring data. In Chapter 20, virtual reality environments will also be discussed in a similar context. This section examines some of the specific techniques which have been studied for visualizing information.

Much of the work on information visualization has been performed at Xerox. Robertson, Mackinlay, and Card (1991) state that almost all information to be displayed on a computer can be classified as either unstructured, linear, or hierarchical. An example of a linear structure for data would be one in which the data are arranged temporally. On some desk tops, the data can be found only by locating the temporal "strata" of related items. In other words, by finding other items that may have been placed in the pile at about the same time, one should be able to find the item being searched for since it should be at the same level in the pile.

Visualization of linear structures has been accomplished through a technique called the perspective wall (Mackinlay, Robertson, and Card, 1991). A perspective wall (see Figure 11-14) is a two-dimensional display of the data which has been folded over at both sides. The information in the middle panel is that which is being focused on, so it appears with the highest resolution and detail. The information displayed on the two side panels is displayed in less detail and provides the context for the middle panel. If needed, the information on the side panels can be brought to the middle panel for a more detailed search.

Hierarchical data includes such things as file structures or organizational charts. Sometimes the hierarchical data is best represented from top to bottom and sometimes from left to right. Xerox has developed two visualization techniques: the cone tree for top-to-bottom hierarchies (see Figure 11-15), and the cam tree for left-to-right hierarchies (this representation would be similar to that shown in Figure 11-15 except that the hierarchy is from left to right). The cone tree starts with the highest-level node at the top of the screen, and the lower-level nodes are represented towards the bottom. The cam tree has the highest-level node to the left, and the lower-level nodes to the right. Both of these techniques involve several perceptual distance cues to make the 2-D representation on the screen appear to be 3-D: the closer objects are larger and brighter than those farther away; shadows provide some perspective; and a "fisheye" perspective reduces the size and acuity of the items in the periphery. Clarkson (1991) says that these methods have been used to display huge amounts of data, such as 600 directories holding 10,000 files and 650 nodes of an organizational chart, so

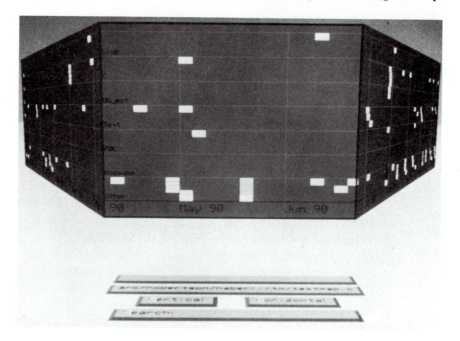

Figure 11-14. The information visualizer (Mackinlay et al., 1991) for linear structures of information, called the perspective wall (the computer color display has been reproduced in black and white here). Most detail occurs in the middle panel; the side panels provide context. The user can move to anyplace on the perspective wall while retaining the context. (Copyright 1991, Association for Computing Machinery, Inc. Reprinted by permission.)

that it all can be visualized easily. The organizational chart required 80 pages of documentation in its paper version.

Moving around in the hierarchies can be accomplished by selecting nodes with a mouse. The node which is selected along with the neighboring nodes are brought to the front of the structure. The whole structure, being three-dimensional, may have to be rotated to accomplish this. The operations which can be performed on the hierarchies are conceptualized by using a gardening metaphor (Robertson, Mackinlay, and Card, 1991). Operations such as pruning or growing allow the hierarchy to be reduced or expanded.

The area of using graphics for data visualization is still in its infancy. More

and different kinds of representations need to be studied. The goal of these techniques is to reduce the huge amounts of data that need to be presented on a display so that it is in a form that can be easily viewed and manipulated.

Graphics for Abstract Information

A challenge for interface design using graphics is to utilize graphical displays for nonspatial or abstract information. One method is the use of metaphors and analogies; these techniques were introduced in the previous chapter. The metaphor provides a spatial organization to the display, as one of the advantages of this approach, but it carries the excess baggage of pos-

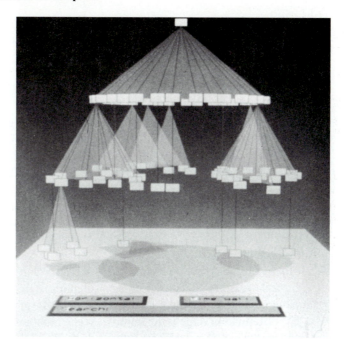

Figure 11-15. The cone tree (Robertson et al., 1991) from Xerox for representing hierarchical data. This is also a color display which has been reproduced in black and white for this figure. (Copyright 1991, Association for Computing Machinery, Inc. Reprinted by permission.)

sible overextension and misunderstandings. To use graphics for nonspatial information, the designer must determine how to organize the information on the display. Simply using an organized table, which provides some amount of spatial information, can increase user performance close to levels of physical representations using graphics (Tullis, 1981). Organization of nonspatial information can also occur through the use of display devices such as hierarchical structures and networks; Billingsley (1982) used some of these techniques for menu displays. Dimensional structures or hierarchical structures can be determined by acquiring knowledge from experts using multidimensional techniques. This was done by Caldwell and Eberts (1989) for C programming

languages, and the spatial structure of the display used for an interface design was determined from the spatial structure of the multidimensional output. Other examples of acquiring knowledge about a task, such as expert systems (Posey and Eberts, 1989), and then designing graphical displays to be compatible with that acquired knowledge, can be found in Eberts and Posey (1990).

Another example of graphics for abstract information is its use in deductive proofs in mathematics. In textbooks, mathematical proofs are usually shown in linear structures. However, many of these proofs have a nonlinear structure which can be shown on computers using animation and graphics. Kaltenbach and Frasson (1989) demonstrated a method to use a partially animated network representation to facilitate understanding of complex mathematical deductive proofs. They did not, however, experimentally validate this method when compared to text.

Graphics have also been used for teaching other kinds of abstract information such as mathematics (DuBoulay and Howe, 1982; Forchieri, Lemut and Molfino, 1983) and music (Lamb, 1982).

Graphics for Metaphor Instantiation

In Chapter 10, the importance of graphics in the use of metaphors was discussed. Recall that in the theory three stages of metaphorical reasoning were defined: instantiation, elaboration, and consolidation. The instantiation stage is the important stage for the use of graphics for interfaces incorporating a metaphor. Instantiation is the recognition or retrieval of something known which can be targeted to the new computerized domain. In an interface design, the appropriate metaphor must be instantiated and this can be augmented through the use of icons or pictures. As examples using the desktop metaphor, all the pictures or icons associated with a desk top would assist the instantiation of the desktop metaphor: the folders, the calculator, the clock, the appointment book, and the trash can.

For some time, a debate has been occurring whether or not pictures and graphics are needed for metaphor instantiation (see Gittins, 1986). Perhaps the metaphor can be instantiated just as easily using words which can access the knowledge structure associated with the metaphor. In any case, graphics in the form of icons can be used for metaphor instantiation; other display techniques such as words

are perhaps almost as good. Further research on these issues is needed.

PROBLEMS WITH GRAPHICS DISPLAYS

Merely using graphics without carefully designing the display will not be useful and, in some cases, can be detrimental to performance. There are three general situations in which graphics can be detrimental to performance: (1) when the use of graphics degrades the performance of the display to such a degree as to be annoying; (2) in a training environment when the operators may form an overreliance on the pictures so that the task could not be done without the graphic augmentation; and (3) when graphics may be incompatible with the code of representation of the task. A related problem to the first is that graphics displays may require excessive screen space. With graphics, the screen can become cluttered quickly so that relevant information may be difficult to locate.

Graphics May Degrade Performance of the System

An experiment by Gould and Finzer (1982) illustrates the first two of these possible pitfalls for graphics displays; in this section, the problem of degrading performance will be discussed. In algebra problems, some students have difficulty translating the natural language text of the problem into some meaningful representation. A possibility is to use graphics to show how this translation can be done. The Gould and Finzer experiment examined the possibility of animating various time-rate-distance problems, a class of problems typically seen in algebra, using relevant pictures such as places, travelers, speedometers, odometers, and clocks.

Providing students with this kind of display for learning algebra problems had some advantages. The students were better able to draw pictures of the situation than a control group who did not have the graphics and the animation. This could be expected from the kinds of experiences they had with the display. Gould and Finzer also claimed that the students provided with the graphics could visualize the problem better. This did not, however, seem to enhance performance. When compared to the control group in how well they could form the underlying algebraic problems, no differences occurred. Similar to the Tullis (1981) experiment, the students in the graphics condition claimed they liked their displays better than those in the nongraphic control condition, but this preference did not always allow for better performance.

One problem with the animation was that the students claimed that it was too slow. They had to wait, watching the screen, while the animation ran its course. As an example, there would be little to do while they watched a car move across the screen.

When animation is used, it should be used to compress the time of a task instead of increase it. As an example, signals moving across a radar screen in real time can be difficult to perceive. Research has shown that performance improvements can be achieved by time-compression of the display, realized by holding the displays in computer memory and then showing the memorized displays all at once. For this kind of display the signals have a pattern to them that is easily perceived all at once, while the random noise has no

pattern to it (Bloomfield and Little, 1985; Scanlan, 1975). Similarly, for an air intercept task where two planes must determine the correct paths to intercept, speeding up the task so that the spatial patterns can be seen easily will enhance performance and the perceptual skill of the trainee (Schneider, 1981).

Users May Become Overly Dependent on the Graphics

The second problem with the blind use of graphics is that the user may become overly dependent on the graphics so that if the task is performed without the graphics then performance will suffer. In the Gould and Finzer (1982) task, the purpose of the display was to train the students so that they could perform time-rate-distance tasks better than if they had not had the training. One reason why performance improvements were not seen could be because students were never forced to perform the task without the graphics and, thus, were never trained to think independently from the graphics display. One of the principles of training from human factors is that augmenting cues, such as the animation of the time-rate-distance problems, should be presented on only some of the trials so that the students are forced to do some trials without the augmentation (Eberts and Brock, 1988; Gordon, 1968; and Wheaton, Rose, Fingerman, Korotkin, and Holding, 1976). As an example, Lintern (1980) displayed a highway-in-the-sky augmenting cue in a flight simulator for training pilots how to land an aircraft (see Figure 11-16). The augmenting cue would only appear on the screen when the pilot was off-track; when on-track the cue was not displayed. This provided feedback

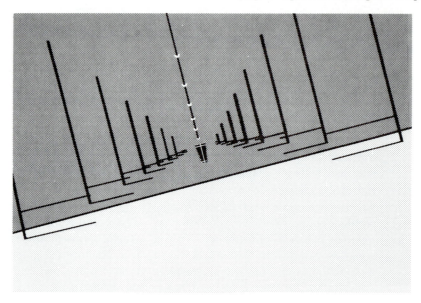

Figure 11-16. The highway-in-the-sky display from Lintern and Liu (1991). A path is provided for the pilot through the augmenting cues. If the pilot is on track, then the cues can be removed; if off track, the cues are displayed and assistance is provided to the pilot trainee. Reprinted with permission from Human Factors, Vol. 33, No. 4, 1991. Copyright 1991 by the Human Factors and Ergonomics Society, Inc. All rights reserved.

when needed; the pilots did not, therefore, become dependent on the augmenting cues. In a tracking task, Eberts and Schneider (1985) provided augmenting graphic cues on every other trial. After practice with this kind of display, the subjects could perform the task without the graphics because they had learned to visualize the cue even when it was not shown. If the graphics had always been shown, the subjects would not have been forced to develop the visualization skill.

Although some uses of graphics can impede the task, such as by slowing down the performance of the system and allowing the user to become too reliant on the graphics, these same liabilities can be turned into assets if done properly. The above examples have shown how graph-

ics can be used in compressing time so that the users are better able to see the spatial patterns and understand better the operation of complex systems. The examples also surveyed some techniques for augmented feedback that ensures that the users do not become overly reliant on the graphics but, over time, can come to visualize how the graphics would have appeared on the screen. This helps to train the users for complex problem solving even without the use of the computer.

Graphics That Are Incompatible

The last problem with graphics is that their use may be incompatible with the central processing code of the task. The compatibilities of graphics with central processing was discussed in an earlier section of this chapter; the flip side is that graphics may be incompatible with some tasks. From Chapter 8, we know the code of representation for central processing could be either verbal or spatial. If spatial, then the stimulus should be spatial or, in the context of computer displays, an analog picture. If verbal, then the stimulus should be textual. In this case, a textual representation on the screen would be most appropriate.

It is difficult to think of many tasks to be computerized which are purely verbal. Tasks involving abstract information could be termed verbal. Sometimes concepts do not lend themselves to spatial representations and can only be discussed verbally. When editing text, some of the task seems to be verbal in nature so that the most compatible display could possibly be textual. This means that commands could be presented textually instead of in a graphical representation. In fact, most people would be hard-pressed to find graphics representations of command names when text editing. Some parts of text editing, such as navigating through the text or searching for sections of text, are spatial. These navigation techniques must remain in a graphics representation.

Another example of a verbal task would be representing the ideas which may be discussed in a meeting. If meetings are to be computerized, as is occurring in electronic meeting rooms (see Chapter 25), then these ideas can be presented in a textual format. Sometimes ideas cannot be placed into pictures easily. This was demonstrated empirically for a computer-supported cooperative work task where coauthors were required to com-

ment on a piece of text which was being written cooperatively (Chalfonte, Fish, and Kraut, 1991). The coauthors were restricted to comments which were either text or speech. When examining the comments, the ability to vocalize allowed the coauthors to comment on higher-level concerns, such as social communications, while those restricted to text only commented on local problems of the task, such as grammar and spelling. The speech communication output allowed the coauthor to concentrate more on the other coauthor in a social manner rather than just through the content of the shared task.

SUMMARY

The use of graphics in interface displays is becoming more and more important. For many of the tasks that we perform, we conceptualize these tasks spatially. For the display to be compatible with this spatial representation, graphics must be used. This chapter discussed many of the ways in which graphics can be used to enhance usability of the display.

As emphasized throughout this chapter, incorporating graphics will not automatically enhance usability. If the graphics provide an organization to the data, then other organizing means, such as the use of tables, will provide the same kinds of benefits as graphics. In some cases, graphics can actually degrade usability. If the display is slowed down by the graphics, then performance on tasks will suffer. If the user learns to depend too much on the graphics display, then performance improvements cannot be achieved. By carefully designing the displays, however, both of these problems can be overcome.

QUESTIONS

1. Make a list of tasks that are spatial. Explain why they are spatial. Make a list of tasks that verbal. Explain why they are verbal.

2. Computer graphics is only one part of direct manipulation displays. List the other important characteristics of this class of display.

3. Choose a task such as setting a VCR to record a particular program. Explain how the following characteristics could be utilized in this interface.

   a. Use of graphics for information organization.

   b. Making the invisible visible. First, explain what could be considered invisible in this task. Next, explain how this could be made visible through the use of graphics.

   c. Use of graphics for representing physical systems.

   d. Use of icons.

4. Which problem with computer graphics did the concept of the highway-in-the-sky for training pilots how to land overcome? How does the highway-in-the-sky overcome this problem?

5. For each of the following computer graphics advantages, explain how nongraphics displays can accomplish the same goal. If you cannot find a way to use nongraphics displays for accomplishing the goal, then explain how graphics may be unique in applications for that particular concept.

   a. Information organization

   b. Making the invisible visible

   c. Icons

   d. Representations for physical systems

   e. Information visualization

   f. Abstract information representations

   g. Metaphor instantiation

6. For each of the following pieces of data, indicate if the cone tree, the cam tree, or the perspective wall would fit the data best. Justify your answer.

   a. An organizational chart

   b. The card catalogue information from a library

   c. The database of movie information from Chapter 24

   d. A database of personal recipes

   e. An address book

   f. An organization of animal species

   g. Television program times

7. Chapter 10 discussed the use of metaphors and analogies in interface design. As emphasized in that chapter, an important part of a metaphor is its spatial component. In most cases, a metaphor has a spatial component.

Determining whether the popularity and success of interfaces, such as the desktop metaphor, is due to the use of a metaphor or the use of graphics is difficult.

In this chapter, the success of graphical interfaces was attributed to several features and characteristics of these kinds of displays, among them the ability to organize information, to make the invisible visible, to use icons to represent concepts, to represent physical systems, or to visualize information. Discuss how metaphors and analogies also have the same advantages and features. Use the metaphor examples from Chapter 10 to illustrate your points. Finally, try to think of metaphors which are not spatial in nature and, thus, would not utilize a graphical interface.

CHAPTER 12

WORKLOAD ASSESSMENT

INTRODUCTION

Recall from Chapter 8 on human information processing that attention was an important component of the model. Attention could be applied to the information processing at several of the stages: perception, decision and response selection, response execution, and working memory. Attention is needed in information processing to perform the functions of the processing; with no attention, the information will not be processed. If the computer user becomes overloaded, because of too much information which must be processed, then information may be not attended to and performance will suffer. Cognitive research in this area has two general application areas for human-computer interaction: design of the task and monitoring of the user to determine possible overload. The applications in both of these broad areas will be discussed. In this discussion, it is important to understand some of the theoretical considerations on human attention to provide an important foundation for the applications. HCI applications of attention are most appropriate for complex computerized systems, such as nuclear power plants, cockpits, and process control plants, in which the operator may not be able to perform all the tasks at one time.

TASK DESIGN ISSUES

In complex human-computer interaction, such as with an airplane cockpit or a nuclear power plant, the designer has to make many kinds of decisions for the multiple controls and displays. For which displays should auditory stimuli, such as a warning buzzer, be used, and for which displays should visual stimuli, such as a red warning light, be used? Should information be displayed on one panel, or should that information be divided between two or more panels? Should auditory and visual displays be used at the same time? Answers to these questions can be found by examining the theories of attentional resources.

Metaphors have been used to understand the theory of attention and to generate hypotheses which can be tested in the theory. Two general metaphors have been used to describe attention: attention as a searchlight and attention as a limited resource. Both of these metaphors will be discussed along with examples of how this cognitive concept of attention is important in human-computer interaction tasks.

Attention as a Searchlight

One of the earliest metaphors for describing attention was in terms of a searchlight. The momentary direction of the searchlight is the attention. The focus of the searchlight is that information which is in momentary consciousness. In other words, everything in the beam is processed, whether we want to or not, and everything outside the beam is not processed.

This searchlight metaphor helps to explain several attentional phenomena which have been researched. People have a capability to divide attention between two or more different tasks under some conditions; under other conditions, attention must be focused on the task. As an example, attention must be divided when driving the car and listening to the radio. Driving a car under high traffic conditions and not being able to hear the radio, even though it may be on, is an indication of focused attention on the driving. Using the searchlight metaphor, the breadth of the beam is analogous to whether attention is spread or focused.

Another attentional phenomenon is that of switching attention (Moray and Fitter, 1973) or selective attention. To use the driving example again, the driver cannot pay attention to all parts of the driving environment at one time. The driver may shift attention from the car in front, to the traffic 200 yards in front, to the traffic in the rearview mirror, or to the traffic in both sideview mirrors. All of these cannot be attended to at one time. The driver selects the events which will be attended. To return to the searchlight metaphor, selective attention is analogous to the brain controlling the hand that moves the searchlight. The time taken to switch the beam from one location to another is the time needed to switch attention.

All of these attentional phenomena, although performing vital functions in information processing, can place severe limitations on information processing. To ensure that the computer user does not come up against these limitations, they must be understood, and the equipment and task must be designed so that the limitations do not cause serious problems. Divided attention can fail when we are unable to divide our attention between all the stimuli or tasks which we wish to pursue. In other words, we have a limited

ability to time-share between tasks. Some tasks, just by their nature, are difficult to perform together.

Focused attention is needed to concentrate on one source of information in the environment. This can fail, however, because people tend to be distracted by other events. In some situations, the operator may be unable to focus attention on a particular display if distracting information is present in the environment. As an example, in a failure in a nuclear power plant, several indicators may go off at once. When this happens, the operators often turn off the distracting auditory displays so they can focus on finding the source of the problem. By turning off the auditory alarms, however, other important information may be missed.

Selective attention is needed to select the appropriate aspects of the environment to process. Selective attention can fail, though, in some cases. In baseball, the batter tries to pick up the rotation of the ball in order to determine whether the pitcher has thrown a fast ball or a curve ball. The pitcher intentionally tries to destroy the batter's selective attention abilities by having the batter follow the motion of the arm instead of the motion of the ball. Breakdowns occur when the person selects the wrong event to be attended.

Using the searchlight metaphor of attention, the most likely source of applications for human-computer interaction tasks is in terms of attention switching, specifically, trying to design the display so that attention does not have to be switched. Attention switching costs can occur through several different means. A cost is associated with switching between modalities (LaBerge, VanGilder, and

Yellott, 1971) when a person must switch, as an example, between the visual and auditory modalities. A cost is also associated with switching between two tasks, sometimes referred to as multiplexing (Polson, Wickens, Klapp, and Colle (1989). Moray (1984) has indicated that attention switching occurs between stimuli, events, and tasks, and that a mental model of the information and timing of the events must be incorporated in order to successfully perform this attention switching. This important role of the mental model emphasizes similar points to those discussed in Chapter 7.

Attention switching can be facilitated through the use of integrated displays which allow the information to be combined on the same channel so that switching is not required. Recall that modality switching was one of the kinds of attention switching that can occur. If all the relevant information which must be integrated occurs in the same modality, then attention switching between modalities should not have to occur. Wickens and Goettl (1985) performed an air traffic control task in which the relevant information was presented using the same modality or different modalities. Performance was better when using the same modality.

Attention switching also occurs when the information is in separate locations on the display. If the information was placed closer, then the switching would not have to occur. In an integrated display (see Figure 12-1), examined by Goodstein (1981) and others, the information is presented on a symmetrical figure, such as a triangle or heptagon, where each point represents some piece of information. When a malfunction occurs, the part of the figure corresponding to the malfunction is elongated. An operator can glance at the display and know that all is functioning well when the display is in a symmetrical form. A glance at the display during a malfunction can easily be perceived because it is no longer in a good form. Performance improvements occur for integrated displays when compared experimentally to the situation in which the operator must combine information from several bar graphs (Carswell and Wickens, 1984a; Wickens, Kramer, Barnett, Carswell, Fracker, Goettl, and Harwood, 1985).

Attention as a Resource

The other metaphor which is used often for describing attentional phenomena is attention as a limited resource (Navon and Gopher, 1979). This metaphor emphasizes the divisibility of attention. Generally, the resources are limited, and attentional resource failures are due to not having enough resources to allocate to a task. In early theories, Moray (1967) proposed that attention was like the limited processing capacity of a general-purpose computer. Task performance depended upon the difficulty of the task or the demand for the limited capacity. If the resources are limited, then something must direct the resources flexibly to the tasks that are consuming them. Moray discussed the possibility of an "executive control" for the allocation of the resources.

As more research was directed to studying attentional resources, researchers discovered that the phenomena were better explained not by one pool of attentional resources but by separate pools of resources. If two or more tasks had to be performed at the same time, performance in this dual task would be based upon

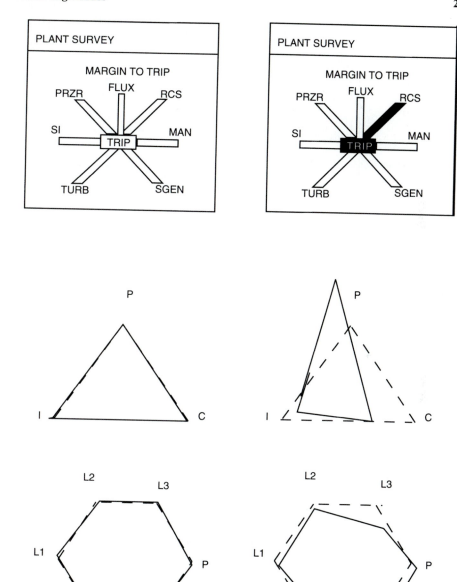

Figure 12-1. Examples of integrated displays adapted from Figure 11-12 and similar to those discussed by Goodstein (1981). The figures in the left column represent normal operations and those in the right column represent malfunctioning systems. The top figure integrates several systems in one display to indicate if any will cause a trip in the nuclear power plant. The middle figure integrates three subsystems, and is thus represented by a triangle, while the bottom figure integrates six subsystems, and is represented by a heptagon.

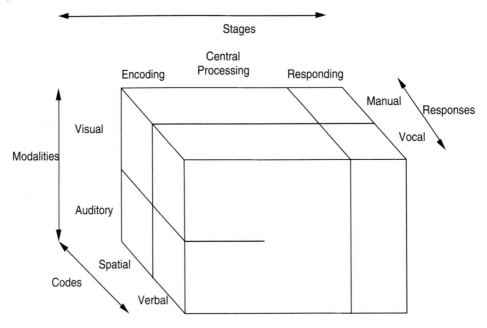

Figure 12-2. The structure of processing resources from Wickens' (1984b) multiple resource theory (reprinted with permission of publisher).

whether or not the resources shared the same resource pool or pulled from different pools. Much work has focused on identifying the structure of these resource pools or the structure of attentional resources.

Wickens (1980, 1984b) has developed a model, called the multiple resource theory, to explain the structure of attentional processing resources. This model tries to account for the allocation of attention and the processing of information in complex tasks, such as piloting an aircraft, in which the operator works in a high-workload environment and has difficulty processing all the possible information. An important part of this multiple resource theory is that different tasks have different representation codes associated with them. In terms of attentional resources, it has been determined (Wickens,

1984b) that tasks with verbal codes and those with spatial codes pulled attentional resources from different "pools," so that these two kinds of tasks could be better time-shared than if the tasks pulled resources from the same pool. Because a positive relation exists between the quality of performance and the amount of resources devoted to a task, performance in these high-workload situations was dependent on the structures of the tasks and on the representation codes of the component tasks.

Wickens (1980, 1984b) has defined this attentional resource structure as having three relatively dichotomous dimensions (see Figure 12-2): two stage-defined resource pools (early versus late processes), two modality-defined resource pools (auditory versus visual encoding), and two resource pools defined by processing codes (spatial versus verbal). The implications of this model for human-computer interaction applications are as follows for each of the dimensions. For the stage-defined resource pools, information is assumed to be processed, following the information processing models considered in Chapter 8, going from encoding (perception) to response execution. From this model, encoding and central processing (cognitive tasks) draw attentional resources from one pool while response execution draws resources from a different pool. Thus, humans would be able to encode or centrally process information at the same time as a response from previous information is executed. For the modality-defined resource pools, the human would be able to attend to visual information at the same time that auditory information is attended to. Thus, computer information presentation should be divided between auditory and visual signals to prevent overloading the user. But, this comes with a consequence, as discussed earlier, of having to devote attention to switching between the modalities. Finally, for the processing code resource pools, information can be presented either spatially (e.g., with graphics) or verbally (in textual form). Again, the user would be less likely to be overloaded if both of these resource pools are drawn upon instead of presenting all the information in the form of drawing upon one of the pools.

Applications of the attention-as-resource metaphor have been studied for human-computer interaction tasks. To determine how the execution of two tasks can best be time-shared, the structure of the resource pools must be studied and the two tasks should be designed so that they pull from different pools. Wickens, San-

dry, and Vidulich (1983) designed a flight simulator task whereby the subjects had to use either the visual or auditory modality for determining the flight commands and then enter these commands either through voice or the keyboard while flying the aircraft, which is a visual-based task. By examining the structure of the attentional processing, one can see that separate pools exist for vision and auditory tasks. One would expect that, since the flight task already incorporates vision, using the auditory channel for the flight commands would increase time-sharing performance. The experimental results confirmed the prediction from the model.

In another test of the model, Wickens and Weingartner (1985) had subjects perform a process control monitoring task. This task was assumed to be spatial in nature. By looking at Figure 12-2, one can see that a concurrent verbal task should pull from a different resource pool, thus allowing the time-sharing to occur. Concurrent tasks that were either spatial or auditory in nature were tested when performing the spatial monitoring task. As predicted by the model, performance was better when, according to the model, the tasks pulled from the different resource pools by designing the tasks to be both spatial and verbal.

MONITORING PERFORMANCE

Besides the design of the task, another practical problem is monitoring performance of the user and operator to determine if an overload situation is occurring. This is not important necessarily with small computer systems, in which the user is performing word processing or working with a spreadsheet, but it is an important problem when an operator is monitoring the displays in a process control plant or a nuclear power plant; it is important when a pilot is flying an aircraft. Several techniques have been developed for assessing the workload of the task. These and the possible applications will be discussed.

Assessing the Workload

Several different methods have been developed for assessing the workload of the task. Some of the assessment techniques can only be applied to laboratory studies of workload, while others can be applied to operating systems. When determining which technique to use, O'Donnell and Eggemeier (1988) listed the following selection criteria: sensitivity, diagnosticity, primary task intrusion, implementation requirements, and operator acceptance.

Sensitivity. Sensitivity refers to the capability of the workload assessment technique to detect changes in the levels of workload imposed by the task performance. A sensitive workload measure will be able to reflect the changes in workload. For an insensitive measure, the workload may change to some degree but the measurement would not change. In some cases, a sensitive measurement may not be needed.

Diagnosticity. Diagnosticity is related to the multiple resource theory of Wickens (1980, 1984b) which was reviewed earlier. A measure is diagnostic if it can identify the attentional resource pool for which the task is pulling the resources. As an example, if the measure determines that a task is drawing from the verbal coding resource pool, as opposed to the spatial coding pool, then this measure

will be highly diagnostic. If the identification of the specific pool cannot be made, then the technique has low diagnosticity.

Primary Task Intrusion. Measuring the workload could change the workload itself so that the measure may be inaccurate. If the task has a high workload to begin with, such as piloting an aircraft or troubleshooting a nuclear power plant during an alarm, then measuring the workload by using a technique which has high primary task intrusion would not be safe. Measures taken after the task are less intrusive than those taken during the task.

Implementation Requirements. Implementation requirements refer to the practical constraints of workload measurement due to obtaining and using the apparatus. These constraints include the measurement equipment and the training of personnel to administer the workload measurements.

Operator Acceptance. The concept of validity, in relationship to questionnaire designs, was discussed in Chapter 4. A questionnaire was valid if it measured what it was supposed to measure. Similarly, for workload assessment, a measure is valid if it measures the workload. Since workload is a subjective measure, the operator must accept the measure as being valid or else the measure will not be valid. In addition, the operator must be able to perceive the utility of the measure for it to be accepted.

Workload Assessment Techniques

Several techniques have been used to assess workload. Very few of these have been used for those kinds of tasks which could be called typical of interacting with the computer, such as using word processors, spreadsheets, and databases. Instead, most of these techniques have been applied to complex systems, which are now increasingly computer-controlled. Many of these techniques are most appropriate for a research environment where the workload for various products or systems is investigated. In the following section, the techniques as outlined by O'Donnell and Eggemeier (1988) are discussed, and then some applications of workload assessment in human-computer interaction tasks are examined.

Subjective Measures. Workload can be assessed subjectively by having the user rate subjective feelings of effort or exertion. Many of the same techniques as discussed under questionnaire design in Chapter 4 can be utilized for subjective measures of workload. In particular, one method uses a Likert scale for responses to questions about workload and assertion on a task.

O'Donnell and Eggemeier (1988) discuss some of the other specific methods for subjectively rating workload. One general method incorporates magnitude estimation techniques. In one technique, a standard task is presented with a certain numerical value (e.g., 10) assigned to it. Subsequent tasks are assigned a numerical value in relation to the standard. As an example, if a user was performing a task with one standard interface, this could be assigned a value of 10. Performing the task with other interfaces would be compared to the standard, and then assigned a number in relation to the standard. Another related technique also has the users assign numerical values to the tasks, but no standard is presented and the users must choose their own scale.

For another method, called equal

appearing intervals, users would perform the tasks and then assign the tasks to one of several categories, usually numbered 1-11, based upon the workload. As an example, several tasks could be performed on different interfaces, and then the users would assess their workload and categorize the tasks and interfaces accordingly.

In some application areas, specific subjective scales are available which provide a standardization to the area. As an example, for aircraft-handling characteristics, the Cooper-Harper scale (Cooper and Harper, 1969) is used (see Figure 12-3). Some variations of the scale exist for other tasks, and it could be varied to include more standard human-computer interaction problems.

Subjective measures can be assessed across the criteria discussed earlier. In terms of sensitivity, O'Donnell and Eggemeier (1988) indicate that these measures are capable of discriminating levels of attentional capacity in nonoverload situations. They can be used to assess the relative potential for overload among design options, tasks, or operating conditions. For diagnosticity, the subjective measures are not very diagnostic; they measure a global indicator of workload. A main advantage of subjective measures, however, is that they are not intrusive because they are administered after the task. In addition, the implementation requirements are minimal, usually requiring only paper and pencil as long as prototypes or the target system are available for testing. The operator acceptance should be high because they should see it as a valid measure directly reflecting their subjective feelings of workload.

Primary Task Measurements. Primary tasks measure the actual perform-

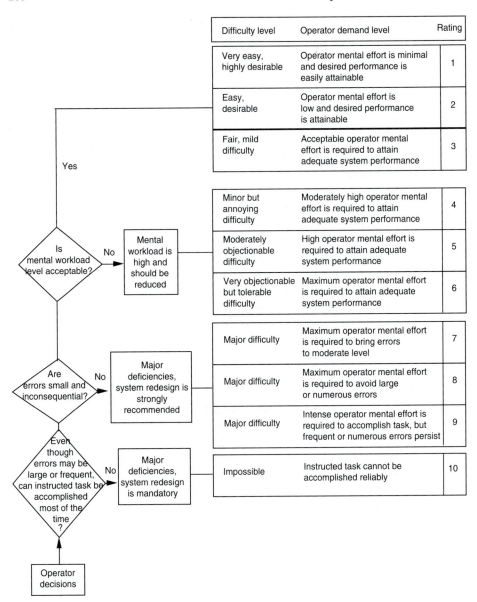

Difficulty level	Operator demand level	Rating
Very easy, highly desirable	Operator mental effort is minimal and desired performance is easily attainable	1
Easy, desirable	Operator mental effort is low and desired performance is attainable	2
Fair, mild difficulty	Acceptable operator mental effort is required to attain adequate system performance	3
Minor but annoying difficulty	Moderately high operator mental effort is required to attain adequate system performance	4
Moderately objectionable difficulty	High operator mental effort is required to attain adequate system performance	5
Very objectionable but tolerable difficulty	Maximum operator mental effort is required to attain adequate system performance	6
Major difficulty	Maximum operator mental effort is required to bring errors to moderate level	7
Major difficulty	Maximum operator mental effort is required to avoid large or numerous errors	8
Major difficulty	Intense operator mental effort is required to accomplish task, but frequent or numerous errors persist	9
Impossible	Instructed task cannot be accomplished reliably	10

Yes

Is mental workload level acceptable? — No — Mental workload is high and should be reduced

Are errors small and inconsequential? — No — Major deficiencies, system redesign is strongly recommended

Even though errors may be large or frequent, can instructed task be accomplished most of the time? — No — Major deficiencies, system redesign is mandatory

Operator decisions

Figure 12-3. An example of a modified Cooper-Harper scale used to assess workload subjectively (O'Donnell and Eggemeier, 1988). Copyright © 1988 by John Wiley & Sons, Inc. Reprinted by permission of John Wiley & Sons, Inc.

ance on the task. The assumption is that as workload increases, the quality of user performance will decrease. This relationship does not hold in all cases, though. Norman and Bobrow (1975) have investi-gated the relationship between perform-ance and workload (see Figure 12-4). They indicate that in some cases, labeled data-driven, performance depends on the qual-ity of the data, and decreasing the work-

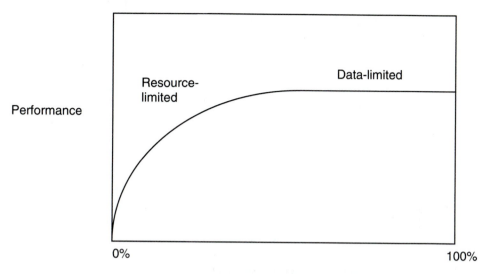

Figure 12-4. An illustration of the relationship between performance and workload. On the part of the graph labeled data-limited, applying more attentional resources to the task will not improve performance. In the other section, however, a monotonic relationship exists between performance and workload (from Norman and Bobrow, 1975, reprinted with permission of publisher).

load by applying more attention to the task will not affect performance. In the other section of the graph, though, where a monotonic relationship exists between performance and workload, the assumption of the relationship between workload and performance will be valid, and primary task measures can be used. Any of the dependent variables for measuring performance of a human-computer interaction task, as discussed in Chapter 4, can be used as the measure for primary task workload assessment. Typically, speed and errors on the task are measured.

In a human-computer interaction situation, primary task workload would be assessed under the following scenario. Two or more interfaces would be tested. A task would be chosen, and this task would be varied with different degrees of workload difficulty. As an example, the calculations in a spreadsheet task may be varied according to difficulty of the calculations.

The calculations could be performed using the spreadsheets on the different interfaces. By looking at performance, such as speed, as a function of task difficulty, it is possible that the relationships may be different for the interfaces. As an example, the relationship could be flat for interface A and sloped for interface B. The conclusion would be that workload could be a problem for difficult tasks on interface B.

In terms of sensitivity, primary task measures are only sensitive to workload changes in the region of the graph of Figure 12-4 which shows the monotonic relationship. These measures are also good for discriminating overload from nonoverload. These measures are not high in diagnosticity; they can only obtain a global measure of workload. Intrusiveness is low because, unlike subjective reports, no additional user report is needed. The only implementation requirements are to have an operational system and a program to store the performance measures, such as speed and errors, on a disk so that it can be analyzed later. For user acceptance, no data have been collected; O'Donnell and Eggemeier (1988) see no reason to expect negative opinions.

Secondary Task Measures. In a secondary task procedure for assessing workload, the user concurrently performs two tasks. The task of central importance is called the primary task and the secondary task is used to measure the workload of the primary task. The secondary task serves as an indicant of the spare attentional capacity from the primary task. The procedure is as follows. The secondary and primary tasks will be performed individually to obtain baseline scores which can be used later as a comparison. Then, the two tasks are performed concurrently. The user is instructed to emphasize either the secondary or primary task. Performance will be measured on both tasks. The degree of the decrement in performance for the two tasks, when compared to the baseline scores, provides a measure of the workload of the task.

The choice of the secondary task is important in this procedure. One requirement is that it should impose a continuous demand on the user. Otherwise, the user could alternate between the primary and secondary tasks so that both tasks were not performed at exactly the same time. Another requirement is that performance on the secondary task should be stabilized before it is used in workload assessment. If performance is changing, then the workload cannot be measured accurately. A final requirement is that multiple resource theory should be used to determine which resource pools are likely to be tapped. The

primary and secondary tasks should pull resources from the same pool. Based upon these requirements, several candidate secondary tasks are available.

One secondary task technique uses a choice reaction time task. In a choice reaction time task, a different response is generated for each stimulus and the reaction time between the onset of the stimulus and the reaction is used as a measurement. As an example, the fingers of one hand may be resting on five keys and a stimulus appears indicating that the key under the thumb should be pushed. The time to push the button, while performing the primary task, is a measure of workload. This task loads on the central processing and response stages.

Another task, called tracking, is a continuous task, much like driving a car, and provides a good secondary task. Typically, a path to follow is provided on the screen, and the user must manipulate some input device, such as a joystick, to follow the path. Deviations from the track can be measured. This task loads on the response stage.

Monitoring is another kind of secondary task technique. In this kind of task, the user tries to detect the occurrence of a particular stimulus from several alternatives. As soon as it appears, a response is made. As an example, the user may be looking for the color green in other colors. This task loads on the perceptual processor.

In a secondary memory task, the user may be provided with a stimulus, such as the letter "H," to be remembered. Then a set of stimuli of several characters can be presented. The user must search through this set to determine if the letter "H" appears. If it does, then a response is made. The task can be made more difficult by requiring the user to remember more than one stimulus, or by increasing the number of stimuli to search through. This task loads mainly on central processing.

Mental math can also be used as a secondary task. The user may be required to perform math operations, such as subtracting or adding numbers, while performing the primary task. This task loads mainly on central processing.

Shadowing is an auditory secondary task. Auditory stimuli are presented, such as a sequence of words or letters, and the user repeats back these stimuli as they are heard. This task loads on the perceptual processor.

In a time estimation task, the user is required to tap at a regular time interval and a specific rate while the primary task is being performed. When overloaded, this becomes a difficult task in that the intervals between taps will become irregular. This task loads almost entirely on the motor processor.

All of these tasks could be used as secondary tasks in the assessment of workload. The choice of task depends on the task loading required. If the visual display of information is being tested, then the tasks that load on the perceptual processor should be chosen; if the cognitive aspects of the task are being investigated, then the tasks that load on the central processing should be chosen.

In terms of sensitivity, secondary task measures can be used to assess non-overload situations. If overloaded, then the tasks become too difficult and cannot be performed. The main reason to use secondary tasks is because it is the only one of the categories of workload measures, except for one physiological meas-

ure, which is highly diagnostic. These measures can be used to pinpoint the locus of the overload. One of the main problems, however, is that they are highly intrusive and are not safe to use in operational environments where increased workload could be a safety hazard. As such, they are most often used in laboratory settings. For the implementation, besides the prototypes or operational systems, the only additional thing needed is the training of the users on the secondary tasks. In terms of operator acceptance, once again, no systematic data are available, but the secondary tasks could distract the users.

Physiological Measures. People exhibit physiological changes with changes in workload. Thus, one method to measure workload is to measure the physiological changes that occur. These measures include the electroencephalograph (EEG), evoked responses, eye functions, cardiac functions, and muscle functions.

The EEG records direct measures of the level of brain activity. This measure is taken by placing electrodes, which are sensitive to electrical activity, on the scalp of the head. When sleeping, one's EEG activity level is very low; when alert and performing a task, one's EEG level is much higher. The variations in the workload of the task will show up as variations in EEG level. Consequently, this provides a global measure of workload.

The evoked response is similar to the EEG measure in that electrodes are placed on the scalp and electrical activity of the brain is measured. In this case, though, the resulting waveform of activity is of particular interest. The waveform is determined from the point of a presentation of a stimulus at time equal to 0. These waveforms have distinct patterns depending on the time after the stimulus presentation, and these patterns are an indication of the processing of the stimulus. Of particular interest is the waveform pattern at about time equal to 3000 msec after the stimulus presentation. This part of the waveform, called the P300, has a higher amplitude than the earlier and later parts of the wave, and it seems to be related to the cognitive processing of the stimulus. The workload of a task can have an effect on the P300 by changing either the latency or amplitude of the spike which occurs at that point on the wave. With high workload, the latency of the P300 could increase and the amplitude could decrease. One of the problems with using evoked responses in on-line workload assessment is that much averaging of the waveforms must occur before an accurate measure of the P300 can be determined. Analyzing the P300 on a single trial is difficult.

Eye functions also change with fluctuations in workload. One change that occurs is the pupil size in relation to workload; the more workload, the smaller the pupil size. One of the limitations to using this technique is that complex and sensitive measuring equipment is needed to detect these changes. The problem becomes even greater when the head is allowed to move around, as would occur during any real-world task. Another change that occurs is in the scanning behavior of the eyes. If the eye must move to scan complex information on one display or over several displays, then under high workload the eye will dwell on one position for long periods of time. Once again, sensitive equipment is needed to take this measure.

One of the simplest physiological measures is the electrocardiogram (EKG) of the heartbeat. The beat-to-beat variability is most related to the workload of the task. This is easy to measure, requiring only that an electrode be placed on the chest near the heart, and it is a nonintrusive measure.

Finally, stress and high workload often operate together. A time-tested method of measuring stress is either through the myoelectric signal of muscle contraction or through surface electromyoelectric signals. This measures the tension in the muscles. Higher tension is an indication of higher workload.

O'Donnell and Eggemeier (1988) indicate that the physiological measures are sensitive to workload changes in nonoverload situations. In terms of diagnosticity, the P300 measure is diagnostic, because it is an indication of cognitive activity, but the other physiological measures are not diagnostic. Intrusion is not a major problem, except for the eye function measurements, because measurements can be taken just on the task itself, with no other tasks required. The implementation requirements can be highly restrictive for some of the measures. In particular, most of the measures require complex, sensitive, and expensive equipment. User acceptance of these techniques has not been assessed. The only potential problem might be in obtaining permission from the users to hook up electrodes and the other apparatus. The eye movement technique is the only one that does not require the attachment of electrodes.

Applications

Applications have been few in those areas that are typically associated with human-computer interaction, such as a single user operating a personal computer. This is, of course, not the only application area for human-computer interaction. Most complex systems are now computerized. Process control plants, nuclear power plants, aircraft, and large ships are just some of the examples of the use of computers in complex systems. There are also cases in which the user may become overloaded, especially when an emergency situation occurs. Overload is important in these cases and cannot be ignored in the design and assessment of the system. In fact, the U.S. government now requires that a workload assessment be performed on some new aircraft before they are allowed to be flown.

Perhaps more applications will be be found as these workload assessment techniques become easier to use and the importance of workload on task interaction is realized. As an example, a potential application exists in adaptive displays (see Chapter 20). Changing or adapting the interface interaction to the workload could be advantageous. It is possible that the wording and tone of help messages could be adapted, depending on the workload and the stress of the user.

Hancock and Chignell (1987) have proposed a model for the integration of mental workload assessment techniques to the control of adaptive interfaces. They argue that the human naturally attempts to adapt to the environment upon the perception that the workload is changing. Again, using the example of driving a car while listening to the radio, a driver under high workload conditions may decide to adapt to the environment by turning off the radio. In some respects, this active adaptation of the environment exasperates the

workload problem in that attentional resources must be devoted to decisions and responses when deciding how to adapt to the environment to reduce the workload and the response required to perform the adaptation. A system that performs these adaptation functions automatically will have characteristics of a natural interface while at the same time reducing the workload required for the adaptation.

Hancock and Chignell (1987) suggest that a system can be built to perform these adaptive functions. The system would include a method to assess the workload and functions to adapt the interface. For assessing the workload, they suggest that the physiological measurement techniques, discussed previously, would be most useful. For adapting the interface, they suggest that a hierarchical decomposition of a task into goals and subgoals, similar to that done for the predictive models of Chapters 14, 15, and 16, could be used to reallocate some of the tasks between humans and machines. No experimental work was performed on this proposal, and no system was built. To achieve the goal of adapting the interface to mental workload, the system must be able to (1) assess workload on-line; and (2) adapt the interface to changing demands. Adapting the interface is considered in more detail in Chapter 20; assessing workload on-line has been considered in an experiment by LeMay and Hird (1986).

LeMay and Hird were interested in assessing the workload of operators controlling and monitoring space probes. As happens with process control or nuclear power plant tasks, many times the equipment is upgraded and the computer operations are centralized, thus increasing the monitoring work and control by the operators. Errors by the operators, due to high workload, could be costly in equipment, in the project development, and in time.

In this study, four methods to determine workload on-line were investigated. In the subjective method, the operators were required to enter a subjective rating, from 1 (low workload) to 7 (high workload), after each subtask. In the time stress condition, ratings using the same scale were again collected, but this time the operators rated the time stress of the task. In the workload ratio condition, the computer automatically determined the ratio of time required to perform the task (set by the experimenter) and time available to perform the task. Finally, in the primary task measurement condition, the time to initialize the task, from the time between keystrokes, was used as the workload measure.

To test the sensitivity of the workload measures, the tasks were varied according to low, medium, and high workload. The low-workload tasks were very routine, requiring little effort. The high-workload tasks were difficult, with random faults included in the system. Sensitivity was investigated by determining whether or not the measures changed over the different workloads. Two of the measures were significant statistically: the time stress rating and the ratio. The other two were nonsignificant and, thus, were less sensitive to changes in workload. Interestingly, errors occurred in the operation of the system, and 78% of the errors occurred in the high-workload condition, indicating that workload does have an effect on performance.

From the results, it appears that the measures with a time stress component were the most sensitive to the changes in workload; the other two measures which examined workload as attentional requirements were less sensitive. This experimentation demonstrates one of the hazards of empirical research. It is possible that the different workload conditions were actually different time stress conditions; no independent measure of workload was taken. Since all the operators were experts, and since the full range of subjective measures for the mental effort were not utilized (most operators reported workload less than a "3"), the results from this study have to be evaluated carefully.

The main point of this experimentation is that workload can be measured on-line and could, possibly, in the future be used to change the task or reallocate the task to other operators, to reduce the workload. The subjective workload is a possible means of evaluating workload but, in a real situation, having operators provide a rating would just increase the workload of the task. We would like to have a measure that is less intrusive. The ratio measurement is not intrusive, but it relies on good estimates of the time needed to perform the task.

The U.S. military services have been interested in application of workload assessment in complex equipment usage. One rudimentary form of determining mental workload is used on-line to adapt the control of machinery. For high-speed aircraft at high-speed turns or dives, the pilot could lose consciousness as the high "g's" restrict the flow of blood to the brain. If brain activity is reduced, indicating the blood flow problem, then automatic control of the plane will occur. One of the goals of this area is to adapt control of the plane to the workload of the pilot.

SUMMARY

The two attentional metaphors can be used in the design of equipment and tasks, especially when the tasks are difficult and the operator may have trouble attending to all the information. On the surface, the two metaphors may seem to offer different suggestions for this design. For the searchlight metaphor, the task should be designed so that the information is integrated or as similar as possible so that time-consuming attention switching is not needed. For the resource metaphor, the task should be designed so that the two tasks are as dissimilar as possible so as to pull from different resource pools. To resolve this conflict, the two metaphors should be applied in different situations. The searchlight metaphor should be applied when the information is from the same task and must be combined with previous information to perform the task. The resource metaphor should be applied when the operator may have to perform more than one task at a time. As noted by Polson et al. (1989), these distinctions may not always be clear. They do provide some overall guidelines, however, in those clear-cut cases.

The assessment of workload will also be discussed in the context of several of the predictive models such as NGOMSL (Chapter 15) and production systems (Chapter 16). These assessments do not equate workload with attentional resources, as do the measures in this chapter, but rather they equate workload with the load on working memory. With the limited capacity of working memory, overloading memory can cause problems. The predictive models can predict this overload problem because they predict the kinds of information needed by the users. The predictive models cannot predict the load on attentional resources, however, and this should be a topic for future research.

QUESTIONS

1. A chemical process has five subsystems which must be monitored by computer: pressure, temperature, outlet valve, intake valve, and water solution level. Show what an integrated display would look like when all subsystems were operating properly. On a malfunction of the intake valve, the temperature would rise and the water solution level would also rise. Show what this malfunction would look like on the integrated display.

2. Name the five methods used to assess workload. Explain how one of these methods is similar to a method used to assess questionnaires.

3. The Cooper-Harper scale is an example of which kind of workload assessment technique?

4. Name three requirements for a good secondary task.

5. Monitoring, when used as a secondary task, will pull resources from which information processing stage resource pool?

6. Are secondary task techniques of workload assessment better utilized in a real-world setting or in a laboratory? Explain your answer.

7. Evaluate the four classes of measures of workload across the following criteria.

    a. Which is best and worst according to sensitivity?

    b. Which is best and worst according to intrusiveness?

    c. Which is best and worst according to diagnosticity?

    d. Which is best and worst according to implementation requirements?

8. Indicate how the criterion of diagnosticity is defined for workload analyses.

9. Name the two aspects of the P300 which indicate high workload.

10. Name the one aspect of electrocardiograms (EKGs) which indicates high workload.

11. Identify the workload assessment technique from the following description.

    a. Look for decrements in the actual performance of the task.

    b. Have a person do a tracking task at the same time as the regular task.

    c. Measurement of the P300 wave is taken.

    d. The Cooper-Harper scale is administered.

    e. The person rates his or her feelings of exertion needed to perform the task.

CHAPTER 13

THE MODEL HUMAN PROCESSOR

INTRODUCTION

The basic tenets of the Model Human Processor of Card, Moran, and Newell (1983, 1986) were presented in Chapter 8 on human information processing. Use of the model indicates the implicit assumptions of the discrete stages models of human information processing. The user of this model must accept the assumptions that processing occurs in stages, that processing in a stage is completed before information is passed to the next stage, and that information flows in a sequential manner from one stage to the next. If these assumptions are accepted, then the model can be used. In particular, if we know the stages that the information must pass through and we know the timing characteristics of those individual stages, then we can add together the timing values to determine an estimate for the total task time. The advantage to this kind of technique is that the database of needed values is reduced. If a computer company wanted to keep a database of the times to perform certain kinds of tasks, such as interacting with menu displays or performing operations on a word processor, the company would have to keep information on all these tasks; the number of tasks could become quite large. We can save time and effort by breaking down these tasks into the specific components and only keeping information on the components. When times need to be determined for the complicated tasks, therefore, the tasks need only be broken down into the individual components, of which we have the relevant timing characteristics. The total time is determined by adding together the times of the individual components. This is the logic behind the Model Human Processor.

PARAMETERS OF THE MODEL HUMAN PROCESSOR

Recall from Chapter 8 that the Model Human Processor is composed of three systems: the perceptual, cognitive, and motor systems. The perceptual and cognitive systems have memories associated with them; the motor system does not have a memory. Several parameters can be used to quantitatively describe these three systems and, thus, make predictions about the timing of information through these systems.

Cycle Time Parameters

One of the most important parameters for determining the timing characteristics of a task is the cycle time, τ, for the three systems. This is the time that it takes for the information to be processed through the stages. While a stage is processing the information, it cannot process any other information. A good example of this is watching a wheel cover, which has some kind of identifying mark, turn around and around on the tire of a moving car (see Figure 13-1). Have you ever noticed how, at a certain speed, it appears that the wheel is going backward instead of forward? The analysis of the cycle times shows why this may occur. Let's say that it takes 150 msec. to process the visual information on

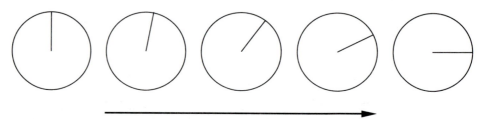

Figure 13-1. The human visual system can only perceive items in little snapshots of information. In watching a wheel move, the snapshots in this example are perceived 2.5 degrees more in the direction that the car is moving. The car wheel appears to be moving forward.

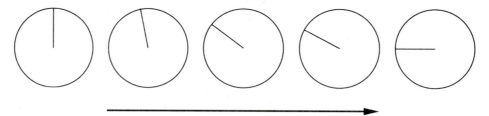

Figure 13-2. In this example, the car wheel has speeded up so that the snapshot receives the information 2.5 degrees in the opposite direction that the car is moving. It appears that the car wheel is moving backward.

the wheel and during this time, no other information can be received and processed. The perceiver has, essentially, snapshots of the wheel moving. Let's say that the wheel in Figure 13-1 is going at such a speed so that every 150 msec. it rotates two times and then 2.5 degrees more. Since the visual system only takes a snapshot of information every 150 msec., it appears that the line on the wheel only moves the 2.5 degrees instead of the full rotation in this time period.

Now let's say that the car has speeded up some so that every 150 msec., the car wheel will move two full rotations and then almost another full rotation, but not quite, of 57.5 degrees (see Figure 13-2). The visual system only takes the 150 msec. snapshots, as in Figure 13-2, so it appears that the line always moves backward 2.5 degrees and that the wheel is moving backward.

The processing times, or cycle times, are important for making predictions about the time needed to perform computerized tasks. Recall from Chapter 8 that the values for the cycle times for the three systems, perceptual, cognitive, and motor, are as follows:

$$\tau_p = 100 \, [50 \sim 200]$$

$$\tau_c = 70 \, [25 \sim 170]$$

$$\tau_m = 70 \, [30 \sim 100] \tag{13.1}$$

The first number represents the most plausible value for the parameter, or the average value. The numbers in brackets represent low and high values for these parameters. These are not really ranges, in the statistical sense, but represent plausible values. As mentioned previously, Card et al. (1983) sometimes refer to the first value as the Middle Man value, the low value as the Fast Man value, and the high value as the Slow Man value.

Memory Parameters

The other parameters of the Model Human Processor are those associated with the memories of the perceptual and cognitive systems. Three parameters describe the processing of information for these memories: the code (κ), the decay time (δ), and the capacity (μ). The code is a nonquantifiable variable referring to the form in which the information is stored in the memory. The decay time is the half-life, which is the amount of time that the information will remain in memory with the probability of retrieval greater than 50%. The capacity of memory is the number of items that can be stored in memory.

For human-computer interaction tasks, the perceptual system has two memories relevant to these tasks: the visual image store (VIS) and the auditory image store (AIS). A definition of these perceptual processors is that information is unprocessed or it is not transformed in any way. Therefore, the code, κ, of both memories is a physical code where information is an unidentified, nonsymbolic analogue to the actual stimulus. This is represented as follows:

$$\kappa_{VIS} = \text{physical}$$

$$\kappa_{AIS} = \text{physical} \tag{13.2}$$

The decay time of these perceptual memories is

$$\delta_{VIS} = 200 \ [90 \sim 1000] \text{ msec.}$$

$$\delta_{AIS} = 1500 \ [900 \sim 3500] \text{ msec.} \tag{13.3}$$

Again, the numbers in the brackets repre-

sent the plausible ranges of values, and the number outside the brackets represents the most likely value. All of these values for the Model Human Processor are taken from experimental studies, and the numbers represent summaries of what are, in many cases, quite clever experiments that were used to determine these values. As an example for the VIS value, Averbach and Coriell (1961) devised an experiment in which the subjects were required to look at a matrix of items, like that in Figure 13-3a. The matrix was only presented for a short period of time, and then all the values in the matrix were blanked out by displaying a mask. In the time period displayed, the number of items in this matrix was too large to remember all of them. After the appearance of a blank white field, a marker would appear pointing to one of the items on the display, as in Figure 13-3b, and the subject was required to identify the item name pointed to by the marker. Of course, when the marker occurs, the items are no longer displayed and the subject does not know where the marker will appear beforehand. The onset of the marker was varied in time. Averbach and Coriell found that the item could still be identified 50% of the time 200 msec. after it was masked, and this value corresponds to the decay rate used in the Model Human Processor. Similar ingenious experiments were performed for the AIS values.

The capacity of the perceptual memories are

$$\mu_{VIS} = 17 \ [7 \sim 17] \text{ letters}$$

$$\mu_{AIS} = 5 \ [4.4 \sim 6.2] \text{ letters} \tag{13.4}$$

The "letters" units are used because this is the form in which the data were collected for the experiments. Letters can refer to

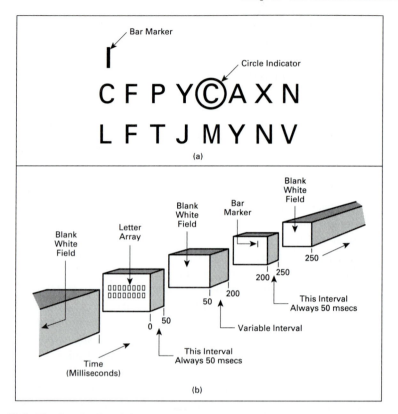

Figure 13-3. The Averbach and Coriell (1961) experiment was used to determine the decay time value for the visual image store in the Model Human Processor. After the onset of the matrix of letters in (a), the matrix was turned off and a marker appeared, either a bar marker or a circle indicator, pointing to one of the values. The time difference between the offset of the letters and the onset of the marker, as shown in (b), was used to determine the decay time of the visual image store. Copyright © 1961 AT&T. All rights reserved. Reprinted with permission.

chunks of information. With these parameters, the characteristics of the perceptual memories are completely specified.

The cognitive memories consist of a working memory and a long-term memory. The working memory (WM) holds information under current consideration and constitutes the general registers of the cognitive processor. Information is coded in two ways in working memory. We usually remember things by the way that they sound, and so the predominant coding is acoustic. Sometimes we code things by the way they look, which is called visual coding. This is represented as follows:

$$\kappa_{WM} = \text{acoustic or visual} \qquad (13.5)$$

The decay time for working memory is dependent on the number of chunks that must be retained:

$$\delta_{WM} \ (1 \text{ chunk}) \ = 73 \ [73 \sim 226] \text{ sec.}$$

$$\delta_{WM} \ (3 \text{ chunks}) = 7 \ [5 \sim 34] \text{ sec.} \qquad (13.6)$$

Information can be retained in working memory indefinitely if the person can rehearse the items; decay will occur for unrehearsed items.

Finally, the capacity of working memory can be described as follows:

$$\mu_{WM} = 7\ [5 \sim 9]\ \text{chunks} \tag{13.7}$$

This value corresponds to Miller's (1956) famous paper on the "magic number plus or minus 2." Subsequent work has found that the capacity of working memory may not be as large as was believed at that time. Working memory only has this capacity if it can be augmented by long-term memory, which may be the case in only some of the applications. Consider the following task. Have someone say to you a series of 15 random digits. In the one-back memory test, you would write down the digit that was said immediately preceding the current digit. As an example, if someone says:

1 2 3 4 5 6 7 8 9

then you would write nothing when 1 is said, you would write down 1 when 2 was said, 2 when 3 was said, and so on. All you would have to remember is one digit back. For the two-back memory test, you would write nothing when 1 and 2 were said; you would write 1 when 3 was said, 2 when 4 was said, and so on. All you would have to remember is two digits back. Of course, in the actual test random numbers would be used. If you perform this test, you will find that remembering two digits is difficult; three digits is almost impossible. The capacity of working memory is smaller than originally thought and can be described as follows:

$$\mu_{WM} = 3[2.5 \sim 4]\ \text{chunks} \tag{13.8}$$

This holds when long-term memory cannot be used.

Long-term memory is the mass of available memory. In most cases, it is conceptualized as a network of related chunks. It is information which retains very little from that originally perceived, and so it has a coding according to its meaning, or semantics, instead of any physical characteristics:

$$\kappa_{LTM} = \text{semantic} \tag{13.9}$$

The information does not decay from long-term memory, and so the decay time is

$$\delta_{LTM} = \text{infinite} \tag{13.10}$$

Finally, the capacity is unlimited:

$$\mu_{LTM} = \text{infinite} \tag{13.11}$$

Some of the above parameters for long-term memory may be somewhat surprising. In particular, we all know that we forget things, yet we say that the capacity is unlimited. Evidence has been collected which indicates that the information is always in long-term memory but the problem is that sometimes it cannot be found. Think of a library. In a library, the books must be placed in the correct position on the shelves or they will never be found in a large library. If a book is put in the wrong place and a person goes looking for that book, it will not be found on the initial search. This does not mean that the book is not stored in the library; it just means that it cannot be found. The same thing happens with long-term memory. The information item may be stored in long-term memory, but we may have forgotten how to retrieve it. In a library, you may happen to find the missing book through browsing in the location of the book. Maybe you have noticed the phenomenon of "browsing" through your memory and then finding information which you thought you may have forgotten.

The capacity of long-term memory is considered to be infinite. In other words, you do not have to worry about learning too much information. Still, people know that trying to learn too much all at once is difficult, so how can capacity be unlimited? The problem occurs again with retrieval cues. When learning something, the person must be careful to develop retrieval cues with the right kinds of links so that the information can be retrieved later. If an item is learned, and then a new item is learned with the same link, it will be difficult to retrieve the earlier learned item. If you are trying to cram for a test, developing the unique links is difficult.

EXAMPLES OF APPLYING THE MODEL HUMAN PROCESSOR

All of the parameters have been specified for the Model Human Processor. The problem now is to use these parameters in predicting times for performing human-computer interaction tasks. Several examples follow. In these examples, we start with relatively simple tasks and then consider complex tasks more closely associated with human-computer interaction.

Simple Examples

First, consider an easy example. A person sits before a computer display terminal. Whenever any symbol appears, the person is to press the space bar. What is the time

between the signal and response? This is similar to just a simple reaction time. To solve the problem, it must be divided into its components and the following steps:

1. τ_p The letter is in the visual image store, then transferred to working memory.

2. τ_c In working memory, a decision is made on the response.

3. τ_m The motor system carries out the response.

Step 1 requires the perceptual system, and so the cycle time is represented by τ_p. Step 2 requires the cognitive system, and so the cycle time is represented by τ_c. Finally, step 3 requires the motor system, and so the cycle time is represented by τ_m. Card et al. (1983) refer to the average value as the Middle Man value, the lowest value in the range as the Fast Man value, and the highest value in the range as the Slow Man value. Using these values, the equation representing the needed time is

$$\tau_p + \tau_c + \tau_m \qquad (13.12)$$

Using the values for the Middle Man model (the average performance times), the estimated time to perform the task is

$$100 + 70 + 70 = 240 \text{ msec.} \qquad (13.13)$$

The estimated time to perform the task using the Fast Man model is

$$50 + 25 + 30 = 105 \text{ msec.} \qquad (13.14)$$

Finally, the estimated time to perform the task using the Slow Man model is

$200 + 170 + 100 = 470$ msec.   (13.15)

Overall, we would expect that the time to perform this task is somewhere within the range of 105 msec. to 470 msec. As pointed out by Card et al. (1983), these results correspond closely to that found in the laboratory, where the range of values is typically between 100 msec. and 400 msec. for this kind of simple reaction time task.

Now consider a second example in which the task is cognitively a bit more difficult. It is essentially the same task as the first example but now the person is shown one of two letters and must determine if the displayed letter is a target or a distractor. To set the target, the person is shown a letter at the beginning of the task, before the timing of the task is started, then is asked to remember that letter. The person is told to push the left button on the keyboard if the displayed letter is the same as the target and the right button if the displayed letter is different from the target, a distractor. Many of the steps are the same as the steps needed for the first example, except for an extra cognitive step. The steps are as follows:

1. The first letter appears (A) (the timing of the task is not yet started).

2. τ_p The second letter appears (A). Transfer the letter from the visual image store to working memory (start the timing of the task).

3. τ_c In working memory, match the second letter to the first letter.

4. τ_c Decide on the response: left button.

5. τ_m The motor system carries out the response of pressing the appropriate button.

Substituting the appropriate processor parameters for steps 2 through 5, the equation estimating the time to perform this task is

$$\tau_p + \tau_c + \tau_c + \tau_m \qquad (13.16)$$

Using the values for the Middle Man model (the average performance times), the estimated time to perform the task is

$100 + 70 + 70 + 70 = 310$ msec. (13.17)

The estimated time to perform the task using the Fast Man model is

$50 + 25 + 25 + 30 = 130$ msec.   (13.18)

Finally, the estimated time to perform the task using the Slow Man model is

$200 + 170 + 170 + 100 = 640$ msec.
(13.19)

Overall, we would expect that the time to perform this task is somewhere within the range of 130 msec. to 640 msec.

Finally, for the third example, suppose that the task is very similar to the previous two except that the person presses the left key if the symbols have the same name (A and a), regardless of the appearance, and the right key if they do not. In the previous two examples, the person was just matching the physical characteristics of the characters; in this example, the person must match the semantic properties of the characters.

In this example, the code of representation of the characters becomes important; this did not need to be considered in the previous examples. Recall that the code of representation of the characters is represented by the κ parameter. For the second example, the operator was shown the target in step 1, and this target could be stored in working memory using a visual representation, which is one of the codes used by the working memory. In step 2, the letter is displayed on the screen and the person must decide, in step 3, whether or not this is the same letter. Since the person is only looking for a physical match, the letters can be compared in working memory according to the visual code.

In this example, however, a physical match will not be able to determine if they have the same name. They could be physically different (the A and a) and still have the same name. The match can only occur at a semantic level, or a level in which the meaning of the letter is considered. The cognitive memory containing the semantic representations is the long-term memory. Therefore, the representation of the semantic meaning of the letter must be retrieved from long-term memory before the comparison can be made. The semantic representation would probably then be coded into an acoustic code in working memory. The retrieval from long-term memory requires an extra cognitive processor not present in the second example.

The steps needed for the name match are as follows:

1. The first letter appears (A) (the timing of the task is not yet started).

2. τ_p The second letter appears

(a); transfer the image from the visual image store to working memory (start the timing of the task).

3. τ_c Have the visual representation in working memory; must retrieve semantic representation from long-term memory.

4. τ_c In working memory, match the second letter to the first letter.

5. τ_c Decide on the response: left button.

6. τ_m The motor system carries out the response of pressing the appropriate button.

Substituting the appropriate processor parameters for steps 2 through 6, the equation estimating the time to perform this task is

$$\tau_p + \tau_c + \tau_c + \tau_c + \tau_m \qquad (13.20)$$

Using the values for the Middle Man model (the average performance times), the estimated time to perform the task is

$$100 + 70 + 70 + 70 + 70 = 380 \text{ msec.} \qquad (13.21)$$

The estimated time to perform the task using the Fast Man model is

$$50 + 25 + 25 + 25 + 30 = 155 \text{ msec.} \qquad (13.22)$$

Finally, the estimated time to perform the task using the Slow Man model is

$$200 + 170 + 170 + 170 + 100 = 810 \text{ msec.}$$
$$(13.23)$$

Overall, we would expect that the time to perform this task is somewhere within the range of 155 msec. to 810 msec. Card et al. (1983) point out that the laboratory tasks for name matches usually take about 70 msec. longer than the physical matches of the second example. This corresponds to our analysis.

Complex Examples

So far, the examples considered for the Model Human Processor have not had much relevancy to human-computer interaction tasks. They have been good, however, for illustrating the application of this model. The next two examples are more relevant. These two examples illustrate how the Model Human Processor can be used to compare different designs of menu displays and different designs for computerized cash registers.

First, consider the example for the design of menu displays for interactive computer programs. An important issue in this area is how to organize the items on the screen. Should all the items be displayed on one screen, or should only a few items be displayed on one and then, depending on the choice, more screens would need to be accessed? This issue is considered in terms of the depth or breadth of the menu items. With all items on one screen the display has high breadth; with items embedded on several screens, the display has depth.

For this example, consider two kinds of organizations. For the high-breadth layout, all 16 menu items are on one screen (see Figure 13-4). For the high-depth layout, four items are on one screen and for any menu choice that is made, the user would then have another choice of four items (see Figure 13-5). In both layouts, the menu item has a number or letter associated with it so that the user would enter a number or letter for the menu choice. Assume that the user knows the menu item needed and is experienced in using this kind of display. We also assume that the user is an expert typist so that key searches on the keyboard are not needed.

First consider the example for the high-breadth display. The following steps would be needed:

1. τ_p perceive item on display and transfer name to working memory

2. τ_c retrieve semantic meaning of needed operation from long-term memory, transfer to working memory

3. τ_c match code from displayed item to needed item

4. τ_c decide on match (yes: go to next step, no: perceive next item)

5. τ_m execute response to choose menu item or execute eye movements to go back to step 1

6. τ_p perceive menu item number and transfer to working memory

7. τ_c decide on key

8. τ_m execute key response

```
        1.     Menu item a
        2.     Menu item b
        3.     Menu item c
        4.     Menu item d
        5.     Menu item e
        6.     Menu item f
        7.     Menu item g
        8.     Menu item h
        9.     Menu item i
       10.     Menu item j
       11.     Menu item k
       12.     Menu item l
       13.     Menu item m
       14.     Menu item n
       15.     Menu item o
       16.     Menu item p


   Enter the number of the menu item:    _____
```

Figure 13-4. An example of the high-breadth display. In this case, all 16 items are displayed on the one screen. To choose a menu item, the user must read through the items, until the desired one is found, and then enter the number of that item.

Steps 1 through 5 must be done (16+1)/2 times on the average, using a serial terminating search, because 16 items are on the screen. Using this, the equation is

$$\text{total time} = (16 + 1)/2 \; (\tau_p + 3\tau_c + t_m) + \tau_p + \tau_c + \tau_m \qquad (13.24)$$

Inserting the Middle Man values, the equation becomes

$$\text{total time} = 17/2 \; (100 + 3(70) + 70) + 100 + 70 + 70 = 3470 \text{ msec.} \qquad (13.25)$$

The main confusion about the above equation may be the multiplication of some of the steps by (16 + 1)/2. This is used because we assume that the user performs a serial terminating search for the menu item. In a serial terminating search, the search ends once the menu item is found. This makes sense, because it would not seem reasonable that the user would continue reading menu items after the desired item was found. If we assume that each menu item has an equal occurrence of being used, then we would expect that the user would stop the search, on the average, at the eighth or ninth item, or after 8.5 items.

To illustrate this further, consider a menu with four items as in the high-depth menu display. If each menu item has an equal probability of being used, then we would expect that the search would stop after the first, second, third, or fourth items

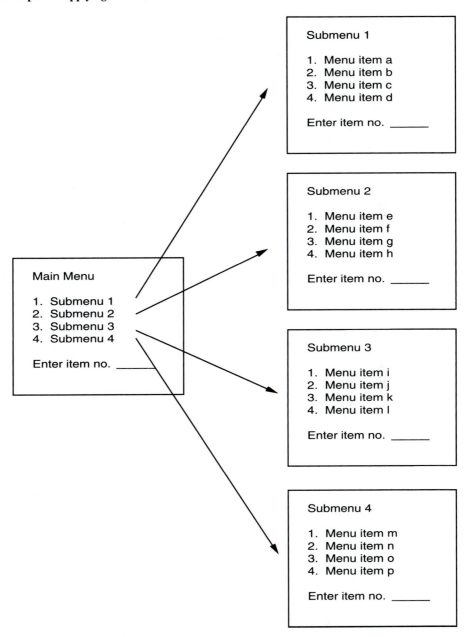

Figure 13-5. An example of the high-depth display. In this case, the 16 items are divided between two levels. On the first screen, four items will appear. The user must make a choice by typing the number of the menu item. Depending on the choice for the first screen, one of the four screens will appear next. If the user chose item 1 on the first screen, then the menu with items a-d will appear on the second screen. If the user chose item 2 on the first screen, then items e-h will appear on the second screen, and so forth. For the high-depth display, the user only has to search four items on a screen, but two screens have to be searched.

with equal probability. To find the average search time, we would just take $(1 + 2 + 3 + 4)/4$, because four searches are occurring and the search could stop at either one with equal probability. This value is $10/4$ or 2.5.

In the general case, a serial terminating search average is found by

$$\frac{\sum_{i=1}^{n} i}{n} \qquad (13.26)$$

However, it can be shown that

$$\sum_{i=1}^{n} i = \frac{n(n + 1)}{2} \qquad (13.27)$$

If we divide through by n, to take the average, then the right-hand side of the equation is

$$\frac{n + 1}{2} \qquad (13.28)$$

This is the general case for the average of a serial terminating search.

Now consider the high-depth menu organization. On the first screen, the sequence of steps would be the same as that above except steps 1 through 5 would be repeated $(4 + 1)/2$ times on the average. Once a choice was made, the second screen would appear. The user would have to repeat all eight steps over again. Assuming the response time of the computer is negligible, the equation would be

$$\text{total time} = 2\,((4 + 1)/2\,(\tau_p + 3\tau_c + \tau_m) + \tau_p + \tau_c + \tau_m) \qquad (13.29)$$

Inserting the values from the Middle Man estimates, the equation is

$$\begin{aligned} \text{total time} &= 2\,(5/2\,(100 + 3(70) + 70) + 100 \\ &\quad + 70 + 70) \\ &= 2380 \text{ msec.} \qquad (13.30) \end{aligned}$$

Using these calculations, we would predict that the high-depth organization would be faster than the high-breadth organization by more than a second.

Finally, consider one last example using the Model Human Processor. Function cash registers are becoming more and more popular, especially at fast food restaurants where the number of items on the menu is relatively small. These kinds of cash registers are replacing the old cash registers which just displayed the 10 digits. Are function cash registers actually faster than the older numerical cash registers? Without performing an experiment, the Model Human Processor can be used to address this question.

For the following example, assume that the user has not memorized the location of items on the function cash register. Assume that all items on the menu are less than $10.00. An ENTER key is used to terminate an entry for the numerical calculator. The timing of the response starts after the customer states an item to be ordered.

First consider the sequence of steps for the function cash register. Assume that this restaurant has n items on the menu and n items on the cash register. The sequence of operations would be:

1. τ_p perceive auditory order from customer and transfer from auditory image storage to working memory

2. τ_c retrieve semantic representation of order from long-term memory and store in working memory

3. τ_c match request in working memory to retrieved item from long-term memory to determine if the order is a valid order

4. τ_c decide on match (assuming a valid request)

5. τ_m execute eye movement to cash register

6. τ_p perceive button on cash register, read label, and transfer label from visual image store to working memory

7. τ_c match label to request

8. τ_c decide on match (if match, initiate movement of hand; if no match, execute eye movement to read label of next button)

9. τ_m execute movement of eye or hand

Steps 6 through 9 would be repeated an average of $(n + 1)/2$ times until a match is found in the serial terminating search through the cash register buttons. The parameters corresponding to these steps are as follows:

$$\text{total time} = \tau_p + 3\tau_c + \tau_m + (n + 1)/2$$
$$(\tau_p + 2\tau_c + \tau_m) \qquad (13.31)$$

Inserting the values from the Middle Man predictions we get

$$\text{total time} = 100 + 3(70) + 70 + (n + 1)/2$$
$$(100 + 2(70) + 70)$$
$$= 535 + 155n \qquad (13.32)$$

Total time is therefore dependent on the number of items on the restaurant menu.

Now consider the numerical cash register. Several possibilities exist for how this task can be performed. In the first possibility, assume that the item ordered is a familiar item for which the operator knows the price without looking it up. Also assume that the operator is an expert typist so that numerical keys do not have to be searched. The sequence of steps would be the following:

1. τ_p perceive auditory order from customer and transfer from auditory image store to working memory

2. τ_c retrieve semantic representation of order from long-term memory and store in working memory

3. τ_c match request in working memory to retrieved item from long-term memory to determine if the order is a valid order

4. τ_c decide on match (assume valid request)

5. τ_c retrieve price of item from long-term memory and store in working memory

6. τ_c decide on digit to enter and store in working memory

7. τ_m execute response for digit

8. τ_c decide if all digits have been entered (if not, go to step 6; if so, task is finished)

Three or four button pushes would be necessary, depending on the price of the item (two for the cents keys, one for ENTER if less than a dollar; one for the dollar digit, two for the cents digits, and one for ENTER if more than a dollar). Assume that the average number of keys is 3.5. In this case, steps 6 through 8 must be repeated 3.5 times. The equation with the parameters entered is

$$\text{total time} = \tau_p + 4\tau_c + 3.5\,(2\tau_c + \tau_m) \tag{13.33}$$

Inserting the values from the Middle Man estimates we get

$$\text{total time} = 100 + 4(70) + 3.5(2(70)+70)$$
$$= 1115 \text{ msec} \tag{13.34}$$

Going back to the function cash register compared to the numerical cash register, the crossover value of n can be determined (the value at which one cash register is better than the other) by setting the equation for the function cash register equal to 1115 msec.:

$$535 + 155n = 1115$$
$$n = 3.74 \tag{13.35}$$

This means that if the restaurant has three items or less, the function cash register is best, and if it has more than three items, the numerical cash register is best.

Now take another case where the operator is not an expert typist and must search for each key on the keyboard. Steps would need to be inserted after step 6 and

before step 7 for searching the keyboard for the digit keys:

6a. τ_m execute eye movements for key

6b. τ_p perceive label on key and transfer from visual image store to working memory

6c. τ_c match key label to digit in working memory

6d. τ_c decide on match (if yes, execute button press response; if no, execute eye movements for search)

6e. τ_m execute movement for button push or eye movements for search

Steps 6b through 6e would be serial terminating so that it would terminate on the average after the (11+1)/2 search (because of the 11 keys on the cash register). The total time for these steps would be

$$\text{total time} = \tau_p + 4\tau_c + 3.5\,(2\tau_c + 2\tau_m$$
$$+ 6(\tau_p + 2\tau_c + \tau_m)) \tag{13.36}$$

Inserting the values for the Middle Man calculations we get

$$\text{total time} = 100 + 4(70) + 3.5(2(70)$$
$$+ 70 + 6(100 + 2(70) + 2(70)))$$
$$= 9095 \text{ msec.} \tag{13.37}$$

Using the above time to find the crossover value for n we get

$$535 + 155n = 9095$$
$$n = 55.23 \tag{13.38}$$

This implies that if there are fewer than 55

items on the restaurant menu, the function cash register would be best. For more than 55 items the numerical cash register would be best.

One could also determine times for the numerical cash register if an item is unfamiliar, in which case the operator would have to look up the price of the item. The calculations would be very similar to those of the function cash register with the added keystrokes for entering the digits on the numerical cash register. In this case, the function cash register would always be faster. To determine realistic comparison times between the two cash registers, a researcher would have to determine how many prices an operator could, on the average, keep in memory. Times for the function cash register could be improved if the keys were grouped according to type (put all the sandwiches in one area). This would reduce the need for a serial terminating search through all the items.

Many other characteristics of the two kinds of cash registers would have to be considered, besides execution time, when evaluating their relative merits. In particular, the function cash register can also keep track of the inventory and determine which items are selling fast. This information can be used to reduce the number of items which must be stored on location. Some of the more sophisticated retail stores make good use of this kind data, thus reducing costs. Numerical cash registers do not have these kinds of advantages. The function cash registers, though, have the added problem that someone must program them to record the item and the correct price. Any price changes must be entered into the system. This extra programming requires more time, and the possibility of errors in the programming

increases. Changing a price would be simpler with a numerical cash register.

SUMMARY

Several examples of how to apply the Model Human Processor to human-computer interaction problems has been presented. The model is very accurate at making estimates, especially for simple tasks. The menu display and the cash register examples are bordering on tasks that are a bit too complicated for the analysis scope of the Model Human Processor. The reason for this is that as the number of cycle time parameters increases, the range of plausible times also increases. When comparing two or more possibilities, such as the function key to digit key cash register or the high-depth to high-breadth menu displays, with many parameters the range of values will overlap to a great degree. For these more complicated examples, the range of values were not included, but they are included as an exercise at the end of this chapter. Nevertheless, we would assume from the model that the average times are important and that the model is good at determining the qualitative relationships (which one is better than the other), even though the actual quantitative time predictions may not be totally accurate.

As with all of the models discussed in this predictive modeling section, different researchers may analyze the task differently, resulting in different parameterizations of the same task. The assumptions, such as the skill level of the operators, are very important considerations also which may result in very different analyses. Any such application of the Model Human Processor must be preceded by a careful task analysis and possibly field interviews of the operators or users to determine which of the assumptions are valid.

Several analysis techniques are considered in this book. The complexity of the task should be matched to the scope of the analysis problem. The Model Human Processor is good for the simple problems; the analysis techniques that follow are good for the more complicated problems. In the following models, the individual components of the task are not at the very atomistic level of cognitive processes, but are at the higher level of keystrokes or goals and intentions. These analysis techniques will be considered next.

QUESTIONS

1. For the cash register problem, use the Slow Man and Fast Man models to obtain values for the two different kinds of cash registers.

    a. What is the overlap of values?

    b. What are the difficulties in determining which cash register is the best?

2. Perform an analysis of the cash registers by grouping the items for the function cash register. How does this change the predictions?

3. The equation describing performance on the function cash register was as follows:

$$\tau_p + 3\tau_c + \tau_m + ((n + 1)/2) (\tau_p + 2\tau_c + \tau_m)$$

Now consider a slightly different

function cash register where the keys on the cash register are color coded by category of the item. As an example, the hamburgers are all coded as red keys; the side dishes, such as french fries, are all coded as green keys; and the drinks are all coded as yellow keys. Each of the categories has six items in it. Use the same assumptions as were used in the earlier cash register analysis, except, in this case, assume that the operator can use the color-coded keys to find the category of the item before finding the specific item in the category. As an example, the operator would search through the three categories by the color coding, and then search through the six keys until the correct one was found. Answer the following questions.

a. Using the above information, write down the equation which would describe performance on the color-coded function cash register described above. You only have to modify the above equation for this new situation. Then, in words, describe what the additions to the equation mean.

b. Which do you think would be fastest: without the color coding or with the color coding? Justify your answer.

4. Performing word processing tasks using the Japanese language is different from the procedures used in typing English or other Latin-based languages. In English, all words are composed of the 26 letters which can be represented easily on a keyboard.

In Japanese, the main alphabet using the kanji system is based upon picturelike characters. To learn to read at a very basic level, someone would have to be able to recognize 2,000 kanji characters; to be highly literate, a person would need to be able to recognize 10,000 characters. Representing this number of characters on a keyboard is infeasible. Because the characters are not composed of basic features, the kanji characters cannot be constructed from smaller units. To make the problem worse, the same pronunciation is used for several kanji characters.

Performing word processing tasks using the kanji characters is problematic. As a goal to alleviate this problem and related ones, three other alphabets have been developed for the Japanese language which are based upon a single character representation for a syllable. These alphabets are called the hiragana, katakana, and romaji alphabets. The Japanese language contains about 40 syllables, and so the words can be constructed from these syllables using these alphabets. The problem is that none of these alphabets has been accepted completely, so that written communication still requires the use of the kanji alphabet.

Japanese companies have developed word processing equipment to construct kanji characters. For this system, the keyboard uses characters from one or more of the alternative alphabets so that all the characters can be represented. The typist enters the syllables of a word using the characters on the keyboard. Since the same syllables can be used in several kanji characters, the system searches a database and determines the kanji characters that match the sound of the word. These kanji characters are then presented on the screen in a menu display. Typically, two to ten kanji characters will match the syllable sounds, and these are then presented in the menu from the most frequently used to the least frequently used. The typist must then choose the correct kanji character from the menu display. This character is then inserted into the text, and the typist must continue this process for all the rest of the words in the text.

a. Use the Model Human Processor to determine the time needed to type in a word using the Japanese word processing system. Assume that a word has two syllables and that five kanji characters will appear in the menu display.

b. Do the task of part a, but perform the model in the general case of having n kanji characters appear on the screen.

c. If a typical English word has five characters, then determine, using the Model Human Processor, the time needed to type a word in English.

d. Do the task of part c, but perform the model in the general case of a word having k characters.

e. When would it be faster to use the Japanese system (e.g., how many items could appear on the menu display) as compared to the English system assuming that a word has five characters?

f. For how many letters in a word would it be the same amount of time to perform the English word processing as to perform the Japanese word processing for a choice of four kanji characters?

5. Some fast food restaurants are offering "meal deals" where, through one order, the customer receives a sandwich, a drink, and french fries. These "meal deals" are usually designated on a cash register by a single digit number. So, instead of having to press three keys, the user only has to press one key. This should make the processing of information faster, enabling more customers to be served in a lesser amount of time. Answer the following questions.

a. Using the model for the function cash register, determine the time needed to perform the cash register functions for a "meal deal." Compare this number to the time needed to perform the same task if each of the items was ordered separately.

b. Assuming that the time between using the cash register and completing a customer's order is 30 seconds, how many more customers could be serviced in a two-hour period if all customers ordered "meal deals"?

c. Assume that each "meal deal" costs an average of $3.00. From part b, how much more money would be received during the two-hour period?

d. Assuming that a worker at the fast food restaurant makes $5.00 an hour, what is the amount of personnel costs which can be saved when a customer orders a "meal deal"?

e. Usually the savings in costs are passed on to the customer. How much could the "meal deal" be reduced in price, as compared to the three items sold separately, to account for the personnel costs which are saved from part d?

6. Different people may perform the menu display task differently. The Model Human Processor can be used to characterize these different task strategies. As an example, a person may transfer from LTM the semantic information about the menu item being searched before the timing of the task begins. Re-analyze the high-breadth and high-depth displays for this kind of strategy.

7. Another variation on the menu display task could occur if the user places both the displayed menu item and its corresponding menu item number into working memory on the same perceptual cycle. Re-analyze the high-breadth and high-depth displays for this kind of strategy.

8. In the menu display example only

two slots of working memory were utilized. The capacity of working memory is, or course, much higher than this and would probably be utilized by the user. For the following situations, re-analyze the high-breadth and high-depth displays and calculate the execution times.

a. Five slots in working memory are utilized (four for menu items and one is needed for retaining the menu item which is being searched).

b. Five slots in working memory are utilized (two for menu items, two for the menu item numbers, and one is needed for retaining the menu item which is being searched).

c. Seven slots in working memory are utilized (three for menu items, three for the menu item numbers, and one is needed for retaining the menu item which is being searched).

CHAPTER 14

GOMS

INTRODUCTION

In many ways, interacting with a computer system is similar to solving a problem. The problem must be decomposed into subproblems, the subproblems decomposed into subsubproblems, and so on. The problem solver must determine the goals and subgoals for attacking the problems. Usually, the means of solving the problem are reduced to a certain set of methods or operators which can be used in the solution, and these are usually specified. As an example, consider how to solve the problem of getting from Lafayette, Indiana, to New York. The present state of the system is that the person is in Lafayette. The goal of the system is to have the person in New York. Further constraints can be placed on this problem by stating when the person has to be in New York, when the person has to be in Lafayette, and the cost of the solution to the problem. Only a few methods are available: by car, plane, train, or bus. If the person decides that plane is the best method, based upon time and cost, then the problem cannot be solved without first decomposing it into subproblems, because no direct flight from Lafayette to New York is available. The person could decompose the problem into two subproblems: first get to Chicago and then get to New York. Each of the methods and operators to solve these subproblems would then have to be considered.

Consider the human-computer interaction task of revising a piece of text. The user must determine the present state

of the text, similar to being in Lafayette, and the desired form of the text at the end of the revision, similar to getting to New York. The user may find that the changes cannot be made all at once but would require an intermediate stage before the solution can be achieved. The changes to the text are restricted to these kinds of commands which can be used on the word processor, so that only certain operators and methods are available to make the changes. Some methods and operators may be more efficient to use than others, or their use may be restricted by the knowledge of the user.

Human-computer interaction tasks have often been described as problem-solving tasks. In such a model, Norman (1986) would say that the user would sequence through the following seven stages in order to solve the problem posed by a human-computer interaction task. To provide an example for these seven stages, consider the problem of a person editing a memo to make it more readable. The seven stages are:

- Establishing the goal (to reorder the paragraphs in the memo to make it more readable)

- Forming the intention (the user may intend to move paragraph 1 behind paragraph 2)

- Specifying the action sequence (this particular word processor may require that the user highlight paragraph 1, use a menu to "cut" the paragraph, move the cursor behind paragraph 2, and then use the menu to "paste" paragraph 1)

- Executing the action sequence (execute the above steps)

- Perceiving the system state (if the word processor shows the changes as they occur, then the user perceives the screen and reads the changed memo)

- Interpreting the state (the user determines the consequences of the changes)

- Evaluating the system state with respect to the goals and intentions (the user evaluates whether the reordered memo makes it more readable)

These stages do not have to be performed sequentially. For example, multiple intentions may be formed before an action sequence is determined. If the evaluation determines that the goal has not been satisfied, then new intentions are constructed.

Formal predictive modeling techniques have also been devised based upon cognitive problem-solving behavior. One of these models, GOMS, described in a book by Card, Moran, and Newell (1983), will be discussed in this chapter. A derivative of the GOMS model, NGOMSL, which is described by Kieras (1988), will be discussed in the next chapter.

THE GOMS MODELS

GOMS, an abbreviation of Goals, Operators, Methods, and Selection rules, was developed by Card et al. (1983) based upon previous work on problem solving

by Newell and Simon (1972). In the Newell and Simon book, the concepts of goals and a goal stack are used to describe how humans solve problems. Their model of problem solving consists of decomposing a primary goal into a hierarchical tree of subgoals with branches of lengths that depend on the degree of subgoal decomposition. At the end nodes of the tree are subgoals to which elementary information processes can be applied. Newell and Simon define elementary information processes to be elemental components of a problem-solving system from which all problem-solving methods are constructed. They use a stack to store the subgoal tree. Two stack operations, "pushing" and "popping," control goal decomposition and application of elementary information processes. The tree is decomposed in a depth-first fashion; thus, only parts of the tree are on the stack at one time. The stack lengthens when a goal or subgoal is split and shortens when elementary information processes are performed. If every subgoal at every level can be split into other subgoals or elementary information processes, then eventually the stack will become empty, at which time the attainment of the primary goal is achieved.

In the GOMS model, human-computer interaction is characterized as one form of problem solving in which the user must solve problems in using a computer to perform a task. The GOMS model includes descriptions of the methods needed to accomplish specified goals. The methods are a series of steps consisting of operators which are elementary perceptual, motor, or cognitive acts. If more than one method is available to accomplish a goal, then the GOMS model includes selection rules that can be used to choose the appropriate method depending on the context.

The GOMS model is actually several models; the basic model and a keystroke model will be discussed in detail in this chapter, which can be used to explain human-computer interaction cognitive behavior at several levels of detail. The basic GOMS model is used to outline the cognitive behavior of a user by decomposing the problem into subgoals and goal stacks. In the next section, this model is discussed. A variant of the basic GOMS model, called the Keystrokes-Level model, was designed to identify observable behavior such as keystrokes and mouse manipulations. This level of the model is especially useful for making specific time predictions based upon simplifying assumptions. The Keystrokes-Level model is discussed in a subsequent section.

THE BASIC GOMS MODEL

Card et al. (1983) based the logic of their GOMS model upon what they called the Rationality Principle. The Rationality Principle states that a person acts so as to attain goals through rational action, given the structure of the task and inputs of information and bounded by limitations on knowledge and processing ability:

Goals + Task + Operators + Inputs +
Knowledge Process Limits

—> Behavior

This states that users rationally attain their goals. It also implies that, similar to the Model Human Processor, there is a small number of information-processing operators underlying the detailed behavior of a particular user. The user's behavior can then be described through a sequence of these operators. If each of these operators can be assigned a time value, then the time the user requires to act is the sum of the times of the individual operators.

Components

The components of the GOMS model can be discussed through an analysis of each letter of its name. The G of GOMS represents the goals of the task. Card et al. (1983) state that a goal is a symbolic structure defining a state of affairs to be achieved and determining a set of possible methods to accomplish it. The goals can serve many purposes. A goal can serve as a memory point that can be returned to upon failure or error. A goal contains information about what is desired, about the methods available, and about what has already been tried.

The O of GOMS represents the operators. Card et al. (1983) define operators as elementary perceptual, motor, or cognitive acts whose execution is necessary to change any aspects of the user's mental state or to affect the task environment. The grain of analysis is dependent on the particular task analysis desired. The perceptual, cognitive, and motor cycles of the Model Human Processor can be considered a very low-level or fine grain of analysis which usually would be too fine a grain to be considered for the GOMS analysis. Usually, the grain of analysis corresponds to observable behaviors such as keystrokes, mouse movements, or user movements (e.g., looking at the screen). User behavior consists of the serial execution of operators.

The M of GOMS represents the methods. The methods describe procedures for accomplishing a goal in terms of operators and other goals. The user usually has a choice of several different methods. A good example is positioning the cursor on the screen. In most word processors and text editors, the user would have several choices for cursor control: arrow keys, a scroll bar on the side of the screen, a search or find function, mouse operations, or commands such as "u" or "d." The user would usually choose the method which is the most efficient for performing the task. If the desired position in the text is far away from the current position, then the user would choose a different method than if the desired position was close to the current position.

The final letter, S, of the GOMS model represents selection rules. To completely specify the user behavior, the choice of methods must be represented in the model. Selection rules are essentially the control structure of the model. This control structure is specified in terms of if-then rules. To use the previous example of cursor control, the methods would be specified through if-then rules. As an example, IF the desired position and the current position are both on the screen, THEN the arrow key method would be used. IF the desired position is on a different screen than the current position, THEN the search command method would be used. These selection rules could be refined based upon the task.

Examples

The GOMS model attempts to capture the goals of the user, how these goals are decomposed into sub- and subsubgoals, and how the observable behaviors, such as keystrokes, are used to satisfy these goals. To further explain the operation of the

GOMS model, it is best to consider an example. Recall the example from Chapter 13 of choosing an item from a menu display for high-breadth and high-depth displays. Consider first the high-breadth display where all menu items are displayed on one screen. The overall goal of this task would be to carry out some kind of command sequence; the command considered in Chapter 13 may be only one unit of this command sequence. We will consider this example in the context of its larger goal. For instance, the user may be in a word processing program and wish to choose the size (e.g., 12 points), font (e.g., Times Roman), and style of the characters (e.g., bold), thus requiring three sequential interactions with the menu displays in order to satisfy the overall goal of setting the type style. Therefore, the highest-level goal implicit in the particular task is to perform the command sequence. This can be represented as follows:

GOAL: PERFORM-COMMAND-SEQUENCE

The single menu item choice from the menu example is one unit of this high-level goal, and each of these units must be considered separately.

The next goal is to perform the unit task of the command, or:

GOAL: PERFORM-COMMAND-UNIT-TASK

To perform this unit task, the user must first determine which command needs to be performed. This is referred to as acquiring the unit task, and then the user must execute the responses by interacting with the computer which carries out the actions needed. This is referred to as executing the task. The latest goal can be decomposed into the following two subgoals:

GOAL: ACQUIRE-UNIT-TASK
GOAL: EXECUTE-UNIT-TASK

Each of these goals must now be satisfied.

To satisfy the acquisition of the goal, the user must determine the next command. This is done by looking at the screen and finding the location of the command on the screen. These actions no longer constitute a subgoal, but they are a series of specific operators used to satisfy the last goal on the stack. The following operators would be needed:

GET-NEXT-COMMAND

The operators are usually characterized by some kind of external action by the user which can be observed; sometimes the operators are internal cognitive actions which cannot be observed. Most of the execution of the operator of getting the command would be unobserved cognitive activities. These activities would correspond to the cognitive processes outlined for this task in Chapter 13: reading the menu items on the screen, matching the menu item to the desired command, and then deciding on the response. For the GOMS model, however, we do not analyze this task at such an atomistic level. All of these cognitive activities can be combined into just the one operator of getting the command. Although this internal cognitive activity cannot be observed, the external action of looking at the screen can be observed, and so it would be associated with this operator.

Once the command is obtained, the acquire task subgoal is satisfied and the execute task subgoal can be attended to. The execution of the task requires that the user enter the one or two digits corresponding to the desired command and then verify that the correct menu item has been entered. Since the menu items number from 1 through 16 for this particular example, the user has the possibility for using two different methods for accomplishing this: entering a single key or entering a string of keys. The selection of the appropriate method depends on the menu item to be entered. If the menu item number is between 1 and 9, then the key method will be used. If the menu item number is between 10 and 16, then the string method will be used. As can be seen, the previous two sentences easily could be converted into selection rules as follows:

IF menu item number is between 1 and 9, THEN use KEY METHOD
IF menu item no. is between 10 and 16, THEN use STRING METHOD

The operators to complete the task can be represented as follows for the key method:

USE KEY METHOD
VERIFY ENTRY

For the string method, the operators to complete the task can be represented as follows:

USE STRING METHOD
VERIFY ENTRY

When this execution of the task is completed, the user is finished with the menu interaction task.

The complete task is usually characterized using the goal stack model, a

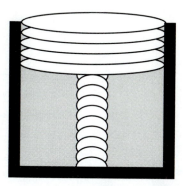

Figure 14-1. A representation of a plate stack which can be used as a metaphor for a goal stack in the GOMS model.

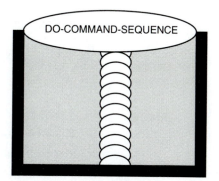

Figure 14-2. Example for popping and pushing goals on a goal stack for the high-breadth menu display. The DO-COMMAND-SEQUENCE goal is the only one on the stack, and it is at the top.

common representation for computer science tasks. A goal stack has two operations associated with it: "pushing" a goal on the stack and "popping" a goal off the stack. A good metaphor for understanding a goal stack is to think of a cafeteria which has a plate stacker for holding the plates that the patrons will use. Many have probably used such a mechanism. The plate stacker consists of a metal box which has a spring underneath the plates to be stacked in the box (see Figure 14-1). As a plate is stacked on the spring, the spring goes down so that the next plate for use is at the top of the box. As a plate is removed, the spring goes up, thus lifting the next plate so that it can be accessed easily. The plate stack is similar to the goal stack such that each plate can represent a goal. The two operations of pushing and popping a goal in the goal stack correspond to the two operations of placing a plate on the stack and removing a plate from the stack. The characteristic of the plate stacker is that plates that are not on the top cannot be removed before the plates on top of them are removed. The goal stack works on the same principle for the goals. In particular, goals are pushed on the stack as they are

acquired. Goals are continually pushed onto the stack until an operator is performed that can pop the goal off the stack. If a goal requires two or more subgoals in order to satisfy the goal, then all the subgoals will be pushed onto the stack on top of the goal. Once a goal is popped through the application of an operator, the topmost goal is analyzed to determine if it has been satisfied. If not, another goal may have to be pushed onto the stack and then popped through the use of an operator. At this time, the topmost goal may be satisfied so that it can be popped. The goal operations are continued until the bottommost goal is exposed.

Figure 14-2 shows the goal stack for the high-breadth menu interaction task for the example of choosing menu item number 10 from the menu display. In step 1, the DO-COMMAND-SEQUENCE goal is at the top of the stack. Prior to the start of the task in this example, other menu interaction command unit tasks may have been completed, but the DO-COMMAND-SEQUENCE goal is not yet complete. To satisfy this goal, another unit task must be

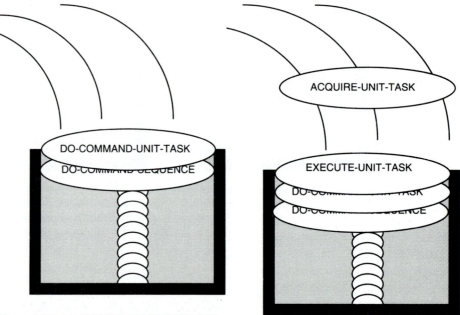

Figure 14-3. DO-COMMAND-UNIT-TASK is pushed onto the top of the goal stack.

Figure 14-4. The topmost goal on the stack cannot be accomplished by an operator so two subgoals, ACQUIRE-UNIT-TASK and EXE-CUTE-UNIT-TASK, must be pushed on the stack.

performed, and this is represented in Figure 14-3 by pushing the DO-COMMAND-UNIT-TASK on the goal stack. No operator is available to satisfy and thus pop this topmost goal so that another set of goals must be pushed on the stack. According to the GOMS model, a unit task is accomplished through the application of two subgoals: the unit task must be acquired, and then it must be executed. Both of these goals, ACQUIRE-UNIT-TASK and EXECUTE-UNIT-TASK, are pushed onto the goal stack with the later occurring goal, EXECUTE-UNIT-TASK, toward the bottom of the stack (see Figure 14-4).

For the topmost goal, ACQUIRE-UNIT-TASK, an operator is available to satisfy it, the GET-NEXT-COMMAND operator, and the application of this operator is represented in the figure. Many unobserved cognitive activities, such as accessing long-term memory (LTM), are

represented by this operator. The only external action associated with this operator is that the user would be looking at the screen. The GET-NEXT-COMMAND operator pops the ACQUIRE-UNIT-TASK goal off the stack in Figure 14-5.

Once ACQUIRE-UNIT-TASK is popped off the stack, the topmost goal is EXECUTE-UNIT-TASK, which was the second subgoal needed to satisfy DO-COMMAND-SEQUENCE (see Figure 14-6). Whenever a goal or subgoal is at the top of the stack, the only operations available for it are to push more subgoals on the top or to pop it with the application of an operator. This goal can be satisfied through the application of two subgoals: MENU-COMMAND and VERIFY-COMMAND. The MENU-COMMAND subgoal is used

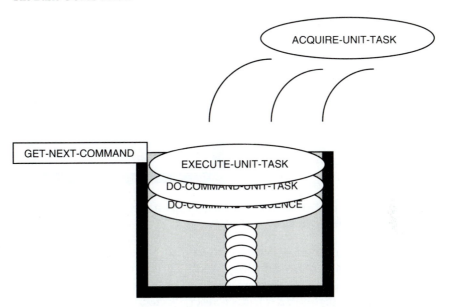

Figure 14-5. The GET-NEXT-COMMAND operator pops the ACQUIRE-UNIT-TASK goal off the stack.

to select a menu item from the screen and then enter the number of the menu item. The VERIFY-COMMAND subgoal is used to verify that the correct number has been entered and then hit the ENTER key. Both of these subgoals are pushed on the goal stack in Figure 14-7.

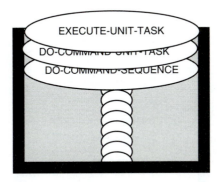

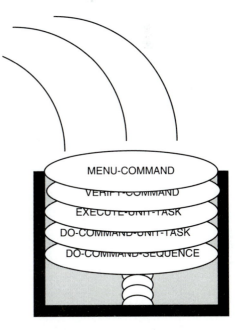

Figure 14-6. The EXECUTE-UNIT-TASK goal must be accomplished because it is now the topmost goal on the stack.

Figure 14-7. The MENU-COMMAND and VERIFY-COMMAND subgoals are pushed on the stack.

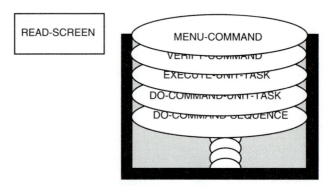

Figure 14-8. The READ-SCREEN operator is applied by reading through the menu items on the screen searching for the target menu item.

Three operators are needed to accomplish the MENU-COMMAND subgoal. The first operator, READ-SCREEN, is performed when the user reads through the menu items on the screen to try to find the appropriate menu item (see Figure 14-8). This menu item is found by matching the menu items read from the screen to the desired menu item, which was accessed from LTM in an earlier step and is now stored in working memory (WM) (see Figure 14-9). The reading and matching process may be performed 10 times, if menu item 10 is the target item. At this point, the user has a choice of two methods: the key method, if the menu item is only one digit long, or the string method, if the menu item is two digits long. The key method would be selected if the menu item number was between 1 and 9; the string method would be selected if the menu item was between 10 and 16. The selection rule for choosing the method should be clear. The external action associated with this operator is that the user hits one or two digits on the keyboard. For menu item 10, the user has chosen the string method (see Figure 14-10). The application of these three operators pops the MENU-COMMAND subgoal from the goal stack.

Once the subgoal is popped, the

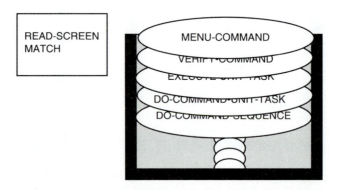

Figure 14-9. The matching of the menu items is accomplished in the working memory of the user.

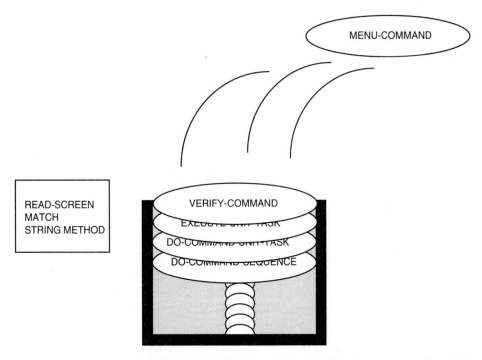

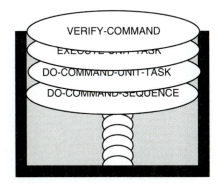

Figure 14-10. The user chooses the string method to enter the two digits for menu item 10 and this pops MENU-COMMAND from the stack.

topmost goal is now VERIFY-COM-MAND (see Figure 14-11). Three operators are needed to accomplish the VER-IFY-COMMAND subgoal. The user must read the screen, decide if the menu item number is correct, and then hit the ENTER

Figure 14-11. The VERIFY-COMMAND subgoal is now at the top of the stack.

key on the keyboard. The external action associated with this subgoal is that the user looks at the echo of the keyboard operations on the screen and then hits the ENTER key on the keyboard if, based upon the feedback, the correct keys were hit. Figures 14-12 through 14-14 show the application of these operators. In Figure 14-14 the last operator is applied, hitting the ENTER key, and this will pop the VER-IFY-COMMAND subgoal from the stack.

Popping the VERIFY-COMMAND subgoal off the stack exposes the EXE-CUTE-UNIT-TASK goal, and this is now completed and can be popped off the goal stack as shown in Figure 14-15. The DO-COMMAND-UNIT-TASK goal is now exposed at the top of the goal stack. This needs no other goals to satisfy it, because it has been acquired and executed, so that

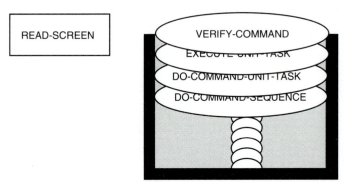

Figure 14-12. The READ-SCREEN operator is applied when the user reads the menu item number, which was just typed in, from the screen.

it too can be popped from the stack as in Figure 14-16. The exposed goal is now the DO-COMMAND-SEQUENCE goal. If this command unit task was the last one in the sequence to perform the overall task, then it too could be popped. If more commands in the sequence are needed, then the next command unit task would be pushed on the stack and the process would begin again.

The goal operations for the high-breadth menu display can be represented more succinctly in Figure 14-17. In this representation, the contents of the goal stack are shown in the second column. This corresponds to the goals and subgoals

which were placed on the goal stack in Figures 14-4 through 14-16. The operators from the goal stack are represented in the third column of Figure 14-17. The external actions associated with the operators are shown in the last column. The high-depth menu display can also be represented using the goal stack model of GOMS (see Figure 14-18). The goal stack is much the same as the high-breadth display, except that the user must make two menu choices for the high-depth display as contrasted to the one menu choice for the high-breadth display. Therefore, the execution of the unit task requires two subgoals to complete, the main menu

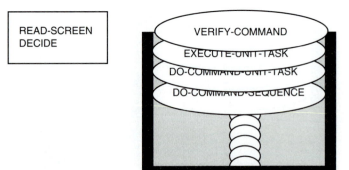

Figure 14-13. The DECIDE operator is used to decide whether or not the entered number is correct.

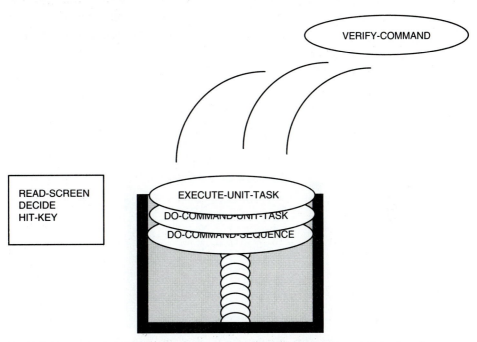

Figure 14-14. The HIT-KEY operator used to hit the ENTER key to confirm that the correct numbers were entered.

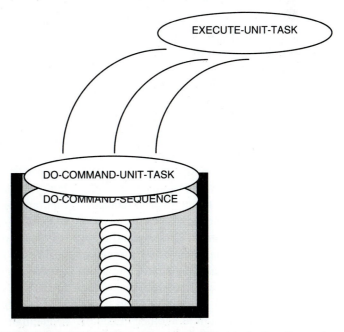

Figure 14-15. The EXECUTE-UNIT-TASK goal is popped off the stack when the previous goals are accomplished.

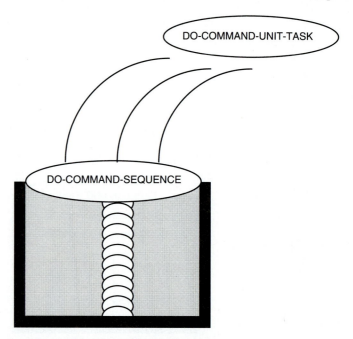

Figure 14-16. The DO-COMMAND-UNIT-TASK goal can be popped off the stack once the previous goals are accomplished. The DO-COMMAND-SEQUENCE is the last goal on the task, and this could be popped if there were no other tasks, besides the menu task, to be performed.

choice and the second menu choice. This is represented in steps 7 through 15. First, the main menu method is used to make a menu choice, and then the second menu method is used. Both use the same operator, the key-method operator.

So far, the goal stack of the GOMS model has been specified, but what is the purpose of this representation? The goal stack can provide the basis for many comparisons of two or more designs: the number of steps, the number of methods, or the number of operators can be used in these comparisons. These quantifiable aspects of the model can be used to measure such important human-computer interaction issues as time predictions, the number of errors, learnability, and transfer from one design to another. Each of these will be considered in more detail.

Execution Time Predictions

Relative time differences in executing the task using the two different menu displays can be considered by counting the number of steps for each display (the step number is shown in the first column of Figures 14-17 and 14-18). A step occurs when a goal is pushed on the stack, popped off a stack, or when an operator is applied. The ordering of the steps is slightly different from that represented by the goal stack operations of Figures 14-4 through 14-16. In the goal stack operations, two subgoals were pushed on the stack in order. As an example, Figure 14-4 showed that AC-QUIRE-UNIT-TASK and EXECUTE-UNIT-TASK were pushed on the stack sequentially. In the summary of these operations in Figure 14-17, these two

Step	Contents of Goal Stack	Operator Executed	Action
1	DO-CS		
2	DO-CS,DO COMM-UT		
3	DO-CS,DO COMM-UT,ACQ-UT		
4	DO-CS,DO COMM-UT,ACQ-UT	GET-NEXT-COMM	access LTM
5	DO-CS,DO COMM-UT		
6	DO-CS,DO COMM-UT,EXE-UT		
7	DO-CS,DO COMM-UT,EXE-UT,MENU-COMM		
8	DO-CS,DO COMM-UT,EXE-UT,MENU-COMM	READ-SCREEN	look at screen
9	DO-CS,DO COMM-UT,EXE-UT,MENU-COMM	USE MATCH METHOD	WM match

. . . Steps 8 and 9 are repeated, on the average, (n + 1)/2 times, or 8.5 times

Step	Contents of Goal Stack	Operator Executed	Action
25	DO-CS,DO COMM-UT,EXE-UT,MENU-COMM	USE KEY METHOD or USE STRING METHOD	enter digits from keys
26	DO-CS,DO COMM-UT,EXE-UT,		
27	DO-CS,DO COMM-UT,EXE-UT,VERIFY COMM		
28	DO-CS,DO COMM-UT,EXE-UT,VERIFY COMM	READ-SCREEN	look at screen, hit ENTER
29	DO-CS,DO COMM-UT,EXE-UT,VERIFY COMM	USE DECIDE METHOD	WM decide
30	DO-CS,DO COMM-UT,EXE-UT,VERIFY COMM	USE KEY METHOD	hit ENTER key
31	DO-CS,DO COMM-UT,EXE-UT		
32	DO-CS,DO COMM-UT		
33	DO-CS		

Figure 14-17. A representation of the goal stack operations for the high-breadth menu display. (Key: CS = command sequence; COMM = command; UT = unit task; ACQ = acquire; and EXE = execute).

subgoals are not pushed on the stack sequentially, rather ACQUIRE-UNIT-TASK is pushed on the stack in step 3 and EXECUTE-UNIT-TASK is pushed on the stack in step 6. Besides this change, the rest of the orderings of the steps are the same as the goal stack operations.

In comparing the high-depth and high-breadth menu displays from Figures 4-17 and 4-18, steps 1 through 9 are the same for both. Starting with step 8, the search process begins for both menu displays, and this is where the two differ. The last three steps of both goal stacks are the same.

As with the Model Human Processor on the menu displays, the number of steps needed for performing the task can be determined in the general case. Recall from Chapter 13 that a search is conducted as a serial terminating search so that it ends when the target menu item is found. If n is the number of menu items on the display, then the number of menu items which must be searched is (n + 1)/2. In the high-breadth display, two steps (8 and 9, displayed in Figure 4-17) are needed for this search process. Therefore, on the average, (2(16 + 1))/2 steps would be needed for this search, or 17 steps. Since the last step before the search began was step 7, the step after the search is concluded will be step 25. On step 25, either the key method or the string method can be used to enter the menu item number, depending on the number of digits in this menu item. The task is finished after 33 steps.

Steps	Contents of Goal Stack	Operator Executed	Action
1	DO-CS		
2	DO-CS,DO COMM-UT		
3	DO-CS,DO COMM-UT,ACQ-UT		
4	DO-CS,DO COMM-UT,ACQ-UT	GET-NEXT-COMM	look at screen
5	DO-CS,DO COMM-UT		
6	DO-CS,DO COMM-UT,EXE-UT		
7	DO-CS,DO COMM-UT,EXE-UT,MENU-COMM		
8	DO-CS,DO COMM-UT,EXE-UT,MENU-COMM	READ-SCREEN	look at screen
9	DO-CS,DO COMM-UT,EXE-UT,MENU-COMM	USE MATCH METHOD	WM match

. . . Steps 8 and 9 are repeated, on the average, $(n + 1)/2$ times, or 2.5 times

13	DO-CS,DO COMM-UT,EXE-UT,MENU-COMM	USE KEY METHOD	enter digit from keys
14	DO-CS,DO COMM-UT,EXE-UT		
15	DO-CS,DO COMM-UT,EXE-UT,MENU-CAT		
16	DO-CS,DO COMM-UT,EXE-UT,MENU-CAT	READ-SCREEN	look at screen
17	DO-CS,DO COMM-UT,EXE-UT,MENU-CAT	USE MATCH METHOD	WM match

. . . Steps 16 and 17 are repeated, on the average, $(n + 1)/2$ times, or 2.5 times

21	DO-CS,DO COMM-UT,EXE-UT,MENU-CAT	USE KEY METHOD	enter digit from keys
22	DO-CS,DO COMM-UT,EXE-UT		
23	DO-CS,DO COMM-UT		
24	DO-CS		

Figure 14-18. A representation of the goal stack operations for the high-depth menu display. (Key: CS = command sequence; COMM = command; UT = unit task; ACQ = acquire; CAT = category; and EXE = execute).

As an example, if the user was searching for the 10th menu item, then steps 8 and 9 would be repeated 10 times for a total of 20 steps in this search. After the search, the next step would be step 28. Nine more steps, including step 28, would be needed, for 36 total steps for this particular search. When finding menu item 10, the string method, instead of the key method, would be used.

The analysis for the number of steps, in the general case, can also be performed for the high-depth menu display of Figure 14-18. As in the previous menu display, the number of steps in the search can be described as $(n + 1)/2$. In this case, however, n is 4 for both the main menu and the secondary menu. Since the search re-

quires two steps, the average number of steps needed for the main menu search would be $(2(n + 1))/2$, or 5 steps. This search would occur in steps 8 through 12, on the average. Steps 13 through 15 would always be present. The next search, for the secondary menu, begins on step 16 and would continue for a total of 5 steps, on the average. Step 21 would be the step after the search. The whole process would be finished on step 24.

For the general case, the high-breadth display should require 33 steps and the high-depth display should require 24 steps. Card et al. (1983) do not make specific predictions for how long each step should take, but we can assume that each step would require about an equal amount of

TABLE 14-1

Methods and operators which have to be learned for the high-breadth display.

Methods and Operators
GET-NEXT-COMMAND
READ-SCREEN
USE MATCH METHOD
USE KEY METHOD
USE STRING METHOD
USE DECIDE METHOD

TABLE 14-2

Methods and operators which have to be learned for the high-depth display.

Methods and Operators
GET-NEXT-COMMAND
READ-SCREEN
USE MATCH METHOD
USE KEY METHOD

time. The NGOMSL analysis, explained in Chapter 15, uses a similar technique to GOMS and finds that 100 msec per step is a good estimate of the time. This estimate could also be used in the GOMS model, but this was not proposed by Card et al., nor has it been tested. From the GOMS analysis of this task, therefore, we would predict that the high-depth display could be performed faster than the high-breadth display. Using the 100 msec estimate for each step, we would say that the high-depth performance would be about 0.9 sec faster than the high-breadth performance. This conclusion is similar to that of the Model Human Processor of Chapter 13. In that analysis, the high-depth display was predicted to be faster by about half a second.

The basic GOMS model, considered above, is best for making qualitative predictions about differences between the tasks. The two other variants of the GOMS model, the Keystrokes-Level model and the Model-UT (for unit task), were designed by Card et al. to make quantitative predictions for the tasks. The Keystrokes-Level model makes these predictions by quantifying values for observable operators; the Model-UT predicts the times by establishing average times for each unit task through experimentation. Each of these models will be considered in later sections of this chapter.

Error Predictions

The GOMS model can be used to determine the methods and operators needed for performing a task. One could assume that the more methods and operators which must be learned, the more chances for making errors on them. Thus, the number of errors should be positively related to the number of methods and operators to be learned.

The number of methods and operators to be learned is not equivalent to the number of steps in the process as used for the execution time prediction. The methods and operators which had to be learned are listed in Table 14-1 for the high-breadth display and in Table 14-2 for the high-depth display. The high-breadth display requires that six methods and operators be learned; the high-depth display requires that only four methods and operators be learned. Based on this, we would predict that the high-depth display would exhibit fewer errors.

In many ways, equating the errors with the number of methods and operators is unsatisfying because it does not provide an analysis for the kinds of errors that would occur. Because of overall similarities between methods and operators, one could expect that confusion may occur, and more errors, if the methods and operators are highly similar to each other. Related to the concept of error predictions is the concept of transfer. In transfer, the user would change from one interactive program to another interactive program, retaining many of the previously learned methods and operators. If the methods and operators are applied to the new interface wrongly, then errors would occur. The issue of transfer, as related to the GOMS model, is considered in the next section.

Transfer

Douglas and Moran (1983) demonstrated how the GOMS model could be used for predicting the kinds of errors which may occur when a person transfers from one interface design to another. In actuality, they analyzed how a person would transfer methods and operators when transferring from a typewriter to a text editor. A typewriter and an interactive computer system have many surface features in common which may cause a person to use similar methods and operators when transferring from a typewriter to a computer. The keyboard is mostly the same between the two, and the computer screen is often designed to look like, and have the same features as, the paper in a typewriter. In most cases, redesigning the similarities between the typewriter design and the design of an interactive program, such as

a word processor, is encouraged, along the lines of a metaphor, so that the user can better understand how to use the interactive program.

Douglas and Moran (1983) used the GOMS model to formulate the methods and operators for the typewriting task. Some of these methods and operators could be applied to a text-editing task with little difficulty. However, some of the operators and methods could not be transferred to the text-editing task without causing difficulty. Because of the similarities between the keyboard for a typewriter and the keyboard for a computer, people would have a tendency to use the typewriter operators on the text-editing task; Douglas and Moran were able to identify 10 misconceptions which could occur when transferring to the text editor. Some of the misconceptions occurred due to the differences between the space bar on a typewriter and the space bar on the text editor. For the typewriter, the space bar can be used to get to a certain location on the paper. As an example, if the user of the typewriter is at the beginning of the line and wishes to get to the middle of the line (40 spaces away), then the user would just hit the space key 40 times. For the text editor, the space bar cannot always be used as a positioning tool, even though it has the same surface qualities as a typewriter space bar. In most new text editors, the user is placed automatically in the insert mode whenever the user does not specify that a new or different mode is to be entered. When in the insert mode, hitting the space bar inserts space characters in the text. The space character is just the same as any other character, such as an "x," but it cannot be seen by the user. As an example, let's say that the text editor user wishes to get to the middle of a line of text, 40 spaces away. If the space key is used in the insert mode, then space characters are being inserted into the text. If 40 space characters are inserted, then the user would still be 40 characters away from the desired text location and the document would be unfavorably altered with the addition of those 40 space characters.

Douglas and Moran (1983) found that the misapplication of typewriter operators to text editor operators resulted in the identification of 10 such operators. In an experimental test of experienced typists transferring for the first time to a computerized text editor, they found that for the 75 errors seen in an experimental validation of the hypotheses on a text editor, 62 of them could be explained due to the misapplication of typewriter operators. Similar analyses could be performed for transferring from one interactive program to another interactive program.

Learnability

The GOMS model was not designed to measure learnability. It is a model which is most useful for skilled users. In fact, novice behavior on computer systems is difficult to predict and is difficult to model. All the analyses performed in the validation of the model by Card et al. (1983) were performed on expert users.

Even though not specifically designed for novices, one could see how the model could be applied to predict the learning time. The more methods and operators to learn, the longer the learning time. As with errors, we would expect a relationship between the number of methods and operators with learnability. By examining Tables 14-1 and 14-2, we can see that the high-depth display should be faster to learn. The NGOMSL and production system models, considered in Chapters 15 and 16, respectively, have developed formal techniques for predicting learning time.

THE KEYSTROKES-LEVEL MODEL OF GOMS

One of the problems of using the GOMS model is that obtaining time predictions for the model could be difficult and time-consuming. For the basic model, no general technique of making time predictions was used. As seen in the next section for the Model-UT, the time predictions are obtained after taking verbal protocols of users, collecting keystroke data, and then determining average times for the unit tasks. This is a detailed procedure which may overwhelm any time savings of GOMS, due to the modeling of performance, over the usual method of experimentally determining the differences between the system. The Keystrokes-Level model of GOMS was designed by Card et al. (1983) to obtain time predictions more easily. Card et al. (1983) referred to this class of models as engineering models because they represent more of a practical design tool.

The Keystrokes-Level model analyzes only the observable behavior such as keystrokes and mouse movements. It does not analyze the non-observable behavior such as the time for acquiring goals. Not estimating the acquisition time could remove a large chunk of the actual time to perform a task. As an example, Card et al. (1983) estimate, based on experimental studies, that acquisition times can be 2 to 3 sec. per unit task if the task is already de-

TABLE 14-3

Time estimates for the operators from the Keystrokes-Level model of GOMS

Operator	Description	Time (sec.)
K	Time varies with typing skill	
	Best typist (135 wpm)	.08
	Good typist (90 wpm)	.12
	Average skilled (55 wpm)	.20
	Average nonskilled (40 wpm)	.28
	Typing random letters	.50
	Typing complex codes	.75
	Worst typist	1.20
P	Point with mouse	1.10
H	Home hands on keyboard	.40
$D(n_D,l_D)$	Draw segment	$.9n_D + .16l_D$
M	Mentally prepare	1.35

fined (such as having a marked-up manuscript). Acquisition times could be 5 to 30 sec. if the task needs to be generated in the user's mind. In addition, the Keystrokes-Level model assumes error-free performance because of the difficulty of predicting the errors and determining the times of errors. The Keystrokes-Level model is used to predict the times given a method; it does not predict the methods.

Card et al. base this level of the model on six operators: K which is a keystroke or mouse button push; P which is pointing to a target on a display with a mouse or some other pointing device; D which is moving the mouse to draw a set of straight-line segments; H which is moving the hands from the mouse to the keyboard; M which is mental preparation for doing an operation; and R which is system response time. Based upon empirical work, Card et al. chose values for operators and

these are shown in Table 14-3. K depends on the experience of the typist. P and H are invariant. D depends on the number of line segments needed (N_D) and the length of the line segments (l_D). M is the only operator which is not observable, and a useful estimate is 1.35 sec. R is not listed because it depends on the particular computer system and the load on the system.

Since M is the only operator which is questionable for when to apply it, Card et al. (1983) formulated rules for its application. An example is that the M operator will only be applied after a chunk; a chunk occurs when an operation is fully anticipated in another operation. This would occur, as an example, when the user is pointing with a mouse and then pushing the mouse button to make a selection. The M operator would occur only at the end of the PK operator combination. This and the other rules are listed in Table 14-4.

TABLE 14-4

Rules for when to apply the M operator for the Keystrokes-Level model

Rule	*Example*
When an operation is fully anticipated in another, M can be chunked with the other operator.	Pointing with the mouse and then hitting the mouse button.
An obvious syntactic unit constitutes a chunk when it must be typed out in full	When using the DIR command (for a directory), the M operator follows the typing of DIR instead of having an M operator after each keystroke.
User will bundle redundant terminators into a single chunk.	If a command is followed by ESC ENTER, the M operator will occur after ENTER.
A terminator of a constant-string chunk will be assimilated into a chunk.	If an ENTER is needed after the command DIR, then the M operator will be after ENTER.

The execution time for a task is found by stringing the operators together for the task, assigning the parameter values to the operator, and then summing the times. Different systems can be compared by examining the final summation of the times. The system with the least amount of time needed for the task is assumed to be the best. Card et al. (1983) validated these times with experiments on expert users and found the predictions to be close to the actual values. The model was especially accurate in predicting the qualitative relationships among the different systems tested.

Examples

As an example of the application of the Keystrokes-Level model of GOMS, consider the high-breadth and high-depth menu interaction task which has been used throughout Chapter 13 and this chapter. In the high-breadth display, the user would be required to search the 16 items on the screen to find the one desired, to enter the one- or two-digit number corresponding to the desired menu item, and then to hit the ENTER key. Using the operators from the Keystrokes-Level model, this would require an M operator for searching the display, one or two K operators for entering the menu item number, and then another K operator for the ENTER key. To apply the model, a few assumptions must be made. First, we will assume that the user is an average skilled typist. Next, we will assume that the 16 menu items have an equal probability of use. The operators needed for the task are as follows:

$$M + K(\text{first digit}) + .44K(\text{second digit}) + K(\text{ENTER}) \qquad (14.1)$$

Since all menu items have the same probability of use, the second digit will be used for items 10 through 16 and these 7 items would occur with a probability of 7/16 or 0.44. Applying the time values for the operators, the predicted time for this task is

$$1.35 + .20 + .44(.20) + .20 = 1.84 \text{ sec} \tag{14.2}$$

This time can be compared to the time prediction of this task using the Model Human Processor which was 3.47 sec. The discrepancy in the predictions occurs because the Model Human Processor explicitly predicts the search time, but the Keystrokes-Level model only provides an estimate of 1.35 sec. for this and other mental tasks. In addition, the time of the keystroke-level analysis is shorter because it only predicts the execution time and not the acquisition time.

A time can also be predicted for the high-depth display. In this one, the user must think about the menu item that is to be entered, enter the single digit from the first menu, and then enter the single digit from the second menu. In this example, we will assume that the user is an expert user so that an M operator is not needed between the first and second keystrokes. In other words, the user would know where to look for the menu item without searching for it on the screen. We assume that the computer is very fast and that the response time, R, between the two menus is negligible, or essentially 0. As in the previous example, we also assume that the user is an average skilled typist. The operators for this task are

$$M + K(\text{digit}) + K(\text{digit}) \tag{14.3}$$

Substituting the values of the operators, the time to perform the task is

$$1.35 + .2 + .2 = 1.75 \text{ sec.} \tag{14.4}$$

This time can also be compared to the time prediction of this task using the Model Human Processor, which was 2.38 sec. Once again, the Keystrokes-Level model predicted a lesser time than the Model Human Processor.

A possibility for making this prediction a little bit more accurate would be to propose that several Ms may occur before the first keystroke. Each M could correspond to the read and match process outlined for the GOMS model. This assumption, however, violates the rules for applying M shown in Table 14-4. The model will not be closer in predictions to the Model Human Processor and GOMS because the 1.35 sec. for search time per item is probably a bit high; it is certainly out of line with the other predictions.

It is interesting to note that the two models make the same qualitative prediction: the high-depth display should be faster than the high-breadth display. The particular time predictions are different as are the differences between the predicted times for the two menu operations.

A relevant question when considering menu displays is whether a keyboard-based computer system is faster or slower than a mouse-based system. The Keystrokes-Level model can be used to compare the menu interaction task using a mouse and using keys. For the mouse-based menu selection, the user sees a list of menu items on the screen, chooses the appropriate item, moves the mouse cursor to the menu item position on the screen, and presses the mouse button. This sequence of operations is as follows:

$$M + P + K \qquad (14.5)$$

For this operation, we are assuming that the task is totally mouse-based so that no homing (the H operator) from keyboard to mouse is needed. For the M operator, mental preparation, the user would look at the screen and choose the appropriate menu item. For the P operator, positioning the mouse, the user would move the mouse cursor to the menu item which was chosen mentally. For the K operator, a keypress, the operator presses the button on the mouse to make the selection. The total time for this task is found by totaling the parameter values for each of the operators. This is 1.35 + 1.10 + 0.20, which totals to 2.65 sec.

The keyboard menu interaction task was determined above. The most relevant comparison would be to the high-breadth display or any display which only uses one screen (the predicted times would be the same). The predicted time in that case was 1.85 sec. This model predicts that the keyboard-based interaction task would be faster for the user. This corresponds to anecdotal evidence from experts who seem not to like to use a mouse because it is so slow. We would assume, however, that the mouse-based task is probably easier to learn for novices. The Keystrokes-Level model has no way of analyzing this, though.

Other Examples

The examples in the previous section were relatively simple, with few keystrokes. Card et al. (1983) provided several examples as applications for the Keystrokes-Level model. Similar examples for slightly different applications are provided in Figures 14-19 and 14-20. The latter figure

is used as a problem at the end of this chapter.

Since direct manipulation displays such as that of the Apple Macintosh are used often nowadays, the examples in these figures focus on direct manipulation tasks. They compare two different systems for manipulating the items from drawings that were already entered. Figure 14-19 shows the methods (in italics) and each of the operators for performing the task. Next to the operators are the times. For K, we assume a skilled typist.

The first task considered is to copy a box (rectangle) to another part of the diagram. This is often referred to as a cut-and-paste operation. Each of the two systems shown in the figure has different methods for performing this task. System A represents a painting program so that the task must be divided into the four methods shown in italics. First, the user must select the area for deletion. The first operator is to reach for the mouse. Since all actions are mouse-based on this interface design, we would assume that the hand is already resting on the mouse so that this action actually does not have to be performed. The next action is to point to the Tools pull-down menu at the top of the screen. One of the icons on this pull-down menu is the select-area icon. The user must move the mouse down to this icon, while still holding down the mouse button, and release the mouse as soon as the pointer is over the icon.

The next method is to select the rectangle on the screen. This is done by moving the mouse cursor to one corner of the rectangle, pushing the mouse button, and then moving the mouse cursor to the opposite corner of the rectangle. This mouse only has one button so that there is

System A

Select area for deletion

Reach for mouse	0H[mouse]	0
Point and select Tools menu	M P[Tools] K[BUTTON-DOWN]	2.65
Point to icon of area-select	P[icon]	1.10
Select area-select	K[BUTTON-UP]	.20

Select rectangle

Point to corner of area	P[corner]	1.10
Enter select mode	K[BUTTON-DOWN]	.20
Point to opposite corner of area	P[corner]	1.10
Select area	K[BUTTON-UP]	.20

Cut rectangle and save in buffer

Point and select Edit menu	M P [Edit] K[BUTTON-DOWN]	2.65
Point to Cut command	P[Cut]	1.10
Select Cut command	K[BUTTON-UP]	.20
Wait for cut	R(0.5)	.50

Paste rectangle in new location

Point to new location	P[display]	1.10
Point and select Edit menu	M P [Edit] K[BUTTON-DOWN]	2.65
Point to Paste command	P[Paste]	1.10
Select Paste command	K[BUTTON-UP]	.20
Wait for paste	R(1.0)	1.00

System B

Reach for mouse	.7H[mouse]	.28
Point to rectangle and select	P[rectangle] K[BUTTON]	1.30
Delete rectangle	M K[Delete]	1.55
Point and select new location	M P[location] K[BUTTON]	2.65
Point and select Edit menu	M P [Edit] K[BUTTON-DOWN]	2.65
Point to Copy command	P[Copy]	1.10
Select Copy command	K[BUTTON-UP]	.20
Wait for copy	R(0.5)	.50

Figure 14-19. Methods and operators for performing an example task. System A represents a painting program and System B represents a drawing program. The predicted times for performing the task are different for the two systems.

no question about which button will be pushed. At this point, the rectangle is highlighted.

The third method is to cut out the rectangle and save in a buffer. This must be done through another pull-down menu display, the Edit menu in this case. One of the items in this menu is to Cut. The user releases the mouse button to select this command. A light system delay of half a second occurs for performing this command.

The final method is to paste the rectangle in a new location. This method is very similar to the third method, except for two things. First, the new location of the rectangle must be chosen by pointing to a location on the display with the mouse. Second, instead of choosing the Cut command in the pull-down menu, the user chooses the Paste command. After the mouse button is released on the Paste command, the rectangle appears at the location chosen.

System B is a direct manipulation drawing program in which each of the figures in the drawing is maintained in memory. This allows for individual items to be deleted as a whole instead of deleting everything in an area as with System A. Because the number of operators is small, they are not divided into separate methods.

When using the drawing program for the same task of moving an existing rectangle, the user must first reach for the mouse. Since it is estimated that 70% of the time the user's hands are positioned over the keyboard instead of on the mouse, 70% of the time the movement, and the H operator, is required. The value for the H operator, 40 sec., is therefore multiplied by .7.

Next, the user points to anyplace on the old rectangle and clicks the mouse button. The rectangle is deleted by pushing the delete key on the keyboard with the hand that is not using the mouse. This figure is saved in a buffer until another deletion replaces it.

To copy the deleted rectangle into a new location on the screen, the user must first point to that location with the mouse and click the mouse button. The copy command is in the Edit pull-down menu. To do this, the user must move the mouse to the Edit pull-down menu, push down the mouse button which displays the rest of the menu, move the mouse to the Copy command while the mouse button is held down, and release the mouse button to select the Copy command. A system delay of half a second occurs while the rectangle is copied in the specified position.

Summing the individual operator times, we can find an estimate for the execution time for each of the two systems: 17.05 sec. for system A and 10.23 sec. for system B. We would predict that System B would be faster to execute by a large margin.

Card et al., 1983, compared three systems for similar kinds of tasks to actual experimental times observed from real users. They found that the predicted times were very close to the actual times. More importantly, the relationships between the predicted performance times and the actual times were always preserved. In particular, if system A was faster than system B which was faster than system C, then these relationships were seen for the actual times. The predicted numbers may be different from the actual times, but the relationships were always the same.

To provide a better statistical basis for the Keystrokes-Level model, some kind of value for the ranges should be evaluated, such as the standard deviation or the standard error. Card et al. (1983) chose to evaluate the standard error for the observed values. A high overlap between the ranges of the values indicates little difference between the systems. Card et al. (1983) should be consulted further to determine how to perform these calculations.

As can be seen from the Keystrokes-Level model estimates for execution times, this model has its advantages and its disadvantages. The advantages are that time estimates can be determined just by knowing the keystrokes that will be needed for a benchmark task. The estimates appear to be reasonable, at least in terms of the qualitative predictions. The disadvantages are that only execution time is calculated. Other important factors besides the number of keystrokes are needed in the evaluation of an interface design. The learnability of the interface may be important. One could expect that the fewer the keystrokes, the less transparent is the interface design and the more difficult it would be to learn. As an example, we could design an interface that could do a whole sequence of commands based upon a single keystroke. Yet, it would be difficult to learn such an interface for many different command sequences. In the example just provided, many of the commands were carried out by pushing one of the mouse buttons. It may be difficult for a user to remember which mouse button to use in which situation because the buttons are unlabeled. Also remember that the estimated times are just for execution times and not acquisition times, and that errors

are not accounted for. The more complex designs could have fewer keystrokes but could cause more errors and may need more time for acquisition of the command. Interface designs should not be chosen only on the time estimates of the Keystrokes-Level model.

The next section examines how the GOMS model can be used to perform design revisions. Other related models, in the next chapters, provide means to estimate other interface design parameters such as learnability and transfer.

MODEL-UT

In some cases, the Keystrokes-Level model may provide an inappropriate level of analysis. It is a good model if interface designs can be specified in terms of the keystrokes. At the conceptual levels of designs, however, specifying such detail would be inappropriate, and probably not needed. A more appropriate level would be at the unit task (UT) level. When discussing the basic GOMS models, unit tasks were examined. Thus, the Model-UT can be used to estimate task times by specifying the unit tasks.

The unit task may be an appropriate level of analysis because it is assumed that for a unit task, the user's behavior is highly integrated and the dependencies between the unit tasks are minimal. Recall that a major assumption of the GOMS model was that different segments of behavior can be seen to be composed of the same few units differently combined. It may be possible to define these units sufficiently independent of each other that the time required by a unit in isolation is a good approximation of the time it requires as part of a sequence. The time prediction

TABLE 14-5
Example for estimating execution times from the Model-UT

Unit tasks	n_{UT}	t_{UT}	n_R	t_R	$n_{UT}t_{UT}$	$n_R t_R$
Place text	4	5	4	6	20	24
Place graphics	4	10	4	8	40	32
Select file	8	15	2	10	120	20
Size graphics	4	5	0	0	20	0
Total	20		10		200	76

would consist of first finding the times for the units (t_{UT}), analyzing the task to determine which unit tasks would occur and how many times within the total task each would occur (n_{UT}), and then summing all of these products. Thus, for each unit task, the product t_{UT} n_{UT} would be determined, and all these products for each unit task would be totaled to determine the time of the total task. If the system response time is large, then this factor would have to be included in the total.

Determining what constitutes a unit task could be difficult. It must be a meaningful unit, it must be highly integrated, and it must be independent of other unit tasks. Many of these decisions are subjective, and so the choice of unit tasks is a subjective matter. Usually a unit task is typified by keystrokes or other types of behavior that are chunked together. If an experiment can be performed measuring the pauses between behaviors, then the choice of unit tasks can be confirmed or disconfirmed (e.g., Robertson and Black, 1986).

The time estimates for a unit task can come from several sources; the source used depends on the availability of information and the amount of time available to perform the analysis. The most exact method to determine the times would be to experimentally determine times for a particular system. This may be impossible, especially if such an analysis is being used for a conceptualized system, one which has not yet been designed or implemented. In this case, the times for unit tasks can be determined from other designs which may correspond closely to the design being conceptualized. We will consider this latter time estimation first.

As an example of this estimation technique, let's say that we are improving a desktop publishing software product. A benchmark task requires that four pieces of text are placed and four pieces of graphics are pasted in place. Each placement of text or graphics requires that the text or graphics files are selected. Each of the graphics must be sized to fit in the available space.

Average execution times for each unit task can be found by simple experimentation on a prototype or by making comparisons to other systems if a prototype does not yet exist. Table 14-5 shows a summary of the unit tasks, the estimated times for each unit task, the number of times that the unit task occurs in the benchmark task, and the system response time for the unit tasks. An estimate for the total time can be found even if the new product does not yet exist or if only some of the unit tasks can be determined experimentally. For the example product, the estimated time for the total task is 276 sec.

For this kind of GOMS analysis, the preferred method of determining the times for the units is to have people perform the task, recording protocols and the time between keystrokes, which can then be used to reconstruct the times of the individual units. Performing this kind of analysis can be very time-consuming. As an example of this method, Card et al. (1983) report an experiment on the use of a CAD system for the design of VLSI (Very Large Scale Integrated) circuits. One subject, an expert on the CAD program called ICARUS, was tested to determine the time units.

In the task, the user was asked to change the arrangement of some of the circuits in the chip to find a more efficient arrangement. The user brought in a detailed sketch of the changes that were to be made. The session was videotaped to obtain a record of performance. One camera was focused on the user and another viewed the screen. Keystrokes, both the name of the keystroke and the time that they occurred, were recorded on a data file. The user was encouraged to talk aloud about what he did as he was doing the task.

Four types of unit tasks were identified from the keystroke and protocol data. The pauses between keystrokes were analyzed and found that they varied between .3 and 80 sec. Anything over 5 sec. was called a pause; pauses divided the events into episodes. The session had 100

episodes with a 25 sec. pause average. The protocol data were used to determine the pauses which could be identified as task acquisitions so that the commands between the pauses could be identified as task executions.

Four types of unit tasks were identified. Draw tasks were used to create new circuit elements on the layout mostly by using Line commands (drawing straight lines from one circuit connection to another on the same layer of the chip) and Flash commands (drawing connections between circuit units on different layers of the chip). Alter tasks moved circuit elements or changed their configuration usually by means of Move commands, Stretch commands, or the Deletion and Drawing commands. Dimension tasks measured the dimensions of the substructures, the distances between circuit elements, or the alignment of elements by using the Distance and Size commands. Check tasks checked the circuit for connectivity, for VLSI design rule violations, or for places that could be spatially compressed.

To determine the times, start and end times for the unit tasks were determined from the data. A unit task may occur several places in the execution of the total task. Therefore, a mean value for each unit task could be determined from all the occurrences of the unit task. In a similar manner, the start and end of a method could also be determined from the keystroke and protocol data. Since the methods also occurred in several places, an average time per method, over several occurrences of the method, could be calculated. Once these values were found for the methods and unit tasks, they could be used for time predictions for variations on the task. The level of analysis of the task depends on the goals of the analysis. The task could be analyzed at the unit task level or at the lower method level. As an example, let's say that the user would enter the task with a different set of changes specified than that for the experimental task. The tasks could be analyzed using the GOMS goal stack analysis, and the unit tasks and methods for this new task could be specified. Since an assumption of the GOMS model is that the unit tasks or method execution times are invariant, then the average times from the previous experimental session could be applied to the new task to predict a time.

If the GOMS analysis is used to predict interaction times, then the more unit task times and method times, the more applicable the model. Much effort may be required to collect these times in a database, but once collected, they could serve as a valuable resource for predicting task times. As an example, Gray (1989) reported that his phone company had collected the times for 8,400,00 unit tasks which then could be used for time predictions of all kinds of tasks.

APPLICATIONS AND TESTS OF THE GOMS MODELS

The GOMS models are a family of models which can be used for very detailed analyses, such as when applying the Model-UT, or for quick global analyses for predicting execution times, such as when applying the Keystrokes-Level model. The applications of these models depends greatly on the skill of the task analyzer. Each person analyzing a task may come up with a slightly different variant of the model. This is not too much of a problem when comparing different systems, as long as the task analyzer was consistent in how the model was applied to the different systems. Some of the later modeling techniques, such as the NGOMSL model (Chapter 15) or the production system models (Chapter 16), attempt to solve this problem. The model has been very influential in human-computer interaction research. Some of the other applications of the GOMS models, and the tests of the model, are considered in the following section.

Design Revisions

The GOMS models can be used to revise a computer design to make it easier to execute, faster to perform, and easier to learn for a user. Card et al. (1983) provided some suggestions for how their models could be used. Some of the important suggestions follow.

1. A basic unit of analysis is the method. When performing a task analysis, all the methods should be determined and written down. The methods should then be examined to eliminate particularly long or awkward methods.

2. An emphasis in these models has been placed on the expert. Make the performance of experts more efficient by eliminating or combining operators.

3. Each interface design will have different methods for performing the same task. Design the set of alternative methods for a task so that the rule for select-

ing each alternative is clear for the user and easy to apply.

4. The interface should be easy to learn. A good technique for learnability is to first design a few general-purpose methods which are easy to learn. A novice would learn these to begin with. Then design alternatives for the user based upon the general-purpose methods. Only when the user has learned the general-purpose methods can knowledge then be extended to the alternatives. In this way, novices can use the system quickly without knowing too much, and they can continue to learn and become more expert by building on this basic knowledge.

Model Validation

Several examples of validation of the GOMS models were presented in the Card et al. (1983) book ranging from text editing to CAD tasks. In the validation of the model, experts would perform the task providing verbal protocols. The computer system would automatically record the keystrokes and the times between keystrokes. The results from these sessions would be compared to predictions from the model. They found that the model could predict the methods used by the user 80-90% of the time on a text-editing task, and it predicted the operators used 80-100% of the time for the same task. For a CAD task, the model predicted an execution time of 1192 sec. while the observed execution time was 1028 sec.

The predictions from the model were very close to the actual times. These should be read with caution, though, because they depend somewhat on the skill of the task analyzer. For predicting the methods and operators, the task analyzer would have to examine the task and formulate the methods and operators for the task. The model only provides very limited procedural information for mapping the task to the methods and operators. When the high predictions for the methods and operators are espoused, this prediction means that most of the times the subjects in the experiments were rational and did not randomly choose methods and operators. This would probably only hold true for novices; an expert would have a difficult time predicting all the methods and operators for a novice.

The prediction for the execution times only considered the time to execute the unit tasks, not the time to acquire the unit tasks. The execution time could only be a small part of the total time, but some may argue that this would be the important component of the task anyway. The acquisition times could vary widely. Without the acquisition times, the execution time forms a kind of ceiling for how fast the task could be performed under optimal conditions. The close correspondence of the predictions to the actual times is due, in part, to the fact that the unit tasks were determined from experimental data, and then the times for each individual unit task were strung together to find a total execution time.

SUMMARY

The GOMS models have been very important in helping researchers trying to understand how a user interacts cognitively with interactive software and in quantifying aspects of the interaction even before the software is prototyped. They have been criticized as being too vague in how to apply them (Kieras, 1988) and only being applicable to error-free performance (Carroll and Olson, 1988). GOMS has provided a good start; more work is being performed to refine and proceduralize these techniques.

QUESTIONS

1. Determine the times for performing the task, represented in Figure 14-20, for systems A and B using the Keystrokes-Level model. Discuss which one should exhibit the fastest execution time. Discuss whether or not this is the best system to use.

2. Perform a Keystrokes-Level model analysis of the predicted execution time for the command-based example and the direct manipulation display given in Chapter 11.

   a. Which interface does the model predict could be executed faster?

   b. How would the results be interpreted if the direct manipulation display was found to be executed faster than the command-based display?

3. Use the Keystrokes-Level model of GOMS to determine which cash register, the function or numerical, would be fastest (see Chapter 13).

4. In a keyboard-based interface, a menu item is entered by typing in the number corresponding to the menu item to be chosen. In a mouse-based interface, a menu item is entered by pointing to the menu item and clicking the mouse button. For a 12 item menu display, with all items having equal probability of being chosen, answer the following questions.

   a. Determine the predicted execution time of the keyboard-based display using the Keystrokes-Level model of GOMS. (Assume an average typist.)

   b. Determine the predicted execution time of the mouse-based display using the Keystrokes-Level model of GOMS. (Assume an average typist.)

   c. Which would be faster, the keyboard-based display or the mouse-based display?

   d. Consider the display that is fastest from part c. Would there be any number of menu items in which the other display would be predicted to be faster based on the Keystrokes-Level model analysis?

Problem: Delete a box (rectangle) with an overlapped line to another part of the diagram, keeping the overlapped line.

System A
Select area for deletion

Reach for mouse	0H[mouse]
Point and select Tools menu	M P[Tools] K[BUTTON-DOWN]
Point to icon of area-select	P[icon]
Select area-select	K[BUTTON-UP]

Select and delete rectangle

Point to corner of area	P[corner]
Enter select mode	K[BUTTON-DOWN]
Point to opposite corner of area	P[corner]
Select area	K[BUTTON-UP]

Cut rectangle and save in buffer

Point and select Edit menu	M P [Edit] K[BUTTON-DOWN]
Point to Cut command	P[Cut]
Select Cut command	K[BUTTON-UP]
Wait for cut	R(0.5)

Select area deletion mode

Reach for mouse	0h[mouse]
Point to place for menu	P[display]
Display menu	K[YELLOW-DOWN]
Expand menu	.5P[icon]
Point to menu icon	P[icon]
Undisplay menu	K[YELLOW-UP]

Redraw damaged line segment

Point and select Tools menu	M P[Tools] K[BUTTON-DOWN]
Point to icon of line	P[icon]
Select line	K[BUTTON-UP]
Point to end of segment	P[end]
Enter drawing mode	K[BUTTON-DOWN]
Draw segment	D(1,2.50)
Exit from drawing mode	K[BUTTON-UP]

System B

Reach for mouse	.7H[mouse]
Point to rectangle and select	P[rectangle] K[BUTTON]
Delete rectangle	M K[Delete]
Point and select new location	M P[location] K[BUTTON]
Point and select Edit menu	M P [Edit] K[BUTTON-DOWN]
Point to Copy command	P[Copy]
Select Copy command	K[BUTTON-UP]
Wait for copy	R(0.5)

Figure 14-20. Methods for operators for performing a task. System A represents a painting program and System B represents a drawing program Use the Keystrokes-Level model to determine which one is fastest to execute.

CHAPTER 15

NGOMSL

INTRODUCTION

NGOMSL, which stands for the Natural GOMS Language, was developed by Kieras (1988) to enable the task analysis using a GOMS-like model to be more specific. As admitted by Kieras, much of the work on NGOMSL is grounded in the appropriate theory and prior research, but determining if it works in practice has not been documented to a great degree. NGOMSL is a proposed procedural method. To analyze a task using the NGOMSL procedure, the interaction of the user with a computer is described in a computer programming-like language. The activities of the user are described in terms similar to the subroutines of computer programming languages. The subroutines, in turn, have decision statements (if...then statements), flow of control statements (goto statements), and memory storage and retrieval statements. Having experience writing computer programs is advantageous for using the NGOMSL task analysis.

Just like GOMS, NGOMSL decomposes a task into goals, operators, methods, and selection rules. A goal is something that a user tries to accomplish and is described as an action-object pair in the form <verb noun>. As an example, the goal of "delete word" would be such an action-object pair.

Operators are actions that a user executes and can be external operators which are observable or can be mental operators which are not observable. Examples of external operators are to press a key or to move a mouse. External operators can also include perceptual operations such as scanning a page. Mental operators must be inferred by the task analyst; examples include recalling information from long-term memory, actively retaining information in memory, and making decisions. In many ways, operators are very similar to goals; the distinction is subjective on the part of the task analyst. The main difference is that a goal is something to be accomplished, while an operator is something that is executed.

A method is a sequence of steps that accomplishes a goal. A step in a method typically consists of either external or mental operators. Each of the statements and the steps correspond to a specific production rule (see the next chapter) so that cognitive complexity can be determined directly from these steps.

Finally, the selection rules are needed if more than one method is available to accomplish a goal. An example of the need for a selection rule, as discussed in Chapter 14, is to determine the method for moving the cursor to a particular place in the text. Selection rules are the same as that for the GOMS model. The information needed for the selection can be formulated in IF-THEN rules for selecting the appropriate method based upon the context.

STRUCTURES AND STATEMENTS OF NGOMSL

The basic structure of the NGOMSL analysis is the method. A method must be

Method to accomplish goal of <goal description>

>   Step 1. <operator>. . .
>   Step 2. <operator>. . .
>   . . .
>   Step n. Report goal accomplished

Method to accomplish goal of <goal description>

>   Step 1. <operator>
>   Step 2. <operator>
>   . . .
>   Step k. Accomplish the goal of <subgoal description>
>   . . .
>   Step n. Report goal accomplished

Method to accomplish goal of <subgoal description>

>   Step 1. <operator>
>   Step 2. <operator>
>   . . .
>   Step k. Accomplish the goal of <subsubgoal description>
>   . . .
>   Step n. Report goal accomplished
>   . . .

Figure 15-1. The three structures for a method (from Kieras, 1988, reprinted with permission of publisher).

specified for accomplishing each of the goals of the task. Accomplishing the method is specified through the steps needed. Three possibilities for this method structure are shown in Figure 15-1 (taken from Kieras, 1988). In this notation, the word in brackets refers to variables which can change depending on the situation. The first statement always states the name of the method in terms of the goal or subgoal which it accomplishes. The steps are operators, goals which must be accomplished through other methods, or the "Report goal accomplished" message. If a step only has an operator, then this represents a low-level operator or primitive at the lowest possible level corresponding to an internal operator or an external operator. This operator is executed, and the step

cannot be decomposed any further. Acceptable operators will be explained later. If a step is a goal which must be accomplished, then the method for doing this must be specified in the steps of another method somewhere in the task analysis. The final step in the method is to report the goal accomplished. This does not have to be the step at the very bottom; depending on the flow of control in the method this step could be located physically elsewhere.

The other structure of the NGOMSL model is a selection rule set. Figure 15-2, taken from Kieras (1988), shows the general structure for a selection rule set. The selection rules are used when the user has a choice of methods to accomplish the goal. The "If," or conditional, part of the rules specifies the conditions which must

Selection rule set for goal of <general goal description>

If <condition> Then accomplish goal of <specific goal description>

If <condition> Then accomplish goal of <specific goal description>

Report goal accomplished

Figure 15-2. General structure for a selection rule set (from Kieras, 1988, reprinted with permission of publisher).

be satisfied for applying the method to accomplish the goal specified in the "Then" part of the rule. The selection rules must be written so that only one of the conditions of the if's is true. The selection rule set can consist of as many rules as necessary for specifying the options. A selection rule always ends with "Report goal accomplished."

The acceptable operators are shown in Figure 15-3. Any of these operators could be substituted in the positions la-

Mental Primitives for Flow of Control

Accomplish goal of <goal description>
Report goal accomplished
Decide: If <operator. . .> Then <operator>
Decide: If <operator. . .> Then <operator> Else <operator>
Goto Step <number>

Memory Storage and Retrieval

Recall that <WM-object-description>
Retain that <WM-object-description>
Forget that <WM-object-description>
Retrieve-LTM that <LTM-object-description>

Primitive External Operators

Home-hand to mouse
Press-key <key name>
Type-in <string of characters>
Move-cursor to <target coordinates>
Find-cursor-is-at <returned cursor coordinates>
Find-menu-item <menu-item-description>

Analyst-Defined Mental Operators

Get-from-task <name>
Verify-result
Get-next-edit-location

Figure 15-3. Acceptable operators for NGOMSL (from Kieras, 1988, reprinted with permission of publisher).

beled <operator> from Figure 15-2. The mental primitives for flow of control are analogous to flow of control statements in computer programming languages. "Accomplish the goal of <goal description>" is analogous to the CALL statement for accessing a subroutine. The "Report goal accomplished" operator is analogous to a RETURN statement which returns control to the calling method or, analogously, the calling subroutine. The Decide operator determines the truth of the operator(s) after the "If" and performs the operator after the "Then" part if the conditional was true. In the second Decide operator, if the conditional was false, then the Else operator is performed. Finally, a goto command can transfer control to another step within the method. As in structured programming, this kind of control should be avoided as much as possible because the flow of control is difficult to determine with too many goto's.

A very important part of the NGOMSL description of a task is the specification of the memory requirements for performing it. The memory storage and retrieval operators specify the operations of working memory (WM) and long-term memory (LTM). WM and LTM have the same cognitive parameters as those explained by the Model Human Processor (see Chapters 8 and 13). From WM, the user can recall, retain, and forget items in this memory. Recall means to fetch from WM and retain means to store the item in WM. Forget means that the item is no longer needed and so can be forgotten. These memory operators are very important for determining the mental workload of the task. Any kind of cognitive processing on information can only occur in WM, so the user may first have to retrieve some

information from LTM before it can be manipulated.

The primitive external operators refer to operators which can be observed. This set of operators may change depending on the particular system being modeled. As an example, some systems may not have a mouse so that the first operator, homing the hand to the mouse, would not be needed. Some systems may require more or different kinds of operators to define their capabilities. As an example, a system may incorporate a touch screen, in which case the operators for this device could be specified.

Finally, the last set of operators refers to mental operators defined by the task analyst. These are mental operations too complicated to be defined in the NGOMSL description. The task analyst has much discretion in the kinds of operators which can be included in this set. Kieras (1988) has suggested the set in Figure 15-3. In some cases, this set may not be specified enough. In particular, verify-result may be defined as a goal instead of an operator so that a method would need to be described for doing this.

EXAMPLES

Kieras (1988) suggests that NGOMSL can be applied in the following steps. The technique should be applied top-down by first describing the top-level goal. The top-level goal is accomplished by a method which will include a series of steps of high-level operators (these could be goals themselves). Each step, or operator, in the high-level goal needs a method by which to accomplish it. The method for accomplishing each step or operator is then specified. The process is continued in this manner until the operators are composed of primitives. A primitive is usually some elementary process such as a keystroke or a cognitive process. The primitive level can change depending on the needs for the task analysis. For example, the following task analyses of high-breadth and high-depth menus carries the task analysis to a low level for the primitives by specifying the memory, match, and decision operators for choosing a menu item. This need not be done in all task analyses. Kieras (1988) provides an operator, called Find-menu-item (see Figure 15-3), which could subsume all the primitive menu operators listed previously. Since two kinds of menus are being compared to determine which is best, a detailed analysis, with low-level or fine-grain primitives, is required. The differences between the menus may only be captured in that detailed analysis. If the focus of the task was not on the menus, but a menu method was a relatively insignificant component of the task, then the higher-level primitive of Find-menu-item could be used to describe the menu operations. The grain of analysis, and the level of the primitives, depends upon the purpose of the task analysis.

High-Breadth Menu Display Example

To show how to apply NGOMSL, we will return to the example of high-breadth and high-depth menu displays. The NGOMSL representation of the high-breadth display is shown in Figure 15-4, and the high-depth display is shown in Figure 15-5. For the high-breadth display, the first goal is to perform all the steps in the command sequence. To accomplish this, five steps must be performed. If a step is a primitive,

then no methods need be specified for that step. If the step is a nonprimitive, then the method for the step must be described fully. In the first method, accomplishing the goal of performing the command sequence, step 1 is a primitive, step 3 is a decision step, step 4 is a control step, and step 2 is a nonprimitive step. Step 2 is the only one in which methods must be described. The step 2 method is described by the second method in the figure. Each of the steps of this method must be primitives, decision steps, control steps, or described by other methods. This continues until all the steps end in primitives.

To better illustrate the processing of the technique, the NGOMSL analysis will be performed step by step for the high-breadth display. The processing starts at the top of the figure with

Method to accomplish goal of executing command sequence

As indicated for the GOMS example, the menu interaction depicted for the high-breadth and high-depth display may be part of a longer command sequence. Notice that the specification of this method has a verb (executing) and a noun (command sequence). The first step of this method is

Step 1. Retrieve-LTM that current item in command sequence is MENU-COMMAND

This is an elementary cognitive process, one of those which was listed in Figure 15-3. We assume that the user is experienced and knows what he or she wishes to accomplish and the commands for accomplishing it. This command sequence is assumed to be stored in long-term mem-

(1a) Method to accomplish goal of executing command sequence

    Step 1. Retrieve-LTM that current item in command sequence is MENU-COMMAND

    Step 2. Accomplish goal of performing the command unit task

    Step 3. Decide: If more commands in command sequence, then Goto 1

    Step 4. Report goal accomplished

(2a) Method to accomplish goal of performing the command unit task

    Step 1. Recall MENU-COMMAND and accomplish goal of locating MENU-COMMAND

    Step 2. Recall N and accomplish goal of enter the menu item number

    Step 3. Recall N and N' and accomplish goal of verify the entry

    Step 4. Forget MENU-COMMAND and report goal accomplished

(3a) Method to accomplish goal of locating MENU-COMMAND

    Step 1. ReadScreen next command line and retain as MENU-ITEM

    Step 2. Decide: If MENU-COMMAND is different from MENU-ITEM then forget MENU-ITEM and Goto 1

    Step 3. Retain that N is number of MENU-ITEM

    Step 4. Forget MENU-ITEM and report goal accomplished

Selection rule set for goal of enter the menu item number

    If N is between 1 and 9, then accomplish goal of do key-method

    If N is 10 or above, then accomplish goal of do string-method

(4a) Method to accomplish goal of do key-method

    Step 1. Press-key N

    Step 2. ReadScreen and retain feedback as N'

    Step 3. Report goal accomplished

(5a) Method to accomplish goal of do string-method

    Step 1. Type-in N

    Step 2. ReadScreen and retain feedback as N'

    Step 3. Report goal accomplished

(6a) Method to accomplish the goal of verify the entry

    Step 1. Decide: If N and N' do not match, then forget N' and accomplish goal of deleting entry

    Step 2. Press-key ENTER

    Step 3. Forget N and N'

    Step 4. Report goal accomplished

(7a) Method for accomplishing goal of deleting entry

    Step 1. Press-key DELETE

    Step 2. Decide: If more digits in entry space on screen, Goto 1

    Step 3. Forget N', recall N, and accomplish the goal of enter the menu item number

    Step 4. Report goal accomplished

Figure 15-4. A representation of the high-breadth menu display using NGOMSL.

(1b) Method to accomplish goal of executing command sequence

Step 1. Retrieve-LTM that current item in command sequence is MENU-COMMAND

Step 2. Accomplish goal of performing the command unit task

Step 3. Decide: If more commands in command sequence, then Goto 1

Step 4. Report goal accomplished

(2b) Method to accomplish goal of performing the command unit task

Step 1. Accomplish goal of issuing MENU-CATEGORY

Step 2. Accomplish goal of issuing MENU-COMMAND

Step 3. Report goal accomplished

(3b) Method to accomplish goal of issuing MENU-CATEGORY

Step 1. Recall MENU-COMMAND and accomplish goal of locating MENU-CATEGORY

Step 2. Recall N and Press-key N

Step 3. Forget N and MENU-CATEGORY

Step 4. Report goal accomplished

(4b) Method to accomplish goal of issuing MENU-COMMAND

Step 1. Recall MENU-COMMAND and accomplish goal of locating MENU-COMMAND

Step 2. Recall N and Press-key N

Step 3. Forget N and MENU-COMMAND

Step 4. Report goal accomplished

(5b) Method to accomplish goal of locating MENU-CATEGORY

Step 1. Retrieve-LTM that the category of MENU-COMMAND is MENU-CATEGORY

Step 2. ReadScreen next command line and retain as MENU-ITEM

Step 3. Decide: If MENU-ITEM is different from MENU-CATEGORY then forget MENU-ITEM and Goto 2

Step 4. Retain that N is number of MENU-ITEM

Step 5. Forget MENU-ITEM and report goal accomplished

(6b) Method to accomplish goal of locating MENU-COMMAND

Step 1. ReadScreen next command line and retain as MENU-ITEM

Step 2. Decide: If MENU-ITEM is different from MENU-COMMAND then forget MENU-ITEM and Goto 1

Step 3. Retain that N is number of MENU-ITEM

Step 4. Forget MENU-ITEM and report goal accomplished

Figure 15-5. A representation of the high-depth menu display using NGOMSL.

ory. This step specifies, through the retrieve-LTM operator, that the command sequence should be transferred from LTM to WM. Once in WM, it is stored under the variable name MENU-COMMAND. Since this step is an elementary cognitive process, it is a primitive and no method need be described for it.

The second step in the method can now be performed, and it states:

Step 2. Accomplish goal of performing the command unit task

The command sequence may not necessarily be a single command but could be a sequence of commands that must be performed one by one. Each command in the sequence is a unit task. This step is not a primitive process, so the methods must be searched to find the one that matches. The second method in the figure shows the steps for accomplishing the goal listed above. At this point, the path through the method structure should be clearer. The path does not flow from top to bottom but jumps around to the different methods in order to accomplish any goals which may have been specified as operators in a method step.

The flow of control is now in the second method of the figure, and it has the following description:

Method to accomplish goal of performing the command unit task

This method has five steps. Step 1 of the second method is as follows:

Step 1. Recall MENU-COMMAND and accomplish goal of locating MENU-COMMAND

MENU-COMMAND was retained in the first method and is fetched, through the use of the recall operator, in this second method. This step is an example of how two operators can be located in one step if, according to Kieras (1988), they do not both have an "accomplish goal" in them. If the operators are relatively simple, then it is likely that a user would combine two in one step. The memory operators of retain, recall, and forget are relatively simple, and these would likely be combined with other operators in one step. The combination of operators would change with user experience; a more experienced user is likely to combine operators in a single step. The task analyst should target the model to some class of user, and, once this class is chosen, it should be used consistently throughout the model.

The accomplish goal part of the step is a nonprimitive method, so the list of methods must be searched to find a match. The third method shows the steps for accomplishing this:

Method to accomplish goal of locating MENU-COMMAND

The MENU-COMMAND has been stored in WM, and the user must search through the menu display until a match is found to the command in the menu items list. This method has four steps. The first step is performed as follows:

Step 1. ReadScreen next command line and retain as MENU-ITEM

MENU-ITEM is a variable which is now being filled by the first menu item on the screen. Step 2 is a decision step:

Step 2. Decide: if MENU-COMMAND is different from MENU-ITEM

then forget MENU-ITEM and Goto 1

In this step, the user matches the MENU-COMMAND to the MENU-ITEM. Since MENU-ITEM was retained in the same method it does not need to be recalled. The match determines if the menu item is the one needed. If it is not, the MENU-ITEM is forgotten, it is no longer needed, and processing returns to step 1 to read the next line on the screen. If they are the same, then the user has successfully found the menu item needed and processing moves to step 3:

Step 3. Retain that N is number of MENU-ITEM

This is a primitive cognitive process that stores information in WM so that no more methods are needed to explain it. N is a variable containing the item number associated with the menu item which matched the desired command. This number has to be stored for later use, when it will be entered to select the menu item. Processing moves to the last step, as follows:

Step 4. Forget MENU-ITEM and report goal accomplished

The specific MENU-ITEM is no longer needed because it has been used to make the match and to find the number associated with it. The goal of locating the MENU-COMMAND on the menu display has been accomplished.

Recall that the goal just completed was called from step 1 of the second method. Processing thus proceeds on to step 2 of the second method:

Step 2. Recall N and accomplish goal of enter the menu item number

N is the number of the command, and it must be recalled from WM before it can be used in the enter menu item goal. For performing this step, two methods are available depending on whether one or two digits are to be entered. If one digit, the operator "Press-key" should be used. If two digits, representing a string, then the operator "Type-in" must be used. To choose between these two methods, a selection rule is specified:

Selection rule set for goal of enter the menu item number

If N is between 1 and 9, then accomplish goal of do key-method

If N is 10 or above, then accomplish goal of do string-method

N between 1 and 9 indicates that only one digit will be entered through a single keypress; N above 10 indicates that a string of two digits must be typed.

The first executable step in the selection rule is:

If N is between 1 and 9

If this conditional is true, the processing continues to the action part of the rule:

then accomplish goal of do key-method

To accomplish this goal, processing proceeds to the fourth method:

Method to accomplish goal of do key-method

This has three steps. The first step is

Press-key N

Press-key is a primitive operator meaning that only one key needs to be pressed; in this case, the key is the digit key corresponding to the menu item number. The second step is

ReadScreen and retain feedback as N'

ReadScreen is also a primitive operator. In this case, it is used to read the echo on the screen of the key which has just been pressed and it stores this variable in WM as N'. N' will be used in a later method to determine if the correct key has been pressed. The last step is

Step 3. Report goal accomplished

This step indicates that the goal has been accomplished and processing can return to the next step from where it was called. In this case, the method was called from the selection rule, and, consequently, the next step in the selection rule is also to report the goal accomplished. Processing then returns to the next step from which the selection rule was called. It was called from step 2 of the second method, so processing would continue with step 3 of this method.

If N was 10 or greater then the second selection rule would have been used. This selection rule is outlined in method 5. It is very much the same as the method associated with the first selection rule, except that a string of digits must be entered. The primitive operator for entering a string is Type-in:

Step 1. Type-in N

In this case, N is a string of two digits, so they are typed in. Steps 2 and 3 are the same as the first selection rule. No matter which part of the selection rule is used, at the end of the method, the menu number is entered into the computer and the user has stored the feedback of the item in WM. Processing returns to the third step of the second method. This third step is

Step 3. Recall N and N' and accomplish goal of verify the entry

N and N' will be compared in the verify entry method, so they must be recalled before the comparison can be made. This is a nonprimitive method which is specified further under the sixth method:

Method to accomplish the goal of verify the entry

This method is accomplished through four steps. The first step is a decision step:

Step 1. Decide: if N and N' do not match, then forget N' and accomplish goal of deleting entry

Let's examine both paths of this decision step, assuming first that the menu item and feedback do not match. Deleting the entry is a nonprimitive step which is described by the seventh, and last, method of the figure:

Method for accomplishing goal of deleting entry

This has four steps. The user hits the DELETE key the number of times required to delete all the entered digits so that the processing will loop until all are deleted. The first step specifies the key for deleting the characters one by one:

Step 1. Press-key DELETE

The second step is used to decide if any more digits or characters are still in the entry space and must be deleted:

Step 2. Decide: if more digits in entry space on screen, Goto 1

If more still need to be deleted, then the goto statement indicates that step 1 should be performed again by pressing the DE-LETE key. If no more digits are present, then processing moves to step 3:

Step 3. Forget N', recall N and accomplish goal of enter the menu item

At this point, processing is returned to the selection rule for entering the menu item number. N is recalled from WM, so the user would still decide to do the key-method or the string-method depending on the value of N. The processing of this selection rule has been detailed earlier in this section and will not be repeated here. At the end of this goal, the user has entered the corrected N and processing returns to step 4 of this seventh method:

Step 4. Report goal accomplished

We will assume that the second entry was correct and that the user would not have to verify the entry again. Therefore, the feedback N' is not needed and can be forgotten. That the user does not verify this second entry may or may not be a valid assumption. Whether or not the user verified the entry again would probably depend on the user, the situation, or the expertise of the user. An exercise at the end of this chapter requires that the model be determined for the situation where the user verifies the entry once again.

The goal of deleting the entry was called from step 1 of the sixth method if N and N' did not match. Step 2 would be processed next. (Note: Remember that step 2 would be called immediately after step 1 of method 6 if N and N' matched.) Step 2 is as follows:

Step 2. Press-key ENTER

The ENTER key is used to indicate that the menu item entry has been verified and is correct. At this point, the user no longer needs to remember the specific item number or the feedback:

Step 3. Forget N and N'

This completes the sixth method:

Step 4. Report goal accomplished

At this point, the menu item number has been entered, so the user can forget the feedback item number, the menu item number, and the MENU-COMMAND. This accomplishes the goal of verifying the entered number.

The task is almost finished. Recall that the verify entry goal was originally called from step 3 of the second method. Since this step has been accomplished, the processing proceeds to step 4:

Step 4. Forget MENU-COMMAND and report goal accomplished

The user no longer needs to keep MENU-COMMAND in memory. Since this goal is completed, processing returns to the step after the command unit task goal was originally called. This is in method 1.

The next step in method 1, step 3, is:

Decide: If more commands in command sequence, then Goto 1

Recall that the command sequence could include many commands of which the just completed command could be only one. Let's assume that this command was the only one in the sequence. In this case, the decision step states that there are no more commands. How this is done has been left purposely vague. It could be spelled out in more detail, but we would have to make assumptions about very low-level cognitive processes which would probably be beyond the useful scope of most modeling of human-computer interaction tasks. Most probably, the sequence of commands would be a list of commands. If no more commands were on the list, then a NULL value would be found for the next command. But, once again, we would usually not have to get this specific. In any case, the third step has now been completed, and processing would proceed to step 4:

Step 4. Report goal accomplished

Method 1 is the highest-level goal so that this would complete the particular command sequence. If in step 3 there were more tasks, then processing would return to step 1 and the next command in the sequence would be retrieved. The whole process would begin again.

Kieras (1988) suggests that even after the NGOMSL representation has been completed, the representation should be examined to make sure that it is complete and the division of steps to methods is plausible. After completing a draft of the NGOMSL analysis, the complete task analysis should be checked for consistency and conformance to guidelines. Kieras (1988) states that the following should be checked:

1. Check on method detail and length. The length of the method should probably be no more than five steps. If it has more than five steps, the method should be divided into other operators. The method

detail should have only one accomplish-goal operator to a step.

2. Check on consistent assumptions about the user's expertise with regard to the number of operators in a step. The rules for the relationship of operators to user expertise are not very clear. Some broad guidelines can be specified. For ordinary or novice users, no more than one external primitive operator should occur in a step. For expert or experienced users, several external primitive operators can be used in a single step if the sequence of external primitive operators is often performed without any decisions or subgoals involved.

3. Identify high-level operators and check that each high-level operator corresponds to a natural goal.

4. Check for consistency of terminology and usage with already defined operators.

The NGOMSL task analysis for the high-breadth menu display has already gone through several revisions before being included in this chapter. It is expected that any task analysis would have to be revised in some way before it was completed.

Perhaps one aspect of the task which could be changed is the method for deleting the entry. If N was 10 or larger, then 2 digits would have to be entered. If only the second digit was entered wrong, then it would make no sense to delete the first digit, the 1, because this digit is correct. The current method specifies that the 1 would be deleted even if it was correct. The modification of this task analysis to include this more accurate specification of the delete entry method is left as an exercise at the end of this chapter.

The NGOMSL task analysis for the high-depth menu display is contained in Figure 15-5. Because of the similarities in the procedures for interacting with a high-breadth menu display and a high-depth menu display, the goals, methods, and operators are similar except for a few changes. The method for accomplishing the goal of executing the command sequence (method 1b) is the same as the corresponding method of the high-breadth display.

The high-depth menu display requires that the user first interact with the main menu to enter the command category and then with the secondary menu display to enter the needed command. For the high-breadth display, the user only has one menu to interact with. Because of this, the command sequence is performed differently between the two menu displays. Method 2b shows the additional steps needed for the main category menu and secondary command menu displays.

Methods 3b and 4b, to accomplish the goal of issuing the menu category and command, are combinations, reorderings, and the result of deletions of some of the methods for the high-breadth display. For the high-depth display, keystrokes are reduced by requiring that only one keystroke be used for entering the menu item number. This can occur because the menu numbers are always less than 10 and so no uncertainty exists about the termination of the response. For the high-breadth menu

display, the number of keystrokes needed is either one or two and the only way for the computer to know when the entry is complete is to terminate it through the use of the ENTER key. Because of this, the user with the high-depth menu display does not have to choose between entering a single digit (the Press-key operator) and entering a string of digits (the Type-in operator). Consequently, the selection rule of the high-breadth display is not needed.

Another use of the ENTER key is that it allows the user to verify the entry before it is terminated. Since no ENTER key is used for the high-depth display, the entry cannot be verified. This may be a bad interface policy for novice users, but we would assume that experts would not need to verify the entry and saving a keystroke would be advantageous. Consequently, the verify entry step is not needed in method 2b. At a later point in the method structure, no delete entry method is provided either.

The methods for locating the MENU-CATEGORY (method 5b) and the MENU-COMMAND (method 6b) are very similar to each other and to method 3a of the high-breadth display. All three are the same except for step 1 of method 5b. This first step is needed for the MENU-CATE-GORY because of the nature of the high-depth display. By dividing the menus into two, a category and a command menu, only one of the menus, the command menu, will correspond to the actual command which is to be executed. The category menu has the categories of the 16 commands. Consequently, the user must search LTM to find the appropriate category for the command. This is achieved in the first step of method 5b. All in all, the high-depth model is similar to the high-breadth model, but with some important differences. Later sections discuss how to use this model to make predictions about using the displays.

The primitives for the cognitive operators on the high-depth and high-breadth menu display analysis were very detailed. As indicated earlier, this level of detail, by spelling out the cognitive operations performed in the choice of the menu items, would probably not be needed in the cases where the menu display was a component of a task and not the main focus of the analysis. A more global operator, such as Find-menu-item would be used. The level of the primitives should be chosen so as to satisfy the goals of the task analysis. Since the goal of the preceding task analysis was to determine which menu display, high-breadth or high-depth, was the best, the differences between the displays could lie in the low-level cognitive operator primitives. Only by analyzing the task at this level will the possible differences be found. Choosing the levels of the primitives is one of the most important choices made by the task analyst.

An Operating System Example

Kieras (1988) presents other examples for applying NGOMSL. One of these examples, for editing text using a Macintoshlike interface, is presented in Figure 15-6. For those familiar with using a Macintosh, the methods should be easy to follow. The task is to move a specified piece of text. The piece of text can be a word or arbitrary text such as two or more words or part of a word. To move this text, the user must position the cursor at the beginning of the text by moving the mouse.

If moving a word, a double click will highlight the word; if moving arbitrary text, the end of the text must be pointed to by the mouse and highlighted by releasing the mouse button which would be down since the selection of the beginning point. A CUT command is issued by moving the mouse to the EDIT pull-down menu and pressing the mouse button. The user must find the CUT command on the pull-down menu, move the mouse to that location, and release the button. Next, the mouse is moved to the location in the text where the cut text is to be placed. The mouse is clicked on this location. The EDIT pull-down menu is accessed again, and, with the mouse button down, the PASTE item is highlighted by moving the mouse over its location. Once the mouse button is released, the cut text is inserted in the specified location.

It would be instructive to go through the methods command by command just to understand how NGOMSL may work. Each goal should have a method of steps or a selection rule set associated with it. Each nongoal operator must be a primitive operator.

APPLICATIONS OF NGOMSL

Kieras (1988) presents several ways in which the NGOMSL model can be applied: estimating execution time; estimating learning times; design revisions; estimating the mental workload of a task; and analyzing the documentation. The procedures for each of these will be reviewed.

Execution Times

Execution time could be dependent on the time to execute the operators and the

Method to accomplish goal of editing the document
>   Step 1. Get next unit task information from marked-up manuscript
>   Step 2. Decide: If no more unit tasks, then report goal accomplished
>   Step 3. Accomplish the goal of moving to the unit task location
>   Step 4. Accomplish the goal of performing the unit task.
>   Step 5. Goto 1.

Selection rule set for the goal of performing the unit task
>   If the task is moving text, then accomplish the goal of moving text
>   If the task is deletion, then accomplish the goal of deleting text
>   If the task is copying, then accomplish the goal of copying text, etc.
>   Report goal accomplished

Method to accomplish the goal of moving to the unit task location
>   Step 1. Get location of unit task from manuscript
>   Step 2. Decide: If unit task location on screen, then report goal accomplished
>   Step 3. Use scroll bar to advance text
>   Step 4. Goto 2

Method to accomplish goal of moving text
>   Step 1. Accomplish the goal of cutting text
>   Step 2. Accomplish the goal of pasting text
>   Step 3. Verify correct text moved
>   Step 4. Report goal accomplished

Method to accomplish goal of cutting text
>   Step 1. Accomplish goal of selecting text
>   Step 2. Accomplish goal of issuing CUT command
>   Step 3. Report goal accomplished

Method to accomplish goal of pasting text
>   Step 1. Accomplish goal of selecting insertion point
>   Step 2. Accomplish goal of issuing PASTE command
>   Step 3. Report goal accomplished

Selection rule set for goal of selecting text
>   If text-is word, then accomplish goal of selecting word
>   If text-is arbitrary, then accomplish goal of selecting arbitrary text
>   Report goal accomplished

Method to accomplish goal of selecting word
>   Step 1. Determine position of beginning of word
>   Step 2. Move cursor to beginning of word
>   Step 3. Double-click mouse button
>   Step 4. Verify that correct text is selected
>   Step 5. Report goal accomplished

(continued on next page)

Figure 15-6. Methods and operators for using an operating system (from Kieras, 1988, reprinted with permission of publisher).

Method to accomplish goal of selecting arbitrary text

      Step 1. Determine position of beginning of text

      Step 2. Move cursor to beginning of text

      Step 3. Press mouse button down

      Step 4. Determine position of end of text

      Step 5. Move cursor to end of text

      Step 6. Verify that correct text is selected

      Step 7. Release mouse button

      Step 8. Report goal accomplished

Method to accomplish goal of selecting insertion point

      Step 1. Determine position of insertion point

      Step 2. Move cursor to insertion point

      Step 3. Click mouse button

      Step 4. Report goal accomplished

Method to accomplish goal of issuing CUT command (assuming that the user does not use command-X shortcut)

      Step 1. Move cursor to "Edit" on Menu Bar

      Step 2. Press mouse button down

      Step 3. Move cursor to "CUT"

      Step 4. Verify that CUT is selected

      Step 5. Release mouse button

      Step 6. Report goal accomplished

Method to accomplish goal of issuing PASTE command (assuming that user does not use command-V shortcut)

      Step 1. Move cursor to "Edit" on Menu Bar

      Step 2. Press mouse button down

      Step 3. Move cursor to "PASTE"

      Step 4. Verify that PASTE is selected

      Step 5. Release mouse button

      Step 6. Report goal accomplished

Figure 15-6 (cont.)

number of cognitive steps involved. The formula used by Kieras (1988), based upon experimentation and modeling of the results, is as follows:

Execution time =

    NGOMSL statement time
    + Primitive External Operator Time
    + Analyst-Defined Mental Operator Time
    + System Response Time

NGOMSL Statement Time =

    Number of NGOMSL statements executed * 0.1 sec.

Primitive External Operator Time =

    Total of times for external operators

Analyst-Defined Mental Operator Time =

    Total of times for mental operators defined by the analyst

1. Retrieve-LTM that current item in command sequence is MENU-COMMAND
2. Accomplish goal of performing the command unit task
3. Recall MENU-COMMAND and accomplish goal of locating MENU-COMMAND
4. ReadScreen next command line and retain as MENU-ITEM
5. Decide: If MENU-COMMAND is different from MENU-ITEM
6. Then forget MENU-ITEM and Goto 1

(Statements 4 through 6 would be executed 12 more times)

43. ReadScreen next command line and retain as MENU-ITEM
44. Decide: If MENU-COMMAND is different from MENU-ITEM
45. Retain that N is number of MENU-ITEM
46. Forget MENU-ITEM and report goal accomplished
47. Recall N and accomplish goal of enter the menu item number
48. If N is between 1 and 9
49. If N is 10 or above
50. Then accomplish goal of do string-method
51. Type-in N
52. ReadScreen and retain feedback as N'
53. Report goal accomplished
54. Report goal accomplished
55. Recall N and N' and accomplish goal of verify the entry
56. Decide: If N and N' do not match
57. Press-key ENTER
58. Forget N and N'
59. Report goal accomplished
60. Forget MENU-COMMAND and report goal accomplished
61. Decide: If more commands in command sequence
62. Report goal accomplished

Figure 15-7. Sequence of steps to choose menu item 14 for the high-breadth display.

System Response Time =

Total time when user is idle

To determine the estimated times, a specific task instance must be used because each specific task may use different statements. Let's run through a time estimate for the high-breadth display when the user is choosing menu item 14.

Figure 15-7 has the sequence of statements that will be executed to choose menu item 14. When making this list, a few things should be noted. First, the "if" and "then" parts of the statements have to be considered as two statements if the condition is true. As an example, statement 44 is a decision statement:

44. Decide: If MENU-COMMAND is different from MENU-ITEM

This is false, so the "then" part of the statement need not be processed. However, if the condition is true, then the "then" part must be executed as a separate statement even though it may be contained in the same step. An example of this occurs in statements 5 and 6:

5. Decide: If MENU-COMMAND is different from MENU-ITEM

6. Then forget MENU-ITEM and Goto 1

In this case they were different, and thus the statement was true, so that the "then" part of the rule could be executed.

At one point the execution is put into a loop (statements 7 through 42) as the user reads the menu items on the display. This corresponds closely to the cognitive processes used for the Model Human Processor for this task. Those steps were not repeated in the figure.

To estimate the times, we need to determine the number of NGOMSL statements, the Primitive External Operator Time, the Analyst-Defined Mental Operator Time, and the System Response Time. The NGOMSL statement time is determined by taking the number of NGOMSL statements executed times 0.1 sec. A total of 62 statements were executed so that this time is 6.2 sec. The 0.1 sec. time is similar to the time needed for a cognitive processor (τ_c) from the Model Human Processor.

Kieras (1988) says that good estimators for the operators are the primitive operator values used by Card et al. (1983) in their Keystrokes-Level model. In this particular example, only three external operators occur: the two digits (14) of the menu item in statement 51 and the ENTER key of statement 57. Recalling the keystroke values from Table 14-3 for an average skilled typist (.20 sec.), the total Primitive External Operator Time is .60 sec.

If Analyst-Defined Mental Operators are included, then these times would have to be determined individually through experimentation or, in the absence of experimentation, values from the Keystrokes-Level model of GOMS or the Model Human Processor values can be used. In this particular case, one Analyst-Defined Mental Operator, ReadScreen, is used 15 times (once in statement 52 and 14 times in the loop of statements 4 through 42). Since this is a relatively primitive process, the perceptual processor (τ_p) from the Model Human Processor can provide a good estimate for this time instead of having to go through the trouble of running an experiment. From Chapter 13, this processor time was 100 msec. Since the ReadScreen occurs 15 times, the Analyst-Defined Mental Operator time is 1.5 sec.

As done in the previous chapters, we will assume that the System Response Time is negligible or equal to 0. Since we are not analyzing the task for any particular system, it is difficult to predict the system response time. If the menu displays were being compared for a particular system, then these times could be determined exactly.

Totaling the execution time, we have the following:

$$\text{Execution Time} = 62 \ (0.1) \text{ sec.} + 0.6 \text{ sec.}$$
$$+ \ 15 \ (0.1) \text{ sec.} + 0$$
$$= 8.3 \text{ sec.} \qquad (15.1)$$

Using the NGOMSL model, we would estimate that the time needed to choose the 14th menu item is 8.3 sec.

Let's determine the estimated execution time for the high-depth display and compare it to the estimated time for the high-breadth display. Figure 15-8 contains the statements needed for choosing menu item m overall by first choosing menu item 4 in the main menu and then menu item 2 in the secondary menu. The execution of this task requires 36 statements. The user has two external primitive operators: the single-digit keystroke for the main menu (statement 19) and the single-digit keystroke for the secondary menu (statement 31). The Primitive External Operator Time is, therefore, 0.4 sec. ReadScreen is the only Analyst-Defined Mental Operator, and it occurs four times for the Category Menu (in the loop of statements 6 through 15) and twice for the Command Menu (statements 24 and 27). Using the 0.1 estimate, the total time for Analyst-Defined Mental Operators is .6 sec. Once again, we assume that the system response time is negligible. The equation for estimating the time is

$$\text{Execution Time} = 36\,(0.1)\text{ sec.} + 0.4\text{ sec.} \\ + 0.6\text{ sec.} + 0 \\ = 4.6\text{ sec.} \qquad (15.2)$$

Comparing this time of 4.6 sec. for the high-depth display to the time of 8.3 sec. for the high-breadth display, we would predict that the high-depth display would be faster to execute by over 3 seconds for choosing menu item 14. These qualitative results are similar to that found for the Model Human Processor and the GOMS models.

In the preceding example, the execution time was solved for a particular case for finding the 14th item; it can also be solved for the general case. The only part that will change in the general case is the number of menu items searched until the correct one was found. Similar to the analyses in Chapters 13 and 14, on the average the menu item will be found, in a serial terminating search, on search number $(n + 1)/2$. With 16 items for the high-

breadth menu display, this would require 8.5 searches. From Figure 15-7, steps 4 through 6 would be repeated, on the average, a total of 8.5 times. This would result in 24.5 steps $((8.5 * 3) - 1)$ for the search to occur. The one step is subtracted from the total because, when the item was found, the "then" part would not be needed. This is statement 6 in Figure 15-7.

The execution of this task, in the general case, requires 45.5 statements: 3 steps before the search begins, 24.5 steps during the search, and 18 steps after the search is completed. The execution time for performing these statements would be

$$45.5 * 0.1 = 4.55\text{ sec.} \qquad (15.3)$$

The external primitive operators are slightly different from the specific case. Whereas the specific case had three keystrokes, two for the menu item number and one for the ENTER key, for the general case, two digits would always be entered: one digit for the menu item and the ENTER key. The second digit would be entered when the menu item number was between 10 and 16. If all items had equal probability of occurrence, then the probability of entering a second digit for the menu item number is 0.44. Using the same estimate of 0.2 sec. per keystroke for an average skilled typist, the time to perform these external operators is

$$(2 + 0.44)(0.2) = 0.49\text{ sec.} \qquad (15.4)$$

ReadScreen is the only Analyst-Defined Mental Operator, and it occurs 12.5 times for the search through the menu items and one time when the entered menu item is being verified. Using the 0.1 estimate, the total time for Analyst-De-

1. Retrieve-LTM that current item in command sequence is MENU-COMMAND
2. Accomplish goal of performing the command unit task
3. Accomplish goal of issuing MENU-CATEGORY
4. Recall MENU-COMMAND and accomplish goal of locating MENU-CATEGORY
5. Retrieve-LTM that the category of MENU-COMMAND is MENU-CATEGORY
6. ReadScreen next command line and retain as MENU-ITEM
7. Decide: If MENU-ITEM is different from MENU-CATEGORY
8. Then forget MENU-ITEM and Goto 2
9 -14 (Statements 6 through 8 would be executed 2 more times)
15. ReadScreen next command line and retain as MENU-ITEM
16. Decide: If MENU-ITEM is different from MENU-CATEGORY
17. Retain that N is number of MENU-ITEM
18. Forget MENU-ITEM and report goal accomplished
19. Recall N and Press-key N
20. Forget N and MENU-CATEGORY
21. Report goal accomplished
22. Accomplish goal of issuing MENU-COMMAND
23. Recall MENU-COMMAND and accomplish goal of locating MENU-COMMAND
24. ReadScreen next command line and retain as MENU-ITEM
25. Decide: If MENU-ITEM is different from MENU-COMMAND
26. Then forget MENU-ITEM and Goto 1
27. ReadScreen next command line and retain as MENU-ITEM
28. Decide: If MENU-ITEM is different from MENU-COMMAND
29. Retain that N is number of menu item
30. Forget MENU-ITEM and report goal accomplished
31. Recall N and Press-key N
32. Forget N and MENU-COMMAND
33. Report goal accomplished
34. Report goal accomplished
35. Decide: If more commands in command sequence
36. Report goal accomplished

Figure 15-8. Sequence of steps to choose menu item m for the high-depth display.

fined Mental Operators is 1.35 sec. Once again, we assume that the system response time is negligible. The equation for estimating the time is

Execution Time = 4.55 sec. + 0.49 sec.
$$+ 1.35 \text{ sec.} + 0$$
$$= 6.39 \text{ sec.} \qquad (15.5)$$

The general case can be determined in a similar way for the high-depth dis-

play. Since each of the two menus has four items, the number of items searched would be $(4 + 1)/2$ or 2.5. Similar to the high-breadth display, the number of steps in the search process would be $(3 * 2.5) - 1$ or 6.5 statements. This search would occur in two places: for the main menu in statements 6 through 8 of Figure 15-8, and for the secondary menu in statements 24 through 26 of the figure. Five statements would precede the first search, seven statements would occur between the two searches, and eight statements would follow the second search. This results in 33 statements total, for an execution time of 3.3 sec. All of the other parameters for the execution time are the same as the specific case. The equation for estimating the time is

$$\text{Execution Time} = 33 \ (0.1) \text{ sec.} + 0.4 \text{ sec.}$$
$$+ \ 0.6 \text{ sec.} + 0$$
$$= 4.3 \text{ sec.} \qquad (15.6)$$

Comparing this time against the high-breadth time of 6.39 sec., the high-depth display is predicted to be faster on average.

Learning Times

Kieras (1988) also reports some experimentation on estimating the learning time for a novice user to learn a task which has been analyzed by the NGOMSL task analysis. He indicates that this is an estimate of "pure" learning time which can be taken as an estimate of minimum learning time. The estimate is determined as follows:

$$\text{Learning time} = (30\text{-}60) \text{ minutes} + 30 \text{ sec.}$$
$$\text{per number of NGOMSL}$$
$$\text{statements} \qquad (15.7)$$

For estimating execution time, a specific task, finding menu item m, had to be executed. In this case, the number of NGOMSL statements refers to the total number of statements in the task analysis independent of any specific task. The learning statements are counted as follows:

1. method title or selection rule title = 1 statement

2. each if-then step or selection rule = 1 statement

3. all other steps = 1 statement

Some may wonder why an if-then rule is counted as one statement for learning time but may be executed in two parts for determining the execution time. For execution time, performance is modeled after how a computer programming language compiler would execute a program. On some execution steps, the "if" part of the rule may be incorrect, which means that the "then" part of the rule is not executed. So, in this case, the "if" requires execution time independent of the second part of the rule, which may or may not be executed. For learning, on the other hand, people are likely to learn both parts of the rule together as one unit. Both have to be associated as one unit because one part of the rule is meaningless without the other part.

The number of statements used for learning time estimation can be determined simply by counting the number of steps of Figures 15-4 and 15-5 and adding one more statement for the method title. For the high-breadth display, the number of statements can be found as follows:

method 1a: title + 4 steps = 5 to learn

method 2a: title + 4 steps = 5 to learn

method 3a: title + 4 steps = 5 to learn

method 4a: title + 3 steps = 4 to learn

method 5a: title + 3 steps = 4 to learn

method 6a: title + 4 steps = 5 to learn

method 7a: title + 4 steps = 5 to learn

selection rule: title + 2 rules + 1 step
= 4 to learn

The grand total is 37 statements which must be learned. For the high-depth display, the number of statements to be learned, calculated in the same way, is 30. We would predict that the high-breadth display would take the following amount of time to learn:

$$\text{Learning time} = 30\text{-}60 \text{ min.} + .5 \ (37) \text{ min.}$$
$$= 48.5 \text{ - } 78.5 \text{ min.} \quad (15.8)$$

The high-depth display would take the following amount of time to learn:

$$\text{Learning time} = 30\text{-}60 \text{ min.} + .5 \ (30) \text{ min.}$$
$$= 45 \text{ - } 75 \text{ min.} \quad (15.9)$$

Because of the 30-60 minute baseline value, nonoverlap in learning times between displays will occur only when the number of NGOMSL statements is very high, which could be the case for many interface designs. When comparing the high-breadth and high-depth displays, the overlap in estimated times is too high, so that it is difficult to determine which one would be easiest to learn with a great degree of certainty.

Gains from Consistency

Kieras (1988) argues that if the methods are designed to be consistent or similar then the learning time will not be as long because the user will be able to determine the pattern of the methods. This is called a gain due to consistency, which can be determined by evaluating the similarities between the methods. Determining similarities depends on the goal description of the method. Recall that the goal description is in terms of a verb-noun pair. Kieras (1988) suggests that to use this technique on methods A and B, either the verb or the

noun term of the goal descriptions of A and B must be the same. If this is the case, then the similar statements in methods A and B are determined by changing the statements of a copy of A to get method B after making a simple substitution of the different goal term in the statements. Kieras (1988) specifies the following steps:

1. Make a copy of A.

2. Identify the single term in the goal specifications of the two methods that is different, change it to a "parameter," and change this term throughout the copy of A.

3. Count how many NGOMSL statements are identical in these methods A and B; these statements are the ones classified as similar and they need to be charged learning time only once.

Let's now apply this technique to determining any gains from consistency for either the high-breadth or the high-depth displays. Examining the verbs and nouns of the goal descriptions of the methods for the high-breadth display shows one possible match between methods 4a and 5a (both have the same verb of "do"). For determining gains due to consistency, the first step is to make a copy of A or, in this case, method 4a (see Figure 15-9). For the second step, the nonmatching verb or noun is parameterized and changed throughout the copy. Since the verbs of these two match, then the noun of method 4a, string-method, will be parameterized. This parameter does not occur elsewhere in the method steps, so no further changes *method 4a*

Method to accomplish goal of do key-method

Step 1. Press-key N
Step 2. ReadScreen and retain feedback as N'
Step 3. Report goal accomplished

changed copy of method 4a

Method to accomplish goal of do string-method

Step 1. Press-key N
Step 2. ReadScreen and retain feedback as N'
Step 3. Report goal accomplished

method 5a

Method to accomplish goal of do string-method

Step 1. Type-in N
Step 2. ReadScreen and retain feedback as N'
Step 3. Report goal accomplished

method 5a

Method to accomplish goal of do string-method

Step 1. Type-in N
Step 2. ReadScreen and retain feedback as N'
Step 3. Report goal accomplished

Figure 15-9. The procedure for determining the gain due to consistency for methods 4a and 5a of the high-breadth menu display.

need to be made. In the final step, count how many statements are the same in methods 4a and 5a. As can be seen, two of the statements are the same.

For the high-depth display, a main category menu is used and then a secondary command menu is used. It would make sense that some of these methods would be consistent because of the two menus used. Examining the verbs and nouns of the goal descriptions, two pairs of matches are found. For methods 3b and 4b, both have the verb "issuing" with the noun differing (MENU-CATEGORY in the first case and MENU-COMMAND in the second case). Similarly, for methods 5b and 6b, both have the "locating" verb with the noun differing in the same way as the previous pair of methods.

We will first examine the similarities between methods 3b and 4b. The first step is to make a copy of A or, in this case, method 3b (see Figure 15-10). For the second step, the nonmatching verb or noun is parameterized. Since the verbs of these two match, then the noun of method 3b, MENU-CATEGORY, will be parameterized. The noun is then changed from

MENU-CATEGORY to MENU-COMMAND in both the original and the copy (see Figure 15-10). In the final step, count the number of statements which are similar between changed method 3b and method 4b. As can be seen from the last figure, all the statements are the same, so this number is 4.

Now examine the similarities between methods 5b and 6b. A copy of the original method 5b is shown in Figure 15-11. Since the verbs match between the methods, then the noun of method 5b, MENU-CATEGORY, is again parameterized. In Figure 15-11 the noun is changed from MENU-COMMAND to MENU-CATEGORY in the changed version of method 5b. Next, in Figure 15-11, the copy is changed until it is similar to method 6b. In this case, step 1 is deleted, all the rest of the step numbers are changed accordingly, and the step number in the goto statement also changes to reflect the deleted step. The number of similar statements between the changed copy of method 5b and method 6b is 4.

This analysis shows that both the high-breadth display and the high-depth

method 3b

Method to accomplish goal of issuing MENU-CATEGORY

Step 1. Recall MENU-COMMAND and accomplish goal of locating MENU-CATEGORY
Step 2. Recall N and Press-key N
Step 3. Forget N and MENU-CATEGORY
Step 4. Report goal accomplished

changed copy of method 3b

Method to accomplish goal of issuing MENU-COMMAND

Step 1. Recall MENU-COMMAND and accomplish goal of locating MENU-COMMAND
Step 2. Recall N and Press-key N
Step 3. Forget N and MENU-COMMAND
Step 4. Report goal accomplished

method 4b

Method to accomplish goal of issuing MENU-COMMAND

Step 1. Recall MENU-COMMAND and accomplish goal of locating MENU-COMMAND
Step 2. Recall N and Press-key N
Step 3. Forget N and MENU-COMMAND
Step 4. Report goal accomplished

method 4b

Method to accomplish goal of issuing MENU-COMMAND

Step 1. Recall MENU-COMMAND and accomplish goal of locating MENU-COMMAND
Step 2. Recall N and Press-key N
Step 3. Forget N and MENU-COMMAND
Step 4. Report goal accomplished

Figure 15-10. The procedure for determining the gain due to consistency for methods 3b and 4b of the high-depth menu display.

display have a gain due to consistency. For the high-breadth display, the original number of statements which had to be learned from the previous section was 37. This results in a learning time of 37 * .5 min. or 18.5 min. above the baseline. If method 4a was learned before method 5a, then the number of statements to be learned could be reduced to 34 (reduced by 1 method title and 2 statements). This would result in a gain due to consistency of 3 statements or 1.5 minutes for this high-breadth display.

For the high-depth display, the original number of statements which had to be learned from the previous section was 30. This resulted in a learning time of 30 * .5 min. or 15 minutes of learning time above the baseline. If method 3b was learned before method 4b, then no learning time would be needed for method 4b because no new statements would have to be learned. Therefore, the number of state-

ments to learn could be reduced by 5 (1 method title and 4 steps) down to 25. If method 5b was learned before method 6b, then the user would learn 6 statements for method 5b (1 method title and 5 steps). Comparing the changed copy of method 5b to method 6b one can see that all the steps and titles are the same, so no new ones would need be learned. Since nothing needs to be learned, the 5 statements from method 6b (1 method title and 4 steps) can be discounted from the total learning time. This would result in a learning time of 20 * .5 min. or 10 minutes of learning time above the baseline. The gain due to consistency for the high-depth display would be about 5 minutes.

The estimation for learning time showed that both could be expected to be learned in about the same time. The analysis for the gain from consistency must be performed to obtain a better estimate of learning time. Because of the consisten-

method 5b

method 6b

Method to accomplish goal of locating MENU-CATEGORY

Method to accomplish goal of locating MENU-COMMAND

Step 1. Retrieve-LTM that the category of MENU-COMMAND is MENU-CATEGORY
Step 2. ReadScreen next command line and retain as MENU-ITEM
Step 3. Decide: If MENU-ITEM is different from MENU-CATEGORY then forget MENU-ITEM and Goto 2
Step 4. Retain that N is number of MENU-ITEM
Step 5. Forget MENU-ITEM and report goal accomplished

Step 1. ReadScreen next command line and retain as MENU-ITEM
Step 2. Decide: If MENU-ITEM is different from MENU-CATEGORY then forget MENU-ITEM and Goto 1
Step 3. Retain that N is number of MENU-ITEM
Step 4. Forget MENU-ITEM and report goal accomplished

changed copy of method 5b

method 6b

Method to accomplish goal of locating MENU-COMMAND

Method to accomplish goal of locating MENU-COMMAND

Step 1. Retrieve-LTM that the category of MENU-COMMAND is MENU-COMMAND
Step 2. ReadScreen next command line and retain as MENU-ITEM
Step 3. Decide: If MENU-ITEM is different from MENU-COMMAND then forget MENU-ITEM and Goto 2
Step 4. Retain that N is number of MENU-ITEM
Step 5. Forget MENU-ITEM and report goal accomplished

Step 1. ReadScreen next command line and retain as MENU-ITEM
Step 2. Decide: If MENU-ITEM is different from MENU-COMMAND then forget MENU-ITEM and Goto 1
Step 3. Retain that N is number of MENU-ITEM
Step 4. Forget MENU-ITEM and report goal accomplished

changed copy of method 5b

method 6b

Method to accomplish goal of locating MENU-COMMAND

Method to accomplish goal of locating MENU-COMMAND

Step 1. ReadScreen the next command line and retain as MENU-ITEM
Step 2. Decide: If MENU-ITEM is different from MENU-COMMAND then forget MENU-ITEM and Goto 1
Step 3. Retain that N is number of MENU-ITEM
Step 4. Forget MENU-ITEM and report goal accomplished

Step 1. ReadScreen next command line and retain as MENU-ITEM
Step 2. Decide: If MENU-ITEM is different from MENU-COMMAND then forget MENU-ITEM and Goto 1
Step 3. Retain that N is number of MENU-ITEM
Step 4. Forget MENU-ITEM and report goal accomplished

Figure 15-11. The procedure for determining the gain due to consistency for methods 5b and 6b of the high-breadth menu display.

method 5b

Method to accomplish goal of locating MENU-CATEGORY

Step 1. Retrieve-LTM that the category of MENU-COMMAND is MENU-CATEGORY
Step 2. ReadScreen next command line and retain as MENU-ITEM
Step 3. Decide: If MENU-ITEM is different from MENU-CATEGORY then forget MENU-ITEM and Goto 2
Step 4. Retain that N is number of MENU-ITEM
Step 5. Forget MENU-ITEM and report goal accomplished

method 3b

Method to accomplish goal of issuing MENU-CATEGORY

Step 1. Recall MENU-COMMAND and accomplish goal of locating MENU-CATEGORY
Step 2. Recall N and Press-key N
Step 3. Forget N and MENU-CATEGORY
Step 4. Report goal accomplished

changed copy of method 5b

Method to accomplish goal of issuing MENU-CATEGORY

Step 1. Retrieve-LTM that the category of MENU-COMMAND is MENU-CATEGORY
Step 2. ReadScreen next command line and retain as MENU-ITEM
Step 3. Decide: If MENU-ITEM is different from MENU-CATEGORY then forget MENU-ITEM and Goto 2
Step 4. Retain that N is number of MENU-ITEM
Step 5. Forget MENU-ITEM and report goal accomplished

method 3b

Method to accomplish goal of issuing MENU-CATEGORY

Step 1. Recall MENU-COMMAND and accomplish goal of locating MENU-CATEGORY
Step 2. Recall N and Press-key N
Step 3. Forget N and MENU-CATEGORY
Step 4. Report goal accomplished

Figure 15-12. This demonstrates that no gain from consistency could be found for methods 3 and 5 of the high-depth menu display because there is no overlap in the statements.

cies in the design of the high-depth display, the estimated learning time will be 6 min. less for this display as compared to the high-breadth display.

One could wonder why methods 3b and 4b were paired instead of methods 3b and 5b, which have the same noun. A quick glance at methods 3b and 4b will show that they have similar statements, while methods 3b and 5b do not. A more formal analysis can be performed on methods 3b and 5b to show that even if the substitutions are made, no statements are similar. Figure 15-12 contains the steps

for analyzing any possible gain from consistency. In the first step, method 5b is shown in the left column and method 3b is shown in the right column. Next, below on the left, method 5b is changed. Since the similarity between methods 3b and 5b is the noun of the goal (MENU-CATEGORY), all occurrences of the verb "locating" must be changed to the verb "issuing." This only occurs in the title of the methods. This change is made. Finally, the changed copy of method 5b is compared to method 3b. As can be seen, no statements match because no changes could be made in the statements. Changing the verb from "issuing" to "locating" results in no gain due to consistency.

Consistency When Alternating Between Interfaces

The preceding analysis involved looking at one part of consistency. Consistency is important because designers generally believe that consistent designs should improve users' productivity by leading to higher performance with fewer errors, which in turn generally lead to improved user satisfaction with the system (Nielsen, 1989). In many cases, though, consistency in user interface designs has been poorly defined, has not been tested through experimental work, and has mostly been advanced through the advocation of broad guidelines.

The preceding analysis for gains due to consistency indicated that the more similar the methods within a task, the higher the gain. This is a good assumption under many conditions. Tanaka, Eberts, and Salvendy (1991) argue, however, that when alternating between tasks, high overlap between the methods of the tasks will result in errors and will slow the execution times. Errors will occur when the user cannot remember which methods go with which task because of the high similarity. As an example, the DOS operating system is command-based such that a directory command is accomplished by entering "DIR." The VMS operating system is also command-based, but it allows the user to enter as many characters of the command as needed to distinguish it from another command. For a directory, the user could enter "DIR" or "DIRECT." In fact, any characters beyond the "DIR"

would be acceptable. Any characters beyond the "DIR" in the DOS operating system are not acceptable. Because of the high overlap in this method, the user could have difficulty remembering which command to use if the user switches between the DOS and VMS operating systems. With the high overlap between methods for these two operating systems, Kieras (1988) would say that they would have a high gain due to consistency.

Under the Tanaka et al. analysis, a user who switches between the DOS operating system and the Apple Macintosh operating system would have little difficulty. As an example, performing a directory on the Macintosh is totally different from the previous example: the user double clicks an icon of a folder to perform a directory. In most of the cases, however, a directory is not even performed because the list of files is always shown on the screen. Because of the little overlap between DOS and the Macintosh operating system, no confusion should occur.

Tanaka et al. used NGOMSL in determining the consistency between interface designs when alternating between interfaces. They quantitatively determined consistency through the use of an NGOMSL task analysis and then counted the number of changes that would be needed to change the methods of one task to the methods of another task. This is much the same analysis as that performed by Kieras to determine the gains due to consistency. The important difference between gains due to consistency and consistency between alternating tasks was in handling the overlap. For alternating tasks, if two task methods were the same except for insertion or deletion of steps, then the tasks were inconsistent; if the two were the same except for replacement of specific words in the steps, then the two were consistent. When tested empirically, execution times with the tasks determined to be consistent were faster than the execution times with those tasks termed to be inconsistent. These differences were noticeable for many trials and were enhanced when the users returned to the tasks after an absence from working with them.

Design Revisions

Kieras (1988) has extended the design revision guidelines suggested by Card et al. (1983) for the GOMS model which were discussed in Chapter 14. They are:

1. Ensure that the most important and frequent goals can be accomplished by relatively easy to learn and fast-executing methods.

2. Try to reduce learning time by eliminating, rewriting, or combining methods, especially to get consistency.

3. If a selection rule cannot be stated clearly and easily, then consider eliminating one or more of the alternative methods.

4. Eliminate the need for operators that retrieve information from LTM which require that the user memorize information, and which therefore may be slow until heavily practiced.

5. If there are WM load problems, see if the design can be changed so the user needs to remember less.

6. Eliminate high-level bypassing operators if possible, especially if they involve a slow and difficult cognitive process.

7. The basic way to speed up execution time is to eliminate operators by shortening the methods. But notice that complex mental operators are usually much more time-consuming than simple motor actions, and so it can be more important to reduce the need for thinking than to save a few keystrokes. In other words, do not reduce the number of keystrokes if an increase in mental operators is the result.

An exercise in the back of the book requires that these design revisions can be performed on an interface design described by a GOMS model.

Mental Workload

Kieras (1988) indicates that mental workload can be considered in several ways and that techniques can be developed for using NGOMSL to quantify these different aspects of mental workload. The techniques for performing these analyses are not very clear and need further experimental work before they can be fully qualified. One aspect of mental workload, the working memory load, is the technique which is the easiest to apply and the technique most easily grounded in empirical validation. Recall from the Model Human Processor that the capacity of working memory was about five chunks with a maximum of nine chunks if long-term memory augmented it. The NGOMSL task analysis specifies when items are retained in working memory and when items are forgotten from working memory. Running through an example task will predict whether or not working memory is overloaded.

As an example of this kind of workload analysis, refer to Figures 15-13 and 15-14 which are copies of Figure 15-7 and 15-8 except these figures have the WM load shown on the right. In this example, we must make several assumptions in order to analyze the WM mental workload. First, the user must keep in WM any variable names. In the figure, the variable names are indicated by all uppercase characters. Second, the user must keep in WM the goal which is being performed and when this goal is accomplished. In the figures, as soon as a goal is to be accomplished, this is indicated in WM by "Executing <goal>". When a goal is complete, two things happen when the statement "Report goal accomplished" is encountered in the NGOMSL analysis: the statement "<goal> accomplished" is stored in WM and, at the same time, the "Executing <goal>" item is removed from WM. Finally, on the very next cycle after the "<goal> accomplished" statement first appears, it is automatically removed from the list.

Two measures can be taken from these two figures. The first would be the peak load on WM. This is found by determining the statements in which the highest number of items are stored in WM. For the high-breadth display, the peak load is 7 items occurring on cycles 52 and 53. For the high-depth display, the peak is 8 items and it occurs on statement 17.

Another measure of workload is the workload density, which is the average amount of items which have to be stored for each statement. This measure can be found by counting the total number of items in memory at each statement and then dividing through by the number of statements. When counting using Figures 15-13 and 15-14, remember that those statements with no memory items listed after them means that the memory did not change but a number still should be counted. As an example, statement 1 of both the high-breadth and high-depth displays has two WM items, but statement 2 has none listed. This means that the two items from statement 1 are retained. The total for statements 1 and 2 is 4 WM items. For the high-breadth display, the total number of items across all statements is 286. The high-breadth display has 62 statements so that the workload density is 4.61. The high-depth display has 185 items to be remembered across 36 steps. In this case, the workload density is 5.14. The high-depth display has a higher workload when measured in terms of peak load and density. This is to be expected because the high-breadth display is meant to be a "flat" display and the high-depth display is meant to have more layers and thus more things to remember. Whether or not these differences are significant would have to be determined experimentally.

Documentation

Kieras suggests that NGOMSL can be used for determining completeness and accuracy of the documentation by comparing the documentation to the procedures of NGOMSL. If the documentation is incomplete, then any omissions should

1. Retrieve-LTM that current item in command sequence is MENU-COMMAND

    1. Executing command sequence
    2. MENU-COMMAND

2. Accomplish goal of performing the command unit task
3. Recall MENU-COMMAND and accomplish goal of locating MENU-COMMAND

    1. Executing command sequence
    2. MENU-COMMAND
    3. Executing command unit task

4. ReadScreen next command line and retain as MENU-ITEM

    1. Executing command sequence
    2. MENU-COMMAND
    3. Executing command unit task
    4. Executing locate MENU-COMMAND
    5. MENU-ITEM

5. Decide: If MENU-COMMAND is different from MENU-ITEM
6. Then forget MENU-ITEM and Goto 1
(Statements 4 through 6 would be executed 12 more times)

    1. Executing command sequence
    2. MENU-COMMAND
    3. Executing command unit task
    4. Executing locate MENU-COMMAND

43. ReadScreen next command line and retain as MENU-ITEM

    1. Executing command sequence
    2. MENU-COMMAND
    3. Executing command unit task
    4. Executing locate MENU-COMMAND
    5. MENU-ITEM

44. Decide: If MENU-COMMAND is different from MENU-ITEM
45. Retain that N is number of MENU-ITEM

    1. Executing command sequence
    2. MENU-COMMAND
    3. Executing command unit task
    4. Executing locate MENU-COMMAND
    5. MENU-ITEM
    6. N

46. Forget MENU-ITEM and report goal accomplished

    1. Executing command sequence
    2. MENU-COMMAND
    3. Executing command unit task
    4. N
    5. Locate MENU-COMMAND accomplished

47. Recall N and accomplish goal of enter the menu item number

    1. Executing command sequence
    2. MENU-COMMAND
    3. Executing command unit task
    4. N

(Continued on next page)

Figure 15-13. Method for determining the workload of the high-breadth menu display.

48. If N is between 1 and 9

1. Executing command sequence
2. MENU-COMMAND
3. Executing command unit task
4. N
5. Executing enter menu item number

49. If N is 10 or above
50. Then accomplish goal of do string-method

1. Executing command sequence
2. MENU-COMMAND
3. Executing command unit task
4. N
5. Executing enter menu item number
6. Executing string-method

51. Type-in N
52. ReadScreen and retain feedback as N'

1. Executing command sequence
2. MENU-COMMAND
3. Executing command unit task
4. N
5. Executing enter menu item number
6. Executing string-method
7. N'

53. Report goal accomplished

1. Executing command sequence
2. MENU-COMMAND
3. Executing command unit task
4. N
5. Executing enter menu item number
6. N'
7. String-method accomplished

54. Report goal accomplished

1. Executing command sequence
2. MENU-COMMAND
3. Executing command unit task
4. N
5. N'
6. Enter menu item number accomplished

55. Recall N and N' and accomplish goal of verify the entry

1. Executing command sequence
2. MENU-COMMAND
3. Executing command unit task
4. N
5. N'

(Continued on next page)

Figure 15-13 (cont.)

56. Decide: If N and N' do not match	1. Executing command sequence 2. MENU-COMMAND 3. Executing command unit task 4. N 5. N' 6. Executing verify entry
57. Press-key ENTER 58. Forget N and N'	1. Executing command sequence 2. MENU-COMMAND 3. Executing command unit task 4. Executing verify entry
59. Report goal accomplished	1. Executing command sequence 2. MENU-COMMAND 3. Executing command unit task 4. Verify entry accomplished
60. Forget MENU-COMMAND and report goal accomplished	1. Executing command sequence 2. Command unit task accomplished
61. Decide: If more commands in command sequence 62. Report goal accomplished	1. Executing command sequence

Figure 15-13 (cont.)

stand out in the comparison. Elkerton (1988) also suggests that the index, table of contents, and headings for the documentation should be organized according to the natural goals of the computer system rather than the specific name provided by the particular system.

Expert/Novice Differences Analysis

An important test of a modeling technique is whether the model can be used to differentiate between novices and experts. It is clear that experts perform tasks differently from novices. Not only are experts faster than novices, they also apparently perform the task with less effort. The main mechanism for differentiating novices and experts with the NGOMSL analysis is

through the combination of operators in steps. As an example of this, one of the statements from the high-depth display is

Recall MENU-COMMAND and accomplish goal of locating MENU-CATEGORY

A novice would be likely to have two steps for this task, recalling the MENU-COMMAND and then accomplishing the goal. Experts are likely to combine several operators in one step. When analyzing a task using NGOMSL, there are no good rules to follow for what level of expertise to combine the statements and what level of expertise not to combine the statements. This is left to the discretion of the individual task analyst. More research is needed

1. Retrieve-LTM that current item in command sequence is MENU-COMMAND	1. Executing command sequence 2. MENU-COMMAND
2. Accomplish goal of performing the command unit task	
3. Accomplish goal of issuing MENU-CATEGORY	1. Executing command sequence 2. MENU-COMMAND 3. Executing command unit task
4. Recall MENU-COMMAND and accomplish goal of locating MENU-CATEGORY	1. Executing command sequence 2. MENU-COMMAND 3. Executing command unit task 4. Executing issue MENU-CATEGORY
5. Retrieve-LTM that the category of MENU-COMMAND is MENU-CATEGORY	1. Executing command sequence 2. MENU-COMMAND 3. Executing command unit task 4. Executing issue MENU-CATEGORY 5. Executing locate MENU-CATEGORY 6. MENU-CATEGORY
6. ReadScreen next command line and retain as MENU-ITEM	1. Executing command sequence 2. MENU-COMMAND 3. Executing command unit task 4. Executing issue MENU-CATEGORY 5. Executing locate MENU-CATEGORY 6. MENU-CATEGORY 7. MENU-ITEM
7. Decide: If MENU-ITEM is different from MENU-CATEGORY	
8. Then forget MENU-ITEM and Goto 2	1. Executing command sequence 2. MENU-COMMAND 3. Executing command unit task 4. Executing issue MENU-CATEGORY 5. Executing locate MENU-CATEGORY 6. MENU-CATEGORY

(Statements 6 through 8 would be executed 2 more times)

(Continued on next page)

Figure 15-14. Method for determining the workload of the high-depth menu display.

15. ReadScreen next command line and retain as MENU-ITEM	1. Executing command sequence 2. MENU-COMMAND 3. Executing command unit task 4. Executing issue MENU-CATEGORY 5. Executing locate MENU-CATEGORY 6. MENU-CATEGORY 7. MENU-ITEM
16. Decide: If MENU-ITEM is different from MENU-CATEGORY	
17. Retain that N is number of MENU-ITEM	1. Executing command sequence 2. MENU-COMMAND 3. Executing command unit task 4. Executing issue MENU-CATEGORY 5. Executing locate MENU-CATEGORY 6. MENU-CATEGORY 7. MENU-ITEM 8. N
18. Forget MENU-ITEM and report goal accomplished	1. Executing command sequence 2. MENU-COMMAND 3. Executing command unit task 4. Executing issue MENU-CATEGORY 5. MENU-CATEGORY 6. N 7. Locate MENU-CATEGORY finished
19. Recall N and Press-key N	
20. Forget N and MENU-CATEGORY	1. Executing command sequence 2. MENU-COMMAND 3. Executing command unit task 4. Executing issue MENU-CATEGORY
21. Report goal accomplished	1. Executing command sequence 2. MENU-COMMAND 3. Executing command unit task 4. Issue MENU-CATEGORY finished
22. Accomplish goal of issuing MENU-COMMAND	1. Executing command sequence 2. Executing command unit task 3. MENU-COMMAND

(Continued on next page)

Figure 15-14 (cont.)

23. Recall MENU-COMMAND and accomplish goal of locating MENU-COMMAND

    1. Executing command sequence
    2. MENU-COMMAND
    3. Executing command unit task
    4. Executing issue MENU-COMMAND

24. ReadScreen next command line and retain as MENU-ITEM

    1. Executing command sequence
    2. MENU-COMMAND
    3. Executing command unit task
    4. Executing issue MENU-COMMAND
    5. Executing locate MENU-COMMAND
    6. MENU-ITEM

25. Decide: If MENU-ITEM is different from MENU-COMMAND
26. Then forget MENU-ITEM and Goto 1

    1. Executing command sequence
    2. MENU-COMMAND
    3. Executing command unit task
    4. Executing issue MENU-COMMAND
    5. Executing locate MENU-COMMAND

27. ReadScreen next command line and retain as MENU-ITEM

    1. Executing command sequence
    2. MENU-COMMAND
    3. Executing command unit task
    4. Executing issue MENU-COMMAND
    5. Executing locate MENU-COMMAND
    6. MENU-ITEM

28. Decide: If MENU-ITEM is different from MENU-COMMAND
29. Retain that N is number of MENU-ITEM

    1. Executing command sequence
    2. MENU-COMMAND
    3. Executing command unit task
    4. Executing issue MENU-COMMAND
    5. Executing locate MENU-COMMAND
    6. MENU-ITEM
    7. N

30. Forget MENU-ITEM and report goal accomplished

    1. Executing command sequence
    2. MENU-COMMAND
    3. Executing command unit task
    4. Executing issue MENU-COMMAND

(Continued on next page)

Figure 15-14 (cont.)

| | 5. N |
| | 6. Locate MENU-COMMAND accomplished |

31. Recall N and Press-key N	1. Executing command sequence
	2. MENU-COMMAND
	3. Executing command unit task
	4. Executing issue MENU-COMMAND
	5. N

32. Forget N and MENU-COMMAND	1. Executing command sequence
	2. Executing command unit task
	3. Executing issue MENU-COMMAND

33. Report goal accomplished	1. Executing command sequence
	2. Executing command unit task
	3. Issue MENU-COMMAND accomplished

| 34. Report goal accomplished | 1. Executing command sequence |
| | 2. Command unit task accomplished |

| 35. Decide: If more commands in command sequence | 1. Executing command sequence |

| 36. Report goal accomplished | 1. Command sequence accomplished |

Figure 15-14 (cont.)

for determining learning characteristics of computer users. It is also likely that experts will have different goal structures from novices (Lang, Eberts, Gabel, and Barash, 1991), but changing the goal structure using NGOMSL is difficult and has not been specified.

COMPARING GOMS AND NGOMSL

The GOMS models and the NGOMSL models are very similar because they both originated from the same source. They were devised to capture the cognitive processing of the user based upon the belief that users will break a problem into goals and subgoals and then determine the

methods and operators for accomplishing these goals and subgoals. As an example of the similarities between the two, a goal stack can be determined from the sequence of statements for the high-breadth and high-depth displays from Figures 15-7 and 15-8. To form the goal stack, whenever a goal is signified by the statement "Accomplish the goal of <goal description>" a goal is pushed on the stack. When the goal is accomplished, signified by the statement "Report goal accomplished," the goal on the top of the stack is removed from the stack. When an operator is used for accomplishing the goal, these are indicated in the appropriate column. These goal stack analyses for the high-breadth and high-depth displays are shown in Figures 15-15 and 15-16.

We will first analyze the goal stack for the high-breadth display (Figure 15-15). A difference between this goal stack and the GOMS goal stack is that the GOMS model requires that a unit task be acquired first and then executed. In the goal stack developed from the NGOMSL analysis, the steps for the acquisition of the unit task are clearly stated through the "Locate MENU-COMMAND" goal. Execution of the unit task corresponds to entering the number and verifying this number. Comparing the goal stack model to the NGOMSL analysis, many similarities exist. The number of cycles shown to accomplish the task is about the same in both analyses. However, the goal stack does not always have as much detail as the statements from the NGOMSL analysis. In particular, the WM details, such as when to recall and forget memory items, are not very specific, so that many of these cycles are not present in the goal stack. One other change is in the decision statements. NGOMSL counts each IF and THEN part of a statement as a separate cycle. The goal stack analysis does not necessarily do this. Therefore, NGOMSL, being more specific than a goal stack analysis usually is, will have more cycles than the corresponding goal stack model. The goal stack model of Figure 15-15 has 57 cycles, while the NGOMSL analysis for the same task has 62 cycles. This does not necessarily mean that the time estimations for the two models will be different, because the GOMS model places no particular time estimate on a cycle in the goal stack. Time estimations are only made through the Keystrokes-Level model or through the Model-UT.

Figure 15-16 shows the goal stack model developed from the NGOMSL analysis of the high-depth display. Once again, the NGOMSL analysis has more cycles (36) than does the goal stack (32 cycles). This can again be attributed to less detail on the VM specifications and the addition of IF and THEN cycles for the NGOMSL analysis.

SUMMARY

NGOMSL is clearly an extension of the GOMS models of Card et al. (1983), and many of the same analyses can be performed using either analysis. Both GOMS and NGOMSL are based upon goals, operators, methods, and selection rules. These are defined in the same way using both models. Both models have mechanisms for making time estimates for tasks which may only be in the prototype stage.

NGOMSL goes beyond the GOMS analysis by combining several of the GOMS models into one integrated model. In particular, the above analysis has shown how the NGOMSL analysis provides a very similar representation to that of the goal stack part of the GOMS analysis. But NGOMSL goes beyond the goal stack model in several ways. First, NGOMSL places a significance on the cycles needed to complete a task, using these cycles as a part of the time estimation equation. NGOMSL integrates the Keystrokes-Level model and the goal stack model of GOMS by specifying clearly the primitive operators which are the same as the Keystrokes-Level operators. An important difference, however, is that NGOMSL has clear mechanisms, through the time estimate of the cycles, to determine exact estimates for the M operator. In GOMS, M is

1. Execute CS		
2. Execute CS, Perform C-U-T		
3. Execute CS, Perform C-U-T, Locate MENU-COMMAND		
4. Execute CS, Perform C-U-T, Locate MENU-COMMAND	ReadScreen	MENU-ITEM
5. Execute CS, Perform C-U-T, Locate MENU-COMMAND	Decide	No Match
6. Execute CS, Perform C-U-T, Locate MENU-COMMAND	Goto 4	
7-42 (Repeat statements 4-6 12 more times).		
43. Execute CS, Perform C-U-T, Locate MENU-COMMAND	ReadScreen	MENU-ITEM
44. Execute CS, Perform C-U-T, Locate MENU-COMMAND	Decide	Match
45. Execute CS, Perform C-U-T, Locate MENU-COMMAND	Retain N	N
46. Execute CS, Perform C-U-T		
47. Execute CS, Perform C-U-T, Enter N		
48. Execute CS, Perform C-U-T, Enter N	Use string-method	
49. Execute CS, Perform C-U-T, Enter N	Type-in	N string
50. Execute CS, Perform C-U-T, Enter N	ReadScreen	N'
51. Execute CS, Perform C-U-T		
52. Execute CS, Perform C-U-T, Verify Entry		
53. Execute CS, Perform C-U-T, Verify Entry	Decide	Match
54. Execute CS, Perform C-U-T, Verify Entry	Press-key	ENTER
55. Execute CS, Perform C-U-T		
56. Execute CS, Perform C-U-T	Decide	More command?
57. Execute CS	Decide	More tasks?

Figure 15-15. Goal stack from NGOMSL for the high-breadth menu display.

1. Execute CS	
2. Execute CS, Perform C-U-T	
3. Execute CS, Perform C-U-T, Issue MENU-CATEGORY	
4. Execute CS, Perform C-U-T, Issue MENU-CATEGORY, Locate MENU-CATEGORY	
5. Execute CS, Perform C-U-T, Issue MENU-CATEGORY, Locate MENU-CATEGORY	Retain-LTM
6. Execute CS, Perform C-U-T, Issue MENU-CATEGORY, Locate MENU-CATEGORY	ReadScreen
7. Execute CS, Perform C-U-T, Issue MENU-CATEGORY, Locate MENU-CATEGORY	Decide
8. Execute CS, Perform C-U-T, Issue MENU-CATEGORY, Locate MENU-CATEGORY	Goto 7
9-14 (Execute statements 6-8 two more times).	
15. Execute CS, Perform C-U-T, Issue MENU-CATEGORY, Locate MENU-CATEGORY	ReadScreen
16. Execute CS, Perform C-U-T, Issue MENU-CATEGORY, Locate MENU-CATEGORY	Decide
17. Execute CS, Perform C-U-T, Issue MENU-CATEGORY, Locate MENU-CATEGORY	Retain N
18. Execute CS, Perform C-U-T, Issue MENU-CATEGORY	
19. Execute CS, Perform C-U-T, Issue MENU-CATEGORY	Press-key N
20. Execute CS, Perform C-U-T	
21. Execute CS, Perform C-U-T, Issue MENU-COMMAND	
22. Execute CS, Perform C-U-T, Issue MENU-COMMAND, Locate MENU-COMMAND	
23. Execute CS, Perform C-U-T, Issue MENU-COMMAND, Locate MENU-COMMAND	ReadScreen
24. Execute CS, Perform C-U-T, Issue MENU-COMMAND, Locate MENU-COMMAND	Decide
25. Execute CS, Perform C-U-T, Issue MENU-COMMAND, Locate MENU-COMMAND	ReadScreen
26. Execute CS, Perform C-U-T, Issue MENU-COMMAND, Locate MENU-COMMAND	Decide
27. Execute CS, Perform C-U-T, Issue MENU-COMMAND, Locate MENU-COMMAND	Retain N
28. Execute CS, Perform C-U-T, Issue MENU-COMMAND	
29. Execute CS, Perform C-U-T, Issue MENU-COMMAND	Press-key N
30. Execute CS, Perform C-U-T	
31. Execute CS, Perform C-U-T	Decide
32. Execute CS	Decide

Figure 15-16. Goal stack from NGOMSL for the high-depth menu display.

estimated to be 1.35. In NGOMSL, M would be equivalent to the number of cycles needed to accomplish the operation. This is most apparent in the number of cycles needed to find the MENU-COMMAND. In GOMS, this time would always be 1.35 sec.; in NGOMSL, this time is dependent on the number of MENU-ITEMs to be searched.

NGOMSL also incorporates the Model Human Processor of Card et al. (1983) through the use of the analyst-defined operators and the specification of the cognitive cycle time to be equal to the statement cycle time. For the analyst-defined operators, estimators in some cases can be found by using cycle times from the Model Human Processor. In the examples provided in this chapter, the perceptual processor cycle time was used for determining the time to read the screen. An alternative method for estimating times is through experimentation. The Model-UT of GOMS is not clearly incorporated in NGOMSL except for this idea of using experimentation to find time estimates for some of the units of the model.

The experimentation associated with the NGOMSL analysis allows many different kinds of estimations not easily possible with the GOMS models. In particular, using NGOMSL one can determine estimates for learning time and gains due to consistency. These are not possible using the GOMS models. Another difference between the two is that GOMS is only applicable to experts, while NGOMSL has some techniques, although they are rather crude at this time, to specify different models for experts and novices.

A problem with these models is that different task analyzers may develop different tasks analyses for the same task.

The procedures cannot be specified completely so that they are invariant across task analyzers. It should be remembered that a task may require several revisions before the analysis is satisfactory. One should not use these models if one expects to find a single model agreed upon by all the task analyzers.

QUESTIONS

1. Modify the NGOMSL analysis of the high-breadth display to include the case where the user only deletes the digits on the screen that are wrong. In other words, if the user enter "15" and wanted to enter "14," currently the model would specify that the user would delete the 5 and the 1, and then enter 1 and 4. A more likely method would be for the user to only delete the 5 and then enter the 4. Perform the modification to show this.

2. Consider the workload problem for the NGOMSL model.

    a. Calculate the peak workload for the high-breadth display if the command sequence had two commands in it.

    b. Calculate the workload density for the high-breadth display if the command sequence had two commands in it.

    c. What is the highest number of commands that could occur in the command sequence without exceeding the five-chunk load of working memory? Determine this for the high-breadth and high-depth displays. What would the user be likely to do if the number of commands in the command sequence caused him or her to exceed the limit? How would the methods be modified to reduce this load?

3. Let's say that an interface contains both high-breadth and high-depth displays. What would be the estimated learning time to learn both at the same time? Would there be any gains from consistency to learn both at the same time? Factoring in any gains from consistency, what would now be the estimated learning time?

4. Rewrite the methods for the high-breadth display so that the user would verify the entry even after the a corrected entry was entered.

5. Task A, using one interface design, requires 40 steps, and Task B, using the same interface, requires 60 steps. Because it is the same interface used for both tasks, the method structure is the same.

    a. What can you say about the differences between the execution times for the two tasks?

    b. What about the differences between the learning times for the tasks?

6. On the Apple Macintosh, one of the functions that can be performed is transferring files from a 3.5" disk to the internal hard disk. For this question, let's say that the user must move two files from a 3.5" disk to the hard disk. To perform this task, the user must pull down one of the menus under the "File" label. A menu is pulled down by moving the mouse to the word "File" at the top left of the screen and pushing down the mouse button. On the screen, the menu appears below the word "File." While keeping the mouse button down, the mouse cursor is moved to the words "New Folder." This is selected by releasing the mouse button. At this point, a folder icon appears in the window and this icon has a label under it that says "New Folder." The user must move the mouse cursor to the "N" of "New Folder" and press the mouse button. While keeping the mouse button down, the mouse cursor is moved to the last letter and released. The name of the new folder, in this case "Transfer," is entered from the keyboard. Pressing ENTER at the end of the name causes the new folder name to be recorded by the system. This name appears underneath the folder icon.

Next, the files from the 3.5" disk must be moved from the disk window to the hard disk window. The user must move the mouse out of the hard disk window and into the 3.5" disk window on the screen. Once the cursor is in this window, the mouse button is pressed and released and the 3.5" disk window is highlighted. The icons of the two files that need to be transferred should now show in the window. The user must move the mouse to one of the file icons and press the mouse button. Without releasing the mouse button, the user moves the mouse cursor to the hard disk window. As the mouse is moved, the file icon moves along with it.

Once the mouse cursor and file are in the hard disk window, the mouse button can be released. A window pops up on the screen indicating that the file transfer is occurring. This file transfer usually takes about 2.5 seconds. The user would then have to go back to the 3.5" disk window to drag another file to the hard disk window. Once this is finished, the task is completed.

Following are the NGOMSL methods for performing this task. You will have to use this analysis to answer questions on the following pages.

A. Method to accomplish goal of transferring files
1. Accomplish goal of opening new file
2. Accomplish goal of moving file
3. Decide: If any more files to transfer then goto 2
4. Forget hard disk window and report goal accomplished

B. Method to accomplish goal of opening new file
1. Accomplish goal of choosing new folder
2. Accomplish goal of naming new folder
3. Report goal accomplished

C. Method to accomplish goal of choosing new folder
1. Move-mouse-cursor to "File"
2. Press-key mouse button
3. Move-mouse-cursor to "New Folder"
4. Release-key mouse button
5. Report goal accomplished

D. Method to accomplish goal of naming new folder
1. Move-mouse-cursor to first part of "New Folder" name below folder icon
2. Press-key mouse button

3. Move-mouse-cursor to last letter of "New Folder" name
4. Release-key mouse button
5. Type-in name of folder and retain folder name (name is "Transfer")
6. Accomplish goal of opening folder
7. Report goal accomplished

E. Method to accomplish goal of moving file
1. Decide: If window bar not highlighted, then accomplish goal of selecting window
2. Accomplish goal of finding file
3. Accomplish goal of dragging file
4. Report goal accomplished

F. Method to accomplish goal of selecting window
1. Recall the location of new window
2. Move-mouse-cursor to new window
3. Press-key mouse button
4. Report goal accomplished

G. Method to accomplish goal of finding file
1. Recall the transfer file
2. Move-mouse-cursor to transfer file icon
3. Press-key mouse button
4. Forget transfer file and report goal accomplished

H. Method to accomplish goal of dragging file
1. Move-mouse cursor to old window
2. Release-key mouse button
3. Verify result (wait for 2.5 seconds for the system to respond)
4. Report goal accomplished

I. Method to accomplish goal of opening folder
1. Move-mouse-cursor to new folder window
2. Press-key mouse button
3. Press-key mouse button
4. Report goal accomplished

a. Write down the steps, by the method and step number (e.g., A1, A2, A3), for transferring two files to the new "Transfer" folder.

b. Determine the execution time for this task.

c. Determine the learning time.

d. Calculate the average workload per step.

e. Are there any good method pairs where a gain from consistency could be achieved? Explain.

f. Using the operators from the Keystrokes-Level model of GOMS, write down the sequence of operators that would be used in the task. Then estimate the execution time for this model.

g. Explain the similarities and differences between the Keystrokes-Level model and the NGOMSL model.

7. Chapter 12 discussed workload assessment techniques. None of these techniques was considered in the NGOMSL model for determining the workload of the task; workload was assessed only in terms of the memory load. Explain how the multiple resource theory could be implemented in the NGOMSL model. What new information would have to be collected in the NGOMSL model in order to determine the workload of a task?

8. Some televisions have the capability to block channels so they cannot be viewed during a certain time period.

If somebody attempts to view the channel, the sound will be muted and the channel will be blocked from view. Normal reception will be resumed after 12 hours. Following is an NGOMSL representation for blocking a channel and then clearing the block before the 12-hour time period is finished.

A. Method to accomplish goal of blocking channel
1. Retrieve-LTM that FUNCTION is BLOCK
2. Accomplish goal of set function
3. Accomplish goal of enter time
4. Accomplish goal of enter channel
5. Report goal accomplished

B. Method to accomplish goal of set function
1. Recall FUNCTION
2. Press-key TIMER/BLOCK
3. ReadScreen and retain as CURRENT-FUNCTION
4. Decide: If FUNCTION not equal to CURRENT-FUNCTION, then forget CURRENT-FUNCTION and Goto 2
5. Forget FUNCTION and report goal accomplished

C. Method to accomplish goal of enter time
1. Retrieve-LTM that time of program to block is TIME
2. Type-in TIME
3. Press-key ENTER
4. Forget TIME and report goal accomplished

D. Method to accomplish goal of enter channel
1. Retrieve-LTM that channel of program to block is CHANNEL
2. Type in CHANNEL
3. Press-key ENTER
4. Forget CHANNEL and report goal accomplished

E. **Method to accomplish goal of clear-ing channel**
   1. Retrieve-LTM that FUNCTION is BLOCK
   2. Accomplish goal of set function
   3. Press-key CLEAR
   4. Report goal accomplished

Keep the following observations in mind when doing the following analyses.

• When setting the function, the first time the TIMER/BLOCK key is pressed it changes to the "clock page." The second time the TIMER/BLOCK key is pressed it changes to the "timer page." The third time the TIMER/BLOCK key is pressed it changes to the "block page," which is the one that is needed to accomplish this task.

• When entering a time, four digits need to be entered for the numerical designation of the time. Also, the timer always starts out on AM. If a PM time is needed, then the AM/PM button needs to be pressed. Assume that half the time you will need to push this button and half the time you will not need to.

• When entering the channel, one or two digits need to be entered, depend-ing on whether the channel is less than or greater than 10. Assume that 30% of the time you would need to enter a channel less than 10.

• Assume that a ReadScreen operator is analyst-defined and requires 100 msec. Assume that the person is an expert typist so that each key press requires 20 msec.

a. List the steps needed to perform the block channel task (not the clear channel). When listing the steps, you do not have to write out the whole step, only the character designation. As an example, the second step in Method B, Press-key TIMER/BLOCK, could be written as B2.

b. List the steps needed to clear a block.

c. Determine the execution time for blocking a channel. Show your work.

d. Determine the execution time for clearing a channel. Show your work.

e. Calculate the learning time for blocking a channel.

g. What would be the gain from consistency, and where would it occur? Show your work.

f. Calculate the workload density for blocking a channel. Show your work.

CHAPTER 16

PRODUCTION SYSTEMS

INTRODUCTION

Production systems have been used to describe how people process and store information. The concept of a production system was developed mostly in the late 1960s and early 1970s, culminating in a book called *Human Problem Solving* by Newell and Simon (1972). This conceptualization has been very influential in many areas: cognitive psychology, cognitive science, computer science, and artificial intelligence. As indicated by the book's name, the purpose of production systems was to determine how people solve problems and to specify these steps in a system resembling, but slightly different from, the computer programming languages of the time which were used to specify the steps for machine problem solving. If the steps could be specific enough, then only a short jump is needed to specify the steps for a machine to solve problems much like a human does. This was an impetus for much of the work in artificial intelligence and the application area of expert systems, although many of the hopes for programming intelligence into machines, similar to human intelligence, have never been achieved totally. Some expert systems, however, have been successful at using a production system to solve problems similar to how a human would (e.g., Garg-Janardan et al., 1987). Two of the most successful expert systems have been developed for computer equipment layout (R1) and for helping to find mineral deposits (PROSPECTOR). Several computer languages, such as LISP, have been

developed to simplify the programming tasks of production systems. Production systems have also been used to model how humans process and store information (Anderson, 1976). Recently, production systems have been used to model how humans interact with a computer system. This chapter describes these kinds of models.

Describing how a production system works is difficult for someone who does not know rule-based programming languages such as LISP. Even knowing popular programming languages such as FORTRAN or C does not help in understanding LISP because of the fundamental differences between them. Before discussing the programming language used for production system modeling in this chapter, an example will be provided for understanding how production systems work. Then, the predictive model for human-computer interaction tasks will be presented. Examples of applications of this model to estimate parameters of human-computer interaction tasks will be presented in the last section.

A METAPHOR FOR A PRODUCTION SYSTEM

One of the best ways to understand how a production system works is to understand it graphically (using the spatial abilities outlined in Chapter 11). The following example was developed by Jack Posey at Purdue University to illustrate how a production system works.

Docks, Ships, and Cargo

Consider the ten objects in Figure 16-1. On the left of each object are two items which have patterns to them. They look sort of like puzzle pieces with the top part of the puzzle piece missing. These will be called docks, similar to where two ships would dock at a harbor. To the right of each object is a rectangular shape which has a pattern to it and is pointing to the right. In this case, both pieces of the puzzle are present, and fit together, and you can see the boundaries of the two pieces by the jagged lines. Using the docking metaphor, the ship has docked by fitting into the correct location.

Some ground rules must be laid before any of the docking and loading can start. "Ships" can dock at the two locations on the left, but only certain kinds of ships can dock. The ships must fit into the dock, similar to two puzzle pieces fitting together, and the pattern of the ship, the fill inside the form which can be called the "cargo", must match the pattern of the dock. When two ships are docked to the left, then the ship to the right can be released from its dock. That ship is now free to float around until it finds a docking berth on the left which matches its contours and fill pattern. We also assume that there is an unlimited supply of ships of each kind. In other words, if several docks all of the same kind are open then all these docks can be filled, even though only one ship of this kind is represented on the paper.

Following these three simple ground rules, the production system can be used to solve a problem. The problem to be solved is to release a ship from the right dock of one of the objects so that the ship has a certain specified contour. When the ship is released, its cargo can be determined by noticing the fill pattern. The goal of the example is to determine the kind of cargo which will be on the ship of a particular contour when it can be released from the dock.

Now look at Figure 16-2. We want to determine the cargo of the ship which has the contour specified. At any particular time, there are free-floating ships that have not yet been docked. These are represented in Figure 16-3. If two of these ships dock, then a ship will be released from the right side of the dock and now that ship is free to dock someplace else. The problem is solved when the ship shaped like that in Figure 16-2 has been released from the right dock with the particular cargo.

Let's start the process. Figure 16-4 shows how all the ships which were free-floating in Figure 16-3 have been docked at all the available locations of Figure 16-1. Six ships can be docked, but only one more ship can be released; the ship from the dock on the upper left corner is now free-floating with the others (see Figure 16-5). At this point, the whole process has completed one cycle in which the docks were recognized so that the ships could dock, and the ship in the upper left was released.

The ship that was just released can dock at two places: the dock second from the top and third from the top (see Figure 16-6). Since the other space at the second from the right top dock was already occupied, the docking of this new ship causes the ship on the right to be released (see Figure 16-7). This ship matches the contour of the ship in which we were supposed to determine the cargo. We can see

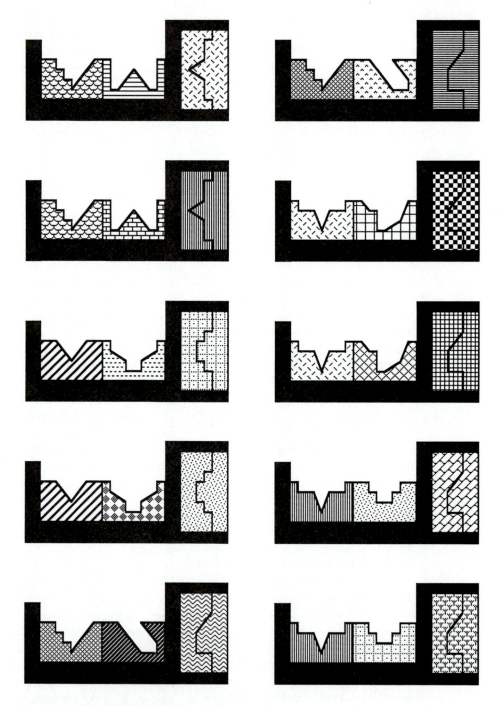

Figure 16-1. Visualization of a production system.

Figure 16-2. The cargo of the ship must be found for the ship of the specified contour.

Initial
Problem
State:

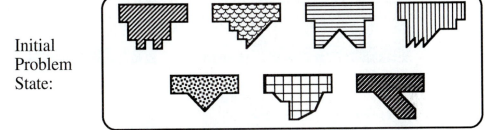

Figure 16-3. The free-floating ships which have not yet docked.

that the problem is now solved and the cargo is represented by the checkerboard pattern. This solution took two cycles.

Three other examples are provided for you to try on your own at the end of this chapter. Some of the examples are more difficult than the others. The simplest kind of problem is if the ships are free-floating to start with, so that you would just have to see where the ships can dock and then determine if the released ships have the same shape. The problem can be solved in one cycle. More difficult problems occur when initially free-floating ships dock to release another ship and then that released ship is needed to release the target ship. The more intermediate steps before the target ship is released, or the more cycles required, the more difficult the problem, and the more time needed to perform this task.

Mapping the Metaphor to Production Systems

The above example illustrates how a production system works, but, of course, a production system does not use docks and ships. Instead, a production system is composed of production rules. The production rules correspond to the objects in Figure 16-1. Each rule has an If part, called the condition, and a Then part, called the action. For the rules illustrated through the example, the two docks on the left side represent the condition and the dock on the right side represents the action. A rule is "fired" when the conditions are satisfied. From the example, this occurs when the two left docks are filled and a ship is released from the right. The result of the action of the rule, the ship that is free-floating, can now be used to fire any of the other rules.

A production rule can have many forms and shapes. In Figure 16-1, only one kind of production rule is shown. In those production rules, both left docks must be filled before the single ship of the right dock is fired. This would have the following form:

IF (left-1) AND (left-2) THEN (right)

The AND is a logical relationship which states that both conditions must be satis-

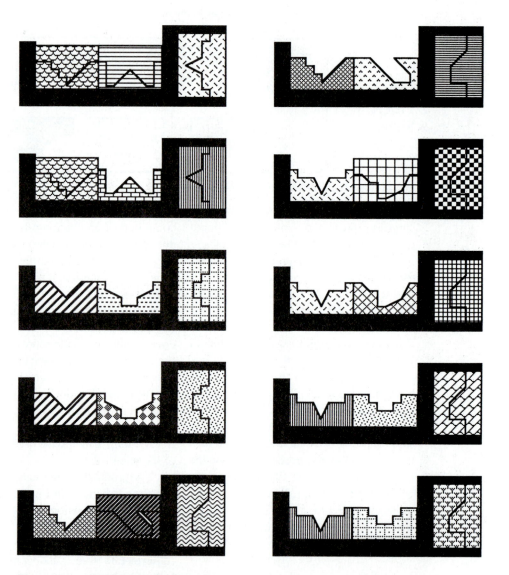

Figure 16-4. All of the free-floating ships have been docked at the available locations.

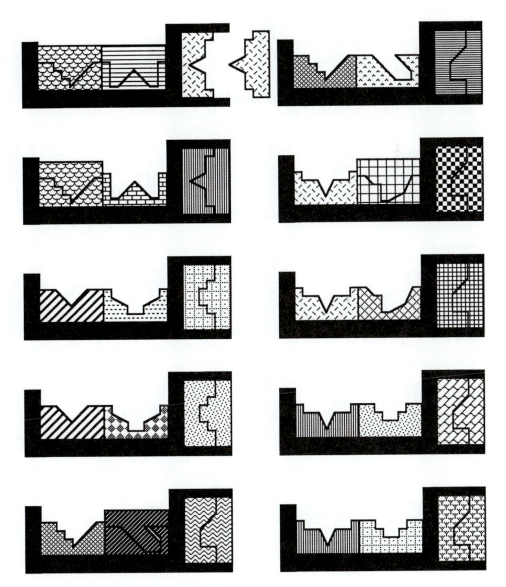

Figure 16-5. One ship is released from the docks.

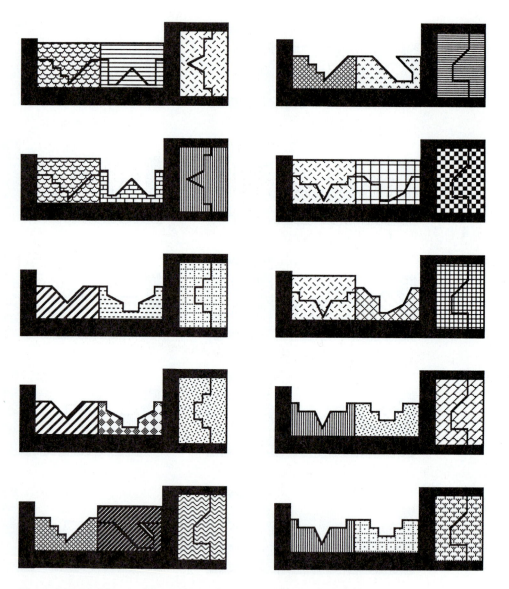

Figure 16-6. On the second cycle, the just-released ship can dock at two places.

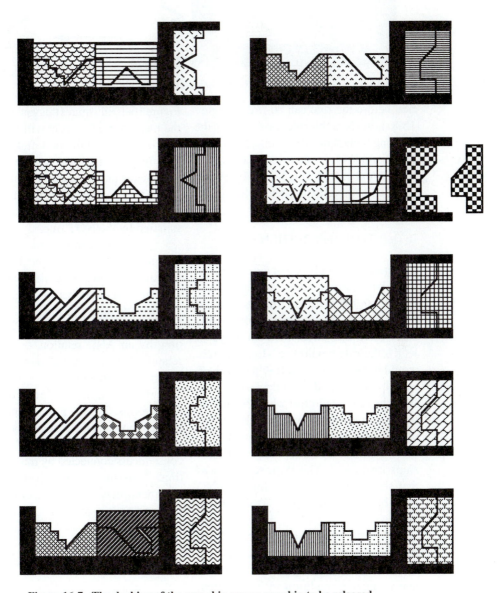

Figure 16-7. The docking of the new ship causes one ship to be released.

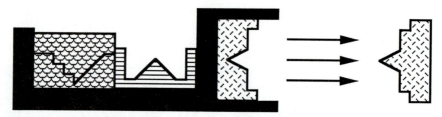

Figure 16-8. An example of an AND rule being satisfied and fired.

fied before the rule can be fired. Figure 16-8 shows how this rule appears using the docking metaphor. Both conditions must be satisfied before the rule can fire.

Another logical relation often used, but not illustrated in the previous example, is the OR relationship:

IF (left-1) OR (left-2) THEN (right)

This means that only one of the conditions must be satisfied before the rule fires. Figure 16-9 shows how this rule would look using the docking metaphor. In this case, there are three different ways in which the rule would fire. In a, the rule would fire when the far left ship is docked; no ship in the middle left dock is needed. In b, the rule would fire when the middle left ship is docked; no ship in the far left dock is needed. In c, the rule would also fire when both the far left and middle left ships are docked. This is the same case as that shown in Figure 16-8 for the AND rule; the two are equivalent in this particular situation.

Finally, a rule can also have a NOT statement in it. Using the metaphor, the NOT means that no ship can be docked for that particular condition to be satisfied. This could have the following form:

IF (left-1) AND (NOT (left-2)) THEN (right)

Figure 16-10 illustrates this statement using the metaphor. This rule will fire when a ship is docked on the far left dock and no ship is docked on the middle left. Although this picture is equivalent to Figure 16-9a, the OR rule is not the same because Figures 16-9b and 16-9c would not be satisfied by the NOT rule.

The rules can become much more complicated than those pictured above. Instead of just the two conditions, there is no limit to the number of conditions. In addition, the left-1 or the left-2 positions may be occupied by another if-then relation, by an AND relation, or by an OR relation. In this case, the rules can become iteratively more complex.

The action of the rule could also take many forms. For the production rules for human-computer interaction modeling, the action often takes the form of a string of consequents connected by the AND relation. This means that several different statements may be released, or fired, once the condition is satisfied.

PRODUCTION SYSTEM MODELING FOR HCI TASKS

Kieras and Polson (1985) developed a production system model for human-computer interaction tasks. This was based upon the GOMS model of Card et al. (1983) and was a precursor to Kieras'

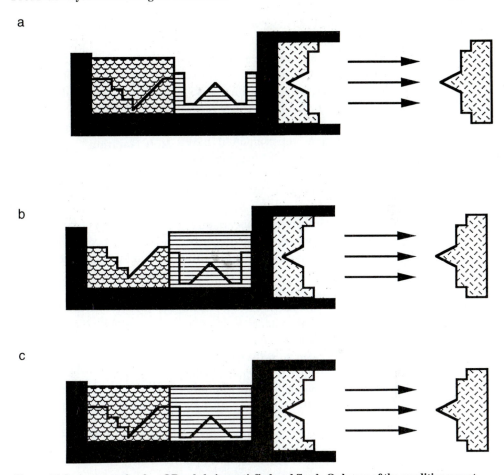

Figure 16-9. An example of an OR rule being satisfied and fired. Only one of the conditions must be satisfied for it to fire. In (a), the far left condition is satisfied, which triggers the firing; in (b), the middle left condition is satisfied, which triggers the firing; and in (c), both conditions are satisfied and it fires. The situation in c is the same as that of Figure 16-8.

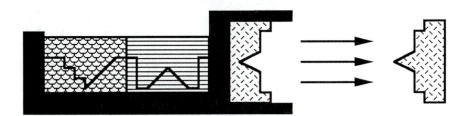

Figure 16-10. An example of a rule firing with a NOT condition. In this case, the rule will fire if the far left condition is satisfied by having a ship docked and if the middle left condition has no ship in it. This is different from the OR of Figure 16-9 in that the OR rule would have fired if a ship had been docked on the middle left.

NGOMSL model. In most ways, the representations between these models are equivalent, especially between production systems and the NGOMSL. With all these modeling choices, the model which is used is a matter of personal preference. Many of the original conceptualizations of the production system representation have been changed from the 1985 paper in order to make the model easier to apply and more invariant from one task analyst to another. The most complete description of how to model human-computer interaction tasks using production systems can be found in Bovair, Kieras, and Polson (1990).

Basic Production Systems

A production system contains declarative knowledge (the facts) and procedural knowledge (how to process the facts). The declarative knowledge is contained in the production rules which, as indicated previously, have the form of

IF <condition> THEN <action>

The procedural knowledge is how the interpreter, that part of the computer program which interprets the programming statements, sequences through the rules. The sequencing occurs through a recognize/act cycle similar to that shown for the ships and docking. In the recognize stage, all of the conditions of the rules are matched against the contents of working memory (WM). To use the metaphor of the ships docking, the matching of conditions occurs through the docking of the ships, and the contents of WM are analogous to the set of free-floating ships of Figures 16-3 and 16-5. The act stage occurs when all the rules that match all the conditions are fired and the interpreter executes the ac-

tions. Analogously, this occurred in the ship example when the ships were released in Figures 16-5 and 16-7. When this is completed, one cycle of the process has been completed.

The Parsimonious Production System Rule Notation

Bovair et al. (1990) found that it was most convenient to represent the production system in terms of the PPS (Parsimonious Production System) Rule Notation which was developed earlier by Kieras. This notation was designed with the following constraints.

1. On any cycle, any rule whose conditions are currently satisfied will fire.

2. Rules must be written so that a single rule will not fire repeatedly.

3. Only one rule will fire on a cycle.

4. All procedural knowledge is explicit in the rules rather than being explicit in the interpreter.

The basic structure of a rule using this notation is

<name> IF <condition> THEN <action>

The name is not functional and is used to assist the programmer in reading the code. The condition is a list of clauses that must all be matched for the rule to be true. The notation for clauses will be described in the following section. The actions are sequences of operators similar to that for the NGOMSL model. These operators can be used to modify working memory, usually so that other rules can fire on the next cycle.

Clauses

The notation conventions for clauses are as follows. Condition clauses have the following form:

(Tag Term$_1$ Term$_2$ ... Term$_k$)

The tag can be one of the following:

> Goal - this corresponds directly to the goals from GOMS or NGOMSL.
>
> Note - this is information kept in working memory over several firings.
>
> Step - this is a control execution sequence within a method.
>
> Device - this is information provided directly from the device.
>
> LTM - this is sometimes used to indicate information stored in LTM.

The terms are used to specify the tags. Each tag has a predefined number of terms associated with it. In the examples used in this chapter, the terms have the following number tags associated with them. As in NGOMSL, each Goal tag has two terms associated with it: the verb or action of the goal and the object of the verb or action.

The Note term has several functions. One function of the Note is to specify the ordering of goals and actions. In some situations, the action of a rule may be to set

a goal and to specify the next step. Since both of these are set, the rule condition containing the goal and the rule condition containing the step will both fire unless a Note is used to limit the firing to only one. This is usually done by including, in the condition with the step, a Note that the goal has been performed so that the rule with the step will only fire after completion of the goal. In the example of the menu displays, the Note is also used to indicate variable values such as for the menu-item number. In this case, the first term of the Note will always be Variable. Finally, the Note is used to set the context of some of the rules and could contain various kinds of information.

The Step term has a structure very similar to the Goal term in that it contains two tags: a verb and an action. It is usually used in conjunction with a Goal to specify how the user is stepping through the different methods steps in the goal.

The Device term is not clearly specified by Bovair et al. (1990) and could probably be left somewhat to the discretion of the task analyzer. In the examples that follow, Device has three tags: the object of the information displayed (usually the User), the location of the relevant information on the screen, and the action required of the information. In some situations, the action is to remember what was displayed on the screen, in which case the user is to add a Note to store in working memory. In one situation, the action is merely to indicate if there are any characters in the location specified.

The LTM term is also not clearly specified by Bovair et al. (1990) and is also left to the discretion of the task analyzer. In the following menu examples, LTM is used to access the command se-

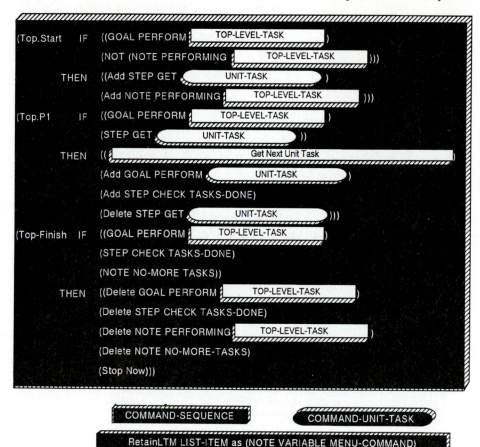

Figure 16-11. A template for the top-level rules in a production system analysis. The pieces at the bottom can be inserted only into certain slots in the template. When all the slots have been filled the rules will be the same as those shown in the beginning parts of Figures 16-14 and 16-16.

quence from LTM or to determine the menu category for the command. It has only one tag which refers to a general description of the information being accessed.

Production System Templates

To keep the task analysis as invariant from one task analyst to another, Bovair et al. (1990) designed a template so that terms for a particular task could simply be put in the template. Such a template is needed

also because of the complex control structure of a production system. Three templates are needed for constructing a productions system: the top-level rules, method rules, and selection rules.

Figure 16-11 contains a representation of a template for the top-level rules. To use the template, the open slots must be filled with information specific to the particular task. In the template, there are three different kinds of slots which must be filled. The short rectangular slot should be filled with the TOP-LEVEL-TASK or, in other words, the highest level goal. For the menu examples of Figures 16-14 and 16-16, the highest goal is to perform the command sequence which is a series of commands for interacting with menu displays. The rectangular piece labeled COMMAND-SEQUENCE can be inserted into the appropriate slots in the template.

The oblong slot must be filled with the first unit task (labeled UNIT-TASK in the template). In the menu display analyses, this has been called COMMAND-UNIT-TASK. The oblong piece at the bottom of the display can be inserted into the oblong slots of the template.

Finally, the one remaining slot is the long rectangular one labeled Get Next Unit Task. The task analyst has much latitude when filling this slot. For the beginning of the menu displays, the menu-command has been retained in long-term memory to be used in the menu item search. The RetainLTM piece at the bottom of the display can be inserted in the long rectangular slot to complete the set of rules. When the three kinds of slots are filled with the appropriate pieces at the bottom of the figure, the set of rules will be the same as those at the beginning of Figures 16-14 and 16-16.

Figure 16-12 contains a representation of a template for a method. The template can be used in two ways. If the method is part of a selection rule, as considered by GOMS and NGOMSL, then the selection rule template in Figure 16-13 must also be used. If not part of a selection rule, then the template of 16-12 can be used alone. The method template works the same way as did the top-level rules template. Only certain pieces fit into the slots of the template, and these pieces must be inserted in all the slots having the

same label and the same size. When the pieces at the bottom of the figure are inserted in the slots, the rules beginning with StartVerifyMethod in Figure 16-14 will have been constructed.

The method illustrated in the template includes several steps similar to the steps in NGOMSL. To specify the steps, MethodRule1 is repeated for the number of steps in the method. The condition part of these steps indicates the overall Goal on the goal stack and the name of the current Step. The action part of the rule indicates the next Step (the Add STEP part) and deletes the current Step so that this rule does not fire again. The real action occurs in the first part: (<DoAct FirstAct>). The action could be one of several kinds. First, it could be another Goal. If it is a Goal, then the condition of the next rule of this method has to have a context Note indicating that the Step cannot fire until this previous Goal has been performed. The action could also be a primitive operator such as a key press or a button action. These operators could be similar to those specified in the Keystrokes-Level model. Once all of the Steps have been completed, the FinishMethod rule is ready to fire.

The final production system template, for a selection rule, is shown in Figure 16-13. As in NGOMSL, this is needed when a choice of methods is available depending on the context. It would have to be used in conjunction with the method template of Figure 16-12. The task analyst must fill in the slots labeled TASK, SPECIFIC CONTEXT, and SPECIFIC-METHOD.

For the example chosen in Figure 16-13, the task is to enter the menu item number n. The TASK is ENTER N. The user has a choice of methods depending on

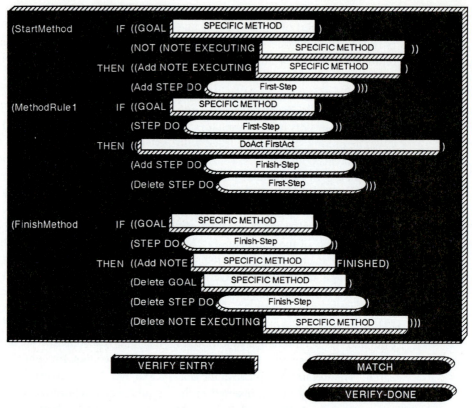

Figure 16-12. A template for the method rules in a production system analysis. As in Figure 16-11, the pieces at the bottom can be inserted only into certain slots in the template. When all the slots have been filled the rules will be the same as those shown in Figure 16-14 starting with the StartVerifyMethod rule.

the specific context of whether n is between 1 and 9 or greater than or equal to 10. If n is between 1 and 9 then the KEY-METHOD is selected. If greater than 9 the STRING-METHOD is selected.

The rules in the template work in the following way. In the SelectMethod, the condition contains the current goal on the goal stack along with two other parts. A variable number of Notes can be used to set the context. The next line, NOT (NOTE EXECUTING TASK), is used to ensure that the SelectMethod rule is fired only the first time through. When the task is executing, it cannot fire. The FinishSelect

fires as soon as the method is completed. In the condition part, it then deletes the Goal and the Note which indicated that the Goal was being performed. The method is specified by the lower part of the template. This will delete the method Goal and indicate that the Goal has been executed. When using this selection rule template, an extra step must be inserted in the FinishMethod rule of the method template. This rule is shown at the bottom of the box. Its purpose is to fire the FinishSelect rule once the method has been completed.

The templates are quite useful for ensuring that the task analysis will be as

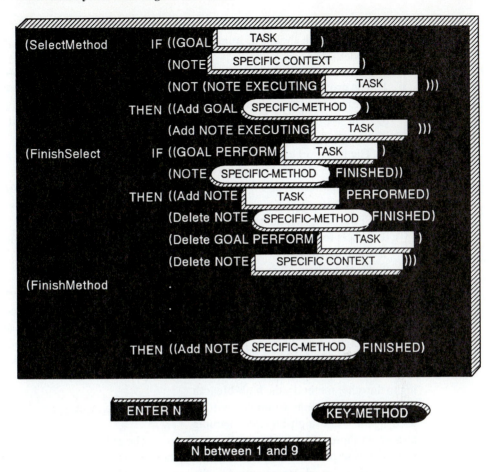

Figure 16-13. **A template for selection rules in a production system analysis. The pieces at the bottom can be inserted only into certain slots in the template. When all the slots have been filled the rules will be the same as those shown in Figure 16-14 starting with the SelectKeyMethod rule.**

invariant as possible over several different task analyzers. It should be remembered, however, that it is just a template, and some of the statements may have to be deleted or others may need to be added. In most cases, however, the structure probably does not have to be changed. The only thing that has to be changed are the Notes specifying the context. One must also make sure that they are deleted in the proper places so that the Notes are available for the context when needed but are not "hanging around" too long, cluttering up the working memory. An intermediate or expert user would be unlikely to allow a cluttered working memory. Also to help with making the analysis invariant, Bovair et al. (1990) formulated nine rules which should be followed in the task analysis. These rules are listed in Table 16-1; examples of how the rules are adhered to are examined in the next section.

TABLE 16-1

The nine rules which should be followed in the task analysis when using a production system model

> 1. The production rules must generate the correct sequence of user actions.
> 2. The representation should conform to structured programming principles.
> 3. The top-level representation for most tasks should have a unit task structure.
> 4. The top-level unit task structure should be based on the top-level goal.
> 5. Selection rules select which method to apply.
> 6. Information needed by a method should be supplied through working memory.
> 7. Sequencing within a method is maintained by chaining Steps.
> 8. Labels for Steps should be based on the action of the rules and should be used consistently.
> 9. Use a lockout Note to prevent a rule from firing repeatedly.

APPLYING PRODUCTION SYSTEMS TO THE MENU DISPLAYS

To compare the production system modeling to the other methods, the high-breadth and high-depth display examples will be used again. The high-breadth example appears in Figure 16-14. As can be seen from the example, each method requires an extensive list of statements for the processing to occur. To understand how it works, recall the analogy of the docking earlier in this chapter: the rule can only fire if all of the conditions are true. In the figure, the conditions are always indicated by two or more statements after the IF. Only one rule should fire at a time. Once a rule fires, the statements in the condition are released to be free-floating. These statements can then dock at any of the other conditions so that another rule can fire. An exception to the free-floating statements is any statement preceded by a NOT. These statements will be true if the statement after the NOT is not true. Thus,

before any statements are free-floating, some of the statements will already be activated. Processing continues until the program is told that all the tasks are completed.

Stepping Through the Example

The only way to completely understand how this production system works is to move step by step or cycle by cycle through the example. Figure 16-15 shows the cycle by cycle analysis for the high-breadth display using the production system of Figure 16-14. Before any processing occurs, there must be one high-level goal that the user has decided to achieve. In this case, the high-level goal is

GOAL PERFORM COMMAND-SEQUENCE

This means that the user has decided that a command sequence, such as backing up a disk, must be performed. This command sequence may have only one command or

(Top.Start	IF	((GOAL PERFORM COMMAND-SEQUENCE) (NOT (NOTE PERFORMING COMMAND-SEQUENCE)))
	THEN	((Add STEP GET COMMAND-UNIT-TASK) (Add NOTE PERFORMING COMMAND-SEQUENCE)))
(Top.P1	IF	((GOAL PERFORM COMMAND-SEQUENCE) (STEP GET COMMAND-UNIT-TASK))
	THEN	((RetainLTM LIST-ITEM as (NOTE VARIABLE MENU-COMMAND)) (Add GOAL PERFORM COMMAND-UNIT-TASK) (Add STEP CHECK TASKS-DONE) (Delete STEP GET COMMAND-UNIT-TASK)))
(Top-Finish	IF	((GOAL PERFORM COMMAND-SEQUENCE) (STEP CHECK TASKS-DONE) (NOTE NO-MORE-TASKS))
	THEN	((Delete GOAL PERFORM COMMAND-SEQUENCE) (Delete STEP CHECK TASKS-DONE) (Delete NOTE PERFORMING COMMAND-SEQUENCE) (Delete NOTE NO-MORE-TASKS) (Stop Now)))
(StartUnitTask	IF	((GOAL PERFORM COMMAND-UNIT-TASK) (NOT (NOTE EXECUTING COMMAND-UNIT-TASK)))
	THEN	((Add NOTE EXECUTING COMMAND-UNIT-TASK) (Add STEP LOOK SCREEN)))
(UnitTask.P1	IF	((GOAL PERFORM COMMAND-UNIT-TASK) (STEP LOOK SCREEN))
	THEN	((Add GOAL LOCATE MENU-COMMAND) (Add STEP ITEM ENTRY) (Delete STEP LOOK SCREEN)))
(UnitTask.P2	IF	((GOAL PERFORM COMMAND-UNIT-TASK) (STEP ITEM ENTRY) (NOTE LOCATE-MENU-COMMAND FINISHED))
	THEN	((Add GOAL ENTER N) (Add STEP DO VERIFY) (Delete STEP ITEM ENTRY) (Delete NOTE LOCATE-MENU-COMMAND FINISHED)))
(UnitTask.P3	IF	((GOAL PERFORM COMMAND-UNIT-TASK) (STEP DO VERIFY) (NOTE ENTER-N PERFORMED))
	THEN	((Add GOAL VERIFY ENTRY) (Add STEP FINISH TASK) (Delete NOTE ENTER-N PERFORMED) (Delete STEP DO VERIFY)))
(FinishUnitTask	IF	((GOAL PERFORM COMMAND UNIT-TASK) (STEP FINISH TASK) (NOTE VERIFY-ENTRY FINISHED))
	THEN	((Add NOTE PERFORM-COMMAND-UNIT-TASK FINISHED) (Delete GOAL PERFORM COMMAND-UNIT-TASK) (Delete STEP FINISH TASK) (Delete NOTE VERIFY-ENTRY FINISHED)

(continued on next page)

Figure 16-14. The production system model for the high-breadth display.

```
                              (Delete NOTE VARIABLE MENU-COMMAND)
                              (Delete NOTE EXECUTING COMMAND-UNIT-TASK)))

(StartLocate        IF    ((GOAL LOCATE MENU-COMMAND)
                           (NOT (NOTE EXECUTING LOCATE MENU-COMMAND)))
                    THEN  ((Add NOTE EXECUTING LOCATE MENU-COMMAND)
                           (Add STEP READ ITEMS)))
(ReadRule           IF    ((GOAL LOCATE MENU-COMMAND)
                           (STEP READ ITEMS))
                    THEN  ((DEVICE USER MENUline (Add NOTE VARIABLE MENU-ITEM))
                           (Add STEP MATCH ITEMS)
                           (Delete STEP READ ITEMS)))
(MatchFalse         IF    ((GOAL LOCATE MENU-COMMAND)
                           (STEP MATCH ITEMS)
                           (MatchWM (NOT (MENU-COMMAND MENU-ITEM))))
                    THEN  ((Add STEP READ ITEMS)
                           (Delete STEP MATCH ITEMS)
                           (Delete NOTE VARIABLE MENU ITEMS)))
(MatchTrue          IF    ((GOAL LOCATE MENU-COMMAND)
                           (STEP MATCH ITEMS)
                           (MatchWM (MENU-COMMAND MENU-ITEM)))
                    THEN  ((Add STEP UPDATE ITEMS)
                           (Delete STEP MATCH ITEMS)))
(UpdateRule         IF    ((GOAL LOCATE MENU-COMMAND)
                           (STEP UPDATE ITEMS))
                    THEN  ((DEVICE USER MENU-ITEMnumber (Add NOTE VARIABLE N))
                           (Add STEP FINISH LOCATE)
                           (Delete STEP UPDATE ITEMS)))
(FinishLocate       IF    ((GOAL LOCATE MENU-COMMAND)
                           (STEP FINISH LOCATE))
                    THEN  ((Add NOTE LOCATE-MENU-COMMAND FINISHED)
                           (Delete GOAL LOCATE MENU-COMMAND)
                           (Delete STEP FINISH LOCATE)
                           (Delete NOTE EXECUTING LOCATE-MENU-COMMAND)
                           (Delete NOTE VARIABLE MENU-ITEM)))

(SelectKeyMethod    IF    ((GOAL ENTER N)
                           (NOTE N between 1 and 9)
                           (NOT (NOTE EXECUTING ENTER-N)))
                    THEN  ((Add GOAL DO KEY-METHOD)
                           (Add NOTE EXECUTING ENTER N)))
(FinishSelectKey    IF    ((GOAL ENTER N)
                           (NOTE ENTER-N FINISHED))
                    THEN  ((Add NOTE ENTER-N PERFORMED)
                           (Delete GOAL ENTER N)
                           (Delete NOTE ENTER-N FINISHED)
                           (Delete NOTE EXECUTING ENTER-N)))
(StartKeyMethod     IF    ((GOAL DO KEY-METHOD)
                           (NOT (NOTE EXECUTING KEY-METHOD)))
```

(continued on next page)

Figure 16-14 (cont.)

	THEN	((Add NOTE EXECUTING KEY-METHOD) (Add STEP DO SINGLE-KEY)))
(KeyMethod	IF	((GOAL DO KEY-METHOD) (STEP DO SINGLE-KEY))
	THEN	((Press-key N) (Add STEP GET FEEDBACK) (Delete STEP DO SINGLE-KEY)))
(KeyFeedback	IF	((GOAL DO KEY-METHOD) (STEP GET FEEDBACK))
	THEN	((DEVICE USER EntryFeedbackLine (Add NOTE VARIABLE N')) (Add STEP FINISH KEY) (Delete STEP GET FEEDBACK)))
(KeyMethodFinish	IF	((GOAL DO KEY-METHOD) (STEP FINISH KEY))
	THEN	((Add NOTE ENTER-N FINISHED) (Delete GOAL DO KEY-METHOD) (Delete STEP FINISH KEY) (Delete NOTE EXECUTING KEY-METHOD)))

(SelectStringMethod	IF	((GOAL ENTER N) (NOTE N greater than 9) (NOT (NOTE EXECUTING ENTER-N)))
	THEN	((Add GOAL DO STRING-METHOD) (Add NOTE EXECUTING ENTER-N)))
(FinishSelectString	IF	((GOAL ENTER N) (NOTE ENTER-N FINISHED))
	THEN	((Add NOTE ENTER-N PERFORMED) (Delete GOAL ENTER N) (Delete NOTE ENTER-N FINISHED) (Delete NOTE EXECUTING ENTER-N)))
(StartStringMethod	IF	((GOAL DO STRING-METHOD) (NOT (NOTE EXECUTING STRING-METHOD))
	THEN	((Add NOTE EXECUTING STRING-METHOD) (Add STEP DO STRING)))
(StringMethod	IF	((GOAL DO STRING-METHOD) (STEP DO STRING))
	THEN	((Type-In N) (Add STEP GET FEEDBACK) (Delete STEP DO STRING)))
(StringFeedback	IF	((GOAL DO STRING-METHOD) (STEP GET FEEDBACK))
	THEN	((DEVICE USER EntryFeedbackLine (Add NOTE VARIABLE N') (Add STEP FINISH STRING) (Delete STEP GET FEEDBACK)))
(StringMethodFinish	IF	((GOAL DO STRING-METHOD) (STEP FINISH STRING))
	THEN	((Add NOTE ENTER-N FINISHED) (Delete GOAL DO STRING-METHOD)

(continued on next page)

Figure 16-14 (cont.)

```
                                      (Delete STEP FINISH STRING)
                                      (Delete NOTE EXECUTING STRING-METHOD)))

(StartVerifyMethod       IF    ((GOAL VERIFY ENTRY)
                               (NOT (NOTE EXECUTING VERIFY ENTRY)))
                         THEN  ((Add NOTE EXECUTING VERIFY ENTRY)
                               (Add STEP DO MATCH)))
(MatchInputFalse         IF    ((GOAL VERIFY ENTRY)
                               (STEP DO MATCH)
                               (MatchWM (NOT (N N'))))
                         THEN  ((Add GOAL DELETE ENTRY)
                               (Add NOTE MORE-DIGITS)
                               (Delete NOTE VARIABLE N')
                               (Add STEP DO TERMINATE)
                               (Delete STEP DO MATCH)))
(MatchInputTrue          IF    ((GOAL VERIFY ENTRY)
                               (STEP DO MATCH)
                               (MatchWM (N N')))
                         THEN  ((Add STEP DO TERMINATE)
                               (Delete STEP DO MATCH)))
(TerminateRule           IF    ((GOAL VERIFY ENTRY)
                               (STEP DO TERMINATE)
                               (NOT (NOTE EXECUTING DELETION)
                               (NOT (NOTE MORE DIGITS)))
                         THEN  ((Press-Key ENTER)
                               (Add STEP VERIFY-UPDATE)
                               (Delete STEP DO TERMINATE)))
(VerifyUpdate            IF    ((GOAL VERIFY ENTRY)
                               (STEP VERIFY UPDATE))
                         THEN  ((Add STEP VERIFY-DONE)
                               (Delete NOTE VARIABLE N)
                               (Delete NOTE VARIABLE N'
                               (Delete STEP VERIFY-UPDATE)))
(FinishVerifyMethod      IF    ((GOAL VERIFY ENTRY)
                               (STEP VERIFY DONE))
                         THEN  ((Add NOTE VERIFY-ENTRY FINISHED)
                               (Delete GOAL VERIFY ENTRY)
                               (Delete STEP VERIFY DONE)
                               (Delete NOTE EXECUTING VERIFY-ENTRY)))
(StartMethod             IF    ((GOAL DELETE ENTRY)
                               (NOT (NOTE EXECUTING DELETION)))
                         THEN  ((Add NOTE EXECUTING DELETION)
                               (Add STEP DO KEY-DELETE)))
(DeleteKey               IF    ((GOAL DELETE ENTRY)
                               (STEP DO KEY-DELETE))
                         THEN  ((Press-Key DELETE)
                               (Add STEP DECIDE MORE-DIGITS)
                               (Delete STEP DO KEY-DELETE)))
```

(continued on next page)

Figure 16-14 (cont.)

```
(DecideMoreDelete       IF   ((GOAL DELETE ENTRY)
                              (STEP DECIDE MORE-DIGITS)
                              (DEVICE USER EntrySpace DigitsPresent))
                        THEN ((Add STEP DO KEY-DELETE)
                              (Delete STEP DECIDE MORE-DIGITS)))
(DecideNoMoreDelete     IF   ((GOAL DELETE ENTRY)
                              (STEP DECIDE MORE-DIGITS)
                              (DEVICE USER EntrySpace NoDigitsPresent))
                        THEN ((Add GOAL ENTER N)
                              (Add STEP DO DELETE-TERMINATE)
                              (Delete NOTE MORE DIGITS)
                              (Delete STEP DECIDE MORE-DIGITS)))
(FinishMethod           IF   ((GOAL DELETE ENTRY)
                              (STEP DO DELETE-TERMINATE)
                              (NOTE ENTER-N PERFORMED))
                        THEN ((Add NOTE DELETE-ENTRY FINISHED)
                              (Delete GOAL DELETE ENTRY)
                              (Delete STEP DO DELETE-TERMINATE)
                              (Delete NOTE VARIABLE N')
                              (Delete NOTE EXECUTING DELETION)
                              (Delete NOTE ENTER-N PERFORMED)))
```

Figure 16-14 (cont.)

it may have several commands involved. In the very beginning, this is the only statement which is free-floating.

The above goal statement can dock at any of the first statements of the top-level method (designated with a Top.Start for the first IF statement). Remember that all of the statements of the IF must be true before a rule can fire. Because no other statements are presently in the problem space (the list of free-floating statements), all of the NOT statements throughout all the methods are true. Only one IF statement has both the goal of the problem space and a single NOT statement, and that is the first IF statement designated by Top.Start (the first cycle):

IF ((GOAL PERFORM COMMAND-SEQUENCE)

(NOT (NOTE PERFORMING COMMAND-SEQUENCE)))

This rule fires and the following statements are added to the problem space:

(STEP GET COMMAND-UNIT-TASK)

(NOTE PERFORMING COMMAND-SEQUENCE)

The Note is an example of a "lockout" Note which is used to ensure that the rule associated with Top.Start does not fire while perform command-sequence is still a goal (this is an example of rule 9 of Table 16-1). A NOT of a true statement is false. The STEP statement indicates which rule should be the next one in the method. This Step can be thought of in the same sense as the steps of the NGOMSL analysis.

For the next cycle, there is only one rule which has the goal (perform the command-sequence) and the step (get command-unit-task): the rule starting with Top.P1 which, consequently, is the only

1. Top.Start	32. ReadRule	42. FinishSelectString
2. Top.P1	33. MatchTrue	43. UnitTask.P3
3. StartUnitTask	34. UpdateRule	44. StartVerifyMethod
4. UnitTask.P1	35. FinishLocate	45. MatchInputTrue
5. StartLocate	36. UnitTask.P2	46. TerminateRule
6. ReadRule	37. SelectStringMethod	47. VerifyUpdate
7. MatchFalse	38. StartStringMethod	48. FinishVerifyMethod
8 - 31 (Rules 6 and 7 are	39. StringMethod	49. FinishUnitTask
fired 12 more times	40. StringFeedback	50. Top-Finish
on no matches)	41. StringMethodFinish	

Figure 16-15. The production model for the high-breadth display cycle by cycle and rule label.

rule which can fire. Once this rule fires, the following statements are added to the problem space:

(NOTE VARIABLE MENU-COMMAND)

(GOAL PERFORM COMMAND-UNIT-TASK)

(STEP CHECK TASKS-DONE)

The MENU-COMMAND variable is found through an analyst-defined operator, RetainLTM. This operator is defined to require two terms: the place where the information is found in LTM (LIST-ITEM) and how the information is tagged in WM (as NOTE VARIABLE MENU-COMMAND). For this operator, we assume that the user has a list of commands (this list may have only one item) and that the user can find the next item on the list through some kind of unspecified mental pointer. This NOTE VARIABLE construction must be used because the scope of variable statements is confined to the method in which it was first assigned. In order for other methods to use this variable, it must be included in a Note which can be stored in WM by the user.

The second statement added a goal to the goal stack Recall from the NGOMSL analysis that an operator can be a primitive operator, such as a key-press, or it can be complex so that a method must be stated for accomplishing the goal.

The Step to check if the tasks are done is largely left unspecified. The user would have to make decisions about whether or not all the commands have been executed for the tasks. When all have been executed then the user makes a mental Note that no-more tasks need be executed.

One statement is deleted from the problem space:

(STEP GET COMMAND-UNIT-TASK)

This ensures that the Top.P1 rule will not fire again.

In this second cycle, both a goal and a step were released, but we must be very careful about which rule fires next because rule 1 of the style rules indicates that the correct sequence of user actions must be preserved. From the NGOMSL analysis of the same task, we know that when a step contains an "Accomplish goal of <goal>" then the processing of the goal must be completed before the next step is processed. The same consideration is used for these production rules. With both a Step and a Goal being released on the same statement, though, how can we ensure that the Goal is accomplished before the Step is performed? This is done through the Notes. In particular, the rule associated with Top-Finish has the following condition:

IF ((GOAL PERFORM COMMAND-SEQUENCE)

(STEP CHECK TASKS-DONE)

(NOT (NOTE NO-MORE TASKS)))

For this condition, the first and second lines are true. The third line, the Note indicating that there are no-more tasks, is false. This can only be fired if the check from Top.P1 shows that no more tasks are needed, which is not true at this point. Thus, this construction accomplishes the same thing as the NGOMSL construction. The only statement that can be fired is the rule associated with StartUnitTask (cycle 3):

IF ((GOAL PERFORM COMMAND-UNIT-TASK)

(NOT (NOTE EXECUTING COMMAND-UNIT-TASK)))

This merely serves to start the method. The statements that fire are another lockout Note, similar to the previous one, and a Step which indicates the next step to perform.

The next rule on the page, UnitTask.P1 (cycle 4), fires because it contains the Step from the previous rule in the condition and the same goal which is now on top of the goal stack:

IF ((GOAL PERFORM COMMAND-UNIT-TASK)

(STEP LOOK SCREEN))

Once this rule fires, the following statements are added to the problem space:

(GOAL LOCATE MENU-COMMAND)

(STEP ITEM ENTRY)

This is another example of a step which fires both a Goal and a Step. Once again, the Goal will be performed first. The Step will be performed after the Goal is accomplished. This is achieved by having a Note in the condition containing the Step for look screen with the Note indicating that the Goal has finished. As is done for every rule, the Step in the condition of the current rule is deleted so that this rule does not fire again on the next round.

Because the next step is locked out due to the Note for finishing the MENU-COMMAND location, processing passes to the locate MENU-COMMAND method (cycle 5) because the following condition is true:

IF ((GOAL LOCATE MENU-COMMAND)

(NOT (NOTE EXECUTING LOCATE MENU-COMMAND)))

The action fires two statements: one locks out the above rule from firing again and the other one specifies the next step. In the next cycle (cycle 6), the following condition is true:

IF ((GOAL LOCATE MENU-COMMAND)

(STEP READ ITEMS))

When this rule fires, two statements are added to the problem space in addition to the deletion of the Step which was used to fire this rule. The first statement is the first example of the Device term which was defined in Table 16-1:

(DEVICE USER MENUline (Add NOTE VARIABLE MENU-ITEM))

From the definition, this operator has three terms. The first term is the target of the information displayed on the device, namely, the user. The second term is the location on the screen in which the user should look for the information. For this step, the user is required to read the menu-item from the screen. The third term is a specification of how this information will be stored. For this particular case, we have specified that the information will be stored as a variable using the name MENU-ITEM. This must be stored in WM because it will be used in a match in a later step. The Note designation ensures the WM storage.

For cycle 7, either the MatchFalse or MatchTrue rule will fire, depending on the outcome of the MatchWM analyst-defined operator. We define this operator as performing a match of specified items in WM. The specified items are listed as the two parameters after the name of this operator. The MatchFalse rule has the following condition:

IF ((GOAL LOCATE MENU-COMMAND)

(STEP MATCH ITEMS)

(MatchWM (NOT (MENU-COMMAND MENU-ITEM))))

Because of the NOT in the statement, this MatchWM identifies a mismatch between the MENU-COMMAND and the MENU-ITEM and will return a true on this mismatch. When finding menu item n, such a mismatch will occur 13 times before the match is found. When the mismatch occurs, the following actions are taken:

THEN ((Add STEP READ ITEMS)

(Delete STEP MATCH ITEMS)

(Delete NOTE VARIABLE MENU-ITEM))

By adding the Step, this means that the processing will return to the above step for reading the next item from the screen. The Step must be deleted so that the present rule does not fire again. The Note must be deleted so that the new MENU-ITEM can be read from the screen and stored in WM.

The MatchTrue has the following statements in its condition:

IF ((GOAL LOCATE MENU-COMMAND)

(STEP MATCH ITEMS)

(MatchWM (MENU-COMMAND MENU-ITEM)))

A match will occur if MENU-COMMAND and MENU-ITEM are the same. For menu item n, this will occur after reading the 14th item on the screen, resulting in the following step being added to the problem space:

(STEP UPDATE ITEMS)

The current step is also deleted from the problem space.

The above rules for the match are somewhat different from the corresponding statement in the NGOMSL model. A decision step was used in the NGOMSL model taking the form of an If-then rule. For a production system, the If-then construction occurs for the rules of the methods to control the flow of control, not as part of an action of a specific rule. Such a decision operator would be illegal or at least awkward for a production system. By using the MatchWM as part of the condition, and having two rules with both possibilities for the match (match or mismatch), the same flow of control can be achieved for the production system as for the NGOMSL analysis. The only difference is that the NGOMSL required three cycles through this part whereas the production system requires only two cycles. In a later section, this potential difference in time estimates using the number of cycles will be discussed in more detail and resolved.

A potential problem for this construction is specifying when the match occurs for the production system. Since the condition statements will fire any time they are true, does this mean that the user is always implicitly performing a MatchWM on each cycle? The answer to this question probably depends on the design of the interpreter (that part of the computer program which is used for controlling the flow of control) or at least the implicit design of the interpreter if none exists. We would probably have to design our interpreter so that a MatchWM would occur only if the two parameters had values associated with them.

To continue with the example, for a match we would be on cycle 33. The match had added an update item Step to

the problem space. The following condition is true (cycle 34):

IF ((GOAL LOCATE MENU-COMMAND)

(STEP UPDATE ITEMS))

The purpose of this rule is to store in WM the corresponding menu-item number so that it can be entered in a later step. The following action accomplishes this:

(DEVICE USER MENU-ITEMnumber (Add NOTE VARIABLE N))

This action uses the Device tag specifying that the User should look at the MENU-ITEM number location on the screen and store the number in variable n. Because it is specified as a Note, this information is stored in WM. The rest of the actions of this rule perform some bookkeeping by deleting the current Step and adding the next Step.

Cycle 35, the FinishLocate rule, is used to perform some of the bookkeeping for the completion of the locate MENU-COMMAND goal. It fires because the following condition is true:

IF ((GOAL LOCATE MENU-COMMAND)

(STEP FINISH LOCATE))

The action deletes this goal from the problem space along with the corresponding execution Note, sends a Note that the goal has finished, and deletes unneeded items from WM (the MENU-ITEM, in this case).

Recall that before the locate MENU-COMMAND goal was specified as an action, a step was also activated, the Step ITEM ENTRY. This Step is part of a condition of a previous method for controlling the sequencing of the command unit task:

IF ((GOAL PERFORM COMMAND-UNIT-TASK)

(STEP ITEM ENTRY)

(NOTE LOCATE-MENU-COMMAND FINISHED))

The Goal of this condition continues to be active. The Step, as mentioned above, was activated before the Goal of cycles 6-35. This condition is activated at this time because, on the previous cycle, the Note was added to WM. When this rule fires, a Goal and Step are activated:

(GOAL VERIFY ENTRY)

(STEP CHECK FINISHED)

The Goal is performed first because the Step is locked out through a Note which will ensure that the Goal is finished before the next Step in the present method is finished. In the same action, the previous Step is deleted and the Note, which indicated that the locate MENU-COMMAND was finished, is also deleted.

This next cycle illustrates how a selection rule works for this production system. The Goal is to ENTER N, and it occurs at the beginning of two methods: SelectStringMethod and SelectKey-Method. Which rule to select depends on the context. Recall that for NGOMSL the context was whether N was between 1 and 9 or greater than 9. In this production system, the context is provided by

(NOTE N between 1 and 9)

for the SelectKeyMethod and

(NOTE N greater than 9)

for the SelectStringMethod.

The selection rules have a slightly different construction from the other methods. The first two rules, the SelectStringMethod and the FinishSelectKey, are extra rules not present in the methods that are not part of a selection rule. The SelectStringMethod will be used to specify the method, in this case the STRING-METHOD, which should be performed based upon the selection rule. The purpose of the FinishSelectString, on cycle 42, is to delete the Goal of the selection rule.

The remaining cycles within the method, cycles 37 to 41, are fairly obvious. The StartStringMethod (cycle 38) is the start place for the method determined by the selection rule. The StringMethod (cycle 39) is used to activate the operator to type in the string of two digits. The StringFeedback (cycle 40) is used to retain the feedback from the typed string. Finally, the StringMethodFinish (cycle 41) performs the bookkeeping for the method by adding a Note that the method is finished, by deleting the Goal and Note of the method, and by deleting the Step which activated StringMethodFinish. Cycle 42 performs similar bookkeeping for the ENTER-N Goal.

Recall that the ENTER N Goal was called from the command unit task method. At the same time, the STEP DO VERIFY was specified. Since the ENTER N Goal has been finished, this next Step, to activate the Goal of verifying the entry, can be performed. This Goal is similar to the other Goals which have already been discussed in detail. Suffice it to say that the cycles for this goal, cycles 43 to 48, check if the number has been entered correctly. Assuming that it has been, processing returns back to the command unit task on cycle 49, which performs the bookkeeping to complete this command unit task.

On cycle 50, processing returns to the top-level task. At this point, the only Goal still active is to perform the command sequence and the active Step is to CHECK TASKS-DONE. If more commands still need to be entered, then another unit task would be available and Top.P1 will fire and all the cycles would be repeated for the next command. If no more commands need to be executed, then Top-Finish will fire and the task will be completed after all the active Goals, Steps, and Notes are deleted.

The production rule system for modeling the high-depth menu display is in Figure 16-16. The sequence of steps needed to find menu item n is shown in Figure 16-17. Once again, this model is very similar to the NGOMSL model except rules are used instead of methods. Recall that the main difference between the high-breadth and high-depth displays is that in the high-depth display the user has to first choose the category of the menu command, from a category or main menu, and then another screen appears on the display with just the four items corresponding to the category. The desired command should be one of these four items if the category was chosen correctly. Many of the rules are the same from the high-breadth to the high-depth menu display. The two differ in the number of screens that must be accessed and the digit entry. Since all menu displays have four items in the high-depth display, only one digit is needed for the entry; no ENTER key is needed for terminating the entry.

Performance Predictions from the Model

For the NGOMSL model of Chapter 15, the techniques were specified for estimating execution time, estimating learning times, performing design revisions, estimating the mental workload of a task, and analyzing the documentation. Since NGOMSL and production systems provide equivalent representations of a task, in slightly different terms, then the same estimations and predictions can be used for production systems. In some ways, however, the representation of NGOMSL has been set up to make these kinds of estimations and predictions easy to perform. To perform these estimations, one could first transfer the production rules into the methods and operators of NGOMSL or convert some of the equations to fit with the production rule parameters. However, the production systems seem to be more appropriate for some estimations than the NGOMSL model. This is especially true of transfer of training experiments. These kinds of estimations will be discussed in greater detail than others later in this chapter.

One technique for utilizing the modeling of users through a production system is to perform a computer simulation on the production rules generated for the particular tasks (Kieras and Polson, 1985; Bovair et al., 1990). A simulation like this is very similar to the process used to sequence the statements in Figures 16-14 and 16-16, except in the simulation, it is done using a computer and an interpreter to specify the flow of control. The simulation will determine many of the same parameters of the task as did the hand simulation of Figures 16-15 and 16-

(Top.Start	IF	((GOAL PERFORM COMMAND-SEQUENCE)
		(NOT (NOTE PERFORMING COMMAND-SEQUENCE)))
	THEN	((Add STEP GET COMMAND-UNIT-TASK)
		(Add NOTE PERFORMING COMMAND-SEQUENCE)))
(Top.P1	IF	((GOAL PERFORM COMMAND-SEQUENCE)
		(STEP GET COMMAND-UNIT-TASK))
	THEN	((RetainLTM LIST-ITEM as (NOTE VARIABLE MENU-COMMAND))
		(Add GOAL PERFORM COMMAND-UNIT-TASK)
		(Add STEP CHECK TASKS-DONE)
		(Delete STEP GET COMMAND-UNIT-TASK)))
(Top-Finish	IF	((GOAL PERFORM COMMAND-SEQUENCE)
		(STEP CHECK TASKS-DONE)
		(NOTE NO-MORE-TASKS))
	THEN	((Delete GOAL PERFORM COMMAND-SEQUENCE)
		(Delete STEP CHECK TASKS-DONE)
		(Delete NOTE PERFORMING COMMAND-SEQUENCE)
		(Delete NOTE NO-MORE-TASKS)
		(Stop Now)))
(StartUnitTask	IF	((GOAL PERFORM COMMAND-UNIT-TASK)
		(NOT (NOTE EXECUTING COMMAND-UNIT-TASK)))
	THEN	((Add NOTE EXECUTING COMMAND-UNIT-TASK)
		(Add STEP FIND CATEGORY)))
(UnitTask.P1	IF	((GOAL PERFORM COMMAND-UNIT-TASK)
		(STEP FIND CATEGORY))
	THEN	((Add GOAL ISSUE MENU-CATEGORY)
		(Add STEP FIND COMMAND)
		(Delete STEP ISSUE MENU-CATEGORY)))
(UnitTask.P2	IF	((GOAL PERFORM COMMAND-UNIT-TASK)
		(STEP FIND COMMAND)
		(NOTE ISSUE-MENU-CATEGORY FINISHED))
	THEN	((Add GOAL ISSUE MENU-COMMAND)
		(Add STEP FINISH TASK)
		(Delete STEP FIND COMMAND)
		(Delete NOTE ISSUE-MENU-COMMAND FINISHED)))
(FinishUnitTask	IF	((GOAL PERFORM COMMAND-UNIT-TASK)
		(STEP FINISH TASK)
		(NOTE ISSUE-MENU-COMMAND FINISHED))
	THEN	((Add NOTE PERFORM-COMMAND-UNIT-TASK FINISHED)
		(Delete GOAL PERFORM COMMAND-UNIT-TASK)
		(Delete STEP FINISH TASK)
		(Delete NOTE ISSUE-MENU-COMMAND FINISHED)
		(Delete NOTE EXECUTING COMMAND-UNIT-TASK)))
(StartCategory	IF	((GOAL ISSUE MENU-CATEGORY)
		(NOT (NOTE EXECUTING ISSUE-MENU-CATEGORY)))
	THEN	((Add NOTE EXECUTING ISSUE-MENU-CATEGORY)
		(Add STEP LOCATE CATEGORY)))

(continued on next page)

Figure 16-16. The production model for the high-depth display.

```
(CatLocateRule      IF      ((GOAL ISSUE MENU-CATEGORY)
                            (STEP LOCATE CATEGORY))
            THEN            ((Add GOAL LOCATE MENU-CATEGORY)
                            (Add STEP CATEGORY KEY-PRESS)
                            (Delete STEP LOCATE CATEGORY)))
(CatKeyRule         IF      ((GOAL ISSUE MENU-CATEGORY)
                            (STEP CATEGORY KEY-PRESS)
                            (NOTE LOCATE-MENU-CATEGORY FINISHED))
            THEN            ((Press-Key N)
                            (Add STEP UPDATE CATEGORY-ITEMS)
                            (Delete STEP CATEGORY KEY-PRESS)
                            (Delete NOTE LOCATE-MENU-CATEGORY FINISHED)))
(CatUpdateRule      IF      ((GOAL ISSUE MENU-CATEGORY)
                            (STEP UPDATE CATEGORY-ITEMS))
            THEN            ((Delete NOTE VARIABLE N)
                            (Delete NOTE VARIABLE MENU-CATEGORY)
                            (Add STEP FINISH CATEGORY)
                            (Delete STEP UPDATE CATEGORY-ITEMS)))
(FinishCategory     IF      ((GOAL ISSUE MENU-CATEGORY)
                            (STEP FINISH CATEGORY))
            THEN            ((Add NOTE ISSUE-MENU-CATEGORY FINISHED)
                            (Delete GOAL ISSUE MENU-CATEGORY)
                            (Delete STEP FINISH CATEGORY)
                            (Delete NOTE EXECUTING ISSUE-MENU-CATEGORY)))
(StartCommand       IF      ((GOAL ISSUE MENU-COMMAND)
                            (NOT (NOTE EXECUTING ISSUE-MENU-COMMAND)))
            THEN            ((Add NOTE EXECUTING ISSUE-MENU-COMMAND)
                            (Add STEP LOCATE COMMAND)))
(ComLocateRule      IF      ((GOAL ISSUE MENU-COMMAND)
                            (STEP LOCATE COMMAND))
            THEN            ((ADD GOAL LOCATE MENU-COMMAND)
                            (Add STEP COMMAND KEY-PRESS)
                            (Delete STEP LOCATE COMMAND)))
(ComKeyRule         IF      ((GOAL ISSUE MENU-COMMAND)
                            (STEP COMMAND KEY-PRESS)
                            (NOTE LOCATE-MENU-COMMAND FINISHED))
            THEN            ((Press-Key N)
                            (Add STEP UPDATE COMMAND-ITEMS)
                            (Delete STEP COMMAND KEY-PRESS)
                            (Delete NOTE LOCATE-MENU-COMMAND FINISHED)))
(ComUpdateRule      IF      ((GOAL ISSUE MENU-COMMAND)
                            (STEP UPDATE COMMAND-ITEMS))
            THEN            ((Delete NOTE VARIABLE N)
                            (Delete NOTE VARIABLE MENU-COMMAND)
                            (Add STEP FINISH COMMAND)
                            (Delete STEP UPDATE COMMAND-ITEMS)))
(FinishCommand      IF      ((GOAL ISSUE MENU-COMMAND)
                            (STEP FINISH COMMAND))
```

(continued on next page)

Figure 16-16 (cont.)

THEN   ((Add NOTE ISSUE-MENU-COMMAND FINISHED)
            (Delete GOAL ISSUE MENU-COMMAND)
            (Delete STEP FINISH COMMAND)
            (Delete NOTE EXECUTING ISSUE-MENU-COMMAND)))

(StartCatLocate   IF   ((GOAL LOCATE MENU-CATEGORY)
                            (NOT (NOTE EXECUTING LOCATE-MENU-CATEGORY)))
            THEN   ((Add NOTE EXECUTING LOCATE-MENU-CATEGORY)
                            (Add STEP ACCESS LTM)))
(AccessLTMRule IF   ((GOAL LOCATE MENU-CATEGORY)
                            (STEP ACCESS LTM)
                            (LTM (MENU-COMMAND category)))
            THEN   ((Add NOTE VARIABLE MENU-CATEGORY)
                            (Add STEP MATCH CATEGORY-ITEMS)
                            (Delete STEP READ CATEGORY-ITEMS)))
(ReadCatRule   IF   ((GOAL LOCATE MENU-CATEGORY)
                            (STEP READ CATEGORY-ITEMS))
            THEN   ((DEVICE USER MENUline (Add NOTE VARIABLE MENU-ITEM))
                            (Add STEP MATCH CATEGORY-ITEMS)
                            (Delete STEP READ CATEGORY-ITEMS)))
(MatchCatFalse   IF   ((GOAL LOCATE MENU-CATEGORY)
                            (STEP MATCH CATEGORY-ITEMS)
                            (MatchWM (NOT (MENU-CATEGORY MENU-ITEM))))
            THEN   ((Add STEP READ CATEGORY-ITEMS)
                            (Delete NOTE VARIABLE MENU-ITEM)
                            (Delete STEP MATCH CATEGORY-ITEMS)))
(MatchCatTrue   IF   ((GOAL LOCATE MENU-CATEGORY)
                            (STEP MATCH CATEGORY-ITEMS)
                            (MatchWM (MENU-CATEGORY MENU-ITEM)))
            THEN   ((Add STEP CATEGORY RETENTION)
                            (Delete STEP MATCH CATEGORY-ITEMS)))
(CatRetentionRule IF   ((GOAL LOCATE MENU-CATEGORY)
                            (STEP CATEGORY RETENTION))
            THEN   ((DEVICE USER MENU-ITEMnumber (Add NOTE VARIABLE N))
                            (Add STEP UPDATE CATEGORY-ITEMS)
                            (Delete STEP CATEGORY RETENTION)))
(UpdateCatRule   IF   ((GOAL LOCATE MENU-CATEGORY)
                            (STEP UPDATE CATEGORY-ITEMS))
            THEN   ((Delete NOTE VARIABLE MENU-ITEM)
                            (Add STEP FINISH CATEGORY-LOCATE)
                            (Delete STEP UPDATE CATEGORY-ITEMS)))
(FinishCatLocate   IF   ((GOAL LOCATE MENU-CATEGORY)
                            (STEP FINISH CATEGORY-LOCATE))
            THEN   ((Add NOTE LOCATE-MENU-CATEGORY FINISHED)
                            (Delete GOAL LOCATE MENU-CATEGORY)
                            (Delete STEP FINISH CATEGORY-LOCATE)
                            (Delete NOTE EXECUTING LOCATE-MENU-CATEGORY)))

(continued on next page)

Figure 16-16 (cont.)

```
(StartComLocate  IF    ((GOAL LOCATE MENU-COMMAND)
                        (NOT (NOTE EXECUTING LOCATE-MENU-COMMAND)))
            THEN        ((Add NOTE EXECUTING LOCATE-MENU-COMMAND)
                        (Add STEP MATCH COMMAND-ITEMS)))
(ReadComRule    IF      ((GOAL LOCATE MENU-COMMAND)
                        (STEP READ COMMAND-ITEMS))
            THEN        ((DEVICE USER MENUline (Add NOTE VARIABLE MENU-ITEM))
                        (Add STEP MATCH COMMAND-ITEMS)
                        (Delete STEP READ COMMAND-ITEMS)))


(MatchComFalse  IF      ((GOAL LOCATE MENU-COMMAND)
                        (STEP MATCH COMMAND-ITEMS)
                        (MatchWM (NOT (MENU-COMMAND MENU-ITEM))))
            THEN        ((Add STEP READ COMMAND-ITEMS)
                        (Delete NOTE VARIABLE MENU-ITEM)
                        (Delete STEP MATCH COMMAND-ITEMS)))
(MatchComTrue   IF      ((GOAL LOCATE MENU-COMMAND)
                        (STEP MATCH COMMAND-ITEMS)
                        (MatchWM (MENU-COMMAND MENU-ITEM)))
            THEN        ((Add STEP COMMAND RETENTION)
                        (Delete STEP MATCH COMMAND-ITEMS)))
(ComRetentionRuleIF     ((GOAL LOCATE MENU-COMMAND)
                        (STEP COMMAND RETENTION))
            THEN        ((DEVICE USER MENU-ITEMnumber (Add NOTE VARIABLE N))
                        (Add STEP UPDATE COMMAND-ITEMS)
                        (Delete STEP COMMAND RETENTION)))
(UpdateComRule  IF      ((GOAL LOCATE MENU-COMMAND)
                        (STEP UPDATE COMMAND-ITEMS))
            THEN        ((Delete NOTE VARIABLE MENU-ITEM)
                        (Add STEP FINISH COMMAND-LOCATE)
                        (Delete STEP UPDATE COMMAND-ITEMS)))
(FinishComLocate IF     ((GOAL LOCATE MENU-COMMAND)
                        (STEP FINISH COMMAND-LOCATE))
            THEN        ((Add NOTE LOCATE-MENU-COMMAND FINISHED)
                        (Delete GOAL LOCATE MENU-COMMAND)
                        (Delete STEP FINISH COMMAND-LOCATE)
                        (Delete NOTE EXECUTING LOCATE-MENU-COMMAND)))
```

Figure 16-16 (cont.)

17. In particular, it can determine the number of cycles and the contents of working memory on any particular cycle. We can simulate the simulation by performing these tasks by hand as long as we do not have too many rules.

Execution times. Just as in the NGOMSL analysis, execution time should be dependent on the time to execute the operators and the number of cognitive steps involved. The formula used by Kieras (1988), based upon experimentation and modeling of the results, can also be used for the production system as follows:

Execution time =
     Production System Cycle Time
     + Primitive External Operator Time
     + Analyst-Defined Mental Operator Time
     + System Response Time

1. Top.Start
2. Top.P1
3. StartUnitTask
4. UnitTask.P1
5. StartCategory
6. CatLocateRule
7. StartCatLocate
8. AccessLTMRule
9. ReadCatRule
10. MatchCatFalse
11-14 (Rules 9 and 10
    are fired 2 more times
    on no matches)

15. ReadCatRule
16. MatchCatTrue
17. CatRetentionRule
18. UpdateCatRule
19. FinishCatLocate
20. CatKeyRule
21. CatUpdateRule
22. FinishCategory
23. UnitTask.P2
24. StartCommand
25. ComLocateRule
26. StartComLocate
27. ReadComRule

28. MatchComFalse
29. ReadComRule
30. MatchComTrue
31. ComRetentionRule
32. UpdateComRule
33. FinishComLocate
34. ComKeyRule
35. ComUpdateRule
36. FinishCommand
37. FinishUnitTask
38. Top-Finish

Figure 16-17. The production model for the high-depth display cycle by cycle and rule label.

Production System Cycle Time =
    Total of times for external operators
    * 0.1 sec.

Primitive External Operator Time =
    Total of times for external operators

Analyst-Defined Mental Operator Time =
    Total of times for mental operators
    defined by the analyst

System Response Time =
    Total time when user is idle

The analysis using the production system should be somewhat similar to the NGOMSL analysis in terms of the number of cycles involved and the overall time estimate for performing the task. As in the NGOMSL analysis, to estimate the times, we need to determine the number of production system cycles, the Primitive External Operator Time, the Analyst-Defined Mental Operator Time, and the System Response Time. The production system cycle time is determined by taking the number of production system statements executed times 0.1 sec.

The number of cycles for the NGOMSL statements and the production system statements should be highly similar. However, some differences between the two techniques occur. The production system has more overhead associated with it in that the rule at the start of a method adds another cycle not present in the NGOMSL analysis (this does not occur in the top-level goal method, though). The NGOMSL analysis has decide operators that are not present in production systems. Usually this does not add an extra step because the false rule will fire and then the true rule will fire to continue. However, on the read menu item/decide on match loop, for the NGOMSL statements three cycles are needed per loop whereas for the production system only two cycles are needed per loop. This occurs because the NGOMSL statements are used to (1) read the screen, (2) decide on a match, and (3) perform the action of the decide statement, returning to the read screen statement, which requires a separate cycle. For the production system in the loop, only two statements are needed: (1) read the screen, and (2) decide on a false match on the nonmatching trials or decide on a true match on the matching trials. The if-then construction is not used on a decide statement; instead, separate rules are utilized.

Because of these differences between NGOMSL and production systems, the number of cycles using both models will not be exactly the same, although the counting of statements in the models could be changed to make them similar. As seen from Figures 16-15 and 16-17, the high-breadth display requires 50 cycles and the high-depth display requires 38 cycles to find menu item n.

As in the NGOMSL analysis, good estimators for the operators are the primitive operator values used by Card et al. (1983) in their Keystrokes-Level model. In this particular example, only three external operators occur: the two digits (14) of the menu item in the StringMethod rule of cycle 39 and the ENTER key of TerminateRule of cycle 46. Recalling the values for keystrokes from Table 14-3 for an average skilled typist (0.20 sec.), the total Primitive External Operator Time is 0.60 sec.

Once again, the Analyst-Defined Mental Operators must be determined individually through experimentation or, in the absence of experimentation, values from the Keystrokes-Level model or the Model Human Processor values can be used. In this particular case, the Model Human Processor is useful for estimating these times. A good method to determine the Analyst-Defined Mental Operators for the model and to estimate times is to look at each cycle and determine if more than one perceptual processor would be used on that particular cycle. As an example, on cycle 32 the following statement is part of the condition of the IF rule:

(DEVICE USER MENUline (Add NOTE VARIABLE MENU-ITEM))

This states that the user would read an item from the screen at the MENUline location and then add this information to WM. This would be similar to the τ_p cycle time for the perceptual processor; the average estimate for this time is 100 msec. In addition, we assume that performing the rule operation itself, since the preceding statement is part of the ReadRule, requires a cognitive processing time. For this Device statement, an extra 100 msec. would be needed and could be counted as part of the Analyst-Defined Mental Operators. These extra times occur in cycles 6 and 34 and also 12 times on the loops of statements 6 and 7 for cycles 8 through 32.

As done in the previous chapters, we will assume that the System Response Time is negligible or equal to 0. Since we are not analyzing the task for any particular system, it is difficult to predict the system response time. If the menu displays were being compared for a particular system, then these times could be determined exactly.

Totaling the execution time, it is

$$\begin{aligned} \text{Execution Time} &= 50\,(0.1)\text{ sec.} + 0.6\text{ sec.} \\ &\quad + 14\,(0.1)\text{ sec.} + 0 \\ &= 7.0\text{ sec.} \qquad (16.1) \end{aligned}$$

Using the production system model, we would estimate that the time needed to choose the 14th menu item is 7.0 sec.

Let's determine the estimated execution time for the high-depth display and compare it to the estimated time for the high-breadth display. Figure 16-16 contains the statements needed for choosing menu item n overall by first choosing menu item 4 in the main menu and then menu item 2 in the secondary menu. The execution of this task requires 38 statements (see Figure 16-17). The operator has two external primitive operators: the single-digit keystroke for the main menu (CatKeyRule of cycle 20) and the single-digit keystroke for the secondary menu (ComKeyRule of cycle 34). The Primitive External Operator Time is, therefore, 0.4 sec. The Device statement, an Analyst Defined Mental Operator which requires an extra perceptual processor time, occurs four times for the Category Menu (ReadCatRule in the loop of cycles 9 through 15) and twice for the Command Menu (ReadComRule in cycles 27 and 29). Using the 0.1 sec. estimate, the total time for Analyst-Defined Mental Operators is 0.6 sec. Once again, we assume that the system response time is negligible. The equation for estimating the time is

$$\text{Execution Time} = 38 \, (0.1) \text{ sec.} + 0.4 \text{ sec.}$$
$$+ \, 0.6 \text{ sec.} + 0$$
$$= 4.8 \text{ sec.} \qquad (16.2)$$

Comparing this time of 4.8 sec. for the high-depth display to the time of 7.0 sec. for the high-breadth display, we would predict that the high-depth display would be faster to execute by over 2 seconds for choosing menu item m. These qualitative results are similar to that found for the other models.

Estimates for execution time can also be found in the general case, instead of only for item n, where we assume equal probability of menu items being chosen. The average can be found for the serial terminating search through the menu items, as has been done in the previous examples for the other models. For the high-breadth display, cycles 1-5 will fire first. The searching through the menu items starts on cycle 7, and two rules fire during the search. These two rules will fire $(n + 1)/2$ times, or 8.5 times on the average. For the search, going through the two rules 8.5 times will require 17 cycles. The UpdateRule will occur on cycle 23, and all the rest of the cycles will be the same as those depicted in Figure 16-15. In the general case, this process will require 39 cycles.

Either two or three keystrokes would be needed to enter the menu item. If each menu item has equal probability of occurring, then this will always require two keystrokes, at 0.20 sec. each, plus 10/16 * 0.20 sec. for the other possible keystroke. The Analyst-Defined Operators, the Device statement, will occur in the search loop 8.5 times. This operator requires an extra 100 msec. to perform. With system response time equal to 0, the execution time for the high-breadth display in the general case is

$$\text{Execution Time} = 39 \, (0.1) \text{ sec.}$$
$$+ \, (0.4 + 0.63 \, (0.2)) \text{ sec.}$$
$$+ \, 8.5 \, (0.1) \text{ sec.} + 0$$
$$= 5.28 \text{ sec.} \qquad (16.3)$$

Using a similar kind of analysis for the high-depth display in the general case, the execution time for the high-depth display is

$$\text{Execution Time} = 40 \, (0.1) \text{ sec.} + 0.4 \text{ sec.}$$
$$+ \, 5.0 \, (0.1) \text{ sec.} + 0$$
$$= 4.9 \text{ sec.} \qquad (16.4)$$

Estimating Learning Time and Transfer Effects. In a transfer situation, a user has already learned one piece of interactive software and then must learn a new piece of interactive software. Usually, it is assumed that the user does not return to the old software. This kind of transfer situation could occur when changing from a UNIX operating system to an Apple Macintosh operating system, as an example. Or, it is likely to occur when a user buys a newer version of software having already learned the older version.

Polson and his colleagues have performed much work on estimating transfer by using production systems (Polson, Bovair, and Kieras, 1987; and Polson, Muncher, and Engelbeck, 1986). Much of this work is summarized in one source by Polson (1988). The main assumption behind the estimation of transfer is that transfer will be large when the overlap between production rules is high. If the overlap between the production rules is low, then transfer will be low. Their results generally support that hypothesis.

In their discussion of production systems, Bovair et al. (1990) also discuss the transfer process. They indicate that transfer of rules can have four possible outcomes:

1. The rule could be identical to an existing rule. In this case, nothing needs to be added to the existing rules already learned and so no additional learning time is called for.

2. The rule could be identical after a trivial generalization. Similar to the NGOMSL analysis of gain due to consistency, the only differences between the new rule and the old rule could be in the verb or noun of the rule. If the verb or noun is generalized, then the rules may be very similar and little learning would be needed for the new rule.

3. The rule could be subsumed under a generalized rule. This is illustrated in Figure 16-20. The generalized rule from Figure 16-19 is now considered as the old rule. The new rule for moving the string can be seen to be a specialized case of the existing generalized rule. Once again, this new rule would require little learning.

4. A rule may be completely new so that full learning is needed to add it to the existing rule set.

Figures 16-18 through 16-20 illustrate the second and third outcomes. In Figure 16-18, assume that the user has learned previously the set of rules starting with StartCategory and ending with FinishCategory (these rules were taken from Figure 16-16). Assume that the user must now learn the rules shown in Figure 16-19 (again, these rules were taken from Figure 16-16). Because the verbs of these two sets of rules are the same, and the rules themselves are highly similar, the new rule (Figure 16-19) can be subsumed under the old rule (Figure 16-18) by changing the word CATEGORY to a variable designation of ?X. This new rule is shown in Figure 16-20. Depending on the context, then, the variable ?X could be replaced by CATEGORY or COMMAND, but the user only has to learn and remember one set of rules. As can be seen from this analysis, the savings in numbers of rules due to generalizing the old rule to include the new rule is five rules. This process is the same as that illustrated in Figure 15-10 using the NGOMSL model which showed the gain due to consistency for Methods 3b and 4b. Bovair et al. provide an example

```
(StartCategory          IF    ((GOAL ISSUE MENU-CATEGORY)
                              (NOT (NOTE EXECUTING ISSUE-MENU-CATEGORY)))
                       THEN   ((Add NOTE EXECUTING ISSUE-MENU-CATEGORY)
                              (Add STEP LOCATE CATEGORY)))
(CatLocateRule          IF    ((GOAL ISSUE MENU-CATEGORY)
                              (STEP LOCATE CATEGORY))
                       THEN   ((Add GOAL LOCATE MENU-CATEGORY)
                              (Add STEP CATEGORY KEY-PRESS)
                              (Delete STEP LOCATE CATEGORY)))
(CatKeyRule             IF    ((GOAL ISSUE MENU-CATEGORY)
                              (STEP CATEGORY KEY-PRESS)
                              (NOTE LOCATE-MENU-CATEGORY FINISHED))
                       THEN   ((Press-Key N)
                              (Add STEP UPDATE CATEGORY-ITEMS)
                              (Delete STEP CATEGORY KEY-PRESS)
                              (Delete NOTE LOCATE-MENU-CATEGORY FINISHED)))
(CatUpdateRule          IF    ((GOAL ISSUE MENU-CATEGORY)
                              (STEP UPDATE CATEGORY-ITEMS))
                       THEN   ((Delete NOTE VARIABLE N)
                              (Delete NOTE VARIABLE MENU-CATEGORY)
                              (Add STEP FINISH CATEGORY)
                              (Delete STEP UPDATE CATEGORY-ITEMS)))
(FinishCategory         IF    ((GOAL ISSUE MENU-CATEGORY)
                              (STEP FINISH CATEGORY))
                       THEN   ((Add NOTE ISSUE-MENU-CATEGORY FINISHED)
                              (Delete GOAL ISSUE MENU-CATEGORY)
                              (Delete STEP FINISH CATEGORY)
                              (Delete NOTE EXECUTING ISSUE-MENU-CATEGORY)))
```

Figure 16-18. Assume that this set of five rules has already been learned by the user and can be designated as an old rule set.

of how the noun of the rule description can be turned into a variable.

The third outcome, subsuming a new rule under an old one, is a related process to rule generalization. In this case, assume that the user has already generalized the rules so that the set of rules depicted in Figure 16-20 is now an old rule. Assume also that the user has to learn a new rule which is very similar to the two that have been generalized, such as Issuing a Menu Subcategory. This new set of rules would not have to be learned, and could be subsumed under the old rule, because Subcategory can be substituted for the variable ?X in the generalized rule depending on the context.

One could argue that the three non-generalized sets of rules considered in these previous examples are not really different rule sets but could be considered as only one set because they are so similar. This would be an alternative way to perform the task analysis. The learning times for the two methods, though, taking into account the transfer times as in this example, would be the same.

Estimations for transfer time are very similar to the estimations of learning time using the NGOMSL analysis. Learning time could just be considered a special case of transfer learning in which the user has no prior rules. Once some rules are learned, then if the new rules to be learned

(StartCommand	IF	((GOAL ISSUE MENU-COMMAND)
		(NOT (NOTE EXECUTING ISSUE-MENU-COMMAND)))
	THEN	((Add NOTE EXECUTING ISSUE-MENU-COMMAND)
		(Add STEP LOCATE COMMAND)))
(ComLocateRule	IF	((GOAL ISSUE MENU-COMMAND)
		(STEP LOCATE COMMAND))
	THEN	((ADD GOAL LOCATE MENU-COMMAND)
		(Add STEP COMMAND KEY-PRESS)
		(Delete STEP LOCATE COMMAND)))
(ComKeyRule	IF	((GOAL ISSUE MENU-COMMAND)
		(STEP COMMAND KEY-PRESS)
		(NOTE LOCATE-MENU-COMMAND FINISHED))
	THEN	((Press-Key N)
		(Add STEP UPDATE COMMAND-ITEMS)
		(Delete STEP COMMAND KEY-PRESS)
		(Delete NOTE LOCATE-MENU-COMMAND FINISHED)))
(ComUpdateRule	IF	((GOAL ISSUE MENU-COMMAND)
		(STEP UPDATE COMMAND-ITEMS))
	THEN	((Delete NOTE VARIABLE N)
		(Delete NOTE VARIABLE MENU-COMMAND)
		(Add STEP FINISH COMMAND)
		(Delete STEP UPDATE COMMAND-ITEMS)))
(FinishCommand	IF	((GOAL ISSUE MENU-COMMAND)
		(STEP FINISH COMMAND))
	THEN	((Add NOTE ISSUE-MENU-COMMAND FINISHED)
		(Delete GOAL ISSUE MENU-COMMAND)
		(Delete STEP FINISH COMMAND)
		(Delete NOTE EXECUTING ISSUE-MENU-COMMAND)))

Figure 16-19. This is a new rule that must be learned after the rule depicted in Figure 16-18.

are similar to those already learned, the transfer model would be relevant. This has the effect of incorporating the gains due to consistency from NGOMSL. Bovair et al. (1990) assume that the transfer time is linearly related to the number of new rules which must be learned.

Consider the learning time or transfer time for the high-breadth display. The total number of rules for the production system describing its operation is 42. Some of the rules are identical, though, and do not need to be counted twice. In particular, the rules starting with SelectKey-Method and SelectStringMethod are very similar. This is a selection rule with the specified methods. The FinishSelectKey

and FinishSelectString rules are exactly the same. The StartKeyMethod, the KeyFeedback, and the KeyMethodFinish rules of the key-method are very similar to the StartStringMethod, the StringFeedback, and the StringMethodFinish rules of the string-method. The only difference between these two sets is that for the key-method the Goal is stated as DO KEY-METHOD while for the string-method the Goal is stated as DO STRING METHOD. The SelectKeyMethod and the SelectStringMethod are different because of the context from the Note. The KeyMethod and the StringMethod are different because of the different operators (Press-key or Type-in) used in the action

(StartCategory	IF	((GOAL ISSUE MENU-?X) (NOT (NOTE EXECUTING ISSUE-MENU-?X)))
	THEN	((Add NOTE EXECUTING ISSUE-MENU-?X) (Add STEP LOCATE ?X)))
(CatLocateRule	IF	((GOAL ISSUE MENU-?X) (STEP LOCATE ?X))
	THEN	((Add GOAL LOCATE MENU-?X) (Add STEP ?X KEY-PRESS) (Delete STEP LOCATE ?X)))
(CatKeyRule	IF	((GOAL ISSUE MENU-?X) (STEP ?X KEY-PRESS) (NOTE LOCATE-MENU-?X FINISHED))
	THEN	((Press-Key N) (Add STEP UPDATE ?X-ITEMS) (Delete STEP ?X KEY-PRESS) (Delete NOTE LOCATE-MENU-?X FINISHED)))
(CatUpdateRule	IF	((GOAL ISSUE MENU-?X) (STEP UPDATE ?X-ITEMS))
	THEN	((Delete NOTE VARIABLE N) (Delete NOTE VARIABLE MENU-?X) (Add STEP FINISH ?X) (Delete STEP UPDATE ?X-ITEMS)))
(FinishCategory	IF	((GOAL ISSUE MENU-?X) (STEP FINISH ?X))
	THEN	((Add NOTE ISSUE-MENU-?X FINISHED) (Delete GOAL ISSUE MENU-?X) (Delete STEP FINISH ?X) (Delete NOTE EXECUTING ISSUE-MENU-?X)))

Figure 16-20. The two rules depicted in Figures 16-18 and 16-19 have been generalized, by changing the word CATEGORY to a variable called ?X, as an indication of transfer of learning.

of the rule. With one rule being the same and three rules similar, if the six rules of one method are learned first then a user would only have to learn two rules of the second method. The number of rules to be learned can be reduced from 42 to 38. The NGOMSL analysis found a similar gain due to consistency.

Consider the learning time or transfer time for the high-depth display. The total number of rules for the production system describing its operation is 33. The rules can be examined to determine if any are identical or similar. As indicated in the example associated with Figures 16-18 through 16-20, to accomplish the goal of issuing the MENU-CATEGORY requires

five rules, as does the goal of issuing the MENU-COMMAND. All five of the rules are similar between the two methods. The only difference between the two sets of rules is that the MENU-CATEGORY goal uses CATEGORY throughout the Goals, Steps, and Notes while the MENU-COMMAND goal uses COMMAND throughout the Goals, Steps, and Notes. When each CATEGORY is changed to COMMAND, or changed to the variable name ?X as in the example, the two methods are exactly the same. Each method has five rules so that when one method is learned before the other, no more rules need to be learned for the second one. A similar situation occurs for the goal of locating the MENU-CATEGORY and the goal of locating the MENU-COMMAND. The only big difference is that the MENU-CATEGORY goal has an AccessLTMRule not present in the MENU-COMMAND goal. For all the rest of the rules, if CATEGORY were changed to COMMAND then the rules would be exactly the same. The locate MENU-CATEGORY goal has eight rules so that if this was learned before the locate MENU-COMMAND method, then the original eight rules are the only ones that need be learned. This analysis shows that the number of rules that need to be learned can be reduced from the 33 by 12 (five for the first analysis and seven for the second analysis). Thus, only 21 rules need be learned.

If learning time is a linear function of the number of new rules to be learned, then we would expect that the high-depth display could be learned faster because a user would only have to learn 21 rules as compared to 37 for the high-breadth display. To estimate actual learning time, the equation from NGOMSL can be used:

$$\text{Learning time} = (30\text{-}60) \text{ min.} + 30 \text{ sec. per number of rules} \quad (16.5)$$

except we base the equation on the number of rules instead of the number of NGOMSL statements. For the learning time, the estimate for the high-breadth display is

$$\begin{aligned}\text{Learning time} &= (30\text{-}60) \text{ min.} \\ &\quad + .5 \,(38) \text{ min.} \\ &= 49\text{ -}795 \text{ min.} \quad (16.6)\end{aligned}$$

For the high-depth display, the estimate is

$$\begin{aligned}\text{Learning time} &= (30\text{-}60 \text{ min.} + .5\,(21) \text{ min.} \\ &= 40.5\text{-}70.5 \text{ min.} \quad (16.7)\end{aligned}$$

This is a very general estimate with a large range. Bovair et al. (1990) used another technique, a multiple regression technique, to determine the equation using experimental data from a text-editing task. They found that the best-fitting equation for the data was

$$\text{Learning time} = 683.2 \text{ sec.} + 34.7 \text{ sec. per number of rules} \quad (16.8)$$

Using this equation, for the high-breadth display, the estimate would be

$$\begin{aligned}\text{Learning time} &= 683.2 \text{ sec.} + 34.7\,(39) \text{ sec.} \\ &= 2036.5 \text{ sec. or } 33.9 \text{ min.} \\ &\quad (16.9)\end{aligned}$$

For the high-depth display, the estimate would be

$$\begin{aligned}\text{Learning time} &= 683.2 \text{ sec.} + 34.7\,(22) \text{ sec.} \\ &= 1446.6 \text{ sec. or } 24.1 \text{ min.} \\ &\quad (16.10)\end{aligned}$$

It should be remembered that this regression equation was found using data from a text-editing task. The best-fitting equation for other tasks may be different. Both analyses show, however, that we could expect the high-depth display to be learned faster by about 10 minutes as compared to the high-breadth display. Although the exact times are only estimates, one has to remember that the learning times or transfer times are linearly related to the number of new rules to be learned. No matter what the time estimates are, we would always assume that the display with fewer rules to be learned, in this case the high-depth display, would be learned faster.

Mental Workload. In the NGOMSL analysis, two measures of mental workload were introduced: the peak workload and the workload density. Each of these was based upon the number of items stored in WM. The production system provides a very detailed description of the items stored in WM and, thus, the same kind of analysis performed on NGOMSL for workload can be used for the production system analysis. In Figures 16-21 and 16-22, the cycles for finding menu item n are shown along with the Notes which are stored in WM. The Notes provide a very precise description of the contents of WM. The peak load for the high-breadth display is seven items, and it occurs for the String-Feedback and StringMethodFinish of cycles 40 and 41. The peak load for the high-depth display is eight items, and it occurs for the CatRetention rule of cycle 17. This is very similar to the analysis from the NGOMSL model.

The other measure of workload, the workload density, is the average amount of items which have to be stored for each statement. This measure is found by counting the total number of items in memory at each statement and then dividing through by the number of statements. For the high-breadth display, the total number of items across all statements is 225. The high-breadth display has 50 statements so that the workload density is 4.50. The high-depth display has 188 items to be remembered across 38 steps. In this case, the workload density is 4.95. Once again, the high-depth display has a higher workload when measured in terms of peak load and density. The workload density will change depending on which menu item is chosen. Determination of the workload density in the general case is left as an exercise at the end of this chapter.

Bovair et al. (1990) performed an experiment on the mental workload for a text-editing task and found that inclusion of this variable in a multiple regression equation did not account for any additional variance in the performance of the subjects. The variables such as the number of cycles used in the execution time, and the number of times that the users looked at the manuscript, accounted for most of the variance. Bovair et al. (1990) indicate that this lack of finding a workload effect on performance could be due to workload being highly correlated with other variables, such as the number of times that users looked at the manuscript, and thus would not account for any more of the variance. An earlier experiment by Kieras and Polson (1985) found an effect for workload. It may not be surprising that no effect was found in the 1990 study. If the workload was within the limitations of WM then we would expect performance would not to be affected. Only when WM load is exceeded, due to poor design of the task, stress, or workload imposed by tasks other than the main computerized task, will performance changes be noticeable.

Expert/Novice Differences Analysis. Differences between experts and novices are more clearly stated using the production system models than using the NGOMSL model. The style rules for the production system were already listed in Table 16-1. These apply only to someone who is not really an expert or a novice, but someone in between. The style rules for novices and experts are slightly different from these original ones. The additions needed for novice behavior will be considered first.

The first addition to the style rules for novice users is
Novice Rule 1: Each overt action requires a separate production rule.

1. Top.Start

1. NOTE PERFORMING COMMAND-SEQUENCE

2. Top.P1

1. NOTE PERFORMING COMMAND-SEQUENCE
2. NOTE VARIABLE MENU-COMMAND

3. StartUnitTask

1. NOTE PERFORMING COMMAND-SEQUENCE
2. NOTE VARIABLE MENU-COMMAND
3. NOTE EXECUTING COMMAND-UNIT-TASK

4. UnitTask.P1

5. StartLocate

1. NOTE PERFORMING COMMAND-SEQUENCE
2. NOTE VARIABLE MENU-COMMAND
3. NOTE EXECUTING COMMAND-UNIT-TASK
4. NOTE EXECUTING LOCATE MENU-COMMAND

6. ReadRule

1. NOTE PERFORMING COMMAND-SEQUENCE
2. NOTE VARIABLE MENU-COMMAND
3. NOTE EXECUTING COMMAND-UNIT-TASK
4. NOTE EXECUTING LOCATE MENU-COMMAND
5. NOTE VARIABLE MENU-ITEM

7. MatchFalse

1. NOTE PERFORMING COMMAND-SEQUENCE
2. NOTE VARIABLE MENU-COMMAND
3. NOTE EXECUTING COMMAND-UNIT-TASK
4. NOTE EXECUTING LOCATE MENU-COMMAND

8 - 31 (Rules 6 and 7 are fired 12 more times on no matches)

32. ReadRule

1. NOTE PERFORMING COMMAND-SEQUENCE
2. NOTE VARIABLE MENU-COMMAND
3. NOTE EXECUTING COMMAND-UNIT-TASK
4. NOTE EXECUTING LOCATE MENU-COMMAND
5. NOTE VARIABLE MENU-ITEM

33. MatchTrue

34. UpdateRule

1. NOTE PERFORMING COMMAND-SEQUENCE
2. NOTE VARIABLE MENU-COMMAND
3. NOTE EXECUTING COMMAND-UNIT-TASK
4. NOTE EXECUTING LOCATE MENU-COMMAND
5. NOTE VARIABLE MENU-ITEM
6. NOTE VARIABLE N

35. FinishLocate

1. NOTE PERFORMING COMMAND-SEQUENCE
2. NOTE VARIABLE MENU-COMMAND
3. NOTE EXECUTING COMMAND-UNIT-TASK
4. NOTE VARIABLE N
5. NOTE LOCATE MENU-COMMAND FINISHED

(continued on next page)

Figure 16-21. The Notes at each cycle for the high-breadth display.

36. UnitTask.P2

1. NOTE PERFORMING COMMAND-SEQUENCE
2. NOTE VARIABLE MENU-COMMAND
3. NOTE EXECUTING COMMAND-UNIT-TASK
4. NOTE VARIABLE N

37. SelectStringMethod

1. NOTE PERFORMING COMMAND-SEQUENCE
2. NOTE VARIABLE MENU-COMMAND
3. NOTE EXECUTING COMMAND-UNIT-TASK
4. NOTE VARIABLE N
5. NOTE EXECUTING ENTER-N

38. StartStringMethod

1. NOTE PERFORMING COMMAND-SEQUENCE
2. NOTE VARIABLE MENU-COMMAND
3. NOTE EXECUTING COMMAND-UNIT-TASK
4. NOTE VARIABLE N
5. NOTE EXECUTING ENTER-N
6. EXECUTING STRING-METHOD

39. StringMethod

40. StringFeedback

1. NOTE PERFORMING COMMAND-SEQUENCE
2. NOTE VARIABLE MENU-COMMAND
3. NOTE EXECUTING COMMAND-UNIT-TASK
4. NOTE VARIABLE N
5. NOTE EXECUTING ENTER-N
6. EXECUTING STRING-METHOD
7. NOTE VARIABLE N'

41. StringMethodFinish

1. NOTE PERFORMING COMMAND-SEQUENCE
2. NOTE VARIABLE MENU-COMMAND
3. NOTE EXECUTING COMMAND-UNIT-TASK
4. NOTE VARIABLE N
5. NOTE EXECUTING ENTER-N
6. NOTE VARIABLE N'
7. NOTE ENTER-N FINISHED

42. FinishSelectString

1. NOTE PERFORMING COMMAND-SEQUENCE
2. NOTE VARIABLE MENU-COMMAND
3. NOTE EXECUTING COMMAND-UNIT-TASK
4. NOTE VARIABLE N
5. NOTE VARIABLE N'
6. NOTE ENTER-N PERFORMED

43. UnitTask.P3

1. NOTE PERFORMING COMMAND-SEQUENCE
2. NOTE VARIABLE MENU-COMMAND
3. NOTE EXECUTING COMMAND-UNIT-TASK
4. NOTE VARIABLE N
5. NOTE VARIABLE N'

(continued on next page)

Figure 16-21 (cont.)

44. StartVerifyMethod	1. NOTE PERFORMING COMMAND-SEQUENCE
	2. NOTE VARIABLE MENU-COMMAND
	3. NOTE EXECUTING COMMAND-UNIT-TASK
	4. NOTE VARIABLE N
	5. NOTE VARIABLE N'
	6. NOTE EXECUTING VERIFY ENTRY
45. MatchInputTrue	
46. TerminateRule	
47. VerifyUpdate	1. NOTE PERFORMING COMMAND-SEQUENCE
	2. NOTE VARIABLE MENU-COMMAND
	3. NOTE EXECUTING COMMAND-UNIT-TASK
	4. NOTE EXECUTING VERIFY ENTRY
48. FinishVerifyMethod	1. NOTE PERFORMING COMMAND-SEQUENCE
	2. NOTE VARIABLE MENU-COMMAND
	3. NOTE EXECUTING COMMAND-UNIT-TASK
	4. NOTE VERIFY-ENTRY FINISHED
49. FinishUnitTask	1. NOTE PERFORMING COMMAND-SEQUENCE
	2. NOTE PERFORM-COMMAND-UNIT-TASK FINISHED
50. Top-Finish	(Empty)

Figure 16-21 (cont.)

An overt action can include a key-press, a mouse manipulation, looking at a manuscript, or looking at a screen. To model novices, each one of these would have to be placed in a separate rule. Other actions manipulating working memory, such as adding or deleting Notes, do not have to be enclosed within separate steps.

The second and last addition to the style rules is

Novice Rule 2: Novices explicitly check all feedback.

The checking of feedback occurs for the high-breadth display in cycle 50 and the StringFeedback rule. If this were a model for an expert, this step would not have been included because we would expect that the ENTER key would be hit automatically without the explicit check.

By examining the production systems for the high-breadth and high-depth displays, it can be seen that modeling was performed with a novice user in mind. It is interesting to note that the production system model is probably easiest to apply to novice users because only having one overt action in a step is a very specific rule to follow, thus reducing the variability of modeling between different task analysts.

The opposites of the preceding two novice rules can be formulated to reflect expert performance. From the second novice rule, we would assume that experts would not explicitly check all the feedback. The rules for checking feedback could be removed thus reducing the number of rules. The production systems for the high-breadth and high-depth displays can be changed to remove these prompts;

1. Top.Start

1. NOTE PERFORMING COMMAND-SEQUENCE

2. Top.P1

1. NOTE PERFORMING COMMAND-SEQUENCE
2. NOTE VARIABLE MENU-COMMAND

3. StartUnitTask

1. NOTE PERFORMING COMMAND-SEQUENCE
2. NOTE VARIABLE MENU-COMMAND
3. NOTE EXECUTING COMMAND-UNIT-TASK

4. UnitTask.P1

5. StartCategory

1. NOTE PERFORMING COMMAND-SEQUENCE
2. NOTE VARIABLE MENU-COMMAND
3. NOTE EXECUTING COMMAND-UNIT-TASK
4. NOTE EXECUTING ISSUE-MENU-CATEGORY

6. CatLocateRule

7. StartCatLocate

1. NOTE PERFORMING COMMAND-SEQUENCE
2. NOTE VARIABLE MENU-COMMAND
3. NOTE EXECUTING COMMAND-UNIT-TASK
4. NOTE EXECUTING ISSUE-MENU-CATEGORY
5. NOTE EXECUTING LOCATE-MENU-CATEGORY

8. AccessLTMRule

1. NOTE PERFORMING COMMAND-SEQUENCE
2. NOTE VARIABLE MENU-COMMAND
3. NOTE EXECUTING COMMAND-UNIT-TASK
4. NOTE EXECUTING ISSUE-MENU-CATEGORY
5. NOTE EXECUTING LOCATE-MENU-CATEGORY
6. NOTE VARIABLE MENU-CATEGORY

9. ReadCatRule

1. NOTE PERFORMING COMMAND-SEQUENCE
2. NOTE VARIABLE MENU-COMMAND
3. NOTE EXECUTING COMMAND-UNIT-TASK
4. NOTE EXECUTING ISSUE-MENU-CATEGORY
5. NOTE EXECUTING LOCATE-MENU-CATEGORY
6. NOTE VARIABLE MENU-CATEGORY
7. NOTE VARIABLE MENU-ITEM

10. MatchCatFalse

1. NOTE PERFORMING COMMAND-SEQUENCE
2. NOTE VARIABLE MENU-COMMAND
3. NOTE EXECUTING COMMAND-UNIT-TASK
4. NOTE EXECUTING ISSUE-MENU-CATEGORY
5. NOTE EXECUTING LOCATE-MENU-CATEGORY
6. NOTE VARIABLE MENU-CATEGORY

11-14 (Rules 9 and 10 are fired 2 more times on no matches)

15. ReadCatRule

1. NOTE PERFORMING COMMAND-SEQUENCE

(continued on next page)

Figure 16-22. The Notes at each cycle for the high-depth display.

2. NOTE VARIABLE MENU-COMMAND
3. NOTE EXECUTING COMMAND-UNIT-TASK
4. NOTE EXECUTING ISSUE-MENU-CATEGORY
5. NOTE EXECUTING LOCATE-MENU-CATEGORY
6. NOTE VARIABLE MENU-CATEGORY
7. NOTE VARIABLE MENU-ITEM

16. MatchCatTrue

17. CatRetentionRule
1. NOTE PERFORMING COMMAND-SEQUENCE
2. NOTE VARIABLE MENU-COMMAND
3. NOTE EXECUTING COMMAND-UNIT-TASK
4. NOTE EXECUTING ISSUE-MENU-CATEGORY
5. NOTE EXECUTING LOCATE-MENU-CATEGORY
6. NOTE VARIABLE MENU-CATEGORY
7. NOTE VARIABLE MENU-ITEM
8. NOTE VARIABLE N

18. UpdateCatRule
1. NOTE PERFORMING COMMAND-SEQUENCE
2. NOTE VARIABLE MENU-COMMAND
3. NOTE EXECUTING COMMAND-UNIT-TASK
4. NOTE EXECUTING ISSUE-MENU-CATEGORY
5. NOTE EXECUTING LOCATE-MENU-CATEGORY
6. NOTE VARIABLE MENU-CATEGORY
7. NOTE VARIABLE N

19. FinishCatLocate
1. NOTE PERFORMING COMMAND-SEQUENCE
2. NOTE VARIABLE MENU-COMMAND
3. NOTE EXECUTING COMMAND-UNIT-TASK
4. NOTE EXECUTING ISSUE-MENU-CATEGORY
5. NOTE VARIABLE MENU-CATEGORY
6. NOTE VARIABLE N
7. NOTE LOCATE-MENU-CATEGORY FINISHED

20. CatKeyRule
1. NOTE PERFORMING COMMAND-SEQUENCE
2. NOTE VARIABLE MENU-COMMAND
3. NOTE EXECUTING COMMAND-UNIT-TASK
4. NOTE EXECUTING ISSUE-MENU-CATEGORY
5. NOTE VARIABLE MENU-CATEGORY
6. NOTE VARIABLE N

21. CatUpdateRule
1. NOTE PERFORMING COMMAND-SEQUENCE
2. NOTE VARIABLE MENU-COMMAND
3. NOTE EXECUTING COMMAND-UNIT-TASK
4. NOTE EXECUTING ISSUE-MENU-CATEGORY

22. FinishCategory
1. NOTE PERFORMING COMMAND-SEQUENCE
2. NOTE VARIABLE MENU-COMMAND
3. NOTE EXECUTING COMMAND-UNIT-TASK
4. NOTE ISSUE-MENU-CATEGORY FINISHED

(continued on next page)

Figure 16-22 (cont.)

23. UnitTask.P2
1. NOTE PERFORMING COMMAND-SEQUENCE
2. NOTE VARIABLE MENU-COMMAND
3. NOTE EXECUTING COMMAND-UNIT-TASK

24. StartCommand
1. NOTE PERFORMING COMMAND-SEQUENCE
2. NOTE VARIABLE MENU-COMMAND
3. NOTE EXECUTING COMMAND-UNIT-TASK
4. NOTE EXECUTING ISSUE-MENU-COMMAND

25. ComLocateRule

26. StartComLocate
1. NOTE PERFORMING COMMAND-SEQUENCE
2. NOTE VARIABLE MENU-COMMAND
3. NOTE EXECUTING COMMAND-UNIT-TASK
4. NOTE EXECUTING ISSUE-MENU-COMMAND
5. NOTE EXECUTING LOCATE-MENU-COMMAND

27. ReadComRule
1. NOTE PERFORMING COMMAND-SEQUENCE
2. NOTE VARIABLE MENU-COMMAND
3. NOTE EXECUTING COMMAND-UNIT-TASK
4. NOTE EXECUTING ISSUE-MENU-COMMAND
5. NOTE EXECUTING LOCATE-MENU-COMMAND
6. NOTE VARIABLE MENU-ITEM

28. MatchComFalse
1. NOTE PERFORMING COMMAND-SEQUENCE
2. NOTE VARIABLE MENU-COMMAND
3. NOTE EXECUTING COMMAND-UNIT-TASK
4. NOTE EXECUTING ISSUE-MENU-COMMAND
5. NOTE EXECUTING LOCATE-MENU-COMMAND

29. ReadComRule
1. NOTE PERFORMING COMMAND-SEQUENCE
2. NOTE VARIABLE MENU-COMMAND
3. NOTE EXECUTING COMMAND-UNIT-TASK
4. NOTE EXECUTING ISSUE-MENU-COMMAND
5. NOTE EXECUTING LOCATE-MENU-COMMAND
6. NOTE VARIABLE MENU-ITEM

30. MatchComTrue

31. ComRetentionRule
1. NOTE PERFORMING COMMAND-SEQUENCE
2. NOTE VARIABLE MENU-COMMAND
3. NOTE EXECUTING COMMAND-UNIT-TASK
4. NOTE EXECUTING ISSUE-MENU-COMMAND
5. NOTE EXECUTING LOCATE-MENU-COMMAND
6. NOTE VARIABLE MENU-ITEM
7. NOTE VARIABLE N

32. UpdateComRule
1. NOTE PERFORMING COMMAND-SEQUENCE
2. NOTE VARIABLE MENU-COMMAND

(continued on next page)

Figure 16-22 (cont.)

	3. NOTE EXECUTING COMMAND-UNIT-TASK
	4. NOTE EXECUTING ISSUE-MENU-COMMAND
	5. NOTE EXECUTING LOCATE-MENU-COMMAND
	6. NOTE VARIABLE N

33. FinishComLocate	1. NOTE PERFORMING COMMAND-SEQUENCE
	2. NOTE VARIABLE MENU-COMMAND
	3. NOTE EXECUTING COMMAND-UNIT-TASK
	4. NOTE EXECUTING ISSUE-MENU-COMMAND
	5. NOTE VARIABLE N
	6. NOTE LOCATE-MENU-COMMAND FINISHED

34. ComKeyRule	1. NOTE PERFORMING COMMAND-SEQUENCE
	2. NOTE VARIABLE MENU-COMMAND
	3. NOTE EXECUTING COMMAND-UNIT-TASK
	4. NOTE EXECUTING ISSUE-MENU-COMMAND
	5. NOTE VARIABLE N

35. ComUpdateRule	1. NOTE PERFORMING COMMAND-SEQUENCE
	2. NOTE EXECUTING COMMAND-UNIT-TASK
	3. NOTE EXECUTING ISSUE-MENU-COMMAND

36. FinishCommand	1. NOTE PERFORMING COMMAND-SEQUENCE
	2. NOTE EXECUTING COMMAND-UNIT-TASK
	3. NOTE ISSUE-MENU-COMMAND FINISHED

| 38. FinishUnitTask | 1. NOTE PERFORMING COMMAND-SEQUENCE |
| | 2. NOTE PERFORM-COMMAND-UNIT-TASK FINISH |

| 39. Top-Finish | (empty) |

Figure 16-22 (cont.)

this is left an an exercise at the end of this chapter.

For the first novice rule, we would expect that the rules would be reduced by compacting the rules into a more efficient rule structure. For the production system modeling, emphasis is placed on making the rule sets more compact rather than generating new specialized methods.

Several techniques can be used for compacting the rules. One technique is based on selection rules. The method and selection rule templates shown in Figures 16-12 and 16-13 has five rules. Much overlap occurs between the SelectMethod and StartMethod and between the Fin-

ishSelect and FinishMethod. Bovair et al. (1990) indicate that experts would reduce this overlap by combining some of the rules. An expert rule template for a selection rule is shown in Figure 16-23, and this can be compared to the templates in Figures 16-12 and 16-13 which were used for constructing the original production system. The SelectMethod and StartMethod rules are combined in addition to the FinishMethod and FinishSelect rules. Similar to Figures 16-12 and 16-13, when the pieces at the bottom of the figure are inserted in the right-sized slots, an expert selection rule and method can be constructed. Figure 16-24 shows the result-

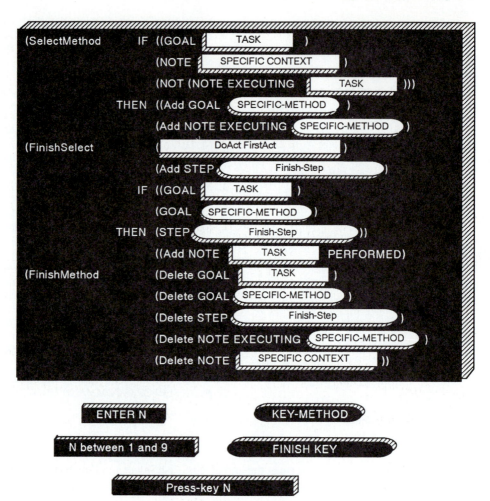

Figure 16-23. A representation of an expert rule template.

ing selection rule and part of the method for the string-method to show how an expert would perform it. Comparing this method to the high-breadth display of Figure 16-14, it can be seen that the number of rules needed can be reduced from five to three (three rules are needed because the KeyFeedback rule from Figure 16-14 is still needed and would be inserted in the template between the SelectMethod and the FinishSelect rules).

The combination of rules for experts can be generalized to other cases besides just the method and selection rule templates described previously. Bovair et al. (1990) describe the situation in which rules can be combined. Rule compacting can occur if two rules, called the preceding rule and the following rule, always occur in succession. In addition, the following conditions must be true:

1. The two rules must not have complementary conditions.

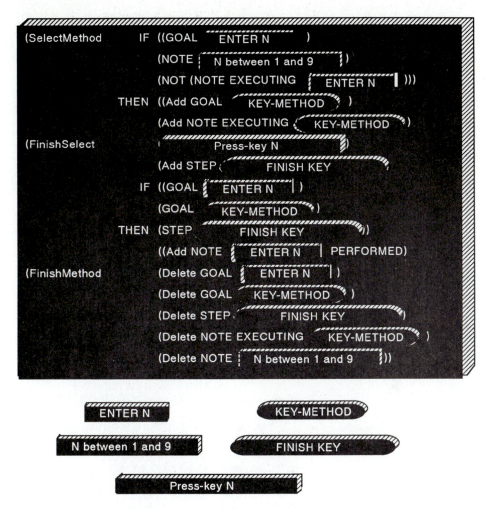

Figure 16-24. Selection rule for the key-method of the high-breadth display to show how an expert would perform it. To obtain this selection rule, the task analyst has only to fill in the slots from the expert rule template of Figure 16-23.

2. The following rule must not be a method return point. If it is a method return point, the control structure of the production system would not be preserved and the outcomes of the models would be different.

3. The following rule must not be a selection rule because this

would also change the control structure.

If these are true, then the two rules which are next to each other can be compacted.

Figure 16-25 illustrates how these three conditions can be used to compact the rules for experts on the high-depth display. An obvious place to look for compacting rules is in the update of the

Old Rules

(StartCategory	IF	((GOAL ISSUE MENU-CATEGORY)
		(NOT (NOTE EXECUTING ISSUE-MENU-CATEGORY)))
	THEN	((Add NOTE EXECUTING ISSUE-MENU-CATEGORY)
		(Add STEP LOCATE CATEGORY)))
(CatLocateRule	IF	((GOAL ISSUE MENU-CATEGORY)
		(STEP LOCATE CATEGORY))
	THEN	((Add GOAL LOCATE MENU-CATEGORY)
		(Add STEP CAT KEY-PRESS)
		(Delete STEP LOCATE CATEGORY)))
(CatKeyRule	IF	((GOAL ISSUE MENU-CATEGORY)
		(STEP CAT KEY-PRESS)
		(NOTE LOCATE-MENU-CATEGORY FINISHED))
	THEN	((Press-Key N)
		(Add STEP UPDATE CAT-ITEMS)
		(Delete STEP CAT KEY-PRESS)
		(Delete NOTE LOCATE-MENU-CATEGORY FINISHED)))
(CatUpdateRule	IF	((GOAL ISSUE MENU-CATEGORY)
		(STEP UPDATE CAT-ITEMS))
	THEN	((Delete NOTE VARIABLE N)
		(Delete NOTE VARIABLE MENU-CATEGORY)
		(Add STEP FINISH CATEGORY)
		(Delete STEP UPDATE CAT-ITEMS)))
(FinishCategory	IF	((GOAL ISSUE MENU-CATEGORY)
		(STEP FINISH CATEGORY))
	THEN	((Add NOTE ISSUE-MENU-CATEGORY FINISHED)
		(Delete GOAL ISSUE MENU-CATEGORY)
		(Delete STEP FINISH CATEGORY)
		(Delete NOTE EXECUTING ISSUE-MENU-CATEGORY)))
(StartCatLocate	IF	((GOAL LOCATE MENU-CATEGORY)
		(NOT (NOTE EXECUTING LOCATE-MENU-CATEGORY)))
	THEN	((Add NOTE EXECUTING LOCATE-MENU-CATEGORY)
		(Add STEP ACCESS LTM)))
(AccessLTMRule	IF	((GOAL LOCATE MENU-CATEGORY)
		(STEP ACCESS LTM)
		(LTM (MENU-COMMAND CATEGORY)))
	THEN	((Add NOTE VARIABLE MENU-CATEGORY)
		(Add STEP MATCH CAT-ITEMS)
		(Delete STEP READ CAT-ITEMS)))
(ReadCatRule	IF	((GOAL LOCATE MENU-CATEGORY)
		(STEP READ CAT-ITEMS))
	THEN	((DEVICE USER MENUline (Add NOTE VARIABLE MENU-ITEM))
		(Add STEP MATCH CAT-ITEMS)
		(Delete STEP READ CAT-ITEMS)))
(MatchCatFalse	IF	((GOAL LOCATE MENU-CATEGORY)
		(STEP MATCH CAT-ITEMS)
		(MatchWM (NOT (MENU-CATEGORY MENU-ITEM))))

(continued on next page)

Figure 16-25. An example of compacting rules for experts.

	THEN	((Add STEP READ CAT-ITEMS) (Delete NOTE VARIABLE MENU-ITEM) (Delete STEP MATCH CAT-ITEMS)))
(MatchCatTrue	IF	((GOAL LOCATE MENU-CATEGORY) (STEP MATCH CAT-ITEMS) (MatchWM (MENU-CATEGORY MENU-ITEM)))
	THEN	((Add STEP CATEGORY RETENTION) (Delete STEP MATCH CAT-ITEMS)))
(CatRetentionRule	IF	((GOAL LOCATE MENU-CATEGORY) (STEP CATEGORY RETENTION))
	THEN	((DEVICE USER MENU-ITEMnumber (Add NOTE VARIABLE N)) (Add STEP UPDATE CAT-ITEMS) (Delete STEP CATEGORY RETENTION)))
(UpdateCatRule	IF	((GOAL LOCATE MENU-CATEGORY) (STEP UPDATE CAT-ITEMS))
	THEN	((Delete NOTE VARIABLE MENU-ITEM) (Add STEP FINISH CAT-LOCATE) (Delete STEP UPDATE CAT-ITEMS)))
(FinishCatLocate	IF	((GOAL LOCATE MENU-CATEGORY) (STEP FINISH CAT-LOCATE))
	THEN	((Add NOTE LOCATE-MENU-CATEGORY FINISH) (Delete GOAL LOCATE MENU-CATEGORY) (Delete STEP FINISH CAT-LOCATE) (Delete NOTE EXECUTING LOCATE-MENU-CATEGORY)))

New Rules

(StartCategory	IF	((GOAL ISSUE MENU-CATEGORY) (NOT (NOTE EXECUTING ISSUE-MENU-CATEGORY)))
	THEN	((Add NOTE EXECUTING ISSUE-MENU-CATEGORY) (Add STEP LOCATE CATEGORY)))
(CatLocateRule	IF	((GOAL ISSUE MENU-CATEGORY) (STEP LOCATE CATEGORY))
	THEN	((Add GOAL LOCATE MENU-CATEGORY) (Add STEP CAT KEY-PRESS) (Delete STEP LOCATE CATEGORY)))
(CatKeyRule	IF	((GOAL ISSUE MENU-CATEGORY) (STEP CAT KEY-PRESS) (NOTE LOCATE-MENU-CATEGORY FINISHED))
	THEN	((Press-Key N) ((Delete NOTE VARIABLE N) (Delete NOTE VARIABLE MENU-CATEGORY) (Add STEP FINISH CATEGORY) (Delete STEP CAT KEY-PRESS) (Delete NOTE LOCATE-MENU-CATEGORY FINISHED)))
(FinishCategory	IF	((GOAL ISSUE MENU-CATEGORY) (STEP FINISH CATEGORY))
	THEN	((Add NOTE ISSUE-MENU-CATEGORY FINISHED) (Delete GOAL ISSUE MENU-CATEGORY)

(continued on next page)

Figure 16-25 (cont.)

```
                                        (Delete STEP FINISH CATEGORY)
                                        (Delete NOTE EXECUTING ISSUE-MENU-CATEGORY)))

(StartCatLocate            IF      ((GOAL LOCATE MENU-CATEGORY)
                                    (NOT (NOTE EXECUTING LOCATE-MENU-CATEGORY)))
                           THEN    ((Add NOTE EXECUTING LOCATE-MENU-CATEGORY)
                                    (Add STEP ACCESS LTM)))
(AccessLTMRule             IF      ((GOAL LOCATE MENU-CATEGORY)
                                    (STEP ACCESS LTM)
                                    (LTM (MENU-COMMAND category)))
                           THEN    ((Add NOTE VARIABLE MENU-CATEGORY)
                                    (Add STEP MATCH CAT-ITEMS)
                                    (Delete STEP READ CAT-ITEMS)))
(ReadCatRule               IF      ((GOAL LOCATE MENU-CATEGORY)
                                    (STEP READ CAT-ITEMS))
                           THEN    ((DEVICE USER MENUline (Add NOTE VARIABLE MENU-ITEM))
                                    (Add STEP MATCH CAT-ITEMS)
                                    (Delete STEP READ CAT-ITEMS)))
(MatchCatFalse             IF      ((GOAL LOCATE MENU-CATEGORY)
                                    (STEP MATCH CAT-ITEMS)
                                    (MatchWM (NOT (MENU-CATEGORY MENU-ITEM))))
                           THEN    ((Add STEP READ CAT-ITEMS)
                                    (Delete NOTE VARIABLE MENU-ITEM)
                                    (Delete STEP MATCH CAT-ITEMS)))
(MatchCatTrue              IF      ((GOAL LOCATE MENU-CATEGORY)
                                    (STEP MATCH CAT-ITEMS)
                                    (MatchWM (MENU-CATEGORY MENU-ITEM)))
                           THEN    ((Add STEP CATEGORY RETENTION)
                                    (Delete STEP MATCH CAT-ITEMS)))
(CatRetentionRule          IF      ((GOAL LOCATE MENU-CATEGORY)
                                    (STEP CATEGORY RETENTION))
                           THEN    ((DEVICE USER MENU-ITEMnumber (Add NOTE VARIABLE N))
                                    ((Delete NOTE VARIABLE MENU-ITEM)
                                    (Add STEP FINISH CAT-LOCATE)
                                    (Delete STEP CATEGORY RETENTION)))
(FinishCatLocate           IF      ((GOAL LOCATE MENU-CATEGORY)
                                    (STEP FINISH CAT-LOCATE))
                           THEN    ((Add NOTE LOCATE-MENU-CATEGORY FINISHED)
                                    (Delete GOAL LOCATE MENU-CATEGORY)
                                    (Delete STEP FINISH CAT-LOCATE)
                                    (Delete NOTE EXECUTING LOCATE-MENU-CATEGORY)))
```

Figure 16-25 (cont.)

memory information (CatUpdateRule and UpdateCatRule). The updates always occur after the key-press, for Cat-UpdateRule, and after a match for the menu item has been found, for UpdateCat-Rule. The conditions of the two rules to be compacted do not have complementary conditions because the Step names are different. Finally, the control structure would not change because no method return points or selection rules are involved in the rules to be compacted. After compacting the CatUpdateRule with CatKey Rule and UpdateCatRule with CatRetentionRule, the two methods are compacted and the whole production system is reduced by two rules. Similar rules to be compacted for experts could be found in other places in the production system.

SUMMARY

The production system studied in this chapter is very similar to the other models studied in the previous chapters. In fact, Bovair et al. (1990) claim that the production system is exactly equivalent to the NGOMSL model or various combinations of the GOMS models. We have seen in this chapter that some of the statements from NGOMSL, especially the decide statements, are difficult to incorporate in a production system, and this can change the estimates for the number of cycles needed for performing a human-computer interaction task. For the most part, though, the production system model is highly equivalent to the NGOMSL model and the two could be used interchangeably. This is especially the case when estimating execution times, learning times, gains due to consistency, and the workload measurements.

With the two models being so highly similar, what are the reasons for using one over the other? NGOMSL has a fairly simple structure so that the model can be formulated and it could be easily understood when shown to someone else. The statements are in a very concise form, although much of the processing and control structure is implicit to the model instead of being explicitly shown. The production system has much more overhead to it. Developing this kind of model is very difficult because it forces the task analyst to be very precise about when the

Notes are to be added and deleted and the kinds of condition statements accompanying each rule. As can be seen when comparing the production system of Figures 16-14 and 16-16 to the NGOMSL models of Figures 15-4 and 15-5, the production system requires many more statements.

It may be useful to use both models during the course of a task analysis. The NGOMSL model is useful for designing the task analysis in the initial stages. It provides the task analyst with a good overall structure, it can be shown to others in the group to get comments or changes, and it is very concise. With less detail, however, the task analyst could possibly become sloppy and make mistakes or not be specific enough. This is why production system modeling would be useful in the next stage. The structure of NGOMSL would provide the task analyst with an overall structure, a specification of the goals, determination of the selection rules, and the primitive operators. This useful NGOMSL structure can then be used as a guide to the overall production system structure. In particular, the goals, operators, methods, and selection rules would already be specified and the task analyst only has to use the templates to fill in the appropriate statements. In so doing, the task analyst is also forced to be very specific about each of the statements, especially the condition statements of the rules, and the adding and deleting of Notes. Many of these kinds of details could have been forgotten through the NGOMSL analysis.

Two advantages of the production system approach over the NGOMSL approach are that it has a good theoretical basis and that it could be used easily in a computerized simulation. Production systems have been shown in the past to be reasonable models of human performance (Anderson, 1976; Newell and Simon, 1972) for tasks other than human-computer interaction. In addition, the production system is, essentially, a computer program that could be run easily in a simulation to obtain measurements and to test the completeness of the analysis.

QUESTIONS

1. Find solutions to the ship, dock, and cargo problems portrayed in Figures 16-26, 16-27, and 16-28. For each, the figure at the bottom must be filled in based upon the fule firings.

2. An alternative construction for cycles 7 and 8 of the high-breadth display would be to combine them so that MENU-ITEM is not stored in WM over several cycles but is read, compared to the MENU-COMMAND, and then forgotten. This could be shown by combining cycles 7 and 8 into one rule as follows:

    ```
    IF    ((GOAL LOCATE MENU-
              COMMAND)
          (STEP READ ITEMS)
          (MatchWM (NOT (MENU-
              COMMAND (DE-
              VICE USER MENU-
              line
          MENU-ITEM)))))
    THEN  ((Delete STEP READ
              ITEMS)
          (Add STEP READ ITEMS))
    ```

The action part of the rule is done just because something needs to be done. The match rule will be as follows:

```
IF    ((GOAL LOCATE MENU-
          COMMAND)
      (STEP READ ITEMS)
      (MatchWM (MENU-COM-
          MAND (DEVICE
          USER MENUline
          MENU-ITEM))))
THEN  ((Add STEP UPDATE
          ITEMS)
      (Delete STEP READ
          ITEMS))
```

This kind of construction is probably most similar to that which Bovair et al. (1990) had in mind for the Device tag. This should be used when information is displayed on the screen. If the information is displayed on the screen, the user need only read the information, make any matches that need to be made in WM, and then the information does not have to be retained in WM because it is on the screen. The following questions address the implications of this change.

a. Do you think that experts would be more likely to use the above rule construction, or would novices? Why?

b. Recalculate the time estimation using the above rule construction.

c. The preceding change to the rules should have implications for the workload estimation. What changes from the original analysis to the preceding construction? Recalculate the workload based upon the construction.

d. Are there any other places in the original analysis where informa-

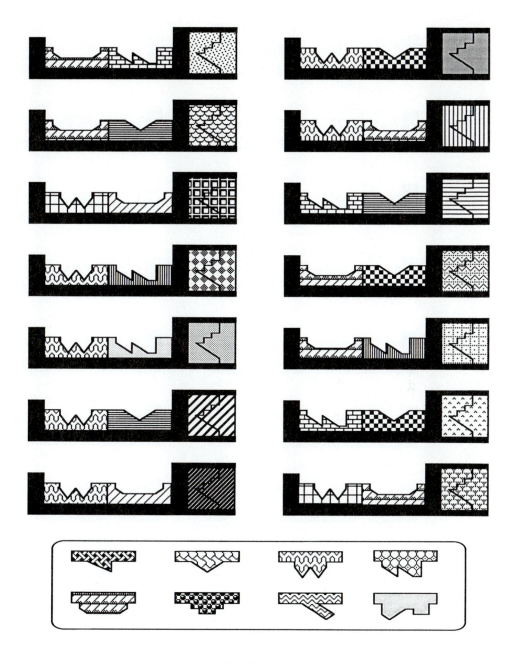

Figure 16-26. Ship, dock, and cargo problem from question 1.

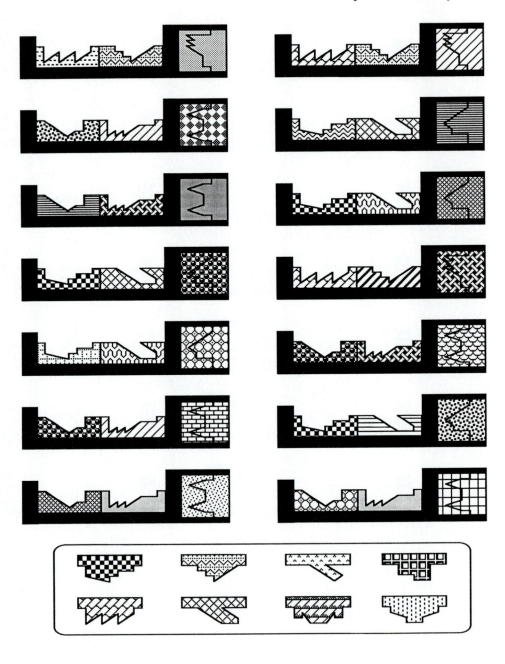

Figure 16-27. The second ship, dock, and cargo problem from question 1.

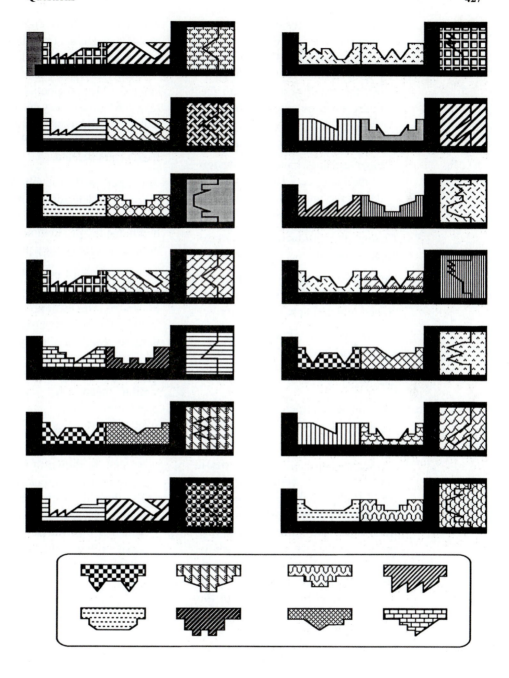

Figure 16-28. The third ship, dock, and cargo problem from question 1.

tion does not have to be explicitly stored in WM but the user could make use of the information displayed on the screen? If so, identify these and perform again the time estimations and the workload analyses.

e. What implication does the Device tag rule change have for the design of the interface? How could you design the interface to reduce the workload of the user?

3. Change the production system to model expert users.

4. Determine the peak workload and workload density for those steps involved in deleting a wrong entry.

5. Determine the workload density for the general case for both the high-depth and high-breadth menu displays.

6. Determine the time estimate for the high-breadth display when deleting an item.

7. A user may be unlikely to verify a menu item entry before hitting the ENTER key. Remove this step from the analysis. Recalculate the execution times, the estimated learning times, and the two workload analyses. Compare this to the high-depth display. This comparison may be fairer because, by the nature of the task, the high-depth display does not allow verification of the entry.

8. Rewrite the appropriate parts of the high-depth analysis so that a user is given the chance to verify an entry. This means that the user would have to enter an ENTER after each menu

item entry. Based upon this new model, recalculate the times for execution, learning, and workload when an item entry does not have to be deleted. Also recalculate these estimates when an entry has to be deleted. Compare these estimates to the high-breadth display with items deleted or not deleted.

9. An expert will probably not verify the entry to determine if it is correct. Rewrite the high-breadth and high-depth display production systems, if needed, to remove any prompts.

10. In Figures 16-18 through 16-20 the method for generalizing rules was illustrated. This method corresponded to the gain from consistency procedure for Methods 3b and 4b illustrated in Figure 15-10 for NGOMSL. Perform rule generalizations in a similar manner for the following problems.

a. Find the set of rules in Figure 16-14 which corresponds to Methods 4a and 5a shown in Figure 15-9. Assume that the user learns Method 4a (the old set of rules) and then learns Method 5a (the new set of rules). Show the rule generalizations which would result in this situation.

b. Find the set of rules in Figure 16-16 which corresponds to Methods 5b and 6b shown in Figure 15-11. Assume that the user learns Method 5b (the old set of rules) and then learns Method 6b (the new set of rules). Show the rule generalizations which would result in this situation.

CHAPTER 17

GRAMMAR REPRESENTATIONS

INTRODUCTION

An interesting research problem in human-computer interaction has been the investigation of techniques to represent the interface languages under a common organizational scheme. In linguistics, this has been done through a production rule grammar (Chomsky, 1964). In computer programming, compilers are designed to translate programming statements into machine code (Lewis, Rosenkrantz, and Stearns, 1976). Several researchers, Moran (1981), Reisner (1981), Young (1981), and Payne and Green (1986, 1989), have developed grammars to describe interactive languages with a goal towards defining a metric for the cognitive complexity and ease of use of these programs.

Grammars were one of the earliest methods used to model human-computer interaction languages. The Reisner (1981) model borrowed many concepts from linguistics by incorporating the BNF (Backus-Naur Form) method. This technique, and others like it, when applied to human-computer interaction tasks can describe complex languages and operating systems in a relatively small number of statements. In many ways, the statements of the grammars are the same as or similar to the production rules discussed in Chapter 16. The BNF grammars emphasized the relationships between the syntax and the actions needed to perform the commands. The Payne and Green grammar, called TAG for Task-Action Grammar, was designed to emphasize the family resemblances among the language elements. In

the following discussion, the Reisner grammar will be discussed first, followed by a discussion of TAG.

REISNER'S GRAMMAR

Generally, a production rule grammar describes a language as a set of rules for specifying correct strings in the language. Linguists have struggled for some time to understand the grammars which underlie languages. Following Reisner (1981), a grammar for a language such as English consists of the following features:

1. a set of terminal symbols (e.g., the words in the language)

2. a set of nonterminal symbols (e.g., invented constructs used to show the structure of the language such as the "noun phrase")

3. a starting symbol (e.g., "S" for sentence)

4. the metasymbols "+", "|", and "::=" (some common meanings for these are "and," "or," and "is composed of," respectively)

5. rules constructed from the above (e.g., S::= noun phase + verb phrase)

The "cognitive grammar," developed by Reisner, uses a similar terminology for describing human-computer interaction languages. The various parts of the above

429

TABLE 17-1
Example of grammar rules (from Reisner, 1981, © IEEE).

---

describe text shape ::= select text background + select text size + describe text typing |
                        select text size + select text background + describe text typing

select text background ::= ADDITIVE BLOCKED SWITCH UP | ADDITIVE BLOCKED
                        SWITCH DOWN

select text size ::= SINGLE-DOUBLE SWITCH UP | SINGLE-DOUBLE SWITCH
                        DOWN

describe text typing ::= initiate typing + continue typing + complete typing

initiate typing ::= symbol operation | typing control operation

typing action ::= symbol operation | continue typing + typing action

symbol operation ::= symbol | symbol operation + symbol

symbol ::= A | B | . . . Z | 1 | 2 | . . . 9 | 0 | ? | . . .

typing control operation ::= SHIFT | | | | | | . . .

continue typing ::= typing action | continue typing + typing action

complete typing ::= NULL

---

grammar, such as words and sentences, can be replaced with human-computer interaction features. In particular, terminal symbols are the actions that a user has to learn and remember, such as hitting a key or positioning a mouse. Nonterminal symbols represent sets of similar actions that can be grouped together, such as sets of drawing actions. The starting symbol is a high-level task to be performed by the user, such as "edit text" for word processing. The metasymbols are the same as in the grammar represented on the previous page. The rules must be constructed for the interaction grammar used; Reisner constructed 101 rules for her particular application.

An Example of the Grammar

An example of a complete section of this production rule grammar is in Table 17-1. In the example, 11 rules are depicted for describing the shape of text. Each nonterminal symbol (the lowercase letters) is defined in terms of other nonterminal symbols or terminal symbols (the uppercase letters or numerals). A terminal symbol means that it can be defined no further. If the definitions are carried all the way through, they ultimately lead to terminal symbols.

A simple run-through of the grammar depicted in Table 17-1 illustrates how it works. First, assume that the overall goal of the user is to describe the text shape. How to do this is described in the first rule. The overall goal, describing the text shape, corresponds to the left side of the statement. The symbol ::= means "is composed of," and the items on the right of this symbol indicate what it is composed of. In particular, describing text shape can be performed in two ways, with the two methods separated by the "|" symbol, meaning "or." Each of the methods is a conjunction of operations which must be performed; the "+" symbol means "and." The "and" feature is similar to the listing of the steps in the NGOMSL model of Chapter 15 or the conjunctions of rules in the production systems of Chapter 16. For the first method, the user must select the text background plus select the text size plus describe the text typing. For the second method, the user must select the text size plus select the text background plus describe the text typing. The difference between the two alternatives is only in the ordering of the first and second items.

Since all the items on the right-hand side of the statement are in lowercase letters, all of these are nonterminal symbols which must in turn be described further by the grammar. Starting with "select text background," the second rule describes how this operation is performed. The user must either put the additive blocked switch up or put it down. Reisner does not fully explain all aspects of this interface, and we can only guess what the additive switch is. Possibly, it is some item on the display which is manipulated directly. In any case, it is a terminal symbol, because of its uppercase letters, and it need not be described further.

The "select text size" operation is described by the third grammar rule. This is composed of two alternatives: putting the single-double switch up or putting it down. Once again, from the description in the paper, we are not sure what this means. It is, again, a terminal operation because it is in uppercase letters.

The only part of the original rule which still needs to be defined is "describe text typing." The description of this is merely a definition of typing in terms of the grammar rules. It could be used to describe any kind of typing task; the rules are not necessarily dependent on the particular application. The fourth rule describes this typing operation as being composed of the conjunction of "initiate typing," "continue typing" and "complete typing." None of these are terminal symbols, because they are in lowercase, and each must be further decomposed.

"Initiate typing" is described in the fifth rule. Reisner separates a symbol operation from a typing control operation. By looking down the list of rules, we see the symbol operation defined as entering one or more symbols. The construction for the symbol operation illustrates how it can be performed iteratively. If only one symbol is needed, then the first part of the disjunction, the "symbol," can be entered. A symbol is associated, from the following rule, with all those characters which are used on the keyboard to type words and sentences. If more than one symbol is to be entered, then the second part of the disjunction, "symbol operation + symbol," can be used. This statement calls itself, providing the iterative capability, so that it can be called continuously until the last symbol in the string is entered.

The second part of "initiate typing," the "typing control operation," incorporates all those keys on the keyboard which are not symbols. Operations such as using the shift key, using the control key, or using the special function keys, can all fall into the category of typing control operations. Typing control operations can only occur one at a time, as evidenced by the rule. This operation does not have the same kind of iterative structure as does the symbol operation, and so, under this grammar, strings of typing control operations cannot occur. In other words, a user would not press SHIFT and then SHIFT again, because the double shift does not accomplish anything. In other tasks, some operations may require sequences of typing control operations and an iterative design for the rule would be needed. As an example, if the task being modeled used arrow keys for cursor control, then an iterative structure for this statement would be needed. Since it is not iterative, the "typing control operation" is defined by terminal symbols such as SHIFT and any others which may be present on the particular keyboard.

Once "initiate typing" has been defined, the next part of "describe text typing," the fourth rule, is to "continue typing." Looking down the list of rules, we see that "continue typing," the next to last rule, has an iterative structure. It is composed of a "typing action," or a "continue typing + typing action." Since "continue typing" calls itself in the second part of the disjunction, it can iterate continuously until no more typing is needed. The "typing action" rule has already been discussed.

Finally, the last part of "describe text typing" is to "complete typing." This is defined in the last rule by the terminal symbol NULL. This means that the user has nothing else to type. The list of things to type is the null set. This part of the task is complete.

Calculations from the Grammar Model

Reisner (1981) used the formal grammar for the interaction language to test two interactive drawing programs to predict which one would be easier to use. This grammar has been used specifically to determine the consistency of the design, defined as the number of rules necessary to describe the structure of some set of terminal strings, and to determine the simplicity of the interaction, defined as the lengths of the terminal strings for particular tasks. Empirical studies on two alternative drawing programs showed that the predictions of the model were accurate; the users found it easier to select the correct actions for the program predicted to be simpler, and the users found it easier to learn and remember the program which was predicted to be consistent. Examples of performing these calculations for the high-breadth and high-depth displays will be performed in a later section of this chapter.

Although not stated explicitly by Reisner, one could assume that execution time for a task could also be determined. Similar to the other models in the previous chapters, execution time would be most likely related to the number of steps needed to perform the task. As each grammar rule is used, this constitutes a particular step. The calculation of the steps needed for the high-breadth and high-depth displays are in a later section of this chapter.

TASK-ACTION GRAMMARS

Payne and Green (1986, 1989) used a very similar grammar, called the Task-Action Grammar (TAG), to investigate consistency in more detail, concentrating on the overall structure of the language rather than individual rules. To accomplish this, TAG represents family resemblances (the overall sentence structure of commands), the degree to which a task language relies on well-learned world knowledge, and the organization of tasks and subtasks. Ease of learning and use depends on the number of simple-task rule schemas, which is based upon the overall structure of the language. Unlike the other predictive models discussed in this section, TAG was designed to make predictions about the relative complexity of designs rather than providing quantitative measures and predictions of performance. In other words, the focus of this model is to generate experimental hypotheses, based upon the model, and then test those hypotheses experimentally. Payne and Green (1989) describe the important aspects of TAG as follows:

1. Identify "simple tasks" that the user can perform without problem solving, and that contain no control structure.

2. Describe simple tasks in a dictionary by sets of semantic components reflecting categorizations of the task world.

3. Rewrite rules which map simple tasks onto action specifications, in which grammatical tokens can be tagged with semantic features derived from the simple-task dictionary. The featural tagging supplies selection restrictions and allows the grammar to capture generalizations, in a way that is the focus of their paper.

The most important aspect of TAG is that it can determine well defined categories of tasks. The tasks with the categories that are well defined are those with the most structural consistency. Arbitrary collections of tasks have poorly defined categories.

Example of a TAG Representation

To help explain some of these concepts, Payne and Green (1989) used TAG to model five commands (copy, rename, copydisk, delete, and create) of the IBM PCDOS operating system (see Figure 17-1). The task-action rule schemas correspond closely to the grammar rules illustrated in the previous section. For the rule schemas, we can see that a task is composed of a name and two parameters: a name, par1, and par2. A name is a nonterminal symbol and is chosen from the five choices based upon the simple task that needs to be performed. As an example, if the task was to delete a file, then the "delete file" in the SIMPLE TASK section of the figure would be found and the features would be noted and matched for the name of the RULE SCHEMAS section (Old = file, New = null, Oldchange? = yes). The name that matches the substitutions maps into the erase command (Payne and Green use —> instead of ::=). The quotation marks, or in some cases capital letters, mean that the symbol is terminal and cannot be further decomposed.

Name has been reduced to a nonter-

TASK FEATURES

Old   file, disk, null
New   file, disk, null
Oldchange?   yes, no

CO-OCCURRENCE RESTRICTIONS

If Old = null THEN Oldchange? not a feature

SIMPLE TASKS

Copy file {Old = file, New = file, Oldchange? = no}
Rename file {Old = file, New = file, Oldchange? = yes}
Copy disk {Old = disk, New = disk, Oldchange? = no}
Delete file {Old = file, New = null, Oldchange? = yes}
Create file {Old = null, New = file}

TASK-ACTION RULE SCHEMAS

Task [Old, New, Oldchange?] —> name {Old, New, Oldchange?}
                                    + par1 [Old] + par2 [New]
name [Old = file, New = file, Oldchange? = yes] —> "ren"
name [Old = file, New = file, Oldchange? = no] —> "copy"
name [Old = file, New = null, Oldchange? = yes] —> "erase"
name [Old = null, New = file] —> "edit"
name [Old = disk, New = disk, Oldchange? = no] —> "diskcopy"
par1 [Old = null] —> NULL
par1 [Old = file] —> drive-id + "filename"
par1 [Old = disk] —> drive-id
par2 [New = null] —> NULL
par2 [New = file] —> drive-id + "filename"
par2 [New = disk] —> drive-id
drive-id —> NULL
drive-id —> "A:"
drive-id —> "B:"
drive-id —> "C:"
drive-id —> "D:"

Figure 17-1. Example of a TAG representation of the IBM PCDOS operating system (from Payne and Green, 1989, reprinted with permission of publisher).

minal symbol, but two more parts, par1 and par2, remain. Decomposing each of these symbols depends on the substitution and matching of the task features which were determined from the simple task. To continue the example, Old = file, so par1 must be mapped into drive-id + "filename". The latter is a terminal symbol, but drive-id is not and must still be decomposed. The last five rules show the five possibilities for drive-id which are all terminal symbols. For par2, New = null, so

command ::= name + oldfile + newfile I name + oldfile I name + newfile
name ::= COPY I REN I COPYDISK I ERASE I EDIT
oldfile ::= drive-id + FILENAME I drive-id
newfile ::= drive-id + FILENAME I drive-id
drive-id —> NULL
drive-id —> "A:"
drive-id —> "B:"
drive-id —> "C:"
drive-id —> "D:"

command ::= name + oldfile + newfile
name ::= COPY I REN I COPYDISK I ERASE I EDIT
oldfile ::= drive-id + FILENAME I drive-id
newfile ::= drive-id + FILENAME I drive-id
drive-id —> NULL
drive-id —> "A:"
drive-id —> "B:"
drive-id —> "C:"
drive-id —> "D:"

command ::= name + par
name ::= COPY I REN I COPYDISK I ERASE I EDIT
par ::= file + par I file
file ::= drive-id + FILENAME I drive-id
drive-id —> NULL
drive-id —> "A:"
drive-id —> "B:"
drive-id —> "C:"
drive-id —> "D:"

Figure 17-2. BNF representation for the five commands of the IBM PCDOS (from Payne and Green, 1989, reprinted with permission of publisher).

par2 will be decomposed into NULL. Since this is in capital letters, this is a terminal symbol and cannot be further decomposed.

TAG is different from BNF-like grammars in one important way: it incorporates task features. This means that family resemblances of commands can be determined instead of showing the mappings for each separate command. As an illustration of this, consider Figure 17-2 which shows three possibilities for what a BNF grammar could look like for the same five commands of the IBM PCDOS. All three possibilities are composed of nine grammar rules, which is considerably fewer than the number of grammar statements needed for TAG. The BNF representation also does not have the task features or the mapping of simple tasks to task features and thus cannot be used easily to determine the family resemblances among the commands.

Constructing a TAG Representation

Payne and Green (1986, 1989) are not very explicit in the specification of applying a TAG representation to a task. They provide several examples, but it is left to the reader to try to extrapolate from the given examples to other tasks. In this section, a more formalized method for applying TAG has been attempted.

Figure 17-3 shows six steps which can be used to apply TAG to the IBM PCDOS problem. In the first step, the structure is written for each of the five commands. This structure is very general in that it does not yet specify the meaning of oldfile and newfile. As can be seen, copy requires two parameters: the file that the user starts with and the name of the file that will be given to the copy. Rename requires two parameters: the original file and the new name for this file. Copydisk requires two parameters: the name of the original disk and the name of the new disk where files will be copied to. Erase requires only one parameter: the name of the file to be erased. Edit requires only one parameter also: the name of the new file to be created.

In step 2, the task analyzer must look at the results from step 1 and try to generalize the command structure so that they can be described in as few overall structure statements as possible. In looking at the step 1 results, we can see that all commands have a command name followed by either one or two parameters corresponding to the files or disks manipulated. If we say that all commands have two parameters and that a parameter may be null (nonexistent), then each command could be conceived as having two parameters and, thus, one overall structure of name plus parameter 1 (the original file or disk) plus parameter 2 (the target file or disk).

In step 3, the task analyzer can place the results of step 2 in a variable/feature relationship. In step 2, two parameters

were identified and the values of those two parameters could change depending on the command; they could be either file, disk, or null. Since the common element of all these, and the element that defines the structure, is whether or not the file or disk is old or new, then Old and New are used for the variable names. The values for the variables are placed to the right for each command.

From step 3, most of the structure of the grammar is already in place. In step 4, the structure is placed into the categories of Task features, Simple tasks, and Task-action Rule schemas. As can be seen from step 3, each of the five tasks has the same kind of structure: the command name followed by two parameters. This kind of structure must be shown in step 4. This is accomplished by indicating that a task, for performing the command, is composed of the three parts of name and two parameters. The variables used for the command are placed within brackets: all the variables which will be used in the decomposition of the task are placed in the left side brackets and the distribution of the variables are placed in the corresponding parts on the right side of the decomposition. This statement with "Task" in it constitutes the main structure of this operating system. Also in this step, the Simple tasks are determined. These Simple tasks are very similar to the concept of a goal from GOMS, NGOMSL, and production systems. They represent, in words, what the user might say when desiring to accomplish some kind of goal using the operating system. The values of the variables for each of the Simple tasks are placed in the brackets. In addition, the variables and possible values are placed under the Task Features heading.

STEP 1 - Start with the commands and their general structure

copy Oldfile + Newfile
rename Oldfile + Newfile
copydisk Olddisk + Newdisk
erase Oldfile
edit Newfile

STEP 2 - Determine if the commands have a general and consistent structure (in this case, two parts with old in the first part and new in the second part)

copy par1[Oldfile] + par2[Newfile]
rename par1[Oldfile] + par2[Newfile]
copydisk par1[Olddisk] + par2[Newdisk]
erase par1[Oldfile] + par2[null]
edit par1[null] + par2[Newfile]

STEP 3 - Place into a variable/feature relationship

copy par1[Old] + par2[New]   Old = file, New = file
rename par1[Old] + par2[New]   Old = file, New = file
copydisk par1[Old] + par2[New]   Old = disk, New = disk
erase par1[Old] + par2[New]   Old = file, New = null
edit par1[Old] + par2[New]   Old = null, New = file

STEP 4 - Generalize by separating into task features, simple tasks, and task-action rule schemas

TASK FEATURES

Old   file, disk
New   file, disk

SIMPLE TASKS

Copy file {Old = file, New = file}
Rename file {Old = file, New = file}
Copy disk {Old = disk, New = disk}
Delete file {Old = file, New = null}
Create file {Old = null, New = file}

TASK-ACTION RULE SCHEMAS

Task [Old, New] —> name [Old, New] + par1[Old] + par2[New]

(continued on next page)

Figure 17-3. Constructing a TAG representation for the IBM PCDOS (from Payne and Green, 1989, reprinted with permission of publisher).

STEP 5 - Expand all parts of task into primitives

TASK FEATURES

Old	file, disk
New	file, disk

SIMPLE TASKS

Copy file {Old = file, New = file}
Rename file {Old = file, New = file}
Copy disk {Old = disk, New = disk}
Delete file {Old = file, New = null}
Create file {Old = null, New = file}

TASK-ACTION RULE SCHEMAS

Task [Old, New] —> name [Old, New] + par1[Old] + par2[New]
name [Old = file, New = file] —> "copy"
name [Old = file, New = file] —> "ren"
name [Old = disk, New = disk] —> "copydisk"
name [Old = file, New = null] —> "erase"
name [Old = null, New = file] —> "edit"
par1 [Old = null] —> NULL
par1 [Old = file] —> drive-id + "filename"
par1 [Old = disk] —> drive-id
par2 [New = null] —> NULL
par2 [New = file] —> drive-id + "filename"
par2 [New = disk] —> drive-id
drive-id —> NULL
drive-id —> "A:"
drive-id —> "B:"
drive-id —> "C:"
drive-id —> "D:"

STEP 6 - Check to ensure that all names are unique (copy and rename are the same); if not, add a feature which will differentiate between the non-unique names

TASK FEATURES

Old	file, disk, null
New	file, disk, null
Oldchange?	yes, no

(continued on next page)

Figure 17-3 (cont.)

CO-OCCURRENCE RESTRICTIONS

If Old = null THEN Oldchange? not a feature

SIMPLE TASKS

Copy file {Old = file, New = file, Oldchange? = no}
Rename file {Old = file, New = file, Oldchange? = yes}
Copy disk {Old = disk, New = disk, Oldchange? = no}
Delete file {Old = file, New = null, Oldchange? = yes}
Create file {Old = null, New = file}

TASK-ACTION RULE SCHEMAS

Task [Old, New, Oldchange?] —> name {Old, New, Oldchange?}
                                                    + par1 [Old] + par2 [New]
name [Old = file, New = file, Oldchange? = yes] —> "ren"
name [Old = file, New = file, Oldchange? = no] —> "copy"
name [Old = file, New = null, Oldchange? = yes] —> "erase"
name [Old = null, New = file] —> "edit"
name [Old = disk, New = disk, Oldchange? = no] —> "diskcopy"
par1 [Old = null] —> NULL
par1 [Old = file] —> drive-id + "filename"
par1 [Old = disk] —> drive-id
par2 [New = null] —> NULL
par2 [New = file] —> drive-id + "filename"
par2 [New = disk] —> drive-id
drive-id —> NULL
drive-id —> "A:"
drive-id —> "B:"
drive-id —> "C:"
drive-id —> "D:"

Figure 17-3 (cont.)

In step 5, all of the nonprimitive parts of the Task-action rule schema must be expanded into primitives. Or, in using the terminology from the BNF grammars, all the nonterminal symbols must be expanded into terminals. Starting to the left on the right side of the rule, the first nonterminal symbol is "name." Since five command names are used in this example, "name" must be decomposed into the five commands. The values for the variables are found within the brackets for each of the commands. The actual command name is enclosed within quotation marks to indicate that it is a terminal symbol and cannot be decomposed further.

The two parameters, par1 and par2, also need to be decomposed into terminal symbols. Par1 always corresponds to the old file or disk or, in some cases, it can be null and does not have to be a part of the command line. The values for the variables are enclosed in the brackets and the decomposition is dependent on the variable value. The "filename" for the decomposition when the value is a file is enclosed within quotation marks to indicate that this is a terminal symbol which must be supplied by the user. NULL, being in capital letters, is also designated as a terminal symbol. The only symbol which is nonterminal is drive-id. The last five statements in step 5 decompose drive-id into terminal symbols. The drive can be designated as NULL, indicating that the default drive is used, or it can be designated as any of the letters between A and D. The decomposition of par2 is very similar.

The last step, step 6, determines whether the combinations of variables and values are unique for each of the simple tasks. In examining the simple tasks, copy file and rename file both have Old equal to file and New equal to file. On these variable-to-value mappings alone, the two commands cannot be differentiated. To differentiate them, a third variable must be introduced which indicates how the two commands are different from each other. To preserve the family resemblance structure of the tasks, this new variable must also be relevant to all the rest of the commands. One difference between copy file and rename file is that a change is made to the old file of rename and no change is made to the old file when copying is performed. If old is present in the other commands, then this feature of Oldchange can be extended to the other commands: copydisk has no change to the old file and delete file changes the old file. Therefore, the variable name of "Oldchange?" can be added to the task features list, to the simple tasks, and to the task-action rule schemas. With this change, the mapping between variable and value is unique for each of the

commands. One further heading must be added to the figure when including the Oldchange? variable: Co-occurrence restrictions. As indicated previously, the Oldchange? could only have an effect when an old file or disk is available for the command. The create file command has no old file or disk to begin with. Therefore, Oldchange? cannot be a feature for this command. The co-occurrence restriction reflects this contingency.

The TAG representation has now been specified for this particular task. These steps should work for most tasks which can be described through TAG. One of the potential problems with TAG, however, is that these steps are not specified very completely by Payne and Green (1986, 1989).

The Use of TAG in Human-Computer Interaction

As mentioned previously, TAG is different from the other predictive models in this section because it does not make absolute performance predictions. Instead, TAG is used mostly to generate hypotheses which can be tested experimentally. TAG can, however, also be used in suggesting design revisions, in determining the consistency of a task, and in evaluating the relative learnability between two or more interface designs.

Design revisions, consistency, and learnability are all evaluated in terms of the top-level rule schema. From the example of Figure 17-1, this top-level rule schema is the rule beginning with the word "Task." An interface is considered to be highly consistent if the whole task can be described using one top-level rule schema, as is the case for the operating system

CONSISTENT INTERFACE

copy sourcefile targetfile
rename sourcefile targetfile
copydisk sourcedisk targetdisk
delete sourcefile
create targetfile

INCONSISTENT INTERFACE

copy sourcefile targetfile
rename targetfile sourcefile
copydisk sourcedisk targetdisk
delete sourcefile
create targetfile

Figure 17-4. Comparison of consistent interface to inconsistent interface.

described in the figure. The task becomes less and less consistent as more top-level rule schemas are needed to describe the task. A consequence of this is that the total number of rules is unimportant; only the number of top-level rule schemas is important for consistency.

Learnability is closely related to the consistency evaluation. An assumption is that most of the learning time is involved in learning the top-level rule schemas and, therefore, learning time is a function of the number of these rules to be learned. Once again, having only the one top-level rule should make the interface of Figure 17-1 easy to learn.

If the interface design contains more than one top-level rule schema, then a revision of the design should be considered. The structure of the commands, if commands are being used, should be evaluated to determine if they can be made more consistent by reducing the number of top-level rule schemas.

An example will illustrate how the above evaluations can be made. In Figure 17-1, the interface for the IBM PCDOS could be described using one top-level rule schema, so this interface would be considered to be highly consistent and easy to learn. No design revisions would be needed. Let's say that we were interested in making an interface design for the IBM PCDOS which was inconsistent and

would be difficult to learn. What would we do? According to the TAG analysis, we would try to construct the language so that we have more than one top-level rule schema.

One way to make the interface inconsistent would be to change the ordering of the parameters based upon characteristics of a particular command or set of commands. As a hypothetical example, consider the commands shown in Figure 17-4. The source file or disk is the file or disk already available when the command is begun; this is similar to the Old variable used previously. The target file or disk is the file or disk which will be the result of the command or the target of the command. As an example, it will be the new file if the result of a copy, or it will be the new file that will be created. The interface design labeled consistent in the figure is consistent because the ordering of the source and target is always the same. Users often use this consistency by saying to themselves "copy sourcefile to targetfile," "copydisk sourcedisk to targetdisk," or "change name of sourcefile to name of targetfile." The word "to" is important to maintain the consistency of the commands.

For the inconsistent interface design, the rename task cannot follow the expression using the word "to." Instead, the command would read something like this: "change the name to targetfile name from the sourcefile name." This expression must use the word "from" between the targetfile and sourcefile in order to make logical sense. So, the user would have to remember that something should be changed <u>to</u> something else for copy and diskcopy and something must be changed <u>from</u> something else for rename. One way to remember this is that if a file is being created, then "to" should be used; if a file is not being created, then "from" should be used.

Everyone would probably agree that the inconsistent interface would be difficult to learn and remember. Can TAG capture this kind of inconsistency? Can it capture the consistency that does exist, namely that the ordering of the parameters is dependent on whether a file is created or not? Figure 17-5 shows the TAG representation of the inconsistent interface. Some changes were made from the consistent interface for the task analysis. First, the most obvious change is that two top-level rule schemas are needed to represent this inconsistent interface, one more than the consistent interface. These top-level rules show that the target-source ordering is used sometimes and the source-target ordering is used at other times for the parameters. The ordering is dependent on whether or not a file is created. This is captured by TAG by designating a variable "Create" and determining the value of the variable (yes or no) depending on the action of the command. In the top-level rules, the first rule is used in the case where files are not created and the second rule is used in the case where files are created.

Some other changes are made from Figure 17-1 to Figure 17-5. As indicated previously, the Old variable is now called

Source and the New variable is now called Target. Using Source, Target, and Create does not differentiate between copy and rename, so another variable, Delete, must be introduced to differentiate between them. The Delete variable designates whether a file is deleted or not. For copy, the source is not deleted, and for rename, the source name is deleted. Each of the variable/value mappings is now unique. All of the other parts of the task analysis are the same between the two interfaces.

Using this analysis, the number of rules is not much different between the consistent and the inconsistent interface: the consistent interface has 17 rules and the inconsistent interface has 18 rules. The inconsistent interface has a 6% increase in the number of rules over the consistent interface. If TAG just considered the number of rules, we would expect small differences in consistency or learnability. As emphasized previously, however, the important evaluatory measure is the number of top-level rules and not the number of total rules. The consistent interface has one top-level rule, and the inconsistent interface has two top-level rules. In terms of percentages, this is a 100% increase in the number of top-level rules for the inconsistent interface as compared to the consistent interface. This one rule increase becomes very important in the TAG analysis.

Payne and Green (1989) conducted an experiment to test the hypothesis that the number of top-level rules is more important in learnability than the total number of rules. They designed one interface, which they hypothesized to be consistent, that could be described using TAG by 28 rules, one of which was a top-level rule. A different interface design, hypothesized to

TASK FEATURES

Source	file, disk,null
Target	file, disk,null
Delete	yes,no
Create	yes,no

SIMPLE TASKS

Copy file {Source = file, Target = file, Delete = no, Create = yes}
Rename file {Source = file, Target = file, Delete = no, Create = no}
Copy disk {Source = disk, Target = disk, Delete = no, Create = yes}
Delete file {Source = file, Target = null, Delete = yes, Create = no}
Create file {Source = null, Target = file, Delete = no, Create = yes}

TASK-ACTION RULE SCHEMAS

Task [Source = file, Target, Delete, Create = no] —> delname [Source, Target, Delete, Create] + tgt [Target] + src [Source]
Task [Source, Target, Delete, Create = yes] —> createname [Source, Target, Delete, Create]+ src [Source] + tgt [Target]
delname [Source = file, Target = file, Delete = no, Create = no] —> "ren"
delname [Source = file, Target = null, Delete = yes, Create = no] —> "erase"
createname [Source = file, Target = file, Delete = no, Create = yes] —> "copy"
createname [Source = disk, Target = disk, Delete = no, Create = yes] —> "diskcopy"
createname [Source = null, Target = file, Delete = no, Create = yes] —> "edit"
tgt [Target = null] —> NULL
tgt [Target = file] —> drive-id + "filename"
tgt [Target = disk] —> drive-id
src [Source = null] —> NULL
src [Source = file] —> drive-id + "filename"
src [Source = disk] —> drive-id
drive-id —> NULL
drive-id —> "A:"
drive-id —> "B:"
drive-id —> "C:"
drive-id —> "D:"

Figure 17-5. Hypothetical disorganized version of IBM PCDOS using TAG (from Payne and Green, 1989, reprinted with permission of publisher).

be inconsistent, could be described by 12 rules, 8 of which were top-level rules. If the number of total rules was important, then learning should take longer for the 28-rule interface than for the 12-rule interface. If the number of top-level rules was important, then learning should take longer for the 12-rule interface than for the 28-rule interface. The results of an experiment supported the predictions from the TAG analysis: learning was faster for the 28-rule interface as compared to the 12-

rule interface. Although the rules used in TAG are not equivalent to the rules used in the production system model considered in Chapter 15, the other models would probably have a difficult time explaining this result for consistency.

In a variation on TAG, Howes and Young (1991) have developed a model in which learnability and consistency can be determined not from specifying all the task-action mappings, as in TAG, but by providing the Programmable User Model (PUM) with examples for how to perform the task. As an example, the PUM can learn how to perform a menu pull-down task when provided with one example. Learnability is assessed by how quickly PUM can acquire the rule for the learning. Consistent interfaces can be learned faster than inconsistent interfaces.

Other TAG Applications

Payne and Green (1989) used the IBM PCDOS application for their examples. In fact, TAG seems to have been developed mostly for command-based operating systems, such as PCDOS, and thus has found much success in this application area. Although command-based interfaces are flexible and generally usable, these have been deemphasized recently with the success of direct manipulation interfaces such as the Apple Macintosh operating system. Thus, a challenge for TAG has been to apply the same kinds of techniques to the interfaces which no longer rely on commands, but rely on direct manipulations and drawing-type tasks.

Many of the recent applications of TAG have been geared more toward direct manipulation interfaces. Schiele and Green (1990) provide a rather informal example

for how TAG has been applied to a drawing task such as MacDraw. In the example, they show the consistencies between drawing rectangles and ellipses in MacDraw, and contrast this to a program which does not exhibit this consistency. The MacDraw program is consistent because only one top-level rule is needed to describe rectangles and ellipses; the inconsistent drawing program needs two top-level rules for these two shapes.

The main part of the Schiele and Green (1990) paper is devoted to a formal analysis of three programs in the Macintosh environment: Multiplan, MacDraw, and MacWrite. Multiplan is a spreadsheet application, MacDraw is a drawing program, and MacWrite is a text-editing program. The analysis using TAG helps to prove why the Macintosh system has been so popular. Apple has provided programming support software, in the form of toolkits, to software developers. These toolkits provide the developers with a certain look to the interface, what is often called the look-and-feel, so that all the Macintosh interfaces incorporate similar features. The TAG analysis shows that these different application programs for the Macintosh are highly consistent even though they perform very different tasks.

Another paper by Howes and Payne (1990) also concentrates on how TAG can be applied to direct manipulation and menu display tasks. This paper also contrasts, in an important way, the TAG model with the GOMS or production system approach. In the latter approaches, Howes and Payne claim that an inordinate amount of attention is focused on the user's preconceived goal hierarchies. This may be inappropriate in many tasks where the user is responding to cues on the display in order to

choose menu item ::= digit operation + complete entry
digit operation ::= digit + digit operation | digit
complete entry ::= ENTER
digit ::= 0 | 1 | 2 | 3 | 4 | 5 | 6 | 7 | 8 | 9

Figure 17-6. BNF grammar representation for the high-breadth menu display.

choose menu item ::= select main menu + select secondary menu
select main menu ::= digit
select secondary menu ::= digit
digit ::= 0 | 1 | 2 | 3 | 4 | 5 | 6 | 7 | 8 | 9

Figure 17-7. BNF grammar representation for high-depth menu display.

formulate a response. In such a case, the goal hierarchy may not be used because the goal or plan cannot be formulated until information is displayed on the screen. Howes and Payne show an example of how TAG can stress these external cues in the formulation of actions. In the high-breadth and high-depth menu displays, discussed throughout this book section on predictive models, an assumption has been that the user has an idea of the steps needed to find and enter the correct menu item. The research by Howes and Payne indicate that this may be an unrealistic assumption; the user may not know what to do until the menu item appears on the screen and the user utilizes this external cue to carry out a response.

APPLICATION OF GRAMMARS TO MENU DISPLAY ANALYSIS

Throughout this section of the book, the models have been used to show how the high-breadth and high-depth menu displays would be modeled and to examine the predictions about human performance which could be made from those models. Since two grammars, BNF and TAG, have been considered in this chapter, two separate representations will be presented.

The BNF Representation

The BNF representation for the high-breadth and high-depth displays is shown in Figures 17-6 and 17-7. Each display can be described by four grammar rules. For the high-breadth display, the overall task is to choose a menu item. This can be composed of a digit operation and a complete entry. Both of these are nonterminal and so must be decomposed further. A digit operation is composed of a digit and a digit operation, providing it with a recursive structure so that it can accept multiple digits or a single digit. If the menu item number is less than 10, then a single digit is needed. If the menu item is 10 or more, then another digit is needed and the digit operation is repeated. On the repeat of the digit operation, the remaining single digit is entered. The specification of a digit is a nonterminal symbol, and the last rule indicates the OR'ed choices for the digits. From the first rule, a complete entry is also a nonterminal symbol. The third rule shows that a complete entry is described by the ENTER key.

The representation for the high-depth display is slightly different. In this case, choosing a menu item involves selecting from the main menu and selecting from the secondary menu. Each selection requires a single digit. A digit is a nonterminal symbol; the last rule shows the terminal symbol possibilities for a digit.

Prediction of Execution Time. Execution time will be predicted by the number of steps needed to complete the task. For the high-breadth display, the following nonterminal steps must be completed to perform the task:

> choose menu item
> digit operation
> digit
> complete entry

This is the case when the user only has to enter one digit for the menu item. If two digits are needed, then the following steps would be performed:

> choose menu item
> digit operation
> digit
> digit operation
> digit
> complete entry

In the one-digit situation, four steps are needed. In the two-digit situation, six steps are needed. If each menu item has an equal probability of being chosen, then the average number of steps needed to perform the task would be:

4 steps + 10/16 (2 steps) = 5.25 steps

For the high-depth display, the following nonterminal steps would be needed to perform the task:

> choose menu item
> select main menu

digit
select secondary menu
digit

This task requires five steps total. From this analysis, we would predict that the high-depth menu display could be performed slightly faster than the high-breadth menu display. Notice that this analysis only accounts for the executable parts of the task, similar to the Keystrokes-Level model of GOMS, and not for the cognitive processing of the task.

Consistency. The grammar can be used to determine the consistency of the design, and Reisner (1981) defined this as the number of rules necessary to describe the structure of some set of terminal strings. In this case, the analysis is very simple. One has only to look at Figures 17-6 and 17-7 and count the number of rules. Both menu displays have four rules, so the model would predict no differences in consistency between the two menu displays. This analysis is slightly different from the consistency analyses for NGOMSL and the production system model, called consistency gains in those cases, in that by the other models predicted that the high-depth display would have higher consistency.

Simplicity. Reisner (1981) also states that the grammar can be used to determine the simplicity of the interaction. This is defined as the lengths of the terminal strings for particular tasks. In Figures 17-6 and 17-7, both the high-breadth and high-depth displays have the same terminal string, so we would expect no differences in terms of consistency between the two displays. What is meant by simplicity? It could mean that a simpler display is faster to execute, and thus it is related to the execution time. Most likely it means that a

TASK FEATURES

digits   one, two

SIMPLE TASKS

Choose a menu item below 10 {digits = one}
Choose a menu item 10 or above {digits = two}

RULE SCHEMAS

Task [digits = one] —> keypress + complete entry
Task [digits = two] —> keypress + keypress + complete entry
keypress —> "digit"
complete entry —> ENTER

Figure 17-8. TAG representation of the high-breadth display.

SIMPLE TASKS

Choose a menu item

TASK-ACTION RULE SCHEMAS

Task —> Menu1 + Menu2
Menu1 —> keypress
Menu2 —> keypress
keypress —> "digit"

Figure 17-9. TAG representation of the high-depth display.

simpler display is easy to learn. Simplicity can be equated with learnability.

The TAG Representation

The TAG representation of the high-breadth and high-depth displays is shown in Figures 17-8 and 17-9. Because this menu operation is so simple, the BNF and TAG representations are very similar: for both models, both displays can be described in four rules. For the high-depth display, the user would have a choice of Simple tasks based upon the menu item number: if below 10 then the variable digits has a value of one; for 10 and above the variable digits will have a value of two. The rule schemas show that two top-level tasks are needed, depending on the number of the menu item. All parts of the top-level task are nonterminal symbols which can be further decomposed. A key-press can be decomposed into a terminal digit, and the complete entry can be decomposed into a terminal ENTER key.

The TAG representation for a high-depth display is shown in Figure 17-9. In this case, there is only one Simple task, which is to choose the menu item. Because of this, we do not need to specify variables and features of the variables. Both Menu1 and Menu2 are decomposed into a single key-press. A key-press must be a digit.

Execution Time. The main focus of the TAG analysis of the task is not on execution time but rather it is on consistency of the task. Thus, Payne and Green (1989) make no predictions about execution time. However, as with the other models, we could make the simple assumption that the model which shows the fewest number of steps needed could be executed fastest. This may be too simple of an assumption, because consistency should also have some effect on execution time. As an example, a task which is consistent could come to be performed with little cognitive processing, and thus very fast, whereas an inconsistent task would need much cognitive processing and thus would be performed slowly.

Just looking at the number of steps needed, we see that the high-breadth display would require the following steps for the nonterminal rules:

> task
> key-press
> complete entry

The preceding steps would hold for one entering one digit. For two digits, the following steps would be needed:

> task
> key-press
> key-press
> complete entry

With equal probability of choosing any menu item, the number of steps needed on average would be

$$3 \text{ steps} + 10/16 \text{ step} = 3.63 \text{ steps} \quad (17.1)$$

The high-depth display would require the following steps:

> task
> Menu1
> Menu2
> key-press

This would require four steps for its operation. Since the high-depth display requires more steps, we would say that this display should be slightly slower to operate when compared to the high-breadth display. This is the only model which makes the prediction in this direction.

Consistency. The TAG representation primarily is designed to capture the consistency differences between the two displays. For TAG, consistency is determined by the number of top-level rules. The TAG analysis shows that the high-depth display is more consistent than the high-breadth display because only one top-level task is needed for the high-depth display and two top-level tasks are needed for the high-breadth display. Even though they both have the same number of rules, the high-depth display should be more consistent. Payne and Green (1989) equate learnability with consistency.

One problem with the TAG representation, and with the other modeling techniques, is that alternative representations making slightly different predictions are also logical. In particular, the high-breadth display could be modeled using one top-level task if the second key-press could take a value of NULL when the menu item number is less than 10. With only one top-level task, the consistencies and learnability of the high-depth and high-breadth displays should be the same. This is an exercise at the end of this chapter.

SUMMARY

The grammars are especially useful for evaluating consistency of the interface design and for offering design revisions based upon consistency. For BNF grammars, consistency is related to the number of grammar rules needed to describe the interface. For the TAG model, consistency is related to the number of top-level rules. In some cases, BNF and TAG may make dissimilar predictions about the consistency of an interface. For the high-breadth display, the BNF grammar predicted no difference between the interfaces while the TAG model predicted a difference. The TAG model corresponded more closely to the predictions of the other models discussed in this section of the book.

Payne and Green (1989) equate consistency with the learnability of the interface. Those displays which are consistent, through a TAG analysis, should be easier to learn than those displays which are inconsistent according to TAG. Experimental results on interfaces hypothesized to be consistent and inconsistent confirmed their predictions.

Out of all the models considered in this section of the book, the grammar models are probably most appropriate for complex systems. The menu interaction task considered in this chapter and the other chapters was probably too simple to model effectively with the grammars. Out of all the models considered, the grammars required the fewest number of statements. One characteristic of the grammars is that they could not be taken to a low level of detail such as eye movements, matching items in memory, or making decisions. Many of the fine-level cognitive activities could not be easily modeled or have not been traditionally modeled using these techniques. This means that if a task has a large component devoted to these kinds of cognitive activities, then some of the other models would be appropriate, especially the Model Human Processor, NGOMSL, or production systems. If the task is fairly complex and the fine-detail cognitive activities are minimal or nonessential to the task, then these grammars can be used.

The grammars also make no predictions about execution time or mental workload. Performance for a particular task could be unimportant if one is just analyzing a large-scale interface design without considering particular tasks or "benchmarks." If mental workload is considered along the lines of consistency, then perhaps the grammars could be altered to consider this concept. The other models did not provide a complete analysis of mental workload.

Table 17-2 compares all the models considered in this section across execution time, learnability, consistency, workload, and expert/novice differences. Some of the models can be used to make these kinds of predictions, and others cannot.

For execution time, the Model Human Processor, the Keystrokes-Level GOMS model, NGOMSL, and production systems can all be used to make quantitative predictions. All of them predict that the high-breadth display will be slower than the high-depth display. The actual estimates vary depending on the model. The Model Human Processor places most of the emphasis on the cognitive processing of the material and little emphasis on its execution. The Keystrokes-Level model, on the other hand, places most of

TABLE 17-2

Comparison of high-breadth and high-depth menu displays for all models

Model	High-Breadth Display	High-Depth Display
Execution Time		
Model Human Processor	3.47 sec.	2.38 sec.
GOMS Goal Stack	33 steps	24 steps
GOMS Keystrokes-Level	1.84 sec.	1.75 sec.
NGOMSL	6.39 sec.	4.30 sec.
Production System	5.28 sec.	4.90 sec.
BNF Grammar	5.25 steps	5 steps
TAG Grammar	3.63 steps	4 steps
Learnability		
Model Human Processor	No prediction	No prediction
GOMS Goal Stack	6 methods	4 methods
GOMS Keystrokes-Level	No prediction	No prediction
NGOMSL	48.5-78.5 min.	45-75 min.
Production System	33.4 min.	23.6 min.
BNF Grammar	No difference (4 rules)	No difference (4 rules)
TAG Grammar	2 top-level rules	1 top-level rule (easier)
Consistency		
Model Human Processor	No prediction	No prediction
GOMS Goal Stack	No prediction	No prediction
GOMS Keystrokes-Level	No prediction	No prediction
NGOMSL	1.5 min. gain	5.0 min. gain
Production System	Reduce 43 rules to 39	Reduce 34 rules to 22
BNF Grammar	4 rules	4 rules
TAG Grammar	2 top-level rules	1 top-level rule (more consistent)
Workload		
Model Human Processor	No prediction	No prediction
GOMS Goal Stack	No prediction	No prediction
GOMS Keystrokes-Level	No prediction	No prediction
NGOMSL	Peak of 7 items	Peak of 8 items
	Density of 4.61*	Density of 5.14*
Production System	Peak of 7 items	Peak of 8 items
	Density of 4.50*	Density of 4.95*
BNF Grammar	No prediction	No prediction
TAG Grammar	No prediction	No prediction
Expert/Novice Differences		
Model Human Processor	Use Fast Man model	Use Fast Man model
GOMS Goal Stack	No prediction	No prediction
GOMS Keystrokes-Level	Only typing skill	Only typing skill
NGOMSL	Combine steps	Combine steps
Production System	Combine rules	Combine rules
BNF Grammar	No prediction	No prediction
TAG Grammar	No prediction	No prediction

*not the general case, for item 14

the emphasis on the execution, not the cognitive processing. NGOMSL and production systems emphasize both aspects of the task about equally.

The GOMS Goal Stack model and the two grammar models do not make specific time estimates for executing tasks. Execution time depends on the number of statements or steps needed to execute the task. For the GOMS Goal Stack, the high-breadth display should be slower because it requires 33 steps as compared to the 24 steps of the high-depth display. For the grammars, the modelers do not state explicitly the relationship between number of steps and the execution time, one can only assume the implicit relationship. The BNF grammar predicts that the high-breadth display has more steps and, thus, would require more execution time. The TAG grammar makes the opposite prediction. The high-depth display would require more steps. This is the only model that makes this prediction.

The second section of Table 17-2 displays the predictions for learnability of the displays. The GOMS Goal Stack, NGOMSL, production system, and BNF grammar models can all predict learning time by determining the number of rules or methods which must be learned. For NGOMSL and production systems, specific learning time predictions can be made from the number of methods to be learned. The others are not so explicit in the prediction. Three of the models (GOMS Goal Stack, NGOMSL, and production systems) predict that the high-breadth display will require more methods and, thus, will take longer to learn. The BNF grammar model predicts no differences in the number of methods.

The exception to the technique for estimating learnability is the TAG grammar model. TAG equates learnability with consistency of the task. Consistency can be determined through the number of top-level rules for performing the task. Experimentation showed that the number of rules was not a determinant of consistency. From this analysis, the high-breadth display has two top-level rules and the high-depth display has one top-level rule. The high-depth display should be easier to learn. The two other models (Model Human Processor and GOMS Keystrokes-Level) make no predictions about learnability.

The third part of Table 17-2 examines predictions for consistency. NGOMSL and production system models determine consistency through the gains due to consistency. Some methods or rules are highly similar so that they do not need to be learned again. The estimated gain due to consistency can be determined exactly from these two models, and both predict that the high-depth display will have a higher consistency gain. For TAG, because learnability and consistency are the same, the top-level rule is considered. TAG also predicts that the high-depth display is more consistent than the high-breadth display. The BNF grammar predicts no difference between the two displays.

Only the NGOMSL and production system models are designed to predict mental workload of the task. Workload is measured according to the peak workload and the density, or average, workload over all steps. Both predict that the high-breadth display will have less workload.

Finally, some models can be used to determine differences between experts and novices. Only one model, the production system model, has been designed explicitly to determine expert/novice differences. Bovair, Kieras, and Polson (1990) worked out several techniques for combining and compacting rules to capture these differences. To a lesser extent, some of the steps in the NGOMSL model can be combined for the experts. These procedures are not stated explicitly in Kieras (1988), however. Finally, some aspects of the other models capture some of the expert/novice differences. For the Model Human Processor, the Fast Man model could be used for the experts and the Slow Man model could be used for the novices. For the GOMS Keystrokes-Level model, the only skill differences would be in typing speed. The tables provide estimates for keystroke times based upon typing skill.

Each of the models considered in this section of the book can be used for different aspects of the analysis of human-computer interaction tasks. The NGOMSL and production system models are the most comprehensive of all the models; but one could also argue that because of the comprehensiveness of these models, they may only consider surface characteristics of the aspect they are trying to measure. As an example, the workload measures only capture one small part of workload, the load on working memory, because this is most easily determined from the model. Other workload measures, such as the amount of attentional resources required for a task, are not considered. The Keystrokes-Level model can be used for a quick determination of execution times. The grammars are probably best for complex tasks in which consistency of the task is an important characteristic. Placing all the emphasis on consistency, instead of being a comprehensive model, may not be a bad approach because of the importance of consistency in usability of the interface (e.g., Nielsen, 1989).

QUESTIONS

1. Change the grammar in Table 17-1 to incorporate cursor control through the arrow keys on a keyboard. In the rules, the "initiate typing" rule would need to be expanded to include cursor control. Then cursor control would need to be defined. At some point, the cursor control operation must end in terminal symbols.

2. The TAG representation of the high-breadth display can be changed around slightly to incorporate a null key-press for the second key-press of the top-level task if the menu item number is less than 10.

    a. Make this change to the TAG representation of the high-breadth display.

    b. Compare your new representation to the high-depth display. What kind of relative predictions would this make about the relative consistency and learnability of the two displays?

    c. Is there any way to determine from the specification of TAG which model is correct for the high-breadth display: keeping the two top-level tasks or the one top-level task?

3. One of the easiest machines to use is the telephone. It also happens to be one of the most difficult to use if you want to do anything more than just

place a call.   In the following questions, you will be asked to evaluate the current functions for the Purdue phone system (hold, transfer, consultation with campus phone, three-way conference, and camp on busy campus telephone) and design new functions, based upon the principles discussed in this book. The descriptions for the phone functions are as follows.

HOLD

Flash
Touch *12
Hang up

To reconnect
touch #12

3-WAY CONFERENCE

Flash
Touch campus no.
Announce call
Flash

TRANSFER

Flash
Touch campus no.
Announce call
Hang up

CAMP ON BUSY CAMPUS
TELEPHONE

Flash
Touch *11
Hang up
To cancel touch #11

CONSULTATION WITH
CAMPUS PHONE

Flash
Touch campus no.
Consult
Flash

The phone has 12 keys starting with the "1" in the upper left corner and sequencing down.   The "0" on the bottom row is flanked by a "*" key on the left and a "#" key on the right. Use this information to answer the following questions.

a.   Outline how you would evaluate this phone system. You do not have to do the evaluations. You should be able to look at the design and indicate which evaluations would be the most important. You should refer to Chapter 1 to find guidance for how to evaluate the system. (Discuss the predictive models in the next question.)

b.   Which of the predictive models would be best for modeling this telephone system? You do not have to do the modeling. Discuss why these models would be most appropriate.

c.   Which predictive models would be inappropriate for modeling this design? Discuss why these models would be inappropriate.

d.   If you were working on a design team for evaluating and redesigning this phone system, describe the process which could be used to enable the design to be incorporated efficiently and quickly.

CHAPTER 18

HUMAN-HUMAN COMMUNICATION

INTRODUCTION

People communicate with other people in varied and rich ways. When interacting with computer systems, people are much more limited in the methods and techniques which can be used. Under the anthropomorphic approach, in which we try to design human-computer interaction to be as close as possible to human-human interaction, knowing how humans interact with each other can provide ideas about how to design effective human-computer interactions.

Think about the ways that humans interact with one another. We certainly use words to interact with one another; but are the words that we use placed in perfect sentences, or do we use the question form of a sentence when we don't understand or need to ask questions? Ideally, we would like to communicate with each other as we see professionals communicating on television or in other media. A few years back, a large American communications company was testing the consumer acceptability of video conferencing in which a video camera would be used in several different sites to hold meetings among the participants. One of the impediments to acceptability of these systems was the reaction of the high-level executives. When these high-powered people saw themselves on television for the video conferencing, they saw that they were not nearly as professional as the professional entertainers or communicators they were used to seeing on television. They did not have the luxury of teleprompters, profes-

sional make-up, or the studied use of effective mannerisms. They were disillusioned to find that their words did not flow in complete sentences and that their thoughts were often inarticulate. If we communicate with a computer in natural language, would we have to expect that our words could be placed in nice complete sentences which could be diagrammed easily electronically?

Gestures and facial expressions are important in communication with other people. A few years back one of the soft drink companies had a series of commercials on American television of people communicating with each other. We could hear the words of the people but the camera never showed their faces. Instead, the camera would show a close-up of the person's hands which could be used to emphasize ideas or to point in certain directions. The camera would show the legs being crossed or a foot being tapped, and one could see how these movements were essential to the understanding of the words. Gestures and body language are an important method of communication. This point is further emphasized if you watch people talk on the phone. Even if the person on the other end of the phone cannot see what you are doing, people still have a tendency to use hand gestures when talking on the phone. Not even car phones constrain the use of hand gestures. It was disturbing to notice on a busy freeway that a person in one of the cars was driving with one hand holding the phone and the other hand providing the important gestures needed to emphasize the words spoken on the phone. Gestures such as these are often an unavoidable means of communicating with other people. Should this kind of communication be incorporated in human-computer interactions?

Facial expressions are also important in communication. When communicating, we watch the other person's face to receive signs of understanding, encouragement, anger, questioning, and so forth. We base the form of our communication on how we perceive the other person is understanding our words through their facial expressions.

In many cases, the computer plays the role of providing knowledge to the user similar to how a teacher would communicate knowledge to a student. In this case, the computer would have to have similar characteristics to the best teachers. Good teachers know when students have questions before the questions are asked. They know when the students may not even know why they are confused so that an intelligent question cannot be addressed. Good teachers know when the presentation of the material is too difficult for everybody to understand and know that further explanations are needed before moving on to the next material. This can be done by noticing the kinds of facial expressions or gestures that are used to indicate stress. Good teachers know the characteristics of the students so that the material can be presented at the right level of difficulty and so that potential problems in understanding can be addressed before they become problems.

Finally, good communicators seem to have a good understanding of their audience or try to have a set method of understanding their audience before serious communication takes place. Good communicators will often spend the first minutes asking questions of the other person before tailoring the message to a certain person. As an example, the most effective salespeople are usually the ones who know their audience when trying to sell something. They want to tailor their sales pitch to the perceived needs of the customer. When selling a car, the successful salesperson will know the important selling points for a particular kind of customer based upon initial impressions or questions. If a customer comes in with a family, the salesperson could mention safety or comfort. If the customer is single, then performance could be emphasized. When evaluating a car customer, the salesperson will often look to see what kind of car the person drove in to understand the points to emphasize for the next car purchase. In other words, for effective communication, the communicator must have a schema of the other person in order to know what the person needs or what the person knows so that the important information can be filled in. When talking with a foreigner, one must be very careful to construct the words and sentences so as not to rely on communication assuming the same kind of cultural background. Idioms have to be avoided, reliance on common cultural experiences are to be avoided, and obviously shared experiences through the mass media that cannot be expected from someone in another culture are also to be avoided. Spending time in another country can be exhausting due to trying to communicate with others. Many of the ways of communicating which are easy in your own country would have to be explained before communication could occur in another country. You must constantly think whether the people you are

456 Chap. 18 Human-Human Communication

communicating with would have the same kinds of schemas as you. If not, the schemas must be communicated before normal communication can occur. These kinds of experiences can help to explain how difficult communication is with a computer which is, in most cases, just an empty box. Effective communication requires some knowledge of schemas or stereotypical situations. Some effort is being made to make computer communication easier by including this stereotypical information in the computer.

Understanding human-human communication can be an important source of information in the design of human-computer interaction. In some cases, human-human communication has been studied experimentally to determine the characteristics which have to be present in human-computer interaction. The first section of this chapter addresses the use of experiments in human-human communication to define the parameters of human-computer interaction. In this introduction, some of the ways that people communicate with each other have been discussed: using gestures, facial expressions, and by understanding people's schemas.

HUMAN-HUMAN COMMUNICATION EXPERIMENTS

In this methodology, humans interacting with each other in experimental settings, sometimes in natural settings, are used to specify the characteristics needed in an effective computer system. The information collected through this experimentation can then be used in the specifications of human-computer interaction environments. Some of the experiments have

addressed the size of computer vocabularies needed if people are to interact with computers using natural language, the kinds of grammars that can be used, or the ability to communicate strategies among communicators. Instead of addressing these human-computer interaction issues blindly, this experimental method provides a means of defining and specifying important design parameters inexpensively before a prototype or mock-up has been built. In addressing each of these experiments, the experiment will be explained and then the implications for human-computer interaction design will be discussed.

Querying the Computer

In many kinds of human-computer interaction environments, the user must query the computer. For database programs, the computer has many items of information stored in memory. To access these data, the user must be able to address a query using the right kind of words to retrieve the information needed. In a computerized card catalogue in a library, to find the call number of the correct book, the user must be able to ask the right question of the computer to retrieve the needed information. The example in the first chapter showed that this kind of query can be difficult for novice users. Designers would like to be able to design a computer system that is easy to query.

People are fairly good at addressing questions to other people, but we seem to have trouble addressing queries to computers. What is the reason for this? One way to examine this issue is to look at how people address questions to other people. In a natural setting, a source of information about how people ask questions is to study radio call-in shows. Pollack, Hirschberg, and Webber (1982) recorded and analyzed the dialogues that occurred from a radio call-in show. They found that the callers rarely asked the radio host well-formulated questions. Instead, the caller and the host had to formulate the question and spend some time defining the terms.

An implication of this experiment is that addressing a question to a computer could be a very difficult task—more difficult than we would have thought intuitively without doing an experiment. The computer, to be natural, intelligent, and perform like a human, must be able to do more than just answer questions. It may also have to help formulate the question. In interacting with an operating system, the user may not be aware that a functionality exists or that a sequence of commands could be performed more efficiently some other way. As an example, if you work with the UNIX operating system, you may not be aware that there is a command, called common, for comparing two files and listing the common lines. What kind of question would you ask to find this information? A question that you could ask UNIX would be: What does common do? By the time you could ask that question, however, you probably would already know the answer. Formulating the question is the difficult part.

The overall implication of this experiment is that the computer may have to help ask questions before the user can determine the correct question to ask. As an example with UNIX again, you may not be aware that there may be efficient and inefficient methods for performing the same command sequence. You can't ask the computer if there is a more effi-

cient method. Perhaps in a natural setting the communicator would monitor someone to see if they are doing something efficiently. If not, then the communicator would ask if the other person would like to know a more efficient method for performing the command. This has been done for efficient and inefficient computer commands. Eberts, Villegas, Phillips, and Eberts (1991) used a neural network to monitor users performing various kinds of computer commands. If the users were not performing the commands efficiently, then the computer would notice this and ask the users if they would like to use a more efficient command sequence. Most of the users were not aware of these more efficient methods but were able to improve their efficiency through the suggestions of the computer. This shows that by the time the person knows how to ask the question, the answer is no longer needed.

Communication Modes

An important question in designing human-computer interaction is to determine the kind of communication mode to use. In the past, we have been constrained mostly to entering information to a computer through the use of a keyboard. Some advancement has come through the use of a mouse which makes interaction somewhat easier; but is this the best method overall? Humans communicate in so many other ways, as indicated in the introduction to this chapter. What about voice as compared to other communication modes? In the following experiment, several of these communication modes were tested by controlling the communication mode people solved problems together.

In a controlled laboratory setting, Ochsman and Chapanis (1974) tested how humans communicate with each other to try to determine the modes which computers should use in interactions with humans. They tested human communication when solving problems in ten different modes: typewriting, handwriting, video, voice, and various combinations of these modes. In observing the problem-solving performance, Ochsman and Chapanis concluded that problems were solved most efficiently if voice was one of the communication channels used.

The implication of this experiment for human-computer interaction is that communication can be improved if voice inputs are allowed. Many people may have difficulty typing the information through a keyboard. Perhaps the added workload of typing reduced people's abilities to concentrate on the typing instead of just concentrating on the problem solving. Perhaps this is not as much of a problem for good typists.

Vocabulary Size

If a computer is to understand natural language, the computer must have a vocabulary that it recognizes. What is the size of the vocabulary needed? Would the vocabulary be too large so that the storage and retrieval costs would be too high? One way to address these issues would be to design a computer system that interprets natural language and uses different vocabulary sizes in the experiment. Developing these systems could be expensive and time-consuming. An alternative method would be to test people communicating with other people while restricting the vocabulary size.

Kelly and Chapanis (1977) used the human-human interaction model as a source of data for determining the size of a natural language vocabulary needed for a computer to interact with a human when solving a problem. Two-person teams were required to interact with each other while solving a problem. The experimenters recorded the words that the teams used during their solutions. Next, new two-person teams were given the problems and told that they could only use the 300 words utilized most often by the previous teams. In comparing the teams from the restricted word environment to the previous teams from the unrestricted environment, little deficit in problem solving performance occurred.

The implication is that an intelligent computer system designed to understand natural language could perform the task with only a 300-word vocabulary. This is not a size which would be too costly to implement. The vocabulary could be task dependent in that different kinds of problems would require different vocabularies. However, in an experiment on classifying messages on a computerized bulletin board, Habibi and Eberts (1991) found that a 100-word vocabulary was adequate for the computer to understand the messages so that they could be classified in the correct category.

Grammars

Each sentence has a certain kind of grammar in which the words can be placed into nouns, verbs, prepositions, articles, and so forth. In turn, these low-level atoms can be placed in verb phrases, noun phrases, prepositional phrases, and so forth. Chapter 17 explains some of these grammars in more detail, in the context of predicting human performance. In the present context, grammars can be used by the computer to understand natural language sentences. The nouns, verbs, and other parts of the grammar can be put into many different sequences to form acceptable sentences. The more grammars in a natural language understanding system, the more complex and costly the system. How many grammars are needed? Can people still communicate with a computer if the number of grammars is limited?

An experiment by Hendler and Michaelis (1983) addressed these questions by comparing two-person teams with unlimited grammar natural language interactions to teams with limited grammar natural language interactions. They found that in the first hour of the two-hour experiment, the team members using the unlimited grammar solved problems better than the team members using the limited grammar. In the second hour, however, no difference in problem-solving ability could be found between the two groups. They concluded that limited grammar natural language systems could be implemented in computer systems if the users are allowed enough time to become accustomed to the limitations.

The implication from this experiment is that people can learn to communicate by only using a limited number of grammars. A natural language understanding computer system would not have to be able to understand all kinds of grammars but could be programmed to understand only a limited number. The users may require some time in order to determine which grammars are possible. But, users would likely have the capabilities to limit their communications accordingly.

Cognitive Strategies

People have different cognitive strategies for performing a task on the computer. For the experts, these strategies are efficient and allow the expert to perform tasks quickly and with as little cognitive effort on the strategy as possible. For novices, these cognitive strategies may be inefficient and require much cognitive effort just to interact with the computer with little energy left over to solve the problem. The computer system usually provides some feedback on whether the syntax is correct by indicating if the command entered is one that can be recognized by the system. Can the computer provide some information on the goodness of the cognitive strategy employed by the user in order to accomplish the task? Before tackling the issue of whether the cognitive strategy can be recognized by the computer, experimentation must first establish whether or not communication of cognitive strategies for performing a task can occur between two or more people. Also, the experimentation must determine if cognitive strategies can be improved once communication occurs.

To address the above issues, Eberts, Majchrzak, Payne, and Salvendy (1990) designed an experiment in which the cognitive strategies to perform a memo-editing task were identified. The strategies were determined by examining the keystrokes and pauses between keystrokes. The strategies were specified according to the goals and subgoals used to accomplish the tasks. By looking at the transitions between the goals and subgoals, the goodness of strategies could be determined. Individuals were first asked to perform the task individually, and then they were combined into two-person groups in order to perform the task together. The job enrichment was further manipulated. Job enrichment is a term often used in management (Hackman and Oldham, 1975). A highly enriched job is designed to have several core job characteristics: task variety, task identity, task significance, task autonomy, and feedback from others and the job itself. A low enriched job is one that has few of these characteristics so as to be routine and unchallenging, with little feedback, meaningfulness, or responsibility.

A comparison between the goals of the people when performing the task individually and when performing the task in a group was important to the results of the study. The results showed that the group strategy in the enriched environment was a combination of strategies of the individuals; the group strategy was better than the individual strategies. In the unenriched environment, the group strategy was the same as the strategy of the typist when performing the task individually. No sharing of strategies occurred.

The implication of this experiment was that people could communicate strategies when performing the task in a group situation. This kind of improvement will occur only in certain kinds of enriched environments; if there is an unenriched environment, strategy sharing will not occur. Improvement in performance occurs when the people combine strategies to come up with a better strategy. Critiques of the cognitive strategies of the users would be useful for improving the strategies and improving performance. The results indicate that work could proceed on a computer system designed to determine cognitive strategies of the users and

provide a critique on those strategies. A system to recognize cognitive strategies through the use of neural nets has been developed based upon these earlier results (Villegas and Eberts, 1992).

Conclusions About Human-Human Communication

The studies described have shown that the human-human communication model can be used to collect data on the kinds of features needed in a computer system to make interaction with the computer more natural and more intelligent. The underlying assumption of this methodology is that naturalness in interacting with computers, where natural is used metaphorically from human-human interaction, is desirable. Another assumption is that given the chance, humans would want to interact with computers as they interact with people. Some people have questioned these assumptions (see Chapter 3), but most researchers would find them plausible. The examples provided in this chapter only address some of the important human-computer interaction issues. The main purpose of discussing these examples is to illustrate the kind of methodology that can be used to define the parameters in these tasks. As the field advances, or as the research needs change, similar methodologies to those discussed in this chapter could be used for these other issues.

THE "WIZARD OF OZ" METHODOLOGY

In the book the *Wizard of Oz*, by Frank Baum, the "wizard" is trying to appear more powerful than he would seem to be

Figure 18-1. Dorothy encounters the Wizard of Oz. From F. Baum (1987), <u>The Wonderful Wizard of Oz</u>. Reprinted with permission of Books of Wonder, New York, N.Y.

in real life by showing a large disconnected image of himself with a booming voice and special effects such as smoke (see Figure 18-1). When Toto discovers the fraud, by pulling back the curtain, Dorothy and the others are disappointed in the discovery of the illusion, but they find that the wizard has good advice anyway

Figure 18-2. By peeking around the screen, Toto discovers that the Wizard is using gimmicks to appear more powerful than he may actually be without the gimmicks. Dorothy and the others discover, however, that much could be learned from the Wizard even though the reality did not match the appearance. From F. Baum (1987), <u>The Wonderful Wizard of Oz</u>. Reprinted with permission of Books of Wonder, New York, N.Y.

(see Figure 18-2). An experimental methodology for testing natural interface designs has been dubbed the Wizard of Oz technique (Newell, Arnott, Carter, and Cruikshank, 1990), because it works on an illusion also. During experimentation the computer appears to be intelligent by answering direct queries or responding to natural language input. In actuality, the experimenter is sitting behind a "screen," usually in another room, and it is the experimenter who is answering the questions or responding to the natural language inputs instead of the computer. With this technique, important interface design questions can be addressed before going to the expense of programming the computer to exhibit this kind of intelligence.

In many cases, researchers and developers would like to design the computer to be more humanlike but they are not sure whether the cost in developing the interface would justify the human performance improvement with such an interface. Instead of going to the cost of designing the humanlike interface for experimenting with the benefits, they can design the experiment so that it looks like the computer is performing the humanlike functions but it is actually not. The humanlike functions are, instead, performed by humans. In other words, a human performs a function similar to that of a wizard. The participants in the experiment think that they are interacting with a fancy, intelligent interface which can perform amazing functions. In actuality, they are merely interacting with a normal human being, behind an electronic curtain, who tries to simulate the functioning of a more intelligent machine. Several examples of this methodology have been reported in the literature.

The Listening Typewriter

One of the first uses of this technique was in the design of natural language interfaces. As indicated in Chapter 20, designing computerized natural language interfaces is a difficult task. The development time would be in the person-years and would involve a sizeable investment from a company. Are the benefits of natural language worth the cost? To examine this question, Gould, Conti, and Hovanyecz (1983) devised an experiment to examine the feasibility of a listening typewriter. A listening typewriter has some intuitive appeal. Using a typewriter or a computerized word processor requires a good deal of skill by the operator. Sometimes this skill takes years to develop. The dictaphone has been a business office staple for years. Somebody dictates a letter, memo, or some other kind of written correspondence into the dictaphone, and then a secretary-typist transcribes the words into print. Eliminating the transcription phase, by having the computer transcribe the words, is appealing.

The drawback of a listening typewriter is that the secretary may perform many intelligent functions that cannot be performed easily by a machine. The person dictating a message includes many necessary nontext words and many extraneous words that should not be transcribed. As an example, a person may be using a dictaphone and decide that the last phrase starting with the word "As" should be deleted. The secretary is able to differentiate the text from the commands for deleting the phrase, but a computer would have a difficulty doing this. In addition, the person dictating the message has to include punctuation and formatting information. Designing a computer system to perform this kind of task is difficult. Would users accept such a system and make it a viable product in the marketplace? Instead of determining these questions after the research and development costs, the Wizard of Oz technique can be used to perform some usability studies on a listening typewriter before it is prototyped.

Instead of designing a listening typewriter, Gould et al. (1983) situated human "wizards" behind the electronic curtain of the terminal to respond intelligently to the dictation of the subjects in the experiment. The subjects were unaware of this, since they had no Toto to expose this covert operation. The subjects were told that the computer would respond to their natural language dictation but it was actually the confederate of the experimenters in another room responding to the dictation. As soon as the words or commands were spoken by the subject, the confederate would type the word or respond to the command, and this would appear on the subject's screen.

In analyzing the results of the experiment, Gould et al. (1983) concluded that the listening typewriter performance was at least as good as traditional typing or word processing methods. In a questionnaire, the subjects indicated that they preferred the listening typewriter over the traditional methods. Gould et al. (1983) concluded that development of such a system would be worthwhile.

Newell et al. (1990) replicated the Gould et al. (1983) study and found that the task was more difficult than expected. As an example of the difficulty, they reported the following verbatim dictation:

The benefits include space colon dash. Two lines down, number 1 full stop tab. Over yeh two more spaces over, right capital G Government grants for open brackets two spaces small letter I close brackets space capital P Private enterprise ah mmm go back to the open brackets and move everything to the right of the open brackets two spaces that's it. Good Down next line underneath the open bracket.

If you wish to register for this capital M Meeting simply telephone this number comma capital H Hichin that's H i t c h i n space brackets 0462 close brackets space 4747861 space extension 962. Can I change extension to capital E small x small t? O.K. Extension 962 full stop.

This may have been a particularly obtuse passage (the experiment was performed in Great Britain; a full stop is the same as a period in the U.S.). One can see the difficulty in dictating the message if the person has to include all the punctuation and formatting. One can also see the difficulty a person would have in transcribing the message and the even greater difficulty in programming a computer to take these kinds of communications. One could wonder if typing, especially for the punctuation and formatting, would be easier than having to place those symbols into words.

Newell et al. (1990) performed an experiment in with an overt and covert condition. In the overt condition, subjects were instructed that there was a "wizard" behind that curtain and that they were actually talking to a person in this simulation of a listening typewriter. In the covert condition, subjects were instructed that they were talking directly to a machine and the machine was interpreting their messages. Both conditions were done in the same way with a person listening to the subjects' spoken words and typing the words which would appear on the screen.

Newell et al. (1990) found that subjects did not much like the listening type-writer over traditional methods. Preferences for the listening typewriter were slightly higher in the covert than in the overt condition. In other words, when subjects knew that they were not talking to the "wizard," they did not like the system as well. This result helps to show one of the disadvantages of this kind of experiment: the subjects may be so enamored with the supposed technology, the ability of the system to recognize these natural language words, that they may be responding favorably to the technology rather than the ease of use. Results from these kinds of studies should be interpreted with caution.

Multiple Commands

In a command-based system, the computer user must try to recall the appropriate command to enter for satisfying the intention. Sometimes the exact command name is difficult to remember, especially when the user interacts with several different operating systems. As an example, the command for listing the directory may be DIR on one system and LS on another system. The kinds of mistakes that users make are likely to be choosing the wrong command name, synonym. In addition, if the user does not know that the computer can perform a certain function, but thinks that it might, the user may try several different possible command names to determine if any of them work.

It is very difficult to determine the most natural command name. Almost every beginning user will have different words for performing similar functions. Furnas, Landauer, Gomez, and Dumais (1987) investigated spontaneous word

choices for new users on five tasks and found that two people favored the same term with probability less than 0.20. This means that in most cases, 80-90 percent failure rates will be exhibited if new users are required to try to determine a designer's favorite word choice for performing a function.

A design technique to solve this problem would be to have the computer operating system recognize several different synonyms for the same command. Wixon, Whiteside, Good, and Jones (1983) used a Wizard of Oz technique for recognizing commands for an e-mail system. Novices to the task were given no help, no documentation, and no instruction; they were instructed to attempt the task using any commands they thought appropriate. If the system did not recognize the command, then a hidden operator interpreted it and provided the communication. Over time, 1070 commands were used. The system had 7% recognition in the beginning; each command that it could not recognize was added to the list of commands and recognized in later trials. After 67 subjects, the system could recognize 76% of the commands. This represents an interesting method to develop command synonyms.

Intelligent Help

Another example of the Wizard of Oz technique is in intelligent help systems. Providing help to users is difficult, especially if the help is to provide very specific instructions on the problem and how to fix it. The problem is that users can come up with unique methods for performing tasks which may be wrong. Anticipating these methods, so that help can be provided, is very difficult. In addition, even if the error is anticipated, the user events preceding the error, when the help is needed, may be very different from person to person. Devising a system would be expensive.

Carroll and Aaronson (1988) devised a Wizard of Oz experiment to determine some of the usability issues for intelligent help messages. From a prior study, they determined 13 errors that users are likely to make. They designed two kinds of help: a how-it-works help message which explained the errors; and a how-to-do-it help message which explained the procedures for error recovery. For the 13 errors, canned text was devised which could be presented to the user when the experimenter, monitoring the user, determined that help was needed by the user. If an unanticipated error occurred, then the experimenter would have to devise a help message on the fly.

In the experiment, the subjects were sent 164 help messages; 73 were the canned messages for the anticipated errors, and the remaining 91 were messages constructed on the fly to unanticipated errors. In a debriefing of the subjects, the experimenters claimed that the subjects did not realize during the experiment that the error messages were being generated by a person instead of software. From this experiment, Carroll and Aaronson were able to make many qualitative judgments on the usability of intelligent help messages. The intelligent help system was able to assist the user in some cases. By terming a help system as intelligent, however, the experimenters found that the users would form very high expectations of the system and blame the system for problems that may have been solved easily by the user.

SUMMARY

The important lesson from this chapter should be how to analyze a task. The anthropomorphic approach indicates that the task can be analyzed to determine how the computer can become more human-like, to act similar to how a person would act. This chapter has investigated two of the empirical techniques that can be used under this approach. For both of these techniques, the people in the experiments interact with other people to determine the characteristics and limitations of possible applications in human-computer interaction. For the human-human communication experiments, people solve problems in groups to determine the characteristics of group problem solving with the intention that the computer may someday take the place of the group members. For the Wizard of Oz technique, the people in the experiment are unaware that they are interacting with a person, thinking that the computer is "behind the screen" providing the intelligent help. Important characteristics of intelligent systems can be determined from this type of experimentation.

Both of these empirical techniques have been designed so that characteristics of intelligent computer systems can be determined before incurring the expense of developing the technologies. This should provide cost-savings in the future so that money is not devoted toward tasks that do not work when interacting with humans and that will not work when interacting with computers. The anthropomorphic approach is very dependent on developments in technology. The next two chapters examine these technologies and how they can be applied to human-computer interaction tasks. Chapter 19 examines some of the hardware advances; Chapter 20 examines the software advances.

QUESTIONS

1. Listen to a radio call-in show. Record the number of people who call in. Determine the percentage who call in with well-formulated questions and the percentage of those in which the caller and the host had to formulate the question and spend some time defining the terms. Evaluate how this process proceeded. Discuss the implications of your findings to human-computer interaction issues.

2. Observe people communicating with each other. Record the gestures and facial expressions that were used. Determine the meaning of each gesture or facial expression and how the communication will change depending on these perceived meanings. Discuss the implications of your findings to human-computer interaction issues.

3. The next time you go to a store to make a purchase, be aware of your interactions with an experienced salesperson. What kinds of questions were asked in the very beginning to establish the information needs of you as a customer? How was the succeeding interaction tailored to your needs based upon these questions? Discuss the implications of your findings to human-computer interaction issues.

CHAPTER **19**

NATURAL INTERFACE DESIGN: ALTERNATIVE INPUT METHODS

INTRODUCTION

Besides performing experiments to determine the features needed in interactive computer systems, the mismatches between human-human interaction and human-computer interaction can be analyzed at an intuitive level. This chapter and the next will examine many of the mismatches which occur and some of the ways to improve interactive computing systems. The discussion of natural interfaces is divided into two separate chapters. This chapter discusses natural interfaces in terms of alternative input devices and methods. A very cursory examination of the mismatches between human-human communication and human-computer communication reveals many differences. We do not communicate with other people by using a keyboard, except when communicating by writing letters. We have many varied ways to comunicate with other people: by talking, by using hand gestures, or through facial expressions. This chapter will examine some of the ways to communicate with the computer using the same techniques. Supposedly by incorporating some of the techniques discussed in this chapter, the communication between the user and the computer will be easier because it is more natural.

The next chapter, Chapter 20, discusses natural interfaces in terms of perceptual and cognitive mismatches between humans and computers. The computer provides the user with a view of the world,

the computer world displayed on the screen, and often the view of the world is different from that which we would perceive in a natural setting. For the cognitive aspect of computer interaction, some of the interfaces are becoming more intelligent so that the user's interactions can be viewed intelligently and the interaction adapted accordingly.

At the beginning of the last chapter, several of the mismatches between human-human communication and human-computer interaction were discussed. In human-human communication, people communicate through natural language, speech, hand gestures, and facial expressions. Attempts to incorporate these four capabilities into computer interfaces are discussed in this chapter.

NATURAL LANGUAGE PROCESSING

One of the most obvious mismatches between human-human commmunication and human-computer interaction is that the former makes great use of natural language and the latter does not. For the computer, direct interaction often comes through typing in commands or pointing to a command with the mouse. Try to type in a sentence about what the computer should do, and the computer will not understand. Some attempts have been made for incorporating natural language understanding into computer systems. Such a system would be able to interpret a sentence, and know what to do. In this case, the direct input device would be the computer keyboard, but the user would not be limited to a small set of commands. The next section in this chapter discusses the application of voice input, which could be used in conjunction with natural language processing, for communicating with the computer.

Human natural language processing involves the complex interplay between the meaning of the words, the context of the words, and background knowledge. For effective communication, one communicator must have a conception of the receiver's knowledge structures so the message can be tailored to be understood by that particular person. Often, understanding natural language is described as a process that is both bottom-up, driven from the individual meanings of the words, and top-down, with meanings derived from the context that they appear in. A simple computerized dictionary containing the meanings of words is not enough to understand natural language.

Many reviews of natural language processing exist (e.g., Barr and Feigenbaum, 1981; Burton and Brown, 1979a). Natural language processing is easiest through present technology only if the domain is limited in some way. As an example, SAM (Cullingford, 1981) is proficient at understanding news stories appearing in newspapers but is not applicable to other domains. News stories are an appropriate domain because each story has a certain journalistic structure which tries to identify for the reader the "who, what, where, why, and how" of the incident. Burton and Brown (1979a) describe a natural language processor for a computer-assisted instruction course which is good at interpreting natural language within its particular domain; again it is not applicable to other domains.

Typically, the natural language processor tries to break down the input by "parsing" it into a form which can be interpreted by the computer. Parsing is done through three basic techniques which determine how the computer intelligently understands the input: the use of syntactic rules (such as whether the words are verbs or nouns), semantic rules (interpreting the context and meaning of the word), or pragmatic rules (categorizing the words as acts or objects, as an example, see Schank and Riesbeck, 1981).

As an example of how a natural language processor works, we will consider one of the most successful methods, the pragmatic rules of Schank and Abelson (1977), which nicely illustrates this particular class of natural language understanding. Two important parts of this method are that the computer tries to parse the sentences (i.e., it categorizes the words into primitives) and that it uses world knowledge about stereotypical situations to understand the input. The method is based upon a theory, called the conceptual dependency (CD) theory (Schank, 1975), which explains how people understand sentences. In CD, the computer parses the sentence (or event) by trying to fill in slots which correspond to the following four items: an Actor (the person performing the actions), the Action (what the actor does), an Object (what the action is performed upon), and a Direction (the orientation of the action which is composed of a To and a From component). An important part of the understanding of an input is an understanding of the Action component. Schank and Riesbeck (1981) iden-

TABLE 19-1
Primitive actions and their meanings from the conceptual dependency theory of Schank
and Abelson (1977)

Action	Meaning	Example
ATRANS	Transfer of an abstract relationship	Transfer of possession, ownership, or control
PTRANS	Transfer of the physical location of an object	Take
MOVE	Movement of a body part of an animal by that animal	Shake your head
INGEST	Taking in of an object by an animal to the inside of that animal	Eat
EXPEL	Expulsion of an object by an animal to the ouside of that animal	Spit
MTRANS	Transfer of mental information between animals or within an animal	Read, forget
MBUILD	Construction by an animal of new information from old information	Decide, conclude
ATTEND	Action of attending or focusing a sense organ towards a stimulus	Notice, see
PROPEL	Action of applying a force	Throw
SPEAK	Convey information to another by talking	Talk
GRASP	Hold an object in the hand	Hold, grasp

tify eleven primitive actions which can be used to categorize all the verbs (see Table 19-1 for the primitive actions and their meanings). If an input sentence does not contain all the information to fill in the slots for an event, then the computer will use its world knowledge and characteristics of the primitive action to fill in the missing information.

An important aspect of CD is the ability of the computer to represent, in the same way, two or more sentences which have the same meaning. As an example, consider the two sentences "John gives a book to Mary" and "Mary takes the book from John." The result of the two sentences are exactly the same: Mary has the book. The computer should be able to determine this and does so by trying to fill in slots. For both sentences, the computer starts with the following slots:

action:
object:
direction To:
From:

For the first sentence, the slots would be filled in by the computer as follows:

actor:	John
action:	PTRANS
object:	book
direction To:	Mary
From:	John

For the second sentence, the slots would be filled in by the computer as follows:

actor:	Mary
action:	PTRANS
object:	book
direction To:	Mary
From:	John

The only difference in the sentence representation is the actor or the main focus; the results of the action are identical.

Natural language processing, such as that based on CD theory, would be useful in responding to queries from the user. Since the computer "understands" the world, in some ways, it would be able to answer questions from the user intelligently. For any natural language processing systems, the important concepts are similar to those mentioned in the context of CD. The computer usually fills in sentences with different wordings, but similar meanings must be interpreted in the same way.

Some experimental comparison of natural language systems to other input possibilities has been performed, with ambiguous results. Small and Weldon (1983) compared a restricted natural language database program to a command-based program. They found that performance was better on the command-based program ostensibly because it restricted the input from the users. Hauptmann and Green (1980) compared a restricted natural language interface to a direct manipulation interface. No differences occurred between the two designs. As indicated in Chapters 4 and 6, null results like these are difficult to interpret, however. Napier, Lane, Batsell, and Guadango (1989) compared a restricted natural language interface, which used contextual information, to a direct manipulation menu-based interface. Unlike the others, they found clear performance advantages for the natural language interface. They attributed their results to the greater use of context information. Simple experimental comparisons of different interface modes is difficult because results are dependent on how well the different interface modes have been designed.

VOICE RECOGNITION

The technology of voice recognition devices illustrates the complexity of human speech understanding. Available devices fall into two main classes: speaker dependent and speaker independent. The early voice recognition devices were speaker dependent (e.g., Lea, 1980). Speaker dependent systems can recognize a particular voice only after it has been "trained" by having the speaker go through a vocabulary from two to eight times. For the speaker independent devices, the system is able to understand any speaker of either sex with any dialect and pronunciation. Early systems required that each word be spoken separately with clear pauses between the words. The capabilities of voice recognition systems are increasing rapidly with larger vocabularies available, and the ability to understand more variations within a voice.

Recognizing Connected Speech

Much of the current research effort in this area is devoted to recognizing connected speech in sentences and phrases. Speech recognition of phrases and sentences is tied into natural language processing which is discussed in the next chapter. The problem of speech recognition is even more difficult than natural language processing because, instead of entering the words through the keyboard, so that the words are unambiguous, the words are entered through voice recognition with large uncertainties about the words. In most cases, the connected speech input must be restricted in some way either by devoting the systems to very limited domains or training the speakers to use only certain kinds of sentence structures or vocabularies. The latter appears to be possible because people tend to speak to computers different from how they would speak to other people (Hauptmann and Rudnicky, 1988).

The technology of connected speech recognition devices is changing so quickly that characterizing the capabilities is difficult. In 1988, the SPHINX system developed at Carnegie-Mellon University had an error rate of 29.4% using a 1,000-word vocabulary for recognizing words in sentences (Young, Hauptmann, Ward, Smith, and Werner, 1989). The main challenge of these systems is in trying to limit the search space for disambiguating the words. With a reduced search space, the system can be more accurate and perform faster. One method to reduce this search space, investigated in a system called MINDS, was to incorporate dialogue knowledge, user goals, and plans in order to understand what was said in a limited domain. When tested, the MINDS system was shown to have a low error rate of 3.5% for 200 sentences from 10 speakers (Young et al., 1989). This was a very limited domain, though, and as the domain is increased, the error rate should also increase.

Experimental Evaluations of Voice Recognition Systems

Voice recognition devices have been compared experimentally to other input devices such as keyboards and mice. Some of the experiments performed can be categorized as either positioning experiments or tracking experiments. In the positioning experiments, the computer users are required to move a cursor on a screen so as to position it at a specific location. In a tracking experiment, the computer user is required to follow some kind of moving path on the screen or to follow a moving cursor on the screen. As an example, driving a car is a tracking task because the driver must follow the path of the road which appears through the windshield. For two of the positioning experiments (Gould and Alfano, 1983; Haller, Mutschler, and Voss, 1984), the voice input was the slowest; the Haller et al. experiment found in addition that the error rate was highest for the voice input. The one experiment on using voice input for tracking (Mountford and North, 1980) found that voice input was good for tracking when compared to keyboard input. In this particular case, the use of keyboard input as a comparison to the voice was a curious choice; it is doubtful that voice input would have fared as well against the joystick or trackball in this context.

The above experiments on positioning indicate that merely using speech as an alternative to other forms of input without considering carefully the task or design of the computer system will be unsuccessful. More recently, Martin (1989) has reviewed the literature in this area and performed more experimentation concluding that voice input has an advantage over other forms of input under two conditions: (1) it is faster than typed input; and (2) it increases the user productivity by providing an additional response channel. In Martin's experiment, she compared voice input, in the context of a very large scale integration (VLSI) chip design package, to typed input, full-word input, single key-presses, and mouse clicks. Generally, the longer the input, the more beneficial the voice input when compared to these others. Thus, voice input held advantages over the typing and the full-word input. Some advantages for voice input were seen when compared to the single key-presses. Voice input showed no advantage over mouse inputs.

Listening Typewriters

Voice input as an alternative to typing would intuitively provide a very natural interface. People naturally use speech in most communication. Typing, on the other hand, is something that has to be learned over long periods of time. Most people can speak faster than they can type. Some languages, such as Japanese and Chinese, are difficult to type because of the large number of characters that are needed. In Japanese, a reader would typically need to know 2000 characters in order to read a newspaper. Placing all these characters on a keyboard is impossible. The alternative, essentially a menu-based typing system, is very slow. Japanese research, especially, has emphasized the development of speech-based typewriters. Recently, some commercial voice typing systems have been developed and marketed, although with little success at this point either because of the price of the system or the limited vocabularies.

IBM recently announced a voice-operated system, called VoiceType, which allows people to operate the computer through the spoken word. Instead of having the system recognize each possible word, the system will produce up to 1,000 keystrokes for a single word command. This kind of system would be especially useful for producing form letters or when pulling up frequently used text or data. IBM claims that VoiceType can be about three times faster than typing, at least for certain kinds of typing tasks. It can adapt to a user's voice, has a base vocabulary of 5,000 words, and can be programmed to recognize 2,000 more. At this time, the system is being targeted toward impaired users who have lost the use of their hands and arms. It compares favorably with other available methods for these users.

Advantages

An advantage for voice typing is that voice can be one input of a multimodal interface so that several tasks could be done at once. Martin (1989) suggests that this is advantageous because the computer user could be speaking to a computer while the hands are free to perform other tasks such as opening mail or leafing through reference materials. Voice input is especially important in situations in which the number of responses for operating something is high. As an example, a pilot in a cockpit must use hands for performing several of the piloting tasks and feet are used for others. If the task of a pilot is increased, then input can no longer be channeled through the hands or the feet because these are already overloaded and no longer available. Voice input provides an alternative input mode.

To illustrate how this can be advantageous, Honeywell was working on a research project in the early 1980s involving a computerized manual for maintenance. In maintenance work, the worker must have the hands available to perform the maintenance. Holding a book or some kind of box of buttons for a response would slow the maintenance task or make it impossible to perform. To solve these problems, a helmet-mounted display was developed to show the maintenance tasks which had to be performed. The worker interacted with the computer through voice input so that the hands could be used exclusively for manipulating the tools. This illustrates that when several different kinds of responses are required, voice input may be a useful alternative. For single-mode computer responses, such as mouse clicks, voice input does not usually outperform these other kinds of input modes.

GESTURES

In the lexicon of computer interfaces, people will often say that we have "pointed" to a certain location on the screen through the use of a mouse or that we point to a certain location on the screen by moving the cursor controlled by arrow keys on the computer. Although pointing is a very natural task to perform (e.g., we point to things in the real world all the time), are we really pointing when we use mice and keyboards? For the mouse, we must reach over and grasp the mouse, manipulate the mouse, watch the cursor on the screen, and then, while simultaneously watching the cursor and moving the mouse, manipulate the cursor until it is pointing to the right location. For keyboards, we must look at the screen cursor, look at the desired location on the screen, decide how to get there (up, down, right, or left), find the appropriate arrow key, and then press the key. If the direction is changed, then the whole process must be repeated. In the real world, pointing with a finger to a certain location is much simpler. For keyboards and mice, pointing is merely a metaphor for the sequence of actions which actually occurs. Why not design a natural interface where the user can actually point with a finger to the location on the screen?

An interactive technique based on gestures has been a focus of research in recent years. A gesture can be described as any movement by the hand resulting in a meaningful motion. Under this definition, a gesture could be a simple movement, such as pointing to a screen, with the purpose, as an example, of choosing a menu item. A gesture could incorporate using a stylus to handwrite a character or word on the screen so that the computer can interpret it as a character. A gesture could also be moving the hand to grasp an item displayed on the screen or in space and then manipulating that item in some way. Some of these methods for interpreting gestures will be discussed.

Touch Screens

A touch screen is used to point to locations on the screen either for cursor control or for choosing items on the screen. Usually it looks just like a regular computer terminal, except it has a built-in mechanism for determining the screen location of the touch. It produces an input signal in response to a touch or movement of the finger at a place on the display. Touch screens operate in two basic ways: the overlay method responds to touch pressure on the screen, and the signal method works by generating a response when a signal is interrupted by the placement of the finger on the display.

A touch wire display is an example of an overlay. Horizontal and vertical wires are set in transparent sheets placed on the display so that a signal is produced when the wires are touched at an intersection. The main disadvantage of this kind of screen is that touches are not always reliably detected and the wires may obscure parts of the display.

An alternative overlay technique uses plastic pressure-sensitive displays. When pressure is applied, two surfaces touch, an electrode pair shorts, and a circuit is completed. The position of the touch is indicated by the horizontal and vertical position of the electrode pair which is activated. A disadvantage of this type of display is that the overlay itself may reduce the amount of light which is transmitted through the screen. In addition, the plastic sheet overlay may be easily damaged.

For the signal displays, two basic kinds of signals can be generated: light or sound. For the infrared light beam displays, light emitting diodes (LEDs) are paired with light detectors and placed along all sides of the display. When touched, two light beams (a horizontal beam and a vertical beam) are interrupted and the resulting x- and y-coordinates for that position are calculated. The disadvantages of this kind of screen are the following. The resolution of the touch screen is limited to the number of light beams included. Visual display terminals (VDTs) are curved because of the requirements of the display tubes, so that the light beams can be far away from the screen. If the finger is placed at an angle when touching the screen, the light beams will be broken at coordinates different from the place the screen is touched. Additionally, inadvertent activation may be a problem because activation occurs when the light beam is broken, not when the finger actually touches the screen. This problem is exacerbated with the curved screens.

For the acoustic devices, a glass plate is placed on the VDT and ultrasonic waves are generated on the glass by transducers placed along both the x- and y-axes. When a waveform is interrupted, the horizontal and vertical waves are reflected back and detected by the transducer. The x and y coordinates are calculated based upon the time between wave transmission and detection. The advantages of this kind of display are that the acoustic device does not obscure the display and they allow higher resolution than do infrared devices. The disadvantage is that anything may break the sound wave, such as dirt or scratches on the screen.

The advantages of touch screens are the following. The main advantage is that choosing a location on the screen by touching it alleviates the problem of having an intermediary to perform the pointing. If pointing with a mouse, the mouse sits on the desk and moves a cursor on the screen which is remote from where the input takes place. Using arrow keys on the keyboard is even worse because movement is restricted to one of the four directions. Again, the action of the user is remote from the action on the screen. By touching the screen, there is a direct relationship between the action of the finger (touching the screen) and the action on the screen (performing a positioning action to the touched location).

A second advantage is that the only movement which is required by the user is a natural pointing movement. Everybody knows how to point; it is a very natural response which requires no skill. Typing, as a comparison, is not as natural and requires a long training period before this kind of action can be used successfully. Because of the naturalness of the response and the ease of pointing, user acceptance of touch screens for gesture input should be high.

Touch screens have some disadvan-

tages. The main disadvantage is that lifting the hand to input information constantly could cause fatigue. One of the reasons for the use of keyboards and especially mice is that hand lifting is not required. For the mouse, the hand can rest directly on the mouse which reduces the fatigue. A related problem is that the finger or arm may block the screen when it is being touched.

Another problem is that the resolution of a touch screen is limited by the size of the finger. If the resolution was small, then a finger would activate several coordinates at one time. This limited resolution means that touch screens may be inappropriate for the selection of small items such as a single character. This means that touch screens may be good for some kinds of pointing tasks, but they would certainly be inappropriate for a task such as typing if the user had to use one finger at a time to touch the characters on the screen to enter the words. A recent experiment, however, has indicated that this resolution problem may not be as bad as originally indicated. Sears and Shneiderman (1991) found that users could activate a single pixel on the screen with the finger, and touch screens were accurately used at about four pixels (about a quarter the size of a single character).

A final problem is that touching the screen can cause smudges and dirt on the screen. Seeing the screen is a problem, in any case, because of problems due to the contrast of the characters to the background and glare from lights or outside windows. The smudges on the screen would make these screen vision problems even worse.

The listing of the advantages and disadvantages shows that touch screens are appropriate for some kinds of input tasks and inappropriate for others. Touch screens are best for working with data which are already displayed on screen. They would be highly appropriate for interacting with menu displays; they provide an alternative to mouse inputs. They are useful when it is time-consuming or perhaps even dangerous to divert attention from the display. With a touch screen, the input can be placed directly on the location of the screen output so that the eyes do not have to be diverted elsewhere. As with other kinds of display designs in which the number of possible inputs is limited, such as direct manipulation displays (see Chapter 11), touch screens could be beneficial in high stress situations because the input does not have to be recalled; it only has to be recognized from the items on the display. Finally, touch screens are highly appropriate in situations in which no training can be required such as shopping malls and bank teller machines.

Gestures incorporating touch screens are inappropriate for inputting graphic information such as drawing programs or painting programs. These kinds of tasks are best for other input devices such as styli or mice. Touch screens are also inappropriate when many items need to be displayed on the screen.

Graphic Tablets and Styli

Graphic tablets, sometimes called data tablets, can also be used for interpreting hand gestures. In this case, graphic tablets are most useful for hand gestures associated with inputting drawings and handwriting. These kinds of devices have many characteristics similar to touch displays except that they are flat and placed on a table in front of or to the side of the display. Some recent innovations in this area have reduced the size of the graphic tablets to very small screens which serve as both output device and input device and can be held in a hand or placed on a table. Generally, a stylus is used to move a cursor or to input the information into the computer. When considering how graphic tablets and styli can be used to input and interpret gestures, both the hardware and software aspects of these devices must be considered. Analysis of the handwriting is considered in the next chapter; the hardware is considered in this chapter.

Most graphic tablets can be categorized as either digitizing tablets or touch tablets differing on whether the stylus or the tablet produces the signal for the position of the stylus. The matrix-encoded tablet is an example of a digitizing tablet. It works through the use of electrical or magnetic fields so that as a special stylus is passed over the tablet, signals are produced by horizontal and vertical conductors or wires in the tablet. A voltage-gradient tablet has conductive sheets which form the surface of the tablet. An electrical potential is applied to the point of the stylus, and a decrease in potential on the plate at the stylus position is measured to calculate the location of the stylus.

For an acoustic digitizing tablet, the stylus generates a spark at its tip and the sound impulses are detected by microphones on the sides of the tablet. By determining the delay between the time the sound originated and its reception by the microphones, the coordinate values can be calculated.

An acoustic touch tablet also works with acoustic waves but does not require the use of a stylus. High-frequency waves are produced on a glass surface and when interrupted by a finger or pen they are reflected back to the tablet edge. The delay between the wave generation and reception is used to calculate the coordinates. This device is very similar to acoustic touch screens.

Finally, a multilayer tablet has two or three conducting sheets so that when these sheets are pressed together by a stylus or finger an electrical potential is generated and the coordinates can be calculated.

The advantage of graphic tablets is that the movement of the stylus or the finger on the tablet is very natural to users. The graphic tablet is virtually the only input device which may be used for drafting or free-hand sketching. Since people are very familiar with writing or drawing, the same kinds of natural movements are used for the tablet. Unlike the touch screen, the user's hand does not cover any part of the display and arm fatigue is not a big problem for a graphic tablet.

The main disadvantage of graphic tablets is that, in comparison to the touch screen, they do not allow for direct eye-hand coordination. Another disadvantage is that large tablets may take up space on a crowded work surface.

Handwriting Devices

In recent years, some small devices have come on the market which allow the users to write on them with a stylus or pen, and then the device recognizes the characters from the free-hand writing (see Figure 19-1). To create such a device and make it commercially feasible, the roadblock has always been creating the ability to recognize the handwriting. The same character can appear very different depending on the person writing and the context of the character. Handwriting can be recognized in two ways: by identifying the features of a character or by recognizing the pattern of the character.

Identifying the features of a character has been the traditional technique for handwriting recognition. Consider the character T. The features of a T could be characterized as follows: top horizontal line, middle vertical line, and line intersection at top-middle. The character Y has some similar features: middle vertical line, slanting middle to left line, slanting middle to right line, and intersection at middle-middle. To recognize these characters, the device must first digitize the image; categorize the features as, for example, lines, curves, or intersection points; and then compare the features of the image to the feature list to find a match. This method can be effective as long as the handwriting is clear enough for feature identification. Figure 19-2 contains a comparison of the characters H and A. The only differentiating features are how much the lines on A are slanting and how much the lines on H are vertical. Only subtle differences may exist between the two. In the next figure, the context of the words would allow a person to identify the letters. Handwriting identification can be more accurate by including this context.

A disadvantage of handwriting devices using feature identification is that identifying the character based upon partial information is problematic. This bottom-up approach of feature to character is not amenable to identifying the whole pattern without a reliance on the individual features. Another problem is that the whole process of digitizing and matching

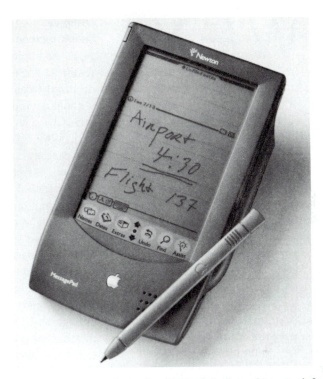

Figure 19-1. The Apple Newton is a device in which a stylus is used to enter information into the computer. The Newton has software which recognizes and interprets the handwriting. (Figure courtesy of Apple Computer Inc.)

features in the list could be time-consuming, because of the sequential nature of the task, and these delays could be disruptive to the user.

The alternative technique for handwriting recognition is to use neural networks for recognizing the pattern of the character (see Chapter 9 for the discussion of neural nets). Several different techniques could be available for using neural nets to recognize characters—an example of this technique is shown by Pittman (1991)—but they basically follow the same pattern. First, the character must be digitized, and usually the digitized image is encoded according to dots in a matrix (see Figure 19-3). Second, the digitized images are used to train a neural net, with the

input nodes being the digitized image and the output node being the name of the character. The more training examples for a character, the better the generalizability of the net to different variations on a character. The training of the net is used to specify the weights of the connections between the nodes. Once trained, the neural net can be used to recognize new characters that it has never seen before.

The Neocognitron model (Fukushima, 1987, 1988a, 1988b; Fukushima, Miyake, and Ito, 1983) is an example of a neural net which has been trained to recognize handwritten characters (see Figure 19-4). This work has shown that: (1) the net can learn to pick up the relevant features; (2) it can separate

WHY

WHY?

CAT

Figure 19-2. The letters H and A can be very similar to each other if not drawn properly. The lower figure shows how there is no identification confusion if the context of the letters in a word is provided unambiguously.

and identify characters even though they overlap in the input provided to the net; (3) partial characters can be recognized; and (4) it can recognize characters in all kinds of orientations. Figure 19-3 illustrates some of the characters the Neocognitron model of the net can recognize.

The advantage of using neural nets to recognize characters is that the net stores information about the character by its overall pattern instead of specific attributes of the character. The handwritten character could be missing a specific feature and, as long as the pattern was the same, the net could still identify the character. Another advantage is that identification of the character can be very fast. An overall advantage of neural nets is that the information is processed in parallel instead of the serial methods used for most

computer programs. The feature identification method requires the step of mapping the digitized image to individual features. The neural net directly maps the digitized image to the character pattern without having to first recognize the features.

Why should handwriting recognition devices be advantageous as an input device? After all, handwriting is relatively slow at least compared to expert typists, and handwriting can be very fatiguing. The main advantage lies in the compactness of the handwriting devices. For a regular computer, the keyboard requires a certain amount of physical space because a minimum number of keys is required and each key must be large enough, at least a finger width. Writing the characters is an alternative to entering the characters through the keyboard. Without the need for the keyboard, the weight and size of the computer can be drastically reduced. The initial handwriting device products have touted the portability of the device.

It is doubtful that handwriting devices will ever replace the use of keyboards on computers. They have some very specific uses, however. Handwriting devices are especially useful for jobs that require the worker to be mobile and to enter information on a form. As an example, these devices have been designed for and used by police officers. Much of the work of a police officer is filling out forms. The advantage to these portable devices is that a police officer does not have to return to the office to fill out the forms. The form can be displayed directly on one of these portable devices, the information can be entered directly on the form through the handwriting, and the whole

Figure 19-3. A neural net such as the Neocognitron can recognize characters similar to these even though they are degraded or in varying locations (see Fukushima, 1988b).

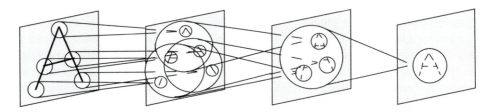

Figure 19-4. The neural net maps the dots from the A into an output corresponding to the character. The different levels of the network focus on extracting important features from the characters (from Fukushima, 1988a, reprinted with permission of publisher © 1988 IEEE).

process can be computerized. These devices have other applications for mobile jobs such as a worker on a factory floor performing inventory by filling in a computerized form.

Complex Gestures

The discussion of gestures in this section has been limited to relatively simple gestures such as touching a screen or graphic

Off   On

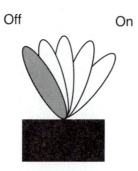

Figure 19-5. An example of a complex gestural interface in which the user must move the finger so as to flip a toggle switch. As the finger is moved from left to right, the toggle switch moves as indicated until it rests at the on position to the right.

tablet, or using a pen or stylus to handwrite characters. These same kinds of interactions could be performed by other input devices such as mice or keyboards. Most gestures used naturally in the real world are more complex. Since pointing and gesturing are such natural acts, recent interface design research has investigated the use of complex gestures for interacting with a computer.

Dannenberg and Amon (1989) have developed a Gestural Interface Designer which has a collection of controls displayed on the screen which are coupled to input from pointing and gesture-sensing devices. As an example, a toggle switch could be represented on the screen and this switch would be "flipped" by the movement of the fingertip across the switch in the right direction (see Figure 19-5). A knob could also be portrayed on the screen and the amount of rotation of the knob is dependent on the amount of rotation in the user's hand when the knob is "grabbed" and "rotated." Obviously, the interface would have to be designed so that the gestures are interpreted; in other words, a

toggle switch cannot be rotated and a knob cannot be flipped.

Dannenberg and Amon (1989) emphasize that the problem in the design of a complex gesture interface is in the recognition of the gestures and the handling of multiple events. For some gesture interpretations, the input device (such as a touch screen) is similar to a normal touch screen except that it can record multifinger touches at one time. Their interface prototyping system has a parser used to interpret the different kinds of movements.

Data Gloves

The complex gestures of the preceding section were limited to those in which the screen was touched either by the hand or by a stylus or pen. Many gestures are three-dimensional; however, in order to input three-dimensional gestures, data gloves have been devised (Zimmerman, Lanier, Blanchard, Bryson, and Harvil, 1987). A data glove looks like a normal glove that fits over the hand and fingers. Several sensors are placed throughout the glove in order to sense the movements that are occurring and the position of the glove in three-dimensional space. Through the use of data gloves, movements such as grabbing and grasping can be interpreted.

An example of the use of data gloves to recognize hand gestures was provided by Murakami and Taguchi (1991). For that application, they trained a neural net (see Chapter 9) to recognize the 42 characters in the Japanese finger alphabet from input provided by a data glove. The recognition rate was dependent on the number of examples in which it was trained and the skill of the people doing the signing. The recognition rate ranged from 47.8%

when trained on 42 patterns from un-skilled signers to 98% when trained on 206 patterns from skilled signers. This method shows the potential for recogniz-ing hand gestures using neural nets.

Data gloves are often incorporated with 3-D perceptual devices as a means of interaction. Some of these will be consid-ered in the next section.

Virtual Reality

Virtual reality has achieved much notice in the past few years. In a virtual world, everything is computer graphics or soft-ware. The hardware is minimized or is nonessential. As an example of a virtual world, the U.S. Air Force has been con-ducting research on virtual cockpits. The physical form of a virtual cockpit is bar-ren: nothing is there. For a pilot to interact with the cockpit and control the plane, the pilot must perceive the world through visual images from cameras placed on the outside of the aircraft and computer-gen-erated graphics interposed on top of the camera output. The pilot has the images displayed on a helmet-mounted display. To solve the problem of limited display resolutions, a computer monitors the head movements of the pilot and displays the outside scene accordingly. As an ex-ample, if the pilot looks to the left, then the computer displays the scene which would be observed to the left. A 1,000 x 1,000 pixel display, therefore, could appear to be much larger to a pilot because it essen-tially extends in all directions.

Just as the pilot does not have to see out of a virtual cockpit, the panels, dis-plays, and controls of the cockpit do not have to be present in a physical form. All of these can be represented by computer

graphics. These soft displays can be coupled with a data glove, similar to that discussed in the preceding section. If the pilot needs to push a button on the soft display, the pilot would move his hand in the direction of the image of the button on the helmet-mounted display. The data gloves incorporated by the virtual cockpit are slightly different in that they not only interpret the 3-D coordinates of the hand but they also can provide pressure to the fingers and hands for tactile feedback. As the soft button is "pushed," the data gloves will place a pressure on the fingertip to provide the important tactile information of pushing a real button.

The virtual cockpit is advantageous because the whole world of the cockpit is programmable through software and not restricted to the hardware; it can be easily reprogrammed for any updates or changes. Most modern cockpits are very complex, and the space of the controls and displays is very limited. With a virtual cockpit, no space is needed in that one panel can be displayed in the same physical location of another panel just by changing the mode. Some behavioral work is needed to deter-mine if this would cause confusion to a pilot. Using the analogy to the real world, we know that only one thing can occupy one position in the physical space. Virtual realities have no such constraints.

The author has had the chance to interact with a virtual reality. This system included 3-D goggles which were used to make the scene displayed on a large screen to appear in three dimensions. It was also outfitted with data gloves which could be used to grasp items. In this world, a space shuttle could be seen in three dimensions moving around in the background. The user could "grab" the space shuttle by

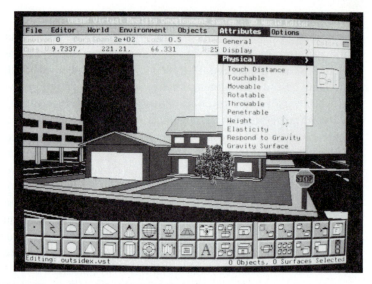

Figure 19-6. An illustration of the VREAM World Editor which is used to program and develop virtual reality applications. To make development easier, each object in the virtual world has certain properties which can be specified by the programmer instead of programming these properties for each object and application. The pull-down menu shows some of the properties. (Photo courtesy of VREAM, Inc., 2568 N. Clark St. #250, Chicago, IL.)

moving an open hand to the place where the space shuttle occurred at that time and then closing the hands. Once grabbed, the space shuttle could be "thrown" by moving the hand back, moving it forward, and then releasing the fingers at the appropriate time. The space shuttle would then appear to move in the direction it was thrown. The technology used to achieve this virtual reality is quite impressive. More usability studies, however, need to be performed on these systems. The author had difficulty with this particular system in being able to determine where the space shuttle was located in reference to the z-coordinate (the coordinate from the user to the screen).

Much research and development activity is being performed on virtual reality software and hardware. Fast advancements are being made. VREAM, Inc. has developed software in which virtual reality will run on a PC-based machine. Figures 19-6 and 19-7 illustrate how this software works. In Figure 19-6, the VREAM World Editor is shown. This is used to program the interface for a virtual reality application. Icons and direct manipulations lessen the development time. The VREAM Runtime System, depicted in Figure 19-7, runs the application that was developed and programmed earlier.

Virtual reality certainly could find a niche if the technology problems can be worked out. Imagine being able to learn how to repair an automobile by "shrinking" and "walking around" the different parts of an automobile through a virtual reality system. You may be able to "touch" different parts of the car and determine the effect of the manipulation. Or imagine "traveling" to other parts of the world

Figure 19-7. An illustration of the VREAM Runtime System which is used to run the developed virtual reality applications. The user manipulates the picture of the hand to grab and interact with objects in the three-dimensional world. Three-dimensionality can be represented by using special glasses to actually see three dimensions or, in the absence of this special equipment, by how the hand on the screen is obscured or not obscured by the objects in the scene. (Photo courtesy of VREAM, Inc., 2568 N. Clark St. #250, Chicago, IL.)

through a virtual reality system without having to leave the room. If we can travel to other parts of the world, then perhaps we can travel to other time periods as well. Teaching history would no longer be through reading books and looking at pictures but would occur through experiencing the time period. It is very easy to be carried away by the promises of the technology. Whether these can be achieved in the near future is difficult to predict.

Some people see virtual reality as a solution to world problems. Some animal rights activists would like to eliminate zoos because of the supposed mistreatment of the zoo animals. As an alternative to zoos, one group has proposed a virtual reality zoo in which the animals are no longer experienced in their live state but are experienced through virtual reality images. A zoo patron could experience the animals up close and personal without the danger associated with a live encounter. In such a world, the animals would not need to be kept in a zoo. But without the need for animals, would animals be termed unnecessary because they already exist in the virtual reality? Many times the technology changes bring about the need for new thinking on social and ethical problems.

FACIAL EXPRESSIONS

Facial expressions are used in human-human communication. When communicating with another person, we watch the other person's face very closely to obtain cues for interpreting the communication. An examination of the places on another person's face in which the eyes fixate reveals the areas on the face which provide the most communication information. Most of the eye fixations are on the eyes and the mouth. Consequently, these provide the best cues in communications and will be discussed in this section.

Computer Perception of Facial Expressions

Is it possible for a computer to watch the user, much as a person watches another person when communicating? Japan's NTT has been investigating methods for a computer to watch the user and then mimic the facial expressions and movements of the user. In this system, a video camera is pointed toward the face of the user. The computer takes the video images and digitizes them, so that they can be interpreted by the computer. The computer changes these digitized images into a stylized image of the face. As the position of the mouth changes, to a smile from a frown, as an example, the stylized image on the monitor changes to mimic that facial expression. As the orientation of the head changes, the stylized image on the monitor will also change.

This facial expression technique is targeted in the immediate future as a method of inputting the kind of simple but specific information that people use when communicating. As an example, a person using an automatic teller machine could answer a query by nodding the head for "yes" or shaking the head for "no." Other kinds of inputs are also possible. Since voice recognition is a problem for most systems, the auditory signals from the voice could be augmented by movements of the mouth; the computer would be performing a method of lip-reading. For ambiguous auditory signals, the lip-read-

ing could provide enough information to differentiate between words.

This kind of system could also be used for adapting the displays, based upon the facial expression. Just as people may adapt their words based upon facial expressions, this computerized version could also be used in adaptation of the interface. As an example, puzzlement is usually accompanied by a certain facial expression. If the computer perceives this, then the interface could be adapted accordingly with more information and better help messages. Impatience is accompanied by specific expressions. If the computer perceives impatience, then the computer could adapt the display by speeding up the interaction.

Many facial expressions may be unrelated to the task. A computer which perceives facial expressions would have to be able to differentiate essential from nonessential movements. What happens when the user is carrying on a conversation with another person while interacting with the computer? Perhaps, the computer would query the user before deciding on the input or the adaptation. As an example, the automatic teller could indicate that you indicated "yes" when you shook your head. In this scenario, how would the user acknowledge that this was correct? By another shake of the head, or would the interaction ultimately need some kind of key input? Would people feel comfortable communicating through head movements and not using the unambiguous keyboard or menu input? Would people feel comfortable knowing that a computer was watching every move that they made?

A main advantage to keyboard input or mouse pointing to menu items is that they generate unambiguous responses. People feel comfortable with this. The inputs will always retain some ambiguity when using facial expressions for input. Perhaps computer perception of facial expressions will be confined mostly to augmentation of the input signals. This would involve the lip-reading, which augments voice recognition, and adapting the display based upon the perception of facial expressions. While the technology is being developed for the computer to perceive facial expressions and movements, many questions remain before this can be a viable interaction technique.

Eye Gazes

The NTT system for perceiving facial expressions of the user did not incorporate a specialized subsystem for perceiving the user's eyes. In human-human interaction, eyes are an important element in the communication. By following someone's eyes, we can tell what that person is interested in by the direction of the gaze. A computer interface could watch the user's eyes and then interpret the communication either through specific inputs or augmenting other inputs.

Erica (Hutchinson, White, Martin, Reichert, and Frey, 1989) is an example of an interface which uses eye gazes to interact with the computer. Erica is a computer workstation which has hardware to digitize and record a picture of where the user is looking. This is done by illuminating the user's face with a harmless near-infrared light source. The user's eyes reflect part of the light back to a video camera which records the location of the gaze. Two reflections of the eye are taken. One of the reflections is from the corneal sur-

face of the eye and is termed the glint. Another of the reflections is from the pupil of the eye and is termed the bright eye. The direction of the user's eye gaze is then determined by the relationships between the glint and the bright eye.

Erica learns the relationships between the glint, the bright eye, and the location of the gaze on the screen by having each user run through a calibration program. In this program, the user gazes at set locations on the screen while the computer records the video image of the glint and bright eye. An algorithm analyzes the relationships between the three parameters in order to calibrate the system for individual users.

One of the main limitations of the system is that the resolution and accuracy of the gaze detector is not very high. For the Erica system reported, the screen was segmented into nine separate parts (in a 3 x 3 matrix) and a gaze could be detected as falling in any one of those nine areas. In addition, this Erica system had no ability to monitor head movements of the user. With any kind of head movement, the Erica system would have to be calibrated again with the new location. At some point in the future, Erica could be combined with a head movement sensor to solve this problem.

At the present time, Erica and other eye gaze systems are best utilized by physically and vocally disabled people who do not have any other methods of independent communication and control. Unfortunately, for some of these people, head movements are not possible so that the head movement sensor is not needed. This kind of system could potentially be applied to other kinds of human-computer interaction.

SUMMARY

One of the most important points of this chapter is that human-computer interaction can be enhanced by analyzing the mismatches between human-human communication and interacting with the computer. Through a comparison of traditional techniques for interacting with a computer, three mismatches have been analyzed in this chapter: voice recognition, hand gestures, and facial expressions. All of these are important modes of communication for people; the technology is advancing to a point that these could be important modes when communicating with a computer.

These modes of communication can be used as inputs, much like hitting a key on the keyboard, or they can be used to augment the communication. Some of the methods discussed in this chapter, such as using a touch screen, can be used as substitutions for other input devices such as the mouse or a keyboard. If touching a menu item on a display, the response will be unambiguous. The handwriting recognition devices can be used as substitutions for keyboards if the information to be entered is not long and complicated. Voice recognizers can be used for simple words, such as "yes" or "no" with little problem.

In other cases, the use of these devices should be confined to being an augmentation for other inputs. Facial expressions could be used to adapt the interface. Perhaps some of these techniques could be used in conjunction with some of the measures of mental workload, discussed in Chapter 12, to assess the workload and then adapt the display. Facial expression could be an indication of stress. Changes in the voice could also be an indicant of stress. These two measures correlated would provide a better indication of workload and stress than any single measurement. They could be used to lip-read, thus augmenting voice recognition devices.

Many of the gestures and facial expressions discussed in this chapter could be culture-related. An indication of "yes" could be an indication of "no" in another culture. Even worse, an acceptable hand gesture in one culture could be an obscene hand gesture in another culture. Much anthropological work has been performed to determine these cultural differences. Some actions seem to be inborn and do not require any training (Morris, 1977). This anthropological information could find a technical use in these new interaction techniques.

For this augmentation and adaptation to occur, we must be able to understand what needs to be adapted. We need to obtain other information about the user in order to individualize the information presented. These and other topics are discussed in the next chapter on the software aspects of natural interaction designs. In this same context, the important analysis technique is how to analyze the task to find the mismatches between human-human communication and human-computer interaction.

QUESTIONS

1. Examine an anthropological textbook and list some of the differences in gestures which are related to the different cultures.

2. Use a computer system and record all the different kinds of facial expressions exhibited during the interaction

with the computer. For each, describe the facial expression and the context in which it occurred. For each item, indicate how the computer could have adapted had it known your particular facial expression.

3. Go to a computer center where many people are interacting with computers. List all the facial expressions and hand gestures that are being used in that setting.

4. Use the conceptual dependency theory from Schank and Abelson to parse the following sentences.

   a. John gives the plate to Mary.
   b. Mary takes the plate from John.
   c. Mary gives the plate to John.
   d. Mary sees John with the food.
   e. John tells Mary to eat.
   f. Mary takes the food to the table.
   g. John gives Mary a fork.
   h. Mary takes the fork from John.
   i. Mary grabs the fork.

5. Get a story from a newspaper. From the story, pick out the who, what, where, why, and how. Ask a question of the computer about some aspect of the story. Show how the computer would answer the question by indicating which part of the answer would come from your question and which part of the answer would be present in all the answers.

6. Get a passage from a book. Show how SAM would not be able to understand this information.

7. You are in charge of designing equipment for the factory floor. You want to design a computer that will assist the user in taking inventory when moving around on the factory floor. Explain which of the input methods discussed in this chapter would be most appropriate for this computer. Explain why this device would be most appropriate.

8. Describe how you would design a driver training simulator using virtual reality.

CHAPTER 20

NATURAL INTERFACE DESIGN: PERCEPTUAL AND COGNITIVE MISMATCHES

INTRODUCTION

The most important part of this chapter, also emphasized in the last chapter, is to illustrate the anthropomorphic approach to interface design. Under this approach, the computerized task must be analyzed to determine how it is different from the task, as it is or as it would be performed in a natural setting, without a computer. The mismatch between the computerized task and the natural setting provides clues for how the human-computer interaction can be made more natural and user-friendly.

In this chapter, the anthropomorphic approach is discussed in terms of perceptual and cognitive mismatches. A perceptual mismatch occurs when the computer presents a version of the visual scene different from that which we perceive naturally. The computer screen can be conceptualized as a window to the computer world, and we should be able to move around that scene and manipulate it. The perspective in the computer world should match the perceptual perspectives we are familiar with when moving around in a natural setting. Just as we would not design a window on the real world with colored filters so that the grass is always blue and the sky is green, we would not want to skew the computer world so that the perceptual relationships are unnatural. This is what happens in some cases, though, and this perceptual aspect is examined in this chapter by discussing the display movement and perspective.

The computer interface can also be made more natural by attributing the computer with some cognitive abilities which we assume will be present when communicating with another human. Two analogies can be used. First, the computer should be able to have some of the communication skills that are expected when a teacher communicates with a student. In this case, the teacher is analogous to the computer and the user is analogous to the student. The computer has information which can be conveyed to the user, about how to use and communicate with the computer, and the computer should be able to provide some intelligent assistance with the task. Second, the computer should be able to adapt to the user much like a salesperson adapts to a customer. In this case, the computer is analogous to the salesperson and the user is analogous to the customer. By understanding what the user needs or knows, the computer should be adaptable to fulfill those needs and thus satisfy the user. A good salesperson understands the needs of a customer, or sometimes creates a need, and then provides the services or the products to satisfy the needs.

Making the computer world similar to the natural world has some of the same advantages as does the use of metaphors (see Chapter 10). Since we already know how to interact with the natural world, portraying it on the computer screen can reduce the time needed for learning how to interact with the computer world. With proper design, and the proper analysis of the task, there is no need to force the user to learn how to interact with the world anew.

In this chapter, three topics will be discussed. Display movement and perspective analyzes the view through the window of the computer and determines the mismatches between this view and a view through a real window in the natural world. User assistance with a task examines ways in which the computer can play the role of a teacher and offer assistance or advice when performing the task. The adaptable interfaces section examines how the interface can be adapted to better fit the needs of the user.

DISPLAY MOVEMENT AND PERSPECTIVES: SCROLLING AND STROLLING

To determine the most natural way to view the computer world, the interface designer must go inside the head and perceive the world from that perspective. The movement of the world from the observer's perspective may not be how you think it might be initially. As an example, when you turn to the left, which way does the world move in front of your eyes? It moves to the right. This kind of perspective can be used when scrolling through a manuscript or strolling through the file space. The following examines some of the advantages and disadvantages of changes in the perspectives.

Scrolling

Displayed information can have two perspectives: the view from inside the person's head looking out on the world, often termed inside-out; or the view from out-

side the person's head looking down on the world, often termed outside-in. The two different perspectives mean entirely different things in terms of the display of information. Take, as an example, driving a car. Consider making a left turn when you are driving the car. If you were looking down on the car from the sky, as obviously you would not be, you would be able to see the car moving in the left direction when turning. Since you are inside the car, you would not be able to get that perspective. Instead, with your perspective, when the car moves to the left, the visual scene, moving across the windshield of the car, moves in the right direction. Sometimes this perspective is difficult to visualize, but it is the only perspective that we have of the scene. From the outside-in, movement of the steering wheel in the left direction results in movement of the car to the left; from the inside-out, movement of the steering wheel in the left direction results in movement of the visual scene to the right. The outside-in perspective preserves compatibilities (see Chapter 8), but the inside-out view may be more natural because that is the way that we view the world from inside the head.

The inside-out/outside-in problem has occurred frequently in human factors before human-computer interaction became a research area. In a plane's cockpit, the orientation of the plane is represented by either a moving horizon or a moving plane perspective (see Figure 20-1). A moving horizon perspective is inside-out. A representation of the plane appears on the screen. When controlling the plane up, the moving horizon moves down as the real horizon does when viewed from the cockpit. When controlling the plane down, the moving horizon moves up.

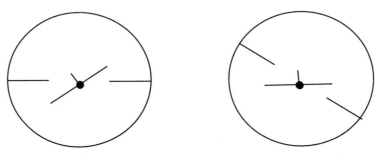

Figure 20-1. The moving plane display (on the left) and the moving horizon display (on the right) inside a cockpit.

The moving plane display is outside-in. The horizon remains stationary, in this case, and the plane on the display moves in response to control inputs. When the pilot controls the plane to move up, the plane on the display moves up in respect to the stationary horizon. If the control moves down, the plane moves down.

Which kind of display to use, inside-out or outside-in, has always been controversial. To navigate in the world, pilots often have to take the perspective of how they are moving in relation to the rest of the world, an outside-in perspective, and not the view from the cockpit (Roscoe, 1980). Sometimes, when using an inside-out perspective, pilots experience control reversals; they think that, based upon the displayed information, they have made the wrong kinds of display input (Roscoe, 1980). The advantages to the inside-out display are that it may be more natural and the display can be more compact. If moving around in the perspective of the world, the displayed information could be huge. If moving around in the limited visual span from inside the cockpit, the display is limited by where the pilot is looking.

The perspective problem has parallels for the display of movement for interface design research. One controversial issue has been the direction of the scrolling on the screen. Two perspectives can be taken, analogous to the inside-out and outside-in perspectives. For one perspective, the user can think of the screen as a moving window with the text being stationary behind the window (see Figure 20-2). If you want to move up, you think of the moving window moving up on the stationary screen. But, when moving up, the text would scroll down the screen. For the other perspective, scrolling (see Figure 20-3), you would think of the screen as being stationary and the text scrolling behind the screen. In this case, scrolling down would mean that the text moves down the screen.

The issue for the moving window or the scrolling occurs with the assignment of command names to the movement. If "up" is assigned to the movement, does it mean to move up on the page, with a moving window, or does it mean that the text should scroll up? If it means moving up on the page, then the physical movement of the text on the screen would be in the downward direction. If it means the scrolling direction moving up toward the top of the screen, then you would find yourself at a location farther down in the text.

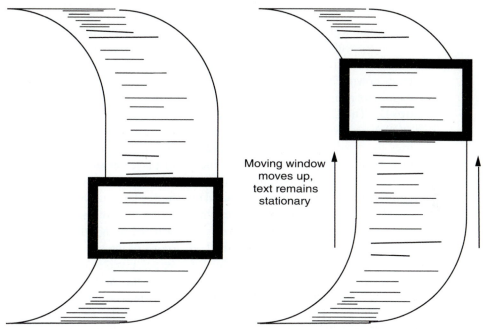

Figure 20-2. For the moving window perspective, the text is stationary and the computer screen is like a window that moves over the text. Up means that you move up the text.

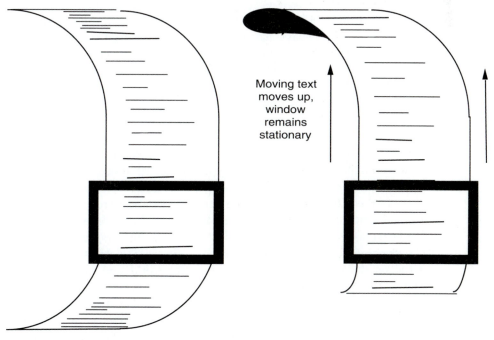

Figure 20-3. For the scrolling perspective, the text moves and the screen window remains stationary. Up means that the scroll, or the text, moves in the upward direction.

The moving window/scrolling problem occurs with all text editors. The "vi" editor, a popular editor on the UNIX system, can illustrate the problem. To move up or down when text editing, two commands are available: control-U and control-D. The U and D represent UP and DOWN, respectively. The "vi" editor uses the moving window perspective so that moving up means to move to a location higher in the manuscript. This perspective appears to be the one preferred by users. Bury et al. (1982) tested the moving window and scrolling perspectives and found that the moving window method allowed the best performance. In this experiment, however, all the subjects were novices. The results could be somewhat different for experts.

Strolling

Recently, a shift in the perspective of many computer displays has been attempted. In the past, most displays have been outside-in. For the desktop displays (see Chapter 10), the items are on the desk top and the user looks down on these items. This perspective works fine as long as the desk top is small and not much detail is needed. Think about your own desk top, however. If the desk top is large, then your eyes would have to move to scan all the items on the desk top. To look at one item in more detail, you would have to move the item closer or move your head closer. As soon as the eyes are scanning the material on the desk top, the perspective shifts to an inside-out perspective.

The virtual reality displays utilizing the Rooms interface, discussed in Chapter 10, use an inside-out perspective (e.g., Clarkson, 1991). For those perspectives,

the user can move through the items on the display so that the perspective remains the same as if the user was moving his or her eyes to scan the items. The advantage of this approach is that it allows more information to be displayed in a more compact space. Displaying the whole world would take a large screen; displaying only that in which the eye scans reduces the amount displayed at any one time.

Information on the screen can also be displayed to correspond naturally to the physiology of the eye. The eye is constructed so that the images falling on the retina of the eye, the central portion, can be perceived in more detail. The periphery of the eye has fewer receptors, and so the detail cannot be perceived. Mackinlay et al. (1991) have designed a computer display to have similar properties to the physiology of the eye. The information manipulated by the user to be in the middle panel of the display is shown in higher detail; that information on the two side panels of the screen is shown in less detail, thus providing a context (refer back to Figure 11-15). The two side panels are folded away from the middle panel providing a 3D effect to the 2D display. This kind of information display would be well suited to database retrieval problems in which the context could be searched to make sure that all the relevant information is found during the search.

There are two advantages to the inside-out perspective in screen design. The first is that this is the way that we view the world, and so this may be the most natural perspective. The second advantage is that it can limit the amount of information which must be presented on the screen. Picture a pilot in a cockpit. If the cockpit was sealed off, but the outside world was presented through television images, then the number of screens would have to be large, incorporating all the space in the cockpit. Only a small part of the display would be viewed at any particular time by the pilot; the rest of the screens are essentially wasted. If, on the other hand, the pilot had a screen in front of his face, then as the pilot moves his head, the information on the screen could change depending on the direction of the head. One medium resolution display could handle all of the display requirements, but the software load would be higher because the computer would have to track head movements and decide which parts to display on the screen. An inside-out perspective on the computer screen conserves space in a similar way.

The advantage to the outside-in perspective is that it preserves the compatibilities between input and output. When we move the steering wheel to the left, we think of the car moving in the left direction. Our mental model of the task has to be from the perspective of moving through the world, instead of how the visual scene moves across the visual field.

Both perspectives have advantages. Perhaps a way to incorporate both would be to provide the user with a choice of perspectives. Perhaps, with different perspectives, the user could come to understand the computer world more fully.

ASSISTANCE WITH A TASK

The teacher/student analogy can be used to anthropomorphize the human-computer interactions. The computer plays the role of the teacher, and the user plays the role of the student. The teacher/computer knows what can be done on the computer and must try to convey to the student/user how to do it. Understanding how good teachers teach or tutor can provide ideas for understanding how to make the interaction with a computer more natural and intelligent.

Collins and Stevens (1981) undertook an extensive study to understand how the good teachers teach. An important part of teaching is for the teacher to have a model of the students' knowledge. A teacher must understand that model by asking probing questions; a teacher must be aware of the kinds of misconceptions that can occur and determine if any of the students have those misconceptions. Once a teacher understands the model of the student, then the missing information must be presented to the student, and topics can be skipped that the student already knows.

Burton and Brown (1979b) describe many tutoring rules which they have developed in their design and implementation of the WEST program to teach children arithmetic skills. The tutoring rules are based upon two major problems: deciding when to interrupt the student's problem-solving activity and what to say once it has been interrupted. In another application of implementing tutoring rules, O'Shea (1978) designed a CAI lesson to teach quadratic equations where the tutoring rules were incorporated in a production rule system (production rules are explained in Chapter 17). Based upon the interactions with the student, the rules in the system can be changed and the tutoring techniques can be modified along the way.

All of these tutoring programs use a model of the teacher as the goal for computerizing these techniques so that tutoring can be performed with little human intervention. Two aspects of this analysis can be applied to human-computer interaction tasks to provide assistance: determining what the user knows and deciding how to convey that information. Most of the work has been performed on the former; little work has been done on the latter.

One of the most important jobs of teachers is to be able to interpret and categorize the misconceptions that the students have. The computer can perform a similar function by interpreting and categorizing the kinds of errors made by the users. Understanding the errors is difficult for the computer. The syntax errors, such as using the wrong punctuation in a command, are probably the simplest for the computer to understand. If the computer finds a syntax error, the message is usually "syntax error." No attempt is made to understand or interpret the error. Many times the error indicates an underlying misconception with the user's mental model of the task. Providing simple error messages may not help and could actually hurt.

Attempts are being made to place more intelligence in the interpretation of errors by the computer. One method which has been used is to have the computer act intelligently, like an expert computer tutor, by encoding the expert's knowledge as a series of rules. This has been done for UNIX operating system help messages (Jerrams-Smith, 1989). For this procedure, the knowledge acquisition technique of protocol analysis (see Chapter 7) was used. Novice UNIX users were asked to perform tasks providing protocols along the way. The protocols, along with a detailed log of the users' actions on the computer, were analyzed by expert UNIX users. The errors were then categorized, and the experts indicated what they would do to correct the errors for each of the categories.

The important thing about the Jerrams-Smith study is how the experts' knowledge is encoded by the computer system so that it can be applied to interpreting users' errors. The experts' knowledge is encoded as a series of production rules (see Chapter 17). Following is an example of a rule:

IF   The current line has the same command as the previous line
The arguments on the two lines are equivalent
One of the arguments is of the repeated-file type
It is this argument which provides the only difference between the two lines

THEN   The hypothesis is that the user was unaware that both filenames could be supplied on the same line

This rule is an example of a conjunction; the ANDs are left out of the IF statement to make the code easier to read. This rule determines whether or not the user knows that more than one file name can be used on one command line. As an example, if several files have to be removed, then the expert user would type

rm file1, file2, file3, file4

where "rm" means to remove the file. A novice user would be likely to remove one file, then the next file on the next command line, and so forth. This is a very inefficient method. The above rule checks to see if this has occurred.

As another example of a rule, consider the following:

IF   Command is invalid
          The string *help* appears
          somewhere in the line
THEN   The hypothesis is that the user
          needs some general
          information on how to find
          help

One of the most frustrating aspects of using a computer is when you require help but you need help in trying to find help. The preceding rule tries to determine when the user may need this help.

Rules similar to those depicted have been incorporated into an intelligent help system to determine when the user is making errors and to offer advice on how to perform the command correctly. For this help system, a user would perform the tasks as usual. Each command line from the user is checked for spelling mistakes and then the rules are activated. Each command line is checked to determine if any of the rules fire. If a rule fires, then a help message will appear on the screen offering advice on a better way to perform the command.

This intelligent help message system was tested experimentally. One group of subjects performed UNIX commands using the intelligent help and another group, the control group, performed the UNIX commands without any computerized help. The results showed that the group provided with the intelligent help had fewer errors, attempted and completed more operations, and used fewer commands than did the control group. The fewer commands means that the treatment group was able to perform the task more efficiently.

This method shows one way that a computer can offer assistance intelligently on a task. The technique of developing this assistance is important. First, a problem is identified and users, typically novices, perform the task so that specific knowledge about the problem can be acquired. In this case, knowledge was acquired through the protocols. Second, the errors must be identified, classified, and specified. In this case, the errors were classified by experts and then specified in terms of production rules. Third, the computer must be programmed to monitor the performance of users trying to identify the errors so that assistance can be provided. In this case, each command line was analyzed by the computer to determine if any of the rules would fire. If so, appropriate assistance would be provided by the user.

The Jerrams-Smith research shows that a computer can develop a user model, similar to the student models developed by experienced teachers, so that errors can be classified and misconceptions can be corrected. The teacher/student analogy should be used for other aspects of human-computer interaction, and this could provide research impetus in the future. As an example, Collins and Stevens (1981) found several different strategies for how good teachers convey information to students. As an example, they found that teachers use counterexamples, hypothetical cases, and entrapment strategies to force students to examine their knowledge about the situation. Typically, in human-computer interaction, the feedback to the user will be on the order of "here is the way to do it." This does not help the user build up a good mental model of the task. Some of these teaching strategies can be used; the interface developer can discover these potential beneficial techniques by examining the mismatches between the human-human communication and human-computer interaction similar to that done in this section by studying the teacher/student interactions.

ADAPTABLE SYSTEMS

People are adaptable. When communicating with someone else, we try to adapt the communication to the person. Good salespeople are especially adept at adapting to the communication needs of the customer. This section surveys many of the methods that can be used to make the computer adaptable.

Adaptable systems are human-computer interfaces which change automatically to meet the changing needs of users. Two aspects of the current situation make adaptable systems necessary. First, novices and experts require different features in a computer system. For example, a system which provides much feedback and assistance for a novice will annoy and encumber an expert. An adaptable system would avoid this problem by providing assistance for the novice but not for the expert unless requested. Second, computer technology is changing so rapidly that many companies cannot afford to update their systems every year. An adaptable interface would enable people to use programs or equipment with different computers.

A good or intelligent interface according to James (1981) is ". . . concerned with human patterns of learning, using, remembering and forgetting." He recommends defining three concepts before the design of any interface. First, the users

must be defined, second, the nature of the task must by identified and defined, and third, the interface should be defined in both machine and user terms. Innocent (1982) believes it should take a user a minimum of effort to personalize a system. The optimum situation would be a system which adapted automatically to the user based on the pattern of the user's responses.

User-Controlled Adaptable Systems

One of the simplest methods for designing adaptable systems is to have the users control the adaptability. Existing adaptable systems rely on fairly simple techniques for user control. Present adaptable systems include adaptable input devices, interfaces, and terminals. Some parameters of input devices, such as their gain, can be adapted by the user. For terminals, many times they can emulate other popular terminals, functions such as cursor blinking can be turned on or off, and special programmable function keys are available.

For many interfaces, some of the functionality can be adapted by the user. For the Apple Macintosh operating system, the user can control the view of the files for a directory. Under one view, the file structure looks like a desk top with folders and papers represented by icons lying on the table top (see Figure 20-4). For this view, the files are directly manipulable in that the icons can be moved and placed anywhere on the table top. For another view (see Figure 20-5), the same files can be represented by words alphabetically in a vertical list. The files are more compact under this view, but the user loses the ability, because of the alpha-

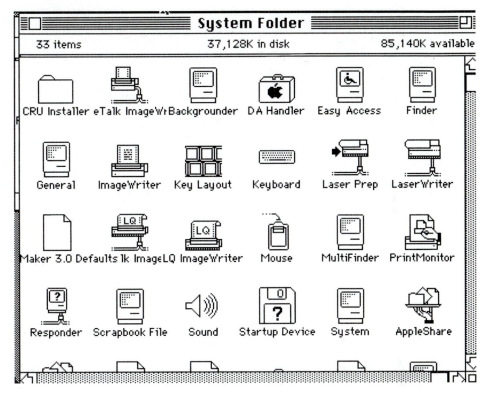

Figure 20-4. The user adaptable interface for the files of an Apple Macintosh. One view shows the files as icons.

Name	Size	Kind	Last Modified	
AppleShare	44K	Chooser document	Thu, Sep 7, 1989	12
AppleShare Prep	2K	AppleShare docu...	Thu, Jun 11, 1992	4:0
AppleTalk ImageWriter	44K	Chooser document	Sat, Apr 30, 1988	12
Backgrounder	6K	System document	Sat, Apr 30, 1988	12
Clipboard File	0K	System document	Sun, Jun 20, 1993	9:0
CRU Installer	--	folder	Sun, Jun 14, 1992	10
DA Handler	8K	document	Wed, Mar 7, 1990	12
Easy Access	4K	Startup document	Tue, Sep 5, 1989	12
Finder	108K	System document	Thu, Jul 30, 1992	1:
Font/DA Mover	38K	application	Thu, Oct 8, 1987	12

Figure 20-5. The user can choose to display the files alphabetically for the Apple Macintosh system.

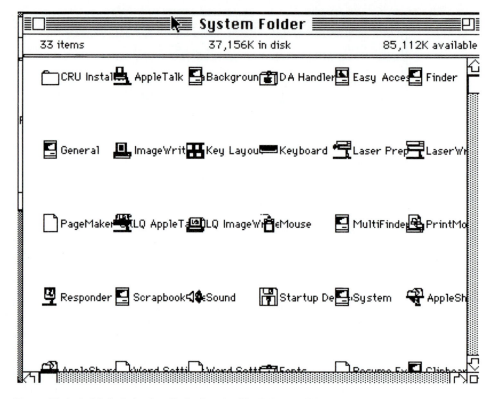

Figure 20-6. A third choice for displaying the files is by small icon.

betizing requirement, to directly manipulate the file icons within the window. Still
another view (see Figure 20-6) utilizes
small icons which compact the file specifications while still retaining some of the
direct manipulation characteristics. The
view is dependent upon the preferences of
the user and perhaps the constraints of the
user's file space. As an example, a file
space with many files could be best represented under the two compact views while
a folder with only a few files could be best
represented by the full icons.

Another adaptable characteristic
from the Apple Macintosh operating system, and other systems, is the menu size.
The user can either specify that the short
menus or the full menus will be shown.

The short menus show the commands
which will be used most often by the user.
By displaying the short menus, the user
can minimize the travel of the mouse
because on these pull-down menus, the
user must first push the mouse button
while located on the menu title in the title
bar, hold the mouse button down when the
menu appears, move the mouse to the
desired commands, and then release the
mouse button to choose the command.
The shorter the distance for moving the
mouse, the faster the command operation.
Also recall from Chapters 13-17, the
fewer commands to read, the faster the
interaction. The full menus include more
commands, some of which are not used
very much except for more specialized

```
#         Switch to user root to get the prompt
#
cd
#
set path=( $HOME/.commands . /usr/games /usr/dwb          \
#          /usr/X                                         \
           /usr/new/X11 /usr/new/X11R5                    \
           /usr/new /usr/ecn ~/bin /usr/ucb /bin /usr/custom \
           /usr/spectrum/rardin/Rroff/rroff              \
           /usr/local /usr/bin /usr/new/bin               \
           /usr/ecn/X11R4/bin                             \
           /usr/rtingres/bin )
#
#  Set default printer
#
setenv PRINTER gd
#
alias   X         "(source ~/.Xstartup) > /dev/null &"
alias   xlock     `xlock -m "Patience is a virtue" `shorthostname`:0´
alias   logout    exit
```

Figure 20-7. Customizing the interface for UNIX through the .cshrc file. This example shows a partial .cshrc file: the paths are used to traverse the file structure pathways so that the complicated paths do not have to be entered each time; a default printer is set; and the aliases are used to substitute one command sequence for another.

tasks. With the full menus, the user has more functions available but the mouse operation to choose a command could take longer.

The UNIX operating system also has many ways in which the interface can be customized and adapted by an individual user. Many of the adaptability functions are performed when creating and including a file called the .cshrc. One of the main forms of adaptability is to specify aliases for commands (see Figure 20-7). In this file, the user can specify that the command to be performed when a command name not in the UNIX command space is entered. As an example, a user may be used to entering "dir" to perform a directory but, in UNIX, the directory command is "ls." The user could include the following line in the .cshrc file:

  alias ls dir

This means that if "dir" is entered, and since UNIX has no command under that name, then it will search the .cshrc file to find possible aliases. It finds that "dir" is

an alias for "ls," and so it carries out the "ls" command. In this file, the user can also specify the prompt that will appear while the system is waiting for a command. A popular prompt is to show the current pathway for the directory of the system. Without this prompt, the user may have trouble remembering the current directory.

An obvious problem with user controlled adaptability is that the user may not know that these kinds of changes can be made to the interface. In many cases, the novices are the most likely group needing adaptability, but they are the least likely to be able to determine how to perform these adaptability functions. In fact, Rosson (1984) found that experienced users, such as computer programmers, were more likely to make use of the adaptable features of the computer than less experienced users such as nonprogrammers or secretaries. Walther and O'Neill (1974) argue that novices do not want to expend the mental effort to learn how to tailor the system to their needs.

On the other hand, adaptability by the user provides the user with much control over the system. Many times the user is the only one who knows when he or she is ready to adapt to a different interface characteristic. It also eliminates the need for the computer to have to determine these needs. If the computer does this task poorly, then the interface could be even more confusing than it has to be.

Kantorowitz and Sudarsky (1989) argue that the important aspect of an adaptable system for interface modes is that the underlying modes all be described using the same language and descriptors. Thus, when the user decides to change from one mode to another, the transition is easier because the underlying representation is the same. They designed a prototype for an interface which adapted between menu displays and command-based displays. This kind of system was easily implemented, but no experimental results were reported on its perceived ease of use.

Adaptability on Expertise Level and User Model

Experts and novice computer users have different requirements of an interface, and often these requirements are not compatible. The expert usually places an emphasis on speed of interaction and so would not like to have to enter long commands, read through long menu displays, or be saddled with long and wordy help or error messages. The novice, on the other hand, would probably like to have as much information as possible about what the computer is doing through either explicit help or error messages; the novice would probably find menu displays the most useful and would not mind entering long

commands if they were easier to remember. Basing the adaptability upon the expertise level of the user seems plausible.

To do this, the computer must be able to determine the expertise level of the user, which can be done by devising a user model. Rich (1983) provides a three-dimensional analysis of user models. This analysis helps describe the different approaches to user models and should help in their formation. Each of the three dimensions contains two levels. The first is the number of people being modeled. Models can be of a single user or a collection of models of individual users. The second is the origin of model specifications. In one instance the designer or user specifies the models and in the other instance inferences about the user are made by the system. The third is user characteristics. Characteristics are either long-term or short-term. Long-term characteristics refer to user attributes such as intelligence, educational background, and job skills, whereas short-term characteristics refer to transient attributes such as the topic of the previous sentence or the time of day.

Rich delineates two methods for designing user models. The first is a method of inferring single facts one at a time. The second is a method which enables the inference of clusters of facts all at once. Facts about the user can be inferred either by studying how individuals use computer commands or by deriving user characteristics through the use of stereotypes. This latter method has advantages when designing systems whose primary users are novices.

Brajnik, Guida, and Tasso (1990) also provide a classification of user models but argue that user models can be classified across four dimensions: implicit vs. explicit; given vs. inferred; static vs. dynamic, and canonical vs. individual. The first two dimensions are distinctions based more upon how they were programmed rather than representing different classes of models. The implicit/explicit dimension, as used by Brajnik et al., refers to the modularization of the software. An implicit user model is one that has been hardwired into the software so that it does not change. An explicit user model can be programmed as a separate module in the code so that it can be accessed and changed easily. The given/inferred dimension refers to how the model is constructed through the software. A given model is defined and coded by the programmer with the rest of the program. An inferred model is constructed automatically during the operation of the program without any intervention by the programmer.

The other two dimensions have more to do with the kind of user model rather than the programming characteristics. A static model remains unchanged during the execution of the program. A dynamic model, on the other hand, will change with the interaction. It could change according to queries addressed to and received from the user; it could change according to how the user interacts with the system; or it could change according to the knowledge exhibited by the user. A canonical/individual dimension is much the same as the individual/group distinction made by Rich (1983). A canonical model identifies the characteristics of a class of users without referring to individual deviations from the stereotype. The individual models include both those characteristics similar to the class of users and those characteristics which distinguish the individual from the

stereotype. This is the only dimension which is related directly to the dimensions specified by Rich (1983).

There appear to be very few user models described in the literature which actually have been implemented. Rich (1983), however, describes a user model called GRUNDY which operates from stereotypes in recommending books. The procedure is interactive and GRUNDY revises its initial user stereotype by incorporating user's responses to suggested titles. After several suggestions, thus allowing for possible revisions of the user mode, GRUNDY can recommend titles successfully.

Another system, called the Adaptive Graphics Analyser (Holynski, 1988), uses machine learning techniques to understand the user and adapt the graphics presentation to the individual needs and preferences of the user. To understand the need for such a system, Holynski contrasts the preferences of an architect and an artist. The architect must think about functionality and plausibility of a design while an artist only cares about the appearance. The Adaptive Graphics Analyser attempts to adapt to these individual models of the graphics use.

Brajnik et al. (1990) have developed an explicit, inferred, dynamic, and individual user model for adapting the natural language interaction in a program which retrieves documents from a database (see Chapter 24 for more information on this model). A book by Browne, Totterdell, and Norman (1990) describes the Adaptive Interface Design (AID) process.

More work on this topic has been performed in computer-assisted instruction (CAI) lessons where the computer tries to form a user model to individualize each student's lessons. In CAI, the computer must be able to detect and correct the misconceptions of students about certain situations. As an example, Stevens et al. (1979) analyzed the kinds of misconceptions students have about weather systems with the goal of designing a CAI lesson to "debug" these misconceptions. The misconceptions of students are incorporated in a user model that the computer keeps of each individual student. Five general methods are in use to ascertain what a student knows. The first two methods used, topic marking and the context modes, are relatively simple approaches. In the topic-marking approach, the system keeps track of the information presented to the student. For the context model, the extent of the student's knowledge is inferred from the dialogue and questions input by the student. An example of this approach is an interface developed by Sleeman (1985) for teaching students about the medical diagnoses performed by the expert system called NEOMYCIN. Through a series of queries to the user, the program determines a user model which specifies the kinds of explanations which will be given subsequently to the user.

Two other methods, the bug and overlay approaches, compare the user's knowledge with the knowledge of an expert. For the bug approach, student knowledge is characterized in terms of the bugs or misconceptions the user has about the subject. User performance is compared with a variety of bugs until the best match is found. For the overlay approach, user knowledge is characterized as a subset of an expert's knowledge. Once the user demonstrates the correct facts or rules contained in the expert's knowledge, the user is considered to have acquired those

facts. An example of this method is a program called WURSOR III (Goldstein, 1982) in which a person plays a game to try to kill the dangerous animal called a WUMPUS. The skill level, and thus the interaction in the game, is changed by comparing the user model to an expert model.

The fifth method, generative modeling, is a relatively new approach. Instead of looking at the particular facts acquired, the student's knowledge is characterized in terms of the plans used to solve a particular problem. The computer instruction is then organized according to these perceived plans; factual misconceptions are corrected and feedback is tailored to the particular student's conceptions. This kind of user model was developed in an adaptive interface called AID (Totterdell and Cooper, 1986) in which different feedback would be provided to the user depending on the user's goal. This approach had only mixed success.

In testing user models in CAI, researchers have found little or no evidence for improvement in performance of user model groups when compared to control groups (see Eberts and Brock, 1988, for a discussion). In addition, Maskery (1984) found that when the interface changes to a higher expertise level, the user can find this very disruptive and exhibit more errors and longer performance times. More work is needed to determine how to make this transition more graceful.

Adaptability on Cognitive Abilities

Although adaptability based upon user cognitive characteristics has elicited much speculation, finding documentation of workable systems has been difficult.

Norcio and Stanley (1989) suggest several cognitive-based user characteristics upon which the interface can be adapted. Many of these abilities are the same as those discussed earlier in the book under the cognitive approach.

One cognitive ability that could possibly be used for interface adaptability is spatial ability. Norcio and Stanley (1989) report an experiment by Yallow (1980) in which high or low spatial ability individuals were presented with either spatial or verbal formats. Those with high spatial abilities performed better with the spatial format, and those with low spatial abilities performed better with the verbal format.

Individual differences may also occur for attentional strategies such as the ability to distribute and allocate attentional resources (Norcio and Stanley, 1989; see also Chapter 12). Norcio and Stanley claim that adapting systems on this ability may be most relevant for windowing systems. With windows, the users can perform several tasks at one time. If individuals do not have the ability to distribute and allocate attention, parallel windowing could be confusing.

Another cognitive ability has been termed field-dependent and field-independent. Field-dependent people tend to look at the task as a whole without analyzing individual parts. They tend to accept the task as it is, relying on the general organization of the material as it is presented, and tend to be very passive in their problem solving and learning. Field-independent people decompose the task into parts, ignoring those parts which are irrelevant to the task. They actively try to reorganize the material and take an active approach to problem solving and learning. They are the ones likely to form a mental model of the situation and change that model through experience. In an experiment on field-dependent and field-independent people using the UNIX operating system, Coventry (1989) found that field-dependent people were less likely to know the command and more likely to ask for help without making any attempt at the task. Field-independent people were more likely to attempt the task and make errors rather than ask for help. Coventry suggested that the help messages should adapt to the cognitive style of the user.

In the chapters on predictive modeling, we assumed that users form goals and plans for interacting with the computer. It is possible that individuals have different abilities to perform this cognitive activity, and that there can be good planners and poor planners. Norcio and Stanley (1989) report a study by Goldin and Hayes-Roth (1980) who suggest that the interface should be adapted so that the poor planners are given assistance with generating plans.

Adapting on Task Characteristics

Depending on the task, some interfaces can be specialized to make interaction easier. As an example, Greenberg and Witten (1985) devised a database for an on-line telephone directory. The computer program tracked which telephone numbers an individual used most often. The most frequently used telephone numbers were then made easier to access through the database. Unlike some of the other adaption schemes, no information about the user is needed; the interface learns about the special needs of the user from the interactions. Other task-specific adaptability could also be considered.

Conclusions About Adaptable Systems

Norcio and Stanley (1989) list some of the positive and negative aspects of adaptive interfaces. For the negative aspects, the user may not be able to develop a coherent model of the interface or an accurate mental model if the interface is always changing. The user may not develop a clear understanding of the relationships between the user input and the system output. Second, the user may develop a feeling of loss of control over the interactions. This will only occur, however, for the automatically adapting systems and not the user-controlled adapting systems. Some users may not like having the computer indicate which interface is best; they may have been perfectly happy with the configuration before the adaptation occurred. Norman (1986) suggests that interfaces should be seen as tools; they should not be designed with too much intelligence in them. A tendency may be to over-automate. People like to have control over the design; with too much intelligence, the user will not have enough control and will quickly lose interest. Finally, adaptive interfaces are more complex and thus costly to design. Poorly designed adaptive interfaces could cause more problems than they solve. Adaptive interfaces have a higher computational overhead and could potentially slow the speed of interaction with the user.

The main advantage of adaptive systems is that the system can be personalized to the individual's cognitive style, information needs, or task requirements. If the individual needs certain kinds of information, the computer should be able to provide it. For those adaptive systems which allow the individual to control the adaptation, users can come to feel that they have control over the system. Norman (1986) claims that users need to have all kinds of control over the system. Adaptation holds the promise of making the interface suitable for all kinds of users ranging from novices to experts. Much of this promise, however, is still to be achieved.

SUMMARY

This chapter has surveyed some of the techniques for making the computer world more natural to the user. By analyzing the mismatches between human-human communication and human-computer interaction, research and development ideas for making interfaces more natural and user-friendly can be found and analyzed. One important aspect of most of this work is the search for methods to make the computer more intelligent. In this chapter, in the UNIX help system example, expertise resided in the production rules which were formulated from experts analyzing novice protocols. Expertise in a computer system can also be incorporated through other methods such as neural nets.

A problem with incorporating intelligence or fancy graphics in computer systems was the development costs and the computer processing costs. Performing protocols and formulating rules is costly; the computer must be able to process information quickly to intelligently analyze the inputs or to display the fancy graphics. Computer processing costs are being reduced, and techniques are constantly being researched for decreasing the development costs. The barriers are being eliminated for implementing these kinds of systems.

QUESTIONS

1. Test several word processing programs to determine if they use a moving window or moving text perspective. For each specify what up and down mean.

2. In teleconferencing people are located in different rooms at remote sites. They have a meeting through the transmission of television images and sound. If several people are located in one room, then a television camera, usually mounted to a motor in a corner of the room, must be controlled by somebody so that it can focus on everybody in the room. The television is controlled through a joystick, so moving the joystick in one direction operates a motor which moves the camera to point in a different direction. This presents a control perspective problem. The designers of such a system can either design the control to be an inside-out or outside-in display relationship between the movement of the joystick and the image that moves across the television screen.

a. Explain how to design the television camera control so that the relationship between the joystick movement and the movement of the image across the television screen is outside-in.

b. Explain how to design the television camera control so that the relationship between the joystick movement and the movement of the image across the television screen is inside-out.

CHAPTER 21

AFFORDANCES, CONSTRAINTS, AND WORLD KNOWLEDGE

INTRODUCTION

In his interesting book called *The Pyschology of Everyday Things*, Don Norman states that "much of our everyday knowledge resides in the world, not in the head." This may not seem like such a radical idea; but, when taken from the context of this textbook, it is. This is an idea which is totally different from the cognitive approach. Recall from the cognitive approach of Chapter 7 the important concept of a mental model. The computer users form a mental model of how the computer operates by interacting with the computer. In that case, we assume that the knowledge of the computer resides in the head. The further assumption is that by understanding this cognitive ability, we can understand how to design the interface.

The techniques discussed for predictive modeling were all based upon modeling cognitive activity. The models can be used to determine the cycle times for perceptual, cognitive, and motor activities; they could be used for determining the load on the cognitive short-term storage; and they could be used to predict the learning time based upon the number of methods which had to be learned and, thus, had to reside in the head. For the grammar models, we had to understand the cognitive activity of the user which decomposes the parts of the interaction. All of these activities reside in the head instead of the world.

The material discussed in this chapter is the antithesis to some of these other approaches. The advocates of this chapter's approach state that many of the everyday tools or objects that we use have knowledge contained in them, merely from their design, about how they can and should be used. When these tasks are changed to computer tasks, the design loses much of that self-contained knowledge. Each computer task, therefore, must be evaluated to determine the desired properties. The implication of this is that general purpose interfaces, following general principles, cannot be designed. In the general purpose interface, the task specificity of the design is, of course, lost. The only general principle of interface design, therefore, is that there are no general principles.

If there are no general principles for interface design, then a textbook like this is not needed. Of course, I would not advocate such a radical position. There are, however, several interesting concepts that can be used in interface design by analyzing how world knowledge can reside in the computer interface in order to make interaction with the computer easier and more natural.

THE IMPORTANCE OF WORLD KNOWLEDGE

Having the knowledge reside in the world instead of the head is a very important concept for computer interaction. When using the computer, we would like to be able to just sit down, look at the computer, and know how to use it. This is not always possible. For one thing, on many computers we cannot even determine how to turn the thing on. The on/off buttons are usually on the back of the machine, not visible to the user. Why not put the button in the front? When looking at the on/off buttons, what does a 0 and a 1 mean? Does the 0 mean that the computer is already on and nothing has to be done, or does it mean that it is doing nothing and therefore is off? There must be a better way to label it. For most of the tools that we use in the everyday world, we do not need instructions for how to use them. We can look at a hammer and determine how to use it just by the way it looks. We can look at a fork, a knife, and a spoon and see which functions are appropriate for each. The ideal is to design these kinds of features into a computer.

The response from a designer may be that the computer user can surely remember just one more thing, such as "1" means that the computer is on (I had to look at the back of my computer while word processing to determine that this was the case). The chapter on human information processing (Chapter 8) showed that our short-term memory is limited and we should avoid situations where it is overloaded. The chapter on the NGOMSL model (Chapter 15) showed how to calculate load on memory, with the idea that the interface design should be changed if these calculations determine that the load is too high. By designing the knowledge into the object, instead of placing it in the head, the memory load can be reduced.

We already have to remember enough things that have no basis in world knowledge that we are becoming overburdened. We have to remember our address, both at work and at home. We have to

remember telephone numbers: our work and home, our spouse's work phone, plus any friends and stores that we wish to commit to memory. ZIP codes are difficult, especially with the relatively new plus four extension in the United States. We have to remember computer log-ons and where we may have stored our important files. If we're a member of an interactive network, we have to remember a different log-on with a different password. If on the system, and using it for making plane reservations, we must remember a different password for that system. We have to remember PINs (personal identification numbers) for automatic teller machine cards, telephone credit cards, and bank credit cards. We have to remember Social Security card numbers. When we come to a gas station, first we must remember which side of the car the gas tank is on and then, if paying by credit card, we must remember the license plate number. The list can go on and on. People should not have to needlessly tax their memory just because of poor design. If possible, the designer should not fall to the temptation of saying that, surely, people can remember one more thing. The next sections of this chapter present some methods and examples for removing this temptation.

AFFORDANCES

The first place to start for learning how to design world knowledge into the interface is in a design principle from Norman's book. Norman (1988) states that the term affordances refers to "the perceived and actual properties of the thing, primarily those fundamental properties that determine just how the thing could possibly be used." The best way to consider this definition is to look at some examples.

Affordances in Everyday Things

Norman (1988) provides several examples of affordances in everyday things: a chair affords support and so is for sitting; glass is for seeing through and possibly for breaking; wood is used for solidity; flat surfaces are used for writing on; plates are for pushing; knobs are for turning; slots are for inserting things into; and balls are for throwing or bouncing. When these affordances are used, then no experience or instructions are needed to operate the machine or tool. If the design does not have affordances, then experience or instructions are needed.

Consider some tools that we commonly use. A fork contains affordances. One end of the fork has prongs that are sharp and the other end has a flat, usually curved surface. The fork contains the knowledge about how to use it. The sharp end is used for stabbing the food and the flat end is used for holding the fork. Chopsticks may require training or instructions because they do not contain the same kinds of affordances. One end is not appreciably sharper than the other or flatter than the other so that we do not know which end to hold. (Actually, either end can be used: the smaller end for normal eating and the larger end for retrieving food from a communal dish.) It is not obvious how to pick up the chopstick; no part of the chopstick fits into the cavity between the thumb and the index finger. Finally, we may not know that two chopsticks are needed and that they both should be used in the same hand. In fact, most people who do not know how to use chop-

stick, or have never seen anybody using chopsticks, would probably place one chopstick in each hand because the affordance would be two chopsticks and two hands so that both should be used.

Consider some other designs. A favorite example of Norman's (1988) is the door. A door should be a simple enough tool for everyone to operate, yet, for some designs, we still may have problems. Most doors only open one way, and the affordances of the handles should indicate that direction. If the door is to be pushed from one direction, then this affordance should be contained in the door mechanism. A way to do that is to have a horizontal bar that cannot be grasped. For this kind of bar, nothing else can be done to it except pushing. Another possibility is to just have a steel plate on the door. From the other side of the door, the person must pull the door to open it. Obviously, the horizontal push bar or the steel plate would not work for pulling. A vertically placed handle, that can be grasped, provides the affordance of pulling.

When you think back to the doors that you have encountered, a surprising number of them are poorly designed. (Is it surprising, then, that computer interfaces are poorly designed?) Many doors have a push bar that can also be grasped which spans the total width of the door. Many times, you do not know which side of the push bar to push and end up pushing the wrong side with no results. The push bar should clearly show the mechanism for opening the door, or the bar should only be on the side of the door which opens. In a better design, some push bar doors have larger pads, providing an affordance for pushing, on the side that should be pushed.

Another example of an affordance

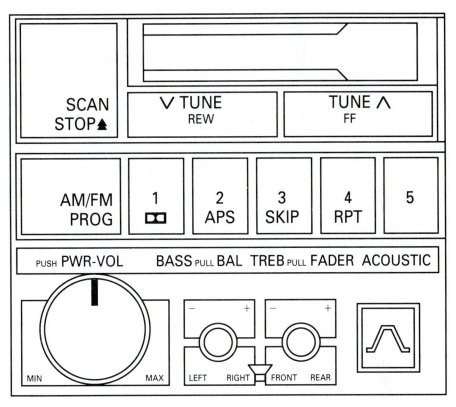

Figure 21-1. On a car radio, the affordance of the knob is to turn it. Many car radios have knobs that have to be pushed for on/off functions.

can be found in the knob for a car radio. In this case, the affordance of a knob is to turn it (see Figure 21-1). In most cases, the car radio knob is used for the volume control, so that when it is turned, the volume changes. Some knobs perform a dual purpose, however. On many of the latest car radios, the knob is also used to turn on the radio by pushing it. This violates the affordance for a knob; a button should be used instead for pushing. In this case, however, convenience trades off with affordances. The push knob is used because it saves space on the car radio and because the volume can be left at a suitable level and never changed. By pushing the knob, the volume does not have to be adjusted. In the older design for radios, rotating the knob to the left turned off the radio. The next time the radio was turned on, however, the radio volume would have to be set again. Many people would say that the convenience of the push knob outweighs the bad affordance of having to push a knob. These people would say that car radio users should be able to remember the function of the push knob. The designer should always remember, however, that having the knowledge reside in the world instead of the user's head is advantageous.

Another example of an affordance

Figure 21-2. A button on the interface can be designed with the affordance of pushing by depicting it as being raised above the surface so that it can be pushed down.

causing problems is the affordance of flat, porous, smooth surfaces for writing on. In fact, my copy of Norman's book provided an affordance for one of my children. On several pages of the book, purple crayon scrawl appears. In most large cities, graffiti is a problem on large flat surfaces. Norman (1988) suggests that part of this problem could be alleviated by removing the affordance. Instead of plywood for walls, Norman suggests that glass be used, since it provides an affordance of looking through, or that rougher surfaces be utilized. The glass solution offers another affordance problem, in that glass also has an affordance for breaking.

Affordances in Interface Design

Since so many simple things must have instructions to use, it is not surprising that computers are often difficult to use. In fact, one of the main problems with a computer is that it removes the tools one step further away from any affordances which may be present in the physical or mechanical form of the object. When using a word processor, we are removed from the paper affordance of a flat object or the pencil or pen affordance. Instead, we only have a flat window screen with a keyboard in front of it. How do we make the keyboard work? What do we write on? An old joke goes: How do we know when an Indiana University (choose your own

rival school) student has been using the word processor? Answer: When the screen has white-out on it.

Gaver (1991) has provided some examples of affordances for interface designs. Recall from Chapter 2 the button widgets in which the mouse cursor is moved to point to the button and then the button is "pushed" by pushing the mouse button. Buttons in the natural world contain affordances for pushing in that they are usually raised above the surface so somebody could easily see that they can be moved downward with a push of the finger. The same kind of affordance of being raised above the surface can be designed into a button on a computer interface (see Figure 21-2). The buttons in the figure provide an affordance of pushing.

Gaver (1991) also introduces the concept of sequential affordances. The natural world example that he uses is one in which a handle is provided for a door. The handle provides an affordance for grasping. If it is a handle which must be turned downward to open the door, then random movement of the hand may provide a tactile affordance that it can be moved down. Similarly, the scroll box on an Apple Macintosh demonstrates a sequential affordance (see Figure 21-3). The box in the scroll box indicates something that can be grabbed with the mouse because it appears white on a gray background. The gray background provides

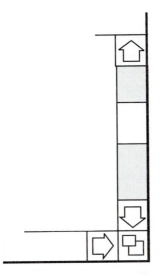

Figure 21-3. A scroll bar provides a sequential affordance. The box indicates that the scroll bar can be grabbed, and the movement of the box indicates that the scroll bar can be moved up and down.

some constraints for movement of the scroll bar. If a user "grabs" the scroll bar, then random movement of the mouse would reveal that the scroll bar could be moved up or down while it was grabbed. The design of the box for the scroll bar can be contrasted with the boxlike design of the push button. The push button had a three-dimensional element to it to indicate pushing; the scroll bar box should be designed with the pathway to indicate that it can slide in the direction provided by the pathway.

The cut and paste command also provides an example of a sequential affordance. Merely through the name of this sequence of commands, the user can determine that two operations must be performed: the cutting and then the pasting. The name of the command also provides some information about the correct ordering of the command sequence. In many

ways, affordances are similar to the concept of metaphors discussed in Chapter 10.

How can an interface designer know which affordances should be associated with the interface design? This is a difficult question at this time. Probably the best that we can do is provide many examples of how affordances are used. Determining general principles is difficult. Each specific case must be analyzed separately. When an affordance exists and is designed into the interface, it becomes obvious. Sometimes, trying to determine the affordance for a particular situation is extremely difficult.

CONSTRAINTS

Another important concept in designing knowledge in the world is that of constraints. Norman (1988) states that the world naturally restricts the allowed behavior of operations on objects such as the order in which parts go together and the way that objects can be manipulated. Norman presents many examples of these. These ideas can also be applied to interface design; the examples can be extrapolated to interface issues.

Constraints in Everyday Things

One of the more common examples of a design constraint is in a pair of scissors. The scissors will cut properly only if the blades are in the correct orientation. To ensure that people do not hold the scissors in the wrong direction, the holes for the fingers have been designed so that only one position is possible, at least, if the person is right-handed. One of the holes is round so that the thumb is the only finger

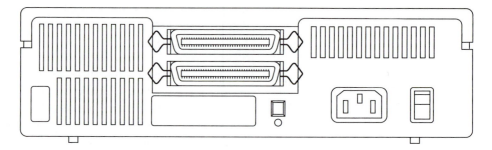

Figure 21-4. A connector has a built-in constraint by making the shape asymmetrical. The plug can only be inserted one way.

that will fit; the other hole is oval shaped so that both the index finger and forefinger will fit in the hole. If the person tries to hold it the other way in the right hand, the constraints ensure that it will not fit.

Another example of constraints occurs in connectors. When plugging one item into another, most times the connection has to be plugged in at the correct orientation; all the connections must line up for it to work properly. On computer systems, and other electronic devices, it is especially important that the correct connections be made. Constraints can be used to ensure that no wrong connections can be made. By designing an asymmetrical plug, so that it only fits in one orientation, the connections cannot possibly be done wrong (see Figure 21-4). On a computer system which has many connections on the back, such as for power supply, keyboard, networks, and printers, if each connection is different, so that one will not fit in the other, then the machine could not possibly be connected wrong. Some computers use these kinds of constraints in the design. The modern electrical plug also usually has a designed constraint so that the polarity is correct; one prong is bigger than the other so that it can only fit in one way.

Without these kinds of constraints, problems can occur easily. Severe damage could occur for electronic equipment if it is not properly connected. One of the failures to use constraints occurs in speaker wire. Since speaker wire must often be cut by the consumer in order to get the correct lengths for the particular stereo setup, proper plugs incorporating constraints are not always possible. For the speakers, the polarity must be correct: the red connector on the stereo must be connected to the red connector on the speaker and the two black connections must be connected. Because the strands of wire are used in the connection, the polarity can easily be wrong, which will degrade the signal to the speaker. Some speaker wire has no differentiation between the strands. Other wire at least has some color coding, either through copper and silver strands or by marking the plastic insulation in some way. This color coding cannot be called a constraint, but, at least, with the difficulty of incorporating a constraint on the connection, it offers some improvement in the design. Without the constraints, connecting the speaker wire is a hit or miss proposition.

A final constraint has to do with the gas tanks in cars. When cars in the United

States switched from leaded to unleaded gas, the designers had to make sure that leaded gas was not used for cars designed for unleaded gas. Since leaded gas is often cheaper than unleaded, the temptation was strong to use the leaded gas. To get around this problem, the designers used a constraint: the nozzle from the gas pump for leaded gas is larger than the hole in the car's gas tank so that the wrong gas cannot be used. Unleaded gas can still be used in vehicles equipped for leaded gas.

Constraints for Computer Systems

If constraints are used properly for computer systems, then it should be difficult for the user to make errors or to perform operations that should not be performed. Interface designs use constraints to a large degree.

One of the most popular constraints is the menu display. With the menu display, the user is constrained to use only those operations which are displayed on the screen. This is different from a command-based display, in which the user can enter any command, either part of the lexicon or not part of the lexicon. As an example, if the user is using a DOS operating system there is nothing to constrain the person from entering ls, a UNIX command, instead of the correct DOS command of DIR. The UNIX command would be wrong in this context. For menu displays, the user is constrained to the items appearing on the menu so that many erroneous entries are impossible. This means that typing errors are impossible, and the confusion between computer systems may be reduced.

Another example of a constraint occurs when menu items are "grayed" out

if they are not functional at a particular time. On the Apple Macintosh computer, most of the interaction is through pull-down menus and mouse clicks. In some contexts, however, certain commands are invalid and cannot be used. For a command-based interface, the users would be able to make errors by entering erroneous commands through the keyboard. On the Macintosh and other computers, however, a constraint is used so that this cannot be done. On the pull-down menus, for those commands which are impossible in the particular context, the command will be grayed out by using a font which only faintly shows the command name. The constraint is that this command is no longer usable, but it is somewhat visible only as a place holder so that the ordering of the other commands does not change. If the user tries to click on this menu item, nothing happens. As an example, consider the cut and paste command for Microsoft Word on the Macintosh. If no text has been cut, then the text obviously cannot be placed and so this command should be unusable. This is conveyed to the user by graying out the paste command (see Figure 21-5). In this case, the user does not have to remember that paste cannot be performed before cut; this knowledge is contained in the world, on the computer screen, through the grayed out command.

Another constraint, often seen as an irritant, is when the computer queries users to make sure that they actually want to do what they indicated. Some computer operations, if performed, are difficult or impossible to recover from if the user did not mean to do them. As an example, deleting a file is an operation which is not recoverable. Formatting a disk is also an operation which is impossible to recover

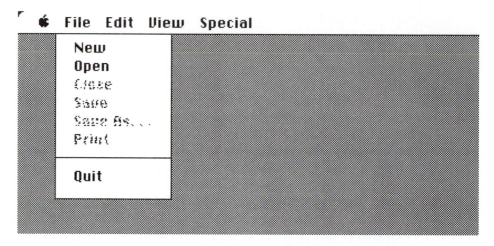

Figure 21-5. A command is grayed out if it cannot be used. In this illustration, a file has not yet been opened. Many of the commands require that a file be opened before they can be applied. As an example, you cannot save or print a file if a file is not open. These nonoperable command names are grayed out.

from. If the user performed these commands erroneously, then the consequences of lost material would be great. Many computer systems constrain the user so that these kinds of operations cannot be done except with difficulty. This is done by displaying the question "Are you sure?" on the screen and forcing the user to say yes or no.

This particular constraint is controversial. Many users do not like the extra time and extra operations needed to answer the question. An experienced user may start to anticipate the question and respond to it automatically so that it loses its constraining abilities. There are those times, however, when a user has been happy that the constraint appeared so that noncorrectable errors could be averted before they occurred.

Through the use of constraints, the computer interface can come closer to its ideal: an environment where it is impossible to make an error. If the possible responses are constrained through the menu display, then only those commands that are possible can be entered. If the menu selections are constrained by the context, through graying out inappropriate commands, then errors can be averted before they occur. But, using constraints does not provide us with the perfect interface. Pointing and clicking on a menu item is slower than typing command names with few letters in them. Having menu items, and a hierarchical menu structure, provides a constraint on the sequencing of commands and, thus, an inflexibility in the kinds of interactions. Finally, constraining potentially destructive commands slows down the overall interaction and provides annoying messages if you know you are right. As emphasized in the next section, designing an interface is a practice in finding the perfect trade-off, if such an ideal exists, instead of the perfect interface. Constraints may be good in some situations, but not good in others.

TRADE-OFFS

Placing knowledge in the head requires a trade-off. Like most computer interface design issues, no one design is perfect in all situations. By choosing one or the other, the designer is losing some good things but gaining others. Norman (1988) indicates that placing knowledge in the world, such as placing information on the computer screen, has the desirable properties of being easy to retrieve whenever the information is displayed, requires no learning if affordances and constraints are present in the design, and can be very easy to use by a novice from the beginning.

The trade-off is that using world knowledge can be inefficient and unaesthetic, especially because the display would become more cluttered if all the information has to be present on the computer instead of in the user's head. Users can be very efficient if the commands can be easily retrievable from memory. If users have to search through a display to find the important information, then the interaction process will be slow and the display may have to be too cluttered to be aesthetically pleasing.

Norman (1986) has portrayed this trade-off in slightly different terms as a trade-off between space and time. A display can be complete and informative but this would take more space on the display and more time to display. It would, however, help the user to understand the interface and may address important questions about the interface. An alternative is to save the space and time by displaying less information. This interface would be faster to use, but the user may find that important questions may not be addressed from the interface design.

How well the interface designer handles these trade-offs for the particular application is a measure of the success of the interface. Affordances can be used to increase the retrievability and ease of use, at the same time reducing the learning. Constraints can be used to reduce the possible kinds of errors that can be made. By examining the human activities, in the next section, the design can be customized to the particular activity and environment. The designer must always be sure, however, that the inefficiency is not at an intolerable level and that the displays are not too cluttered. Finding the right trade-offs for these kinds of design issues can be enhanced by knowing the important issues, such as affordances and constraints, but the good design depends on the ability of the designer to subjectively determine the point on the trade-off which is appropriate for the particular application and user environment.

HUMAN ACTIVITY ANALYSIS

Many of the same points made by Norman (1986, 1988) were also reiterated by Brodker (1989) with a few enhancements. Even more so than the work by Norman, Brodker emphasizes the application rather than the general case. Interfaces should be designed for the context of the groups of users. Hutchins, Hollan, and Norman (1986) came to a similar conclusion when they stated that if the interface is good the users should feel like they are in the application instead of using the computer.

Brodker (1988) bemoans the artifacts that computer users have to endure when using the computer as a tool. She uses the example of a journalist whose main job is to write an interesting and factual news story. To accomplish this task on a computer, however, the journalist must not only concentrate on the story but must also concentrate on how to use the computer. The activity of writing the story should take precedence over the activity of using the computer, but, as often occurs, the story could be diminished if too much emphasis has to be placed on using the computer.

Once the journalist is finished writing the story, a typesetter must lay out the story. Typesetting is a different activity from journalism, with different needs from the computer. The typesetter must have the tools for cutting and pasting the article, for trying different configurations on the page, and for visualizing the finished article on the page. Different human activities make different demands on the computer interface. The journalist would not have to know all the functions needed by the typesetter; the typesetter would not have to use the functions incorporated by the journalist.

The human activity defines the interface. The features of the interface cannot be determined without knowing the human activity that it is to be used for. General principles, which should be valid for all interfaces, are invalid from the perspective of this human activity approach. Specific interfaces for specific applications should be used.

Norman (1986) discusses the trade-off between general purpose interfaces and specific purpose interfaces. With a general purpose interface, the user could perform several tasks by knowing just a few commands. This is a very efficient and powerful design concept. With a specific interface design, the user would have to know different interfaces for different applications. Knowing one interface would not necessarily transfer to another interface. This is inefficient, but, if the interface is designed with the appropriate affordances, learning the interface would not be such a detriment to performance. Brodker states clearly that specific interface designs are the best, but she does not back up this claim with empirical evidence.

Finally, the implication from the Brodker (1989) discussion is that interface design must be extended to include the organizational structure and environment of the job. Using the journalism example, once again, merely designing an interface for journalism is inappropriate. Separate interfaces must be designed for each particular task within the overall journalism job. The journalists need one kind of interface, the typesetters need another.

SUMMARY

Norman (1988) states that for the programmer to design an interface so that the knowledge is in the world is particularly difficult. The programmer is certainly a computer expert and sometimes an application expert. As such, the programmer has internalized the relevant knowledge to be in the head. Since the programmer is a user also, the assumption is that all users will have the knowledge residing in the head, as does the programmer. Because a trade-off exists between the ease of the task (with knowledge residing in the world) and the efficiency of the task (with knowledge residing in the head), the programmers are likely to assume their own experiences as models for the user and trade off ease of use for efficiency by residing the knowledge in the head. Because they already have the knowledge and, thus, the computer application is easy for them, they would not necessarily see this as a trade-off, but as the only logical way to design the interface. Designing the interface so that the knowledge resides in the world, or in the interface in this case, may be difficult and unnatural for the designer. This kind of design may require a conscious effort, either by the designer or management, so that the knowledge is placed in the interface.

The problem with this approach is the difficulty with specifying how to design affordances and constraints into the interface, and how to base the interface design upon the specific human activity instead of the general case. Brodker (1989) emphasizes that the interface design should not be taken out of the context of how it will be used. Each specific case requires a new approach to the design.

Although Brodker (1989) claims that her approach is a theory of human activity, it really is not, and this is part of the problem with its application. Developing a theory is an iterative process: an organizing set of explanations is proposed for a group of empirical data which were not previously able to be explained together, and then, from the theory, new hypotheses could be generated, new data collected, and the hypotheses tested. The theory is ultimately grounded in empirical data, not anecdotes, and hypotheses are testable. Instead of data, Brodker presents anecdotes. Instead of generalizing over many pieces of data, Brodker says that no generalizations can be made. Instead of presenting a theory that is testable, Brodker presents a shifting target.

Saying that this approach is not a theory does not discount it totally. Instead, the material in this chapter presents ideas which should certainly be considered in the interface design. Without a theoretical approach, however, generalizing on how to apply these ideas is difficult. The best that can be done is to present examples, as was done, about how the ideas have been incorporated in other designs. This is more of a case-studies approach to interface design, rather than a theoretical approach. By knowing some of these examples, affordances, constraints, and human activity could possibly be applied to future interface designs.

QUESTIONS

1. Look back at the widgets shown in Chapter 2. For each widget, consider if it has any affordances or constraints associated with it. If it contains neither, discuss how affordances and constraints could be designed into it. If it contains affordances or constraints, discuss what these are.

2. Compare the affordances in the design of a book to the affordances, or lack of affordances, when reading text off a word processor on a computer. Explain how some of the affordances of the book could be incorporated into the word processor.

3. Consider the design of a calculator. How could you design affordances and constraints into the calculator to improve its design?

4. Many examples of affordances and constraints occur for noncomputerized products. Each of the following

items or products was good for either incorporating affordances or constraints. For each, indicate if the item adheres to affordances or constraints, and then indicate why it is a good design.

a. Scissors

b. The balance and fade adjustments on a car radio using a joystick

c. A stove top which has the burners arranged in a square and the control knobs also arranged in a square

d. Fork

5. Indicate if the following descriptions are for affordances or constraints in product design.

a. A knob which is used for pushing, instead of turning

b. On an electrical plug, one prong is larger than the other, and so it can only be placed in the outlet one way

c. Using plywood for covering the walls in a subway station

6. Each of the following items or products was bad for not incorporating proper affordances or constraints. For each, indicate the affordance or constraint that the item has, and explain how these run counter to the intended operation of the items.

a. The fade and balance on a car radio using knobs for both

b. The stove top in which the burners are in a square but the control knobs are in a straight line

CHAPTER 22

FEEDBACK AND HELP MESSAGES

INTRODUCTION

When a person performs any kind of task, feedback must be provided for task improvement. If no feedback is provided, learning will not occur. This has been known for a long time in experimental psychology. An early experiment by Trowbridge and Cason in 1932 experimentally investigated four feedback conditions: a control condition where no feedback was provided; irrelevant feedback where a nonsense word was provided; qualitative feedback (right or wrong); and quantitative feedback (amount off the target). These four conditions were compared in a task in which the subject had to hit a target which could not be seen. The results were compared to the control condition. Irrelevant feedback hindered performance, the qualitative feedback improved performance slightly, and the quantitative feedback had the most positive effect on performance. The implication for human-computer interaction design is that the user should be given as much relevant feedback on performance as is possible or adequate for the task.

Early computer systems were notorious for their feedback or lack thereof. The compilers for programming languages were especially difficult. As an example, one compiler would number the errors, with a summary statement indicating the problem. Error 1 was fairly specific: "statement number does not exist, called from line 25." But as the numbers got higher, the programmer learned that the feedback became less and less specific:

Error 63 stated: "Illegal trap." This meant, essentially, that the compiler had no information about what went wrong.

A popular compiler for the programming language C can also provide confusing feedback. C allows on-line comments to be enclosed within single quotation marks. The compiler counts as part of the comment everything up until the next quotation mark which it interprets as an end quote, even if this quotation mark is on another program line. If the programmer leaves out the end quote for the comment, the compiler counts everything until the next beginning quote as a comment, and the next comment is counted as part of the executable code of the program. The compiler provides feedback which says "Undefined variable." If the programmer is not aware of the missing quotation mark, then she or he may examine variable names for long periods of time to see if they are illegal in some way. Many times, the feedback occurs on a line of the program which is far away from the missing end quote. This is a case of the feedback being misleading and causing the programmer longer recovery time than if more specific feedback were given.

Sometimes the feedback is intentionally or unintentionally unfriendly. Whenever a user error occurs, the interface designer should not conceptualize it as the user being stupid or untrained; it should be conceptualized as a problem in the design. One of the most common feedback phrases used to be "Illegal entry." This sounds intentionally unfriendly; in most cases, this is a felony. The un-

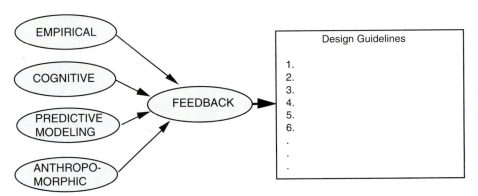

Figure 22-1. Design guidelines can be formulated by applying the four approaches to the design of feedback and help messages.

friendliness can be unintentional also. One operating system prefaced much feedback with the letters KMON, which, although never explained, possibly stood for keyboard monitor. A user could think that it stood for "come on, you dummy."

For a successful interface, feedback must be considered carefully. Feedback can take many kinds of forms in human-computer interaction and so the interface designer is faced with many options and possibilities. How are feedback choices to be made? Where should research, either in the library or in the laboratory, be directed? The four approaches to human-computer interaction, outlined in the previous sections, can be used to address these issues. From these four approaches, design guidelines can be formulated (see Figure 22-1).

EMPIRICAL APPROACH

The empirical approach is usually the first one to be used. The interface designer should determine what has been done previously and evaluate the validity of those results based upon a knowledge of good empirical methods. The research

literature should be searched first. If more empirical validation is needed, then laboratory studies may need to be conducted. In the following survey of the literature, in many cases, it is difficult to determine what should be included under the empirical approach and what should be included under the other approaches. Within the cognitive, predictive modeling, and anthropomorphic approaches, the ultimate test of the subapproaches must be determined empirically. Studies on feedback are included under the empirical approach if the experiments were conducted mostly in the absence of a theoretical basis.

Shneiderman has been most productive at applying the empirical approach to feedback issues. In one study, Shneiderman (1982) examined the ability to debug computer programs when the specificity of the feedback was manipulated. Similar to Trowbridge and Cason (1932), performance improved with increased specificity. In a somewhat related study, Shneiderman tested whether outputting a question mark or a simple error message provided the best feedback on an error. He found that the more specific feedback, the simple error message, was best.

Shneiderman also investigated the tone of the feedback by manipulating the error messages to be hostile, neutral, or courteous in tone. In a programming task, the accuracy of the programmers in responding to these messages was evaluated. He found that errors using courteous message feedback were responded to more accurately than the neutral message feedback. No other differences occurred. Surprisingly, the accuracy on the task was not improved significantly by using courteous messages when compared to the hostile messages.

A problem with providing feedback is that the time taken to read the feedback could be too long. In some cases, the user may know already that an error has occurred and feedback will not be needed. Recall from the discussion of widgets in Chapter 2 that some feedback windows are displayed on the screen and the user must move the mouse and perform a button click, to remove the feedback window, before any other operations can be performed. In other cases, using the feedback may be just too time-consuming to be practical. The time-consumption of the task must be traded off with the consequence of the error. If the user is not forced to respond to the error feedback, and is allowed to continue, the result may be extremely time-consuming or even impossible to recover from. If the user is forced to respond by clicking the feedback window on each error, then this can be time-consuming and annoying to experts especially.

A slightly different situation from error feedback is the use of help messages. For help messages, the user has not necessarily committed an error, but he or she may not know what to do next. Several experiments have been conducted to determine how help feedback should be provided.

An early experiment (Dunsmore, 1980) indicated that on-line help could even be detrimental to performance. Subsequent experimentation has indicated that the important aspect of the situation is not whether or not on-line help is provided but the form of the on-line help. If the on-line help is not good, the help will not be useful. Magers (1983) improved the on-line help in several ways: reducing the verbiage in the help message; making the message more specific to correcting the errors; providing examples; and introducing better ways to access the help such as through a specific key and dependent on the context. With these new methods, user performance improved significantly. In another study, Cohill and Williges (1982, 1985) found that help messages are best, in terms of time and error, if the user initiates them.

Most of the empirical work points to one overall conclusion: the feedback should be as specific as possible. This was found in the Shneiderman study, when tested specifically, and it was found more indirectly for the help messages in the Magers (1983) study. The Magers study, however, failed to isolate this particular feature of help messages, instead, including this as just one aspect of good feedback. Figure 22-2 summarizes the guidelines from the empirical approach.

COGNITIVE APPROACH

In the chapters on the cognitive approach, several subapproaches were considered: mental models and cognitive goals, human information processing, neural net-

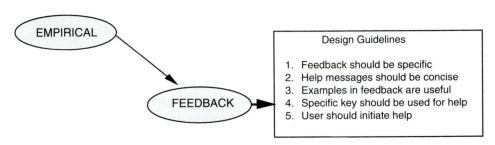

Figure 22-2. The design guidelines from the empirical approach.

works, metaphors and analogies, spatial reasoning and graphics, and attentional resources. Each of these subapproaches provides some means to determine and predict the kind of feedback which would be best for the user.

Mental Models

Recall from Chapter 7 that the mental model is built up through interactions with the display representation which provides the user, along with off-line documentation, the only view of the conceptual model of the system. The conceptual model, used by the programmer to build the system, is an accurate and complete underlying model of the system. The goal for an interface designer is to try to convey the conceptual model, in its accurate, consistent, and complete form, to the user. Feedback is one of the display devices in which this information can be presented to the user. With poor feedback, the mental model of the user will be inaccurate, inconsistent, and incomplete.

As an illustration of this, take, as an example, the mental model of the calculator which is built up through interaction. Norman (1983) has studied the mental models of users and concluded that they were inaccurate, incomplete, and inconsistent. The calculator conveys very little information about its conceptual model through feedback to the user. Most of the interactions in the calculator mental models could be attributed directly to the lack of feedback. One of the misconceptions was that the "clear" key may have to be hit several times in order to clear the operation. If feedback was provided by showing the sign of the operation on the display, then the calculator users would know, at least for some calculators, that the first clear clears the number and the second clear clears the operation. The calculator users were also reluctant to use the memory for storing often-used variables. If the contents of the memory could be displayed on the calculator, through the use of feedback, the users might have a better understanding of what is in memory, where it is, and how it is removed.

A relationship exists between the developed mental model and the feedback received by the user. The calculator example provides a good illustration of this relationship. Other examples would also illustrate it. The mental model is related to other topics under the cognitive approach, in particular, the spatial and graphics subapproach. Further examples of the use of feedback will be provided in that section.

Another important topic in the mental models section of Chapter 7 was that of

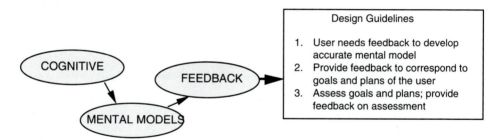

Figure 22-3. The design guidelines from the cognitive mental models approach.

goals, plans, and intentions in human-computer interaction. Under the cognitive approach, an assumption is that the user forms goals or intentions and then the actions are chosen to satisfy these goals or intentions. This was also a very important concept in the predictive modeling section for the GOMS, NGOMSL, and production system models. It should also be a consideration when providing feedback to the user. Goals can be used in two ways: by providing goal information in the help messages or by assessing the goals and providing information about the adequacy of these goals. The first way is much easier to implement than the second method.

A main assumption of the cognitive approach is that computer users form goals of the task. In the past, much of the feedback and help message information was in terms of the syntax of the task. In other words, the feedback provided information when undefined command names were used or the parameters of the command were wrong. As indicated by Shneiderman (1987), this kind of syntax information is needed for some systems but increases the difficulty of the task. An alternative is to provide semantic information, which could include the goal information. We would assume that the

information about the goal to be performed would be very compatible with how the user is thinking about the task. Thus, the information provided in the feedback should be compatible with those cognitive goals.

Elkerton (1988) discusses several of the methods that can be used to provide goal information to the user in help messages. The goals correspond to the kinds of tasks that the users may be performing instead of more abstract concepts. As an example used by Elkerton, if help messages are being provided then the messages could indicate how to type, edit, print, and delete the manuscript. All of these should correspond to high-level goals which may be performed by the user.

Assessing the goals on-line is a more difficult problem. In a limited domain, Carroll and Carrithers (1984) demonstrated that goals could be assessed and feedback provided to the users. This feedback could be used for error recovery. However, Carroll (1985) shows that the goal feedback is limiting; it provides no information on the procedures for recovering from the error. In many cases, especially for experts, this procedural information is all that is needed. Figure 22-3 summarizes the guidelines from the cognitive mental models approach.

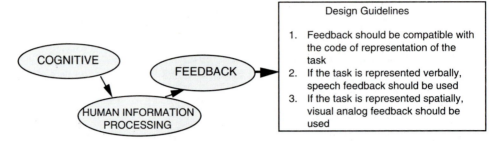

Figure 22-4. The design guidelines from the cognitive human information processing approach.

Human Information Processing

The most important aspect of human information processing which can be applied to feedback is the concept of S-C-R compatibility (Wickens, Sandry, and Vidulich, 1983) which, you may recall from Chapter 8, stands for stimulus-central processing-response compatibility. This approach emphasizes that the stimulus, the central processing, and the response must all be compatible. Recall that four types of representation codes typical in a computer environment are: (1) text (visual modality, verbal code); (2) speech (auditory modality, verbal code); (3) sound localization and pitch (auditory modality, spatial code); and (4) analog picture (visual modality, spatial code). In terms of feedback, therefore, for tasks with a verbal representation code, the most compatible feedback would be speech. For tasks with a spatial representation code, the most compatible feedback would be visual analog, or graphics. Thus, by knowing the representation code used in central processing, the compatible feedback can be specified.

The feedback should be compatible with the representation code of the task. Boehm-Davis, Holt, Koll, Yastrop, and Peters (1989) investigated the relationship between instructions and the repre-sentation code of the task. They showed that performance will be better if the instructions are in the same form as the task. As examples, if the task is a textual task, then the instructions should be in text. If the task is spatial, then the instructions should be spatial. Instructions, in this case, were not exactly the same as feedback in that feedback is given in response to behavior and instructions precede the interaction. It has many of the same characteristics as feedback, however, and this concept can be extended to feedback in general.

The compatibility of feedback with the representation code of the task must be exploited in more applications. Much of the feedback in the past has been visual textual. Since many of the tasks probably have a spatial code to them, this kind of feedback would not be compatible with the task. More work needs to be done on providing spatial feedback, in terms of graphics, to the users. Figure 22-4 summarizes the guidelines from the cognitive human information processing approach.

Neural Networks

One of the challenges of providing feedback on-line to subjects is for the computer to recognize when feedback is needed. This recognition problem has many characteristics similar to the recognition problems, such as in visual character recognition (Fukushima, 1987, 1988a, 1988b; and Fukushima, Miyake, and Ito, 1983) or speech recognition (Sejnowski and Rosenberg, 1987), that neural networks have been very successful at addressing (see Chapter 9). When a feedback advice system provides assistance on the kinds of commands to use, the system would have to recognize a wide range of responses. It would have to recognize commands separated in time and possibly by other nonessential commands. As an example, the user may perform several file manipulation commands which could be combined into one more efficient command. In between the file manipulation commands, the user may check the contents of the directories which would constitute a nonessential command separating the more important commands; it would have to be ignored by the system. The advice system would also have to recognize synonymous but incorrect command names. For example, the user may not realize that the correct command name is "ls" and may enter "dir" instead.

An experiment was conducted to use a neural net to monitor user behavior when utilizing the UNIX operating system, determine when feedback advice could be provided, and then provide the feedback to the users in real-time (Eberts, Villegas, Phillips, and Eberts, 1991). The UNIX operating system is very powerful, because of its flexibility, but it is difficult to use. Many people who know how to use UNIX only bother to learn a small subset of the possible commands. Consequently, using only a small subset of commands, inefficient command sequences are exhibited. The problem with improving

performance for these users is that sometimes they do not know that more efficient command sequences are available or they do not want to make the effort to learn what these are. A feedback advice system would have to solve both of these problems: it would have to monitor users' performance to determine if a better method is available and it would have to offer advice so that the users would not have to exert much effort in learning the new commands.

A neural net was trained to map inefficient and efficient UNIX command sequences into feedback advice to indicate to the user either that the command sequence was the most efficient that could be used or to provide a suggestion for how to perform the command sequence more efficiently. If the net turned on an efficient advice output node, feedback was provided to the user that the most efficient command sequence was used. If the net turned on an inefficient advice output node, advice was provided to the user on how the command sequence could be performed more efficiently. Results showed that the net had a hit rate of 88%, a miss rate of 12%, and no false alarms. When a group of subjects receiving the advice was compared to a group with no advice and a group with no advice but off-line help, the advice group was three times better at finding the most efficient commands.

This experiment showed that the advice could be provided on-line in real time because of the speed of the neural net in propagating through the commands. The use of neural nets has much potential in quickly providing feedback to users in real time. Figure 22-5 shows the guideline from the cognitive neural net approach.

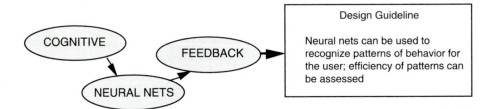

Figure 22-5. The design guidelines from the cognitive neural nets approach.

Metaphors and Analogies

Not much research has been reported on applying metaphors and analogies to feedback issues, but some possibilities exist. Once again, this analysis demonstrates how the four approaches can be used to define new areas of research and applications in the area of human-computer interaction.

Recall from Chapter 10 that analogies and metaphors are used to present the new information, on how to interact with the computer, in terms of old information already known to the user, such as how a desk top may be arranged. This was shown to be a very powerful device so that the user could quickly understand how the computer system works. The negative side of providing metaphors and analogies is that no perfect match between the computer system and the metaphor ever exists. The user must know which parts provide the match and which parts do not. The user must not overextend the metaphor into areas in which it is not applicable.

From this brief summary, one can see that feedback using analogies and metaphors can be utilized in two ways: through feedback that explains the methods in terms of the metaphor and by providing intelligent feedback when the system senses an overextension of the meta-phor. First, feedback could be provided in terms of the metaphor. As an example, a common feature of the desktop metaphor is to have a wastepaper basket icon in which files can be discarded. Feedback could be provided by providing the following help message: "Just like a regular wastepaper basket, the wastepaper basket icon can be used to throw away unwanted files by picking up the unwanted file by moving the mouse cursor to the file and pushing the mouse button. With the mouse button down, the waste can be carried to the wastepaper basket by moving the mouse. The waste can be released in the basket by releasing the mouse button." The feedback should show the mapping between the old information, the metaphor, and the new information, the computer operations.

Carroll and Aaronson (1988) used a metaphor when providing intelligent help message feedback to users when they were instructed to construct a form on the screen and then fill in that form with specific information. Messages were constructed to inform the user how the system worked. The users were instructed to think of the form using a metaphor which most of us are unfortunately too familiar with: a tax form. This experiment was exploratory and the experimenters did not compare this metaphor feedback technique to other possible kinds of feedback.

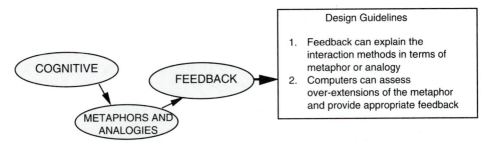

Figure 22-6. The design guidelines from the cognitive metaphors and analogies approach.

Second, an intelligent interface should be able to provide feedback to the user if it determines that a metaphor over-extension is occurring, which, when using a metaphor, could be a likely event for a novice. Using the same wastepaper basket feature as an example, a user may think that the garbage from the wastepaper basket will only be removed at night, or when specified by the user, much like a real wastepaper basket. Most systems incorporating this icon have a removal policy not readily apparent to the user. Earlier files may be removed when new files are placed in the basket, or the files may be removed during other computer operations seemingly unrelated to the wastepaper basket. The user may think that the file can be retrieved from the wastepaper basket up until the point that the computer is turned off. In the initial stages of use, the computer could provide feedback to the user on information about the removal policy and how this policy may be different from that which could be expected if the metaphor was not overextended. If the user tried to retrieve a deleted file which was already removed from the wastepaper basket, then feedback could again be provided informing the user how the metaphor was overextended.

For all these possible applications, the important thing is that the feedback should be consistent with the metaphor or analogy. The user should be shown the mappings between the new information and the old information. Possible overextensions should be anticipated and corrected through the feedback. Figure 22-6 summarizes the guidelines for the cognitive metaphors and analogies approach.

Spatial Reasoning and Graphics

As shown in Chapter 11, many people prefer to think of computer tasks spatially. A computer program can be conceptualized spatially, and position within a document in a text-editing task can be conceptualized spatially. One of the purposes of direct manipulation interfaces was to eliminate the possibilities of errors occurring and, in the process, lessen the need for feedback. Feedback can still be provided on direct manipulation displays incorporating the spatial characteristics of these displays.

Shneiderman (1987) has speculated how spatial feedback can be used in programming tasks. In the introduction to this chapter, one of the examples of poor feedback was in terms of the single quotation marks for on-line comments. Sometimes the programmers would forget to close the comment with a quotation mark at the end. A similar situation is closing the parentheses when the left parenthesis is used but the right parenthesis is forgot-

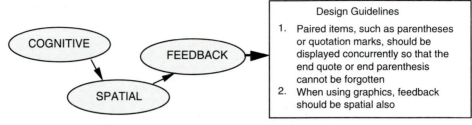

Figure 22-7. The design guidelines from the cognitive spatial approach.

ten. This is an important issue in most programming languages, but an especially important issue in a programming language such as LISP in which parentheses perform such an essential role in the structure of the program. Shneiderman suggests that programming languages should be provided in an environment such that whenever a left parenthesis is entered into the program, the right parenthesis automatically appears on the screen. The contents can be typed in between the two parentheses. Whenever the programmer deletes one of the parentheses, the other is deleted automatically also. The same thing could be done for the quotation marks for the comments. This is a form of spatial feedback because the programmer is provided with a spatial representation of the demarcations of the required punctuation.

Another programming problem discussed in the beginning of this chapter was the feedback in which the program compiler indicated that an error occurred on a certain line number some place in the program. This kind of feedback is textual, whereas the programmer could think of the program spatially. A solution to this problem is not to refer to the program line by number, but for the compiler to place the editor at that position in the program so that the error must be corrected before continuing with the rest of the program. Context, by including the surrounding program lines, should also be displayed. Perhaps a map of where this occurs within the program would also be advantageous. Many recent compilers have eliminated the line number designation for errors and they place the editor at the line in which the error occurred.

Another feature of Chapter 11 was that for physical systems with a spatial component to them, graphics can provide a representation of the system. Within these kinds of systems, the feedback should be in terms of the graphics representation of the system. Instead of providing feedback that a fault has occurred on subsystem 303, the spatial feedback can be provided by showing a representation of the system, and some graphics indication of the fault occurring in subsystem 303, but it does not have to have this number indication any longer. Figure 22-7 summarizes the guidelines from the cognitive spatial approach.

Attentional Resources

Interfaces should be designed so that the primary activity of using the computer is not forgotten. When writing a paper, the primary activity should be the writing process and not typing or performing the computer commands. If the typing and computer operations grab too many of the attentional resources, then enough resources will not remain for the primary writing task and writing will be worse than if doing it by hand. In a CAD task, the primary purpose of the task should be the design process. Again, if the computer operations require too many attentional resources, the design will not be as good as if it had been done using drafting pen and paper.

Feedback is similar to the situations described above. Feedback is important for improving performance, but it should not be designed so that it grabs too many attentional resources and the primary task suffers. If the feedback is too wordy, then the user will have to spend some time and resources on decoding the message; the primary task may suffer as a result. Perhaps this is one of the reasons that the empirical results showed that specificity of the feedback was most important. Being specific to the task or the behavior of the user, the attentional resources are still devoted to the task or behavior, instead of the mechanism of the feedback.

Some of the discussions in the previous sections can also be described in terms of attention, especially focused attention. Previously, feedback was hypothesized to be effective if it uses the current metaphors or analogies and if it is designed within the context of the graphics. Attention would have to be divided, with performance decrements, if feedback did not fit in these contexts.

Many of the present computer systems, with multiple windows and multiple processes, place even more of a demand on attentional resources. Interface designers must be more vigilant in these designs so that overload does not occur. With multiple windows and processors, the users can start a process in one window on the screen and then move to another window to perform another operation. As an example, a user may start a long program compiling in one window, and while it is compiling, the user's e-mail can be read in another window. Or, when writing a document, the user may bring up the document in one window, and then bring up another window with information, such as references or other papers, which could be included in the document.

These multiple windows and processes are very powerful and can save time because several tasks can be performed at one time. No longer is the user required to perform tasks in a linear fashion. With this increased flexibility also comes a possibility that the user will be overloaded and forget what was being done or the particular point at which a task was suspended. Miyata and Norman (1986) suggest that computer interfaces should incorporate remindings to reduce the load on the user and consequent errors. A reminder is feedback that indicates the suspended task is ready for further processing. They indicate that in the real world, reminders are utilized often: dirty dishes in the sink; a phone call from a friend about an appointment; or the sound of a boiling teakettle.

Miyata and Norman suggest that an ideal reminder should have five characteristics: inform the user when conditions are ready for resumption of a suspended or backgrounded activity; remind the user when something has to be done immediately; not distract from the current activity; continuously or periodically list activities that have been suspended or backgrounded; and help resumption of an activity by retrieving the exact previous state of the activity and showing it to the user.

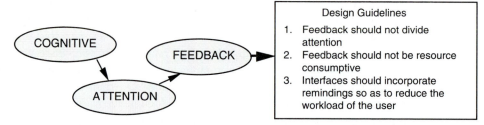

Figure 22-8. The design guidelines from the cognitive attention approach.

Many of these characteristics are present in current computer interfaces. The use of windows satisfies some of these criteria. When using a window, the user can leave a window, open up a new window, perform some kind of operation, and then return to the previous window. The contents and appearance of this old window will not have changed so that the previous process can be resumed in the exact state in which it was left. In some cases, a window will appear on the screen when a backgrounded activity has been finished. The user should have the capability of responding to that information directly or it can remain on the screen until the current activity is finished. If several activities are occurring at the same time, the user can be reminded of this by the number of windows on the screen at any one time. For most interfaces, a window manager decides where a new window will be placed on the screen so as not to obscure all the rest of the windows. The parts of windows on the screen will remind the user that the other processes are occurring and can be attended to at the appropriate time. Besides the window manager, the user usually has the option of moving the windows or opening the windows to organize windows on the screen so that the important processes and windows may be more prominent. The user should be allowed the flexibility to do this.

By reminding the user that other processes are occurring and by allowing the user to retrieve the suspended context of the process, the potential attentional overload is reduced. Current interface practices, with multiple windows and processes, increase the productivity of the user with the potential of increasing the overload and errors. The above techniques can be used to reduce the attentional overload. Figure 22-8 summarizes the guidelines for the cognitive attentional resources approach.

PREDICTIVE MODELING APPROACH

The predictive modeling approach, as explained in Section IV, is used to predict user performance such as execution time, learnability, memory workload, and transferability. If an interface designer has a choice of feedback methods to use, the predictive modeling approach could be used potentially to predict which would be best in terms of performance. Some of the proposed benefits of feedback, such as assisting and accelerating the learning process, are not captured by the models. For execution time and learnability, especially, providing more methods which have to be learned through interaction with the feedback will increase execution time and learnability, according to the GOMS

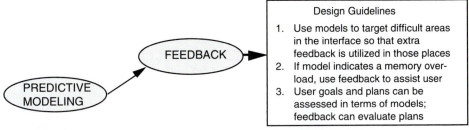

Figure 22-9. The design guidelines from the predictive modeling approach.

(Chapter 14), NGOMSL (Chapter 15), and production system models (Chapter 16). These predictions must be interpreted cautiously, however, because the positive aspects of feedback, such as reducing errors and learning time, cannot be modeled easily. Experimental confirmation of longer execution times for feedback, however, has been shown by Dunsmore (1980).

As pointed out by Elkerton (1988), instead of using the predictive models for predictions of performance with the feedback present, the predictive models would probably be best for pinpointing those parts of the interaction which will be most problematic for the user. If the analysis indicates that one part will be particularly difficult to learn, because of the number of methods to be learned, then this part should be targeted for feedback to assist the learning. If the analysis indicates that one part will require long times to execute, possibly because of system response times, then this is a target for using feedback to inform the user what is happening in these long delays. If the analysis indicates that memory may be overloaded at a certain point, then feedback can be used to assist the user.

It is possible that providing feedback to the user can help to change the method structure of the task or the rules which govern user behavior. If the meth-

ods or rules can be reduced, through appropriate feedback, then the execution time and learning time would be reduced. Predicting the effect of feedback on methods and rules would be a more difficult analysis than normally done, but the models have the potential for estimating the positive changes in behavior when feedback is provided.

An excellent example of the application of a predictive model to a feedback system is one developed by Hoppe (1988) which is called TOP for Task-Oriented Parser. TOP is based upon the TAG model (see Chapter 17), and it uses this model to parse sequences of user actions into the goals or plans that are being employed by the user. If the user requires help, or if the system determines that a task can be done more efficiently, TOP can be used to provide this feedback and assistance in terms of the user plans, or what the system thought that the user was doing. Figure 22-9 summarizes the guidelines for the predictive modeling approach.

ANTHROPOMORPHIC APPROACH

One of the topics under the anthropomorphic approach was assistance with a task. This is essentially what this chapter on feedback has been about, so there is much overlap between this chapter and that previous discussion in Chapter 20. The anthropomorphic approach offers other suggestions for designing feedback into the interface.

Human-Human Communication

In Chapter 18, one method to analyze the interface and determine the interface features was to examine human-human interaction. Since the assumption was that human-human communication was natural, and most human-computer interaction was unnatural, then by examining the differences between the two, and applying principles from human-human communication to human-computer interaction, the interface can be made more natural. The same kind of approach can be taken with feedback.

One area in which human-human interaction has been examined to determine how better and more natural feedback can be provided to users is in the communication between teachers and students (see Chapter 20). One of the problems with providing feedback, also identified by Miyata and Norman (1986), is when the feedback should be provided. If provided at the wrong time, important mental processes of the users may be interrupted (Burton and Brown, 1979b). In many cases, the student does not know how to phrase the question to the teacher, but the teacher knows when a problem has occurred (e.g., Collins and Stevens, 1982). In most cases, the teacher knows how to guide the student so that the missing information, and only this relevant information, is provided to the student. Some teachers are more effective at these techniques than others.

If we can understand how good teachers perform these feedback functions, then we could possibly apply these techniques to computer-based feedback. This was the premise of the approach used by Collins and Stevens (1982) as discussed in Chapter 20. They found that good teachers could provide the appropriate feedback to students, such as counterexamples or hypothetical cases, so that the students could understand their mistakes. Human-human communication can be investigated to determine the most natural methods for providing feedback to the users.

Facial Expressions and Gestures

In Chapter 19, some of the novel input devices for natural interfaces were discussed. In that discussion, many examples of feedback occurring in the natural world were provided. The importance of gestures and facial expressions in communication with other people was discussed. As examples, when communicating, we watch the other person's face and body to receive signs of understanding, stress, questioning, and so forth. We base the form of our communication on how we perceive the other person is understanding our words through their facial and gestural expressions.

To utilize gesture and facial communication in feedback, some mechanism is needed to interpret these forms of communication in the user. The computer must be able to analyze the gestures and facial expressions of the user. The first step in this process is to have a camera take a video of the user so that the facial expressions can be interpreted. This is in the initial stages of development at some companies. The capability to mimic the user in terms of head movements, eye blinks, and mouth movements has been achieved. The next step is to analyze these movements and change the feedback dependent on this analysis. This has not yet been accomplished.

Chapter 19 also discussed how gestures can be interpreted and used in the interface design. These gestures were mostly confined to meaningful gestures for interaction such as would occur through interaction devices. The nondirect gestures, besides those for directly interacting with the device, would be the most important to analyze for feedback. However, with most devices requiring input through the hands, the possibilities for other nondirect gestures is limited. As an example, with your hands on the keyboard, you could not very easily do hand movements based upon what you were writing. For this reason, facial expressions would provide the best clues to how to provide feedback.

Natural Language

An important discussion on the usefulness of natural language for interface design occurred in Chapter 19. Natural language has an important place in feedback. One of the difficulties with natural language interfaces, discussed in Chapter 19, is that the syntax and vocabulary of the language must be limited so that the computer can understand it. Some work has been performed to provide feedback information about how the natural language must be limited. In addition, whereas natural language was used in Chapter 19 as a form of input, for feedback it can be used as a form of output. Thus, instead of emphasizing the understanding of natural language from the input side, for feedback the computer must be able to generate natural language.

Feedback can be made more specific if it is provided in natural language form, adapted to the user. Also, natural language generated feedback can be used to answer user questions.

Zoltan-Ford (1991) argues that the low recognition rates of computers for natural language is due to the variety of ways in which the user interacts with a computer in natural language. For typical command-based or direct-manipulation interfaces, the form of the interaction is very constrained so that the variety does not occur. Natural language interfaces can be made more successful through a higher recognition rate if the forms of the natural language are limited. The computer communication to the user about how to limit the natural language inputs is the focus of Zoltan-Ford's research.

Zoltan-Ford (1991) believes that the kinds of feedback provided by the computer to the natural language inputs can be used to shape the user to respond to the computer in the limited natural language methods that the computer can understand. She studied some ways to provide feedback to shape the user to interact with a certain vocabulary and phrase length. For one method, the premise was that the user would use the output from the computer as a model for the inputs. For the other method, the premise was that error message feedback could be used to shape the natural language interaction of the subject. Results showed that the error message feedback was more successful in shaping the natural language input than was modeling the output message. Even though the modeling of output was not as successful as the other, the partial success shows that making the output message consistent with the desired form of the input can be used to assist some of the shaping.

Natural language generation can be used to answer questions in natural language or can be used to provide advice and feedback to users in the natural language syntax that should be natural and easy to understand. Mykowiecka (1991) recently reviewed the status of natural language generation. The use of natural language generators most compatible with providing feedback are the systems that answer users' questions. He indicates that the existing systems in this area are very limited to a particular knowledge base or specialization. Such a system would have to be able to do the following: "guess" the user's goal in order to give the most appropriate answer; adapt a dialog style to the user's level of knowledge; and find the best way for expressing goals in a particular context.

For a natural language generation system to be successful, Mykowiecka (1991) indicates that it must have the following characteristics: knowledge about the world, syntactic and semantic knowledge about a language, and vocabulary. Knowledge about the world is needed so that the system can know the facts which need to be communicated to the user. Many of the existing systems use various forms of semantic nets to represent the world knowledge. A semantic net has nodes and arcs connecting the nodes similar to the neural nets discussed in Chapter 9. A semantic net is different in that the nodes usually represent objects and the arcs represent some kind of relationship between the nodes. As an example, the animal world can be placed in a semantic net by including the animal hierarchy. The sparrow, bird, and animal nodes would

be related by "is a" relationships between sparrow and bird and between bird and animal. With this semantic net, the system could reason that a sparrow is an animal even though no direct arc links the two. Other knowledge representations have also been used.

According to Mykowiecka (1991), knowledge about the language should contain the following information: a method of organizing texts, rules of building compound sentences, rules of ordering sentence elements, and principles of choosing words and establishing agreement of word forms. As can be seen, the problem of natural language generation is more than just the syntax of a sentence, for example, where to place the verb and the noun. Instead, the problem lies in the structure of the sentence and the relationships of the sentences in the text.

Finally, for the vocabulary, a natural language generator must have access to a dictionary or lexicon which must contain all the forms of the words. The spelling of the single and plural forms of the words must be provided. The different tenses of the words must be known. The problem is not just knowing the word, but rather the form and spelling of the word which will fit in a particular situation.

Mykowiecka (1991) has identified two natural language generators which have been developed to answer questions in natural language. One system, called XPLAIN (Swartout, 1983), was developed to answer questions about the rules in an expert system rule base. This was limited to a very specific domain. The other system, called Kafka (Mauldin, 1987), is a bit more general and could be applied to many different kinds of dedicated systems. Kafka has the capability to

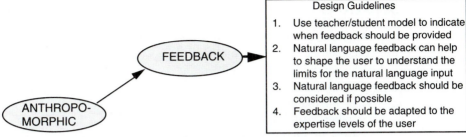

Figure 22-10. The design guidelines from the anthropomorphic approach.

generate only one English sentence, which is quite a bit easier than generating multiple sentence text.

Adaptable Interfaces

An important topic of Chapter 20 was adaptable interfaces. The interface can be designed to adapt to various characteristics of the user or the situation. In essence, this is the purpose of most of the applications mentioned in this chapter on feedback. By knowing the mental model of the user, the feedback can be adapted to the mental model. By knowing the attentional requirements of the current task, the feedback can be adapted so as not to further overload the user. By determining the facial expression, the system can interpret understanding or stress and adapt feedback accordingly. Natural language generators provide a means to adapt the interface to the particular context and question generated by the user.

Shneiderman (1987) has also suggested that the feedback and help messages should be adapted to the expertise level of the user. He suggests that experts may need to be reminded only that they made a particular mistake with very few words. Novices may need more information such as the nature of the error and how to recover from the error. This would require more words and information. Experts would not like to have to read these lengthy explanations each time, and the short messages may not have enough information for the novices to recover from the errors.

Figure 22-10 summarizes the guidelines for the anthropomorphic approach.

SUMMARY

The purpose of this chapter was to illustrate how the different approaches can be used to address the feedback issues of interface designs. Many different methods are available; some of this research by others has been discussed. This discussion was also important for generating new ideas not yet tested by others. Certainly, not all these discussed methods would need to be used in providing feedback to the user. They could be used at different times in the design process. As an example, the anthropormorphic and cognitive approaches were good for generating ideas for the kinds of features to be included in the feedback. The predictive modeling approach could also be used in this context, to determine the places in the interface design in which feedback may be most needed. The experimental approach could then be used to test various kinds of designs.

QUESTIONS

1. Many times a person will have one computer at work and a different computer, with a different operating system, at home. Transfer errors occur when alternating between the two computers. Assume that a person has an IBM PC at work using a DOS operating system and a workstation at work using the UNIX operating system. On DOS, the command for displaying the directory is DIR and for UNIX, the appropriate command is ls. Design a help message to provide feedback when the user inadvertently gets confused about which operating system is being used. Can you see a solution to this problem, without resorting to help messages, either in the design of a direct manipulation display or in the design of the command itself?

2. Use the design guidelines of Figure 22-2 to design feedback and help messages for the situation described in problem 1.

3. Use the design guidelines of Figure 22-3 to design feedback and help messages for the situation described in problem 1.

4. Use the design guidelines of Figure 22-4 to design feedback and help messages for the situation described in problem 1.

5. Think of a metaphor for the situation described in problem 1 and then design a feedback/help message to incorporate this metaphor.

6. Use the design guidelines of Figure 22-10 to design feedback and help messages for the situation described in problem 1.

7. For the situation in problem 1, design three feedback messages that are either courteous, friendly, or unfriendly.

CHAPTER 23

MENU DISPLAYS

INTRODUCTION

Menu displays are one of the most common forms of interaction modes available, for many reasons. They appear to be easy to use in that almost anybody can use menus without training or documentation. Some of the devices which have been developed, such as automatic teller machines, must be operated with no training or documentation, and these devices most often use menu displays. Menu displays are also an essential part of the direct manipulation interface mode.

As indicated in Chapter 2, menu displays can come in several forms utilizing many different kinds of inputs. Some interfaces are totally menu-driven. The interface will begin with a main menu; the menu choice from this main menu determines which other menu to display; and all the functioning is performed through the menus (see Figure 23-1). Another alternative, direct manipulation interfaces, do not rely solely on menus, but menus are an integral part of this interaction method. Screen space is also provided for directly manipulating items, such as files and folders. In this design, the menus are often displayed as pull-down menus (see Figure 23-2). Unlike the menu-driven displays, all menu choices are not shown with the pull-down menus; only the main topic or category of the menu is displayed on the screen. Once the category is chosen, then the menu items are displayed typically in the screen space reserved for directly manipulating the screen items.

Several different methods to interact with the menu displays have been incorporated. The purpose of the menu display is to display the choices, and the user must choose one of the items. One method is to provide a number or letter designation for each item (see Figure 23-3). A place on the screen is provided for entering the character or characters through keyboard input. If all items can be described by a single character, such as the 10 digits or the 26 alphabetic characters, then an ENTER key entry is not needed to terminate the response. If more than one character is used, then the ENTER key entry is needed. Sometimes, even if not needed for signifying the end of an entry, the ENTER key is used so that the user has time to read the response before it is entered.

One of the problems with designation of the menu items by characters is that the characters may have little relationship with the menu item. The user is not directly responding to the menu item but is using some intermediate designation, the character, in the response. One method to solve this problem, used in some menu displays, is to have the user enter the first letter of the menu item. This provides a better relationship between the menu item and the response and is advantageous for an experienced user who may not read through the menu items any more but only respond with the character from memory. It is much easier to remember to enter "d" for delete than to remember that this is response "4." An obvious problem with this approach is that all the menu items may not start with different letters. This problem has been solved by choosing

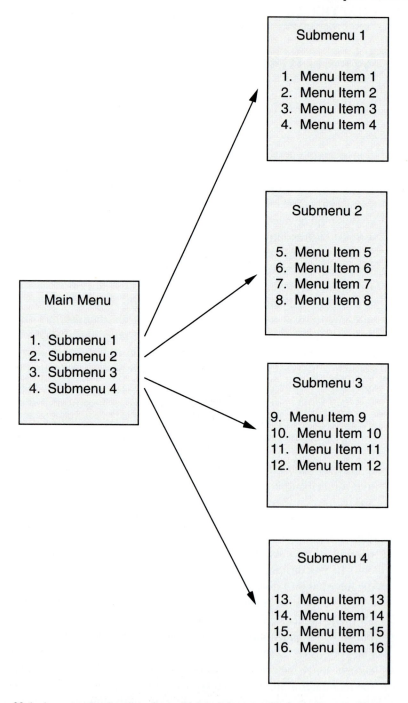

Figure 23-1. An example of an interface which is driven totally through menu displays. A main menu will appear on the screen. Through the choice of a menu item, submenus can then appear.

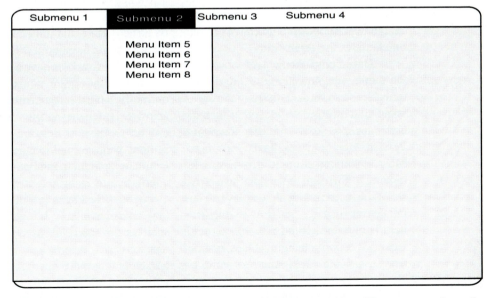

Figure 23-2. The pull-down menus from a direct manipulation display. The top screen shows the categories for the menu items and the bottom screen shows menu items pulled down for one of the categories.

```
Main Menu


1. Submenu 1
2. Submenu 2
3. Submenu 3
4. Submenu 4


Enter Menu Choice:  2
```

Figure 23-3. The choice for the menu item can be entered by typing the character or characters corresponding to the desired menu items.

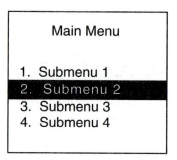

Figure 23-4. When an item is pointed to, it videoinverts as a highlighting technique.

unusual names for the command, a name whose only relationship to the function seems to be the uniqueness of the starting letter. Another possibility is to use a letter other than the first one, and designate this letter on the screen through some kind of highlighting. This alternative could be confusing if you try to remember which menu items have the first letter as the designator and which items have the second letter as the designator.

The other method class for choosing the menu item is to point to the desired item. This can be done through the use of some kind of input device, other than the alphanumeric keys on the keyboard. Several input devices have been used. Most keyboards contain arrow keys for moving right, left, up, and down. All could be used in menu displays. The interaction usually starts with the first item being highlighted possibly through video-inversion, changing black characters on a white background to white on black or changing white characters on a black background to black on white (see Figure 23-4). Highlighting can also be performed by changing the font, by chang-

ing the characters from regular to bold-face, by underlining, or by placing an "x" or some other designation in front of the menu item. As the arrow keys are entered, the highlighting follows the direction of the keys. If the down arrow key is entered, then the next item down is highlighted and the highlighting of the above item is turned off. Some menu displays have items in two or more columns so that the right/left arrow keys can be used. If items are in just one column, the left/right arrow keys can be turned off so that only appropriate directions could be entered. Most menu displays with arrow keys have a wrap-around function. If the bottom item is highlighted currently, and the user enters the down arrow key, then the highlighting will wrap around to the top item on the display. Similar wrap-around occurs for moving from the top item to the bottom item. An alternative to using the arrow keys, and useful on those keyboards in which arrow keys are not available, is to designate keys such as "d" and "u" as down and up, respectively. A problem with this approach is that these keys may not be devoted to menu functions, as arrow keys can be, because they would have to be used for other kinds of text. The interface may have to incorporate modes, such as a menu mode and a text mode, which could cause the interface to become unnecessarily complex and prone to errors.

Having a menu mode should be avoided, if at all possible. Norman (1986) provided much anecdotal evidence to indicate that modes are a cause of many human errors. In some cases, modes are needed to differentiate between commands and text. Commands provide instructions to the computer. If writing text, the computer must know what is to be inserted into the text and what is to be acted upon as commands. If, during word processing, the user entered "2" for menu choice 2, then the computer could interpret this as a "2" that should be entered as text. For some interfaces, the only choice is to respond to the menu, so multiple modes are not needed. In other situations, entries could be either commands or text. One means of solving this problem is to use mode keys. Menu items could be chosen by holding down a key, such as the control key, while the menu choice is entered. This solves the problem of initiating and terminating modes, but the user must remember that the control key is to be used.

An alternative, and popular, input method is to use the mouse, and several methods are available for choosing the item. As the mouse is moved, the mouse cursor moves on the screen. When the mouse cursor moves over the menu item, and the mouse button is clicked (sometimes two clicks are needed), then the menu choice is accomplished. In another method, if the mouse cursor moves over a menu item, then the menu item will become highlighted and a single mouse click is needed for the choice or a ENTER key entry could activate the choice. For pull-

down menus, the menu is typically displayed by pressing the mouse button, and it continues to be displayed as long as the mouse button is down. When moving the mouse cursor down through the items with the mouse button down, if the cursor passes over a menu item, that menu item is highlighted. A choice is made when the mouse button is released and the highlighted item is chosen.

Other more unusual input devices have been used for pointing to menu items. For a touch screen, the screen can be activated, and, by touching the menu item with a finger or some other object, the choice is entered. Light pens accomplish much the same purpose, but, instead of using a finger, a special light pen is used. A stylus, on a digitizer tablet, can also be used to make the choice. Some displays have special function buttons pointing to each of the choices on the screen. These are especially popular in automatic teller machines. They must be designed carefully, however, so that the buttons are close enough to the menu items so that the user can see which button corresponds to which item (see Figure 23-5). An even better design displays the menu item directly on the button to be pushed.

With so many choices of interaction available, the user may have difficulty remembering which interaction method is used with which menu. Of course, within an application the menu choice methods should all be consistent. Flexibility can also be designed into menu displays so that the user has a choice of interaction methods. A mouse-based pointing system can also incorporate arrow keys or first-character designations. Menu choices designated by characters can also be chosen through the use of arrow keys. The

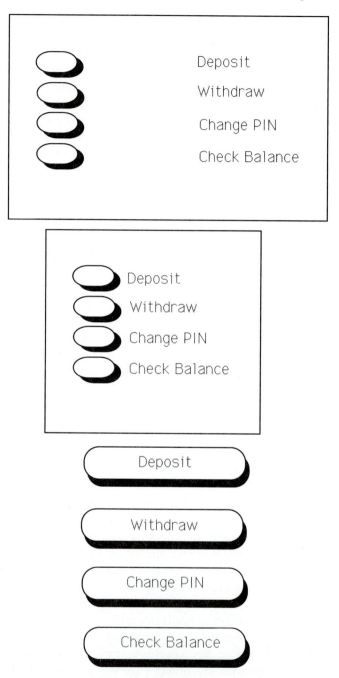

Figure 23-5. This shows three examples for how buttons are used to point to menu displays. The top example is difficult to use because the menu items are so far away from the buttons. The middle example is easier, with the menu item close to the button. The bottom example is even better by displaying the menu item directly on the button.

permutations of choices can be large.

By using multiple methods, much is gained and little is lost. Certain people may just prefer a certain method to interact with menu displays. Some people, through interacting with other systems, may only think that one method exists. In some contexts, one method may be faster than another. As an example, the Keystrokes-Level model of GOMS (Card et al., 1983) showed that the time to move from the keyboard to the mouse is 0.40 sec. So, if the hand is already on the keyboard, then keyboard methods could save that 0.40 sec if the hand did not have to move to the mouse. Similarly, if all operations are mouse-based, choosing menu items with the mouse would be faster than using the keyboard. The only thing that is lost is a little bit more programming time to incorporate all the methods.

Another issue for menu displays are the items that are displayed in the menu. In some cases, the context dictates that certain menu items are not possible. As an example, in a cut-and-paste operation, an item can be pasted only after it has been cut. So, if the item has not been cut, then the paste operation should be disabled in some way. In Chapter 2, examples were provided of how items could be "grayed" out by changing the font. Some menus will just not include, in any form, the menu item which is not possible.

Menu displays are used quite often in many different kinds of interface designs. The interface designer must determine when to use menu displays, instead of the alternative interface modes, and how to design the menu display if used. Once again, the four approaches can be used to address these issues.

EMPIRICAL APPROACH

Under the empirical approach, two issues are important. First, other interface modes are available such as fill-in-the-blank, parametric, and direct manipulation (Shneiderman, 1980, 1987). The empirical approach can be used to determine which is best in which situations. Second, incorporation of a menu display means choosing particular features for the menu. The empirical approach can be used to determine which features are best.

Empirical Comparisons to Other Interface Modes

Shneiderman (1980) outlined four different kinds of interface modes. Menu selection is the same as that which has been discussed above; but the other three, command, fill-in-the-blank and parametric, have not been discussed previously in any detail. A fourth interface mode, direct manipulation, has been developed extensively since the Shneiderman book and has been discussed in Chapter 11.

For command-based displays, the user must enter through a keyboard the full name of a command or a partial name in order for the computer to perform the functions. To perform this task, the user must remember the relevant commands and enter the syntax correctly. Parameters can be used with some commands to perform more specialized functions. As an example, the command "copy" requires two other parameters in order to perform the function: the file to copy (the old file) and where to copy the file (the new file). These files must be in the correct order, following the command name, or the command will be performed wrong. Some interfaces only require that a partial command name be entered, as long as that part which is entered can distinguish it from all the other possible command names. As an example, entering "co" would not be enough characters to distinguish the name from "concatenate," but entering "cop" would. With some practice, users can remember the least amount of letters to enter. The fewer characters to enter, from the Keystrokes-Level model (Card et al., 1983), the faster the interaction.

At one stage, most computer operating systems utilized command-based displays. Some users liked these kinds of interfaces because they are fast for the experts, they are flexible because of the large number of commands and parameters, and they can be very powerful. Much research has been performed on methods to improve command-based displays such as through the choice of command names (Dumais and Landauer, 1981; Scapin, 1981), by methods to enter the commands, and by manipulating how the computer interprets the command (Wixon, Whiteside, Good, and Jones, 1983). In recent years, direct manipulation and menu displays have become more popular at the expense of the command-based displays. Many of the old command-based displays can be converted into direct manipulation displays. From Digital Equipment Corporation, DECWindows has been used to turn the command-based VMS operating system into a direct manipulation display. DOS is a command-based display used widely on PCs; Microsoft Windows 3.0 provides this command-based display with more of a direct manipulation feel. UNIX is a very powerful, but complicated, command-based interface. X Windows

has been used to convert the commands into direct manipulation. Command-based displays will only be discussed further in relation to menu displays.

Fill-in-the-blank displays can also be referred to as form fill-in displays. For these displays, the user is queried and must respond to the queries. As an example from Shneiderman (1980), the user may be required to enter information about a student, and the interaction could occur as follows:

READY FOR GRADE LEVEL?
JUNIOR
GRADE POINT AVERAGE?
3.47
MAJOR?

The user must enter items in those spaces that are underlined. A form fill-in is very similar, except the display looks like a form and certain fields are available for entering the specific information without scrolling on the screen. Some situations, such as entering the grade point average, cannot be performed easily using menu displays because the choices are so numerous. Other situations, such as entering the grade level, could be performed alternatively with a menu display.

The parametric interface mode is not used to a great extent, but it has some advantages in terms of speed of entry. The example from Shneiderman (1980) is entering information at an airline ticket counter. The following could be entered:

A21AUGJFKLAX

This is shorthand for determining any flight information on August 21 for flights between JFK airport in New York and LAX airport in Los Angeles. The advantage of this kind of interface mode is that it is very fast and the operators feel that they have great control over it. The disadvantage is that training is needed to remember all the abbreviations. Some of the information could not easily be placed on menu displays because the number of items, for example, airports, would be too large to place on the screen.

An experiment by Gade et al. (1981) has compared menu interface modes to other possible command-based input methods. The menu system tested in this experiment used cursor positioning by hitting error keys to move the cursor from boxes associated with a menu item. When the cursor was in the appropriate box, the ENTER key was hit and the choice was made. The menu interaction was compared to three other kinds of interaction. In the typing with edit feedback condition, users typed in the appropriate code for each item in the defined format referring to a dictionary of legal codes and their definitions as needed. The typing with error correction was similar but, when an invalid entry was typed, the system assumed a typing error and tried to correct it. Four kinds of typing errors could be corrected: transposition of two adjacent letters, insertion of an extra letter, omission of one letter, or substitution of one incorrect letter. If the computer determined a possible correction, the correction was displayed and the user could either confirm the correction or retype the correct entry. If no correction was determined, then the user had to retype the command. In the last condition, typing with autocompletion and English option, the English definition could be typed in place of the code and when the user thought that enough characters had been typed to distinguish

the command from other commands, then the autocompletion button could be pushed and the rest of the command would be entered automatically.

The results showed a 30% decrease in errors when selecting from menus as compared to typing with edit feedback, which was the simplest command-based interaction. This difference was significant statistically. None of the other methods were different statistically from the menus. In the time to interact, no differences occurred across the different methods. A majority of subjects (62%), however, preferred the menu interaction when compared to the other methods. The error corrector and the autocompletion were not completely satisfactory. The error corrector was used 4.7 times on average per subject in the four-hour experiment. It decreased errors by 11% when compared to the edit feedback condition. The autocompletion was not very popular in that subjects only averaged 6.5 uses out of 106 opportunities. Some subjects complained that it confused them, but the people who did use it could become fairly fast and proficient at the task.

This experiment lasted four hours, so the results can be generalized only to novice subjects. It is possible that experts would perform differently on some of the displays, showing more improvement with the command-based displays than they could with the menu displays. Anecdotal evidence (Iseki and Shneiderman, 1986) indicates that experts believe that they can use commands faster than they can use menus, but this experiment did not test experts. Evidence of that was found for the autocompletion in which some of the subjects were becoming proficient with this method. Also, the error corrector only caught some of the simple syntax errors. The more difficult errors are logic errors. These would include choosing the wrong command, choosing a command which would be correct with another system but wrong with this one, or choosing a synonymous name. These are difficult errors to determine automatically.

Comparisons of Menu Features

Once the choice of a menu display has been made, the interface designer must still determine the features to incorporate in the menu design. Some of these feature choices have been investigated through experimentation: the depth vs. breadth of the menu and the design of embedded menus.

Depth vs. Breadth. The depth vs. breadth of menus was introduced as the common example for the predictive models in Section III. Recall that a menu system has high breadth if the menu items are placed on one screen. A menu system has high depth if only a few items are placed on one screen, and the user must move through many screens in order to make the menu choice. The screens higher in the hierarchy provide category designations for the lower hierarchical screens. For high-breadth displays, the user must read more items to find the appropriate item, but this requires fewer responses. For the high-depth displays, the user has fewer items to read but must make more responses. The length of the menu item will influence the reading time, thus having a large effect on high-breadth displays. The kind of response, especially the number of keystrokes if this method is used, would have a large effect on response time for the high-depth displays.

Miller (1981) investigated manipulations of depth and breadth. In this kind of research, a convention for designating the breadth and depth of the menu has been used in which the number of items on a screen is signified first and then the number of levels is signified second. Miller had four manipulations: 2-6 (2 items over 6 levels), 4-3, 8-2, and 64-1. The 2-6 was the highest depth and the 64-1 was the highest breadth. When measuring speed and accuracy, Miller found that subjects were slower and less accurate with the 2-6 and the 64-1; these were the values at the extremes for the depth and breadth. The conclusion from this study is that medium depth or breadth displays should be utilized.

Kiger (1984) performed a similar experiment but also tested user preferences for the menus. He had subjects interact with the following menus: 2-6, 4-3, 8-2, (4-1+16-1) (4 choices at level one and 16 choices at level two), and (16-1+4-1). To make a menu choice, the subject would have to enter the alpha character (e.g., "B") corresponding to the menu item and then hit the ENTER key.

The results for the speed and accuracy were somewhat similar to the Miller (1981) results. The 2-6 was the worst (38.23 sec.), the 4-3 was in the middle (21.74 sec.), and the 8-2 (15.64 sec.) was about the same as the remaining two. The only difference from the earlier study was that the 4-3 was significantly different statistically from the 2-6 in this study but not in the Miller study. The accuracy followed a similar pattern.

For the ratings on ease of use, the subjects felt that the high-depth display was the most difficult to use when compared to all but the (16-1+4-1) display.

The 8-2 and 4-3 displays were about equal in ease of use. Overall, the subjects preferred the 8-2 and 4-3 over the others.

A conclusion from this study, without the highest breadth (64-1) display, is that displays with medium depth and breadth are both faster to use and preferred by the users. One problem with this study is that the 2-6 display, the highest depth, had to be designed in unnatural ways in order to fulfill the requirement of high depth. As an example, the subjects had to make the following selections at each of the six depths: (1) education & science; (2) science; (3) science; (4) science news; (5) chemistry & physics; and (6) physics. The choices were redundant, and it could appear that the choices were meaningless and had no effect, such as moving from level 2 to 3. With the redundancy, confusion could have occurred. As a comparison, to make the same response in the 4-3 display, the subjects would make the following responses: (1) science; (2) science news; and (3) physics. Less redundancy occurs, and each item has more information content. The artificiality of the experiment could have had a large effect on the results. These results must be interpreted cautiously in light of this possible confound of understandability with depth of the display.

The final conclusion of the Kiger (1984) study was that breadth was better than depth in menu construction. He did not, however, test the high-breadth condition (64-1) as did Miller (1981). By including that condition, Miller's conclusions are probably more accurate in that the extremes of depth or breadth should be avoided. Menus of medium depth or breadth are faster and are preferred by users. Kiger's results showed, somewhat

unintentionally, that menu organization through the semantic meaning of the items and path are important to performance and usability.

Menu Organization. Menu organization can refer to which items are grouped under which menu category. With pull-down menus, menu category is important because only the category name is displayed continuously, and not the individual menu items. If the menu item does not match the category name, then the user may have to search through several pull-down menus before the desired item is found. Sometimes the category of the item can change from software version to software version. As an example, the "find" command, for finding a certain word or set of characters, was under the category heading of "search" in one version of a word processing software. In a later version, "find" was now under the category of "utilities." Is "find" part of searching or is it part of utilities? This change was made because new utilities were added to the new version, and room on the display was no longer available. Practical considerations play a part in category organization.

Organization of menus is also important to menus which are displayed continuously on the screen. From Section III on modeling, we know that reading time had a large effect on execution time. Reading time could be reduced if the user no longer had to read the items serially. With some kind of semantic organization to the items on the screen, the user could learn where the desired menu item was located, based upon the context of the other items in that area, and then skip to that area of the display. Some experimentation has been performed on this issue.

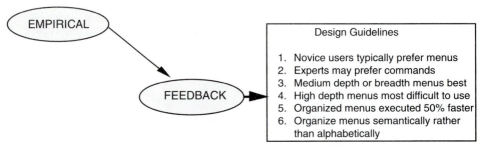

Figure 23-6. A summary and illustration of the design principles as applied to menu displays when using the empirical approach.

Liebelt, McDonald, Stone, and Karat (1983) investigated the effect of organized and disorganized menu displays on execution time. In the organized displays, the menu items were grouped according to category, and in the disorganized displays, the menu items were organized randomly. Results showed that the organized displays could be performed about 50% faster, and the confusion, as evidenced by the time needed to select a menu item, was reduced significantly.

Another possibility for menu organization is by alphabetic characters instead of semantic organization.   Alphabetic organization was compared to random or semantically meaningful organizations by McDonald, Stone, and Liebelt (1983). Once again, the results showed that the semantic organization was faster than the random or the alphabetic.

The above experimentation indicates that semantic organization of the menu items is most important, when compared to disorganized or alphabetic arrangements. Another consideration, discussed in the section on predictive models, is that the most-used menu item should be at the top of the list. This would reduce execution time because the user would not have to read through all the items and would not have to move the mouse very far to make the choice. No experimentation has been

performed comparing this feature to other features, although the predictive models would show clear performance advantages. This exercise is performed later in this chapter.

A summary of the design guidelines from the empirical approach is shown in Figure 23-6.

COGNITIVE APPROACH

Many researchers argue for the advantages of menu display over other alternatives by invoking cognitive explanations. In particular, one of the main advantages of menu displays is that the user can utilize recognition instead of recall. Much research in cognitive psychology has shown that people are much better at recognizing items than recalling items (Dallett, Wilcox, and D'Andrea, 1968; Paivio, 1971; and Standing, Conezio, and Haber, 1970). For menu displays, the possible commands and functions are displayed on the screen so that the user only has to recognize the appropriate command. With command-based systems, the user must recall the correct command or function and then enter that command so that it is correct syntactically. This places a larger load on memory. Research has found that experienced users of menu displays cannot even recall the names of the menu items because they rely so much on recognizing the items on the display (Mayes, Draper, McGregor, and Oatley, 1988).

Another cognitive advantage for menu displays is that they can be designed to organize the decision making of the user (Koved and Shneiderman, 1986). Through the hierarchical organization of the menu display, the user can be guided about how to categorize the functions through the names of the menu screens at each level. This would be especially useful for novices, because they would probably need this kind of organization in their decision making. Perhaps this method may become more restrictive to experts, who need to think of the functions under different organizations depending on the circumstances.

In the following sections, some of the other applications of the cognitive approach to menu display design are discussed. This discussion follows the organization of Section IV. Not all of the subapproaches have been applied to menu display design; the subapproaches of mental models, neural nets, and attentional resources will not be discussed.

Human Information Processing

The main application of human information processing to menu design is in the information processing limitations as outlined in the human information processing models. As a summary of experimental evidence, the models indicate that the short-term memory limitations are around three to nine chunks of information. Kiger (1984) argues that the depth/breadth issue in menu design can be related to this limitation. The results from his study, and others, indicate that the

number of items displayed on a menu screen should be in that region of seven to nine items, which uses the more expanded estimate of the Model Human Processor when long-term memory assists working memory.

As an example of this limitation, if an interactive program had 15 menu items, then the designer should consider decomposing these items into three separate displays of five items each. A main menu, on the first screen, would be used to access the three displays. Having five menu items is within the limitations of working memory. A high-breadth display of 15 items would exceed this limitation.

Metaphors and Analogies

In some sense, menu displays are just a metaphor in action. The term menu refers to the menus we are all familiar with in restaurants. With a restaurant menu, we have several categories of selections, such as appetizers, entrees, desserts, and drinks. Items can be selected under each of the categories. By understanding how to perform operations in this familiar knowledge domain of restaurant menus, we can understand how to perform computerized menu operations.

Not much research has been reported on specifically applying metaphors and analogies to menu design issues. One possibility for applications of metaphors and analogies is in the choice of names for the menu items. The names can be used to support other metaphors or to support an analogy local to the items. As an example, popular menu item names within a word processing system are "cut" and "paste." Both of these names support the analogy that the computer system is performing operations similar to that which could be done with scissors and glue. By looking at the menu item names, the user can determine quickly the functionality by applying the knowledge of these familiar tools to the new computer task. Norman and Chin (1989) have discussed some ways in which menu items could be improved by more effectively using the analogy to restaurant menus.

Spatial Reasoning and Graphics

One of the problems with menu displays is that the interaction with the menus is usually in a different place on the screen from the item that is being manipulated. As an example for a direct manipulation word processor, if the user is changing a word in text, then the word is usually highlighted with a mouse, by pressing the mouse button while the cursor is on the first letter, moving the mouse to the last letter, and releasing the button. Then, the function, such as delete or copy, is chosen through a pull-down menu which is usually located at some different location on the screen. When the user has to move from the spatial location of the manipulation, the word which has been highlighted, to another location to perform the function, this violates one of the principles of direct manipulation. The manipulation of the objects should always be performed in the spatial location, or close to the spatial location, of the object.

This problem should be solved by displaying the menus so that the spatial context of the object is maintained. The location of the menu could be variable and context-dependent so that the menu is displayed as close to the manipulation as is possible. For the text-editing example,

this could be achieved by displaying the menu underneath the word to be highlighted. In word processing systems, when a word is highlighted then this implies that an editing command will be performed on it, and these editing commands are very limited. No other kinds of operations could be performed after highlighting a character, word, or phrase. These editing commands could be displayed in a menu directly underneath or above the word which has been highlighted. By doing this, the spatial location of the manipulation is preserved and the user does not have to move the mouse long distances, which can save execution time.

Koved and Shneiderman (1986) make a distinction between embedded and explicit menus. Explicit menus are the kind which have been reviewed mostly in this chapter where both the items in the menu and the position of the menu are invariant. Embedded menus can have menu items which change, depending on the context, and the positioning of the menu can change so as to be located spatially close to the item that is being manipulated. Koved and Shneiderman list several examples of embedded menus.

One kind of embedded menu discussed by Koved and Shneiderman (1986) is to have words highlighted in text. Each of the highlighted words represents a menu item that can be chosen to find more information about the item. This is how hypertext systems work. Once a highlighted word is chosen, more information can be found about the word, and this information is presented in text form. The new text, in turn, also contains highlighted words that can be chosen for more information. Reading is different in this kind of environment in that the user does not have

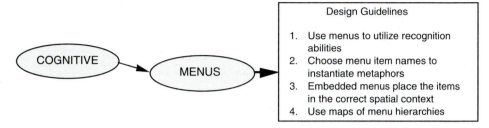

COGNITIVE → MENUS →

Design Guidelines

1. Use menus to utilize recognition abilities
2. Choose menu item names to instantiate metaphors
3. Embedded menus place the items in the correct spatial context
4. Use maps of menu hierarchies

Figure 23-7. A summary and illustration of the design principles as applied to menu displays when using the cognitive approach.

to go through the text linearly but can jump from section to section depending on the desired information. Some evidence indicates that users have trouble with this nonlinear kind of reading and often end up trying to straighten out the hypertext. This kind of menu system is advantageous spatially because the menu items can be chosen in the spatial location that they appear in the text instead of having another location for an index of appropriate words.

Another example from embedded menus by Koved and Shneiderman (1986) is used in spell checkers. Spell checkers are often incorporated in word processors to search the text for misspelled words, and they then allow the user to change the spelling. Some checkers only find possible misspelled words while others find the words and then suggest corrections for the words. Koved and Shneiderman present an example where the possible corrections for the word are presented in a menu underneath the misspelled word. The most likely choice is presented at the top of the menu, and the less likely choices are presented in descending order. This is an embedded menu because the spatial location of the menu changes, depending on the location of the misspelled word, and the items vary depending on the possibilities for the misspelled words. Once again,

this method has spatial advantages because the user does not have to go to a different location on the screen in order to make the change.

Another spatial subapproach issue for menu displays is how the users keep a mental spatial map of where they are in the menu display. For menus with multiple screens and levels, the location of the user could become confusing. The user may not realize how many levels must be traversed before the desired menu item is reached and may not realize how to get back to the beginning. Some menu displays have dealt with the spatial orientation problem by always listing the previous menu screen which occurred at the higher level. Billingsley (1982) has investigated using a spatial map in order to orient the users in deep menu displays.

A summary of the design guidelines from the cognitive approach is shown in Figure 23-7.

PREDICTIVE MODELING APPROACH

The example used throughout the discussion of the predictive modeling approach, as explained in Section IV, was a menu example on predicting the execution time, learnability, memory workload, and transferability of the different menu displays.

This example shows very clearly how these predictive models can be used in the interface design process. In the following discussion, these models will be used again in light of the empirical results of the depth/breadth trade-off. In addition to this issue, the predictive models could also be used to help determine the placement of items in the menu and as a comparison to the other possible interface modes. To show how the predictive models can be applied, the depth/breadth trade-off for those menus considered in the empirical section and the placement of items in the menu will be discussed for each of the relevant models. Previously, using the notation from the depth/breadth trade-off experiments, in Section IV menu configurations of 16-1 (16 items in one level) and 4-4 were considered. The experiments examined 2-6, 4-3, 8-2, and 64-1 configurations. For each of the relevant models, the execution time will be predicted for these four configurations.

Model Human Processor

Recall that the Model Human Processor of Card et al. (1983) was used to predict performance on high-breadth and high-depth displays. First recall the example for the high-breadth display. The following steps were needed:

1. τ_p perceive item on display and transfer name to working memory

2. τ_c retrieve semantic meaning of needed operation from long-term memory; transfer to working memory

3. τ_c match code from displayed item to needed item

4. τ_c decide on match (yes: go to next step; no: perceive next item)

5. τ_m execute response to choose menu item or execute eye movements to go back to step 1

6. τ_p perceive menu item number and transfer to working memory

7. τ_c decide on key

8. τ_m execute key response

In these steps, steps 1 through 5 must be done $(n+1)/2$ times on the average where n is the number of items on the screen at each level. The number of levels of the menu display must also be considered. If k is used to represent the number of levels, then all eight steps must be repeated k times. Using this, the equation in this general case is

$$\text{total time} = k((n + 1)/2 \, (\tau_p + 3\tau_c + t_m) + \tau_p + \tau_c + \tau_{m)} \quad (23.1)$$

Inserting the Middle Man values, the equation becomes

$$\text{total time} = k((n + 1)/2 \, (100 + 3(70) + 70) + 100 + 70 + 70) \quad (23.2)$$

By reducing and combining terms, the equation becomes

$$\text{total time} = 190kn + 430k \text{ msec.} \quad (23.3)$$

This equation can be used conveniently for the notation of depth and breadth. The notation can be designated as n-k, and the execution times for the 2-6, 4-3, 8-2, and 64-1 menu configurations can determined. For the 2-6 configuration, the predicted time is total time = 190 (6) (2) + 430 (6)

$\qquad$ = 4860 msec. $\qquad$ (23.4)

For the 4-3 configuration, the predicted time is

total time = 190 (3) (4) + 430 (3)

$\qquad$ = 3570 msec. $\qquad$ (23.5)

For the 8-2 configuration, the predicted time is

total time = 190 (2) (8) + 430 (2)

$\qquad$ = 3900 msec. $\qquad$ (23.6)

For the 64-1 configuration, the predicted time is

total time = 190 (1) (64) + 430 (1)

$\qquad$ = 12,590 msec. $\qquad$ (23.7)

The predictions from this model follow the relationships among the empirical results almost perfectly. The results are much the same as the Miller (1981) results in that the two extremes of depth (2-6) and breadth (64-1) were the worst. Much like the empirical results, the high breadth was considerably worse than the high depth. The Miller results also found no statistical difference between the 4-3 and 8-2, and from the predicted models, these are fairly close. The predicted execution times are slightly different from those of the Kiger (1984) results in that Kiger found that the 8-2 configuration was significantly faster than the 4-3 configuration, and the predicted results for the 4-3 are faster than the predicted results for the 8-2 configuration with the Model Human Processor. The prediction times are considerably lower than what was found in the other results: the predicted times ranged from around 3.5 sec. to 12.5 sec.; the em-

pirical times ranged from around 18 sec. to 38 sec.

The serial terminating search assumes that all menu items have an equal probability of being the menu choice. If the items are configured so that the highest probability items are placed at the top of the list and the lower probability items are placed at the bottom, then the serial terminating search assumptions are no longer valid and the average search times could change. Consider the case for a 6-1 configured menu in which the six items, starting at the top, have the following probabilities of being chosen: 0.5, 0.25, 0.1, 0.05, 0.05, and 0.05.

First, consider the equal probability case where each item has a 1/6 probability of being chosen. Recall from Chapter 13 that in a serial terminating search with each item having equal probability, steps 1 through 5 must be done (n+1)/2 times on the average where n is the number of items on the screen, in this case 6, at each level. On average, 17/2 or 3.5 items must be searched to find the match. This occurs because if the choice is the first item, then 1/6 (1) items would have to be searched; if the choice was the second item, then 1/6 (2) items would have to be searched; and so on up to 6 items. Totaling those, the sum would be 1/6 (1 + 2 + 3 + 4 + 5 + 6) or 21/6. This reduces to 3.5 items. With k equal to 1, the search time is

$$\text{total time} = 3.5\,(\tau_p + 3\tau_c + t_m) + \tau_p + \tau_c + \tau_m$$
$$(23.8)$$

Inserting the Middle Man values, the equation becomes

total time = 3.5 (100 + 3(70) + 70) + 100

$\qquad$ + 70 + 70

$\qquad$ = 1570 msec. $\qquad$ (23.9)

Next, consider the case where the items are ordered from top to bottom starting with the highest probability item at the top. In this case, fewer items on the average would need to be searched. Using the probabilities from the top, the average number of items which had to be searched could be determined from the following:

$$0.5 (1) + 0.25 (2) + 0.1 (3)$$
$$+ 0.05 (4) + 0.05 (5) + 0.05 (6)$$
$$= 2.05 \text{ items} \qquad (23.10)$$

Inserting this value into the equation, the total time needed to find the item on the average would be

$$\text{total time} = 2.05 (100 + 3(70) + 70) + 100$$
$$+ 70 + 70$$
$$= 1019 \text{ msec.} \qquad (23.11)$$

With the menu organized according to probability of using the item, the execution time can be reduced by about a half second.

If the menu display is designed poorly, then it is possible that the highest probability items may be at the bottom of the display. The items could be turned around completely so that the six items have the following probabilities of occurring: 0.05, 0.05, 0.05, 0.1, 0.25, and 0.5. For this poor design, the average number of items searched before the desired item is chosen would be

$$0.05 (1) + 0.05 (2) + 0.05 (3)$$
$$+ 0.1 (4) + 0.25 (5) + 0.5 (6)$$
$$= 4.95 \text{ sec.} \qquad (23.12)$$

Inserting this value into the equation, the total time needed to find the item on the average would be

$$\text{total time} = 4.95 (100 + 3(70) + 70) + 100$$
$$+ 70 + 70$$
$$= 2121 \text{ msec.} \qquad (23.13)$$

With this poor menu design, the execution time is increased by about a half second over the equal probability case.

There are limits to the increases and reductions in execution times. The two extremes would be if the first item had a 100% probability of occurring or if the last item had a 100% probability of occurring. With the first item at 100%, the execution time would be 720 msec. and with the last item at 100% the execution time would be at 2,520 msec. By changing the probabilities, and ordering the menu items differently, all predicted execution times would fall between those ranges.

GOMS Model

Making explicit time predictions for execution was difficult for the GOMS model in Chapter 14. The Keystrokes-Level model of GOMS was used to make explicit predictions, but search time was captured under the mental operator, so that the model did not differentiate between the number of items that had to be searched on a screen. Predictions were made solely on the basis of keystrokes or other kinds of external operators. For menus of different breadth and depth, performance would then be dependent on the number of levels, since each level requires another keystroke.

Assuming that the menu display has a number starting with 1 associated with each menu item, and the menu choice has to be terminated by the ENTER key, the time predictions for the 2-6, 4-3, 8-2, and 64-1 configurations can be predicted. If each search is associated with a mental operator (M), and each keystroke is represented by the K operator, the 2-6 configuration would require the following amount of time:

$$6 (M + K(\text{digit}) + K(\text{Enter})) \qquad (23.14)$$

Six levels are used, so that searching and pressing the two keystrokes must be performed at each level. Substituting 1.35 sec. for the M operator and 0.2 sec. for the K operator, the equation becomes

$$6 (1.35 + .20 + .20) = 10.5 \text{ sec.} \qquad (23.15)$$

For the 4-3 configuration, three levels must be traversed. The increase in the number of menu items has no effect on the M operator, by the assumptions of the model. The predicted time is

$$3 (M + K(\text{digit}) + K(\text{Enter})) \qquad (23.16)$$

Making the time substitutions, the equation becomes

$$3 (1.35 + .20 + .20) = 5.25 \text{ sec.} \qquad (23.17)$$

For the 8-2 configuration, two levels must be traversed. The predicted time is

$$2 (M + K(\text{digit}) + K(\text{Enter})) \qquad (23.18)$$

Making the time substitutions, the equation becomes

$$2 (1.35 + .20 + .20) = 3.5 \text{ sec.} \qquad (23.19)$$

For the 64-1 configuration, the menu display is all on one screen. Since all items cannot be designated by nine digits or fewer, the number designation for items 10-64 would have to contain two digits. With all items of equal probability, the probability that two digits would be needed

in the choice is 55/64 or 0.86. The predicted time is

$$M + K(\text{first digit}) + .86 \ K(\text{second digit}) \\ + K(\text{Enter}) \qquad (23.20)$$

Making the time substitutions, the equation becomes

$$1.35 + .20 + .86 \ (.20) + .20 = 1.92 \text{ sec.} \qquad (23.21)$$

The predictions of the model are based solely on the number of levels traversed. Without including the mental search time as a variable, the Keystrokes-Level model is not very good at predicting execution time. The empirical results of Kiger (1984) and Miller (1981) showed that the extremes of depth and breadth were the slowest. The Keystrokes-Level model only predicts that the higher the depth, the slower the execution time, which is not a valid assumption. The predictions of the Keystrokes-Level model could be made more accurate by substituting the result from the Model Human Processor for the M operator. Since the Model Human Processor only determines the mental time, and the Keystrokes-Level model only determines the external execution time, combining the two makes sense and would help to make them both more accurate.

When the Model Human Processor and the Keystrokes-Level model are combined, then the predictions for the menu configurations are as follows. For the 2-6 configuration, 12 keystrokes would have to be added to the result of the Model Human Processor prediction so that the prediction is 7,260 msec. For the 4-3 configuration, six more keystrokes would have to be added to the Model Human Processor results for a total of 4,770 msec.

For the 8-2 configuration, four more keystrokes would have to be added for a total of 4,700 msec. Finally, for the 64-1 configuration, two more keystrokes plus the 86% probability of the second digit would be added to the Model Human Processor result for a total of 13,160 msec. These results more closely approximate the absolute values of the empirical results. In addition, the 4-3 configuration is now slower than the 8-2 configuration, which was found in both the Miller (1981) and Kiger (1984) experiments.

In a similar way, the Keystrokes-Level model would not be able to predict the effects of varying the ordering of the menu items dependent on the probability of occurrence of each item. By combining the Model Human Processor results with the Keystrokes-Level model, however, predictions could be made.

NGOMSL Model

The NGOMSL model was used to predict execution times of menu configurations in Chapter 15. Two different models were determined for the high-depth and high-breadth displays. The high-breadth display used a model in which each menu item was designated by a single or double digit. The response was terminated by pressing the ENTER key. Before the ENTER key, the choice could be verified to determine if it was correct. Because of the fewer items on each screen, the high-depth display used a method whereby only one digit could designate a menu item. Pressing the digit key terminated the choice so that no verification was possible. In the following discussion when comparing the different configurations, the model from the high-breadth display, with the possi-

bility of two digits, verification, and the ENTER terminator, will be used.

Recall that execution time for the NGOMSL model is determined as follows:

Execution Time =
  NGOMSL statement time
  + Primitive External Operator Time
  + Analyst-Defined Mental Operator
    Time
  + System Response Time

NGOMSL Statement Time =
  Number of NGOMSL statements
  executed * 0.1 sec.

Primitive External Operator Time =
  Total of times for external operators

Analyst-Defined Mental Operator Time =
  Total of times for mental operators
  defined by the analyst

System Response Time =
  Total time when user is idle

For the different menu configurations, the total number of statements executed is dependent on the number of levels, or k. In addition, 3 of the 21 statements, statements 4-6 from the figure, must be executed dependent on the number of menu items on the screen, or n. Therefore, a general case for the number of statements executed, at 0.1 sec. for executing each statement, will be

NGOMSL statement time =
  $0.1 \, (k \, (18 + 3(n+1)/2))$ sec. (23.22)

The only primitive external operator is the press-key operator. This occurs two times in the 21 statements. Therefore, the general case is

Primitive external operator time = 2k (.20)
(23.23)

The only analyst-defined operator is the ReadScreen operator. This occurs twice: once in statement 4 and once in statement 12. Statement 4 is in the loop for when the items are read and must be multiplied by n. Therefore, the general case is

Analyst-defined mental operator time =
$$k (1 + (n+1)/2) \qquad (23.24)$$

In this example, we will assume that the system response time is negligible. It is possible that the system response time will have a large effect on the high-depth displays in this kind of research, but since we are not modeling any particular kind of system, the system response time cannot be determined.

Using the above information, the total execution time in the general case is

Execution Time = 0.1 (k (18 + 3((n+1)/2))) + 2k (0.2) + 0.1 (k (1 + (n+1)/2)) sec.
(23.25)

Through reductions, the following is found:

Execution time = 2.5 k + 0.2 kn sec.
(23.26)

Substituting in the values for the n and the k, the predicted execution time for the 2-6 configuration is 17.4 sec., for the 4-3 configuration it is 9.9 sec., and for the 8-2 configuration it is 8.2 sec. The 64-1 configuration requires an extra keystroke, because of the 0.86 possibility of an extra digit, and it requires one more statement, because the if statement for the n > 9 is the second if statement in the sequence.

Therefore, the following must be added to the equation for this configuration (k = 1):

0.86 k (0.10) + 0.86 k (0.20) = 0.26 sec.
(23.27)

Therefore, the 64-1 configuration has a predicted execution time of 15.56 sec.

The predictions from the NGOMSL model are fairly accurate. More than the Model Human Processor, the absolute times are close to the experimental times of Kiger (1984) and Miller (1981). If the system response time is significantly large, then the absolute times would be even closer; Kiger did not report the system response times so this cannot be determined. The relationships between the times are preserved also.

The NGOMSL model can be used to show how menu items with different probabilities of occurring should be ordered in a menu. For the six-item menu used in the Model Human Processor example, the same probabilities can be used: 0.5, 0.25, 0.1, 0.05, 0.05, and 0.05. By using the same kind of analysis as was used for the Model Human Processor, the user would have to search, on average, 2.05 items. This can be substituted for the (n + 1)/2 term from the previous equation of execution time, resulting in the following equation:

Execution Time = 0.1 (k (18 + 3(2.05))) + 2k (0.2) + 0.1 (k (1 + 2.05)) sec.   (23.28)

Since k = 1, through reductions the execution time can be found to be

Execution Time = 3.12 sec.   (23.29)

With the equal probability items, and searching through an average of 3.5 items, the predicted execution time is 3.70 sec. With the ordering of the menu items going from lowest to highest in the display, the predicted execution time would be 4.28 sec. Once again, ordering the items according to highest probability of occurrence can reduce the predicted execution time.

Production System Models

The production system models, discussed in Chapter 16, can use the same equation for execution time as that of the NGOMSL model. Although the models are very similar, production system models require more overhead than does the NGOMSL so that the number of statements and the execution times are slightly different.

Again, for the different menu configurations, the total number of statements must be executed by the number of levels, or k. Two of the 25 statements, statements 7 and 8 from the figure, must be executed dependent on the number of menu items on the screen, or n. Therefore, a general case is that the number of statements will be

$$\text{Statement time} = 0.1 \ (k \ (23 + 2(n+1)/2)) \text{ sec.} \quad (23.30)$$

The only primitive external operator is the press-key operator. This occurs two times in the 25 statements. Therefore, the general case is

$$\text{Primitive external operator time} = 2k \ (.20) \quad (23.31)$$

The only analyst-defined operator are the UserDefine statements. They occur twice: once in statement 7 and once in statement 15. Statement 7 is in the loop for

when the items are read and must be multiplied by n. Therefore, the general case is

$$\text{Analyst-defined mental operator time} = k \ (1 + (n+1)/2) \quad (23.32)$$

In this example, we will once again assume that the system response time is negligible.

Using the above information, the total execution time in the general case is

$$\begin{aligned} \text{Execution Time} = \\ 0.1 \ (k \ (23 + 2((n+1)/2))) + 2k \ (0.2) + \\ 0.1 \ (k \ (1 + (n+1)/2)) \text{ sec.} \quad (23.33) \end{aligned}$$

Through reductions, the following is found:

$$\text{Execution time} = 2.95 \ k + 0.15 \ kn \text{ sec.} \quad (23.34)$$

Substituting in the values for the n and the k, the predicted execution time for the 2-6 configuration is 19.5 sec., for the 4-3 configuration it is 10.65 sec., and for the 8-2 configuration it is 8.3 sec. The 64-1 configuration requires an extra keystroke, because of the 0.86 possibility of an extra digit, and it requires one more statement, because the if statement for the $n > 9$ is the second if statement in the sequence. Therefore, the following must be added to the equation for this configuration ($k = 1$):

$$0.86 \ k \ (0.10) + 0.86 \ k \ (0.20) = 0.26 \text{ sec.} \quad (23.35)$$

Therefore, the 64-1 configuration has a predicted execution time of 12.81 sec.

The execution times for the production system model are less than those for the NGOMSL model. This occurs because the statements that are in a loop, when reading through the menu items, can be done in one fewer step for the production system. The predicted times follow the same relationships as those in the NGOMSL and the experiments of Kiger (1984) and Miller (1981).

Production systems could be used to predict the ordering effects, similar to that done for the Model Human Processor and NGOMSL. This exercise will not be completed in this discussion because the results would be similar to that of the NGOMSL analysis.

Grammar Models

Howes and Payne (1990) use the TAG predictive model to model performance on pull-down menus. They argue that a weakness of the GOMS-related models and earlier versions of the grammar models is that they cannot model how the information that is represented on the display is processed by the user. As seen from the above discussions of the GOMS-based models, the goals and the methods, both cognitive activities, are the main influence on the execution time predictions. Using the Mayes et al. (1988) finding that even experienced users do not remember the menu item names for pull-down menus, Howes and Payne conclude that all the information to perform the task cannot be located entirely in the head but much of the information must be located on the display itself. In fact, a good interface design, as discussed in Chapter 21, may have most of the knowledge located on the display. Howes and Payne were interested in expanding the TAG model to incorporate this display-based knowledge.

Howes and Payne (1990) present an example of the find command from the MacWrite word processor. MacWrite makes extensive use of pull-down menus, so that the menu items are hidden from view until the category name of the menu is clicked. From the Mayes et al. (1988) results, we would expect that the users would not remember the name of the menu item, but only the general class. The GOMS-based models, discussed in the previous sections, all indicate that the user would have to be able to recall the name of the menu item for the model to work. From Howes and Payne (1990), the TAG description of the "find" command is as follows:

Task[Op = find]—>

    action(point,display_item([Op= find], [class = menu-bar])

    action(drag,display_item ([Op= find],[class = menu-bar; class = pull-down, location = below; class = text])

    action(type,target)

    action(type,ENTER)

The above grammar states simply that the task is to perform the "find" operation. Four actions are required for this command. The first action is a mouse action pointing to the appropriate menu-bar item under which the "find" operation should be found. The second action is to drag the mouse, through the menu items, until the appropriate item is found. The third action is to type in the target character, word, or phrase that the user wishes to find. The last action terminates the typing of the target by hitting the ENTER key.

The important aspect of the above TAG description is that the user does not have to know the name of the command in order to perform the "find" function. Howes and Payne (1990) use all kinds of methods to describe the command, without actually indicating the name of the command. The information that the user may have is more of a fuzzy representation of the command such as that it is on the pull-down menu; that the exact location is unknown (the user knows only that it is "below" the menu-bar); and that the command is written in text. The best match for this frame of knowledge is the command that the user chooses. The user does not have to recall exactly the command name, only recognize a name from the menu choices. The frame representation used for the recognition process is the first attempt for the predictive models to specify some of the features present in this process.

Conclusions

The predictive models have been shown to provide predictions of execution times which are quite close to the actual findings from the Kiger (1984) and Miller (1981) experiments. In all cases, the relationships between the predictions have been very similar to the relationships of the experimental results. With the NGOMSL model, the absolute times were very similar to the absolute experimental times.

The predictive modeling approach has some advantages over the experimental approach in that the predictions may be somewhat "purer" than the experimental times. The experimental times have other factors represented in the times such as semantic meaning of the items, prefer-

ences for certain kinds of displays, and artificiality due to experimental constraints. The predictive modeling estimations are free of these factors, unless the modeler wishes to include some of these aspects in a new model of the process. With some work, the models could be changed to incorporate something like semantic meaning of the items.

Predictive models must be able to capture the knowledge inherent in the display. The discussion of Chapter 21 indicated that this kind of knowledge is important in effective interface design. Howes and Payne (1990) have modified the TAG model to incorporate this kind of interactive information; similar modifications are needed for the other predictive models.

A summary of the design guidelines from the predictive modeling approach is shown in Figure 23-8.

ANTHROPOMORPHIC APPROACH

The anthropomorphic approach has only a few applications for menu displays. Menu displays are thought to adhere to this approach because of its ease of use. In the real world, we use several different kinds of displays which are similar to menu displays. The most obvious example is restaurant menus. In some sense, books can be conceptualized as natural menu systems. The table of contents represents the highest-level menu. Once a chapter is chosen, then the sections within a chapter can also be selected. The process can continue through subsections and sub-subsections. Through interaction with these objects in the natural world, we are better able to understand how computer menu displays work.

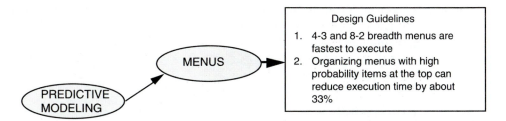

Figure 23-8. A summary and illustration of the design principles as applied to menu displays when using the predictive modeling approach.

One of the most natural actions that people perform is the pointing action. Menu displays use this action extensively. If the user desires to select a certain item, the item is pointed to by one of several methods. This is a natural response utilized in the real world.

A subapproach under the anthropomorphic approach is to adapt the display to the user or the task. McDonald, Dayton, and McDonald (1988) performed studies on the relationships between the menu organization and the tasks. They found that for different kinds of tasks, different menu organizations were optimal in terms of performance. They suggest that this finding can be used to adapt the organization of the menu to the particular task. They did not, however, attempt to incor-porate this adaptability into a computer system and test its use and feasibility.

A summary of the design guidelines from the anthropomorphic approach is shown in Figure 23-9.

SUMMARY

The purpose of this chapter was to illustrate how the different approaches can be used to address the issues for designing menu displays. Most of the applications have been found under the experimental and predictive modeling approaches. The predictions of the models showed that these two approaches made similar suggestions. The cognitive and anthropomorphic approaches were used to a lesser degree in menu displays. These approaches were

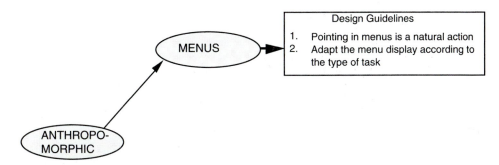

Figure 23-9. A summary and illustration of the design principles as applied to menu displays when using the anthropomorphic approach.

important, however, to show how menu displays reduced the cognitive load of the task, through recognition of menu items, and how the menu displays are natural and easy to use.

QUESTIONS

1. In a menu display of five items, the probabilities of the items being chosen are 0.4, 0.25, 0.2, 0.1, and 0.05, respectively, for items 1 through 5.

   a. Using the Model Human Processor, determine the predicted execution time for this kind of display.

   b. Assume that the designer changed the order so that the highest probability item was last on the list, the lowest probability was first on the list, and the order of the others changed accordingly. Calculate the predicted execution time using the Model Human Processor.

   c. What is the difference between the optimal order of items and the worst sequencing?

2. Kiger (1984) included menus designated as (4-1+16-1) (4 choices at level one and 16 choices at level two) and (16-1+4-1).

   a. Explain in words what a (16-1+4-1) display is.

   b. Using the Model Human Processor, calculate the predicted execution time for the (4-1+16-1) display.

   c. Using the Model Human Processor, calculate the predicted execu-

tion time for the (16-1+4-1) display.

   d. (2) Why are the Model Human Processor predicted times faster than the predicted times from NGOMSL?

   e. (2) Why are the predicted times from NGOMSL generally faster than the actual times from the experiments?

3. With an 8-2 display, there are 8 items on the first screen and 8 items on the second screen. Overall, on the second screen, the user has 64 choices. As an example, if the user chose item 1 on the first screen, then choices 1-8 would come up on the second screen. If the user chose item 2 on the first screen, then choices 9-16 would come up on the second screen. Finally, if the user chose item 8 on the first screen, then choices 57-64 would come up on the second screen. Assume that each of the 64 choices has the following probabilities of being chosen:

Items 1-16	.03/item
Items 17-32	.015/item
Items 33-48	.01/item
Items 49-64	.0075/item

Remember that with 64 items all having equal probability of being chosen that, on average, 32.5 items would be searched before the item was found ($(n+1)/2$). With the 8-2 display, which has two layers, how many items would have to be searched, on average, before the target menu item was found?

CHAPTER 24

DATABASE APPLICATIONS

INTRODUCTION

Databases can be very important to the productivity of individuals, companies, and organizations. With many companies, the amount of information is so great, and the need to share that information exists so strongly within the company, that databases of products, equipment, and resources become essential to the efficient operation of a medium-sized or large organization. One part of the company needs to know what another part of the company is doing. As an example, one division of a company may have already developed a product which could be used by another division in their product development. Without the possibility of communication between the divisions, ostensibly through a database, work may be duplicated within a company, reducing productivity. Also, a company may need to track the equipment used by individuals or keep personnel files on employees. When selling products, a detailed customer profile in a database can be very important to personalize the service to the customer.

For those individuals with personal computers, three computer applications are popular: word processors, spreadsheets, and database programs. In some cases, the distinctions between the three become blurred. Individuals may need a database to keep track of tax information and organize household information such as recipes, inventories of household goods, and even video movies.

Most of the databases in use today are relational. Date (1986) indicates for a relational database, the user conceptualizes the data as tables (see Figure 24-1). Typically, the rows of a table are referred to as the records and the columns are regarded as the fields. Operations can be performed on the tables by extracting columns or rows from the table to form new tables. Figure 24-2 shows how a new table is formed by specifying the columns to be output (the MOVIE and DIRECTOR columns) and then specifying a value for an entry. The operations can become more complicated when the logical relationships are used. Figure 24-3 shows an example where the movies that have Hepburn as the female lead AND Tracy as the male lead are searched and displayed; this list is the intersection of the two kinds of leads, and entries are chosen for the table if both parts of the AND are satisfied. The above AND table would be different from the table that has Hepburn as the female lead OR Tracy as the male lead (see Figure 24-4). This table is a result of the union of the two leads, and the entries are included in the table if only one of the leads is as specified. Finally, a NOT relationship can be used. Figure 24-5 shows the table formed from those movies in which the female lead is Hepburn and the male lead is other than (NOT) Tracy. Some data may be better represented by a structure other than tables, and the more popular structures are inverted lists, hierarchic, and network representations (Date, 1986).

Using a database can be difficult. In a database retrieval, the user must formulate retrieval information from a data source which is usually quite large and difficult to

MOVIE COLLECTION

MOVIE	YEAR	DIRECTOR	MALE LEAD	FEMALE LEAD
Adventures of Robin Hood	1938	Curtiz	Flynn	de Havilland
African Queen	1951	Huston	Bogart	Hepburn
Big Sleep	1946	Hawks	Bogart	Bacall
Bringing Up Baby	1938	Hawks	Grant	Hepburn
Captain Blood	1935	Curtiz	Flynn	de Havilland
Desk Set	1957	Lang	Tracy	Hepburn

Figure 24-1. An example of a relational database for a movie collection. A relational database is represented as a table; the rows are termed the records and the columns are termed the fields.

MOVIE COLLECTION

MOVIE	DIRECTOR
Adventures of Robin Hood	Curtiz
Captain Blood	Curtiz

SELECT MOVIE, DIRECTOR
FROM MOVIE COLLECTION
WHERE DIRECTOR = CURTIZ

Figure 24-2. A new table is constructed based upon the query at the bottom of the figure. The query asks for a list of the movies directed by Curtiz.

MOVIE COLLECTION

MOVIE	MALE LEAD	FEMALE LEAD
Desk Set	Tracy	Hepburn

SELECT MOVIE, FEMALE LEAD, MALE LEAD
WHERE (FEMALE LEAD = HEPBURN) AND (MALE LEAD = TRACY)

Figure 24-3. The query at the bottom of the figure utilizes a logical AND. It asks for the intersection of the movies which have Hepburn as a female lead and Tracy as a male lead.

envision. Borgman (1984) warns that this kind of task is inherently a complex task. It involves the articulation of an information need, often ambiguous, into precise words and relationships that match the structure of the system being searched. In a computer search, the user must apply two types of knowledge: knowledge of the mechanical aspects of searching (syntax and semantics of entering search terms, structuring a search, and negotiating through the system) and knowledge of the conceptual aspects. The conceptual aspects include when to use which access

```
MOVIE COLLECTION
MOVIE              MALE LEAD       FEMALE LEAD

African Queen      Bogart          Hepburn
Bringing Up Baby   Grant           Hepburn
Desk Set           Tracy           Hepburn

SELECT MOVIE, FEMALE LEAD, MALE LEAD
WHERE (FEMALE LEAD = HEPBURN) OR (MALE LEAD = TRACY)
```

Figure 24-4. The query at the bottom of the figure utilizes a logical OR. It asks for the union of the movies which have Hepburn as a female lead or Tracy as a male lead.

```
MOVIE COLLECTION
MOVIE                 MALE LEAD            FEMALE LEAD

African Queen         Bogart               Hepburn
Bringing Up Baby      Grant                Hepburn

SELECT MOVIE, FEMALE LEAD, MALE LEAD
WHERE (FEMALE LEAD = HEPBURN) AND (NOT (MALE LEAD =
       TRACY))
```

Figure 24-5. The query at the bottom of the figure illustrates a logical NOT. It is for the movies which have Hepburn as a female lead and do not have Tracy as a male lead.

points, ways to narrow and broaden search results, alternative search paths, and distinguishing between no matches due to a search error and no matches because the item is not in the database.

Typical computerized database manipulations require the use of a query language. Ehrenreich (1981) defines a query language as a set of syntactic and lexical rules with which the user can question the computer. Query languages belong to the class of computer languages commonly referred to as "nonprocedural" or "very high level." In nonprocedural languages, the user declares what the program is to accomplish without stating how it is to be accomplished. One of the features of a database query language that

makes it more difficult for the casual user to learn easily is the complicated syntax. In this language, each word in the syntax means complex operations for the computer, some of which are shown to the user. Hence the vocabulary used is small but powerful.

A difficult aspect of database retrievals is that the user does not know if the retrieval has been performed correctly and all the relevant information has been retrieved. An error could occur because the user performed the search incorrectly, because the information was stored incorrectly in the database, or because the search utilized was incomplete. Many people have probably performed a database retrieval in a library to find books under a certain topic. After specifying the words in the topic, the results of the search will display several books. The user cannot be entirely certain that these represent all the books under the topic. It is possible that related topic words, synonymous with that specified on the earlier search, could have been used to store the information about other books. The user cannot be certain that all the relevant books are displayed because of the uncertainty about whether the search was done correctly and completely or whether the books were stored originally under the correct topic words.

Database retrievals have several potential usability problems, which makes this an interesting topic in the study of human-computer interaction. First, a database is needed because the amount of information is so large. Because of this, it becomes difficult for a user to understand the content of the database and the structure of the items. Second, the syntax for database retrievals has often been difficult to learn and to apply. The user has to understand the logical connectors (i.e., AND and OR), the search categories, the commands, and how to string all these together in a specified sequence with, possibly, punctuation. Third, the user has difficulty determining the source of errors. Syntax errors would be relatively easy to understand. But logic errors, such as using the wrong logical connector or topic word, are difficult to localize. The results of the search may be correct in the exact terms the user specified, but the user may have erred in the specifications for the search and not realize the mistake. Because the search was completed, the user would be likely to accept the results without question.

Approaches to database interface design have attempted to correct some of these usability problems. The following discussion organizes this research according to the empirical, cognitive, predictive modeling, and anthropomorphic approaches. Much of the research has occurred using the cognitive and anthropomorphic approaches.

EMPIRICAL APPROACH

Many experiments have been conducted on databases. Most of the experimentation falls under one of the other approaches, however, so that the experiments will be discussed in those contexts. Database retrievals require extensive cognitive functioning by the user, and so many of the techniques developed have been discussed in relation to the cognitive approach.

COGNITIVE APPROACH

A database retrieval relies heavily on the cognitive functioning of the user. Therefore, many of the cognitive subapproaches from Chapter 7 have been applied to database interface design. Each of these will be discussed.

Mental Models

Mental model research has been applied in two ways to database applications: methods to assess the mental models of database applications and the relationship between the displayed information and the mental model developed.

Marchionini (1989) was interested to determine how database searches changed when using print and when using electronic computerized searches. He had high school students perform searches either using a printed encyclopedia or an electronic encyclopedia on a computer.

Electronic searches provide more features than the manual searches using the printed encyclopedias. In particular, the electronic searches can make use of hypertext features. For hypertext, certain words may be highlighted in the encyclopedia, and these words represent further topics which could be read just by activating the highlighted words. Hypertext encourages the use of nonsequential reading patterns, in which only the relevant information is read. Printed material encourages sequential reading. The hypertext feature could be useful in eliminating irrelevant material, but the subjects may have trouble operating a nonsequential mental model when all the previous training with printed material has been in the development of sequential-reading mental models.

The mental models of the subjects were determined through observer notes, audio protocols, interviews, and keystrokes in the electronic searches. Results showed that some of the subjects just used the print models to guide their electronic searches, not taking full advantage of the hypertext features. Most of the subjects used some of the electronic hypertext features, although not to a great extent. Only a few of the subjects showed an ability to adapt the existing print mental models to good electronic mental models. In terms of time performance, Marchionini (1989) found that subjects using the electronic searches took more time, posed more queries, and examined more articles. Marchionini concludes that interface designers must take into account previous mental models and adapt the displays to emphasize the differences between electronic searches and searches performed on printed material.

Katzeff (1990) investigated how mental models are formed in full-text database retrievals. During the manipulations, subjects in the experiment were required to think aloud, and these thoughts were collected as protocols. The protocols provided information about the underlying mental models. Katzeff (1990) determined that the users passed through three stages: construction, testing, and running. In the construction stage, subjects use the system to address questions they may have about how the system works. Through the feedback, the subjects are able to fill in gaps for the developing mental model. During this construction stage, the subjects try to understand how to use the feedback to address the questions. As an example, one subject receives feedback about the record number of a database item and says: "Record 116...If it had been 'record 1' I would have thought I was at the beginning...." This protocol indicates that the subject is still trying to understand the relationships between the input and the feedback provided by the system.

In the testing phase, the subject has already constructed parts of the mental model and determines whether to confirm or reject it. Criteria for confirmation or rejection are formulated and, in a partial run of the model, the feedback is compared to the evaluation criteria. As an example, the protocol for one of the subjects was as follows: "I will probably get the same article, the next time if [the focus-area] appears.... No, it is the next article....I should have done this 'expand' in between in order to stay within the same article. . . ." In this case, the evaluation criteria was whether or not the same article was retrieved. Since the feedback indicated it was not the same article, the test of the model indicated that the mental model constructed was incorrect.

The final stage is the running stage. In this stage, the subject uses the mental model to predict the outcome of a query instead of using the feedback. The subject will decide on the input and then mentally run the model to indicate the outcome. The mental model is refined by comparing this predicted outcome to the actual feedback. The following protocol demonstrates this: "If I now type 'next' I will get the next [focus-area] if there are any more . . .otherwise I will get a new article . . .which I do. That would mean that there are no more expert systems in this third article. . . ." The subject chooses an input, next, and predicts the outcome, either obtaining the next focus-area or getting a new article depending on the items in the database. The subject has formed a model of the database, and the outcome is used to further refine that form.

One of the important aspects of the Katzeff (1990) article is the relationship between the system feedback and the formation of the mental model. If the feedback is poor, the mental model will be incorrect. Another important aspect is the indication of the dynamics of the mental model. During the construction and testing stages, the mental model is constantly changing. To understand the database system, the subject must be able to get to a stage where the model can be run mentally and the outcome can be predicted through the model. The user must have an understanding so as to know what to expect from the system.

Eberts and Bittianda (1993) used the assessment of mental models of databases in a slightly different way. In this case, the mental model assessments were used to determine the preferences for interface designs. In this study, three groups of subjects were trained on different inter-face designs: a command-based interface using text, a direct manipulation interface, and a combined interface in which both the commands and direct manipulations were shown. In this latter interface, the subjects alternated between using commands and direct manipulations. In addition, when the command was entered, the corresponding spatial manipulations would be shown automatically on the display. In previous research, preferences for interface designs are usually assessed through questionnaires. This approach is problematic because the subjects may be responding to the most familiar interface or the one which uses the fanciest technology. In the Eberts and Bittianda research, the interface preference was determined by assessing which mental model was used by the subjects on the combined interface: a mental model based upon commands or a mental model based upon direct manipulations. This could be determined by matching the mental models of the combined group to the mental models of the command or direct manipulation groups to determine which provided the best match.

Mental models were assessed after training by having the subjects transfer to new tasks, not performed previously, in which they had to utilize their mental models. In one transfer task, the subjects were asked to explain the input which would produce a given output. This tested how well the subjects could run their mental model. In another transfer task, the subjects were asked to expand the interface by allowing for an OR relationship, a relationship not trained previously. In a third assessment, subjects were asked to expand the database by adding another section to the information.

Results showed that the mental model

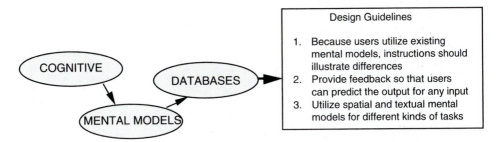

Figure 24-6. A summary and illustration of the design principles when using the mental models cognitive subapproach.

depended somewhat on the task, and that some of the subjects had the flexibility to utilize two mental models to perform the task. Subjects preferred the direct manipulation mental model when running the model for predicting the input which would produce the given output. They also preferred to use the direct manipulation mental model when adding new information to the database. Subjects split, however, in their preference when expanding the interface for the OR relationship. This was a characteristic which could be incorporated easily into a command-based interface, but with more difficulty into a direct manipulation interface. The subjects that could incorporate the direct manipulation model and then the command-based model were more accurate than those utilizing only one mental model. This research showed that providing subjects with multiple mental models through the design of the interface could be advantageous.

The other application of mental models for databases has been in the relationship between interface design and the development of mental models. The discussion in Chapter 7 indicated that users develop mental models of the application through the displayed information and the documentation. Several different display

methods have been used, emphasizing different kinds of mental models, and performance has been assessed. This research can be discussed both under the topic of mental models and the other cognitive subapproaches. In the remainder of this section, the different kinds of mental models will be discussed only briefly, with more extensive discussion under the appropriate subapproach. The principles derived from the mental model subapproach are summarized and displayed in Figure 24-6.

The displayed information has utilized metaphors and graphics, with the corresponding effects on the developed mental models assessed. Katzeff (1988) investigated the performance effects when subjects were given three different models: a table metaphor, a set model using Venn diagrams, and a set model with a general logic explanation. These three were compared to a no-model condition. The table model could be classified as a metaphor, and the set model could be classified as a spatial model. Eberts and Bittianda (1993) provided subjects with two models: a command-based text model and a direct manipulation model. The direct manipulation model utilized the desktop metaphor along with graphics and spatial manipulations. Davis (1990) con-

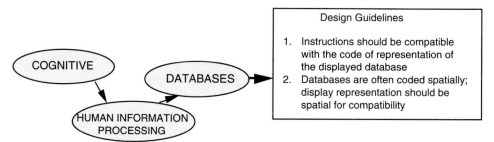

Figure 24-7. A summary and illustration of the design principles when using the human information processing cognitive subapproach.

centrated on the documentation instead of the computer display and showed that for relational databases subjects performed better if the documentation displayed the relations in table or graphical (spatial) form instead of textual form. Conceivably, the spatial form of the documentation was more compatible with the subjects' mental models of the database. Each of these will be discussed in more detail in the next sections.

Human Information Processing

An important aspect of human information processing which has been applied to databases is the concept of S-C-R compatibility which has been discussed in Chapter 8 and in Chapter 22 for feedback. The Boehm-Davis, Holt, Koll, Yastrop, and Peters (1989) work, discussed in Chapter 22, investigated the relationship between instructions and the representation code of the task for databases. They showed that performance will be better if the instructions are compatible with the task. Textual instructions should be provided with textual tasks, and spatial instructions should be provided with spatial tasks. Databases can be either in a textual form or a spatial form, and this form should be compatible with the other information presented to the user.

The Davis (1990) experiment also demonstrates compatibility, but in this case, compatibility between the stimulus and the central processing (the S and C of S-C-R compatibility). We would assume that the central processing of the database task is spatial in nature, so that the other stimuli, such as the instructions, should be in the same form as the central processing.

The principles derived from the human information processing subapproach are summarized and displayed in Figure 24-7.

Neural Networks

Neural networks appear to be a likely candidate for database applications. A few experiments on applications have been conducted, with good results. Neural networks are useful because they work in parallel and can be extremely fast. In addition, neural networks are used primarily for pattern recognition tasks, such as in vision or audition. In some ways, database retrievals are pattern recognition tasks because the database could be given a pattern of key words to match and the data retrievals could be based on partial matches instead of exact matches. In many cases, the user may not know the exact match and thus would be interested in matching patterns to find likely matches.

Stanfill and Kahle (1986) demonstrate the potential speed of computers using neural net techniques to distribute the processing and work in parallel. By using a connectionist machine, one that uses computing which is distributed and parallel, large databases (a database containing 31,994 documents was tested) can be searched very quickly. A sequential machine would not be able to perform some of these searches.

Stanfill and Kahle (1986) use a free-text search method. In a free-text search, the database program searches the documents for arbitrary combinations of words in the documents. This can be contrasted to a keyword search in which human indexers are required to read all the documents and assign keywords to them based upon a limited vocabulary. Advantages to the free-text approach are that the user does not have to rely on an index to access the article correctly, the interface can be easy to use because the lists of words are unlimited, and the user may be able to find documents which are classified in ways that could not be anticipated by an indexer. Problems with the free-text search are that it could fail to retrieve all the documents or that it could deliver too many irrelevant documents. The advantage to the keyword approach is that the search is more focused. The problem with this approach is that different indexers may come up with different keywords for the same article so that the searches become unreliable.

A neural net approach solves some of the problems associated with the free-text searches. In this approach, the inputs are all possible words in the documents. The outputs are the documents. The user interface involves browsing on the part of the user. The first step is to enter a list of words as the input. The computer then searches the database to find a pattern match for those words and delivers the relevant documents. The user then browses through these documents marking each one as "good" or "bad." Based upon this information, the computer initiates a new search and delivers a refined list of documents. The process can continue until the relevant documents are identified.

Mori, Chung, Kinoe, and Hayashi (1990) also investigated a neural net technique for document retrievals from a database using a keywords approach. They argue that users often do not know the keywords so that the user and the computer must cooperate to determine the correct keywords to find the relevant documents. A neural net approach can assist in this cooperation. Also, they argue that the search should be based not upon individual keywords but upon the relationships between keywords. As an example, consider the word "mouse." A mouse can be an animal, or, in the computer context, it can be an input device. If the words "mouse" and "input device" were entered as keywords, then the search would include documents on mice in relation to computers. A good database search should consider the relationships between the keywords.

In the Mori et al. (1990) document retrieval interface, the first step for the user is to input a set of keywords. In the second step, the program inputs these words to the neural net and retrieves the documents that are mapped from the keywords. In the third step, the user evaluates the retrieved documents and assigns each document a grade from 1 (no connection to query) to 6 (close connection to query). In the fourth step, the system tries to adapt to the user by using the ratings from the

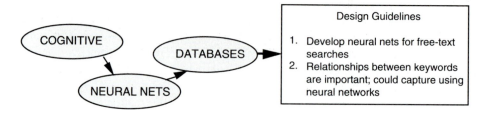

Figure 24-8. A summary and illustration of the design principles when using the neural network cognitive subapproach.

previous step to reduce the difference between the inferred result and the user's intended query. In the fifth step, the system revises the set of keywords from the initial step. The process can repeat itself until the user is satisfied with the results.

Five subjects performed a document retrieval task using the neural net database. The system was successful in adapting to the user and cooperatively retrieving the appropriate documents. The database retrieved an average of 72.3% of the relevant documents as compared to only 14% on the first try. This result is difficult to interpret, however, because the researchers did not include a control group of subjects using the document retrieval without the neural net. One could expect that the subjects would be able to narrow the search without assistance of the neural net, and one cannot determine if the search narrowing would be faster with or without the neural net. The method, though, seems promising and more evaluation is needed.

Figure 24-8 summarizes and illustrates the design principles when using the mental models cognitive subapproach.

Metaphors and Analogies

Metaphors and analogies allow the applications to be learned faster because the user can apply the old familiar information to the new unfamiliar situation. Just as in operating system design, an important metaphor for database applications has been the desktop metaphor.

In many ways, the desktop operating system seen on many computers today is a database application. One of the main purposes of the desktop metaphor is to organize the file structure so that the user can retrieve and manipulate those files. The user has to determine where to store the files—files can be stored in folders and folders can be stored in other folders—and then remember how to retrieve the appropriate file from the database of files and folders. If you think about your own desktop, retrieving papers or folders in the physical world can result from many different cues. You may organize the desktop by location; certain kinds of papers go at one location on the desk. A naturally occurring organization has to do with temporal cues. The papers worked on most recently will be at the top of the pile. So, if you are trying to find a paper and can remember when you worked on it, then it can be retrieved based upon the "strata" it appears on. The database retrieval of the files in an operating system utilize the desktop metaphor.

In the Eberts and Bittianda (1993) experiment, a metaphor of a filing cabinet was used for organizing the database

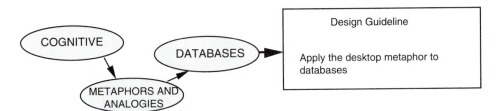

Figure 24-9. A summary and illustration of the design principles when using the metaphor and analogies cognitive subapproach.

concepts and for organizing the graphical display. The metaphorical relationships between the filing cabinet and the database were as follows: the cabinet was analogous to the complete data structure of the database; the drawers in the cabinet were analogous to the broader divisions of data structures; the folders were analogous to the actual data sets; and the sheets of paper in each file were analogous to the records in the data sets. The results showed that, when given a choice, subjects preferred to use a mental model based upon the desktop metaphor when performing certain kinds of tasks.

An experiment by Raymond, Canas, Tompa, and Safayeni (1989) designed a desktop metaphor for a database interface. In that interface, users could directly manipulate database items on the screen and stack them in piles. These spatial piles, representing categories, could be named by the user. Generally, the interface was successful, yet it was not as easy to use as a noncomputerized version of the task.

Metaphors can be used in other creative ways. Shneiderman (1987) reports on an interface design using a Rolodex metaphor. On many desk tops, the Rolodex is a standard feature. It is composed of cards, typically containing alphabetized addresses, that have a slot so that they can be inserted on or removed from a plastic frame. The inserted cards form a partial circle or a whole circle. To find the address, the person can flip through the cards until the correct one is found. Shneiderman (1986) provides an example of a computer interface which incorporates this idea. The interface looks like a Rolodex which contains cards. By clicking buttons on the display, the user can move forward or backward through the cards until the correct one is found. All information is shown on the cards. This is a very simple kind of database retrieval problem without many of the search features common to other kinds of database interfaces. This would not be a very practical solution for large databases; but the simplicity of the interface and the use of an underlying metaphor makes it an easy-to-use interface for small databases such as addresses for personal use.

Figure 24-9 summarizes and illustrates the design principles when using the mental models cognitive subapproach.

Spatial Reasoning and Graphics

Many of the examples of database interfaces used in the previous section on metaphors could also be discussed in this section on spatial reasoning and graphics. The direct manipulation displays using

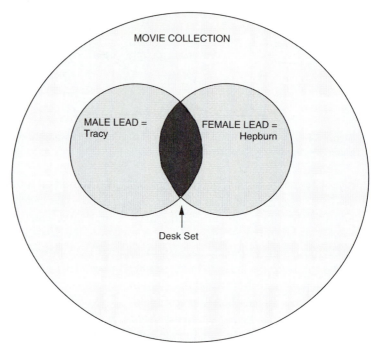

Figure 24-10. Representation of the AND relationship in Venn diagrams. The shaded areas in the figures represent that part of the database which would be included in the AND relationship. The relational database from Figure 24-3 is used in this illustration.

the desktop metaphor rely on the graphics to make the screen look like a desk top so that the metaphor can be instantiated by the user. The Rolodex metaphor was also an example of the combination of graphics and metaphors. In most cases, it is difficult to determine if enhanced performance is due to the use of the metaphor or to the use of graphics because they usually occur together.

One graphical interface for databases does not require a metaphor. A Venn diagram is an abstract, yet spatial, representation of relationships used in mathematics. For a Venn diagram, a set is an abstract entity which could be used, in this case, to represent the data in a database. The set is usually represented as a circle. By having several sets, represented as circles, the logical relationships of AND, OR, and NOT can be represented through the shading in the circles. The logical relationship of AND can be represented by overlapping two circles and then shading all the areas inside the two circles. Figure 24-10 shows a possible Venn diagram representation of the query of Figure 24-3 which utilized the movie collection database. The logical relationship of OR can be represented by overlapping two circles and then just shading the overlap; Figure 24-11 shows a possible Venn diagram for the query of Figure 24-4. The more complicated relationship of Figure 24-5, utilizing a NOT and an AND, can also be represented by Venn diagrams (see Figure 24-12). In this way, the logical relationships can be better understood through the spatial use of Venn diagrams.

An important component in data-

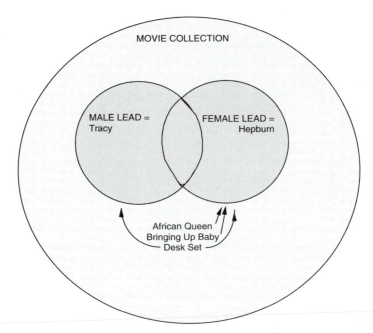

Figure 24-11. Representation of the OR relationship when using Venn diagrams. The relational database from Figure 24-4 is used in this illustration.

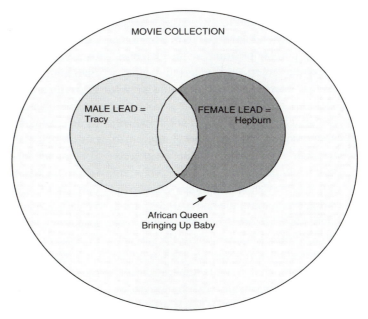

Figure 24-12. Representation of the logical NOT when using Venn diagrams. The relational database from Figure 24-5 is used in this illustration.

bases is the logical relationships. Because Venn diagrams can be used to illustrate logical relationships, they have been investigated in database interface designs. Michard (1982) compared a traditional text-based query language interface to one using graphics in the form of Venn diagrams. For the Venn diagram interface, subjects indicated the logical relationships by pointing to parts of the Venn diagram. Results showed that the graphical interface allowed subjects to make fewer logical relationship errors.

Some evidence seems to indicate that database retrieval tasks always contain a spatial component in that users must try to remember where they are when searching a database. Vicente and Williges (1988) found that subjects with low spatial ability were getting lost in a hierarchical database file system. This could mean that these users need some kind of spatial or graphical assistance with the task so that they do not become lost. They designed an interface which provided a partial map and analogue indicator of the users' current position in the database. When this interface was tested against a textual interface, some performance advantages for the graphics were obtained. The graphical interface did not, however, assist the low spatial subjects more than the high spatial subjects in that no interaction occurred between spatial ability and interface design. Parts of the evidence indicate that some of the low spatial subjects were assisted with the graphical interface because the variability among the subjects in the graphical interface was reduced when compared to the textual interface.

An experiment by Greene, Devlin, Cannata, and Gomez (1990) found only a weak relationship between performance on a relational database query task and spatial performance. The strongest indicant of performance was not spatial reasoning but logical reasoning. This could be expected due to the strong logical component of database queries. Users must be able to understand how to use logical AND, OR, and negation operators either singly or in combination. Greene et al. found that using a typical relational database language, called SQL, the better the subjects' performance on a standardized cognitive test measuring reasoning ability the better the performance on the database query task. When the interface was redesigned, however, to place less of an emphasis on the logical components of the task, then little or no relationship between reasoning ability and database performance was seen. When designing database interfaces for the general population, the less dependence on cognitive abilities, the better the design.

The visualization techniques discussed in Chapter 11 are also forms of databases using a spatial structure. The cone tree and cam tree visualizations are used because they can present much information on one computer screen. A problem with a database search is visualizing where you are in the search and being able to determine any other parts of the database which may be related to your search. By having all this information on the screen, and seeing the context on the screen, then these problems are solved. These visualization structures could become very important in database retrievals as they become researched and applied.

Recall from the discussion of mental models in Chapter 7 that the mental model is formed both from the information displayed on the screen and on the documentation. The previous examples of spatial reasoning applications have focused on screen information displays. Other experimentation has researched the use of graphics in documentation. Katzeff (1988) investigated the use of Venn diagrams in documentation. Similar to the use of Venn diagrams by Michard (1982) in an interface design, in the Katzeff experiment the Venn diagrams were confined to explanations in the documentation. Experiments showed that subjects could perform queries better after receiving the documentation with the Venn diagrams when compared to documentation with no graphics or documentation explained in terms of textual tables. The understanding of logical relationships was assisted through the use of the Venn diagrams.

Davis (1990) investigated other types of graphical presentations of documentation for relational databases. In typical documentation, since relational databases are often conceptualized in table form, the documentation usually shows the fields as rows and a description of the data type for each field. The problem with this textual table form of documentation is that it does not show the relationships within the table or among the different tables. Davis examined two main graphical methods of providing these relationships in the documentation. One type, called a data structure diagram, showed the fields with the data types listed below the field name (see Figure 24-13). Arrows then show the relationships between the fields and the data items. Another method, called the entity-relationship, contains much the same kind of information except that the spatial structure resembles more of a flowchart (see Figure 24-14). When separate groups of subjects were provided with the typical textual documentation or the different kinds of spatial documentation, performance was better with the spatial documen-

tation. No statistical differences between the different spatial documentations were observed.

As indicated in a previous section, the Boehm-Davis (1990) experiment found that spatial or graphics documentation is not always the best. The best form of documentation depends on how the subjects conceptualize the task. If the task is conceptualized textually, then textual documentation is best. If conceptualized spatially, then spatial documentation is the best. Davis (1990) did not determine how subjects were conceptualizing the task. One cannot always assume that graphical or spatial presentation of documentation would be best in all situations.

Figure 24-15 summarizes and illustrates the design principles when using the spatial cognitive subapproach.

Conclusions from the Cognitive Approach

Database queries are different from many of the other interface interactions because of the reliance and emphasis on the cognitive ability of logical reasoning. The Greene et al. (1990) experiment indicated that logical reasoning ability was the main cognitive determinant of performance when making queries on a database. They demonstrated how to design a database interface to reduce the reliance on logical reasoning ability. In their interface, queries were generated by concrete examples, with no reliance on logical relationships, such that the system could determine the query from the examples. Consider an example from the database of movies, directors, male leads, and female leads shown in Figure 24-1. In the typical SQL query language, a query would look like this:

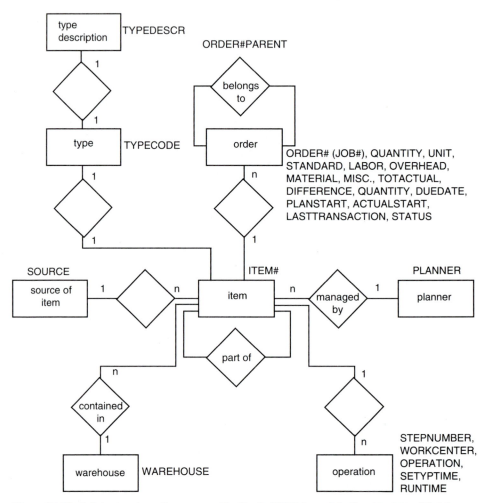

Figure 24-13. A data structure diagram used by Davis (1990) to explain the structure of databases. This shows the database structure in a spatial relationship (reprinted with permission of publisher).

```
SELECT   Name
  FROM   Movie
 WHERE   (Female lead = "Hepburn"
    OR   Male lead = "Tracy")
   AND   Director = "Huston"
```

In this query, the syntax, such as the parentheses and the punctuation, has to be done correctly for the query to be valid. It also shows the reliance on the logical operators OR and AND. In English form, this query means: Find all movies with either Hepburn as the female lead or Tracy as the male lead, and which were also directed by Huston.

Greene et al. (1990) demonstrate how to perform the same kind of query with less of a reliance on logical reasoning ability. In this interface, the query is entered without the logical operators, as follows:

Movie, Female lead = Hepburn, Male lead = Tracy, Director = Huston

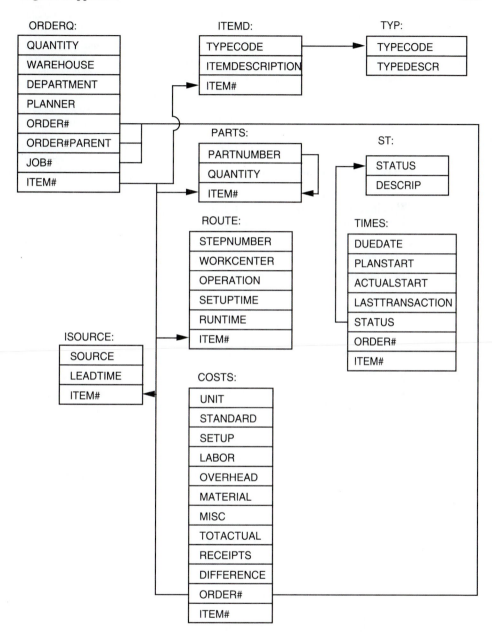

Figure 24-14. An entity-relationship structure used by Davis (1990) to explain the structure of databases. This shows the database structure in a spatial relationship (reprinted with permission of publisher).

Of course, this query would be inadequate to generate the correct response because the system does not know the logical rela-tionships between Hepburn, Tracy, and Huston. To obtain these, the system gen-erates an example truth table (see Table

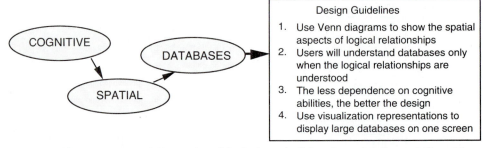

Figure 24-15. A summary and illustration of the design principles when using the spatial cognitive subapproach.

24-1) in response to the query listed in the preceding text. The user must go through the rows of the table and indicate which one(s) should be included in the response. The logical operators do not have to be used; the system infers them based upon the responses.

Assume the user wanted the database records in response to the query specified earlier: Find all movies with either Hepburn as the female lead or Tracy as the male lead, and which was also directed by Huston. The reader should look through Table 24-1 and determine which record would be designated as an example of the query and which ones should not. Each record is a possibility dependent on the logical relationships between the items in the fields.

To satisfy the query, the user would choose the first record. None of the other records has the correct logical relationships needed for the query. After this

example is chosen, the computer would go through the rest of the database to determine if any other records are available which satisfy the relations. As a point of fact, the *African Queen* was the only movie made which satisfies this query. More examples of this technique are provided as questions at the end of this chapter.

Another important cognitive feature in other interface designs, especially direct manipulation displays, has been the reliance on recognition instead of recall. For most database queries, the user must recall the query. The interface designed by Greene et al. (1990) indicates how a query can be designated through recognition instead of recall. The subject does not have to really know the syntax. By providing the possible examples in the table, the user has to merely go down the list and recognize which ones are examples of the query and which ones are not examples.

Other cognitive subapproaches were

TABLE 24-1

An example of a table generated to determine the logical relationships

Movie	Year	Director	Male Lead	Female Lead
African Queen	1951	Huston	Bogart	Hepburn
Bringing Up Baby	1938	Hawks	Grant	Hepburn
Desk Set	1957	Lang	Tracy	Hepburn

also shown indicating the importance of these. Metaphors, especially the desktop metaphor, were shown to be helpful in improving the ease of use of the database interface. This metaphor, and others like the Rolodex interface, utilize graphics. Graphics were also used as a map for the users so that they get some indication of the structure of the data. Taken together, the cognitive approach has been very successful in increasing the usability of database interfaces.

PREDICTIVE MODELING APPROACH

The predictive modeling approach, as explained in Section IV, predicts performance of a user such as execution time, learnability, memory workload, and transferability. If an interface designer has a choice of feedback methods to use, the predictive modeling approach could be used potentially to predict which would be best in terms of performance. No examples were found for how the predictive models were applied to database interface design. Some of the possible applications could be quite simple. As an example, one could use the Keystrokes-Level model of GOMS (see Chapter 14) to predict whether a command-based database interface would be faster than a direct manipulation interface. Other simple applications of the models are also possible.

This database application area could be somewhat problematic for the application of these models, however. As indicated in the previous section, one of the determinants of ease of use of the database system is the understanding of the logical relationships in the database. The predictive models cannot predict this kind of confusability or compare two database

programs on the basis of learnability of the logical relationships. More specific cognitive models would have to be developed to address these issues. The predictive models are too general to achieve meaningful results.

ANTHROPOMORPHIC APPROACH

The 1950s Katharine Hepburn / Spencer Tracy movie called *Desk Set* is an example of where a computerized database was compared to a human database, thus illustrating the anthropomorphic approach for database designs. Katharine Hepburn played the head of a research department in a company. When an employee called the research department with a question, Hepburn and her workers would interpret the question, look up the answer in the reference books, and report back to the questioner. This was a very efficient and easy-to-use method because the questioner was communicating directly with a human so that the questions could be vague and they could still be answered. Spencer Tracy was an efficiency expert who was trying to replace the research department with a computer. Once replaced, however, the employees found that the computer was much more difficult to use than Hepburn's group. As an ultimate test, the human research department was compared to the computer in speed and accuracy of the answers to questions. Needless to say, the humans won, the computer blew up in coughs of smoke, and Spencer Tracy and Katharine Hepburn fell in love.

Some gains in naturalness of the interfaces for database applications have been made, but the gains have probably not been great enough to cause you to fall in love with your database program. The gains should be great enough to at least not cause you to end up hating your program. By looking at how humans interact with other humans on database-type queries, however, insights can be achieved for improving the ease of use of database interfaces.

Human-Human Communication

In some ways, interacting with a database is not analogous to communicating with another person but it is analogous to communicating with yourself. The brain can be seen as a vast database, and the person employs various kinds of strategies in order to retrieve information from that database. Some psychologists believe that once information is stored in long-term memory that it is never lost. Our failures to retrieve information from long-term memory are due to a breakdown in the retrieval mechanism instead of a loss of memory. By investigating some of these retrieval strategies, we can come to understand how databases could be designed to make the retrieval of information from a database more natural.

Williams and Hollan (1981) conducted an experiment on how people retrieve information from long-term memory. They took college student volunteers and asked them to try to retrieve from long-term memory everybody in their high school class. When the subjects were first asked this question, they thought they could retrieve only a few of the names. Indeed, in the first couple minutes most people could only recall a few names most probably associated in memory as close friends. The interesting part of the experiment was that Williams and Hollan had asked to obtain the yearbooks of the subjects, and they gave the students the whole semester to complete the task. They were instructed

to use as many strategies as possible and to write down the names as they remembered them. Think about how you would do this task if asked to do so.

The subjects kept track of their strategies for retrieving the names of their high school classmates. Some of the strategies are probably typical of how database manipulations are performed on computers. In particular, any of the strategies which are associated with categorizations of the classmates are typical of computerized databases. People may have an organization in long-term memory of associating names with categories such as friends, club members, members of sports teams, or members of social cliques. To retrieve this information, the person only had to retrieve the category and then retrieve the names associated with the category.

Some of the other strategies were interesting and not easily associable with computerized database retrievals. In particular, one strategy was to picture yourself walking down a street in your home town. As you pass the houses in this simulated walk, you try to remember the names of the people who live in the houses. Another strategy was very similar. Picture yourself sitting in a high school classroom and then "look" around the classroom trying to remember the faces. Then associate the faces with names. To perform this task, the subjects found that they had to use many different strategies. In so doing, the subjects found that the information about high school classmates' names was not lost from memory, but almost all the names could be retrieved given the time and creative use of retrieval strategies.

One of the problems with computerized databases is that they restrict our retrieval strategies to just a few simple ones. We do not have the richness of strategies that we can incorporate naturally for retrieving information from our own memories. In emphasizing the anthropomorphic approach, we can see some possibilities for new interface designs. One interesting possibility is for an interface to be designed so that we can walk around the data in three dimensions much as the subjects walked down the street to retrieve classmates' names. Although not the main purpose of the virtual realities discussed in Chapter 11, a possibility is to use virtual reality techniques in database retrievals. Instead of using different keywords in the search, the user would walk around the three-dimensional space to find the appropriate data. The user could take certain paths to try to find the appropriate datum. This would work for some types of concrete databases, but it would not work for other kinds of more abstract information.

The experiment by Raymond et al. (1989) showed how the interface design can limit the use of natural database organization schemes. In that experiment, the interface was designed to be as easy to use as possible, incorporating the desktop metaphor and direct manipulation techniques. Subjects organized the data into categories by moving the items into stacks. Retrieval of the items from the categories revealed how the computerization of the task affected retrieval strategies. For the noncomputerized retrieval, subjects could go directly to the item to retrieve it. For the computerized search, the subjects had to go through the intermediate category items in order to find the item. This resulted in increased time and a reduction of item hits for the computerized version of the task. A conclusion from this study is that natural retrieval strategies should be investi-

gated before a computerized version is completed so that the computerized version will allow the natural strategies to occur.

Another finding from the Raymond et al. (1989) study was the form of the natural categorization of the items in the database. They found that no subjects had categories which were more than three levels deep. Users may have difficulty with databases designed to be several levels deep.

Let's return now to the Williams and Hollan (1981) study on how people retrieve information from long-term memory. The previous paragraphs have discussed how the interface designs for databases can be limiting so that various cognitive retrieval strategies cannot be utilized. Williams and others (Williams, 1984) designed a database interface called RABBIT to incorporate one of the cognitive strategies for retrieval into a database. The particular strategy has been called retrieval by reformulation. This strategy has the following characteristics: retrieval by reconstructed descriptions; interactive construction of queries; critique of example instances; and dynamic perspectives.

In retrieval by reconstructed descriptions, the user formulates a query by describing the object being sought. In the next step, the interactive construction of queries, the computer and the user cooperate to try to narrow interactively the search in the database. The database provides some examples of retrievals, and the user can then critique these examples through the use of commands which can expand or narrow the search. Finally, the perspectives allow the user to look at the data in different ways depending on the information needs of the user. As can be seen, this retrieval search strategy corresponds in some ways to the long-term memory search strategies used by people, but more can be generated and incorporated in database interfaces of the future.

Natural Language

When we ask a person questions about something this other person knows, we usually find it fairly easy to obtain an answer. This is merely the database retrieval problem in which the interface between the person asking the question and the person answering the question is a natural language voice recognition system. Developing a database retrieval system incorporating the same features could possibly result in a natural, easy-to-use interface.

Young, Hauptmann, Ward, Smith, and Werner (1989) reported a system called MINDS, for Multi-modal, Interactive, Dialog System, which could understand speech in a continuous natural dialogue. MINDS uses dialogue knowledge and user goals and plans to understand the continuous speech. The particular application investigated by Young et al. was interaction with a database containing information on U.S. Navy ships. An example of the dialogue is contained in Figure 24-16. Recognition of the words was very accurate, but the authors did not compare this method with other possible database assessment methods.

One of the things that is significant about MINDS is that it uses speech recognition along with natural language processing. Other database retrieval systems utilize natural language processing inputted textually through a keyboard instead of by voice recognition. Brajnik, Guida, and Tasso (1990) developed a natural

language interface for retrieving documents from a database. This interface adapted the natural language interaction dependent upon a user model. This interface will be discussed more fully in the next section.

In an experiment in which natural language was used as though typing on a keyboard, a specialized query language was found to be performed better by subjects than the natural language input (Small and Weldon, 1983). A problem with natural language is that it does not constrain the user to appropriate responses; the language itself offers all kinds of possible interactions which may not be supported by the software. The user must learn the limitations of the language. With a specialized command language, like that studied by Small and Weldon, the constraints offered by the syntax and the commands can actually help the users to understand the limits of the software.

Another problem with a natural language interface is the difference between the use of "and" in natural language and its formal use in logical relationships. In natural language, "and" can mean either the union or intersection of two sets, while in formal logic "and" should only mean the intersection of the sets and "or" should mean the union of the sets. As an example, if you were searching a library database and indicated that you would like to see book topics on computers and human factors, this command may be difficult to understand or ambiguous to the user (Ogden and Kaplan, 1986). In the context of natural language this could mean that you would like all books on computers in addition to all books on human factors. Or, it could mean that you would like all books on the use of human factors for computer systems. In formal logic, the

List the casualty reports for ships in the
Persian Gulf?

> *Gridley is in the Persian Gulf. Harpoon missile is disabled.*

What's its mission?

> *Gridley's mission is escort.*

Show me Gridley's required capabilities.

> *Harpoon missile, Phalanx gun, SPS-10 radar are required*
> *capabilities.*

Let me see all Leahy-class cruisers in the
Persian Gulf.

> *England is a Leahy-class ship. It is a cruiser. It is in*
> *the Persian Gulf.*
> *Gridley is a Leahy-class ship. It is a cruiser. It is in the*
> *Persian Gulf.*

What is the mission for England?

> *England's mission is transport.*

Priority?

> *England's mission importance is 1.*

What are her capabilities?

> *It has Harpoon missile.*
> *It has Phalanx gun.*
> *It has SPS-10 radar.*
> *It has torpedo tubes.*
> *It has SM-2 missile.*

Does England have any CASREPS?

> *Nothing found in the database.*

**Figure 24-16. An example of the natural language database called MINDS (Young et al., 1989).
Copyright 1989, Association for Computing Machinery, Inc. Reprinted by permission.**

statement would mean to search for all books on human factors in computer systems.

This ambiguity of "and" is a difficult problem for users to overcome if they encounter a natural language interface for databases. The users are likely to assume that the computer has similar intelligence characteristics to humans. If a human heard the ambiguous request, the questioner and the answerer would probably discuss the issue between themselves to determine which meaning was used in the query. Ogden and Kaplan (1986) suggest a similar scenario for database interfaces. They suggest that the computer should prompt the user for the correct classification.

Adaptable Interfaces

Possibilities for adaptable interfaces have been discussed in the context of some of the other subapproaches. Under the neural net subapproach, the Mori et al. (1990) retrieval system for databases, using the neural net, could adapt to the particular keywords used by the user. Vicente and Williges (1988) showed that the database retrieval problem requires spatial knowledge and that low spatial users have difficulty with database retrievals. Adapting the interface based upon spatial ability was a possibility in that low spatial subjects would get special assistance with the task through the use of graphics and high spatial subjects would get the normal interface. Results showed, however, that the graphics assistance helped both high and low spatial subjects, so adaptively providing the low spatial users and not the high spatial users with the graphics would actually deprive high spatial users of benefits to performance.

Brajnik et al. (1990) investigated the possibility of incorporating user models in a database interface so that the interface could adapt on characteristics of the user model. The user model was constructed upon three sources of information: a general profile of the user, an information retrieval profile, and user knowledge. Figure 24-17 shows an example user model from Brajnik et al. This technique incorporates information into a frame. A frame is a structure which has slots to be filled in as the system determines the relevant information. In the beginning of the session, the computer queries the user about the profile information by, as an example, asking the user about what kind of degree the user has and when it was obtained. This information is then entered into the

slots FIELD and DATE in the Educational Background section of the General Profile frame. Other kinds of information, such as that contained in the Information Retrieval Profile, are elicited from the methods the user incorporates to retrieve information from the database in previous sessions.

The user model in the Brajnik et al. (1990) article is used to assist the user in searching for the appropriate documents in the database. This is accomplished by knowing what the user has searched for in the past and interactively determining, through a natural language interface, whether the documents retrieved are sufficient to satisfy the search. By incorporating the user model, the natural language interface can act more intelligent by tailoring the language and the questions to the individual.

Figure 24-18 summarizes and illustrates the design principles when using the anthropomorphic approach.

SUMMARY

The example in the first chapter of this book was on the problems associated with a database retrieval in a library setting. For a database program in particular, it seems very easy to design a poor program which is difficult to use and understand. This chapter has demonstrated how the four approaches, but especially the cognitive and anthropomorphic approaches, could be and have been applied to database programs. Emphasis needs to be placed especially on making the logical relationships easy to understand and natural to use.

As interactive systems evolve, the divisions between the different categories of application programs have become blurred. An operating system tradition-

GENERAL PROFILE
    EDUCATIONAL BACKGROUND
        FIELD: computer science
            DEGREE: Ph.D.
            DATE: 1978
    PROFESSIONAL BACKGROUND
        FIELD: computer science
            POSITION: researcher
            SINCE: 1982
    INFORMATION RETRIEVAL BACKGROUND
        EDUCATION: medium
        TRAINING: medium
        EXPERIENCE:
            TYPE: user
            MODE: assisted
            SINCE: 1987
    PERSONAL TRAITS
        COMMUNICATION
            LEVEL: concise
            QUALITY: precise
        ATTITUDE: cooperative

INFORMATION RETRIEVAL PROFILE
    NORMAL EXPRESSION OF NEEDS
        DOMAIN: computer science
            ACCURACY: high
            COMPLETENESS: average
            ATTITUDE: browsing-oriented
        DOMAIN: others
            SOURCE OF PROBLEM: write paper
            GOALS LEADING TO SEARCH:
                discover something,
                fill gaps in knowledge,
                review literature
    NORMAL SEARCH REQUIREMENTS
        DOMAIN: computer science
            SEARCH OBJECTIVES: high precision
            LIMITS
                DATE: 1975
                LANGUAGE: English
                TREATMENT: theoretical, technical
            OUTPUT FORMAT
                FIELDS: title, authors,
                affiliation, date, abstract
                MODE: off-line
            PREFERRED DATABASES: INSPEC,
                NTIS, COMPENDEX

USER KNOWLEDGE
    SUBJECT DOMAINS
        DOMAIN: computer science
            COVERAGE: high
            DEPTH: high

(continued on next page)

Figure 24-17. An example user model for database retrievals (from Brajnik et al., 1990, © IEEE).

```
DATABASES
      NAME: INSPEC
            TOPIC: known
            TERMINOLOGY: well-known
      NAME: NTIS
            TOPIC: known
            TERMINOLOGY: not known
      NAME: COMPENDEX
            TOPIC: known
            TERMINOLOGY: well-known
INFORMATION RETRIEVAL SYSTEMS
      NAME: ESA-IRS
            FUNCTIONS: known
            LANGUAGE: well-known
      NAME: DIALOG
            FUNCTIONS: known
            LANGUAGE: unknown
INFORMATION RETRIEVAL ACTIVITY
         SEARCH SESSION STRUCTURE: known
         APPROACHES: citation pearl growing, most
                                 specific first
         TACTICS: exhaust, reduce, pinpoint,
```

Figure 24-17 (cont.)

ally has been associated with the commands for performing operations on a system and the directory structure for storing files. Recently, an operating system is becoming more and more associated with a database of file directories and application programs. The user must be able to access the application program from its storage location. The Rooms interface from Xerox (discussed in Chapter 10) could be associated with an operating system, but its main function seems to

be to allow users to access the commands easily by storing them in identifiable rooms. The visualization techniques discussed in Chapter 11 are a method to store large directory files in a display form which makes it easy for the user to move around in and see the context of the files. Perhaps because these techniques deviate so greatly from the database programs from the past, we do not associate them with the database term.

Another application area which can

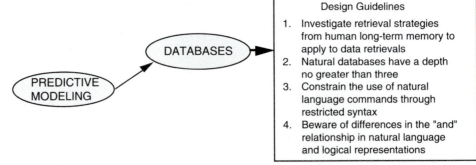

Figure 24-18. A summary and illustration of the design principles when using the anthropomorphic approach.

be conceived as a database is the hypertext programs. Hypertext has not been discussed a great deal in this book. Hypertext is a computerized book which has enhanced properties due to the computerization of its features. Instead of having to read through the text sequentially, hypertext encourages a nonsequential activity of reading. On a page of hypertext, as an example, several words or phrases may be highlighted. If the reader needs to find out more information about the word or phrase, then the user can very simply click on the word or phrase and the text explaining the concept appears on the screen. From a database perspective, the system retrieves the information from a database when the word or phrase is selected. This kind of application blurs the distinction between the display of computerized text and database retrievals.

One of the keys to making database manipulations easier is to fool the user into thinking that it is not a database program at all but merely the natural way of accessing needed information. Too much emphasis on the logical relationships and the manipulations lose the naturalness.

QUESTIONS

1. Do the following for natural retrieval strategies. (1) Try to retrieve information about the topics in the following subquestions. Specify the natural retrieval strategies you use to fetch this information from long-term memory. (2) Specify how these strategies could be incorporated into databases utilizing the issues discussed in this chapter. For this specification, make use of drawings and sketches. (3) Also indicate how the database concepts discussed in this chapter may not be able to incorporate your memory retrieval strategies.

a. All the books you have read in the last five years.

b. All the movies you have seen in the last two years.

c. Everybody in your high school graduating class.

d. All the restaurants you have eaten at in the last two years.

2. A language translation firm needs a database for retrieving previous translation jobs to aid translators with technological and field-specific vocabulary. Currently, the translations reside in the attic with no cataloguing available for the database. The firm needs to be able to access translated articles according to (1) source language, (2) target language, (3) job number, (4) translator's name, (5) firm client, (6) topic of article, (7) date of translation, and (8) length of job in words. A sample database for this problem is shown at the bottom of the page (see Table 24-2). Based upon this database, and for each of the following searches, (1) construct queries similar to those shown in Figure 24-2 through 24-5, (2) construct the Venn diagrams as shown in Figures 24-10 through 24-12, (3) construct an entity-relationship structure as shown in 24-14, and (4) construct a truth table as in Table 24-1.

a. Search for the job numbers on cordless phones that had a source language of English.

b. Search for the job numbers that had Japanese as either the source or the target language.

c. Search for the job numbers that had a target language of English and a source language of French or German.

d. Search for the job numbers that had topics on cordless phones and were translated into Japanese.

3. Consider the query discussed earlier in this chapter:

Movie, Female lead = Hepburn, Male lead = Tracy, Director = Huston

From Table 24-1 and for each of the queries in the following subquestions, indicate the record or records which provide an example of the query.

a. Find all movies with Hepburn as the female lead and Tracy as the male lead, and which were not directed by Huston.

b. Find all movies with Hepburn as the female lead or Tracy as the male lead, and which were not directed by Huston.

c. Find all movies with Hepburn as the female lead or Tracy as the male lead or Huston as the director.

d. Find all movies with Huston as the director or Tracy as the male lead, and which had Hepburn as the female lead.

e. For parts a through d, each pattern of logical relationships between the items in the fields should have a unique specification of records. If not, then the logical relationships cannot be determined. Think of an example of a query, including the logical relationships, which would generate the same examples as one of those in parts a through d. How would the computer set the logical relationships in this case?

TABLE 24-2

Sample database for translation article access for problem 2.

Date	Job#	Source	Target	Length	Firm	Translator	Article Topic
4-12-91	125	French	English	2,000	Madison Metals	Jane	computer desks
3-30-92	128	German	English	3,000	Ennis Electronics	Hans	cordless phones
11-10-92	129	English	Japanese	5,000	Tri-Comm	Ishi	cordless phones
10-9-90	130	Japanese	English	2,000	NorComm	Ishi	computers
6-12-90	135	English	German	2,500	Madison Metals	Hans	phone desks
5-29-89	101	Japanese	English	3,000	Ennis Electronics	Ishi	switches
4-04-90	140	English	French	1,500	Tri-Comm	Jane	switches

CHAPTER 25

GROUPWARE

INTRODUCTION

Many of the previous applications of computers on the job have only considered one person working alone to accomplish a task. In actual organizations, this is usually not the case, of course. A person is usually part of a team that is organized to accomplish an overall task. The concept of a team in U.S. business is becoming increasingly important (Johansen, 1988). Each individual could still perform only part of the task on the computer, but it might be possible to design a computer system and an interface so that the group task could be accomplished more efficiently for a group of people sharing a computer system. Just as much of the prior research discussed in this book has utilized the results and theories from cognitive psychology or science to guide the design, research on groups of people working together on a computer system can utilize the results and theories of social psychology or management science to guide the designs. The software and hardware environment together, when people are working in groups, is often termed groupware. This chapter considers some of these theories and the resultant design principles as they apply to groupware.

The efficiency of an organization in the future could be dependent on how well the organization is networked together and the workers can communicate with each other through the computer network. One of the goals of this book, stated in the first chapter, is to increase the productivity of white collar workers through the effective design of computer interfaces and systems. If the white collar worker spends little time using the computer on individual projects or tasks, then little room is left for increasing efficiency. White collar workers spend much of their time interacting with other people; one survey stated that 30-70% of the time of some workers is spent in meetings (Panko, 1964). Even those heavily involved in computer system design and applications spend much time working with others; DeMarco and Lister (1987) found that 70% of the time working on a computer system development project was spent working with other people. Groupware applications work toward making the interaction with other people more efficient.

Consider the following scenario that could occur in the not-too-distant future; in fact, parts of the following example already exist. A certain company has a product that has been on the market for a number of years and the time has come to make a design change to it. During the years that it has been on the market, one division of the company has been receiving suggestions or complaints from the customers and has compiled electronically a list of how the product possibly could be improved. Using this list as a starting point, several people are invited to a brainstorming session in which ideas will be generated for modifying the product. Instead of brainstorming in a traditional meeting, participants use a group decision support system (GDSS) in which each person generates ideas in front of a computer terminal, and these ideas are sent to all participants for reactions to them. From the meeting, general guidelines for the modifications are summarized and sent electronically to a concurrent engineering design team. This team can again use a tool similar to the GDSS in order to provide further design specifications. This team may include a designer, a manufacturing engineer, and other specialists so that the modified product not only satisfies the design specifications but also is easy to manufacture. After the GDSS meeting, a computer-aided design (CAD) system is used in the product design. This CAD system is different, however, in that several designers have access to the same schematic of the design and any changes will occur for all the systems of the people working on the design. Once the product has been designed using the CAD system, it is sent electronically to a computer-assisted manufacturing (CAM) system and the machines are retooled and reconfigured so that the new product can be manufactured as automatically as possible. The specifications of the design are sent automatically to the salespeople so that they can start interacting with customers about the new product. Any comments from the customers are sent electronically to the central clearinghouse, and the process begins again.

The use of groupware does not have to be limited solely to industries or advanced technologies. It seems that modern life, at least modern American life, is missing some of the personal interactions which used to occur, as an example, at the local cafe. People used to visit the cafes so that they could interact with other people. Some of the technologies which are now available in the home seems to have re-

moved the need to get out of the house and interact with others. We have 70-channel television cables providing a wide array of entertainment choices. The availability of recent films on videotape, and the sophistication of some of the home video systems, means that people no longer have to leave their homes to view good films with good video and audio. Even when visiting a restaurant, the social interactions seem to be limited to the waiter or waitress.

Just as technology has destroyed some of these social interactions, the groupware technology can help to restore them. Some cafes in the San Francisco area now have computer terminals at tables which are hooked into a network of computer terminals at other cafes in the area. A customer in the cafe has merely to sign on to the computer, type in some comment, and the message is sent to other customers at other locations. These other people can respond to the comment, or generate new comments, and the interactions can escalate. Sometimes lively conversations can occur. Recently, a discussion on this network made national news. At one of the cafes, a waitress refused to serve a customer because he was reading a *Playboy* magazine at the table. This action was observed and a comment was placed on the network. Other people at other locations started commenting pro and con about the situation. Perhaps in a situation like this, people would be willing to make more outrageous comments because people are not conversing face to face. Certainly much is lost when the face to face contact is missing; but the conversations can change in other positive ways.

The use of electronic bulletin boards has recently been popularized. Computer users can communicate with others by posting messages on an electronic bulletin board and then having people respond to the messages. The Prodigy computer service has around two million subscribers, and all these subscribers have the potential to correspond with one another. These bulletin boards offer an easy means to obtain feedback. As an example, the Prodigy service has an entertainment bulletin board. Television show executives have found that signing on to Prodigy and reading the bulletin board messages about a particular show provides feedback on the successes or failures of that show. In the last presidential election, presidential candidates responded electronically to questions submitted through the bulletin board services.

TYPES OF GROUPWARE

The preceding examples illustrate many different aspects of groupware, such as electronic mail (e-mail), electronic bulletin boards, GDSS, and computer supported cooperative work (CSCW). Each of these will be discussed in more detail and related back to the examples to place them in context.

Electronic Mail (E-Mail)

E-mail is used presently in many organizations and has been successful for many years now. In e-mail, messages can be sent to another person electronically, usually over the telephone lines. An e-mail message is typically structured so that the sender of the message indicates to whom the message will be sent. The message can also be sent to groups of people, and some e-mail systems allow the user to predefine a group by a single name so that when the message is sent all the members of the predefined group will receive the message. Each message typically has a topic which is specified by the sender.

When received by another person, messages will be tagged by this header information so the words used in the header could provide important context for the receiver. After the header, the sender enters the text of the message. Once received by another person, this user has several options after reading the message. The message could be deleted so that a copy is no longer available. Some systems provide an automatic means to save the message. The receiver of the message could be expected to reply to the sender on some aspect of the message. Some systems have a method to reply easily, such that the address is entered automatically, the header information is retained from the previous message, and the user has only to enter the new text. In the context of the previous example, e-mail could have been used to invite participants to the meetings, to send the meeting agenda materials to the participants before the meeting, or to ask specific questions of individuals within the organization.

One of the important issues with e-mail is how to facilitate transfer of information among the users without overloading the user (Malone, Grant, Lai, Rao and Rosenblitt, 1987). A problem is that some users may be inundated with messages that can be classified as "junk mail." One method for performing this filtering is to use distribution lists. In a distribution list, users with similar topic interests are placed on a list and whenever a question arises on this topic or information sharing is needed, the e-mail message is sent to all members on the distribution list. This kind of filtering is left to the members of the distribution list to ensure that only messages relevant to the topic area will be distributed.

Another solution to the filtering problem is to incorporate database methods to search for particular keywords. Just as a database user can search a database by listing a set of keywords, for e-mail the database could be the incoming e-mail messages. The user would specify certain keywords relevant to the topic area, and then a databaselike program would search the e-mail messages to find the appropriate messages. This method has the advantage that the user has control over the topics that are to be searched, but has the problem of possibly finding too many messages or the message not using the particular words in the keyword list. Other filtering methods besides these two are considered under the cognitive approach section in this chapter.

Electronic Bulletin Boards

Electronic bulletin boards have many characteristics similar to e-mail except that the messages are not sent to individual users or groups of users but can be stored in a central location and accessed by many different people. The messages in an electronic bulletin board are organized into topics and subtopics. If a user has a general question, or a comment to an earlier question, then a message can be posted on the bulletin board. This message usually has some number associated with it and is summarized by a brief header. Users can read the messages and they may respond to them. Messages are saved on the bulletin board for a specified number of days and then are deleted. Bulletin boards

are used heavily in the academic community and the computer industry. If a person has some kind of hardware or software problem, as an example, that person can post a message to determine if anybody else has had a similar problem and can offer a solution to the problem. This method reaches more people than could be reached potentially through the use of e-mail.

Bulletin board messages have much the same structure as e-mail. They usually contain a header, which is a summary of the message in a few words, and the text. When another user responds to a bulletin board message, the header information is usually retained for this new message so that people using the bulletin board can track the messages and the topics.

Group Decision Support Systems (GDSS)

GDSS has received much attention in the last few years as a means for increasing the quality of group decisions while at the same time decreasing the time needed to make a decision. Although research in this area has occurred through many different research groups, one of the best-known facilities is the PLEXSYS project at the University of Arizona (which has been sponsored largely by IBM). Although a GDSS can come in many forms, using the PLEXSYS system as a model, the configuration includes the facility, a human facilitator, software tools, and hardware (Liou and Nunamaker, 1990). The facility is the room in which the group activities take place and it is designed, through control of noise, design of furniture, and lighting, so that it provides a setting within which people can work

Wall Mounted
Projection Screen

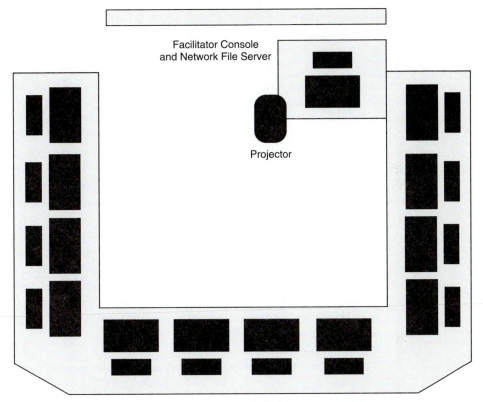

Facilitator Console
and Network File Server

Projector

Figure 25-1. The setting for a GDSS at the University of Arizona. Each participant has access to a computer terminal to enter and respond to comments, and the messages are sent to the other participants.

comfortably on complex problems (see Figure 25-1). The software includes various group support tools which are matched to the focus of the particular group meeting. Tools can include capabilities such as brainstorming, analyzing issues, and voting. PLEXSYS has over 20 such tools. The hardware includes individual workstations which are networked together through a central file server, printers, and presentation media such as a large centralized screen for displaying information to the whole group.

One of the most important aspects of the GDSS, at least for PLEXSYS, is the human facilitator. The facilitator can have three roles: a group leader who guides the group to achieve objectives of particular sessions, a chauffeur who serves as the intermediary between the group and the GDSS software, and an assistant in the use of computer technology (Liou and Nunamaker, 1990). The facilitator is very important to the operation of the group. Usually the facilitator and the proponent of the meeting meet four days before to plan a one-day meeting. The job is very difficult; all facilitators at IBM go through a long training period, because they must manage the technical work at the same time as helping with the content organization. IBM has found the need to keep the person out of meetings for an unspecified time after a meeting to prevent burnout.

A GDSS has several potential advantages when compared to traditional face-to-face meetings. One of the advantages is that all the participants can participate in parallel. In a traditional meeting, one person talks, everybody is supposed to listen, and then somebody else talks. In a GDSS situation, a comment is received from a participant, and this comment can be sent to everybody in the meeting. Because of the large number of comments received in the PLEXSYS system, comments are not sent to everybody but only a random sample of participants. Instead of having only one comment, several people can comment by entering messages all at the same time. Because these messages occur in parallel, one or two people cannot dominate a meeting.

Another advantage of a GDSS is the anonymity of the participants. Although the comments of the participants could be labeled by the contributor, most GDSS do not provide this kind of label. Therefore, ideas can be evaluated for their own merits, instead of the contributor being evaluated. The anonymity may also allow people to contribute more freely without fear that their ideas will not be accepted.

Important considerations for GDSS are to compare the results from a GDSS-supported group to that of a nonsupported GDSS group, and to determine the conditions under which a GDSS-supported group will be the most effective. As occurs when evaluating any new technology, the effectiveness depends on many factors, so global statements about effectiveness are difficult. Much of the research in this area will be reviewed under the empirical approach of this chapter.

In the context of the preceding product design example, a GDSS could be utilized at many points. Brainstorming has been one of the most effective tools of the GDSS, and it is one of its most popular applications. In the preceding example, a brainstorming session was needed to get ideas for the design modifications. In addition, a GDSS meeting could be used for the concurrent engineering when the design specifications are formulated. Although most GDSS applications occur with all participants in the same room, this need not be the case if everybody cannot be present physically. Instead, participants can be at different sites, and the meeting could occur with little disruption.

Computer Supported Cooperative Work (CSCW)

In many ways, CSCW is similar to GDSS. They both are groupware tools that can be used to structure and handle electronic meetings. CSCW has an important component, however, that is not present on most GDSS tools. CSCW typically includes tools so that several people can work on one document or drawing at the same time. As an example, if several people are collaborating to write a manuscript, a CSCW tool can be used so that all participants are working from the same manuscript and can make changes to the manuscript which are seen by the others in the group. One of the most advanced CSCW systems is the Colab project developed at Xerox (Stefik, Foster, Bobrow,

Kahn, Lanning, and Suchman, 1987).

Stefik et al. (1987) describe two tools that are used in Colab: Cognoter and Argnoter. Cognoter is a tool which assists in preparing presentations, such as for talks at conferences, from an electronic meeting. For Cognoter, the meeting is divided into three stages, brainstorming, organizing, and evaluation, and the software tools are used to assist the process of these three stages.

In the brainstorming stage, meeting participants are encouraged to freely contribute ideas that should be included in the presentation. All participants may enter ideas simultaneously, and, because the free exchange of ideas is encouraged, no ideas may be deleted from the screen. The software supports these functions. Ideas are entered on the screen by clicking a mouse button at the location to be entered. A brief summary of the idea is then entered in the space. The body of the idea, its presentation in more detail, can then be shown by clicking the mouse on the idea summary and a window with the idea body will appear on the screen (see Figure 25-2). Because the ideas have not yet been organized, no structure is provided for these ideas. No deletion operations can occur in this stage of the meeting.

In the organizing stage of the meeting, the ideas from the brainstorming stage must be organized into groups and linked. The software tools allow for these to occur easily. Through mouse operations, the meeting participants can indicate which items should be grouped together. Mouse operations also allow links to be drawn between the two ideas. The links are shown on the display as lines between the ideas. The links and groupings are usually preceded by some discussion from the

members about which items should be linked and grouped (see Figure 25-3).

Evaluation is the final stage of the meeting. In this stage, ideas are reorganized, missing information may be filled in, and irrelevant information may be deleted. From the organizations of the previous stage, the participants can see clearly how the presentation is being organized. Using operations similar to those in the previous two stages, new ideas can be filled in to improve the presentation. Also, this is the first stage in which deletion of ideas is allowed, so that the participants can eliminate ideas that no longer fit into the structure. At the end of this stage, the product is an outline for a presentation or manuscript that can then be used by the participants to write a finished product (see Figure 25-4).

Argnoter is another Colab tool described by Stefik et al. (1987). In some ways it is similar to the Cognoter tool except that it is used more for situations in which alternatives are being considered. At Xerox, the particular purpose of the tool is for writing proposals. For Argnoter, the meeting is again divided into three stages: proposing, arguing, and evaluating.

In the proposing stage, proposals are brought up in windows which can appear on the workstation. These proposals can either be public, in which all meeting participants can see them, or private, in which an individual may work on it before turning it public. Word processing tools are available for working on these proposals.

In the arguing stage, the meeting participants can respond to the proposals by presenting arguments that are either pro or con. Through mouse operations,

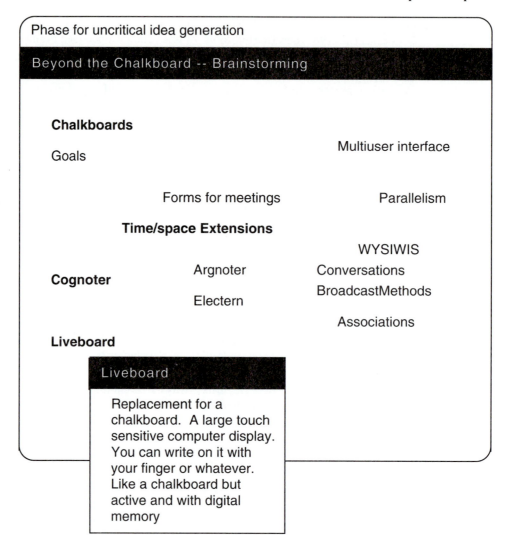

Figure 25-2. In CogNoter, the ideas are placed on the screen and specific ideas can be brought up in a window by clicking the mouse on the idea name. The idea appears in the window (Stefik, et al., 1987). Copyright 1987, Association for Computing Machinery, Inc. Reprinted by permission.

each argument will be associated with a particular proposal. All participants can produce arguments, and these arguments are made public.

In the evaluating stage, the meeting participants review the arguments and then evaluate the proposals. Tools are available to select and rank evaluation criteria.

Some of the other examples of CSCW will be discussed in subsequent sections. CSCW can also be used as support for collaborating on drawing and for communicating ideas through the use of whiteboards. Applications of the four approaches to groupware are discussed in the next sections.

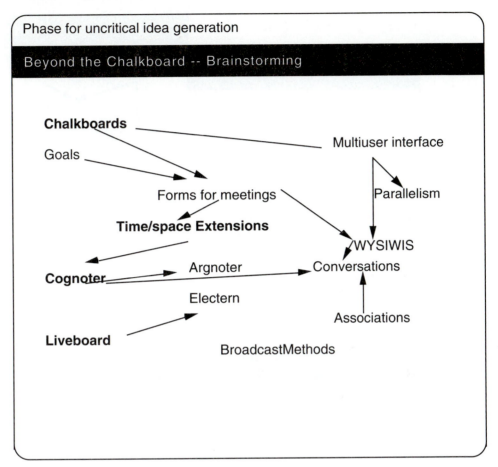

Figure 25-3. From CogNoter, the ideas are linked and organized by the participants. The links are shown by drawing the arrows (Stefik, et al., 1987). Copyright 1987, Association for Computing Machinery, Inc. Reprinted by permission.

EMPIRICAL APPROACH

For a computer technology such as CSCW which is still in its infancy, much of the research follows the empirical approach. Using this approach, one of the first questions is whether or not the new technology is effective when compared to traditional techniques. If this occurs, then other questions address under what conditions the technology is effective and ineffective.

Effectiveness has been evaluated for GDSSs in three ways: quality of the decisions, time to make the decision, and effect on group processes such as domination by one or more group members. Several studies have shown that decisions using a GDSS are better than those made by non-GDSS-supported groups (Gallupe, 1985; Lewis, 1982; and Steeb and Johnston, 1981). Gallupe (1990), however, reports many cases, especially those which were tested in a laboratory setting, in which GDSS-supported groups did not produce better decisions than non-GDSS-

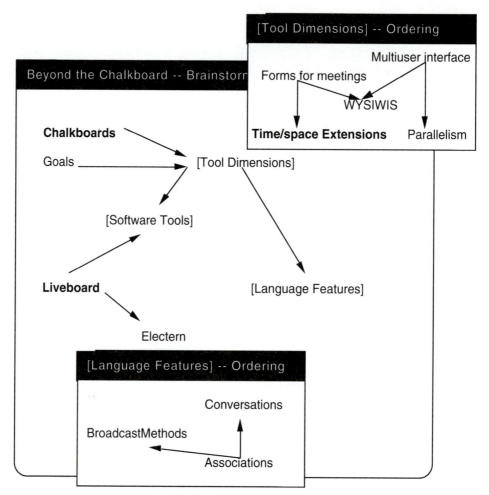

Figure 25-4. Items can be reorganized and clustered into groups. The group can decide to delete some of the ideas. This provides the form for the presentation (Stefik, et al., 1987). Copyright 1987, Association for Computing Machinery, Inc. Reprinted by permission.

supported groups. When contradictory results like these occur, one possibility is that GDSS is only effective under certain kinds of conditions; research has been devoted to determining those conditions.

Dennis, Nunamaker, and Vogel (1989) have summarized some of the conditions under which GDSS-supported groups will be effective and ineffective. They noticed that most GDSS-supported groups generally are effective in field settings but not in laboratory experiments, and they speculated on the characteristic differences between laboratory settings and field settings. One of the important differences is that field settings tend to use larger groups (10-30 participants) and the participants usually have nonoverlapping knowledge. A subsequent experiment by Dennis, Valacich, and Nunamaker (1990) examined the size of a group which could be supported by a GDSS. In a non-GDSS-supported environment, the effective size of a group for making decisions is about five to six people (Dennis et al., 1990). Because the GDSS allows the participants to operate in parallel, the size of the effective groups can be increased. Dennis et al. (1990) studied three sizes of groups: 3-member, 9-member, and 18-member. They found that the larger groups generated more ideas and were more satisfied with their work than were the smaller groups. It should be emphasized, though, that the idea generation per person did not increase with larger groups (it stayed around 11 for the session), but the fact that there were more people in the larger groups meant more total ideas. In a non-GDSS environment, larger groups would cause the participation per group member to decrease.

The complexity of the problem is also important to the effectiveness of the GDSS. Gallupe (1985) found that GDSS-supported groups were effective when solving complex problems and not when solving simple problems. This could possibly be related to the size of the group. Simple problems could be solved by fewer people, which would mean that a GDSS would not be needed in the support of a larger group. More complex problems require the use of more people, some with specialized knowledge, so that GDSS support would be needed.

Nunamaker, Vogel, Heminger, Martz, Grohowski, and McGoff (1989) have performed the most detailed study comparing the worker-hours needed to reach a decision in a GDSS environment when compared to regular meetings. In 29 field studies, they found that the percent savings, in worker-hours, using a GDSS system ranged from 31% to 84% with a mean of 56%. The worker-hours determined from the GDSS could be determined directly from the recordings of the meetings, but the regular meeting worker-hours were only estimated by an expert who considered how long it would take to reach the decision that was reached in the GDSS system. The accuracy of this estimate could be questioned.

In terms of group processes, Dennis et al. (1989) found that participants made only one verbal comment about every 94 minutes and that most of the time was spent interacting with the computer with comments inputted in a range from once every 1.75 minutes to once every 5.5 minutes. GDSS tends to equalize participation so that the most dominant members do not control the decisions of the group (Lewis, 1982; and Nunamaker, et al., 1989). The participant equalization comes with a problem, though, in that the contributions of the best group member can be suppressed in the group. Gallupe (1990) found that the best individuals could make better decisions alone than when in the GDSS environment. To make this kind of comparison, though, the decision must be one that could be made individually. Nunamaker et al. (1989) found that group performance seemed to be independent of participants' typing skills or familiarity with computer technology.

Most of the empirical work on groupware has been performed in the GDSS area. Very little work has been performed on the other systems. Similar kinds of evaluations of groupware technology are needed for the other systems such as CSCW and bulletin boards. Figure 25-5 illustrates the principles that can be derived from applying the empirical approach to groupware.

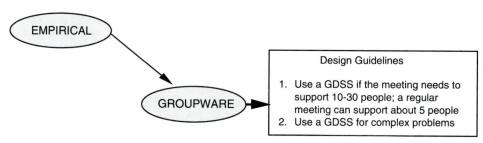

Figure 25-5. Principles which can be derived from the empirical approach.

COGNITIVE APPROACH

When examining the cognitive approach, several subapproaches need to be considered: mental models and cognitive goals, human information processing, neural networks, metaphors and analogies, spatial reasoning and graphics, and attentional resources. Each of these subapproaches will be examined in terms of contributions to groupware.

Mental Models

Mental models can be analyzed in terms of how different mental models may effect the functioning of the group in a collaborative situation. The research on GDSSs indicates that complex problems are supported better in a GDSS environment than are simple problems. This could be related to the need to have people with different viewpoints, or different mental models of the task, participate in the group design.

A study by Bringelson (1991) manipulated the participants of a GDSS according to the mental models of the members. In one condition, all members had similar mental models of the design task. In another condition, participants had different mental models of the situation. The mental models affected the resultant design, and the group with the different mental models reflected those models in the design.

Human Information Processing

One of the most important aspects of human information processing, which was not discussed fully in Chapter 8, was the importance of filtering. As the information is processed by the human, it is filtered so that much of the information is lost; only the relevant information is processed all the way through the system. All of the models discussed in Chapter 8 have some means to filter information. In the Model Human Processor, the perceptual subsystem receives information which is unfiltered to a great extent. When the stimulus information is stored in the sensory stores of the perceptual subsystem, the code of representation of this information is physical, or unfiltered. When passing to the cognitive subsystem, however, much of the information is lost. In fact, the purpose of the sensory stores is to hold the information so that the system can filter out the irrelevant information.

In the Wickens model of human information discussed in Chapter 8, an important component of the model was the attentional resources. The limitation on the amount of attentional resources means that only some of the information will be processed further, and thus the irrelevant information will be filtered out. If you are in a crowded room trying to listen to conversations, then you must make a decision about which conversation to follow in which part of the room. When attention is applied to that conversation, then other conversations at other locations will be filtered out. The ear is still receiving that information, but the information is not processed further due to the filtering that occurs. As an indication that the filtered information is still received, if someone says your name in a conversation you were not attending to, then your name will get through the filter and you will respond to it. If you were not hearing this information when your name was said, then you would never be able to respond to it. But, since you could respond to it, this means that the information was coming in but was being filtered at some later stage.

If we did not filter information, then we would become so overloaded that we could not possibly function in the world. The world would be a mass of uninterpretable sounds that would be meaningless. Only in a perfectly quiet environment would we be able to do anything, and we certainly cannot expect the environment to remain quiet. However, we can still operate in a noisy environment because of our ability to filter information.

Sometimes it seems that the computer environment is a noisy environment. It would be nice if we could just sit back, have information come over the computer screen, and have our automatic filter supply us with only the relevant information. But it does not work this way. Some people receive so much e-mail that reading through it to find the important messages is a daunting task. People who use electronic bulletin boards are bombarded with a plethora of messages so that finding the relevant messages can be difficult.

Fischer and Stevens (1991) reported a small study that they ran on the users of one of the most popular bulletin boards called Usenet. In analyzing Usenet, they found that the six most popular newsgroups contain about 3,000 messages in a typical month. The users that they studied indicated that they would like to view more of the topics but the great number of messages prevented them from doing so. Our human information processing filter will not work if we have to read a message line by line off a computer terminal. If our filter will not work, then we need some other means to filter the information for us.

Malone (1987) was one of the first to recognize the relationship of the cognitive human information processing theories to the information filtering problems for groupware applications. Malone developed a method to filter information on e-mail and has termed his filtering system the Information Lens (e.g., Malone, Grant, Lai, Rao, and Rosenblitt, 1988). The Information Lens works upon the principle of semistructured messages which are of an identifiable type and contain fields in which text can be entered. Different kinds of e-mail messages may have different structures and different fields. As an example, Figure 25-6 shows the structure for a message announcing a meeting. A pop-up window on the left side has three menu choices: fill in information based upon a default, explain the particular field, or provide a list of alternatives for filling in the field. As can be seen from the figure, the information needed for conveying the meeting announcement is provided in the structure. Figure 25-7

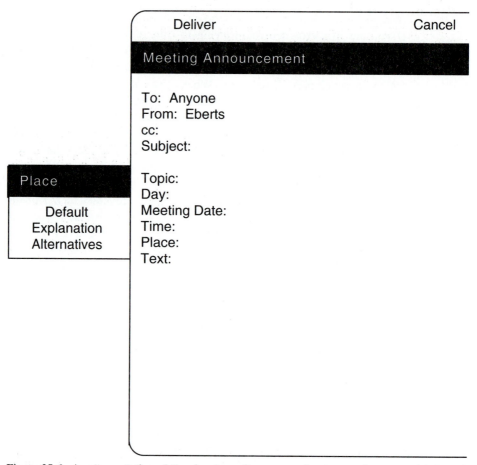

Figure 25-6. A representation of the structure of a message for announcing a meeting for the Information Lens.

shows how the fields could be filled in for a particular meeting announcement. The e-mail user potentially has many different structures to choose from when sending a message. Some capability has been provided for the user to define the structures for e-mail messages.

Different kinds of messages will have different kinds of structures and fields; these patterns are called message templates. When sending a message, the user must first select a template, specific to the kind of message sent, and then fill in the fields on the template. To be successful,

the user must be aware of the different kinds of messages and the templates which are available for these messages. If the wrong template is chosen, the message information will not fit into the structure.

The structure of the message does not filter the information directly; the filtering is performed on the receiver's end. Since the structures of the messages have been defined and confined through the templates, rules can be developed for searching the fields and routing messages depending on the information in the fields. As an example, the "From" field indicates

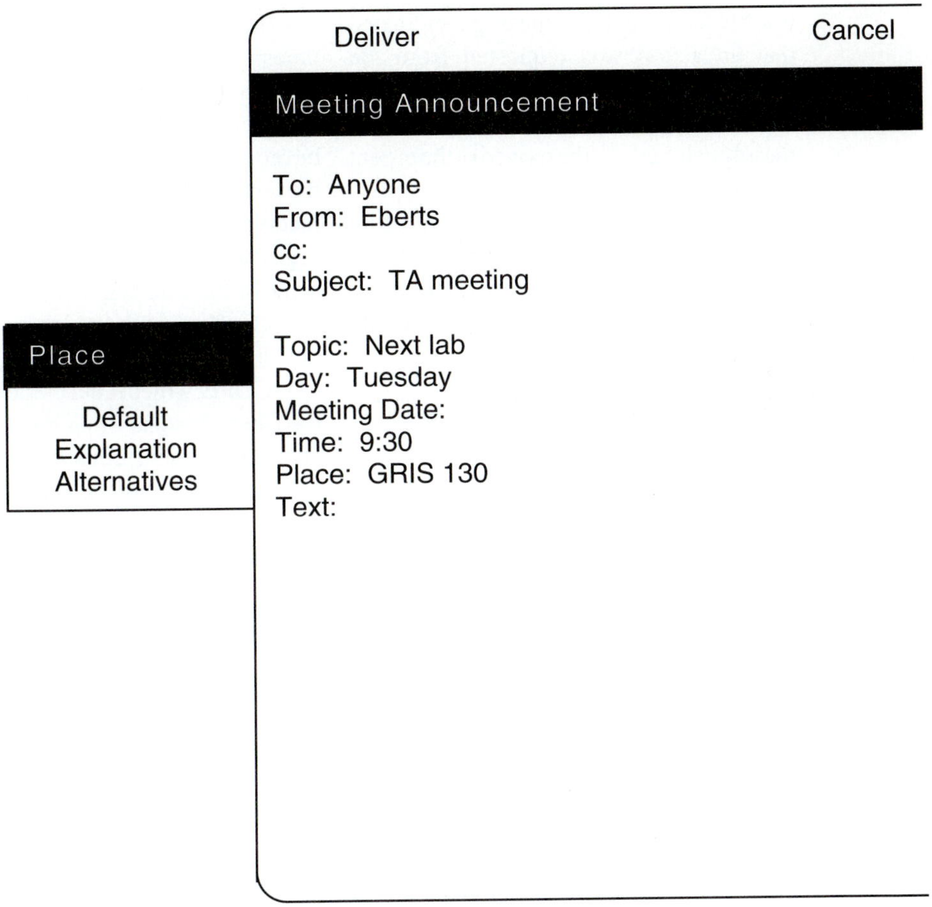

```
/‾‾‾‾‾‾‾‾‾‾‾‾‾‾‾‾‾‾‾‾‾‾‾‾‾‾‾‾‾‾‾‾‾‾‾‾‾‾‾‾‾‾‾‾‾‾‾‾‾‾‾‾‾‾
            Deliver                                    Cancel

  ▓▓▓▓▓▓▓▓▓▓▓▓▓▓▓▓▓▓▓▓▓▓▓▓▓▓▓▓▓▓▓▓▓▓▓▓▓▓▓▓▓▓▓▓▓▓▓▓▓▓▓
  Meeting Announcement


  To: Anyone
  From: Eberts
  cc:
  Subject: TA meeting
```

Place
Default
Explanation
Alternatives

```
  Topic: Next lab
  Day: Tuesday
  Meeting Date:
  Time: 9:30
  Place: GRIS 130
  Text:
```

Figure 25-7. For the Information Lens the fields of the meeting announcement have been filled in by the sender of the message.

who the message is sent from. A simple rule for the information in this field would be if the message is from your boss or some other important person, then assign a high priority to the message and read it quickly. The following shows an example of this set of rules:

> IF   From: Yang, Thomas
> THEN Set Characteristic: VIP
> IF   Message type: Action request
>   Characteristics: VIP
> THEN Move to: Urgent

In this case, if a message is from a boss, such as Yang or Thomas, then the message is moved to the urgent folder.

The Information Lens can also handle meeting requests through rule construction. The following shows an example of this:

> IF   Message type: Action request
>   Action deadline: Today,
>   tomorrow
> THEN Move to: urgent

In this case, the template which had been

used to construct the message indicated that an action was requested from the sender and that the deadline is today or tomorrow. The rule indicates that this message should also be moved to the urgent folder.

If a secretary takes care of meeting schedules, then the rules can be modified to route the messages to the appropriate person. The following shows an example of this:

IF   Message type: Meeting
         proposal
      Sender: Not Brenda

THEN   Resend: Brenda

The template for the message in this case was for a meeting proposal. The secretary, Brenda, schedules all the meetings. The message is routed automatically to Brenda for scheduling. The rules in any of these examples can be modified somewhat by the user to enhance the message routing and classification capabilities.

Malone et al. (1988) suggest that this Lens system can be incorporated into a larger system, such as a computerized calendar. For meeting announcements, the time of the meeting could be entered automatically on the user's computerized calendar. If the time slot on the calendar had already been filled by another appointment, then a message could be sent back automatically to the sender requesting a different time.

As argued by Fischer and Stevens (1991), Malone's Information Lens system has placed a good deal of the filtering burden on the sender of the message instead of the receiver. The receiver of the message is responsible for constructing the filter that is used to classify and priori-

tize the messages, but the filter is useless unless the sender uses the templates to construct the e-mail messages. Fischer and Stevens argue that the senders may not be motivated to go to the extra effort to use the templates, because the benefit is to the receiver. Only the receiver of the messages would be likely to pay the cost to achieve the filtering benefits.

Fischer and Stevens (1991) have developed a filtering system, called IN-FOSCOPE, which reduces the cost of using the filter. Instead of an e-mail filter, Fischer and Stevens constructed a filter for bulletin board users. Bulletin boards have many of the same characteristics as e-mail, since they both are messages which are sent and received by users, but bulletin boards are different in that the user does not necessarily have a recipient in mind when the message is sent.

The filter developed by Fischer and Stevens (1991) uses a slightly different cognitive science concept to make decisions about the messages which should be stored or deleted. They use Anderson's (1990) Rational Analysis of Human Memory to assist in making these decisions. Anderson indicates that the probability that an item in memory will be needed at a later time is a function of three effects: frequency, recency, and spacing. Frequency refers to the number of times that the item has been used in the past. Recency refers to the amount of time since it has been used. Spacing refers to the distribution of usage over time. One could expect that the same three effects are important for analyzing the need to select newsgroups within a bulletin board and then to read messages from that newsgroup. A filter using these three effects could be used to prioritize messages within a

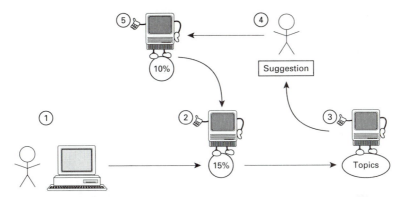

Figure 25-8. Agents assist the user in filtering bulletin board messages (Fischer and Stevens, 1991). Copyright 1991, Association for Computing Machinery, Inc. Reprinted by permission.

newsgroup. As an example, if messages within a newsgroup have been read frequently, then the filter will assign these messages a higher priority to display on the screen. If messages within a newsgroup have been read recently, other messages from this newsgroup would also receive a high priority.

The users of INFOSCOPE do not have to construct the filters themselves. Instead, the filter is constructed and modified through the use of agents. Agents are collections of rule-based heuristics which monitor the behavior of the user in relation to the messages received by the user to construct rules. The rules allow the system to be personalized to the particular user and, in consultation with the user, can assist in the modification of the rules used for the filter. Figure 25-8 shows how the filters can work. In 1, the user is perusing messages in a newsgroup. The agent in 2 recognizes that the user only reads 15% of the messages in a particular newsgroup. This is judged to be too low a number by the agent. This agent tells agent 3 to start gathering messages which may be more interesting to the user. Once these messages have been gathered, agent 3 sends a

suggestion to the user, in 4, indicating that more interesting messages have been found because the user had not been reading many messages. The user can either accept this suggestion or not. If it is not accepted, then agent 5 must try to determine why the suggestion was not accepted and modify the behavior of the other agents. In this example, the suggestion was not accepted by the user and agent 5 modifies agent 2 by setting the threshold at 10% for finding more interesting messages.

The INFOSCOPE example shows an important use of the cognitive approach. In this example, the filter tries to mimic the operation of human memory to perform some of its functions automatically and naturally. In many ways, this approach is similar to that used in the RABBIT database (see Chapter 24) which incorporated human memory retrieval strategies as a basis for the design of database retrievals.

Neural Networks

The application in the preceding section was on filters for e-mail and bulletin board messages. Habibi and Eberts (1991) have applied neural nets to filter messages for

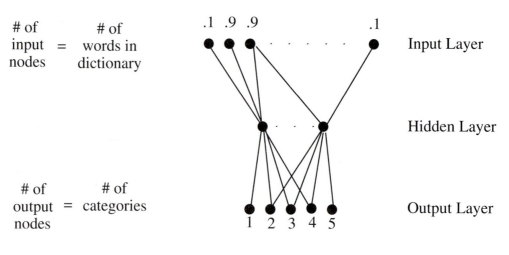

Figure 25-9. The neural net for filtering information on bulletin board messages. The inputs to the neural net were the dictionary of words. The outputs were classifications of the messages. The user may be interested in only some of the categories.

bulletin boards. Whereas the Fischer and Stevens (1991) INFOSCOPE used statistical methods, by tracking the frequency, recency, and spacing, to filter the messages, the Habibi and Eberts neural net bases the filtering on the content of the messages. In this case, message content was determined by a dictionary of words associated with categories of bulletin board messages.

Figure 25-9 depicts the neural net used for filtering messages to categories of subtopics. If the net can classify messages into subtopics, then the subtopics can be used to personalize the choice of topics for each user. The dictionary words were used as inputs, 30 nodes were in the hidden layer, and the five subtopics were used as outputs. For each news posting, the input nodes from the dictionary were turned on if the news posting contained the word corresponding to the particular input node; the node remained off if the news posting did not contain the word corresponding to the particular node.

An important issue is the choice of the words in the dictionaries. Habibi and Eberts (1981) researched two different methods for constructing the dictionary (see Figure 25-10). The words in the dictionary were taken from two news postings from each of the five topics to construct the dictionaries. First, the words and characters from the postings are sent through a filter that replaces all nonalphabetic characters with a carriage return, converts the remaining characters to lowercase, and sorts the words. The result is two output files. Second, the words in the output files are compared, and the words that are the same from the two files are sent to common word file 1. Up to this point,

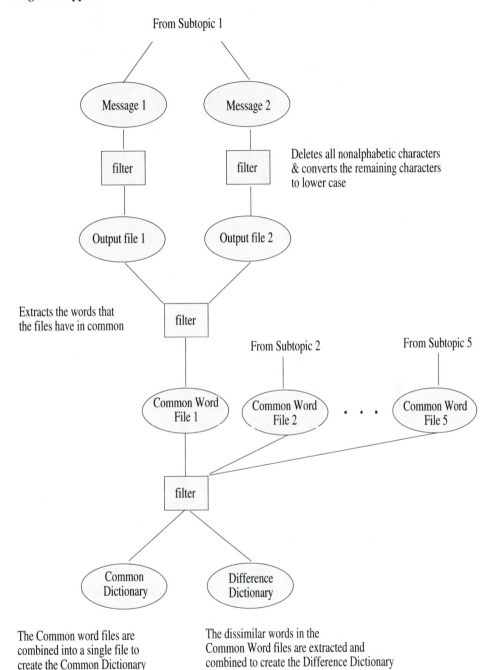

Figure 25-10. The method for constructing the two different kinds of dictionaries. One method was based upon the words that were the same in the messages, and another method was based on the words that were different.

the same procedure is followed for the other four subtopics resulting in four more common word files. Finally, the words from all five common word files are sent through the last filter. This filter is used differently depending upon the type of dictionary that is constructed. For the Common Dictionary, all the words from the common word files are combined into the one dictionary. For the Difference Dictionary, only those words that are dissimilar in the five common word files are included in the dictionary.

After training the net to categorize the messages into the subtopics, the net was tested on messages that it had never seen before. Results showed that the Common words dictionary approach was better than the Difference dictionary. Out of 64 samples, the Common words dictionary correctly categorized 60 of the messages and the Difference words dictionary correctly classified 53 of the messages. Further experimentation showed that the net could be used to filter messages on other dimensions besides just content. An emotive dimension, where the messages had an emotional tone to them instead of content, could be classified by the net. In many cases, bulletin board users would want to ignore the emotional messages and just read those with high content. This kind of information can be filtered out using the neural net.

Besides this example for using neural nets for filtering information, other potential applications exist. Schneider and Detweiler (1987) have developed a neural net model for human information processing. Testing of the model indicates that it can closely simulate actual human information processing. An im-

portant component of the model is the ability of the net to construct a filter through training. Some of the items, if they are consistently responded to, will be processed automatically and pass through the filter. Other items, if not responded to consistently, will not attain automatic processing and could be lost. This model, or the ideas inherent in the model, has potential to be used as a filter for messages in bulletin boards and e-mail.

Spatial Reasoning and Graphics

Spatial organization can be applied to groupware by organizing the information on the screen. Typically, the bulletin boards have to be displayed on many different kinds of terminals, so that they cannot use special computer-dependent graphics; instead they must rely on simple scrolling. This kind of display makes it difficult for the user to see the threads of messages that occur naturally. Most bulletin boards have an organizational structure which is difficult for the user to perceive as the messages scroll down the screen. For bulletin board messages, the sender of a message must specify words or phrases in a subject field at the top of the message. If another user responds to the message, then it automatically places an "Re:" on the message and repeats the subject field. This means that this message is in response to the earlier message. By reading the subjects of the messages, a user can determine the threads of conversations that are occurring. Some messages will get many responses, and then the responses can also be responded to.

Tracking the threads of conversation through the subject at the top of the message is difficult because of the lack of

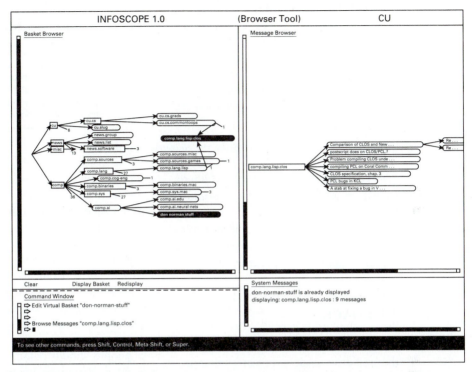

Figure 25-11. An example of the spatial structure used by INFOSCOPE to show the threads of organization in the bulletin board messages (Fischer and Stevens, 1991). Copyright 1991, Association for Computing Machinery, Inc. Reprinted by permission.

organization to the messages. Fischer and Stevens (1991) have developed a spatial organization for INFOSCOPE by providing a hierarchical structure to the messages. The structure is determined from the subject phrases and the "Re:" label in the subject field. For an example, see Figure 25-11. The messages at the top of the hierarchy will be the first designations of the subject. Below this top node will be those messages that have "Re" plus the subject at the top; these are messages responding to the original subject. A response to a response can also be received, and these will be designed as "Re: Re:." This structure can continue with further responses. A user of this system can see quickly the threads of conversation and pick out the ones that may be of interest.

This kind of spatial organization can also be applied to other groupware such as e-mail and GDSS. For e-mail, the same kind of subject sentence is usually required, and the user could store messages depending on the thread of conversation. For GDSS, a "subject" field could be required to make it easier to track the different threads of conversation in the decision-making process.

Attentional Resources

Attentional resources have already been discussed in the human information processing section. As discussed previously, overload of messages is a problem for e-

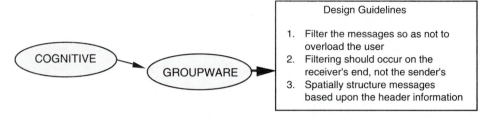

Figure 25-12. Principles derived from the cognitive approach.

mail and bulletin board users. Methods were discussed in the previous sections for filtering these messages.

Figure 25-12 illustrates the principles that can be derived from applying the cognitive approach to groupware.

PREDICTIVE MODELING APPROACH

Groupware will provide a challenge for the predictive models. In many situations, the tasks can be modeled just from the perspective of a single user. When using e-mail or bulletin boards, a single user is seated in front of a terminal and the interactions are the same as considered in Section IV. For other kinds of groupware, the interactions are not so simple because of the group aspect. For CSCW tasks, several people may be working on one task at a time; for GDSS, several people are participating in the decision process. The predictive models cannot be applied easily to these situations.

ANTHROPOMORPHIC APPROACH

The anthropomorphic approach is concerned with the ways that people communicate with each other and how this communication can be applied to human-computer interaction. The primary purpose of groupware, however, is for people to communicate with each other with the support of the computer. In this way, the study of human-human communication is the study of groupware.

One of the main purposes of groupware is to allow people at remote sites to interact with each other just as if they were together in the same room. Thus, how people communicate in the same room can be an important source of data for defining how people should communicate at remote sites. By comparing the remote site interactions to the same-site interactions, the effectiveness of groupware can be evaluated. In meetings, people interact in many ways; one of the most obvious ways is through speech communication. Another way to interact is by drawing items on a shared whiteboard. Sometimes two or more people collaborate to write a paper or report together. In other situations, people may collaborate on drawings. The groupware for some of these situations will be analyzed.

Human-Human Communication

Whittaker, Brennan, and Clark (1991) studied a CSCW situation in which people could share work through the use of a central whiteboard. Participants using the shared whiteboard could type or draw inputs on the screen and these inputs would

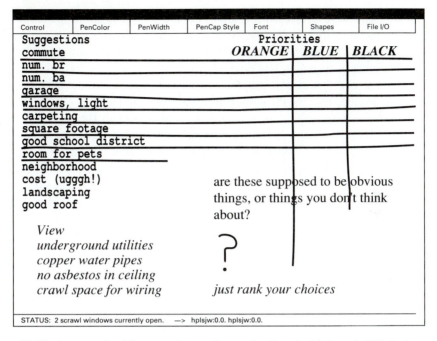

Figure 25-13. An example of the group interaction on the shared whiteboard. This is the status of the screen halfway through the session (Whittaker et al., 1991). Copyright 1991, Association for Computing Machinery, Inc. Reprinted by permission.

be shared with the rest of the participants in the group. Through experimentation, they found that the inputs in this shared whiteboard environment fell into three classes: artifacts, which were lists, tables, calendars, and matrices; prose, consisting of text; and deixis, consisting of drawing, pointing, selecting, and voting in reference to existing inputs on the whiteboard.

Figure 25-13 shows an example of a brainstorming session using the video whiteboard. The different fonts indicate different participants' inputs. The drawn table is an example of an artifact. The text in the bottom right is an example of prose. The question mark is an example of a deixis.

One of the main findings from the Whittaker et al. (1991) study was that the CSCW situation differed from normal human-human communication. First, the CSCW environment supported parallel activity on the part of the participants; 41% of the inputs were made in parallel with inputs of other participants. In normal conversation, only 5% of the conversation is in parallel (Levinson, 1983). The parallel activity allows more work to be performed during a smaller amount of time because people can do more things at one time.

A second difference between the CSCW environment and normal communication was less of an emphasis on the speech channel and more emphasis on artifacts for the CSCW (Whittaker et al., 1991). When a speech channel was added to the whiteboard, participants still made use of artifacts, probably because of the perception that these kinds of spatial structures were an effective means of communication. When the CSCW environment with speech was compared to the one without speech, a few other changes occurred. The use of prose on the screen dropped because the participants with the speech capability were performing this function through the prose. Certain kinds of activities, such as negotiation, were performed more effectively with the speech capability. This study shows that merely studying human-human communication may not always provide insight to the groupware environment. Human-human communication does provide a context, however, for analyzing the differences between the two situations.

Probably the most important consideration for CSCW is the policy for how to handle changes to the work in progress. As an example, if one person in the group decides to make a change to a manuscript being worked on by the group, how should this change be accepted by the other group members? Who should make the final decision about the proposed change? One way to attack this problem is to understand how these policies are set in non-CSCW settings. This becomes an anthropomorphic issue. Although some work has been done on this issue (e.g., Dewan and Choudhary, 1991), more work needs to be done.

Group Activities

For many of the group activities, groupware is being developed to allow these activities to occur with participants at remote sites. Some of these have already been discussed in other contexts. The following discusses some other examples of groupware.

People spend much of their time at meetings. If people from different locations are meeting, then the cost can be expensive to bring them together. Using an electronic meeting system, people can stay at their remote sites and still participate in the meetings. Sometimes electronic meetings are referenced under the banner of GDSSs, which have been discussed in a previous section. GDSSs have some advantages over regular meetings, as discussed earlier, because the participants can operate in parallel, the responses can be anonymous, and the effective size of a meeting can be increased. More needs to be understood about the structures of meetings so that the developed software can support these structures.

When people get together, they will often use a whiteboard, with colored felt pens, to communicate to others within the room. Once again, groupware attempts to support this activity at remote sites. One system which has been developed is called VideoWhiteboard (Tang and Minneman, 1991). Figure 25-14 shows a schematic of the VideoWhiteboard. Each person draws upon a projection screen using standard felt markers. A video camera at one site captures the images from the translucent projection screen and transmits the image to the video projector of the other participant. A video projector projects the image onto the screen. In addition to seeing the marks from the other participant, a shadow of the other person can also be seen through the projection screen. This shadow, through the use of gestures, can provide many cues to the shared work. In addition to the video channel, the two participants also have an audio connection to each other.

Another groupware tool has been

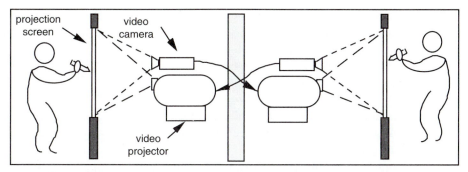

Figure 25-14. An example of the VideoWhiteboard. People at remote sites can share ideas over the whiteboard (Tang and Minneman, 1991). Copyright 1991, Association for Computing Machinery, Inc. Reprinted by permission.

developed for collaborative drawing tasks, and it has been termed Commune (Minneman and Bly, 1991). In Commune, each user has a shared drawing surface which can be drawn upon with a stylus. When a participant draws on the surface, the image is shown on all the screens simultaneously. In this way, the finished product and design is a result of the collaborative work of all the participants.

Much of this work is still in its infancy. Under the anthropomorphic approach, more work could be done to determine how people collaborate in natural settings, and this work could be applied to the design of groupware. Research and theories in social psychology, especially the interactions within groups, can be used to help guide some of this research and design.

Figure 25-15 illustrates the principles that can be derived from applying the anthropomorphic approach to groupware.

SUMMARY

The research on groupware represents a technology which is still developing. Not much work has been performed on this technology in the context of the four approaches. For the empirical approach, much of the work on groupware has been supported by very loose experiments and anecdotes (e.g., Tang and Minneman, 1991; Minneman and Bly, 1991). More effort has been devoted to applying the

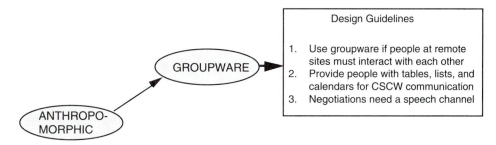

Figure 25-15. An illustration of the principles that can be derived from applying the anthropomorphic approach to groupware.

cognitive approach to groupware, especially in terms of developing automatic filters when a user is overloaded with messages. The predictive modeling approach could be applied in traditional ways by concentrating the efforts on the interface design for one person within the group. Applying these modeling techniques to the group is more difficult. Finally, the anthropomorphic approach provides much promise in its applications to groupware. By analyzing groups in natural settings, without computer support, much can be known about how to support the participants with technology. More work needs to be done on applying social psychology theories to the design of groupware.

QUESTIONS

1. Name the groupware tool (e.g., GDSS) which corresponds to the following situations.

    a. Participants, about 15-20, interact on a brainstorming session through networked computer systems.

    b. Someone has a hardware problem and posts a message to seek solutions to this problem.

    c. Five people work together electronically on the same file to compose a report.

    d. In a concurrent engineering meeting several people, with diverse backgrounds, provide ideas for a product design.

2. Name several reasons why a GDSS session will be more productive than a traditional meeting.

3. Consider the CSCW task of composing a report electronically where everyone in the group could have access to the same report. The policies for allowing changes to the manuscript are very important in this situation. One possible policy would be for all changes to occur only after a change was agreed to by the designated leader of the group. Write down all the other kinds of policies that you can think of for how the group members can interact, and decide on changes, when writing the report.

REFERENCES

Allen, R. (1990). User models: Theory, method, and practice. *International Journal of Man-Machine Studies, 32,* 511-543.

Anderson, J. A. (1983). Cognitive and psychological computation with neural models. *IEEE Transactions on Systems, Man, and Cybernetics, SMC-13,* 799-815.

Anderson, J. R. (1976). *Language, memory, and thought.* Hillsdale, NJ: Erlbaum.

Anderson, J. R. (1983). *The architecture of cognition.* Cambridge, MA: Harvard University Press.

Anderson, J. R. (1990). *The adaptive character of thought.* Hillsdale, NJ: Erlbaum.

Anderson, J. R., Greeno, J. G., Kline, P. J., and Neves, D. M. (1981). Acquisition of problem-solving skill. In J. R. Anderson (Ed.), *Cognitive skills and their acquisition* (pp. 191-230). Hillsdale, NJ: Erlbaum.

Atkinson, R. C., and Juola, J. F. (1973). Factors influencing speed and accuracy of word recognition. In S. Kornblum (Ed.), *Attention and performance, Vol. IV.* New York: Academic.

Ausubel, D. P. (1968). *Educational psychology: A cognitive approach.* New York: Holt, Rinehart & Winston.

Avner, A. R. (1979). Production of computer-based instructional materials. In H. F. O'Neil (Ed.), *Issues in instructional systems development.* New York: Academic (pp. 133-180).

Averbach, E., and Coriell, A. S. (1961). Short-term memory in vision. *Bell System Technical Journal, 40,* 309-328.

Baecker, R., Small, I., and Mander, R. (1991). Bringing icons to life. *Human Factors in Computing Systems Conference Proceedings, CHI'91* (pp. 1-6). New York: ACM.

Bainbridge, L. (1974). Analysis of verbal protocols from a process control task. In E. Edwards and F. P. Lees (Eds.), *The human operator in process control* (pp. 146-158). New York: Halsted.

Barr, A., and Feigenbaum, E. A. (1981). *The handbook of artificial intelligence.* Los Altos, CA: Kaufman.

Bayman, P., and Mayer, R. E. (1983). A diagnosis of beginning programmers' misconceptions of BASIC programming statements. *Communications of the ACM, 26,* 677-679.

Bayman, P., and Mayer, R. E. (1984). Instructional manipulation of users' mental models for electronic calculators. *International Journal of Man-Machine Studies, 20,* 189-199.

Benbasat, I., Dexter, A. S., and Todd, P. (1986). The influence of color and graphical information presentation in a managerial decision simulation. *Human-Computer Interaction, 2,* 65-92.

Bewley, W. L., Roberts, T. L., Schroit, D., and Verplank, W. L. (1983). Human factors testing in the design of Xerox's "Star" office workstation. In A. Janda (Ed.), *Human factors in computing systems.* New York: ACM (pp. 72-77).

Billingsley, P. A. (1982). Navigation through hierarchical menu structures: Does it help to have a map? *Proceedings of the Human Factors Society, 26,* 103-107.

Bloomfield, J. R., and Little, R. K. (1985). Operator tracking performance with time-compressed and time-integrated moving target indicator (MTI) radar imagery. In R. E. Eberts and C. G. Eberts (Eds.), *Trends in ergonomics/Human factors, Vol. II* (pp. 219-223). Amsterdam: North-Holland.

Boehm-Davis, D. A., Holt, R. W., Koll, M., Yastrop, G., and Peters, R. (1989). Effects of different data base formats on information retrieval. *Human Factors, 31,* 579-592.

Boose, J. (1984). A framework for transferring human expertise. In G. Salvendy (Ed.), *Human-computer interaction* (pp. 247-254). Amsterdam: Elsevier.

Borgman, C. L. (1984). Psychological research in human-computer interaction. *Annual Review of Information Science and Technology, 19,* 33-64.

Bovair, S., Kieras, D. E., and Polson, P. G. (1990). The acquisition and performance of text-editing skill: A cognitive complexity analysis. *Human Computer Interaction, 5,* 1-48.

Bower, G. H. (1972). Mental images and associative learning. In L. Gregg (Ed.), *Cognition in learning and memory.* New York: Wiley.

Brajnik, G., Guida, G., and Tasso, C. (1990). User modeling in expert man-machine interfaces: A case study in intelligent information retrieval. *IEEE Transactions on Systems, Man, and Cybernetics, 20*, 166-185.

Bringelson, L. S. (1991). *Group mental model transfer.* Unpublished Ph.D. Dissertation, School of Industrial Engineering, Purdue University, West Lafayette, IN.

Broadbent, D. E. (1958). *Perception and communication.* Oxford: Pergamon.

Brodker, S. (1989). A human activity approach to user interfaces. *Human-Computer Interaction, 4*, 171-195.

Browne, D., Totterdell, P., and Norman, M. (Eds.) (1990). *Adaptive User Interface.* London: Academic.

Burton, R. R., and Brown, J. S. (1979a). Toward a natural language capability for computer assisted instruction. In H. F. O'Neil (Ed.), *Procedures for instructional system development* (pp. 272-313). New York: Academic.

Burton, R. R., and Brown, J. S. (1979b). An investigation of computer coaching for informal learning activities. *International Journal of Man-Machine Studies, 11*, 5-24.

Bury, K. F., and Boyle, J. M. (1982). An on-line experimental comparison of two simulated record selection languages. *Proceedings of the Human Factors Society, 26*, 74-78.

Bury, K. F., Boyle, J. M., Evey, R. J., and Neal, A. S. (1982). Windowing versus scrolling on a visual display terminal. *Human Factors, 24*, 385-394.

Caldwell, C. D. (1993). Mental models of C programming languages. Unpublished manuscript.

Caldwell, C. D., and Eberts, R. E. (1989). Interactive graphics display design based on the mental models of experts and novices: Evaluating users' knowledge acquisition. In G. Salvendy and M. J. Smith (Eds.), *Designing and using human-computer interfaces and knowledge based systems* (pp. 271-277). Amsterdam: Elsevier.

Campbell, D. T., and Stanley, J. C. (1966). *Experimental and quasi-experimental designs for research.* Chicago: Rand McNally.

Card, S. K. (1989). Human factors and artificial intelligence. In P. A. Hancock and M. H. Chignell (Eds.), *Intelligent interfaces: Theory, research and design* (pp. 27-48). Amsterdam: Elsevier.

Card, S. K., Moran, T. P., and Newell, A. L. (1983). *The psychology of human computer interaction.* Hillsdale, NJ: Erlbaum.

Card, S. K., Moran, T. P., and Newell, A. L. (1986). The Model Human Processor. In K. R. Boff, L. Kaufman, and J. P. Thomas (Eds.), *Handbook of perception and human performance, Vol. II* (pp. 45:1 - 45:35). New York: Wiley.

Card, S. K., Robertson, G. C., and Mackinlay, J. D. (1991). The information visualizer, an information workspace. *Human Factors in Computing Systems Conference Proceedings, CHI'91* (pp. 181-188). New York: ACM.

Carroll, J. M. (1982, November). The adventure of getting to know a computer. *IEEE Computer*, 49-58.

Carroll, J. M., and Aaronson, A. P. (1988). Learning by doing with simulated intelligent help. *Communications of the ACM, 31*, 1064-1079.

Carroll, J. M., and Carrithers, C. (1984). Blocking errors in a training-wheels system. *Human Factors, 26*, 377-390.

Carroll, J. M., Mack, R. L., and Kellogg, W. A.. (1988). Interface metaphors and the user interface design. In M. Helander (Ed.), *Handbook of human-computer interaction* (pp. 67-85). Amsterdam: Elsevier.

Carroll, J. M., Mack, R. L., Lewis, C., Grischkowski, N., and Robertson, S. (1985). Exploring exploring a word processor. *Human-Computer Interaction, 1*, 283-307.

Carroll, J. M., and Olson, J. R. (1988). Mental models in human-computer interaction. In M. Helander (Ed.), *Handbook of human-computer interaction* (pp. 45-65). Amsterdam: Elsevier.

Carroll, J. M., and Thomas, J. C. (1982). Metaphor and the cognitive representation of computing systems. *IEEE Transactions on Systems, Man, and Cybernetics, SMC-12*, 107-116.

Carroll, J. M., Thomas, J. C., and Malhotra, A. (1980). Presentation and representation in design problem-solving. *British Journal of Psychology, 71*, 143-153.

Carswell, C. M., and Wickens, C. D. (1984). *The integration of information from analog-visual display: The role of dimensional integrality* (Technical Report). University of Illinois Engineering, Psychology Laboratory, EPL-84-2/NASA-84-3.

Cassel, R. N., and Cassel, S. L. (1984). Cassel computer literacy test (CMLRTC). *Journal of Instructional Psychology, 1*, 3-9.

Chalfonte, B. L., Fish, R. S., and Kraut, R. E. (1991). Expressive richness: A comparison of speech and text as media for revision. *Human Factors in Computing Systems Conference Proceedings, CHI'91* (pp. 21-26). New York: ACM.

Cheng, T. T., Plake, B., and Stevens, D. J. (1985). A validation study of the computer literacy examination: Cognitive aspect. *AEDS Journal, 18*, 139-152.

Chin, J. P., Diehl, V. A., and Norman, K. L. (1987). *Development of an instrument measuring user satisfaction of the human-computer interface* (Technical Report CAR-TR-328 & CS-TR-1926). College Park, MD: University of Maryland, Human/Computer Interaction Laboratory.

Chin, J. P., Diehl, V. A., and Norman, K. (1988). Development of an instrument measuring user satisfaction of the human-computer interface. In *Proceedings of CHI '88 Conference on Human Factors in Computing Systems* (pp. 213-218). New York: ACM.

Chomsky, N. (1964). *Syntactic structures.* The Hague, The Netherlands: Mouton.

Clarkson, M. A. (1991, February). An easier interface. *Byte, 6* (2), 277-282.

Cohill, A. M., and Williges, R. C. (1982). Computer-augmented retrieval of HELP information for novice users. *Proceedings of the Human Factors Society, 26*, 79-82.

Cohill, A. M., and Williges, R. C. (1985). Retrieval of HELP information for novice users of interactive computer systems. *Human Factors, 27*, 335-344.

Collins, A. M., and Loftus, E. F. (1975). A spreading activation theory of semantic processing. *Psychological Review, 82*, 407-428.

Collins, A. M., and Quillian, M. R. (1969). Retrieval time from semantic memory. *Journal of Verbal Learning and Verbal Behavior, 8*, 240-247.

Collins, A., and Stevens, A. L. (1982). Goals and strategies of inquiry teachers. In R. Glaser (Ed.), *Advances in instructional psychology, Vol. 2* (pp. 65-118). Hillsdale, NJ: Erlbaum.

Cook, T. D., and Stanley, J. C. (1979). *Quasi-experimentation: Design and analysis issues for field settings.* Chicago: Rand McNally.

Cooke, N. J., and Schvaneveldt, R. W. (1988). Effects of computer programming experience on network representations of abstract programming concepts. *International Journal of Man-Machine Studies, 29*, 407-427.

Cooper, G. E., and Harper, R. P. (1969, April). The use of pilot ratings in the evaluation of aircraft handling qualities (NASA Ames Technical Report NASA TN-D-5153). Moffett Field, CA: NASA Ames Research Center.

Cooper, L. A. (1975). Mental rotation of random two-dimensional shapes. *Cognitive Psychology, 7*, 20-43.

Cooper, L. A., and Shepard, R. N. (1975). Mental transformation in the identification of left and right hands. *Journal of Experimental Psychology: Human Perception and Performance, 1*, 48-56.

Coventry, L. (1989). Some effects of cognitive style on learning UNIX. *International Journal of Man-Machine Studies, 31*, 349-365.

Cowan, N. (1988). Evolving conceptions of memory storage, selective attention, and their mutual constraints within the human information-processing system. *Psychological Bulletin, 2*, 163-191.

Cullingford, R. (1981). SAM. In R. C. Schank and C. K. Riesbeck (Eds.), *Inside computer understanding* (pp. 75-119). Hillsdale, NJ: Erlbaum.

Dallett, K., Wilcox, S. G., and D'Andrea, L. (1968). Picture memory experiments. *Journal of Experimental Psychology, 76*, 312-320.

Dannenberg, R. B., and Amon, D. (1989). A gesture based user interface prototyping system. *Proceedings of the ACM SIGGRAPH Symposium on User Interface Software and Technology.* ACM: New York.

Date, C. J. (1986). *An introduction to database systems.* Reading, MA: Addison-Wesley.

Davis, J. S. (1990). Experimental investigation of the utility of data structure and the E-R diagrams in database query. *International Journal of Man-Machine Studies, 32*, 449-459.

Davis, R., Buchanan, B., and Shortliffe, E. H. (1977). Production rules as a representation for a knowledge-base consultation program. *Artificial Intelligence, 8*, 15-45.

De Kleer, J., and Brown, J. S. (1981). Mental models of physical mechanisms and their acquisition. In J. R. Anderson (Ed.), *Cognitive skills and their acquisition* (pp. 285-305). Hillsdale, NJ: Erlbaum.

DeMarco, T., and Lister, T. (1987). *Peopleware: Productive projects and teams.* New York: Dorset.

Dennis, A. R., Nunamaker, J. F., and Vogel, D. R. (1989). GDSS laboratory experiments and field studies: Closing the gap. *Proceedings of the IEEE 22nd Annual Hawaii International Conference on System Sciences*, 300-309.

Dennis, A. R., Valacich, J. S., and Nunamaker, J. F. (1990). An experimental investigation of the effects of group size in an electronic meeting environment. *IEEE Transactions on Systems, Man, and Cybernetics, 25*, 1049-1057.

Dewan, P., and Choudhary, R. (1991). Flexible user interface coupling in a collaborative system. *Human Factors in Computing Systems Conference Proceedings, CHI'91* (pp. 41-48). New York: ACM.

Dickson, G. W., DeSanctis, G., and McBride, D. J. (1986). Understanding the effectiveness of computer graphics for decision support: A cumulative experimental approach. *Communications of the ACM, 29*, 40-47.

Douglas, S. A., and Moran, T. P. (1983). Learning text editor semantics by analogy. In A. Janda (Ed.), *Human factors in computing systems* (pp. 207-211). New York: ACM.

DuBoulay, B., O'Shea, T., and Monk, J. (1981). The black box inside the glass box: Presenting computing concepts to novices. *International Journal of Man-Machine Studies, 14*, 237-249.

DuBoulay, J. B. H., and Howe, J. A. M. (1982). LOGO building blocks: Student teachers using computer-based mathematics apparatus. *Computers & Education, 6*, 93-96.

Dumais, S. T., and Landauer, T. K. (1981). Psychological investigations of natural terminology for command and query languages. In A. Badre and B. Shneiderman (Eds.), *Directions in human/computer interaction* (pp. 95-109). Norwood, NJ: Ablex.

Dunsmore, H. E. (1980). Designing an interactive facility for non-programmers. In *Proceedings of the ACM Computer Conference* (pp. 475-483). New York: ACM.

Eberts, R. E. (1985). Four approaches to human-computer interaction. In *Proceedings of the IEEE Systems, Man, and Cybernetics Conference* (pp. 615-619).

Eberts, R. E. (1987). Human computer interaction. In P. A. Hancock (Ed.), *Human Factors Psychology* (pp. 249-304). Amsterdam: Elsevier.

Eberts, R. E., and Bittianda, K. P. (1993). Preferred mental models for direct manipulation and command-based interfaces. *International Journal of Man-Machine Studies, 38*, 769-785.

Eberts, R. E., and Brock, J. F. (1988). Computer-based instruction. In M. Helander (Ed.), *Handbook of human-computer interaction* (pp. 599-627). Amsterdam: North-Holland.

Eberts, R. E., and Eberts, C. G. (1989). Four approaches to human computer interaction. In P. A. Hancock and M. H. Chignell (Eds.), *Intelligent interfaces: Theory, research and design* (pp. 69-127). Amsterdam: Elsevier.

Eberts, R. E., Majchrzak, A., Payne, P., and Salvendy, G. (1990). Integrating social and cognitive factors in the design of human-computer interactive communication. *International Journal of Human-Computer Interaction, 2*, 1-27.

Eberts, R. E., and Posey, J. W. (1990). The mental model in stimulus-response compatibility. In R. W. Proctor and T. G. Reeve (Eds.), *Stimulus-response compatibility* (pp. 389-425). Amsterdam: Elsevier.

Eberts, R. E., and Schneider, W. (1985). Internalizing the system dynamics for a second-order system. *Human Factors, 27*, 371-393.

Eberts, R. E., Smith, D., Dray, S., and Vestewig, R. (1982, August). A practical guide to measuring transfer from training devices to weapon systems (Final Report to the US Army Research Institute for the Behavioral and Social Sciences). Minneapolis: Honeywell Systems and Research Center.

Eberts, R. E., Villegas, L., Phillips, C., and Eberts, C. G. (1991). User assistance for UNIX commands using neural net modeling. In *Proceedings of the Second Workshop on Neural Networks: Academic/Industrial/NASA/Defense* (pp. 723-730).

Eberts, R. E., Villegas, L., Phillips, C., and Eberts, C. G. (1992). Using neural nets for user assistance in HCI tasks. *International Journal of Human-Computer Interaction, 4*, 59-77.

Ehrenreich, S. L. (1981). Query languages: Design recommendations derived from the human factors literature. *Human Factors, 23*, 709-725.

Elkerton, J. (1988). Online aiding for human-computer interfaces. In M. Helander (Ed.), *Handbook of human-computer interaction* (pp. 345-364). Amsterdam: North-Holland.

Embley, D. W. (1978). Empirical and formal language design applied to a unified control construct for interactive computing. *International Journal of Man-Machine Studies, 10*, 197-216.

Ericsson, K. A., and Simon, H. A. (1980). Verbal reports as data. *Psychological Review, 87*, 215-251.

Fairweather, P. G., and O'Neal, A. F. (1984). The impact of advanced authoring systems on CAI productivity. *Journal of Computer-Based Instruction, 11*, 90-94.

Ferguson, E. S. (1977). The mind's eye: Nonverbal thought in technology. *Science, 197*, 827-836.

Finlay, J., and Beale, R. (1992). Pattern recognition and classification in dynamic and static user modelling. In R. Beale and J. Finlay (Eds.), *Neural networks and pattern-recognition in human-computer interaction* (pp. 65-89). New York: Ellis Horwood.

Fischer, G., and Stevens, C. (1991). Information access in complex, poorly structured information spaces. *Human Factors in Computing Systems Conference Proceedings, CHI'91* (pp. 63-70). New York: ACM.

Fitter, M. (1979). Towards more "natural" interactive systems. *International Journal of Man-Machine Studies, 11*, 339-350.

Fitts, P. M. (1954). The information capacity of the human motor system in controlling the amplitude of movement. *Journal of Experimental Psychology, 47*, 381-391.

Fodor, J. A., and Pylyshyn, Z. W. (1989). Connectionism and cognitive architecture: A critical analysis. *Cognition, 28*, 3-71.

Forchieri, P., Lemut, E., and Molfino, M. T. (1983). The GRAF system: An interactive graphics system for teaching mathematics. *Computers & Education, 7*, 177-182.

Fukushima, K. (1987). Neural network model for selective attention in visual pattern recognition and associative recall. *Applied Optics, 26*, 4985-4992.

Fukushima, K. (1988a, March). A neural network for visual pattern recognition. *IEEE Computer*, 65-75.

Fukushima, K. (1988b). Neocognitron: A hierarchial neural network capable of visual pattern recognition. *Neural Networks, 1*, 119-130.

Fukushima, K., Miyake, S., and Ito, T. (1983). Neocognitron: A neural network model for a mechanism of visual pattern recognition. *IEEE Transactions on Systems, Man, and Cybernetics, SMC-13*, 826-834.

Furnas, G. W., Landauer, T. K., Gomez, L. M., and Dumais, S. T. (1987). The vocabulary problem in human-system communication, *Communications of the ACM, 30*, 964-971.

Gade, P. A., Fields, F. A., Maisano, R. E., and Marshall, C. F. (1981). Data entry performance as a function of method and instructional strategy. *Human Factors, 23*, 199-210.

Gaines, R., Lisowski, W., Press, S., and Shapiro, N. (1980). *Authentication by keystroke timing: Some preliminary results*. Rand Report R 256-NSF. Santa Monica, CA: Rand Corporation.

Gallant, S. I. (1988). A connectionist expert system. *Communications of the ACM, 31*, 152-169.

Gallupe, R. B. (1985). *The impact of task difficulty on the use of a group decision support system*. Unpublished doctoral dissertation. University of Minnesota.

Gallupe, R. B. (1990). Suppressing the contribution of the group's best member: Is GDSS use appropriate for all group tasks? *Proceedings of the IEEE 23rd Annual Hawaii International Conference on System Sciences, Vol. III*, 13-22.

Garg-Janardan, C., Eberts, R. E., Zimolong, B., Nof, S. Y., and Salvendy, G. (1987). Expert Systems. In G. Salvendy (Ed.), *The handbook of human factors* (pp. 1130-1176). New York: Wiley.

Garner, W., Hake, H. W., and Eriksen, C. W. (1956). Operationism and the concept of perception. *Psychological Review, 63*, 149-159.

Gaver, W. W. (1991). Technology affordances. *Human Factors in Computing Systems Conference Proceedings, CHI'91* (pp. 79-84). New York: ACM.

Gentner, D., and Gentner, D. R. (1983). Flowing water or teeming crowds: Mental models of electricity. In D. Gentner and A. L. Stevens (Eds.), *Mental models* (pp. 253-271). New York: Academic.

Gentner, D., and Stevens, A. L. (Eds.) (1983). *Mental models*. New York: Academic.

Gittins, D. (1986). Icon-based human-computer interaction. *International Journal of Man-Machine Studies, 24*, 519-543.

Goldin, E. E., and Hayes-Roth, B. (1980). *Individual differences in planning processes*. Office of Naval Research Note #N-1488-ONR.

Goldstein, I. P. (1982). The genetic graph: A representation for the evolution of procedural knowledge. In D. Sleeman and J. S. Brown (Eds.), *Intelligent Tutoring Systems* (pp. 51-77). New York: Academic.

Gomez, L. M., Egan, D. E., and Bowers, C. (1986). Learning to use a text editor: Some learner characteristics that predict success. *Human Computer Interaction, 2*, 1-23.

Goodstein, L. P. (1981). Discriminative display support for process operators. In J. Rasmussen and W. B . Rouse (Eds.), *Human detection and diagnosis of system failures* (pp. 433-449). New York: Plenum.

Goodstein, L. P., Andersen, H. B., and Olsen, H. E. (Eds.) (1988). *Tasks, errors and mental models*. London: Taylor & Francis.

Gordon, N. B. (1968). Guidance versus augmented feedback and motor skill. *Journal of Experimental Psychology, 15*, 566-568.

Gould, J. D. (1981). Composing letters with computer-based text editors. *Human Factors, 23*, 593-606.

Gould, J. D., and Alfano, L. (1983). Revising documents with text editors, hand writing recognition, and speech recognition systems. *Proceedings of the Human Factors Society, 27*, 831-833.

Gould, J. D., Conti, J., and Hovanyecz, T. (1983). Composing letters with a simulated listening typewriter. *Communications of the ACM, 26*, 295-308.

Gould, L., and Finzer, W. (1982). A study of TRIP: A computer system for animating rime-rate-distance problems. *International Journal of Man-Machine Studies, 17*, 109-126.

Gray, W. E. (1989). GOMS meets the phone company, or, Can 8,400,00 unit-tasks be wrong? ACM SIGCHI Interactive Poster Material.

Greenberg, S., and Witten, I. H. (1985). Adaptive personalised interfaces — a question of viability. *Behaviour and Information Technology, 4*, 31-45.

Greene, S. L., Devlin, S. J., Cannata, P. E., and Gomez, L. M. (1990). No IFs, ANDs, or ORs: A study of database querying. *International Journal of Man-Machine Studies, 32*, 303-326.

Grudin, J. (1989). The case against user interface consistency. *Communications of the ACM, 32*, 1164-1173.

Guastello, S. J., and Traut, M. (1989). Verbal versus pictorial representations of objects in a human-computer interface. *International Journal of Man-Machine Studies, 31*, 99-120.

Haber, R. N. (1974). Information processing. In E. C. Carterette and M. P. Friedman (Eds.), *Historical and philosophical roots of perception, Vol. I* (pp. 313-333). New York: Academic.

Habibi, S., and Eberts, R. (1991). Using neural networks to categorize bulletin board messages. In C. H. Dagli, S. R. T. Kumara, Y. C. Shin (Eds.), *Intelligent engineering systems through artificial neural networks* (pp. 947-952). New York: ASME.

Hackman, J. R., and Oldham, G. R. (1975). Development of the Job Diagnostic Survey. *Journal of Applied Psychology, 60*, 159-170.

Haller, R., Mutschler, H., and Voss, M. (1984). Comparison of input devices for correction of typing errors in office systems. *Proceedings of the Interact '84 Conference, First IFIP Conference on Human-Computer Interaction, 1*, 218-223.

Hancock, P. A., and Chignell, M. H. (1987). Adaptive control in human-machine systems. In P. A. Hancock (Ed.), *Human factors psychology* (pp. 305-345). Amsterdam: North-Holland.

Hansen, W. J., Doring, R., and Whitlock, L. R. (1978). Why an examination was slower on-line than on paper. *International Journal of Man-Machine Studies, 10*, 507-519.

Hanson, S. J., and Kegl, J. (1987). PARSNIP: A connectionist network that learns natural language grammar from exposure to natural language sentences. *Proceedings of the Ninth Annual Conference of the Cognitive Science Society* (pp. 106-119).

Hauptmann, A. G., and Green, B. F. (1980). A comparison of command, menu-selection and natural language computer programs. *Behaviour and Information Technology, 2*, 163-178.

Hauptmann, A. G., and Rudnicky, A. I. (1988). Talking to computers: An empirical investigation. *International Journal of Man-Machine Studies, 28,* 583-604.

Hayes, P. J., and Reddy, R. (1983). Steps toward graceful interaction in spoken and written man-machine communication. *International Journal of Man-Machine Studies, 19*, 231-384.

Hebb, D. O. (1949). *The organization of behavior.* New York: Wiley.

Hendler, J. A., and Michaelis, P. R. (1983). The effects of limited grammar on interactive natural language. In A. Janda (Ed.), *The human factors of computing systems* (pp. 190-192). New York: ACM.

Hollan, J. D., Stevens, A., and Williams, N. (1980). STEAMER: An advanced computer assisted instruction system for propulsion engineering. Paper presented at the Summer Simulation Conference, Seattle.

Holynski, M. (1988). User-adaptive computer graphics. *International Journal of Man-Machine Studies, 29*, 539-548.

Hoppe, H. U. (1988). Task-oriented parsing: A diagnostic method to be used by adaptive systems. In *Proceedings CHI'88 Human Factors in Computing Systems* (pp. 241-247). New York: ACM.

Howes, A., and Payne, S. J. (1990). Display-based competence: Towards user models for menu-driven interfaces. *International Journal of Man-Machine Studies, 33*, 637-655.

Howes, A., and Young, R. M. (1991). Predicting the learnability of task-action mappings. *Human Factors in Computing Systems Conference Proceedings, CHI'91* (pp. 113-118). New York: ACM.

Hutchins, E. L., Hollan, J. D., and Norman, D. A. (1986). Direct manipulation interfaces. In D. A. Norman and S. W. Draper (Eds.), *User centered system design* (pp. 87-124). Hillsdale, NJ: Erlbaum.

Hutchinson, T. E., White, K. P., Martin, W. N., Reichert, K. C., and Frey, L. A. (1989). Human-computer interaction using eye-gaze input. *IEEE Transactions on Systems, Man, and Cybernetics, 19*, 1527-1534.

Huttenlocher, J. (1968). Constructing spatial images: A strategy in reasoning. *Psychological Review, 75*, 550-560.

Innocent, P. R. (1982). Towards self-adaptive interface systems. *International Journal of Man-Machine Studies, 16*, 287-299.

Irani, E. A., Matts, J. P., Long, J. M., and Slagle, J. R. (1989). Using artificial neural nets for statistical discovery: Observations after using backpropagation, expert systems, and multiple-linear regression on clinical trial data. *Complex Systems, 3*, 295-311.

Iseki, O., and Shneiderman, B. (1986). Applying direct manipulation concepts: Direct Manipulation Disk Operating System (DMDOS). *Software Engineering Notes, 11*, 259-264.

James, E. B. (1981). The user interface: How we may compute. In M. J. Coombs and J. L. Alty (Eds.), *Human-computer interaction.* London: Academic.

Jenkins, J. P. (1984). An application of an expert system to problem solving in process control displays. In G. Salvendy (Ed.), *Human-computer interaction* (pp. 255-260). Amsterdam: Elsevier.

Jerrams-Smith, J. (1989). An attempt to incorporate expertise about users into an intelligent interface for Unix. *International Journal of Man-Machine Studies, 27*, 269-291.

Johansen, R. (1988). *Groupware: Computer Support for Business Teams.* New York: Free Press.

Johnson-Laird, P. N. (1981). *Mental models.* Cambridge, England: Cambridge University Press.

Jones, O. (1989). *Introduction to the X Window System.* Englewood Cliffs, NJ: Prentice Hall.

Joyce, R., and Gupta, G. (1990). Identity authentication based on keystroke latencies. *Communications of the ACM, 33*, 168-176.

Kahneman, D. (1973). *Attention and effort.* Englewood Cliffs, NJ: Prentice Hall.

Kaltenbach, M., and Frasson, C. (1989). DYNABOARD: User animated display of deductive proofs in mathematics. *International Journal of Man-Machine Studies, 30,* 149-170.

Kantorowitz, E., and Sudarsky, O. (1989). The adaptable user interface. *Communications of the ACM, 32,* 1352-1358.

Karat, C-M. (1991). Cost-benefit and business case analysis of usability engineering. Tutorial presented at the ACM SIGCHI Conference on Human Factors in Computing Systems, New Orleans, LA, April 28-May 2.

Karat, C-M. (1992, November). Cost-justifying human factors support on software development projects. *Bulletin of the Human Factors Society, 35* (11), 1-4.

Katzeff, C. (1988). The effect of different conceptual models upon reasoning in a database query writing task. *International Journal of Man-Machine Studies, 29,* 37-62.

Katzeff, C. (1990). System demands on mental models for a fulltext database. *International Journal of Man-Machine Studies, 32,* 483-509.

Keele, S. W. (1973). *Attention and human performance.* Pacific Palisades, CA: Goodyear.

Kelly, G. A. (1955). *The psychology of personal constructs.* New York: Norton.

Kelly, M. J., and Chapanis, A. (1977). Limited vocabulary natural language dialogue. *International Journal of Man-Machine Studies, 9,* 477-501.

Kessel, C. J., and Wickens, C. D. (1982). The transfer of failure-detection skills between monitoring and controlling dynamic systems. *Human Factors, 24,* 49-60.

Kieras, D. E. (1988). Towards a practical GOMS model methodology for user interface design. In M. Helander (Ed.), *Handbook of human-computer interaction* (pp. 67-85). Amsterdam: Elsevier.

Kieras, D. E., and Polson, P. (1985). An approach to the formal analysis of user complexity. *International Journal of Man-Machine Studies, 22,* 365-394.

Kiger, J. I. (1984). The depth/breadth trade-off in the design of menu-driven user interfaces. *International Journal of Man-Machine Studies, 20,* 201-213.

Koved, L., and Shneiderman, B. (1986). Embedded menus: Menu selection in context. *Communications of the ACM, 29,* 312-318.

Kozar, K. A., and Dickson, G. W. (1978). An experimental study of the effects of data display media on decision effectiveness. *International Journal of Man-Machine Studies, 10,* 494-505.

Kruskal, J. B., and Wish, M. (1978). *Multidimensional scaling.* Beverly Hills, CA: Sage.

LaBerge, D., VanGilder, P., and Yellot, S. (1971). A cueing technique in choice reaction time. *Journal of Experimental Psychology, 87,* 225-228.

Lachman, R., Lachman, J. L., and Butterfield, E. C. (1979). *Cognitive psychology and information processing.* Hillsdale, NJ: Erlbaum.

LaLomia, M. J., and Sidowski, J. B. (1990). Measurements of computer satisfaction, literacy, and aptitudes: A review. *International Journal of Human-Computer Interaction, 2,* 231-253.

Lamb, M. (1982). An interactive graphical modeling game for teaching musical concepts. *Journal of Computer-Based Instruction, 9,* 59-63.

Landauer, T. K. (1987). Relations between cognitive psychology and computer system design. In J. M. Carroll (Ed.), *Interfacing thought: Cognitive aspects of human-computer interaction* (pp. 1-25). Cambridge, MA: Bradford.

Lang, G. T., Eberts, R. E., Gabel, M., and Barash, M. (1991). *IEEE Transactions on Engineering Management, 38,* 257-268.

Langlotz, C. P., and Shortliffe, E. H. (1983). Adapting a consultation system to critique user plans. *International Journal of Man-Machine Studies, 19,* 479-496.

Lea, W. A. (Ed.) (1980). *Trends in speech recognition.* Englewood Cliffs, NJ: Prentice Hall.

Lees, F. P. (1974). Research on the process operator. In E. Edwards and F. P. Lees (Eds.), *The human operator in process control* (pp. 386-425). New York: Halsted Press.

Leggett, J., and Williams, G. (1988). Verifying identity via keyboard characteristics. *International Journal of Man-Machine Studies, 23,* 67-76.

LeMay, M., and Hird, E. (1986). Operator work load: When is enough enough? *Communications of the ACM, 7,* 638-642.

Levinson, S. C. (1983). *Pragmatics*. Cambridge, England: Cambridge University Press.

Lewis, B. N., and Cook, J. A. (1969). Toward a theory of telling. *International Journal of Man-Machine Studies, 1*, 129-176.

Lewis, F. (1982). Facilitator: A microcomputer decision support system for small support groups. Unpublished doctoral dissertation. University of Louisville.

Lewis, P. M., Rosenkranz, D. J., and Stearns, R. E. (1976). *Compiler design theory*. Reading, MA: Addison-Wesley.

Liebelt, L. S., McDonald, J. E., Stone, J. D., and Karat, J. (1983). The effects of organization and type of target for items in menus: The effects of organization and type of target. *Proceedings of the Human Factors Society, 26*, 546-550.

Lintern, G., and Liu, Y-T. (1991). Explicit and implicit horizons for simulated landing approaches. *Human Factors, 33*, 401-417.

Lintern, G., Roscoe, S. N., and Sivier, J. F. (1990). Display principles, control dynamics, and environment factors in pilot training and transfer. *Human Factors, 32*, 319-327.

Liou, Y. I., and Nunamaker, J. F. (1990). Using a group decision support system environment for knowledge acquisition: A field study. *Proceedings of the IEEE 23rd Annual Hawaii International Conference on System Sciences, Vol. III*, 40-49.

McCarroll, T. (1991, August 12). What new age? *Time, 138* (6), 44-46.

McClelland, J. L. (1979). On the time-relations of mental processes: An examination of processes in cascade. *Psychological Review, 86*, 287-330.

McDonald, J. E., Dayton, T., and McDonald, D. R. (1988). Adapting menu layout to tasks. *International Journal of Man-Machine Studies, 28*, 417-435.

McDonald, J. E., Dearholt, D. W., Paap, K., and Schvaneveldt, R. W. (1986). A formal interface design methodology based on user knowledge. *Proceedings of Human Factors in Computer Systems, CHI'86*, pp. 285-290.

McDonald, J. E., Stone, J. D., and Liebelt, L. S. (1983). Searching for items in menus: The effects of organization and type of target. *Proceedings of the Human Factors Society, 27*, 834-837.

MacIntyre, F., Estep, K. W., and Sieburth, J. M. (1990). Cost of user-friendly programming. *Journal of Forth Application and Research, 6* (2), 103-115.

Mackinlay, J. D., Robertson, G. C., and Card, S. K. (1991). The perspective wall: detail and context smoothly integrated. *Human Factors in Computing Systems Conference Proceedings, CHI'91* (pp. 173-179). New York: ACM.

McKeithen, K. B., Reitman, J. S., Rueter, H. H., and Hirtle, S. C. (1981). Knowledge organization and skill differences in computer programmers. *Cognitive Psychology, 13*, 307-325.

MacLean, A., Bellotti, V., Young, R., and Moran, T. (1991). Reaching through analogy: A design rationale perspective on roles of analogy. *Human Factors in Computing Systems Conference Proceedings, CHI'91* (pp. 167-172). New York: ACM.

Magers, C. S. (1983). An experimental evaluation of on-line HELP for non-programmers. *Proceedings CHI'83 Human Factors in Computer Systems* (pp. 277-281). New York: ACM.

Malone, T. W. (1981, December). What makes computer games fun? *Byte*, 258-277.

Malone, T. W. (1987). Computer support for organizations: Toward an organizational science. In J. M. Carroll (Ed.), *Interfacing thought: Cognitive aspects of human-computer interaction* (pp. 294-323). Cambridge, MA: MIT.

Malone, T. W., Grant, K. R., Lai, K-Y., Rao, R., and Rosenblitt, D. (1988). Semistructured messages are surprisingly useful for computer-supported coordination. In I. Greif (Ed.), *Computer-Supported Cooperative Work: A Book of Readings* (pp. 311-331). San Mateo, CA: Kaufmann.

Malone, T., Grant, K., Lai, K., Rao, R., and Rosenblitt, D. (1987). Semistructured messages are surprisingly useful for computer-supported coordination. In I. Greif (Ed.), *Computer-supported cooperative work: A book of readings* (pp. 311-331). San Mateo, CA: Kaufman.

Mantei, M. M., and Teory, T. J. (1988). Cost/benefit analysis for incorporating human factors in the software lifecycle. *Communications of the ACM, 31*, 428-439.

Marchionini, G. (1989). Making the transition from print to electronic encyclopedias: Adaptation of mental models. *International Journal of Man-Machine Studies, 30,* 591-618.

Martin, G. L. (1989). The utility of speech input in user-computer interfaces. *International Journal of Man-Machine Studies, 30,* 355-375.

Maskery, H. S. (1984). Adaptive interfaces for naive users - An experimental study. In *Proceedings of the the IFIP Conference, Interact '84* (pp. 343-350).

Mauldin, M. L. (1987). Semantic rule based text generation. In *The 10th International Conference on Computational Linguistics.* Palo Alto, CA: Stanford University.

Mayer, R. E. (1975). Different problem solving competencies established in learning computer programming with and without meaningful models. *Journal of Educational Psychology, 67,* 725-734.

Mayer, R. E. (1976a). Some conditions of meaningful learning for computer programming: Advance organizers and subject control of frame order. *Journal of Educational Psychology, 68,* 143-150.

Mayer, R. E. (1976b). Comprehension as affected by structure of problem representation. *Memory & Cognition, 4,* 249-255.

Mayer, R. E. (1978). Advance organizers that compensate for the organization of text. *Journal of Educational Psychology, 70,* 880-886.

Mayer, R. E. (1980). Elaboration techniques for technical text: An experimental test of learning strategy hypothesis. *Journal of Educational Psychology, 72,* 770-784.

Mayer, R. E., and Bromage, B. K. (1980). Different recall protocols for technical texts due to advance organizers. *Journal of Educational Psychology, 72,* 209-225.

Mayes, J. T., Draper, S. W., McGregor, M. A., and Oatley, K. (1988). Information flow in a user interface: The effect of experience and context on the recall of MacWrite screens. In D. M. Jones and R. Winder (Eds.), *People and computers IV.* Cambridge, England: Cambridge University Press.

Meister, D. (1986). *Human factors testing and evaluation.* Amsterdam: Elsevier.

Michard, A. (1982). Graphical presentation of boolean expressions in a database query language: Design notes and ergonomic evaluation. *Behaviour and Information Technology, 1,* 279-288.

Miller, D. P. (1981). The depth/breadth tradeoff in hierarchical computer menus. *Proceedings of the Human Factors Society, 25,* 296-300.

Miller, G. (1956). The magical number 7, plus or minus two: Some limits on our capacity for processing information. *Psychological Review, 63,* 81-97.

Minneman, S. L., and Bly, S. A. (1991). Managing a trois: A study of a multi-user drawing tool in distributed design work. *Human Factors in Computing Systems Conference Proceedings, CHI'91* (pp. 217-224). New York: ACM.

Minsky, M. (1975). A framework for representing knowledge. In P. H. Winston (Ed.), *The psychology of computer vision* (pp. 211-277). New York: McGraw-Hill.

Miyata, Y., and Norman, D. A. (1986). Psychological issues in support of multiple activities. In D. A. Norman and S. W. Draper (Eds.), *User-centered system design* (pp. 265-284). Hillsdale, NJ: Erlbaum.

Moher, T., and Schneider, G. M. (1982). Methodology and experimental research in software engineering. *International Journal of Man-Machine Studies, 16,* 65-67.

Molzberger, P. (1983). Aesthetics and programming. In A. Janda (Ed.), *Human factors in computing systems* (pp. 247-250). New York: ACM.

Montag, M., Simonson, M. R., and Maurer, M. M. (1984). *Test administrator's manual for the Standardized Test of Computer Literacy and Computer Anxiety Index.* Ames, IA: Iowa State University.

Moran, T. P. (1981). The command language grammar: A representation for the user interface of interactive computer systems. *International Journal of Man-Machine Studies, 15,* 3-50.

Moray, N. (1967). Where is attention limited? A survey and a model. *Acta Psychologica, 27,* 84-92.

Moray, N., and Fitter, N. (1973). A theory and measurement of attention. In S. Kornblum (Ed.), *Attention and performance IV.* New York: Academic.

Mori, H., Chung, C. L., Kinoe, Y., and Hayashi, Y. (1990). An adaptive document retrieval system using a neural network. *International Journal of Human-Computer Interaction, 2*, 237-242.

Morris, D. (1977). *Manwatching*. New York: Abrams.

Mountford, S. J., and North, R. A. (1980). Voice entry for reducing pilot workload. *Proceedings of the Human Factors Society, 24*, 185-189.

Moyer, R. S. (1973). Comparing objects in memory: Evidence suggesting an internal psychophysics. *Perception & Psychophysics, 13*, 180-184.

Murakami, K., and Taguchi, H. (1991). Gesture recognition using recurrent neural networks. *Human Factors in Computing Systems Conference Proceedings, CHI'91* (pp. 301-305). New York: ACM.

Mykowiecka, A. (1991). Natural language generation — An overview. *International Journal of Man-Machine Studies, 34*, 497-511.

Napier, H. A., Lane, D. M., Batsell, R. R., and Guadango, N. S. (1989). Impact of a restricted natural language interface on ease of learning and productivity. *Communications of the ACM, 32*, 1190-1198.

Navon, D., and Gopher, D. (1979). On the economy of the human processing system. *Psychological Review, 86*, 214-253.

Newell, A., and Simon, H. (1972). *Human problem solving*. Englewood Cliffs, NJ: Prentice Hall.

Newell, A. F., Arnott, J. L., Carter, K., and Cruikshank, G. (1990). Listening typewriter simulation studies. *International Journal of Man-Machine Studies, 33*, 1-19.

Nielsen, J. (Ed.) (1989). *Coordinating user interfaces for consistency*. Boston: Academic.

Norcio, A. F., and Stanley, J. (1989). Adaptive human-computer interfaces: A literature survey and perspective. *IEEE Transactions on Systems, Man, and Cybernetics, 19*, 399-408.

Norman, D. A. (1983). Some observations on mental models. In D. Gentner and A. L. Stevens (Eds.), *Mental models* (pp. 7-14). Hillsdale, NJ: Erlbaum.

Norman, D. A. (1986). Cognitive engineering. In D. A. Norman and S. W. Draper (Eds.), *User centered system design* (pp. 31-61). Hillsdale, NJ: Erlbaum.

Norman, D. A. (1988). *The psychology of everyday things*. New York: Basic Books.

Norman, D. A., and Bobrow, D. (1975). On data-limited and resource-limited processing. *Journal of Cognitive Psychology, 7*, 44-64.

Norman, D. A., and Rumelhart, D. E. (1970). A system for perception and memory. In D. A. Norman (Ed.), *Models of human memory* (pp. 19-64). New York: Academic.

Norman, K. L., and Chin, J. P. (1989). The menu metaphor: Food for thought. *Behaviour and Information Technology, 8*, 125-134.

Nunamaker, J. F., Vogel, D., Heminger, A., Martz, B., Grohowski, R., and McGoff, C. (1989). Group support system in practice: Experience at IBM. *Proceedings of the IEEE 22nd Annual Hawaii International Conference on System Sciences*, 378-386.

Ochsman, R. B., and Chapanis, A. (1974). The effects of 10 communication modes on the behavior of the teams during cooperative problem solving. *International Journal of Man-Machine Studies, 6*, 579-619.

O'Donnell, R. D., and Eggemeier, F. T. (1988). Workload assessment technology. In K. R. Boff, L. Kaufman, and J. P Thomas (Eds.), *Handbook of perception and human performance, Vol. II, Cognitive processes and performance* (pp. 42:1—42:49). New York: Wiley.

Ogden, W., and Kaplan, C. (1986). The use of *and* and *or* in a natural language interface. *Proceedings of the Human Factors Society, 30*, 829-833.

O'Shea, T. (1978). A self-improving quadratic tutor. *International Journal of Man-Machine Studies, 11*, 97-124.

Paivio, A. (1971). *Imagery and verbal processes*. New York: Holt, Rinehart and Winston.

Palmer, S. E. (1975). The effects of contextual scenes on the identification of objects. *Memory & Cognition, 3*, 519-526.

Panko, R. R. (1964). Office work. *Office Technology and People, 2*, 205-238.

Pask, G., Scott, B. C. E., and Kallikourdis, D. (1973). A theory of conversations and individuals (Exemplified by the learning process on CASTE). *International Journal of Man-Machine Studies, 20,* 373-419.

Payne, S. J., and Green, T. R. G. (1986). Task-action grammars: A model of the mental representation of task languages. *Human-Computer Interaction, 2,* 93-133.

Payne, S. J., and Green, T. R. G. (1989). The structure of command languages: An experiment on task-action grammar. *International Journal of Man-Machine Studies, 30,* 213-234.

Pittman, J. A. (1991). Recognizing handwritten text. *Human Factors in Computing Systems Conference Proceedings, CHI'91* (pp. 271-275). New York: ACM.

Pollack, M., Hirschberg, J., and Webber, B. (1982). User participation in the reasoning process of expert systems. *Proceedings of the National Conference on Artificial Intelligence.* Pittsburgh, PA: AAAI.

Polson, M. C., Wickens, C. D., Klapp, S. T., and Colle, H. A. (1989). Human interactive informational processes. In P. A. Hancock and M. H. Chignell (Eds.), *Intelligent interfaces: Theory, research and design* (pp. 129-164). Amsterdam: Elsevier.

Polson, P. G. (1988). The consequences of consistent and inconsistent user interfaces. In R. Guindon (Ed.), *Cognitive science and its applications for human-computer interaction* (pp. 59-108). Hillsdale, NJ: Erlbaum.

Polson, P. G., Bovair, S., and Kieras, D. E. (1987). Transfer between text editors. In P. Tanner and J. M. Carroll (Eds.), *Human Factors in Computing Systems Conference Proceedings, CHI'87* (pp. 27-32). New York: ACM.

Polson, P. G., Muncher, E., and Engelbeck, G. (1986). A text of a common elements theory of transfer. In M. Mantei and P. Orbeton (Eds.), *Human Factors in Computing Systems Conference Proceedings, CHI'86* (pp. 78-83). New York: ACM.

Posey, J. W., and Eberts, R. E. (1989). Effects of display mode on the development of mental models through rule-based expert system interaction. In G. Salvendy & M. Smith (Eds.), *Designing and using human-computer interfaces and knowledge-based systems* (pp. 271-277). Amsterdam: Elsevier.

Power, M., Lashley, C., Sanchez, P., and Shneiderman, B. (1984). An experimental comparison of tabular and graphic data presentation. *International Journal of Man-Machine Studies, 20,* 545-566.

Press, L. (1971). Toward balanced man-machine systems. *International Journal of Man-Machine Studies, 3,* 61-73.

Proctor, R. W., and Reeve, T. G. (Eds.) (1990). *Stimulus-response compatibility.* Amsterdam: Elsevier.

Quillian, M. R. (1968). Semantic memory. In M. Minsky (Ed.), *Semantic information processing.* Cambridge, MA: MIT Press.

Rasmussen, J. (1985). The role of hierarchical knowledge representation in decision making and system management. *IEEE Transactions on Systems, Man, and Cybernetics, SMC-15,* 234-243.

Raymond, D. R., Canas, A. J., Tompa, F. W., and Safayeni, F. R. (1989). Measuring the effectiveness of personal database structures. *International Journal of Man-Machine Studies, 31,* 237-256.

Reisner, P. (1981). Formal grammar and human factors design of an interactive graphics system. *IEEE Transactions on Software Engineering, SE-7,* 229-240.

Rich, E. (1983). Users are individuals: Individualizing user models. *International Journal of Man-Machine Studies, 18,* 199-214.

Robertson, G. C., Mackinlay, J. D., and Card, S. K. (1991). Cone trees: Animated 3D visualizations of hierarchical information. *Human Factors in Computing Systems Conference Proceedings, CHI'91* (pp. 189-194). New York: ACM.

Robertson, S. P., and Black, J. B. (1986). Structure and development of plans in computer text editing. *Human-Computer Interaction, 2,* 201-226.

Rohr, G., and Keppel, E. (1984). Iconic interfaces: Where to use and how to construct. In H. W. Hendrick and O. Brown (Eds.), *Human factors in organizational design and management* (pp. 269-275). Amsterdam: North-Holland.

Roscoe, S. N. (1980). *Aviation psychology.* Ames, IA: Iowa State University.

Rosenberg, C. R. (1987). Revealing the structure of NETtalk's internal representations. *Proceedings of the Ninth Annual Conference of the Cognitive Science Society* (pp. 537-554).

Rosenberg, C. R., and Sejnowski, T. J. (1986). The spacing effect on NETtalk, a massively-parallel network. *Proceedings of the Eighth Annual Conference of the Cognitive Science Society* (72-89).

Rosenberg, D. (1989). Cost-benefit analysis for corporate user interface standards: What price to pay for a consistent "look and feel." In J. Nielsen (Ed.), *Coordinating user interfaces for consistency* (pp. 21-34). New York: Academic.

Roske-Hofstrand, R. J., and Paap, K. R. (1986). Cognitive networks as a guide to menu organization: An application in the automated cockpit. *Ergonomics, 29,* 1301-1312.

Rosson, M. B. (1984). The role of experience in editing. In B. Shackel (Ed.), *INTERACT'84* (pp. 225-239). Amsterdam: Elsevier.

Rouse, W. B., and Morris, N. M. (1986). On looking into the black box: Prospects and limits in the search for mental models. *Psychological Bulletin, 100,* 349-363.

Rumelhart, D. E. (1980). Schemata: The building blocks of cognition. In R. Spiro, B. Bruce, and W. Brewer (Eds.), *Basic processes in reading: Perception and comprehension* (pp. 33-58). Hillsdale, NJ: Erlbaum.

Rumelhart, D. E., and McClelland, J. L. (1986). *Parallel distributed processing, explorations in the microstructure of cognition, Volume 1: Foundations.* Cambridge, MA: MIT Press.

Rumelhart, D. E., and and Norman, D. A. (1981). Analogical processes in learning. In J. R. Anderson (Ed.), *Cognitive skills and their acquisition* (pp. 335-359). Hillsdale, NJ: Erlbaum.

Scanlan, L. A. (1975). Visual time compression: Spatial and temporal cues. *Human Factors, 17,* 84-90.

Scapin, D. L. (1981). Computer commands in restricted natural language: Some aspects of memory and experience. *Human Factors, 23,* 365-375.

Schank, R. C. (1975). *Conceptual information processing.* Amsterdam: North-Holland.

Schank, R. C., and Abelson, C. K. (1977). *Scripts, plans, goals, and understanding.* Hillsdale, NJ: Erlbaum.

Schank, R. C., and Riesbeck, C. K. (Eds.). (1981). *Inside computer understanding.* Hillsdale, NJ: Erlbaum.

Schiele, F., and Green, T. (1990). HCI formalisms and cognitive psychology: The case of task-action grammar. In M. Harrison and H. Thimbleby (Eds.), *Formal methods in human-computer interaction* (pp. 10-62). Cambridge, England: Cambridge University Press.

Schneider, W., and Detweiler, M. (1987). A connectionist/control architecture for working memory. In G. H. Bower (Ed.), *The psychology of learning and motivation, Vol. 21* (pp. 53-119). Orlando, FL: Academic.

Schneider, W., and Detweiler, M. (1988). The role of practice in dual-task performance: Toward workload modeling in a connectionist/control architecture. *Human Factors, 30,* 539-566.

Schneider, W., and Shiffrin, R. M. (1977). Controlled and automatic human information processing: I. Detection, search, and attention. *Psychological Review, 84,* 1-66.

Sears, A., and Shneiderman, B. (1991). High precision touchscreens: Design strategies and comparisons with a mouse. *International Journal of Man-Machine Studies, 34,* 593-613.

Sejnowski, T. J., and Rosenberg, C. R. (1987). Parallel networks that learn to pronounce English text. *Complex Systems, 1,* 145-168.

Shannon, C. E., and Weaver,W. (1949). *The mathematical theory of communication.* Urbana, IL: University of Illinois Press.

Sharit, J. (1985). Supervisory control of a flexible manufacturing system. *Human Factors, 27,* 47-59.

Sheil, B. A. (1981). The psychological study of programming. *Computing Surveys, 13,* 101-120.

Sheridan, T. B., and Verplank, W. L. (1978). *Human and computer control of undersea teleoperators* (Technical Report). MIT Man-Machine Systems Laboratory.

Shiffrin, R. M., and Atkinson, R. C. (1969). Storage and retrieval processes in long-term memory. *Psychological Review, 76,* 179-193.

Shiffrin, R. M., and Schneider, W. (1977). Controlled and automatic human information processing: II. Perceptual learning, automatic attending, and a general theory. *Psychological Review, 84,* 127-190.

Shneiderman, B. (1980). *Software psychology.* Cambridge, MA: Winthrop.

Shneiderman, B. (1982). Systems message design: Guidelines and experimental results. In A. Badre and B. Shneiderman (Eds.), *Directions in human-computer interaction* (pp. 55-78). Norwood, NJ: Ablex.

Shneiderman, B. (1987). *Designing the user interface: Strategies for effective human-computer interaction.* Reading, MA: Addison-Wesley.

Shortliffe, E. H. (1976). *Computer-based medical consultations: MYCIN.* Amsterdam: Elsevier.

Siochi, A. C., and Hix, D. (1991). A study of computer-supported user interface evaluation using maximal repeating pattern analysis. *Human Factors in Computing Systems Conference Proceedings, CHI'91* (pp. 301-305). New York: ACM.

Sleeman, D. (1985). UMFE: A user modelling front-end subsystem. *International Journal of Man-Machine Studies, 23,* 71-88.

Small, D. W., and Weldon, L. J. (1983). An experimental comparison of natural and structured query languages. *Human Factors, 25,* 253-263.

Smith, E. E., Shoben, E. J., and Rips, L. J. (1974). Structure and process in semantic memory: A featural model for semantic decisions. *Psychological Review, 81,* 214-241.

Smith, P. J., and Janosky, B. (1985). An analysis of human errors in the use of an online library catalog system. In *Proceedings of the IEEE Systems, Man, and Cybernetics Conference* (pp. 273 - 275).

Smith, S. L., and Mosier, J. N. (1984). *Design guidelines for the user interface for computer-based information systems.* Bedford, MA: The MITRE Corp. (also available from the National Technical Information Service, Springfield, VA).

Sperling, G. (1963). A model for visual memory tasks. *Human Factors, 5,* 19-31.

Sperling, G. (1967). Successive approximations to a model for short-term memory. *Acta Psychologica, 27,* 285-292.

Standing, L., Conezio, J., and Haber, R. N. (1970). Perception and memory for pictures: Single-trial learning of 2500 visual stimuli. *Psychonomic Science, 19,* 73-74.

Stanfill, C., and Kahle, B. (1986). Parallel free-text search on the connection machine system. *Communications of the ACM, 29,* 1229-1239.

Steeb, R., and Johnston, S. C. (1981). A computer-based interactive system for group decision-making. *IEEE Transactions on Systems, Man, and Cybernetics, SMC-11,* 544-552.

Stefik, M., Foster, G., Bobrow, D. G., Kahn, K., Lanning, S., and Suchman, L. (1987). Beyond the chalkboard: Computer support for collaboration and problem solving in meetings. *Communications of the ACM, 30,* 32-47.

Stern, K. R. (1984). An evaluation of written, graphics, and voice messages in proceduralized instructions. *Proceedings of the Human Factors Society, 28,* 314-318.

Stevens, A. L., and Collins, A. (1980). Multiple conceptual models of a complex system. In R. E. Snow, P. A. Frederico, and W. E. Montague (Eds.), *Aptitude, learning and instruction, Volume 2* (pp. 96-121). Hillsdale, NJ: Erlbaum.

Stevens, A. L., Collins, A., and Goldin, S. (1979). Misconceptions in student's understanding. *International Journal of Man-Machine Studies, 11,* 145-156.

Stevens, A. L., Roberts, B., and Stead, L. (1983, March/April). The use of sophisticated graphics interface in computer-assisted instruction. *IEEE Computer Graphics and Applications, 3* (2), 25-31.

Sutherland, W. R. (1963). Sketchpad: A man-machine graphical communication system. *Proceedings of the Spring Joint Computer Conference,* 329-346.

Swartout, W. (1983). XPLAIN: A system for creating and explaining expert consulting programs. *Artificial Intelligence, 21,* 285-325.

Switchenko, D. M. (1985). In defense of the traditional (non-icon) interface: A position based on a selective review of the literature. In R. E. Eberts and C. G. Eberts (Eds.), *Trends in ergonomics/ human factors II* (pp. 373-379). Amsterdam: North-Holland.

Tanaka, T., Eberts, R. E., and Salvendy, G. (1991). Consistency of human-computer interface design: Quantification and validation. *Human Factors, 33,* 653-676.

Tang, J. C., and Minneman, S. L. (1991). VideoWhiteboard: Video shadows to support remote collaboration. *Human Factors in Computing Systems Conference Proceedings, CHI'91* (pp. 315-322). New York: ACM.

Totterdell, P. A., and Cooper, P. A. (1986). Design and evaluation of the AID adaptive front end to Telcom Gold. In M. D. Harrison and A. F. Monk (Eds.), *People and computers: Designing for usability.* Cambridge, England: Cambridge University Press.

Trowbridge, M. H., and Cason, H. (1932). An experimental study of Thorndike's theory of learning. *Journal of General Psychology, 7,* 245-258.

Tullis, T. S. (1981). An evaluation of alphanumeric, graphic, and color information displays. *Human Factors, 23,* 541-550.

Umanath, N. S., and Scamell, R. W. (1987). An experimental evaluation of the impact of data display format on recall performance. *Communications of the ACM, 31,* 562-570.

Umphress, D., and Williams, G. (1985). Identity verification through keyboard characteristics. *International Journal of Man-Machine Studies, 23,* 263-273.

Vicente, K. J., and Williges, R. C. (1988). Accommodating individual differences in searching a hierarchical file system. *International Journal of Man-Machine Studies, 29,* 647-668.

Villegas, L., and Eberts, R. E. (1992). Implementing a neural network for a cognitive text-editing task. In R. Beale and J. Finlay (Eds.), *Neural networks and pattern-recognition in human-computer interaction* (pp. 267-284). New York: Ellis Horwood.

Walther, G. H., and O'Neill, H. F. (1974). On-line user compute interface—the effect of interface flexibility, terminal type, and experience on performance. *National Computer Conference*, pp. 379-384.

Wheaton, G. R., Rose, A. M., Fingerman, P. W., Korotkin, A. L., and Holding, D. H. (1976). *Evaluation of the effectiveness of training devices: Literature review and preliminary model* (Research Memorandum 76-6). Alexandria, VA: U.S. Army Research Institute for the Behavioral and Social Sciences.

Whittaker, S., Brennan, S. E., and Clark, H. H. (1991). Co-ordinating activity: An analysis of interaction in computer-supported co-operative work. *Human Factors in Computing Systems Conference Proceedings, CHI'91* (pp. 361-367). New York: ACM.

Wickens, C. D. (1980). The structure of attentional resources. In R. Nickerson (Ed.), *Attention and performance VIII* (pp. 239-257). Hillsdale NJ: Erlbaum.

Wickens, C. D. (1984a). *Engineering psychology and human performance.* Columbus, OH: Merrill.

Wickens, C. D. (1984b). Processing resources in attention. In R. Parasuraman and D. R. Davies (Eds.), *Varieties of attention* (pp. 63-102). Orlando, FL: Academic.

Wickens, C. D. (1987). Information processing, decision-making, and cognition. In G. Salvendy (Ed.), *Handbook of human factors* (pp. 72-107). New York: Wiley.

Wickens, C. D., and Goettl, B. (1985). The effect of strategy on the resource domains of second order manual control. In R. E. Eberts and C. G. Eberts (Eds.), *Trends in ergonomics/human factors II.* Amsterdam: North-Holland.

Wickens, C. D., Kramer, A., Barnett, B., Carswell, M., Fracker, L., Goettl, B., and Harwood, K. (1985). *Display/cognitive interface: The effect of information integration requirements on display formatting for C3 display* (Technical Report). University of Illinois Engineering Psychology Laboratory and Aviation Research Laboratory, EPL-85-2/RAD-85-1.

Wickens, C. D., Sandry, D. L., and Vidulich, M. (1983). Compatibility and resource competition between modalities of input, central processing, and output. *Human Factors, 25,* 227-248.

Wickens, C. D., and Weingartner, A. (1985). Process control monitoring: The effects of spatial and verbal ability and current task demands. In R. E. Eberts and C. G. Eberts (Eds.), *Trends in ergonomics/human factors II.* Amsterdam: North-Holland.

Williams, M. D. (1984). What makes RABBIT run? *International Journal of Man-Machine Studies, 21*, 333-352.

Williams, M. D., and Hollan, J. D. (1981). The process of retrieval from very long term memory. *Cognitive Science, 5*, 87-119.

Wilson, J. R., and Rutherford, A. (1989). Mental models: Theory and application in human factors. *Human Factors, 31*, 617-634.

Wixon, D., Whiteside, J., Good, M., and Jones, S. (1983). Building a user-defined interface. *Human Factors in Computing Systems, CHI'83* (pp. 24-27). New York: ACM.

Woodworth, R. S. (1938). *Experimental psychology.* New York: Holt.

Yallow, E. (1980). *Individual differences in learning from verbal and figural materials.* School of Education, Stanford University, Aptitudes Research Project Technical Report No. 13, Palo Alto, CA.

Young, L. R. (1969). On adaptive manual control. *IEEE Transactions on Man-Machine Systems, MMS-10*, 229-331.

Young, R. M. (1981). The machine inside the machine: Users' models of pocket calculators. *International Journal of Man-Machine Studies, 15*, 51-85.

Young, S. R., Hauptmann, A. G., Ward, W. H., Smith, E. T., and Werner, P. (1989). High level knowledge sources in usable speech recognition systems. *Communications of the ACM, 32*, 183-193.

Ziegler, J. E., and Faehnrich, K-P. (1988). Direct manipulation. In M. Helander (Ed.), *Handbook of human-computer interaction* (pp. 123-133). Amsterdam: Elsevier.

Zimmerman, T., Lanier, J., Blanchard, C., Bryson, S., and Harvil, Y. (1987). A hand gesture interface device. *Proceedings of the ACM Society on CHI+GI* (pp. 189-192). New York: ACM.

Zoltan-Ford, E. (1991). How to get people to say and type what computers can understand. *International Journal of Man-Machine Studies, 34*, 527-547.

Author index

SUBJECT INDEX

Adaptive graphics analyser, 503
Adaptive interfaces or systems, 273, 498-506,
    537
  cognitive abilities, 504-505
  databases, 588-590
  evaluation, 506
  expertise, 502-504, 537
  feedback, 537, 588
  menus, 563
  task characteristics, 505
  user-controlled, 498-502
Affordances
  card catalogue system, 7
  definition, 509-510
  everyday things, 510-512
  interface design, 512-513
Analogies. *See also* Metaphors
  definition, 50-51
Animation, 250, 254-255
Assistance, 495-498
Attention
  divided, 260-262
  dual task, 262-263, 265
  examples, 270-271
  feedback, 530-532
  focusing, 263-264
  groupware, 613-614
  information processing, 260
  limited capacity or resources, 51-52, 166-168,
    169, 260, 262-265
  models, 51-53
  multiple resource theory *(see* Multiple
    resource theory)
  searchlight metaphor, 260-262
  selective or switching, 261-262
  time-sharing *(see* Attention, dual task)

Bit-mapped displays, 20-21, 25
Bits, 169

CAD, 235, 322, 531, 694
CAI (Computer-Assisted Instruction)
  example *(see* STEAMER)
  programming productivity, 6
  tutoring, 495-498
  user models, 502-504
CAM, 594
Cam trees, 252, 578

CAP1, 199, 204
Card catalogue systems, 7-11
Cascade models, 181-182
Cause and effect, 63-66
Channel capacity, 169-170
Chunking, 169-170, 176-177, 280-281, 551
Cluster analysis, 150, 152-156, 158-160
Codes, memory. *See* Human memory
Cognitive processor. *See* Processors
Colab, 598-600
Command-based displays, 20, 545-548, 550-551
  consistency with direct manipulation, 353
  constraints, lack of, 515-516
  databases, 570-572
  difficulty of use, 143-144, 238
  experimental considerations, 69-70
  feedback and help messages, 526
  file selection, 38-39
  menu bar widgets, 41-42
Command names, 57-58, 176, 465
Communication. *See also* Input methods and
    devices
  human-computer, 55-58, 465, 466
  human-human, 55-56, 466, 485-487, 534,
    584-585, 614-617
Compatibilities. *See* Stimulus-response com-
    patibility; Stimulus-central processing-
    response compatibility
Computer
  in consumer products, 1
  on productivity, 3-4
  sales, 2
  usage, 1
Computer interface, 4-5, 19-21
Computerization problems, 1
Computer-supported cooperative work (CSCW),
    595, 598-604, 614-617
Computer usability
  consumer expectations, 5
  cost effectiveness, 5
  effects on sales, 2-3
  illustrations, 6-11
  and productivity, 2-3, 16-17
Conceptual dependency theory, 469-471
Conceptual models, 50, 140-141
Cone trees, 252-253, 578
Confounding variables
  carry-over effects, 83-86, 128-130